Susan Lola Hunter
Rm. 52 Emerson House

Clinical Psychology

THE CENTURY PSYCHOLOGY SERIES

Kenneth MacCorquodale
Gardner Lindzey
Kenneth E. Clark

CLINICAL PSYCHOLOGY
Expanding Horizons

SECOND EDITION

NORMAN D. SUNDBERG
University of Oregon

LEONA E. TYLER
University of Oregon

JULIAN R. TAPLIN
Morrison Center for
Youth and Family Service

New York
APPLETON-CENTURY-CROFTS
Educational Division
MEREDITH CORPORATION

TO RICHARD M. ELLIOTT

ACKNOWLEDGMENTS

Figure 2-1: From H. D. Sargent and M. Mayman (figure on the history of clinical psychology), "Clinical Psychology," in S. Arieti (Ed.) *The American Handbook of Psychiatry*, vol. II, p. 1713. © 1959 by Basic Books, Inc., Publishers, New York.

Figure 4-1: From J. G. Miller (figure illustrating negative feedback), "The Nature of Living Systems," *Behavioral Science*, vol. 16, no. 4, 1971. By permission of James G. Miller, M.D., Ph.D., Editor.

Figure 5-1: From J. B. Chasson (figure illustrating drug effects on anxiety), *Research Design in Clinical Psychology and Psychiatry*, p. 199. Copyright © 1967 by Meredith Publishing Company. By permission Appleton-Century-Crofts, Educational Division, Meredith Corporation.

Figure 5-2: From R. V. Hall, D. Lund, and D. Jackson (Figure 3. A record of study behavior for Rose), "Effects of teacher attention on study behavior," *Journal of Applied Behavior Analysis*, 1968, 1, 1–12. Copyright 1968 by the Society for the Experimental Analysis of Behavior, Inc.

Figure 7-2: Profile sheet of Strong Vocational Interest Blank for Men. Permission granted by James C. Slaughter, Director, Interpretive Scoring Systems, a division of National Computer Systems, Inc.

Figure 10-1: From Paul E. Meehl (chart entitled Causal Chains in Schizophrenia, Minimum Complexity), "Specific genetic etiology psychodynamics, and therapeutic nihilism," *International Journal of Mental Health*, 1972, 1, 10–27. Reprinted by permission of *International Journal of Mental Health*, published by International Arts and Sciences Press, Inc., White Plains, N. Y.

Figure 12-1: From O. I. Lovaas, "A behavior therapy approach to the treatment of childhood schizophrenia," in John P. Hill (Ed.), *Minnesota Symposia on Child Psychology*, vol. I, p. 137. University of Minnesota Press, Mpls. © 1967 University of Minnesota.

D. R. Peterson, *The Clinical Study of Social Behavior*, pp. 121–122. Copyright © 1968 by Appleton-Century-Crofts, Educational Division, Meredith Corporation.

Contents

Preface to the Second Edition

Revising a book after the lapse of a decade is an illuminating experience. One gets an exciting sense of movement. Topics that seemed important ten years ago—assessment and report writing, for example—have receded into the background. Ways of tackling psychological problems barely visible on the horizon ten years ago—behavior modification and community psychology, for example—have come into prominence. Clinical psychology in the early 1960s was like an adolescent at the peak of his powers. By the 1970s clinical psychology is more like a young adult matured by the trials and responsibilities of his first and second jobs.

Choosing a subtitle for the new edition turned out to be unexpectedly difficult. It was clear that the subtitle of the first edition, "An introduction to research and practice," no longer exactly fit what we found ourselves writing. "Toward amalgamation of the helping psychologies?" Too pedantic. "Designing improvement programs for many levels of difficulties?" Too long. "Getting it all together to help people?" Too informal. We wished somehow to suggest that our emphasis is less on the psychologist's role and more on what his clients need, less on traditional tasks and skills, assessment, therapy, and research, and more on a kind of thinking a psychologist can apply to all sorts of situations in which people are seeking more effective ways to live. The new subtitle, "Expanding horizons," is an attempt to express succinctly this shift in orientation.

The book is addressed primarily to the psychology student considering seriously whether he should choose clinical psychology as a specialty, but we hope that it will have value also for graduate students and professional workers in this and related fields. The basic question we have kept in mind as we chose, rejected, and organized material is: What does the student need to know about the work clinical psychologists do? What activities? What knowledge base? What situations? With some regret we omitted detailed coverage of testing and abnormal psychology, topics that should properly receive more extensive coverage in special texts and courses. We tried wherever possible to include case reports and illustrations in order to give the student a feel for what psychologists do in real situations.

We have provided generous referencing to help the reader go on to more extensive explorations of topics. At the end of each chapter we suggest readings to guide those who are interested in more comprehensive discussions of the topics taken up in the chapter. The research summaries are intended to whet the reader's appetite for more information about how psychologists evaluate and improve their practice and how they push back the frontiers of knowledge. We still consider research to be a vital part of clinical psychology—if anything, more important than it was a decade ago. As practice has diversified, research-based knowledge in many branches of psychology has become relevant. Evaluation has taken on new significance now that it is being applied to programs as well as individual treatment. Being knowledgeable about research techniques and findings is an asset even to psychologists who do not themselves conduct any research. It serves to keep generator and user of knowledge in touch with one another.

We view clinical psychology as a very broad field extending from work with children to services for the aged, from severe disorders such as schizophrenia to the attempts at self-growth that adequate people make, from psychological testing to sociopolitical activity, from cooperation with physicians in treating psychosomatic illnesses to cooperation with urban planners in redesigning communities. Clinical psychology, as we see it, overlaps extensively with counseling and community psychology.

Such breadth brings problems of conceptual organization. We have used general systems theory as an organizing framework, but in order not to let this relatively abstract and detached kind of analysis obscure the human aspect of individual lives, we have supplemented it with concepts about development, organized into what we call "possibility theory." We are impressed with the increasing importance of choice in modern society, as other recent writers— Drucker and Toffler, for example—have been. Our image of the person is that of chooser and decision maker, selecting and rejecting from a wide range of life possibilities. Our approach might be described as a "psychoecological" theory taking into account the development of people in environments, environments that consist of symbols as well as physical and social objects, and that require choices as well as adaptive responses. This theory, admittedly still in a rudimentary state, seems to us to be useful in an increasingly complex and interrelated era of human history.

Comparing this edition with the previous one, the reader will find rather little overlap. Few pages have been reused. Eighty percent of the more than 900 references are new. The difference is great enough so that some readers may wish to use the first edition to supplement the second.

One major change is that we are no longer separating assessment and therapy. They are now seen as parts of a single process, developing and implementing "designs for improvement." The changes we have made clearly move clinical psychology away from the medical model, and we use the term "client" more frequently than the term "patient," but we still recognize the value of collaboration between medicine and psychology. We have shortened the section on individual therapy and included much more about work with organizations and communities.

The book consists of three parts. First are five chapters of introduction, history, theory, and research. Second, the main core of the book, introduced by Chapter 6, proposes the merging of assessment with therapy, putting it in the framework of appraisal for image making and decisions, and examining all activities from the viewpoint of payoff for clients. The twelve central chapters deal with the clinical enterprise at the several different levels of intervention. The third and last section consists of three chapters that return to the personal and professional meaning of clinical psychology, ending with what we see as the pluralistic futures for the profession. The appendixes provide supplementary material for those who want more detail on diagnostic systems, tests, clinical reports, and various other topics.

We hope that the reader will find in this book as much pleasure and stimulation as the three of us did in writing it. Over more than three years, as we met month after month to review successive revisions of the chapters, we have enlarged our own concepts about this fascinating area, which we call *Clinical Psychology: Expanding Horizons*.

N.D.S.
L.E.T.
J.R.T.

Preface to the First Edition

The title of this book, *Clinical Psychology: An Introduction to Research and Practice*, suggests immediately its central intention—to present in an organized manner both clinical inquiry and clinical service. Psychology is one of those rare disciplines—in some ways the only one of its kind—that attempts to combine the deliberate scholarliness of the laboratory with the arts and responsibilities of the practical world of human affairs. Some related fields, for instance sociology and social work, physiology and medicine, have split into different disciplines and separate training structures. But clinical psychologists are psychologists first, and as such they need to be prepared to contribute both to the betterment of individual lives and to the advance of general knowledge.

Research and practice are not easy bedfellows. From time to time attempts are made to divorce one part of clinical psychology from the other; a completely happy union appears unlikely if not impossible. Nevertheless, we believe that the great strength of clinical psychology lies in its attempt to accomplish this difficult undertaking—to maintain a lively conversation between the researcher and the practitioner. Improvements in service depend on the discovery and testing of new knowledge; deep and creative insights into human nature—insights of great value to science—come in the intimacy of clinical work with patients. It is true that one man cannot be all things, and an individual clinician must usually emphasize one activity or the other. But the clinician who decides to become primarily a practitioner remains a *consumer* of research. Through his insights and practical "know-how," he can also serve as a questioner and goad to the research psychologists. On the other hand, the clinician who becomes primarily a researcher is constrained to remember the complexity and rich reality of human behavior. Moreover, research is the way to find out what really works. Ultimately, there is nothing so practical as good research.

In this book we have tried to clarify the identity of the developing profession and to outline ways of thinking that will make it possible for the two kinds of clinicians to remain in touch with one another. For these reasons, we have used research examples at the ends of chapters and written special chapters on research in clinical psychology as a whole, on assessment, and on psychotherapy. We have tried to embody a critical concern with research questions in the discussion of each practical topic. Our view of research has been broad, including naturalistic as well as experimental studies, and we have looked at the implications for clinical work in physiological, social, and developmental psychology as well as in traditional areas. Moreover, on the practical side, we have brought cases into almost every chapter and given concrete examples of the kinds of interaction that occur in psychotherapy.

Another of the ways in which we have tried to facilitate the fusion of research and practice is to use a conceptual framework, which, though imprecise in many ways, keeps the length and breadth of human life before our eyes. In the process of selecting concepts and principles as tools to use in understanding clinical work, we arrived at what might be called an organized eclecticism. The whole framework of the book rests on a developmental foundation. We view development as a constantly changing system of relationships—relationships between inner aspects of the individual's personality and relationships of the individual to other persons and to the larger social order. We have placed considerable emphasis on choices and decisions as salient features of developmental processes and have kept constantly in mind the decisions made by both clinicians and patients in the course of clinical work. Both assessment and therapy are considered within this broad developmental framework.

The book is divided into four parts. The three introductory chapters present the problems and principles underlying the rest of the book. The seven chapters on psychological assessment cover the ways in which clinicians arrive at decisions and develop "working images" about patients and their situations. In the nine chapters on psychotherapy we have classified the varieties of psychological treatment on the basis of the kinds of personality change at which they aim rather than on the basis of techniques they use. The final three chapters deal with clinical psychologists as persons and with the profession as it fits into the larger society.

We view this book as a means of introducing the student to a kind of thinking he can apply to the patients and the situations with which he will work rather than as a technical manual from which he can learn skills. Consequently, we have omitted detailed descriptions of tests and the interpretations made from them. We assume that a really extensive coverage of intelligence and personality testing will be an important part of a student's graduate program. Similarly, we decided to omit any detailed discussion of psychopathology. Like testing, it deserves a much more thorough treatment than we could have given it in this book and will also be covered in other phases of a clinician's training. We have, however, tried to provide many illustrations of pathology and tests usage. In the appendix we have listed 50 important clinical tests.

The book is written primarily for the student beginning his graduate work in psychology. We hope that it may also be useful to advanced undergraduates in psychology and to graduate students in related fields such as psychiatry, social work, and education. We hope also that professional workers in the mental health field may find that the book ties together some ideas and research findings and helps them organize the large unwieldy mass of knowledge that has accumulated so rapidly in the sociopsychological professions.

Some readers may wonder which sections each of the authors has written. The book is truly a cooperative venture. It has grown out of ten years of talking and working together in the development of the clinical and counseling programs at the University of Oregon. Though Miss Tyler was responsible for the first drafts on most of the chapters on psychotherapy and Sundberg for the chapters on assessment, each of us has revised and re-revised the other's work so often that the original author has been lost sight of.

It has been exciting to try to organize our ideas about clinical work and the findings of research in this still new and changing field. We believe that clinical psychology, along with the other behavioral sciences, is standing at the dawn of its influence in human affairs. Just as "wars begin and end in the minds of men," so too can the individual mind, as Milton said, "make a heaven of hell, a hell of heaven." Thinking of the promise and the peril involved in trying to help others, we have a feeling of humility as we commit these efforts to print. We hope students will take up the challenge of making sense and science out of this fascinating interplay of service and search.

N.D.S.
L.E.T.

Acknowledgments

This book is the product of many people, and we cannot hope to list all the clients, students, instructors, and colleagues who have been involved one way or another. We are continuing our dedication of the book to Richard "Mike" Elliott, who gave very much of himself to the editing of the first edition. Two of us have known Mike and have learned from him as students. Since the first edition, Mike has died, but his influence, we hope, can still be identified in the present version.

We are also grateful to Gardner Lindzey, who edited this second edition, and to the many people who have read parts of it or written suggestions for the revision of the book. Among those who read parts of the manuscript or made direct contributions to this edition, we wish to acknowledge and thank the following: Morton Bard, Alexander Caldwell, James Farnes, Lewis Goldberg, James Kelly, John Kerrigan, Peter Lewinsohn, James Lindemann, Joseph Matarazzo, Roland Pellegrin, Stanley Pierson, Roberta Ray, Wendell Swenson, and Shirley Terreberry.

We hope that all of those who shared in some way in the preparation of this book, including our families and secretaries, will find a sense of joy and perhaps pride in the result. Even though we have not listed all those who helped, we hope they will know that we are very grateful.

N.D.S.
L.E.T.
J.R.T.

part I

Introduction and Conceptual Framework

chapter 1

Clinical Settings, Clients, and Activities

What do clinical psychologists do? If ever there were a time when it was possible to give a simple, straightforward answer to this reasonable question, that time has long since passed. On the most general level we might say that it is the clinical psychologist's job to understand people and through this understanding to help them handle better the complicated business of living. Such a statement, however, does not even suggest the bewildering variety of tasks and responsibilities psychologists take on. Let us look specifically at several examples of what particular clinical psychologists are doing before turning to a more systematic discussion of the profession.

PEOPLE CLINICIANS SERVE

"Emotional checkups" for preschoolers. Jonathan Dayton was five years old and was to start kindergarten in the fall. In his town a pioneer mental health center conducted a program in "preventive intervention" designed to screen the incoming group of kindergarteners for emotional problems. Jonathan appeared with his mother at the center and was met by two professionals, the social worker and the psychologist, Dr. Harris. The social worker explained that she would see the mother while Jonathan went with the psychologist and played with some toys. (Each staff member saw an equal number of parents and children in this project, and it was this psychologist's turn to work with this particular child.) The psychologist and social worker noted that Ms. Dayton seemed rather anxious about having Jonathan leave her, although Jonathan did not seem to mind.

In the interview with Ms. Dayton the social worker asked questions to elicit the history of Jonathan's development—the time and condition of his birth, the feelings and relationships that had surrounded such changes as weaning, walking, talking, and toilet training. The interviewer gently tried to

3

elicit Ms. Dayton's attitudes about her boy, whom she always called Jonathan, not Johnny or another pet name. At first, Ms. Dayton seemed to need to be reassured often that some problems were not unusual. "Many children *do* find bathroom activities fascinating," said the social worker. Later, less worried about what the interviewer would think, she revealed that she and the children all rather feared Mr. Dayton. At the time Ms. Dayton married him, his social and financial status seemed to answer her long-felt needs. But instead of finding security, she had come to feel that she and the children were inadequate, given the political and social ambitions of her husband—that the family had become just a burden to him. "Jonathan *has* to turn out well," she said. The interviewer interpreted this to mean that she hoped that he would qualify for his father's Ivy League alma mater. The interviewer felt that Ms. Dayton had gained some insight into her situation when, after being asked which parent Jonathan resembled, and how, she said, "Oh, he's more like me. He needs to be liked a lot, too."

Meanwhile, Jonathan and the psychologist were in the playroom. Dr. Harris tried to interest Jonathan in the large dollhouse (which, for boys, he called "our model house") to see what Jonathan would do with the figures representing mother, father, brothers, sisters, and others. After briefly rearranging the furniture, Jonathan tired completely of the house and started asking the psychologist many questions about objects in the room and telling him to do things like throwing a ball or getting some crayons. Jonathan talked a great deal and used words more common to older children. His drawings, done rapidly, also showed considerable knowledge of details. When the hour was up, Dr. Harris found that the social worker's interview with Ms. Dayton was not yet finished. He had not planned to meet longer, and the waiting room was proving to be too small. Jonathan's demands for attention had become very friendly, reminding Dr. Harris of a child's attitude toward a father who has just returned from a long trip. Jonathan hugged the psychologist and begged to be lifted onto his shoulders. Dr. Harris, remembering his own strained back, suggested instead that they go outdoors, where Jonathan interspersed demands to be swung on the swings or play hide and seek with happy, yet unusually affectionate, clinging and hugging.

Over lunch the social worker and the exhausted psychologist compared notes. Both agreed that Jonathan was bright but that the family needed serious attention. They both agreed, too, that Jonathan's friendly but excessive demands for recognition and physical contact, together with his lower than average ability to do things on his own, might become a liability for him in the kindergarten situation. They knew that teachers interact most comfortably with children who have at least some skills in autonomous behavior. A teacher might readily become uncomfortable about a child with such intense demands for physical attention, and this discomfort could easily result in her labeling Jonathan "emotionally disturbed," thus starting a pejorative record for him. Both workers thought that Jonathan's behavior was probably related to his mother's insecurity about herself, to her rather unfeeling demands for Jonathan's future, and to his busy father's comparative neglect.

It was decided that the social worker, in the routine follow-up interview with the mother, would invite her to return for additional interviews in which they could explore some of the ways in which Mr. and Ms. Dayton might more effectively meet each other's needs and develop greater confidence and certainty in loving Jonathan and helping him to be more independent. Jonathan began kindergarten as scheduled.

In this instance, a naive person looking on the psychologist at work might have decided that he was primarily a babysitter and wondered why he needed the many years of study leading to a Ph.D., which most clinical psychologists possess. What was actually occurring was some penetrating observation and analysis of a child's behavior, made possible through knowledge of personality development. The judgments based on this observation entered into the psychological plan for this child.

Randy B and Fairoak School for the Retarded. After a particularly disruptive marital fight, a Mr. and Ms. B applied to the neighboring mental health center for assistance. In the course of exploring the problem, the psychologist, Dr. Cardahl, noted that they had a son, Randy, aged ten, who was a student at Fairoak School for the Retarded.

Fairoak had never had much to do with psychologists. The school functioned on a pitifully small budget, frequently using parent volunteers in a cooperative way. Over the years the staff had developed ways of caring for many retarded children at a very low cost per child. But this meant that new techniques, sometimes even instruction itself, were unavailable to the children in the rather custodial atmosphere. Staff and parents had developed ways of assuring one another that most cases were "hopeless," and they sometimes resorted to rather primitive practices such as tying overly active children to chairs.

Much of the family's difficulty seemed to revolve around Randy. The Bs loved their son, but at the same time they had feelings that he was less than human, a bitter mistake of nature unjustly inflicted upon them. They viewed his existence as spoiling their lives and ruining their futures, yet they felt guilty about these thoughts and fearful about putting them into words. Randy *was* difficult to live with. He could not control bowels or bladder and he could not talk, but he was physically well developed and very active. He caused extra work and extra expense. Because of Randy, parents, brother, and sisters led a very restricted social life. They felt isolated and ashamed.

Dr. Cardahl's treatment team approached the problem on two fronts. While a social worker offered marital counseling, Dr. Cardahl asked the parents if they would be interested in learning ways to change Randy's behavior. Although the parents politely agreed to meet with him they stated their firm conviction: "He's hopelessly retarded." First, Dr. Cardahl taught the parents some of the basic elements of social learning theory, using a programmed instruction book. Next he taught the Bs to observe the child's behavior. This involved breaking a behavior sequence into specific units, such as: child is destructive—father disapproves—mother yells—child ignores parents. Dr. Cardahl's long-range goal was to teach the parents to observe and to control the responses they made to Randy. Along the way many other discoveries were made. For instance, in watching herself interact with Randy on closed-circuit TV, Ms. B counted fifty-one requests and commands that she made in a 20-minute period—almost like background noise for the child. Realizing what she was doing, Ms. B became more careful about making such requests, changing their nature, and reducing their frequency.

Through instruction related directly to Randy and the home situation, the Bs developed new ways of looking at Randy's behavior. After they learned that they could produce even a minor change in his behavior on their own, their fatalistic, negativistic attitudes subsided, and they put more effort into learning behavior-modification techniques, such as keeping graphs and charts, and thinking up new reinforcement strategies. One of the hardest parts of their experience was to think of even a few things to get Randy to do more of. Most of their concern had always been that he stop or do less of the various things that displeased them.

A major difficulty was obtaining the cooperation of Randy's teacher at Fairoak. She felt that the Bs had deserted the Fairoak group in favor of a newfangled treatment in which the children "don't get the love they need." Dr. Cardahl began the long, slow process of offering the teacher some new ways of dealing with problems. Coolly received at first in her classroom, he began by explaining his interest in Randy and seeking the teacher's help in the treatment plan. From this they moved on to ways in which the teacher might find the psychologist's techniques useful in the class as a whole. However, after several months, Dr. Cardahl still reported that while changes had occurred for Randy and the Bs, there was really no change at all in Randy's class at Fairoak.

In this case the psychologist used his knowledge of the learning process to train parents and teachers to initiate procedures that would improve the functioning of a difficult child, at the same time enabling them to become happier and less anxious themselves. He succeeded in accomplishing his objective with the parents but not with the teacher.

Millie, an attractive runaway. Millie had run away and spent several nights with her boyfriend. She wasn't yet sixteen, and her parents were in a turmoil. They remained calm enough to be able to make agreements with her over conditions for her return home from the juvenile detention facility, but then they had no idea of what to do next. Her father suspected, although without much evidence, that the boyfriend's father, himself in deep marital trouble, had abetted the children and furnished them with liquor. The parents immediately forced Millie to submit to a vaginal examination, changing their rationale from a "pregnancy check" to a "VD check" to satisfy the physician. The examination did not end their distress, and Millie's parents, long-time churchgoers, turned to their pastor for answers to a tumult of questions: What has gone wrong? Where have we failed? What should we do now?

The pastor, sympathetic to youth and a "turned-on mental healther," undertook the job of counseling the family. He soon found that while her parents were reasonable enough, Millie manifested some impenetrable hostility of a particularly aggravating, challenging sort. Irritated, fascinated, he pressed on into a crash program of counseling; seeing parents, Millie, and all three for many hours a week. After deciding to release his own mounting anger at Millie in an attempt to get through her pouting, picking, correcting, and muttering, he discovered that she could be a scaldingly vocal and formidable adversary. With her quick slashing tongue, she was capable of making him look incompetent by quoting him out of context.

The pastor called a clinical psychologist in private practice to request that Millie be tested. The psychologist noted the minister's curiously deep involvement in the case. He indicated that a psychological report could be available to the minister only if Millie's father would request testing and sign a release of information. This the father did.

The psychologist first interviewed Millie and her parents, and after the three had been briefed on what to expect, Millie was tested. The psychologist then suggested possibly arranging another meeting to talk about the findings. The psychological assessment revealed Millie's unhappiness; she thought badly of herself and had a pervasive authority conflict and considerable distrust of older people, especially authority figures. She seemed, in short, a rather typical early-delinquent girl. Through his findings and through his observations of this quiet, shy, yet attractive girl who seemed so much in need of help, the psychologist began to piece together a picture of someone who would attract help from parent figures, and would then disappoint them or let them down.

Recommending a course of action for Millie became only part of the psychologist's task. He also tried in a friendly way to help the minister become aware of his lack of caution and his need to behave differently on the basis of increased knowledge. The psychologist was able to include some "pointers" such as "Millie is the kind of person who makes unwary helpers feel they can give her special help or be like parents to her. She cannot now meet the needs of such people. . . ." The report emphasized that the running away episode was only one ripple in an ongoing stream of family interaction. Other topics mentioned included possible courses of action, possible areas for counseling, and possible ways to build clear, unambiguous understandings between parents and daughter. Requirements for the type of relationship that would be needed to reach some of the goals were added, so that the minister and parents could make informed decisions and work toward Millie's emancipation and toward harmony with her in the future.

Here we see the psychologist mainly as an evaluator of persons and family relations. Using his specialized tools to find out what comprises an individual's personality, he could describe this girl in terms that would enable others to act in constructive ways toward her. He attempted to improve the quality of the help others in the community were giving her.

Marie, a depressed and desperate woman. Marie had grown up as the oldest child of a large farm family. Her father was a cold, austere German, interested in amassing more farm land and running the family as economically and efficiently as possible. Her mother seemed to be either sick or busy with a new baby most of the time. Consequently, Marie became the hardworking housekeeper for the family. When she married John Williams at an early age, she continued this role, keeping a neat house, devoting herself to the care of her three children, and finding little time for enjoying the "frivolities" of life. Her husband, whom she found attractive because he had the warmth and conviviality she lacked, became increasingly dissatisfied with her overattention to household and family work, and started to go out more and more on drinking bouts with business friends.

In her early fifties Marie found herself essentially alone. Her children had grown up and left home. Her husband was working or out with his business friends most of the time. She had no friends of her own. In the next few years, things became worse. She began to think that her husband was gone so much because he had found someone else. She suspected a certain secretary at the office. When on one occasion she saw the secretary buying a present in a men's clothing department, she thought her suspicions were confirmed. Still, she did not want to question her husband because she feared he might become angry. For a time she turned to prayer and for a time went to church every day, but this did not erase her fears. As she grew increasingly depressed and distracted, she did not want to leave the house. All day she lounged around in a bathrobe. She let her gray hair become straggly and began to have trouble getting to sleep. She thought that there was something wrong with her stomach, perhaps a nameless disease, cancer or worse, and ate very little. Mr. Williams, aware of this gradual change, tried different things—encouraging her to go out, buying a new television set, praising any moves she made toward improving the house. When sometimes he became angry, she would just look away. He got sleeping pills for her when she refused to go to the doctor herself. She, however, became more and more disturbed. She roamed the house at night and in her desperation would sometimes wake him up. She started saying that life was not worth living. When he failed in all his attempts to get her to see a physician or go to a hospital, Mr. Williams finally inquired from the county health department as to how he might force his wife to see someone. They suggested that he sign commitment papers. When he did so, she became extremely angry, since the act confirmed her fears that her husband was trying to get rid of her so that he could marry his secretary. Mr. Williams then called an ambulance. His wife was overpowered, given a sedative, and taken to the county psychiatric ward.

The psychiatric examination resulted in a diagnosis of involutional psychosis, and a course of electroconvulsive therapy was prescribed. After twelve treatments Marie was much more relaxed and less concerned with her worries. While on the ward, a psychologist invited her to participate in a group therapy meeting, where she became acquainted with other patients her age who were also suffering from loneliness and despair. Although she said little in the group, she felt some interest in the patients. She began to pay more attention to her appearance. After she was dismissed she continued to return to the community hospital for group therapy every week. With the encouragement of her therapist, she became involved in some of the ladies' groups at her church. Gradually, Marie again began to find a place for herself in life.

In this case the psychologist did not play a role in the decision on the initial treatment of a person with an acute emotional disturbance, but came into the picture after that stage was past, as a therapist or specialist in bringing about personality improvement through stimulating constructive associations with other people.

A program for chronic patients. Every day the patients on the locked side of Ward 3, a 120-bed psychiatric ward in a veteran's hospital, were visited by the psychiatrist, psychologist, the social worker, and the head nurse, leaders of the ward's treatment team. The psychologist, Dr. Q, watched some of the patients coming out of acute phases of their disorder and progressing to the unlocked side of the ward. But some patients never seemed to change. There was a hard-core group, most of whom had been in the hospital for more than ten years. Dr. Q decided to try something bold in an effort to induce change in some of these patients. Drawing on his knowledge of small-group interaction and behavior modification, he proposed a program for the patients. He proposed forming a group of six men. The group was to do a task and be rewarded according to the group's performance. The proposal was received with considerable skepticism by the rest of the staff, mostly because Dr. Q proposed that this small patient group undertake a complicated and lengthy project *and* that they be responsible for their own attendance.

How, other staff members asked, could a group of chronic patients like these possibly avoid making a complete mess of hospital grounds if they tackled the job of building masonry cold frames (which are like foundations of small buildings) for the horticulture department? And as if the building of the cold frames were not enough, Dr. Q actually proposed that these men cast their own masonry blocks, starting with dry materials. He began by listing carefully all that his proposal involved, such as its general scope, contingencies for handling troubles of various kinds, a defense of the basic rationale, possible locations for the cold frames, and so on, and then he set about winning approval from the chief psychologist, the ward team, the hospital administration, the other staff who would be involved (such as teachers of crafts and gardening and hospital engineers), and, finally, from the patients themselves.

After many weeks of slow administrative preparation, the small group began to function. Each week a member's money and passes depended on how well the group had done. Progress was slow and irregular, but gradually the pile of acceptable blocks grew large enough to begin the digging and leveling for foundations. Despite more objections from the staff, Dr. Q insisted that the group do the site alignment and leveling on their own after receiving instruction. At about this time, one of the group "leaders," who had shown rapid progress in taking responsibility and motivating less responsive patients, went on extended absence from the hospital. Another group member then became increasingly apathetic. This threatened to wreck the group because his decreased productivity reduced group rewards. In Dr. Q's weekly meeting with the group, he stressed only that the group knew what the consequences of working or not working were. Despite prophecies of doom from other staff members, he did not change the group rules. Ultimately the group restabilized, accepted replacements for members who had obtained discharges, and finished six cold frames some nine months after starting. Of the ten patients who had been members of the group at various times, four made unpredicted and substantial gains. One resident of fourteen years was able to get along in a halfway house outside using his own funds, and three others improved somewhat. In the remaining three patients no lasting gains were apparent.

Dr. Q would have preferred to have carried out a more scientific experiment using carefully measured criteria for improvement, as well as examining in more detail the project's differing effects on patients with different types of pathology and personal histories. But this project was a minor addition to his other duties. Furthermore, it is always difficult to do rigorous research within ongoing treatment programs. Despite its shortcomings as a publishable investigation, Dr. Q felt that the effort had been worthwhile even for the patients who gained only the dignity of a temporary improvement in their functioning within the hospital.

What the psychologist was doing primarily here was to try out an idea he had about how some people usually considered hopeless might be helped, thus increasing the basic knowledge upon which his efforts and those of other psychologists rest. Although not rigorous and well controlled, the project was essentially research. Even though it was difficult, the psychologist managed to initiate a process that could lead to innovation and improved service to patients.

Introduction to Allen, a troubled young serviceman. Allen Ward was unable to perform his duties effectively because either he was nervous, irritable, and jumpy, or else he was dopy or sleepy. His sergeant wanted to punish Allen, but the commanding officer—with whom Allen worked closely—decided to send him to a neighboring mental health center so that no disciplinary or psychiatric entries would blot Allen's record. Allen's contact with the clinic, his history and treatment, are dealt with in some detail in Chapter 6.

Jonathan, Randy, Millie, Marie, the Ward 3 patients, and Allen are only a few of millions of people who have varying needs for psychological assistance. For a more complete picture we would need to mention many more, such as the following: Harold, a pedantic and withdrawn high school student who was diagnosed as schizophrenic; Vera, a middle-aged woman who had become an alcoholic; Mick, a rebellious adolescent who had been arrested and brought before the juvenile authorities several times for stealing cars; Margaret, who had such high blood pressure that she had to give up her job and reorient her life; Hank, a former safe cracker, who had become morose and touchy at his prison job; Bill, an adolescent heroin addict; Sally, a little brain-injured girl who was having a hard time learning to read; Johnny, who had severe asthma that appeared to be of psychogenic origin; and a group of university students who want to learn better social skills. There are many, many more of all ages showing disorders of all degrees of severity, coming from all kinds of families and backgrounds, and manifesting all kinds of talents and abilities. They are seen in a variety of settings and receive many different types of service from the psychologist and his colleagues.

SETTINGS, CLIENTS, AND ACTIVITIES OF THE CLINICIAN

The vignettes seem to have very little in common, at least as far as the role of the clinical psychologist is concerned. In addition there are many other roles played by clinical psychologists in the broad sense, including many counseling psychologists and related professionals with graduate training. (For an examination of training and relation to others performing similar services, see the last three chapters of this book.) The rest of this chapter is designed to serve as a useful intermediate step toward the system to be developed in later chapters. Using this intermediate framework, we locate the clinician's professional life along three general dimensions, the *setting* where he works, the actual *activity* he carries out, and the *clients* he serves. The examples illustrate several different combinations:

	Setting	Client(s)	Activities
Jonathan	Mental health center	Town's pre-school children one at a time	Screening, case finding
Randy	Mental health center and day care center for mentally retarded children	Retarded boy's parents and his teacher	Teaching behavior-modification skills, consulting
Marie	State hospital	Depressive adult	Group therapy
Millie	Private practice	Resource person and his client	Assessment and consultation
Ward 3	Veteran's Administration Hospital	Group of long-term (chronic) patients	Designing and operating a small-group program

As a lively and growing profession, clinical psychology has been entering a wide range of settings, client groups, and activities. Each of the three dimensions is subdivided in terms of traditionally acknowledged roles and responsibilities, but can make room for others about which all psychologists would probably not agree. The scope and limits of the settings, groups, and activities will be considered in turn, as we get an overview of the profession's movements in recent years.

Diversifying Settings

The number of settings in which clinical psychologists work has increased in recent years. Beginning with child guidance clinics, mental hospitals, and psychiatric facilities, especially veterans' hospitals, psychologists have found their way into all the various mental health facilities. Private practice settings and university psychology clinics and counseling centers are well established. Clinical psychologists have moved into mental retardation facilities, correctional institutions, and agencies working with juvenile delinquents. Settings have been expanded to include alcoholic treatment centers. Moving in another direction, some clinical psychologists have gone into industrial consulting, assisting with the evaluation of executives and the improvement of functioning organizations. This list of settings, although not exhaustive, illustrates the diversification among settings which has occurred. Older notions that the clinician was employed where there was concern with "mental problems" may have to give way to a newer notion that clinicians work in settings where there is concern about human resources and maximizing human potential, interpreted very broadly.

One minor feature of settings to be noted at this point is that the setting determines whether we use "patient" or "client" when referring to the person we seek to serve. Medical settings have historically used the term "patient"; hence settings related to medicine, or employing physicians, or those which "treat" individuals generally follow the "patient" tradition. Counseling centers and community agencies or any setting that is seen as being involved *with* the person rather than treating him, tend to prefer the term "client." In this book we shall most often use the broader word, "client."

Expanding Clientele

One might characterize recipients of the clinician's services simply as people—singly, in pairs, or in larger groups. This broad formulation would not always have been appropriate. In the past an overwhelming majority of clinical psychologists' efforts have consisted of direct service to single individuals. A few clinical psychologists have gradually moved from concern with a single client, a patient whom they saw face to face, to a concept of a group of people as the client. Couples and whole families can be clients of the clinical psychologist, whose aim may be to change patterns of interaction within that small social-psychological system. Client groups with more members may include school classes, all the patients in a physician's practice whom their doctor considers to be disturbed, or psychiatric wards. The clinician has come to expand his concern to very large groups, such as the delinquent children of a particular county in consultation with large organizations or in working for change in procedures and laws. Similarly, a mental health consultant to a state board of education might view his ultimate client group as "all the children of my state." Although, in one sense, the board of education is his client, the psychologist must think of the needs and possibilities of the larger clientele of the organization if he is to serve them well.

Expanding Activities

One of the first answers the man on the street might give if asked what a clinical psychologist does would be "testing." In former decades giving, scoring, and interpreting tests—summarized by the term *assessment*—took up a major part of the psychologist's time. After World War II, psychologists became accepted as therapists. They also engaged in research activity, which was heavily emphasized in their training. Roles have been further expanded by such factors as broader definitions of mental health, increasing emphasis on public health, and new treatment approaches derived from learning theory. It is now an accepted conclusion that the clinical psychologist should contribute wherever his skills prove useful.

In recent years there has been increasing emphasis on *consultation.* Consulting is an activity that takes many forms (and involves the clinician in a multitude of settings, such as schools and physician's practices). We distinguish between two major kinds of consultation, *case-directed* and *program-directed.*

Case-directed consultation. Case-directed consultation, sometimes called clinical consultation, has two distinct subdivisions: *consultative service*, which involves direct service to the client or patient, and *practitioner consultation*, with which the clinician only contacts a resource person (the consultee) about the patient. For an example of the first kind, a patient is referred for a psychological examination. The psychologist interviews him and administers tests, subsequently communicating his findings to a psychiatrist who has asked for the information. As an example of the second variety of consultation, a minister might ask for discussion and critique of his plans for dealing with a parishioner who is disturbed. The clinician confers *only* with the minister, and never sees the patient in question. Distinguishing between consultative service and practioner consultation turns out to be important in practice because so many more people can receive services through practitioner consultation than through consultative service.

Program-directed consultation. Program-directed consultation occurs when the objective of the consultation is to establish or improve a *system* rather than to help a particular individual. For example, a clinician might be asked by a school principal to review and comment on the way in which his school handles children with behavior problems. A good deal of consultation begins as consultative service, and, through the agency's developing trust in the clinician, moves toward program consultation. The major consultation is most frequently provided by psychologists working in private practice, consulting firms, and community mental health settings, but the institutional psychologist also consults in connection with the design and implementation of programs of treatment and training and the evaluation of such programs. Dr. Q's work with the Ward 3 patients illustrates a small-scale program. A larger one might be to help design a program to reduce the recidivism rates of a state's institutions for delinquent youth, one that would be feasible and politically acceptable. Frequently the program designer has to be especially skilled in his dealings with both professionals and nonprofessionals from other disciplines because he must earn their support and share their concerns if he expects them to operate the new program with conviction and dedication.

As clinicians get older and more experienced, the community tends to invite and pressure them to become administrators and teachers and to give up direct service to clients. Clinicians often become supervisors of clinical students or teachers in nearby universities—activities that are readily accepted by most clinical psychologists. But the role of administrator that frequently beckons the senior clinician may elicit less enthusiasm (a phenomenon we shall examine in more detail in a later chapter). As a group, clinicians do not seem sufficiently sensitive to the tremendous impact

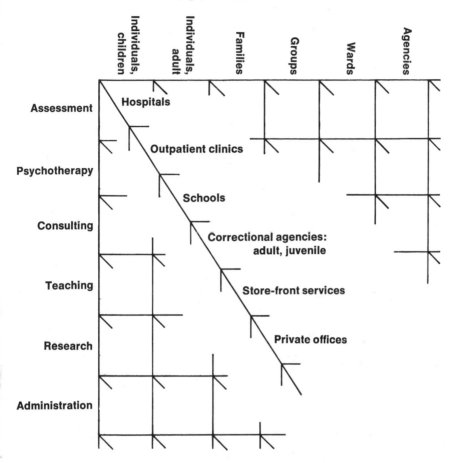

FIGURE 1-1   Settings, clients, and activities in the work of clinical psychologists.

administrative decisions have on patients. Whatever his preferences, the clinician can look forward to opportunities to move into teaching, supervision, or administration. One survey (Goldschmid et al., 1969) reported that 21 percent of clinical psychologists spent more than one third of their time in one of these three activities.

Frequent Setting–Client–Activity Combinations

The foregoing paragraphs have briefly suggested some of the settings, some of the activities, and some kinds of clients with which clinical psychologists may be concerned. Figure 1-1 illustrates many of the kinds of SCAs. The uncompleted three-dimensional cube of settings, clients, and activities prompts us to see a range of possible combinations and to think of the present and future extent of each dimension. It is important to recognize that every activity cannot be carried on in every setting with every client. Each setting, each activity, and each client may have a likely "mate" on one or both of the other dimensions. Consultation and programming, for instance, are activities suited to clients consisting of large groups. Mental retardation settings are most likely to call for activities based on one particular perspective, such as behavior modification; service to low-income clients who are sufferers from psychological crisis is likely to have strict requirements for setting and location, if the clients are to avail themselves of the service.

What, then, are the most frequently occurring setting–client–activity combinations? Surveys of the work settings and practices of clinical psychologists begin to point to some general answers, although they are ambiguous in two ways. First, surveys have examined setting and activity dimensions, but have not ordinarily addressed themselves to the question "Who is the client?" Second, the complexity of the sampling task makes it hard to generalize about results. Any survey that aims to ascertain what clinical psychologists are doing, and within what settings, necessarily reflects some of the characteristics of the particular sample surveyed. Differences between samples on matters such as geographic location, age, and educational attainment of respondents may account for rather different overall survey results.

One survey (Beier, 1973*) found that 100 University of Utah clinical psychology Ph.D.'s reported their positions as follows: universities, 27 percent; postdoctoral fellowships, 8 percent; research, 20 percent; private practice, 8 percent; service positions, 25 percent; and community agencies, 12 percent. Rather different results from a sample somewhat more representative of clinicians in general in age range and geographical distribution, came from a study by Goldschmid et al. (1969), who reported the settings of 241 members of the division of clinical psychology of the American Psychological Association engaged in full-time work. They were: private practice, 28 percent; college or university, 17 percent; community clinic or hospital, 16 percent; university medical center, 11 percent; other, 11 percent; Veterans' Administration, 10 percent; state hospitals, 7 percent. As for percentages of their time given to various activities, Goldschmid and his colleagues reported that individual psychotherapy took up the most, with 34 percent of the sample spending one third or more of their time in this activity. The next most frequent activities are research (12 percent) and teaching (11 percent), followed by administration (6 percent), supervising (4 percent), and consulting (3 percent). These data showed that a clinician seldom spends more than one third of his time in any one activity and also that a variety of activities (diagnostic interview, objective tests, projective tests, consulting, teaching, research, supervising, administration) are participated in by more than 60 percent of the respondents.

*Personal communication.

Trends

One way of assessing trends in the field from surveys is to ask such questions as: What are the respondents now doing that they were not trained for? What training do respondents now say they wish they had had? The Goldschmid study indicates that many more clinicians are involved in community psychology family therapy, and behavior therapy than had received training in these areas. Goldschmid's respondents indicated that their training in "treatment procedures as preparation for current work" was less than adequate. The survey concluded by noting the increasing tendency to utilize group and "systems" approaches directed at the family and the community. The authors felt that their results reflected the need for training programs to provide a broader base of theory and methods to help psychologists meet the problems they face at the organizational level of intervention. Comments of respondents to Beier's Utah survey similarly mentioned the lack of community mental health courses, and requested greater emphasis on social action.

It is difficult to assess the degree to which the social, community, or systems orientations are becoming accepted by psychologists in mental health settings. The Chicago survey of mental health professionals by Henry et al. (1968), for instance, showed that only 8 percent of the clinical psychologists designated their therapeutic orientation as "social–community." The accompanying classification of job activities did not include consultation. On the other hand, some newer mental health centers have made it plain that they intend to function mainly as consultants and to minimize direct services (e.g., psychotherapy, casework) by their professionals. Such centers benefit their community primarily through community organization, systems improvement, and consultative skills.

The preceding sections have cast the professional roles of the clinical psychologist into a scheme of setting, client, and activity (SCA). They have suggested how diverse the combinations of SCAs are, what the most frequent ones require, and how they are changing over time. Besides the influence clinical psychologists themselves have in shaping the SCAs open to them, powerful factors in society operate to determine what settings, clients, and activities will emerge. These factors play a large part in determining what the training, the behavior, the interests, and the paychecks of clinical psychologists will be like.

SOCIAL FACTORS DETERMINING SCA PATTERNS

This section will discuss some of the social factors in our complex social fabric that facilitate or limit the development of SCAs. Such a list cannot be exhaustive, but it illustrates how diverse are the influences that determine the career patterns available to clinical psychologists.

Legislation and Government Programs

The enactment of laws and the activities and decisions of branches of the government influence SCAs in several ways. The first is by *what they provide*. Several movements have been launched through the enactment of federal and state laws in the United States. The extensive and diversified mental health center network, for example, occurred as the result of the "bold new approach" championed by the late President Kennedy. Similarly, state laws and state budgets control a high proportion of SCAs in mental hospital, mental retardation, and penal systems, and affect others by their provision of matching funds for various federal and foundation programs. Yet another example is the creation of the National Institute of Mental Health, the United States Public Health Service, and Veterans Administration programs, organizations which, because of their "purse string" functions, exercise extensive control over many of the research and training aspects of clinical psychology. On the state level, the provision of jobs for psychologists in state institutions is related to legislation, administrative conception of programs, and civil service definitions of positions for psychologists.

Second, legislation influences by what it *prohibits*. Laws about behavior have the effect of creating a pool of behaviors that stand out, namely, those behaviors which have been defined as illegal. The various law-making bodies considering such behavior provide an array of reactions to the offender: "punishment," "cure," or "rehabilitation." Putting these solutions into effect creates a variety of SCAs, in prisons, parole and probation offices, and mental hospitals. Because of the ways laws are written, there will be work with child abusers and homosexuals, and there will be evaluative research. We can see how arbitrary the client pool and the SCAs created by legal prohibitions become when we imagine what would happen, say, to all those youths referred as "emotionally disturbed" because of marijuana involvement, if marijuana were declared legal.

Third, legislation influences by *what it defines*. The definitions contained in legal statutes have a bearing on the SCA picture. Definitions of mental illness and mental retardation determine who will be found in the respective institutions. The public laws defining veteran status and eligibility for veterans' benefits affect the Veterans' Administration SCA by defining the population and even by having something to say about what may happen to eligible members. The definition of eligibility for welfare services, shifting with the politics of the country, makes certain psychological services available for some people but not others.

Fourth, legislation influences by *what it permits*. The private practice of clinical psychology is regulated in many states by certification or licensing laws that fix the requirements for legal recognition of psychologist and state what a person so recognized may call himself and do. Many states protect the confidentiality of what clients tell clinicians as they do with ministers and physicians; others do not. All states do not permit psychologists to prescribe drugs or carry out somatic treatments which are the prerogative of physicians.

Professional Role

What the clinical psychologist does, and where and to whom he does it, depends to a considerable degree on what he means to the others on whom he depends most vitally, on other professionals and administrators. He cannot simply declare what he wants his role to be: his notion of his role must be reasonably similar to the ideas others have in order for many types of employment situations to exist at all. For example, on the "psychiatric team," a term usually denoting a psychiatrist, a psychologist, a social worker, and perhaps a psychiatric nurse working in an in-patient or out-patient setting, notions of who leads the group are rarely open to question (the leader is usually the psychiatrist), and many other aspects of treaters' roles are fixed and defended. For instance, it is the nurse who will give the medication and the social worker who will see the family. A central question, then, becomes: What services is the psychologist *seen* as being able to give? The perspective others have of him influences not just his role on the psychiatric team but the kinds of referrals that will be made to him in almost any setting. Should we hire a psychologist in this setting? Is this an activity a psychologist could do? Is this an appropriate group for a psychologist to work with? That psychologist in private practice—what services can he give that would help patients and families in my pediatric practice? All these are questions that do much to determine SCAs for psychologists and depend a good deal on the perspective others have of clinical psychology. Just as laws change and evolve, so does the role of the psychologist vis-à-vis other professionals. Psychologists realize that they depend in many ways on being seen as useful members of the network of helpers. It is up to the psychologist to develop a variety of ways of keeping co-workers' ideas of clinical psychology up to date.

Professional role is influenced by the factor of economic rewards. Most of what psychologists do are services for which they will be paid (although typically they also do some voluntary work). They tend to work in settings where someone, clients or employer, will provide a competitive combination of income, fringe benefits, and job security. The traditional laws of supply and demand, of people going where the perceived reward is greater, account in large measure for the fact that several sectors of clients, such as the poor, the retarded, and the antisocial, have been so short of psychological services. When we look at the impact economic factors have had on the development of our field of knowledge over the span of several decades, we can see that the well-developed areas have had a sound economic foundation; other areas are unexplored because they have been able to provide little in the way of economic support.

Professional Peer Pressure

A good deal of the professional life of the psychologist is regulated or codified by boards of professional affairs, state licensing boards, and the like. For instance, a psychologist might like to serve in a ghetto-area storefront clinic, if clients could know beforehand that his fees are only $2 per hour. The psychologist considers that fee low enough to be afforded by everybody needing service and high enough to make clients feel they are not receiving charity, but if most psychologists in other areas are working for $25 an hour, there may be a need to contend with their reactions; it is likely that such problems can be solved, but they do need attention. Peers also monitor ethical practices, a topic to be covered in detail in Chapter 20.

Location of Training, Location of Practice

Training institutions usually have their own particular perspectives, directions of interest, and special emphases. Midwestern universities have been associated with the phrase "dustbowl empiricism," for instance, while many Eastern institutions have emphasized psychoanalytic theory. Moreover, in the community of professional practice, norms may vary widely. Long-term psychotherapy, for instance, might mean more than the standard four-year classical psychoanalysis in one area of the country and more than three months in another. Certain areas of the country prefer particular theoretical orientations, such as Freudian or Sullivanian. Setting—client—activity combinations are thus somewhat dependent on geographic factors as they relate to a "local culture."

MAJOR DIFFERENCES IN SCAs

Prevention Versus Remediation

As elaborated in Chapter 2, clinical psychology grew up in settings where persons with deviant behavior were treated. It naturally focused on helping individuals to return to a state of better functioning, that is, remediation. As will become apparent, vast bodies of literature have sprung up around this task, which have occupied a central place in clinicians' efforts. More recently, however, epidemiological studies such as Srole et al. (1962) and Leighton (1959) have begun to indicate how very prevalent various psychological disorders are in the community. Srole, for instance, indicates that up to one-third of Manhattan children are in need of some kind of psychological services. Plainly, there is neither manpower nor funds to remediate with present methods even a fraction of these children. One approach to problems of this size is the preventive or public health method, in which group-administered procedures are used to prevent problems from arising. An early example of the public health approach came from London, where a well on Broad Street was passing contamination and disease to its users. Authorities controlled the problem by removing the handle from the pump. In an analogous fashion, the report of the Swampscott conference on community psychology (Bennett et al., 1966, p. 1) said: "Today the mental health frontier is shifting from the treatment of illness to its prevention, and to the positive promotion of mental health. Increasingly, the mental health professions are delivering services to the community—not just responding to the onset of pathology." Although there are now many voices proclaiming the usefulness of such methods in psychology, the question of just which mass procedures to apply in preventing which psychological problems is only just beginning to be studied systematically.

The concept of prevention rather than remediation is persuasive, even pressing, because of the size of the task and the relatively few trained personnel available. But a central problem in using preventive approaches for psychological difficulties is that effectiveness is difficult to demonstrate. Are there fewer marital crises or child-rearing problems among those who, as students, had had some kind of preventive intervention, such as a class, some group work, or some sessions with a counselor? At present we cannot begin to answer such questions.

Another problem for prevention lies in the political realm. Programs aiming to limit the number of children born to demonstrably inadequate mothers, programs attempting to guarantee rudimentary rights of infants, programs trying to help emotionally deprived marriage partners meet each others' needs without producing emotionally deprived babies—all of these would seem manifestly reasonable and worthy efforts to prevent psychological problems. Yet each runs into difficulties over some aspect of legally guaranteed individual freedoms. Preventive programs can sometimes be construed as taking sides in conflicts between the interests and values of individuals and those of larger social groups, or between one social or political group and another. Widespread public support for preventive programs is thus often difficult to obtain.

Nonetheless, if there is any orderly and predictable onset for even a few psychological difficulties, it would seem only reasonable that clinical psychologists give more attention to clients whose functions are currently unimpaired, but who have been shown to be highly vulnerable to psychological difficulties. Psychologists must try to use available techniques to prevent problems from arising rather than to wait for pathology to show up so that they can treat it. In their research they must work on identifying and preventing conditions in individual, family, and community systems which are later associated with mental health problems.

The central problem for remediation is the often-cited fact that manpower presently available constitutes only a fraction of what would be needed to meet present needs. Some observers have noted that with present methods of utilizing manpower, proposed programs can scarcely be staffed at all. Furthermore, the evidence indicates that the persons who are going without services in the present situation of partial coverage are in general those who are poor members of minority groups, and those with the more severe disorders.

In addition to the practical difficulties involved in applying remediation strategies, there is another issue inherent in the use of such strategies. Do people use services more often because the services are available? Do more "problems" appear because more people to "cope" with them come on the scene? Ryan (1969) points out that the number of mental health professionals in the Boston area is several times the national average. The use of mental health services seems to be more a part of the Boston way of life than it is in many other cities. It is incumbent upon such services to show that they are doing more than encouraging public dependency. In short, there would seem to be reason to think that the system of help which is offered may influence the perspectives and the behavior of the people who will use it. For all of these reasons it is important for the clinical psychologist to recognize that there are extensive social and cultural components in the definition, discovery, and presentation of psychological problems.

If we leave the familiar clinical world of remediation and enter the relatively uncharted areas of prevention and public health we must approach our tasks in a different manner. Many of the assumptions underlying traditional clinical-counseling programs seem to stand in opposition to the public health and preventive approaches, especially when the traditional programs emphasize the diagnosis of underlying disorders and when preventive approaches may involve social action. But it seems that many of the traditional skills, such as interpersonal sensitivity, assessment skills, and research competence, are essential in community settings as in other kinds of programs.

All varieties of intervention cannot be adequately summarized within the simple dichotomy of prevention and remediation. There is, for instance, the question: How *much* change does the intervener hope to see once an intervention is instituted? Another issue is how *committed* is the professional to achieve changes in the patient? Yet another concern might be: At *which stages* of disorder process does the intervention apply?

In practice, discussions about prevention and remediation may be affected by the public pressure for increasingly obvious results. Did program X decrease the number of chronic patients in the hospital? Does a detached worker decrease juvenile delinquency and committment rates from his area? Are the patients you return to the community more productive and better adjusted than before they came to your agency? Criteria are increasingly pragmatic, and much of the remediation that is currently used seems to be closer to amelioration—making a problem somewhat better—than to "cure" of a condition.

The press to meet these publicly identified needs and meet them as effectively as possible seems to have led to a variety of techniques. For the most part, these involve both prevention and remediation. Service to people in crisis is a good example. Emergency services, always a requirement of a federally supported community mental health center, and increasingly offered in the general hospital, are in a way a compromise between prevention and remediation. Plainly the problem or crisis need some remediation, but the early detection and intervention and more persistent follow-up is also designed to *prevent* further disorganization or decompensation and to minimize the disruption in the patient's family system.

One purely ameliorative technique that aims to meet needs effectively is that of *management*. Management connotes taking the kind of action that will elevate or maintain the client's level of functioning without assuming that the client's need for service will thus be ended. Gurel (1967) argues for the management concept in schizophrenia. It is, in fact, being put to use by several mental health centers, which maintain many otherwise chronic patients on medications and provide assistance and guidance in various aspects of living, especially employment. Another example of the management technique is the stabilization of heroin addicts on methadone, a procedure that does not cure the addiction but removes the need for money to buy heroin, and provides an opportunity for social readjustment.

Figure 1-2 summarizes many of the things we have been discussing. Along the bottom, points of disorder and positive functioning are indicated. Along the vertical axis, different kinds of psychological assistance range from keeping full-blown impairments minimal to creating opportunities for highly effective functioning. The three lower forms can be roughly related to the useful distinctions of Caplan (1964) about kinds of prevention, which, however, focus on breakdown and disorder. The encircled clinical activities illustrate the range of disorder and well-being over which they extend.

We can see that prevention and remediation are not necessarily opposing activities, rather that they both form part of the patchwork of problem-centered or pathology-centered approaches to service. We must keep in mind that not all of clinical psychology is concerned with problems or pathology. Some psychologists ask simply: How can things be made better for people? Figure 1-2 is an attempt to remind us that there must be a place in our

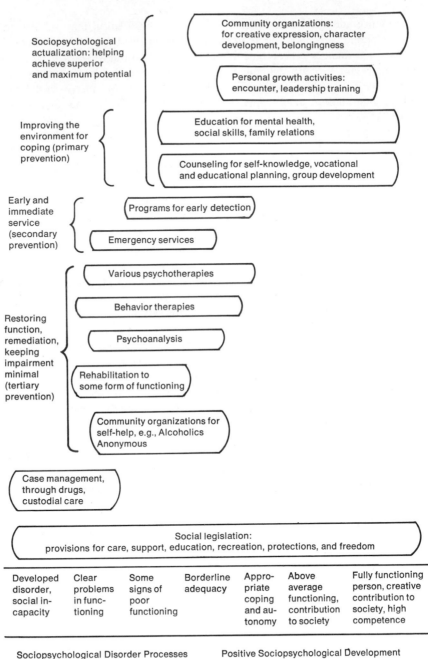

Sociopsychological actualization: helping achieve superior and maximum potential {

Community organizations: for creative expression, character development, belongingness

Personal growth activities: encounter, leadership training

Improving the environment for coping (primary prevention) {

Education for mental health, social skills, family relations

Counseling for self-knowledge, vocational and educational planning, group development

Early and immediate service (secondary prevention) {

Programs for early detection

Emergency services

Restoring function, remediation, keeping impairment minimal (tertiary prevention) {

Various psychotherapies

Behavior therapies

Psychoanalysis

Rehabilitation to some form of functioning

Community organizations for self-help, e.g., Alcoholics Anonymous

Case management, through drugs, custodial care

Social legislation: provisions for care, support, education, recreation, protections, and freedom

Developed disorder, social in- capacity	Clear problems in func- tioning	Some signs of poor functioning	Borderline adequacy	Appro- priate coping and au- tonomy	Above average functioning, contribution to society	Fully functioning person, creative contribution to society, high competence

Sociopsychological Disorder Processes In Patients and Clients

Positive Sociopsychological Development In All Citizens

FIGURE 1-2 Breadth of concern of various forms of psychological assistance.

thinking for activities that aim to enhance the quality of life, to improve people's assets to help them define their identities, and to encourage them to use their potential boldly. A person might recover from one of the severe psychological disorders such as schizophrenia and still not be very adequately developed psychologically. The statement "Mental health isn't the opposite of mental illness" is another way of pointing out the differences, although those terms are themselves somewhat ambiguous. Viewed in the light of Figure 1-2, the prevention-versus-remediation issue concerns itself entirely with processes of breakdown and disorder and, as such, misses the broader issue of improving psychosocial functioning for everyone, the processes indicated on the right half of the diagram. Clinical psychology's traditional closeness to medicine seems to be largely responsible for the problem-centered approach, while the emerging concepts about enhancement stem from such sources as learning and development theories, counseling psychology, humanistic psychology, and the broadened concern with organizations and community systems.

Voluntary Versus Nonvoluntary Clients

The distinction between setting—client—activity patterns designed to prevent disorders, and patterns that emphasize the remediation of disorder, can easily be exaggerated. An important distinction more often ignored is between SCAs serving voluntary patients or clients and those serving nonvoluntary patients or clients.

The framework of laws within which we all live permits each of us a great deal of latitude in our conduct—for instance, in deciding what we shall buy. When it comes to obtaining psychological services on a voluntary or self-interest basis, people have demonstrated a willingness to select for themselves from a diversity of approaches: psychoanalysis, extended psychotherapy, encounter groups, and sensitivity groups, to name only a few. As long as vendors and purchasers agree about their respective roles (and remain within legal and ethical limits) we acknowledge their right to contract with one another for psychological services, chiropractic treatments, religious retreats, or extended dancing lessons. The psychologist selling his services to voluntary consumers seems to be bound not only by legal and ethical codes but also by the nature of his arrangements with the client.

However, not all who receive psychological services do so voluntarily. The court-committed patient at the state hospital is an obvious example. Boys in a forest camp for delinquents whose supervisor has decided on a particular psychological group experience for them, or welfare mothers whose caseworker wants them to form a therapy group with a psychologist—these people are also to a degree involuntary participants. In families coming to clinics, one member, such as the child, may come against his will.

What principles guide psychological services in such cases? Plainly, the legal and ethical considerations always apply, but the client, in the most extreme case, has no say about what is to be done with him. Mutual understanding about service between psychologist and client may be impossible. The psychologist's responsibility thus becomes divided between the involuntary recipient and the agency that is contracting for the services.

Similarly, we can mention the "visibility" of the psychologist's potential assistance to clients. The psychologist invariably favors a particular perspective or activity and his certain special competence. He may feel, for instance, that "being in touch with your own values" is good, or that "working through the transference" is at the core of good service, or he may like to organize and conduct particular kinds of groups. But if the client cannot agree that he wishes such treatment, and if the employer has hired the psychologist for a general task, such as "make psychotic patients better," is the psychologist free to "do his thing?"

Our basic viewpoint is that the burden on the psychologist in such a situation is an exceptionally heavy one. For one thing, he should explain the planned procedures to the client and obtain his self-generated motivation as much as possible. He must also be aware of the behavioral criteria toward which he encourages his clients, because it is usually by some behavioral criterion that they first lost their freedom. The criteria of positive mental health, although rather arbitrary and poorly agreed upon, do assert that the first goal of helping services should be to promote freedom of choice, usually acknowledged to be an essential human characteristic. It matters little in such applied tasks whether the patients "worked through the transference," "encountered each other," or whatever. The important question is: Were they more effective in the community afterward? Did our intervention move them toward being equal to peers who had not spoken incoherently, stolen a car, or gone on welfare?

We must remember that our theoretical ideas were developed as ways to understand and to help people. In serving the involuntary client we must continually check the effectiveness and efficiency of our methods in doing the task most needed—restoring autonomy and effective functioning in the community. Only clinical research, particularly research on the effectiveness of programs, will provide the psychologist with a guide for services to nonvoluntary clients. Only through such knowledge can he remind himself that he isn't just "doing his thing."

We should keep in mind that when an agency requests or authorizes particular services, the request or authorization may reflect only things like willingness to pay the psychologist, or the agency's traditions. The psychologist always bears the burden of examining the worth of his service. We should keep in mind also, if keeping our focus on purely empirical evidence seems objectionable, that the other major method of determining the worth of a service, professional consensus about what constitutes good practice, involves some rather severe pitfalls. In medicine, good practice has included a host of activities which, when examined systematically for their actual effect upon the client, were found to be sadly wanting. Bloodletting, for example, was sustained by professional consensus until empirical knowledge of its effects discredited it.

The clinical psychologist must be increasingly prepared to deal with nonvoluntary clients who have not suffered any loss of civil freedoms. Nonvoluntary clients show up in many settings, such as a school system whose superintendent has decided that a particular psychological group experience would be good for the school principals. The principals may attend unwillingly only because they know that not attending might seriously jeopardize their professional standing. In this example, the loss of freedom arises from the principal's subordinate position in a hierarchy, not from a behavioral deficiency. Nonetheless, the psychologist is responsible for telling such clients about the procedures so that they can react by their own "informed judgment," and only if the psychologist has empirical data is he in a position to be fully responsible to the involuntary clients involved in his particular offering or program.

For further elaborations of settings, clients, and activities and for current discussions of developments in clinical psychology, the reader is urged to see the journals and books listed in Appendix A. Of special importance are the *American Psychologist* and *Professional Psychology*.

SUMMARY

Clinical psychologists in the 1970s are doing a wide variety of things. The framework within which these diverse concerns can be classified is a three-dimensional structure of settings, clients, and activities. In recent years the number increased greatly, to include agencies and organizations broadly concerned with the development and utilization of human resources as well as clinics, hospitals, and mental health facilities. The number and variety of clients has increased to include organizations and large groups as well as individuals and small groups. In recent years there has been increasing emphasis on consultation. Consultative service, in which the clinician carries out a service to the patient, can be distinguished from practitioner consultation, in which he provides information or advice to another professional person about a client, or attempts to establish or improve a whole system or organization. Surveys have indicated that some SCA combinations occur much more frequently than others. Social factors that influence the emergence and development of SCAs are legislation and government programs, professional roles as defined partly by other professional persons, peer pressures, and training programs. The major distinctions that can be made among SCAs have to do with whether the objective is remediation or prevention and whether the clients are voluntary or involuntary. Many of these considerations about the work of psychologists and the developments in the profession will be taken up again in the last chapters of this book.

SUGGESTED READINGS

Kaplan, B. (ed.). *The inner world of mental illness*. New York: Harper & Row, 1964.

Kaplan presents thirty-one accounts of the experience of psychosis and other forms of mental disorder. In the introduction, Kaplan asserts that the patient's experience is worthy of study, not as something foreign to himself but as a meaningful action he has chosen. Among the several reports from former mental patients are excerpts from the famous books by Clifford Beers and William Leonard. Another source of personal accounts of coping and adjustment is Peter Madison's book (1969) on personality development among college students; in this book a perceptive psychologist analyzes the autobiographies of students. Literary accounts of various forms of neurosis and psychosis are presented by Rabkin (1966) in twenty-eight selections from authors such as Kafka, Dostoevsky, Shakespeare, Sartre, Cather, and Proust. Rabkin points out that literature sometimes produces a greater understanding of people than psychological reports do because writers strive for the creation of an emotive richness and subjective wholeness, whereas psychologists seek to be analytic and objective.

Among other excellent personal accounts, see Goethals and Klos, *Experiencing youth* (1970). A patient and her therapist both present their views in *Mary Barnes: Two accounts of a journey through madness* (Barnes and Berke, 1971).

Rotter, J. B. *Clinical psychology*, 2nd ed. Englewood Cliffs, N. J.: Prentice-Hall, 1971.

This short book is a good brief introduction to those who have little knowledge of clinical psychology. It answers the public's oft-raised questions about the difference between psychologists and psychiatrists and about the nature of the clinical psychologist's work. It discusses clinical psychology as both an art and a science and raises questions about the validity of current practice. There is a brief introduction to Rotter's important social learning theory.

Lubin, B., and Levitt, E. E. (eds.). *The clinical psychologist*. Chicago: Aldine-Atherton, 1967.

Lubin and Levitt present a useful variety of topics ranging over history, training, roles, interprofessional relations, ethics, and international aspects of clinical psychology. The reader will find many of the fifty-one articles by leading clinicians excellent background for this chapter and subsequent ones.

Cowen, E. L., Gardner, E. A., and Zax, M. *Emergent approaches to mental health problems*. New York: Appleton-Century-Crofts, 1967.

This book has an unusually good collection of chapters describing new programs in the middle 1960s. Of particular relevance are the chapters at the beginning and end summarizing the issues and trends in the field of mental health. The book covers such topics as manpower needs and programs, college students as companions for the mentally ill, neighborhood services, and prevention programs in the schools.

Shoben, E. J. Toward a concept of the normal personality. *American Psychologist*, 1957, *12*, 183—189.

Shoben presents a way of thinking about personality that does not have psychopathology as a central focus. He works toward a model of integrative adjustment characterized by self-control, personal responsibility, social responsibility, democratic social interest, and ideals.

Sarbin, T. R., and Mancuso, J. C. Failure of a moral enterprise: attitudes of the public toward mental illness. *Journal of Consulting and Clinical Psychology*, 1970, *35*, 159—173.

The authors assert that the mental health movement has failed to sway the public to view mental illness and behavioral deviancy with the same nonrejecting valuations as somatic illness. Although the public tends to reject persons diagnosed as mentally ill, it is more tolerant of deviant behavior when not described with mental illness labels. Labeling people as mentally ill is an enterprise at odds with established ways of handling deviancy in the community.

For a critique which argues that the public does accept the medical model, see Crocetti et al. (1972). Sarbin and Mancuso give a rejoinder (1972).

The American Psychologist and *Professional Psychology*

These two journals are the major resources for the background and development of the clinical profession. *The American Psychologist* is the major voice of the APA and is issued to all members. *Professional Psychology*, which started in 1969, devotes itself to " . . . applications of research, standards of practice, interprofessional relations, innovative approaches to training and to the delivery of services." A majority of articles spell out aspects of settings, clienteles, and activities of psychologists. As an illustration of new areas psychologists need to enter, see David's discussion (1970) of population planning, counseling, and consultation. See Appendix A for a listing of many other journals relevant to clinical psychology.

chapter 2

The Evolution of Clinical Psychology

In the first chapter we looked at the settings, clientele, and activities of clinical psychologists as they are functioning in our time. In this chapter we will explore the origins and contexts within which clinical psychology developed. We can view the profession as having evolved like a plant or animal in an ecological system—nourished by its environment and contending with adversities. Such an exploration should give us a sense of the external and internal forces that shape a profession and should help us understand present conditions and anticipate future developments.

A LONG PAST, A SHORT HISTORY

In these days of rapid change, it helps to remember consistencies and to feel a kinship with earlier times. Whether we look at 1920 or 1890 or 300 B.C., we find men faced with many of the same problems, adjusting to their environments and coping with social pressures. Technology and social organizations look radically different now, and man lives longer, but there is little or no evidence to indicate that modern man differs biologically from his ancestors, and it appears that people have always had the same kinds of personal and family problems as we have now. The Greek and Elizabethan plays speak to us today as they did to our predecessors hundreds of years ago. The *Panchatantra*, a collection of animal fables from India that antedated Aesop, with such folk wisdom as the story of the fox and the grapes, reminds us that people used psychological defense mechanisms and played interpersonal games in those times as well as now.

Still today's ways of promoting mental health and providing other human services differ dramatically from the counsel given at Delphi, the medieval trials of witches, and the shaman's rituals. One of the differences is that we now have science-based professions such as clinical psychology. This specialty is one of several "helping professions"—social work, psychiatry, clinical psychology, and related professions dealing with problems of human behavior. The fortunes of clinical psychology have been bound up with those of the other human services as man has changed his concepts about altering disturbed behavior and improving the quality of life. The decision makers at different times have allocated the analysis and treatment of behavioral problems to different segments of society—sometimes to religious leaders, sometimes to educators, and sometimes to medical men.

In this brief overview of the historical development of clinical psychology, we hope the reader will catch something of its great motivating forces. Sometimes these forces reflect humanitarian and rational trends in the prevailing religions or philosophies. Sometimes they relate to the exciting thrust and counterthrust of theoretical assertions uttered by bold personalities. Sometimes they are related to the invention of new techniques, such as tests or therapeutic procedures. Sometimes they result from organizational efforts within the profession or related professions. Always these motivations relate to the surrounding context and "spirit of the times," the *Zeitgeist*, with its enthusiasms and sociopolitical forces and its great events, such as war and depression, which control the allocation of rewards both monetary and psychological.

Modern scientific psychology and its clinical subdivision officially began in the latter part of the nineteenth century. However, they grew out of deep roots in the past, as Figure 2-1 suggests. The words "psychology" and "clinical" have Greek origins. "Psychology" comes from "psyche," the word for soul or mind, and "logos," the word for reason or thought. "Clinical" comes from "kline," meaning bed, and "klinikos," the adjective pertaining to bed, and then through the Latin and the French, and thus signifies the sickbed and the personalized medical teaching that occurs in places where the sick are treated.

Throughout the centuries, many great thinkers, beginning in classical Greece with Thales (born 640 B.C.), developed the scientific ways of looking at man and nature that became the foundation of twentieth-century psychology. Aristotle (born 384 B.C.) would be considered the first psychologist because of his observations about sensations and thought, although the word "psychology" was first used in the sixteenth century by a German, Melancthon (LaPointe, 1970). Throughout the centuries, also beginning in Greece with Hippocrates (born 460 B.C.), philosopher—physicians developed a medical approach to abnormal psychological phenomena that eventually superseded the prevalent supernatural and demonological approaches and made it possible to apply scientific knowledge to the treatment of the deranged. Weyant (1967) argues that Lycurgus, the king who instituted the high discipline of Sparta, was the father of applied psychology—the first systematic behavior modifier. The historical record is anything but an account of steady progress. During some periods, such as the era of superstitions that followed the collapse of Greco-Roman civilization, only a few enlightened thinkers held to scientific conceptions. But the ideas survived even in the heyday of witchcraft trials during the fifteenth and sixteenth centuries, and eventually they reemerged. The rational and libertarian ideas leading to the American and French revolutions also produced humanitarian figures like Pinel, who removed the chains on mental patients at La Bicêtre in the 1790s.

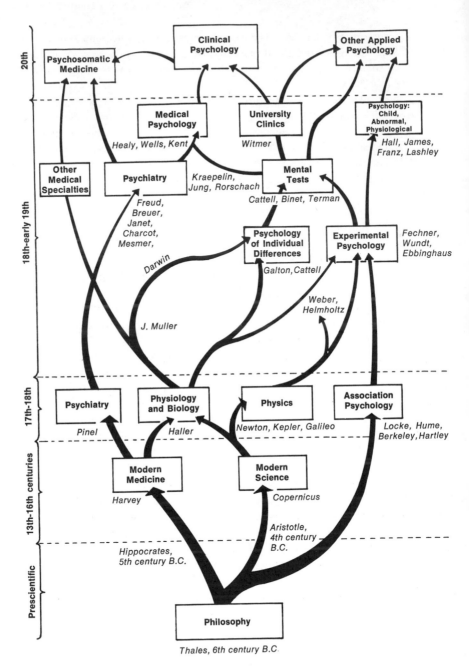

FIGURE 2-1 Major fields and persons leading toward clinical psychology. (From Sargent and Mayman, 1959, p. 1713.)

We cannot go into this long prehistory of clinical psychology and psychology here. Those who are interested can turn to Boring's (1950) history of psychology and the books mentioned in Suggested Readings at the end of the chapter. We take up our account at the time when clinical psychology began to take shape as a separate profession, the closing years of the nineteenth century.

In the nineteenth century the groundwork was being laid for the emergence of many new forms of human activity. Three broad developments defined the *Zeitgeist*. One was the emergence of "modern" society, characterized by large organizations and increasingly bureaucratic and impersonal relations in many areas of life. Traditional family ties and identifications with villages and the land were disrupted as people migrated to the cities, to work in factories. Governments and social organizations took on new responsibilities to handle the physical and psychological disruptions industrialization had produced.

The second was the firm establishment of science particularly experimental science. Putting their faith only in demonstrated evidence from observations, physicists, chemists, biologists, and many others were building a respected and promising corpus of knowledge. Helmholtz, Fechner, Galton, and others began to formulate systematic psychological laws. The credit for the first psychological laboratory went to Wilhelm Wundt in 1879 at Leipzig. William James, about this time, started a demonstration laboratory at Harvard.

The third aspect of the nineteenth-century spirit was the beginning of a general cultural and intellectual reorientation in European and Western life. The dominant model for looking at man in the eighteenth and early nineteenth century, the concept of a liberal, rational, simply hedonistic individual, was recognized as increasingly inadequate to explain human behavior. The romantic movement in art, architecture, music, and literature was one reaction. Intellectuals by the end of the century were interested in the irrational and the perverse, incorporating primitive symbols, images, and myths in their thinking, and exploiting such mysteries as hypnosis—man's psychic hinterland. In this exciting climate of search for new human territory and for new modes of human service, clinical psychology was born.

THE PERIOD OF ESTABLISHMENT, 1890–1919

The Spirit of the Times

The turn of the century was a time of ferment, reform, and social creativity. Almost all the basic concepts, methods, and organizations of clinical psychology have their origins in that period—psychoanalysis, behaviorism, community efforts, intelligence testing, personality inventories, projective techniques, psychological clinics, and the professional organization of psychologists. These developments occurred in a climate of both optimism and outrage. Men and women saw abuses and believed that something could be done to get rid of them.

It was a period of economic expansion and, until 1914, of relative peace. The European countries and the United States established and strengthened colonies and outposts all over the world, bringing back ideas as well as objects of trade. Some men, through fierce competition, were becoming giants of industry and commerce. Inventors startled and stimulated the imagination of the world with the automobile, airplane, and wireless transmission of signals. Artists experimented with new combinations and forms—impressionism, cubism, musical atonality, a wild eclecticism in architecture, the first skyscrapers. In science Einstein's theory of relativity initiated a revolution in physics. Millions saw education as the royal road to improvement of the world and to advancement of individual status. In the United States many colleges were established, and Americans began turning from Europe to their own universities for Ph.D. degrees.

Accompanying this enormous growth were some alarming side effects, such as those reflected in the plays of Ibsen and Shaw. Uncontrolled industry produced sweatshops, exploitation of child labor, company-controlled towns, and monopolies with strangleholds on many areas of business. Natural resources were wasted with little thought of consequences. The migration of Europeans to the United States—over eight million in the first decade of the twentieth century—produced deplorable slums in New York and other major cities. Many city governments were controlled by corrupt bosses. These conditions, together with the optimistic belief that it is possible for man to improve his lot, laid the ground for many reform movements. Some took a legal and political shape—antitrust and child labor laws. Theodore Roosevelt led the fight for conservation. Merit systems for selecting government officeholders reduced the power of bosses. By the end of this period the feminist movement had succeeded in obtaining the vote for women in the United States. Enthusiastic reformers were also advocating prohibition as a cure for alcoholism.

In this period of activism new social agencies and kinds of human services were developed to meet the problems people saw. Mass education created a need to screen out children who could not profit from schooling, a task Binet accomplished in France by putting together the first intelligence tests. School problems also called for the establishment of special educational services. The breakdown of family life among immigrants contributed to the rise of delinquency, and clinics were established to deal with it. The sexual repressiveness of Victorian times was one of the factors leading to the development of Freud's psychoanalysis.

In the late 1880s and early 1890s, the first settlement houses were started: Toynbee Hall in London, the University Settlement in New York's lower East Side, the Henry Street Settlement and Jane Addam's famous Hull House in Chicago. These places attracted young intellectuals, many of them women social workers and ministers, who lived in the depressed neighborhoods and served in a variety of ways as good neighbors. At this time they were not bound by the constraints of professionalism that later arose. They organized youth clubs, started university extension classes, and worked actively for political reforms. Although psychologists were rarely associated with settlement houses, they can learn much from them. Levine and Levine (1970, p. 73) have written "If history provides any model for the contemporary community mental health movement, it is the settlement house of the Pre-World War I period." The authors indicated that the settlement movement was destroyed by the "antisocialistic" conservatism of the 1920s and the development of more-structured professional training standards.

Following a different approach, Clifford Beers wrote of the deplorable treatment of the mentally ill. He spoke from experience, for he had been confined to an asylum himself. With the support of William James and the famous psychiatrist Adolf Meyer, he launched the mental hygiene movement. He built on the great humanitarian tradition of the earlier reformer, Dorothea Dix, who dramatically, in the middle 1800s, had stumped the United States and Europe for improvement of asylums and prisons. Hers was a style that has not been equaled in recent times.

Development of Clinical Psychology

This period was especially significant in the history of clinical psychology, as it marked the beginning of many lines of development in ideas and concepts, techniques and practice, and organizational arrangements. Table 2-1 summarizes these salient events.

Important books by major theorists—James, Freud, and Watson—came out during this period. Others, by Dewey, Adler, Jung, McDougall, and the early Gestalt psychologists, have also been influential. "Schools" of psychological thinking came into existence, and major issues and controversies arose. The most important of these, perhaps, was whether psychology is the study of mind or the study of behavior.

There were important new tools, techniques, and practices. Binet's invention of the intelligence test, and the adaptation of intelligence tests to group administration by World War I psychologists were major events. Jung's free-association technique and Woodworth's Personal Data Sheet initiated personality assessment. Freud's psychoanalytic technique, with the variations and adaptations other early workers contributed, launched the practice of psychotherapy on its way. The first psychological clinic for children was organized by Witmer. (For reports on its early activities, see Witmer, 1907, and Brotemarkle, 1931.)

The professional organization of psychologists began with the founding of the American Psychological Association in 1892, with an initial membership of thirty psychologists. Clinical psychologists set up a special section of the organization in 1917.

In summary, it can be said that during the period from 1890 to 1919 clinical psychology was established and laid claim to its basic settings, clientele, and

TABLE 2-1   Significant Events for Clinical Psychology, 1890–1919

Historical context	Psychological theory and research	Assessment	Psychotherapy and intervention	Settings and organization
	1890, William James's *Principles of Psychology*	1890, J. McKeen Cattell introduces term "mental tests"		1892, APA founded; G. Stanley Hall, first president
1893, at Chicago World's Fair, Jastrow demonstrates psychological measures				
1895, Marconi invents wireless telegraphy			1895, Breuer and Freud publish *Studies in Hysteria*	
	1896, John Dewey's critique of the reflex arc as unit of psychology			1896, first psychological clinic founded by Witmer
1898, Spanish-American War; Boer War	1898, Torres Straits expedition (Rivers, McDougall, Myers), first study of preliterate people using psychological instruments			

1899, Sharp reviews existing "mental tests," finds them of limited usefulness

1899, Freud's *Interpretation of Dreams*

1900, Teddy Roosevelt elected promising "a square deal," trust busting, conservation
1901, New York School of Social Work started, the first of its kind
1903, First airplane flight, by Wright Brothers

1903, Janet describes psychasthenia

1904, concept of general intelligence, proposed by Spearman

1904, Freud's *Psychopathology of Everyday Life*

1905, first intelligence test, published by Binet and Simon in Paris; Jung's word-association test published

1905, Japan defeats Russia in Russo-Japanese War

1905, "Classes" for mental patients, precursors of group therapy, given by Pratt ard Worcester in Boston

1906, Parsons publishes first book on vocational guidance

1906, Pavlov gives address on conditioned reflex in London

1906, *Journal of Abnormal Psychology* established by Morton Prince
1907, The journal *Psychological Clinic* started by Witmer

TABLE 2-1 Significant Events for Clinical Psychology, 1890–1919 (continued)

Historical context	Psychological theory and research	Assessment	Psychotherapy and intervention	Settings and organization
	1908, Ross publishes first book using term *Social psychology*		1908, Beers publishes *A Mind That Found Itself*, founds first American mental hygiene society	1908, Goddard offers first psychological internships at Vineland Training School, New Jersey
1909, Peary reaches North Pole	1909, Freud, Jung, and Ferenczi speak at Clark University			1909, Healy establishes Juvenile Psychopathic Institute in Chicago
1910, Flexner's Carnegie Foundation critique of medical education in U.S. and Canada		1910, Kent–Rosanoff Free Association Test		
1911, Sun Yat-sen proclaims China a republic		1911, Goddard's version of Binet-Simon test published in U.S.	1911, Bleuler's *Dementia Praecox*	1911, Adler breaks with Freud, initiates Individual Psychology
1912, Wilson elected president				
1913, Ford starts automobile assembly line	1913, Watson proclaims "Psychology as a Behaviorist Views It"			
1914, Archduke assassinated at Sarajevo; World War I begins				

38

1915, German U-boats sink *Lusitania;* Flexner addresses National Conference of Charities and Corrections: "Is Social Work a Profession?"

1917, U.S. enters World War I; Russian Revolution begins; Mary Richards's *Social Diagnosis,* first major book on casework
1918, Armistice ends World War I

1919, U.S. Senate votes against joining League of Nations; Prohibition enacted

1916, Terman's Stanford-Binet test published
1917, Army Alpha and Woodworth's Personal Data Sheet developed for screening recruits

1917, Healy and Bronner organize Judge Baker Guidance Center in Boston

1918, National Community Chest organization established
1919, Section on Clinical Psychology formed in APA

39

activities. It was not on a very firm foundation at this time and had already begun to develop the organizations and training procedures it needed. But psychological clinics had been started in some universities, and psychologists were working in some child service agencies and some mental hospitals. By the end of the period they had demonstrated their abilities to carry on large-scale testing and research. Aside from military work, clients with whom clinicians worked were mainly children, especially children with educational and learning problems and juvenile delinquents, but some work had been initiated with adult mental patients. Psychologists emphasized intelligence testing but they had given some attention to personality investigation. They conducted a great deal of educational guidance. At the same time, some psychologists in Europe were working with Freud to become "lay analysts." All in all, clinicians were well on the way to establishing their professional identity.

THE PERIOD OF CONSOLIDATION, 1920–1945

The Spirit of the Times

If the turn of the century was a time of establishment and reform for clinical psychology, the decade of the 1920s and much of the rest of the period up to World War II constituted a time of consolidation of efforts already begun. The term "Roaring Twenties" applied to an era of speakeasies, the Charleston, bobbed hair, and debates over free love. The term suggests an emphasis on individual expression—not experimental social change. The Great Depression motivated extensive efforts to reduce unemployment through the new programs of the middle 1930s. Social work training and activities were vastly enlarged: a social worker, Harry Hopkins, was prominent in the Roosevelt administration, and the New Deal took up the reform movement which had been interrupted by World War I (Ferguson, 1969, p. 74). With a few exceptions psychologists did not respond to the widespread social needs of the depression as they did to the military needs of World Wars I and II. (The Employment Stabilization Research Institute at the University of Minnesota, organized in the early 1930s, was one notable exception, and E. L. Thorndike's concern for the city in his study of 1939 was a little-noted forecast of the interests of the 1960s). In the United States both world wars were followed by periods of fanatic "Americanism." Both saw the imposition of loyalty oaths to identify "Communists." In the 1920s the Ku Klux Klan terrorized Negro, Jewish, and Catholic citizens in the North as well as the South. In this repressive atmosphere, restrictions on immigration designed to maintain Northern European supremacy were passed, and even labor unions took conservative positions (Levine and Levine, 1970, pp. 232–233). In such an atmosphere there is little enthusiasm for experimental social programs and institutional reform. So, in the main, the 1920s set a conservative tone for clinical developments, leading to emphasis on the treatment of individuals by professionals.

In the natural sciences and engineering, many innovations and discoveries occurred. Insulin was discovered. Viruses were isolated for the first time. Antibiotics and other medicines became available to prolong life. Radios became cheap enough to be very common, even in the homes of the poor. Electronic technology developed rapidly under the stimulus of war support for applied research. In 1939 the atom was split for the first time, and before World War II was over, the awesome power of nuclear fission was used to destroy life on a greater scale than had ever been possible. Detergents, insecticides, and jet planes were developed. Computers began to revolutionize the processing of information.

World War II began after a series of provocative actions by nationalistic dictators. Mussolini came into power in Italy in 1922, Hitler in Germany in 1933. Japan invaded Manchuria in 1931 and China in 1937. Italy attacked Ethiopia in 1935, and the League of Nations, optimistically started after World War I, was unable to do anything except talk. Unprepared or unwilling to fight, the Western powers concurred in Hitler's annexation of the Sudeten borderlands of Czechoslovakia, but in 1939, when Hitler attacked Poland, Great Britain and France declared war. By the end of 1940, Hitler had conquered most of Western Europe, but in turning to the East he was finally stopped deep inside Russia. When Japan attacked Pearl Harbor on December 7, 1941, the United States declared war in both Europe and Asia.

Development of Clinical Psychology

One of the effects of Hitler's racial policies was to bring to the United States large numbers of Jewish intellectuals, among them outstanding psychologists such as Lewin, Rank, Adler, Wertheimer, Kofka, Kohler, Klopfer, and Goldstein. These refugees accelerated the progress of American psychology. Another effect was to increase the emphasis researchers and theorists placed on social and motivational problems, for the Nazi barbarisms showed how thin was the veneer of civilization covering brutal and savage forces.

Table 2-2 summarizes what was occurring in clinical psychology during this quarter century. As far as ideas and theories are concerned, the major development was the greatly increased influence of Freudian psychoanalysis. The ideas of men who had broken with Freud, especially Adler, Jung, and Rank, were also widely circulated. An important theoretical offshoot of Freudian theory was the development of ego psychology, focusing on the aspect of personality that copes actively with the world. Behaviorism became the dominant theory in psychology as a whole, and Gestalt psychology was influential, but their effects were not to be felt strongly in clinical psychology until the next period. Issues and arguments from the previous period persisted.

An enormous number of assessment devices were developed and placed on the market: tests for measuring intelligence, special abilities, school achievement, and personality characteristics. Originated by a Swiss psychiatrist, the Rorschach inkblot procedure was introduced to America in the early 1930s. (See an

TABLE 2-2 Significant Events for Clinical Psychology, 1920–1945

Historical context	Psychological theory and research	Assessment	Psychotherapy and intervention	Settings and organization
1920, U.S. Constitution amended to give women the vote	1920, Freud's *Beyond the Pleasure Principle*	1921, Rorschach's *Psychodiagnostik*		1921, Commonwealth Fund begins demonstration child guidance clinic program
1922, Mussolini assumes office in Italy	1922, Kretschmer proposes typology of three temperaments based on body build		1922, In Vienna, Moreno founds spontaneity theater, Adler starts clinics for problem children and parents	1922, J. McKeen Cattell founds Psychological Corporation
	1923, Piaget's *Language and Thought of the Child*		1924, Mary Cover Jones reports use of behavioral therapy—the case of Peter	1924, American Orthopsychiatric Assocaition founded; Healy, first president
		1925, Gesell's *Mental Growth of the Pre-School Child* 1926, Florence Goodenough's Draw-A-Man		

1927, Lindbergh flies Atlantic; Stalin takes over in Russia

1929, New York stock market collapses, initiating Depression

1932, F.D. Roosevelt elected; launches New Deal

1928, Spranger introduces personality-typology-based values, basis for later inventory by Allport and Vernon

1929, Berger records human electroencephalography (brain waves); Boring's *History of Experimental Psychology*

1932, Tolman's *Purposive Behavior in Man and Animals*

1927, E. K. Strong develops Vocational Interest Blank

1930, Grace Arthur's Arthur Point Scale of Performance Tests

1928, Dreikurs introduces Adlerian family counseling in U.S.

1932, Melanie Klein's *The Psychoanalysis of Children*

1927, Morton Prince founds Harvard Psychological Clinic

1931, first American residential treatment center for children founded, the Emma Pendleton Bradley Home

1931, Clinical Section of APA appoints committee on training standards

TABLE 2-2 Significant Events for Clinical Psychology, 1920–1945 (continued)

Historical context	Psychological theory and research	Assessment	Psychotherapy and intervention	Settings and organization
1933, Hitler becomes Chancellor of Germany; U.S. repeals prohibition; Federal Emergency Relief Administration set up.				
			1934, Slavson starts "activity group therapy," Moreno publishes "Who Shall Survive?" initiating sociometry	
1935, U.S. Congress passes Social Security Act; Works Progress Administration replaces FERA		1935, Christiana Morgan and Henry Murray publish Thematic Apperception Test (TAT)		
1936, Soviet Union abolishes psychological tests		1936, Doll's Vineland Social Maturity Scale; Louttit's *Clinical Psychology*	1936, Cerletti and Bini in Italy develop electroshock therapy	

1937, von Bertalanffy initiates general systems theory; Gordon Allport's *Personality, A Psychological Interpretation*; Anna Freud's *The Ego and the Mechanisms of Defense*; Karen Horney's *The Neurotic Personality of Our Time*

1937, Samuel Beck publishes manual for Rorschach technique; Terman and Merrill publish revision of Stanford-Binet

1937, Moniz of Portugal performs psychosurgery on psychotics; lobotomy introduced to U.S. by Freeman and Watts

1937, Williamson and Darley publish *Student Personnel Work*, describing newly established student counseling service at University of Minnesota; Clinical Section of APA disbanded and American Association for Applied Psychology formed

1938, APA sets up committee on Scientific and Professional Ethics

1938, Hitler takes over Austria

1938, Skinner publishes *Behavior of Organisms*; Murray and Harvard colleagues publish *Explorations in Personality*; Kallmann publishes studies on heredity of schizophrenia

1938, Lauretta Bender introduces Bender-Gestalt Test; Thurstone develops Primary Mental Mental Abilities Test; Buros initiates series of *Mental Measurements Yearbooks*

TABLE 2-2 Significant Events for Clinical Psychology, 1920–1945 (continued)

Historical context	Psychological theory and research	Assessment	Psychotherapy and intervention	Settings and organization
1939, Germany invades Poland; World War II begins	1939, Dollard and Yale colleagues publish *Frustration and Aggression*; American Psychiatric Association develops diagnostic system; Faris and Dunham relate psychotic breakdowns to socioeconomic areas in Chicago; E. L. Thorndike publishes *Your City* 1940, Sheldon's *The Varieties of Human Physique*	1939, Wechsler's Wechsler-Bellevue test; L. F. Frank proposes term "projective techniques" for Rorschach, TAT, Bender, and variety of other personality devices 1940, Committee of psychologists develop Army General Classification Test; Kuder publishes Preference Record 1942, B. Klopfer and Kelley produce scoring technique for Rorschach		
1941, Japanese bomb Pearl Harbor; U.S. enters war; USSR enters war against Germany	1941, Korzybski's *Science and Sanity* initiates semantic therapy			

1942, Carl Rogers's *Counseling and Psychotherapy*

1943, MMPI published by Hathaway and McKinley

1944, Reunification of APA; AAAP disbanded

1945, Connecticut passes first certification law for psychologists; F. C. Thorne founds *Journal of Clinical Psychology*

1943, Hulls' *Principles of Behavior*; Lewin's study using group methods to change wartime food habits; Kanner identifies syndrome of early infantile autism

1944, J. M. Hunt edits *Personality and Behavior Disorders*

1943, Italy surrenders

1945, Germany and Japan surrender; United Nations established

47

account of the Rorschach pioneers by Beck, 1972.) The Thematic Apperception Test grew out of Murray's extensive investigations of personality at Harvard. Projective devices, named such by Frank in 1939, began to proliferate. Assessment became a major activity of psychologists.

The treatment efforts of psychologists, not generally accepted as psychoanalysts because they lacked medical degrees, were still predominantly educational in nature. Child guidance clinics organized during the 1920s and 1930s were generally staffed by teams made up of psychiatrists, social workers, and psychologists; the role of the psychologist was to provide diagnostic testing, interviewing, and educational treatment. During World War II, however, psychologists began to enlarge their therapeutic activities to include hypnosis, psychoanalytically oriented therapy, speech therapy, and reeducation of the brain-damaged. With the publication of Rogers's book in 1941, nondirective, or client-centered, therapy began. The demands for psychotherapy arising from World War II accelerated the movement of psychologists into this field of endeavor.

The place of clinical psychologists in relation to psychologists as a whole changed somewhat with the organization of a separate association in 1937, the American Association for Applied Psychology, and again in 1944 with the reorganization of the APA to include both scientific and professional interests. Professional standards began to be specified, but major developments of training programs, ethical codes, and certification laws did not occur until the next period.

During this important period, clinical psychology had progressed from testing alone to therapeutic treatment, from a major affiliation with education to a major affiliation with medicine, from a concentration on children to a heavy emphasis on work with adults, from the use of assessment indices mainly for measuring intelligence and achievement to the use of many diverse procedures for exploring personality. Clinicians, with whatever school they affiliated, had come to realize that persons are too complex for a simple explanation or single method. Their backgrounds in research and their affiliation with university psychology made for some skepticism about any assessment or treatment technique; they looked for evidence of its effectiveness. The clinician's search for identity was sharpened by both cooperation and combat with the medical profession. A new profession had taken form.

THE PERIOD OF RAPID PROFESSIONAL GROWTH, 1946–1959

The Spirit of the Times

The ending of World War II brought millions of men and women back to their homes or, in the case of many refugees, to new homes. Although there was great celebration and relief that the war was over, the radioactive clouds circulating around the earth from Hiroshima, Nagasaki, and the subsequent atomic tests continually reminded mankind that some human relationships would spell the difference between life and death for all. A few American psychologists responded to the concern about international relations; Gardner Murphy worked for the United Nations, and Charles Osgood did research on international peace and conflict resolution. Later many psychologists participated in the Peace Corps or used Fulbright—Hayes awards to work in other countries. Despite more international knowledge and concern than after World War I, and in spite of the creation of the United Nations, wars continued. The Korean "police action" took the lives of more than fifty thousand American men. At home, fear of communism led to the repressive tactics of Joseph McCarthy and the clamor for loyalty oaths in universities. As after World War I, the nation seemed to combine an antisocialist with an antiintellectual attitude. This changed only when the Soviet Union put the first earth satellite, Sputnik, into orbit in 1957. Then the nation again awoke to its need for scientific development and trained intelligence, and the federal government began to pour billions of dollars into the education of scientists.

The period after World War II did provide fertile ground for the flowering of what has been called the Second Industrial Revolution, marked by the appearance of machines designed to process not energy but information (Rapaport, 1968, p. xix). All wars consume tremendous resources in the manufacture of hardware, but the important difference in military machines of World War II and the subsequent Cold War as compared with earlier wars was the use of complex control mechanisms and related sensing and processing systems. This development was accompanied by related theories—cybernetics and general systems theory.

The 1950s were often referred to as the "age of anxiety." Psychotherapy and psychoanalysis were popular subjects in films. Books about the "organization man" (Whyte, 1956) and the "man in the gray-flannel suit" expressed the sense of restriction and conformity that many people felt despite the general prosperity. Psychologists' studies of conformity showed how readily people accepted the opinions of others. Psychologists also started to study the opposite characteristic, creativity, more extensively than ever before, spurred on by the need to keep up with Russian progress in science and engineering. The public and some professionals also became greatly concerned about the communist "brainwashing" of captured servicemen in Korea.

In the middle and later 1950s some young people reacted against the conformist society. Some participated in the Beatnik movement in San Francisco, the small forerunner of the Hippie movement of the 1960s. Others became activists and worked for civil rights in the South. A landmark in the struggle of blacks for civil rights was the Supreme Court decision in 1954 that ruled "separate but equal" schools unconstitutional. Psychologists like Kenneth B. Clark (later the first black president of the APA), influenced that decision by testifying about the damaging effects of segregation.

Consumer goods were produced in abundance—processed food, home appliances, large automobiles with tail fins, and countless gadgets. The predominant new development in communication, television, was eagerly adopted by the mass of society, creating a whole new way of life. Studies showed that children were soon spending more time in front of what some called the "boob tube" than in the classroom. Some of the consumer goods even became subjects for a new art form—Pop Art—in which common items like soup cans, hamburgers, and toilets were painted or made into sculpture. In the absence of strong industries in other countries after World War II, American factories deluged the world with what was derisively labeled the "Coca-Cola culture." The theatre of the absurd made apparent the meaninglessness and happenstance quality of modern life.

The general affluence led to an increase in the number of automobiles, superhighways, and jet planes. This mobility contributed to the breaking of family ties. The already high divorce rate climbed higher.

In the postwar period both business and science found the fantastic data-processing powers of computers helpful and profitable. Modifications and improvements came at breakneck speed. Psychologists found they could do hundreds of correlations in the time it had previously taken to do one.

The minor emphasis on social reform during this period and the great concern with individual anxieties was accompanied by strong support for traditional mental health services and for training in the helping professions. There was also a great deal of research on the physiological bases of abnormal behavior. Although no real breakthrough occurred, with the possible exception of the discovery of genetic anomalies in mongoloid retardates, a discovery was made that strongly influenced treatment procedures. In 1952 a plant used for folk medicine in India, rawolfia serpentina, was found to yield a chemical, reserpine, which had tranquilizing effects. In the next few years thousands of studies were done on this and other mind-altering drugs, including LSD. For the age of anxiety, tranquilizers seemed to provide an answer.

Development of Clinical Psychology

It was during this period that clinical psychology really came into its own as a profession. Some of the most significant events that determined its shape are listed in Table 2-3. It was a time of intense theoretical, methodological, and professional activity.

Theoretical thinking and research activity brought about some rapprochement between the clinic and the laboratory. There were numerous attempts to bring the dominant psychoanalytic theories, especially as they made an increasing place for ego functions, into alignment with experimental work on learning, thinking, perception, and memory. Important research on sleep and dreaming was carried on. Sensory deprivation, or too little stimulation, was shown to have a damaging effect on personality functioning. Theoretical concepts from sources other than Freudian psychoanalysis also influenced psychologists' thinking. Harry Stack Sullivan, Erich Fromm, Karen Horney, and especially Erik Erikson emphasized social factors in the development of personality. Existentialism began to permeate the thinking of many clinicians who were not completely satisfied with the philosophical assumptions of psychoanalysis.

TABLE 2-3 Significant Events for Clinical Psychology, 1946–1959

Historical context	Psychological theory and research	Assessment	Psychotherapy and intervention	Settings and organization
1946, Congress passes National Mental Health Act	1946, Asch's study of impression formation and social pressure	1946, Rapaport's *Diagnostic Psychological Testing*		1946, APA starts publication of *American Psychologist*; Veterans Administration initiates training program for clinical psychologists
1947, India and Pakistan partitioned, become independent				1947, Educational Testing Service established; American Board of Examiners in Professional Psychology (ABEPP) organized; APA makes recommendations for training programs in clinical psychology, begins examination and approval of programs

TABLE 2-3 Significant Events for Clinical Psychology, 1946–1959 (continued)

Historical context	Psychological theory and research	Assessment	Psychotherapy and intervention	Settings and organization
1948, Truman upsets Dewey	1948, Wiener's *Cybernetics*	1948, Psychologists of the Office of Strategic Services publish *Assessment of Men*; Bell publishes first text on projective techniques 1949, Wechsler Intelligence Scale for Children published		1949, APA holds Boulder conference on graduate education in clinical psychology
1949, Mao Tse-tung and Communists take over in China	1949, Adorno and colleagues publish *The Authoritarian Personality*			
1950, Korean war begins	1950, Fromm's *Escape from Freedom*; Erikson's *Childhood and Society*; first volume of *Annual Review of Psychology*	1951, E. L. Kelly and Fiske publish *The Prediction of Performance in Clinical Psychology*	1950, Frieda Fromm-Reichmann's *Principles of Intensive Psychotherapy*; Dollard and Miller's *Personality and Psychotherapy* 1951, Rogers' *Client-Centered Therapy*	

52

1953, APA publishes *Ethical Standards* and casebook

1956, APA holds Stanford conference on training

1954, Stanton and Schwartz publish *The Mental Hospital*

1955, Frankl's *The Doctor and the Soul*

1952, American Psychiatric Association publishes 2nd edition of *Diagnostic and Statistical Manual*

1954, The APA publishes *Technical Recommendations for Psychological Tests and Diagnostic Techniques*; Meehl publishes *Clinical Versus Statistical Prediction*

1955, Wechsler Adult Intelligence Scale published

1952, Eysenck publishes evaluation survey of psychotherapy; American Psychiatric Association produces first *Diagnostic and Statistical Manual of Mental Disorders*

1953, book of H. S. Sullivan lectures published posthumously as *The Interpersonal Theory of Psychiatry*

1954, Lindzey edits *Handbook of Social Psychology*; Rotter's *Social Learning and Clinical Psychology*

1955, George Kelly's *Psychology of Personal Constructs*

1956, Selye's *Stress of Life*

1953, Eisenhower becomes president; Korean war reduced to a cease-fire; McCarthysm and loyalty oaths

1954, U.S. Supreme Court decides in favor of desegregation of schools

1956, Whyte's *The Organization Man*

TABLE 2-3 Significant Events for Clinical Psychology, 1946–1959 (continued)

Historical context	Psychological theory and research	Assessment	Psychotherapy and intervention	Settings and organization
1957, Russia orbits first earth satellite, *Sputnik*	1957, Hall and Lindzey publish *Theories of Personality*	1957, Cronbach and Gleser's *Psychological Tests and Personnel Decisions*; Gough's California Psychological Inventory; Edwards's *Social Desirability Variable in Personality Assessment*		
1958, National Defense Education Act passed, providing funds for training in counseling and other specialties	1958, Hollingshead and Redlich's *Social Class and Mental Illness*; Jahoda's *Current Concepts of Positive Mental Health*		1958, Wolpe's *Psychotherapy by Reciprocal Inhibition*	1958, APA holds Miami Conference on graduate education in psychology; Albee's *Mental Health Manpower Trends*
	1959, Koch edits *Psychology: A Study of a Science*; Birren edits *The Handbook of Aging and the Individual*	1959, Guilford presents "Structure of Intellect," his theory of intelligence		1959, first APA conference on *Research on Psychotherapy*, reported by Rubinstein and Parloff

54

Tremendous activity occurred also in the area of psychological practice and techniques. There was a great proliferation of new assessment procedures, and the emphasis shifted from the evaluation of intelligence and other abilities to the evaluation of personality. The immensely popular Rorschach method was supplemented by a host of other projective tests in which the subject's free responses to some sort of stimuli were analyzed for evidence about his predilections and problems. Personality inventories were also widely used, especially the Minnesota Multiphasic Personality Inventory. Much of the time and energy of psychologists was channeled into psychotherapy. Although the psychoanalytic orientation and Rogers's client-centered approach were most salient, many other views and practices were tried and publicized.

With all this effort going into assessment and treatment, it was not strange that two skeptical research reports should have struck the profession with the impact of bombshells. Mcchl (1954) brought together research evidence indicating that the predictions clinicians made were not as accurate as those turned out mechanically by a calculating machine using a statistical formula for combining and weighting the data. Eysenck (1952) brought together figures that seemed to show that as many patients recovered from neurotic conditions without psychotherapy as with it. Both conclusions were challenged, and the reports gave rise to prolonged controversy. But they left a residue of deep skepticism about what psychologists were doing. The demonstration by Hollingshead and Redlich (1958) that lower-class people were not receiving their share of the treatment resources generated another kind of discontent.

During this period many important decisions were made about professional standards and organization. Stimulated by the availability of financial support through the Veterans' Administration and the National Institute of Mental Health, the APA initiated procedures for evaluating and approving doctoral training programs in clinical and counseling psychology. In a series of high-level conferences beginning with a very important one at Boulder in 1949 (Raimy, 1950), standards for these training programs were set up. Certification of psychologists for practice was undertaken by the American Board of Examiners in Professional Psychology and by state certifying boards. Increasing numbers of clinical psychologists went into private practice.

The end of the 1950s saw clinical psychology in the United States at a very high point. It was firmly established and growing mightily as a profession. If there were gnawing doubts about the value and validity of its assessment and therapeutic efforts, they did not yet bother the public or most practitioners. During this period, clinical psychology seemed to have accepted the psychiatric medical model. Many clinicians were doing much the same thing that psychiatrists were doing, except for the authorization of hospital commitment of patients and the prescription of drugs and somatic treatments. The doctorate was now the accepted level of training. In taking the medical model, clinicians had vacated much of their earlier concern with schools, children, and educational remediation. Higher prestige and salaries lay with medicine and with private practice than with public education. To some extent the vacuum was filled by increasing numbers of school psychologists, most having only a master's degree. As the demand for psychological services grew in the burgeoning population after the war, colleges of education took more and more responsibility for training, and psychology departments became separated from school programs. Counseling and rehabilitation psychology was also being taught in education and helped to meet the needs for psychological manpower at the doctoral level as well as the master's level. In achieving its high status, clinical psychology seemed in danger of losing touch with education and with lower levels of training. In its emphasis on individual therapy it was losing touch with organizational and community efforts.

A PERIOD OF DOUBTS AND REORIENTATION, FROM 1960 ON

The Spirit of the Times

The ten-year period beginning in 1960 was a hard-hitting decade. Starting with the heady vision of John Kennedy, the United States moved optimistically to attack basic inequities of racism and poverty and, through the Peace Corps, to help other nations. On February 5, 1963, President Kennedy delivered a special message to Congress—"the first occasion where a head of state addressed his country's representatives on the subject of mental health" (Roen, 1971, p. 776). Then war, as it has so often, put the damper on reform. The Vietnam misadventure, along with student protests and rightist—leftist conflicts, tore apart the nation's tranquility and tried its cohesiveness as it probably had not been tried since the great Civil War a century earlier. In the domestic struggles there were also casualties—John Kennedy, Martin Luther King, Robert Kennedy, Malcolm X, and Medgar Evers—all assassinated. Americans could no longer deny what national commissions reported, that the nation was rife with racism and violence.

All these things happened, as if in some absurd drama, while the United States was remarkably prosperous. The annual gross national product reached one trillion dollars at the end of the decade. However, the dollar weakened because of inflation based in large part on the extensive military spending abroad, and major economic moves had to be taken by President Nixon in 1971.

Kennedy's pledge to put Americans on the moon before the end of the decade was realized when Neil Armstrong stepped on lunar soil in 1969. The televised picture of the whole Earth sent back by spacemen became a symbol that Earthmen could not forget—an image of the interdependent system in which we live. As Adlai Stevenson put it (Dubos, 1968, pp. 261—262): "We all travel together, passengers on a little space ship, dependent on its vulnerable supplies of air and soil, all committed for our safety to its security and peace, preserved from annihilation only by the care, the work, and I will say, the love we give our fragile craft."

The image of the interdependent system called attention to the damage being done by those who did not consider the consequences of their actions. The pollution of water and air and even the ocean became cause for alarm before the end of the decade. Fundamental to the problem of pollution are the world population expansion and economic growth. That system image also was in line with the growing concern for the community. The alienation felt by many, especially the young people who did not have ready places in society, led to "communes" and a new "hippie" life style characterized by easy relationships, mobility, relaxed and old attire, and an interest in arts and crafts. The music and long hair of Britain's Beatles became symbols for youth and soon spread around the world. Books on the counterculture (Roszak, 1969) and the "greening" of America (Reich, 1970) proclaimed a new possibility for change in society.

The condition of the alienated mentally ill and the poor cried out for social programs that were more than amelioration for individuals through psycho-therapy or somatic treatment. The "delivery of services," be they medical, educational, or legal, was a major concern during the last half of the decade. The community mental health movement came into being. Compounding the other problems was the severe deterioration of the central parts of cities as wealthy people moved to the suburbs and poor people flocked in.

Another development related to alienation, affluence, and the Vietnam war was the enormous increase in drug usage. The popularity of tranquilizers became translated into other ways of alleviating anxiety—and just plain boredom. Marijuana was used so widely that there was much talk of legalizing it. The use of harder, more dangerous drugs, such as amphetamines and the opiates, also increased; soldiers in Vietnam were able to buy heroin cheaply and some returned home addicts. Major programs to deal with the drug problem came into existence in the early 1970s and new modes for reacting to alienated youngsters, such as free clinics and drop-in centers, were developing all over the country. Many young people, some weary of drugs, turned to fundamentalist religions, mysticism, or Oriental transcendentalism.

In the early 1970s the worries of Americans—and many others in the world, since television carries these worries around the earth—were inflation, war, pollution, the wildness of youth, drugs, violence, and crime. Many Americans seriously looked at their wealthy, technology-based society and wondered how they could have made such a mess of things. Others were more optimistic about the long-established tradition of Americans to be problem solvers as well as problem creators.

Development of Clinical Psychology

Although it is difficult to discuss happenings within a profession while they are still going on, some salient trends can be pointed out. In ideas and concepts,

TABLE 2-4 Significant Events for Clinical Psychology, from 1960 on

Historical context	Psychological theory and research	Assessment	Psychotherapy and intervention	Settings and organization
1960, J. F. Kennedy elected, launches New Frontier			1960, Whitehorn and Betz identify patterns of Strong Vocational Interest Blank responses in therapists who work best with schizophrenics	
	1961, Joint Commission on Mental Illness and Health publishes *Action for Mental Health*; Szasz's *Myth of Mental Illness*; Goffman's *Asylums*			
1962, John Glenn orbits Earth 1963, President Kennedy signs Community Mental Health Act of 1963; Kennedy assassinated		1962, Hoffman's *Tyranny of Testing*		

1964, Johnson defeats Goldwater; Berkeley students protest and riot over free speech; Gulf of Tonkin resolution passes Congress

1965, U.S. initiates bombing of North Vietnam and troop buildup

1968, M. L. King assassinated; Robert Kennedy assassinated; Nixon elected
1969, first men land on moon

1965, Wolman edits *Handbook of Clinical Psychology*

1968, Mischel's *Personality and Assessment*

1969, Rollo May's *Love and Will*

1964, Gerald Caplan presents "crisis theory" in the *Principles of Preventive Psychiatry*; Albert Ellis's *Theory and Practice of Rational-Emotive Psychotherapy*; Schofield's *Psychotherapy, the Purchase of Friendship*; Riessman, Cohen, and Pearl publish *Mental Health of the Poor*

1965, Krasner and Ullman publish *Research in Behavior Modification and Case Studies in Behavior Modification*

1968, Donald Klein's *Community Dynamics and Mental Health*

1965, APA holds Chicago conference on graduate training in clinical psychology; Swampscott conference inaugurates community psychology

1968, American Psychologists for Social Action is formed

TABLE 2-4 Significant Events for Clinical Psychology, from 1960 on (continued)

Historical context	Psychological theory and research	Assessment	Psychotherapy and intervention	Settings and organization
1970, first gene synthesized; students shot in antiwar protests at Kent State and Jackson State; Reich's *The Greening of America*; Toffler's *Future Shock*				1970, George Albee's APA presidential address seriously questions clinical psychology
1971, President Nixon devalues dollar	1971, Skinner's *Beyond Freedom and Dignity*		1971, Bergin and Garfield edit *Handbook of Psychotherapy and Behavior Change*	
1972, President Nixon visits People's Republic of China				1972, S. B. Sarason's *The Creation of Settings and the Future Societies*

recent years have been marked by a decreasing interest in psychoanalysis and a much stronger interest in what research on learning has shown about the direct modification of behavior. One could almost say that B. F. Skinner has replaced Sigmund Freud as the central figure from which clinical efforts radiate. There has also occurred, however, a movement away from scientific theories toward more humanistic approaches, generating such manifestations as encounter groups and the practice of Oriental meditation. Interest in personality theories emphasizing concepts and assumptions rather than habits and behavior is also apparent.

In professional practice there has been a decline in assessment efforts. With the repudiation of the "medical model" of mental illness (discussed elsewhere in this book) it no longer seems important to many psychologists to attempt a diagnosis of pathology by means of personality tests, and there has been increasing public criticism of tests. Assessment techniques based on observation of behavior have gained in popularity. Treatment efforts have increasingly been directed to the improvement of social situations, organizations, and communities, as well as to the modification of maladaptive individual behavior. Community psychology is a going concern. Research in which programs are evaluated has become an important part of the responsibility assumed by some psychologists.

Professional development during this period has been marked by continued growth along with increasing dissatisfaction with the status quo. In the 1960s several new divisions of the APA were organized to serve the particular interests of subgroups of clinical psychologists. Activism became the order of the day, and special political organizations were set up to increase the influence psychologists could bring to bear on decision makers in government.

The decline of the medical model, the uncertain place of psychologists in community work, a general climate of skepticism about professionalism, the questioning of the effectiveness of psychotherapy, and the doubts about the utility of assessment all conspired to raise serious questions about the identity of clinical psychology. These doubts were expressed by George Albee in his APA presidential address in 1970. He decried the heavy influences of both psychiatry and science-minded academic departments on the development of clinical psychology. He called for separate programs, and speculated on the demise of clinical psychology. Other psychologists, less pessimistic about the predominant scientist—professional model, saw the times as an opportunity for many desired changes and the emergence of new forms. Thus a battle raged over the directions the profession should take. In Chapter 20 we shall continue the discussion of the future of clinical psychology.

OVERVIEW OF THE EVOLUTION OF CLINICAL PSYCHOLOGY

As we look back over the history of clinical psychology, several general questions come to mind: What accounts for the rise and growth of clinical psychology? Why is there a greater development of clinical psychology in the United States than in other countries? Why do we have shifts in attention, fads, and ups and downs in the field? What are the sources and conditions for the growth of knowledge and the improvement of practice? What are the "creative tensions" in clinical psychology? Let us explore some possible answers to each of these questions in turn, hoping thereby to contribute to what might be called the "social psychology of knowledge."

What accounts for the rise and growth of clinical psychology? As mentioned at the start of this chapter, answers would certainly include reference to the needs for psychological services generated by the human disruptions in connection with the industrialization and urbanization of society in the last century. Other answers are to be found in the cultural and intellectual *Zeitgeist*, which has raised questions about the meaning of man never pondered in earlier, more traditional times. Here let us look more specifically at clinical psychology as part of general psychology. The emergence of scientific psychology in the last decades of the nineteenth century was part of a worldwide growth of science. Differentiation among branches of science had begun, as it became impossible for men to have detailed knowledge in all areas. Specialization seems to be a rule of growth in a favorable but competitive environment. When psychologists acquired a few useful theories and methods, and let the world know it, society began to ask for more, particularly regarding learning difficulties in school and problems of mental disturbance and behavior deviation. The history of the last century has been the history of rising expectations for education and health, independence from colonial and racist oppression, and freedom from poverty. Governmental actions and revolutions can be seen as ways of coping with people's growing expectations. Less able to rely on traditional family support, people expect public resources to enable them to lead more secure and pleasant lives, and assistance in freeing themselves from anxiety, illness, and other troubles. Psychology has seemed like the science that would help meet some of these expectations. Particularly after World War II, clinical psychology has received sizable governmental support to deal with the problems of mental illness, mental retardation, and delinquency.

Why has clinical psychology developed more in the United States than in other countries? Reisman (1966, p. 355) pointed out that in 1952 it was estimated that there were 18,000 psychologists in the United States, 2,500 in Great Britain, 700 in Japan, and 24 in South America. Berlyne (1968) reported estimates of the proportion of the world's psychologists in the United States ranging from 50 to 80 percent and "a Western European psychologist is not held to have completed his studies or to have won the right to speak authoritatively on psychological matters until he has spent some time at an American university" (p. 447). In many countries clinical psychology is not known as such; physicians carry out whatever work is done with the mentally ill and the neurotic. Henry David, editor of *International Resources in Clinical Psychology* (1964, p. 5), states that "The model of an accredited doctoral level graduate training program with an approved internship, enjoying massive governmental and private support, appears unique to the United States."

Science in general, and certainly applied science, is nested in cultural, socioeconomic, and political values, as viewed by the field called the sociology of knowledge, originated by Mannheim. Gunnar Myrdal (1965) has stated that belief in a scientific knowledge independent of all valuations is naive empiricism. Joan Robinson (1962, p. 1) says, "Economics has always been partly a vehicle for the ruling ideology of each period as well as partly a method of scientific investigation. It limps along with one foot in untested hypotheses and the other in untestable slogans." C. Wright Mills (1943) has argued persuasively that early American sociologists' conceptualizations of social pathology were determined by their reformist value orientations. Since it may be impossible to avoid influence from one's values, it seems especially important to state them as clearly as possible.

Perhaps the preponderance of clinicians in the United States can be attributed to two factors—the strong emphasis on each individual's responsibility for his own welfare, and the country's relative wealth. Influenced by such factors as the individualism of the frontier, the migration of people to this country to achieve freedom, the nature of the Constitution and the Bill of Rights, the Protestant work ethic, Social Darwinism (the belief in socioeconomic survival of the fittest), the breakdown of family life, and the competitive capitalistic system, Americans emphasize the duty of each individual to achieve his own success. They tend to blame the person if he is deficient or deviant in some way, and when he is a trouble to others, they may try to isolate him. Such tendencies are found all over the world, of course, but they may be stronger in this country than elsewhere. The major science concerned with the *individual's* problems is psychology, so it is natural that the country would turn to clinical psychologists and psychiatrists for help. The great wealth of the country has made it possible to support this interest in a sizable way. Berlyne (1968) also attributes American predominance to readiness for change and new ideas, a high level of energy and mobility, the great emphasis on a college education, and the prevalence of philosophies of pragmatism and operationalism.

Despite the fact that this book will naturally draw very heavily on American work in clinical psychology, the writers feel strongly that Americans need to do much more to understand how other countries deal with clinical problems. Brandt (1970) has argued that American psychology reflects American values— especially the emphasis on "doing" rather than "thinking." By avoiding provincialism, people of different backgrounds can learn a great deal from each other and test whether theories and practices generated in one country apply in another. Readers are encouraged to refer to occasional articles in the *American Psychologist* (such as Ardila's on Latin America, 1968; Pandey's on India, 1969; and Whittaker's on China, 1970) and David's reports (1964, 1965), which have brief presentations of the current status of the field in 58 countries. At the time of David's survey, the most highly developed clinical psychology programs similar to those in this country were in Great Britain, the Netherlands, the Scandinavian countries, and Japan. The Soviet Union and other communist countries have emphasized work therapy and social programs as ways of treating disorders. Early Marxists' optimism about the disappearance of mental illness under socialism has not been supported, although it is difficult to make exact comparisons between countries because of differences in definitions of disorder and in record keeping. The heavy emphasis on environmentalism and collectivism in the Soviet Union led to the abolition of psychological tests in 1936 and, as Brozek reports (1969), to weakness in personality theory and research.

Looking over the history of the field, we notice shifts of interest and ups and downs in the growth patterns of parts of the field. Why do these occur? We have noticed that there is a periodic resurgence of some issues—nature versus nurture in the development of intelligence, interest in introspection and perception versus interest in behavior, organic versus environmental causation of schizophrenia and other mental illnesses, concern with individual versus social influences. Dallenbach (1955) compared the popularity of psychoanalytic theory in the 1950s with the popularity of phrenology a century before, emphasizing the cultlike nature of "science." Levine and Levine (1970), Simon (1970), and Reiff (1970) think shifts occur mainly in response to the general sociopolitical climate—whether it fosters reform or conservatism. During reform periods, we try to change society's institutions. We have seen that this occurred before World War I, during the middle and late 1960s, and, to some extent, in the middle and late 1930s. In each of these instances strong support for reform was given by American leaders. All three reform periods have ended in connection with wars—the two world wars and the Vietnam war. Both the reform periods and the war periods provided support for psychology, but the nature of psychologists' activities changed. During reform periods there has generally been a branching out into nontraditional work, especially work with the schools and with social agencies; in more conservative times, clinicians have moved closer to the individualistic and medical model. Reiff upbraids psychologists for responding much more to war than to social needs. William James long ago called for the invention of a moral equivalent to war, noting that only war had been found to motivate entire societies.

Another of the most persistent influences has been the growing self-regulation and professionalization of psychology through training, certification, and development of publications and other means of communication. This general change probably leads to more conservatism. Clinical psychology has more property to protect, so to speak; private practices on which people are economically dependent must not be threatened; public grants on which many state employees and college professors are dependent must be maintained. The growth of the organization itself puts a restraining force on change, but also makes the profession a more dominant factor in the national picture of change or maintenance. Without the strength obtained by professional affiliation, the psychologist would probably be even more dominated by the social institutions, medicine, and industry.

Trends, if not faddism, are evident in the rise and fall of certain areas of psychological publication (Louttit, 1957). We have seen one obvious trend in the rise during the 1940s and 1950s of projective techniques and the relative decline of intelligence tests (Sundberg, 1954, 1961). "Ins" and "outs" in research topics occur, not necessarily in response to rational proof or disproof of theories or hypotheses, but also in response to other influences of considerable power. In academic circles, where advancement in rank is at least partially determined by the mandate to "publish or perish," research workers often scramble into areas where a quick payoff may be expected rather than settling down to attack long-range or complex problems. In colleges of arts and sciences, where clinical subjects are lacking and there are hordes of "captive" students, it is not surprising that short-range studies and problems requiring normal, verbally competent, and middle-class subjects predominate. When a new laboratory is set up or new sources of financial support become available, changes occur in the kinds of problems that are attacked. Frequently scientists decry the over-emphasis on applied research, believing that this leads to neglect of basic research, but the direction from which important additions to knowledge will come is not always determined along such a simple dichotomy as applied versus pure. For instance, Lewin's study during World War II of the influence of group discussion in shifting the meat-using patterns of housewives (1943) had definite consequences in the future development of social psychology. The kind of situation in which the clinical psychologist works naturally has an influence on the selection of research topics and even on the outcome of the research. In one of a very few studies of the social psychology of clinical research, Levy and Orr (1959) analyzed the origins and the findings of 168 studies of validity in the Rorschach test over a five-year period. They found that studies emanating from academic settings, as contrasted with clinical settings, were oriented toward the testing of theories or constructs more than toward relating results to practical criteria and that higher validities turned up in the construct than in the criterion studies. Levy and Orr concluded that it might be very profitable to launch a general investigation not only into processes of research as it is conducted in various settings, but into the biases and personalities of the researchers, and into the pressures and ideologies to which they may be subject.

A more extended analysis would reveal many other influences on the growth and shifts of interest and attention in clinical psychology—public acclaim through literature, television, and films; the differential recruiting of new psychology students from different segments of society; the special interests of powerful individuals, such as President Kennedy's concern for mental retardation; the stimulus given to research and practice by the development of usable and interesting laboratory techniques or tests; the number and nature of conferences psychology holds; and the cultural lag between discoveries and theories and their acceptance by the profession in general.

One final question we will consider is the nature of the sources of new knowledge and improved practice. Do influential new developments in clinical psychology come from inside or outside the field? Do they come from basic science? It is clear, of course, that changes in clinical psychology come from many sources. The fortunes of the field are bound up with psychology in general, with psychiatry and social work and the mental health movement, with education, and with many of the other major organizations of society. The question of internal versus external influence is related to questions previously discussed. As the field grows it becomes more internally controlled; as the general climate of the country shifts it becomes more liberal or more conservative in its outreach. If one looks at other professional groups, one sees similar issues and protests. The impression is that the general orientation with regard to the application of knowledge is strongly determined by the surrounding world; certainly financial support and psychological interest play a big part in what individual investigators and practitioners think. But the methods and manners of application seem to come more from the history and present capability of the field. When projective techniques were popular, there were many Rorschach studies of different forms of mental illness. Now it is behavior-modification technology that is being developed. Occasionally the rare individual strikes out in a new direction and gathers adherents for a new view.

The question as to whether basic or applied research plays a primary role in the advancement of clinical psychology cannot really be answered. Clinical psychology must depend on both. The direction of the flow of knowledge is not one way, from basic to applied. Skinner's work on basic research with animal learning led to operant learning theory, which stimulated the behavior-modification movement. But the work of Freud and of Rogers in the consulting room with clients led to new theoretical formulations and research. Both kinds of research, and more of both, are needed.

Progress in any field reflects the creative tensions under which it operates. Clinical psychology is not a static, rigid structure; it is being pushed and pulled as it moves in its environment. For clinical psychology one major challenge to problem solving is the never-ending urge to be both humane and scientific—to be understanding and empathic but also objective and long-ranging in thought, to be the involved artist but also the detached researcher. This tension arises repeatedly in the APA's conferences, in which the scientific—professional model is attacked and defended. It is reminiscent of the dialectic which William James discerned in all of psychology (and all of science for that matter) between the tender-minded and the tough-minded. The tender-minded romantically seeks "something more" in life—meaning, soul, understanding, wholeness. The tough-minded declares that life is "nothing but" material things, mechanisms, atoms, reflexes, stimuli, and responses. In clinical psychology we see the tensions of assertion and counterassertion between humanists, existentialists, and growth group enthusiasts on one side and behaviorists, strict environmentalists, and organic psychophysiologists on the other. We cannot help but feel that this condition is a healthy one, promoting vigor and a lively scrambling for evidence in an exciting and evolving field.

This brief overview will, we hope, stimulate the reader to give more thought to how a field gets where it is. If we understood history and the cultural context of a field better, we would be able to discern today's hidden agendas, our unstated assumptions, the active trends, and the unfinished business of our time. Furthermore, we might discover that earlier times have confronted similar problems in a way that could give us some insights for dealing with our present dilemmas.

SUMMARY

After noting origins in Greek thought and the setting of the stage for the development of clinical psychology in the nineteenth century, we have explored the evolution of the field through four periods: 1890 to 1919, 1920 to 1945, 1946 to 1959, and from 1960 into the early 1970s. The period of the turn of the century was characterized by a reform spirit and a blossoming of many basic theories in psychology, of which the work of Freud and his followers and the initial proposals of behaviorism by Watson have proved to have the longest effect on the development of clinical psychology. During this period, too, Witmer established the first psychology clinic at the University of Pennsylvania in 1896, coined the term "clinical psychology," and initiated many programs that anticipated much of the subsequent activity in the field. The American Psychological Association was established in 1892. The period of social reform was largely closed by World War I and was succeeded in the 1920s by a conservative trend, which did not, however, prevent the development of individualized treatment, especially in child guidance clinics, and the proliferation of intelligence tests growing out of their successful usage in World War I. In the 1930s projective techniques began proliferating as well as some personality questionnaires. During World War II psychologists were very active in a wide variety of psychological activities. In the postwar era clinical psychology supported by VA and NIMH training funds grew enormously and became the largest division of the APA. Psychoanalysis and projective techniques were now in their heyday. The utility of both psychological assessment and psychotherapy were attacked seriously by Meehl and Eysenck, respectively, whose publications engendered vigorous debate and numerous studies. In the 1960s clinical psychology saw the decline of traditional assessment and the rise of behavior modification. Psychologists responded to the *Zeitgeist* by becoming socially active and developing a lively new area called "community psychology." Clinical psychology entered the 1970s large in numbers, diverse in activities and settings, and seriously questioning its future directions.

SUGGESTED READINGS

Reisman, J. M. *The development of clinical psychology.* New York: Appleton-Century-Crofts, 1966.

Reisman (p. 1−2) defines clinical psychology "as a branch of psychology devoted to the search for, and the application of, psychological principles and techniques that contribute to the understanding of individuals and that may be used to promote their more effective functioning." After a brief reference to roots to be found in the works of philosophers and reformers of the late eighteenth and the nineteenth centuries, Reisman starts a review of each of the seven decades between 1890 and 1960. In each decade he describes the major historical events, the developments related to normal personality functioning, diagnostic techniques, diagnostic formulations, treatment formulations, and professional development. Another excellent reference for an introduction to clinical psychology as well as its development is Mensh's book (1966). In the book are reprints of articles on history by Boring, Brotemarkle, and Watson and some thoughtful discussions of basic issues by leaders in clinical psychology.

Levine, M., and Levine, A. *A social history of helping services.* New York: Appleton-Century-Crofts, 1970.

Murray and Adeline Levine are primarily concerned with what the past history of clinical services for children can teach us about the contemporary community mental health movement. They were shocked to discover that psychoeducational clinics started as innovations recently were actually throwbacks to earlier times; perhaps some of the older services were even better than what we have now. They selected several major developments roughly between 1890 and the mid-1920s: the work of Lightner Witmer, the settlement house movement, the establishment of visiting teachers as the first school social workers, the Gary plan for community use of schools, the Chicago Juvenile Court, Judge Lindsey and the Denver Juvenile Court, and the child guidance clinics started by the Commonwealth Fund in the 1920s. The authors propose the thesis that intrapsychic modes of help are prominent during periods of political and social conservatism, when the "goodness" of the environment is assumed, and situational assistance and extraindividual causation of deviance are emphasized during periods of reform. In the light of this thesis and their evidence for it, they conclude that much of the professionalism that has developed in the helping services has retarded advances in those very services. The articles by Reiff (1970) and Simon (1970) add further fuel to the argument asserting the sociopolitical influences on psychologists' choices for work.

Further considerations of the relation of social science and public policy can be found in Horowitz (1971) and Knapp and Schafer (1970).

Dennis, W. *Readings in the history of psychology.* New York: Appleton-Century-Crofts, 1948.

Wayne Dennis has provided a collection of the original texts from writings of 61 people who have had a great influence on the development of psychology in general. To those particularly interested in clinical psychology and related areas, the following selections would be noteworthy: Aristotle's "On Dreams" (ca. 330 B.C.), Mesmer's "Animal Magnetism" (1779 A.D.), Braid's "The Power of the Mind Over the Body" (about hypnotism, 1846), Galton's "Classification of Men According to Their Natural Gifts" (1869), Cattell's "Mental Tests and Measurements" (1890), "Upon the Necessity of Establishing a Scientific Diagnosis of Inferior States of Intelligence" (1905), Cannon's "Recent Studies of Bodily Effects of Fear, Rage, and Pain" (1914), Terman's "The Measurement of Intelligence" (1916), and Yerkes' "Psychological Examining in the United States Army" (1921).

In a separate article, Margaret Ives (1970) recounts the history of psychological services in Saint Elizabeth's Hospital in Washington, D. C. Established by Congress in 1855, the hospital has offered continuous psychological services since 1907—something of a record.

Shakow, D. *Clinical psychology as science and profession—a forty-year odyssey.* Chicago: Aldine-Atherton, 1969.

One of the great clinical psychologists, David Shakow, has gathered papers from his professional life of over four and a half decades. In the foreword he indicates that his philosophy derives fundamentally from William James, Freud, and a number of his teachers, whose names are familiar in the history of psychology—McDougall, Boring, Wells, and Kent. The first section of the volume deals specifically with aspects of the history and functions of clinical psychology, but in the twenty-seven papers dating from 1938 through 1969, Shakow covers many other topics relevant to this book on clinical psychology— training programs and objectives, relations with other professions, psychoanalysis, and the rewards and frustrations of a psychologist in public service.

Veith, I. Psychiatric nosology: from Hippocrates to Kraepelin. *American Journal of Psychiatry*, 1957, *114*, 385–391.

Because of the importance of psychiatric diagnosis in the history of clinical psychology and in clinical practice, the reader may find this short and interesting article quite useful.

For a more recent critical historical review of psychiatric classification, see Sharma (1970). See also the excellent review of psychiatric diagnosis in Menninger, Mayman, and Pruyser (1963).

Watson, R. I. Psychology: a prescriptive science. *American Psychologist*, 1967, *22*, 435–443.

Watson, an historian of psychology, presents a set of themes or issues that have appeared historically and might provide further guidance and organization of the field of psychology. These "prescriptions" for the attention of the science include such antitheses as conscious versus unconscious mentalism, determinism versus indeterminism, empiricism versus rationalism, mechanism versus vitalism, and peripheralism versus centralism.

Portes, A. On the emergence of behavior therapy in modern society. *Journal of Consulting and Clinical Psychology*, 1971, *36*, 303–313.

Portes, a sociologist, raises the question: Why has behavior therapy emerged as a powerful movement in current society? From the perspective of the sociology of knowledge he sees behaviorism as reflecting the dominant image of man as rational. He suspects that humanistic rebellions, like encounter groups and existential therapy, are mere temporary interruptions of a long-term trend identified by Max Weber, a rationalism that includes bureaucratism, scientism, and impersonal legalism. Portes argues that behavior therapists employ behaviorism as an analogy; actually their aim is nonobservable changes in self-image and perception of the environment. Immediately following this article, Eysenck (1971) responds in opposition, and Portes (1971b) rejoins.

chapter 3

Survey of Working Concepts and Perspectives

The varied course over which clinical psychology has flowed has left a rich legacy of ideas, concepts, and perspectives, many of whose origins we sketched in Chapter 2. Each psychologist is faced with the problem of organizing his knowledge and experience, a problem that is generally approached by selecting a set of concepts from particular theories or schools of thought. The need for organization is so widely felt that a commanding figure like Sigmund Freud, whose psychology approaches a *Weltanschauung* in scope, finds a receptive audience among workers in all the sociopsychological professions. Many, perhaps most, psychologists find their conceptual framework by identifying with one of the theoretical points of view that happen to be prominent in the subculture in which they are immersed. Markedly original thinkers become leaders in psychoanalysis, client-centered therapy, group dynamics, behavior modification, and other varieties of psychology, gathering schools of followers not only because their views have a clarifying utility, but also because of social–political influences that come to dominate professional organizations and training centers. Even when psychologists do not consciously adopt a particular framework or espouse a certain theory, they may nonetheless behave according to its implicit assumptions and principles.

In the case of the scientist, whether he recognizes it or not, theoretical concepts determine what kind of observations he will make and thus what kind of scientific work he will do. A psychologist whose main job is research can feel satisfaction and security in locating a congenial variety of overall theory and adopting it as his basic orientation. If it is inadequate in some respects, his research will demonstrate this inadequacy, and he may get the credit for a constructive modification. If it does not generate all the kinds of experiments that might be done on various problems, he can safely assume that some other experimenter, viewing his world from the vantage point of a different theory, will do them. The time and energy of any one researcher is limited anyway. He cannot do everything.

For the practicing psychologist, however, the existence of conflicting theories poses a real problem. His task is to understand a human being in all his complexity. If he approaches the task using only the conceptual tools provided by one theory, he is almost certain to miss some aspects of the personality he is trying to understand. Orthodox psychoanalysis emphasizes intrapsychic motivation and mechanisms but pays little attention to the influence of social organization. Learning theories of a behavior type focus on what the person is doing but cannot be stretched far enough to reveal his organizing concepts. Theories about the physiological components of emotion are likely to suggest therapies that relieve tension rather than therapies aimed at discovery of unconscious conflicts. If a clinician disregards some aspects of personality because his preferred theory does not sensitize him to it, he may in an individual case overlook a crucially important factor.

Furthermore, a practicing psychologist finds it very difficult to maintain strict theoretical orthodoxy because he is constantly running up against conflicting interpretations of the same observations or facts. Each client he encounters has his own brand of psychological theory, whether or not it is clear and explicit enough so that it could be given a name. Each colleague with whom he works differs from him to a greater or lesser extent in theoretical orientation. It is almost impossible for a clinician to choose a theoretical system and maintain it in its entirety, a fact that may be fortunate. Freud himself was constantly remodeling and elaborating his ideas until the end of his life. Thus there are advantages to the beginning clinician in becoming familiar with concepts from many sources and organizing them into his own personal theory.

Our aim in this chapter is to set forth what seem to us the concepts of personality stressed in present-day theories which are likely to be valuable in this personal theory building. This poses a real problem: Which concepts shall we include? It is obviously impossible to crowd in here all the concepts that can be found in books on psychological theories. What seems important is to include the assumptions *that make a difference* in clinical practice. If assuming one thing rather than another leads the clinician to ask this question rather than that, to look for some things rather than others in a case history, to adopt certain attitudes and ignore other possible ones, to make particular kinds of interpretations, or in general to behave in one way rather than another, these assumptions are important enough to include in the clinician's framework. We have tried to select the concepts that do make such a difference.

It will be obvious to the reader of the following pages that we are not discussing any one of these concepts in sufficient detail so that a person new to the world of psychological ideas could completely grasp its meaning. We are assuming that by the time a student encounters this book he will already have considerable familiarity with such concepts as reinforcement, repression, and introversion. All that we are attempting to do here is to produce an inventory of the concepts an individual clinical psychologist is likely to find himself using and making a place for in the personal theory that undergirds the work he carries on. Some readers may wish to turn directly to Chapter 4.

CONCEPTS FROM EXPERIMENTAL PSYCHOLOGY

Because the training of a clinical psychologist involves first the mastery of a body of research-based psychological knowledge, it is inevitable that concepts growing out of experimental research should be used in his theorizing. One topic that has occupied a central position is *learning.*

Under what circumstances does change of behavior occur, especially these changes that are in line with the organism's needs? The standard formulation in behavior psychology has been in terms of stimulus and response, and its general plan of research was to search for ways of joining responses to stimuli under controlled conditions. Pavlov's experiments showing how the reflex response of salivation in the dog could be attached to a wide variety of new stimuli seemed to the early behaviorists to represent the essence of the process in which they were interested. The *conditioned response* became the prototype of all learning. *Reinforcement* and *extinction, generalization* and *discrimination* became basic concepts, applied in explanation of all sorts of situations. Skinner's research added to Pavlov's concept of conditioned reflexes the new concept of the *operant* response, controlled not by a particular stimulus but by its consequences. These consequences, for which Skinner used Pavlov's term *reinforcement*, have been studied in great detail.

Reinforcement follows particular behaviors perhaps routinely or perhaps sporadically. The importance of "which behavior gets reinforced and when" has drawn attention to *contingencies of reinforcement.* Psychologists sometimes approach a problem by analyzing contingencies and promoting or teaching *contingency management*—identifying behaviors and consequences and promoting ways of having appropriate consequences reliably follow particular behaviors.

Learning theories in the past forty years have become increasingly complex, and their fine points need not concern us here. But every clinician in all his work and his thinking makes use of some of the concepts learning theorists have elaborated. In understanding clients, he is often trying to analyze the stimulus conditions through which a person has come and the responses he has learned to make to them. In treating many conditions he will identify useful responses the client now has in his repertory and attempt to get them attached to the sorts of stimuli the person is likely to meet. Clinicians differ in the extent to which they use the stimulus—response way of conceptualizing their work, but they must all make room somewhere in their thinking for theoretical ideas as to how learning takes place.

Another topic of major concern to experimental psychologists and clinicians alike is *perception*. Research has shown that this is not just an automatic recording of what there is in the organism's environment, but an active sorting and organizing process with its own laws, a process capable of much change and modification.

Unless experimental conditions are deliberately manipulated to make it impossible, what one sees is a *field* differentiated in part as *figure* and in part as *ground*. Things are seen as objects rather than abstract geometrical forms, and these objects appear to be the same objects under all conditions, that is, approximately the same in size, shape, and color even when viewed from different distances, different angles, or in brighter or dimmer lights. A stationary picture followed quickly by another stationary picture of the same figure in a slightly different position will register as perceived movement of the figure from one place to the other. We are all familiar with this phenomenon in motion pictures. The sudden shifts and reversals in perception such as those we find in the familiar Necker cube and Rubin vase illustrated in most elementary psychology textbooks are important to the perception psychologists as evidence of the organizing principles that underlie all our experience. Although most of their research has had to do with rather simple visual phenomena, there is no reason to limit perception to these. Perceptions can be thought of as unconscious as well as conscious, emotional as well as relatively indifferent, learned as well as innate, and as having motivational characteristics.

People differ widely from one another in the way they perceive things. The influence of wishes, needs, and past experiences on what is observed has been a very active research topic in recent years. It is mandatory that the clinician should be thoroughly familiar with the psychology of perception so that he can over and over again remind himself that the persons with whom he works, both clients and colleagues, may be living in quite different phenomenal worlds from his own. One of his first responsibilities to a patient or client is to become as sensitively aware as he can of his particular ways of perceiving the world.

A related field of psychological research, the study of *cognition*, has also provided useful theoretical material for the clinician. Since psychology began, research workers have been interested in *concepts*, the categories into which a person sorts incoming stimulation in order to deal economically with its complexity. George Kelly, for example, built an elaborate theoretical structure on the idea of the *personal construct*, the building block of an individual's basic personality organization. Piaget and his associates have used the word *schema* to refer to the cognitive structures in terms of which an individual experiences and reacts to his world. From cognitive research on problem solving has come another concept that has occupied a central position in the thinking of clinicians, *insight*, the grasping of relationships between the parts of a situation so that organization is possible.

The psychologist's "thinking about thinking" has been greatly influenced by computer technology and information theory. For many psychologists, the concepts *input* and *output* have largely replaced *stimulus* and *response*, and the process occurring between the two is thought of as the operation of an enormously complex computer that has been programmed in a certain way. The concept of *program* is being widely used in the attempt to understand child development, psychopathology, and many other psychological processes. Miller, Galanter, and Pribram (1960) have furnished an excellent example of the application of computer language and information theory to human behavior. The idea that people's plans are like a computer's program is, they show, a useful way to relate knowledge and action together. From this corner of the research world has come also the concept of *feedback*, meaning evaluative information produced at one stage of a complex on-going process that is automatically utilized to change the process in some way. Ultimately theorists writing along these lines begin to speak of ability to revise our own "programs" and thus have a way of conceptualizing complex adaptive behavior and the idea of compe tence.

CONCEPTS FROM THE CONSULTING ROOM

Fully as influential as the concepts arising from experimental research have been those that have arisen from the efforts of gifted psychotherapists generalizing from and organizing what they have observed in working with patients. Standing out as by far the most influential of all these has been Sigmund Freud. His ideas have become woven into the fabric of all our thinking about personality so that it is now next to impossible even to discuss personality without using some Freudian concepts. Freud and the psychoanalytic movement he fathered have stimulated both violent opposition and fanatical adherence. Nowadays few psychologists would deny that psychoanalysis constitutes the single most important personality theory, but few would deny that it needs considerable modification. It will be impossible to do full justice to the breadth of Freud's thinking here. The reader must go himself to Freud's original writings (especially 1913, 1914, 1933, 1949a, 1949b) and the many descriptions of his system by his followers, such as Fenichel (1945), and critical evaluations, such as those of Madison (1961), Hook (1959), and Sears (1943). Here we shall take up only a few of the most important principles that he developed in fifty years of observing and thinking deeply about his patients and himself. He conceived of psychoanalysis as having three areas of contribution: a personality theory, a mode of research into the human mind, and a form of psychotherapy.

The most pervasive of Freud's ideas is the conception of personality as the *interplay of intrapsychic forces.* Psychoanalytic theory places primary emphasis on *motivation* and dynamic interaction. This interaction often takes the form of two forces opposed to each other. The *id*, containing the chaotic primitive animalistic urges, fights for expression and satisfaction of its needs with the *ego* and its subsystem, the *superego*, or conscience. The basic energy of life, the *libido*, a sexualized constructive instinct, was seen in Freud's later writings as opposed to the death instinct, a destructive aggressive urge. The *pleasure principle*, by which a person lives early in life as he strives toward immediate gratification of his wishes and needs, is opposed to the *reality principle*, which allows for the realities of the social and physical world. A clinician using psychoanalytic concepts is constantly aware of the wishing, striving, seeking, searching aspect of people and of the inner conflicts that prevent the expression of their needs and wishes. Laboratory psychologists have also made a place for motivation in their theories, but there it is a less salient concept than in psychoanalysis, and clinical workers tend to use psychoanalytic formulations, which are anthropomorphic and convenient, more than the abstract and technically sounder concepts of the experimentalists.

The second major psychoanalytic idea that has exercised a profound influence on our thinking about personality is the concept of *unconscious processes*. As clinicians we assume when we listen to what a person says about his motives and goals that a large part of his actual motivation is undetected and inaccessible to him. It is only through painstaking attention to the indirect effects and expressions of the unconscious processes that we can get some clues as to what they are. The assumption that much motivation is unconscious is an advantage for the clinician in that it makes apparently irrational behavior at least potentially lawful and understandable.

A third broad Freudian principle that has permeated practically all thinking about personality is the concept of *anxiety* and *defenses against anxiety*. Theorists differ in their ideas about the source of the anxiety that is at the root of all neurotic symptoms, but they would agree fairly well on the proposition that neurotic symptoms and much of normal behavior as well constitute defenses against anxiety, a kind of behavior that serves to keep it within manageable limits. The basic defense mechanism, or as some more behaviorally oriented psychologists call it, adjustment mechanism, is *repression*. Repression is the mechanism by which threatening feelings and impulses are excluded, denied entry to consciousness. Repression occurs because the individual feels threatened, but, it is to be added, the attempted repression is never completely successful. The repressed needs and desires and urges are expressed in roundabout ways, by slips of the tongue, displaced reactions to things, and dream symbols. The expression may take the form of neurotic symptoms. There are, of course, a number of other defense mechanisms which are fairly well known: rationalization, projection, reaction formation.

A fourth contribution psychoanalysis has made to our thinking is emphasis on the critical *importance for personality development of infancy and childhood*. Freud produced convincing evidence that the life of a child is not a time of idyllic bliss and innocence but one when urges are strong and conflicts are many. Freud put particular stress on the notion of *infantile sexuality*, which to him meant a progressive development of children through distinguishable periods of pleasurable erotogenic activities—successively the oral, anal, and genital periods.

Furthermore, his emphasis on the Oedipus complex pointed toward the inevitability of a child's intense longing for affection from the parent of the opposite sex. Along with this concept he postulated castration anxiety, whereby the parent of the same sex could appear to be a powerful threat to the young child. The discovery of such relationships within the family became ground for developing the idea that besides *intra*personal conflicts, there were also *inter*personal relationships and conflicts. Contemporary thinking about therapy, about methods of child training and education, and about ways of analyzing differences between societies and social classes have all been deeply influenced by these Freudian principles.

We might have selected many more psychoanalytic concepts for special mention. Psychoanalysis is an intricate and involved system well worth the study needed to understand it thoroughly or to dissent from it intelligently. The broad principles that we have singled out are some that must be incorporated, or at least dealt with, in almost any personality theory that can be formulated today.

The predominance of orthodox Freudian psychoanalysis has in the judgment of many persons led to an undervaluation of certain useful concepts embodied in modifications of the system. Two major deviations from Freudian conceptualization have been theories centering on cognitive processes and theories emphasizing the social and cultural aspects of personality. The lead in both these lines of deviation was taken by Alfred Adler. Instead of seeing persons as especially to be understood through their intrapsychic conflicts, he asserted that the individual, who is an irreducible whole, could be known through his social goals and his relationships to other people, especially with his family. These taken together distinguish his particular *style of life*, and this, rather than sexuality, betrays his basic motivation. In analyzing any bit of behavior, neurotic or normal, Adler would ask the question: What is this person's *social purpose* (his *Gemeinschaftsgefühl*)? The *guiding fictions* or "mistaken notions" of a person seeking to relate to his fellows are at the basis of his neurosis, if he has one. Many present-day psychologists who do not think of themselves as Adlerians are emphasizing the cognitive and social aspects of personality in their theoretical formulations.

From all the complexities of thinking for which Carl Jung is noted comes one idea that has influenced the work of clinicians belonging to many schools. It is the concept of *creative* or *constructive unconscious processes*. Jung in his doctrine of *individuation* holds that psychological health is a matter of learning to express one's self more completely. Jung, because he is frequently very difficult to follow and even outright mystical in the judgment of most critics, has had rather less influence on American psychology, in which the keynote is empiricism, than on European thinking. Nevertheless, his famous concepts of *introversion* and *extroversion* and the word-association test he developed have had wide influence.

Otto Rank is another psychoanalyst popular with psychologists, who find it natural to think of human motivation more in terms of self-actualization and creative self-expression than in terms of biological drives. His emphasis was on the *will* and on the individual's struggle by separating himself and achieving independence to find his own unique personality and place in the world.

Many sorts of syntheses of these and many other concepts from a variety of personality theories are possible. The more a clinician knows about them, provided he is alert and does not feel the need to maintain a strict theoretical orthodoxy, the better equipped he is for his work. Although it is simpler to seize upon one theory and stick with it, it is likely that the clinician whose mind is open to conflicting evidence and novel hypotheses will accumulate a more useful set of concepts and serve his clients better—at least, this is the hypothesis about professional development that seems to be most likely to be true. Fortunately, personality theorists are becoming at the present time more and more concerned with attempts to reconcile and unify concepts and to put theories to the test. Thus, as time goes along, somewhat easier channels of communication have opened among divergent groups.

Concepts arising from or usually associated with the consulting room are legion; therefore, we have made arbitrary choices. But mention should be made of Rogers's notions that a person gets into difficulty when he gets *out of touch with his own values*. Ellis, borrowing essentially philosophical concepts from Epictetus, the Greek philosopher, has used in his consulting room the idea that human difficulties arise because people accept and act on *irrational ideas*, for example, the idea that everybody must love us and that it is a disaster if they don't.

A final concept from the consulting room that we will mention is that of *crisis*. The psychiatrist Erich Lindemann (1944) is generally credited with recognizing the patterns of adequate and incomplete crisis resolution in relatives of persons killed in the Coconut Grove dance hall fire in Boston. Crisis has been approached from many different perspectives (Darbonne, 1969; Taplin, 1971) but the basic idea is that people become psychologically overwhelmed and that they regain functioning either with increased resources or with impaired resources.

The concept of crisis—or a succession of crises—also forms the cornerstone of Erikson's (1950, 1959) view of personality. In it he postulates eight phases or stages of development, each stage being a crucial choice point or developmental crisis between achievement of the more mature functioning on a new level or turning into unproductive and harmful styles.

The consulting room, and its counterpart, the hospital, have continued to be fruitful sources of ideas for psychological service. Recent ideas from hospitals, notably VA Palo Alto, asserting that good treatment results in adequate community functioning, have given rise to a community readjustment and halfway-house approach. Hopefully the reader will be involved himself in many new attempts to reconceptualize old problems and thus to develop and test different methods of helping people.

CONCEPTS FROM THE STUDY OF GROUPS AND SOCIETY

Much of our knowledge in the human sciences has come not from laboratory experiments but from observation and study of persons in real-life situations. This has been particularly true with regard to the problem of the relationship between the individual and his society. The cultural anthropologists, the sociologists, and the social psychologists are modifying our thinking about mentally ill people and behavior deviation in general. An early instance of an effective sociological approach of this sort is the work of Durkheim. He formulated the concept of *anomie*, a condition without organization or system, the feeling a person may have of not belonging to society, or not having a "place." Durkheim used *anomie* to explain the development of mental aberrations and suicide.

When it was noted that in some cultures psychosis-like behavior was an accepted thing, a reexamination of our ideas about what is "abnormal" was clearly called for. The finding that there is great variation in behavior and in value systems from people to people, and even between social classes and racial groups in a single country, has made us aware of the overriding effects and importance of social influences. In recent years social psychology has developed rapidly and the fields of organizational psychology, environmental psychology, and community psychology have emerged. Sources of stress in communities and in organizations are now inevitably part of the study of etiology of mental illness and health.

If we seek to explain the behavior of individuals, we have to bring in social concepts—we must resort to relating him to one or another group. To say, for example, that someone is a man or a woman is already to have placed him in a group which it is assumed one knows a good deal about, and, because this is so, the individual must also be known to some extent. If you tell his age and his occupation, you are assigning him to other groups. Although, in general, intragroup differences are larger than intergroup differences, it is still true that the successive identification of the groups to which a person belongs enables one to say a great deal about him—so powerful is the standardizing influence of groups.

"Every man is in certain respects like all other men, like some other men, and like no other man" (Kluckhohn and Murray, 1955, p. 53). As individuals, we share much of our world with other people, some things even with other animals—such as the physical environment, with its storms, the features of its terrain, its edible and inedible plants. We also share such physiological needs and limitations as are imposed by hunger, sexual desire, and finite physical strength. With other peoples we may share a common language or common ways of doing things. *Culture* is "a great storehouse of ready-made solutions to problems which human animals are wont to encounter" (Kluckhohn and Murray, 1955, p. 54).

A major conceptual scheme of social psychology is that of George Herbert Mead, whose work is the cornerstone of a system known as *symbolic interactionism*. Mead held that self and mind are social products, coming into being because a person engages in social processes, primarily in communication with other people. He outlined a way in which language serves as one major set of symbols for making up what we call mind and self. He held that action using language symbols can be carried on *within* the person, as well as between people. Later writers in similar vein have called thinking covert speech. Mind, then, is seen as being an importation within the individual of social processes and shared symbols.

He pointed out that a child's self-concept develops from the "reflected appraisals of others." Even when a person is by himself, he has within him effective traces of many of the people he has known and the way they have acted toward him. Although he is not interacting with them at the time, he may behave as if he were. It is not uncommon for a person to feel guilt upon doing certain things that his parents would have punished him for in the past, or to feel a surge of anger at the mere idea of an insult which there is no chance he will ever encounter.

A related idea of more recent vintage is the concept of *cognitive dissonance*, widely employed by Festinger. "No theory in social psychology has stimulated more research than the theory of cognitive dissonance," Zajonc wrote in 1968. It has been demonstrated repeatedly that individuals are motivated to avoid holding incompatible knowledge or opinions. They seek a certain self-consistency. If they become aware of discrepancies, or dissonances, in attitudes or behavior they often shift either their thinking or actions to bring them in line.

A central generalization of the symbolic interactionist perspective is that people behave according to what they believe their situation to be. That is, they behave according to what the situation symbolizes to them in the context of their prior knowledge and experience.

Mead's thought on the sharing of symbols and common understandings has helped provide a foundation for role theory. Sarbin and Allen (1968, p. 489) indicate that the term *role*, borrowed from the theater, "is a metaphor intended to denote that conduct adheres to certain 'parts' (or positions) rather than to the players who read or recite them." In defining particular roles two different things must be kept in mind. One is the *function* the individual has in a group, what he does, the characteristic contribution he makes. The other is the behavior *expected* of the person who fills a defined position in a group. In both its aspects, the actual and the expected, a role cannot be understood unless the group is specified and understood. Any confusion that may arise between the two meanings is dispelled to some degree if we differentiate between *role expectations* (obligations and responsibilities) and *role behavior* (what the person actually does in a given group). The possibilities for *role conflict* develop when an individual is expected to play one role that interferes with his simultaneously playing another role. For instance, role conflict may occur when the father of a family finds that his employer expects him to give up many evening hours to his job while his family expects him to stay at home and do things with them.

Another idea of symbolic interactionism is that people *share* each other's behavior rather than just react to it. When we see an accident victim, we have some idea of what it would be like to be in his predicament. When John says to Joe, "put a log on the fire," they both share aspects of the imagery, the action, and the consequences of a log being put on the fire. *Role taking* is the ability to use linguistic and social symbols to "play over" what it would be like to be in the other person's shoes. Lack of skill in role taking has become a prominent notion in thinking about people who show a high degree of impulsiveness and absence of conscience, such as psychopaths and sociopaths.

Of all concepts in social psychology, role is the one that does most to link the individual with his society or group. The sharing of common symbols lies at the core of what constitutes a group. Such sharing of symbols is the collective agreement or *consensus*, which may concern objects, understandings and expectations, sets of acceptable motives, or roles. Paths along which the sharing takes place are called *communication channels*. These can be formal, like the news media, or informal, like the "grapevine" or the "rumor mill." Knowledge, news, rumor, conventional norms and sentiments, social unrest, and so on, can all be seen as segments of collective behavior, each segment having agreed upon ways of being defined and generated, of being communicated, and of being acted upon.

To date, symbolic interactionism has contributed to the thinking of several prominent psychologists and psychiatrists. The one who has been most influential is Harry Stack Sullivan. It seems likely that it will play an even larger part in clinical psychology as we extend our thinking about matters such as collective mental health and social intervention. Manis and Melzer (1967) or Shibutani (1961) provide good introductions. Although the conceptual system and the language have not been very familiar outside the sociologist's side of social psychology, the present emphasis on communities, social change, and systems intervention calls for new approaches. The symbolic interactionist perspective is a potential asset which the socially concerned psychologist would be well advised to explore.

One feature of modern life which is ignored surprisingly often is the importance of *large organizations* and institutions in directing and controlling the lives of the people who comprise them. Millions of our citizens work for formally organized entities—business corporations, schools, and government. As Max Weber pointed out, it is the ideal of every bureaucracy to have each individual performing assigned duties in an efficient, machinelike manner as set forth in a table of organization. There may be an *informal organization* which modifies and runs counter to the *formal organization*, but when a person joins a given organization, much of his behavior is defined and prescribed. Unless he conforms, at least within limits, he will not be able to retain his position. A nation's way of governing its people is translated down into distinct influences on individual human behavior. Prohibition was associated with large-scale gangsterism in the United States. There were many suicides at the start of the Depression. Changes in tax laws, marriage laws, abortion laws, labor laws, adoption laws, traffic laws, criminal codes, laws governing military service, rationing, and social security affect people directly, as do the provisions the state makes for the aged and mentally ill. The kinds of sanctions that prevent nonwhites in the United States from living in certain districts of town and segregate them in slum areas seem to be related to the rates of occurrence of delinquency and schizophrenia. Increasingly, as we move from the "fire-fighting" of social ills to "fire prevention," the psychologist must be concerned with these community correlates of mental illness and maladjustment.

Another line of thinking comes from the direct observation of people in living situations. Barker (1963, 1968) and his associates have done a long and productive series of studies on the *ecology of behavior*. Ecology is the study of organisms in relation to the environment to which they are more or less successfully adapted. This concept has to do with the ongoing natural interaction of human beings. Barker's methodology was to observe his subjects wherever they naturally go rather than to bring them into a laboratory or to interview them in the usual clinical manner. His work sharpens our awareness of how much goes on in the life of a person even during a single day and how difficult it would be to categorize all that he does in an adequate manner.

Undoubtedly the theorist who has had most success in showing the relations between personality and social phenomena is Kurt Lewin. We have no space here for going into much detail about Lewin's system, accounts of which have been presented by Leeper (1943) and Deutsch (1968). Lewin's most enlightening concept was the *life space*. By this he meant the perceived *psychological environment* rather than the physical environment. What is always required as we attempt to understand a person is that we find out how *he* sees his world, whether or not this view corresponds to that of others who know him or to our own. Whether or not we follow Lewin in calling such personal views of the environment "life space," we use the concept constantly.

It is the great variety of these different approaches to understanding individuals through social concepts which impresses us most and leaves us asking for some way to integrate them. The likelihood that such an integration can be effected in the near future is not great, though many interesting formulations have been proposed. Meanwhile, the clinician will find his observations and reflections on the nature of interpersonal relationships and on the influence of situations on behavior a rich source of ideas and hypotheses.

CONCEPTS FROM INDIVIDUAL DIFFERENCES
AND THEIR MEASUREMENT

The other large body of knowledge that has come mainly from research in the field rather than laboratory investigation is made up of what we have learned about individual differences in psychological characteristics. Once it became apparent, at about the turn of the century, that differences in intelligence could be expressed in quantitative terms, the way was open for work on all sorts of "mental measurements." Tests as devices for measuring psychological characteristics or traits have been given to many millions of people—schoolchildren, soldiers, job applicants, and all sorts of other groups.

If we look at the basic concepts, rather than at the tools of measurement, that have arisen in this line of research, the first that comes to mind is the *trait* concept itself. Like other major ideas that we have been discussing, its origins go back much further than scientific psychology. But our methods of measuring in numerical terms have forced us to ask what it is that we are measuring. We speak of a trait when we single out one aspect of an individual personality, some quality, some ability that he shares with many, perhaps with all, human beings and then measure some performance ("output") believed to be indicative of this quality, or ability, so that we can state in quantitative terms how his performance compares with those of a large population of other people. For example, an intelligence test, by showing us how much below or above average an individual is in the performance of a specified set of tasks under standardized conditions, is supposed to indicate how *much* of the trait intelligence, or problem-solving ability, the individual possesses. Such a device is particularly helpful in situations where the need is to be able to sort out individuals and place or assign each of them to a group or a situation where he will best fit. Clinicians find trait concepts both a help and a hindrance. On the one hand, they must keep in mind this normative evaluative way of looking at persons, for society itself uses it constantly; on the other hand, they must be sensitive to their client's essential nature in an overall nonevaluative way—to his absolute worth as a person.

Even if there were only ten human traits, each of which could be measured on a seven-point scale, the combinations would add up to more than 56,000 kinds of individuals. So it is understandable that the trait concept has of late been combined to an increasing degree with the more significant concept of patterns of traits. This is a move in the direction of expressing individuality in quantitative terms. In many different areas of practice and research, the *trait-pattern* method of describing a person has come into use. Counselors at employment offices look for combinations of scores on the separate tests of the General Aptitude Test Battery for the occupations that require such combinations. The trait-pattern approach is one that the clinician often finds enlightening, and its use will surely be expanded as fast as methods can be devised. (See, for example, the Kulik, Stein, and Sarbin study, 1968.)

The third contribution that work in individual differences has made to our theoretical thinking is not exactly parallel to the others. It is a sort of basic prescription that we apply the *logic of probabilities* to all thinking in this field. The concepts underlying the whole technology of mental testing are statistical concepts based on probability theory. When a psychologist finds, for example, that a mentally retarded child obtains an IQ of 58 on the Stanford-Binet test, he automatically interprets this as a range of scores within which the child's IQ *probably* falls rather than as an exact score. It is such thinking that technical knowledge of individual differences fosters.

CONCEPTS AND PERSPECTIVES FROM RELIGION AND PHILOSOPHY

It is well for psychologists to remember that they are far from being either the first or the only group of professional people who have thought long and deeply about human nature. Philosophers and religious leaders have been concerned for centuries with man—his nature and his needs. Many of their insights are doubtless direct ancestors of what we take to be basic premises. As an applied science, clinical psychology must assume that some conditions and goals are "good" and others undesirable.

May (1969) has called attention to the idea that *concerns about death* and a *search to find meaning* are organizing or motivating factors in human life. In an age crying for "meaning" and "relevance" and shunning death as if it were an obscenity rather than the culmination of life, May's writings, growing out of *existentialist* philosophical concerns, have become increasingly influential.

Much religious thinking has centered around the concept of the *soul*, and the word *psychology* itself is derived from the Greek word for their idea of a soul. In the personality theories of our day, the *self-concept*, or as some writers prefer, the concept of *ego identity*, carries some of the same sort of meaning, though stripped of mystical or supernatural connotations.

It is difficult to discuss the contributions religion makes to the psychologist's thinking in terms of isolated concepts. They can more readily be characterized as perspectives or orientations. Psychologists differ greatly in their ideas about the meaning of *choice, responsibility*, and *freedom*. Mowrer, a major contributor in this area, might have been discussed under "Concepts from Learning Theory," but he parts company with many experimentalists in the emphasis he gives to choice and responsibility. He asserts that disturbances in emotions, such as fear or guilt, *follow* naturally from behavior that is socially or morally deviant, behavior that a person has consciously chosen, and chosen to keep concealed. He uses the term *misbehavior* for such a course of action.

The notion that to change one's emotions one must change one's behavior is opposed to the classical Freudian notion that behavior *follows* from emotions. The concept of personal responsibility enters the picture here because it is the person's own choice (his *mis*behavior) that produces his predicament rather than an emotional illness over which he has no control. Mowrer explains "symptoms" by postulating that they arise from the discomfort or guilt that comes from the misbehavior. He, like many others, views symptoms as behaviors that reflect or handle the inner feelings, but he pinpoints the misbehavior as the root of the problem.

Not unexpectedly, his logic of intervention focuses on behavior and on authentic, honest involvement with others rather than on analysis of feelings. First, the patient must *change the behavior* that originally got him into trouble, that is, his misbehavior. Second, he must change the behavior (his symptoms) with which he has been handling the resulting bad feelings. (It does not follow that with change in the first, improvement in the second is automatic; further misbehaviors, such as dishonesty or duplicity, may have been used in the second coping phase.) This approach differs from the common view that "symptoms" are signs of underlying disorders not of the patient's making, and that an outside expert must make the patient feel better by working on the patient's emotions. Accepting Mowrer's notions leads to the conclusion that "traditional" therapists compound the patient's problems, enabling him to avoid responsibility for himself and his own emotions and deemphasizing the need for behavior change. The growing literature on self-help groups and on nonprofessional workers points to the importance of these concepts.

Although Mowrer makes interesting reference to religious concepts (and in his earlier writings called misbehavior *sin*), the "how" of intervention is derived by identifying the behavior to be changed and the damaged situations that are to be restored. Sometimes—mainly in cases of neurosis (anxieties, guilt) and character disorders (impulsiveness, immaturity)—the parallel with *atonement* or *forgiveness of sin* is plain. Where the symptoms involve interpersonal deviousness or manipulation, some form of interpersonal "making up" is called for *with those who have been mistreated* before an individual can be restored to the esteem of his reference group and thus regain self-esteem.

Mowrer's system is developing, and is still incomplete. It does, however, provide a system of considerable utility to nonprofessional as well as professional workers who are attempting to help people function more adequately. In a time of increasing social disorder, it provides a perspective emphasizing not just the individual's obligations to his society and his fellows, but the personal returns in emotional stability he reaps for "keeping up his membership." It is also interesting from the standpoint that it is one of the few psychological perspectives that is consonant with major aspects of the Judeo-Christian heritage yet is also in tune with some of the most recent efforts toward self-enhancement through authenticity, honesty, and self-disclosure.

The psychologist who has moved farthest from a concern with the "negatives"—sin, guilt, abnormality—to a celebration of "positives"—self-actualization, creativity—is Abraham Maslow (1968, 1971). Maslow is deservedly known as the father of humanistic psychology. Early in his career he became fascinated with highly effective, psychologically healthy people. So, in addition to a well-developed knowledge in clinical and abnormal psychology, he embarked on intensive case studies of "fully human," superior people. He developed a theory of motivation involving a *hierarchy of needs* from basic organismic requirements like air, food, and water to needs for intellectual exploration and creativity. With minimal meeting of *deficiency needs* the person can move to *being needs*. The highest levels result in a full function of greatest humane capacities—the attainment of *self-actualization*. Occasionally the individual attains almost accidentally and without straining a sense of high understanding and deep insight, which Maslow called the *peak experience*. This belief, approaching a religious faith, that men can be *more*, that his truly human nature can be discovered, that human beings can attain much greater understanding of themselves and others than they usually do, has led to the development of what is called humanistic psychology and to a great deal of exploration of ways of attaining peak experiences—sometimes through encounter groups, sometimes through yogi exercises, and sometimes through meditation. This search for transcendence has many parallels in mystical religions of the West and the East.

The attainment of enlightenment has been particularly emphasized in Buddhism and Hinduism. Although Oriental thought has never been successfully combined with Western scientific psychology, Eastern philosophies can tell a student of man a great deal. The goals of life and views of nature and man that have arisen in India, China, and Japan can profoundly question the emphasis that Western science places on physical evidence for truth, on hedonism (as expressed in reinforcement theory), and on atomism as opposed to a deep sense of relation to all life and nature. The Buddhist view is that the aim of man is to overcome all desire. The Hindu Bhagavad-Gita states: "The wise man is not the one who has abstained from action but the one who has given up the fruits of action" (Murphy and Murphy, 1968, p. 81). In sharp contrast with Greek thought, the ultimate end in much of Asian religion is loss of individuality and the attainment of nirvana, a union with the world oneness. Gardner and Lois Murphy in *Asian Psychology* (1968) reach the general conclusion that Oriental approaches, in contrast to Western ideas, are pessimistic about the attainment of a sound mind and a good life. There is a tone of resignation and an acceptance of one's duty and fate. The Murphys draw an interesting comparison between the sudden inspirations of Buddha and Archimedes. Buddha was seeking *within* and Archimedes *without*. They conclude (p. 231) that the force of the Buddhist tradition lies in very *arduous self-examination*, whereas the force of the Western educational tradition lay in training in *direct observation*. It is interesting that the well-known contemporary Japanese psychiatrist Morita, in contrast to

Freud, emphasizes—not introspection and the "baring of the soul"—but ignoring the patient's feelings and egocentricities, and, after a period of isolation, immersing him in nature and in family and community life (Vieth, 1971). Morita therapy, quite foreign to Western ways, relates to Zen Buddhism. Choices for treatment take place in a cultural context, sometimes building on existing cultural tendencies, sometimes trying to counteract cultural stresses.

A significant philosophical and religious issue throughout history has been freedom of will; psychologists, particularly those dealing directly with human beings who might be aided to live fuller and more meaningful lives, must come to terms with the issues involved in values, choice, goals, freedom, and responsibility. The problems of will and freedom periodically return to confront any person who thinks deeply, and psychologists take different stands. (Contrast May's *Love and Will*, 1969, with Skinner's *Beyond Freedom and Dignity*, 1971, for instance.) In doing so, a sort of basic dilemma confronts them. On the one hand, it has been feared that to recognize the reality of freedom and individual responsibility would undermine the determinism that must be postulated if psychology is to be considered a science. On the other hand, to assume that the actions of a human being are completely determined by causal factors in his past history and present situation leads to pessimism concerning the outlook for a person whose background has been extremely unfavorable, and what the practicing clinician needs is optimism and faith in therapy. What psychologists have tended to do is to alternate between the two frames of reference. Boring (1957), in a thoughtful analysis of the problem, justifies this alternation on the grounds that each view of the world is only a sort of model into which we fit events as we observe them, and it is quite legitimate to use different models at different times. Another way to look at the problem is adopted by Feigl (1959). He explains how we often confuse determinism with compulsion. He points out that as we move up the phylogenetic scale, there is more and more *self-determination.* A man, though he, too, may be the product of antecedent conditions, can control much of his behavior through cerebral dispositions equitable with his personality. Feigl arrives at a resolution of the free-will problem in terms of both determinism and individual responsibility. His clarification of the problem will repay study by the clinician who feels doubt, in principle, of the efficacy of a man's trying to behave differently.

The physical concepts about causation that dominated nineteenth-century thinking, when Freud, for example, was beginning to formulate his theory, have given way to much more complex and subtle ideas. The Heisenberg indeterminacy principle, the proposition that the act of observation changes the phenomenon observed, is as important when we deal with human beings as when we deal with electrons. Adopting the limited objective of predicting what individuals will do in probabilistic terms and for a limited time only makes it unnecessary for the psychologist to rule choice and responsibility out of his thinking about a person's life. Powerful new logical and mathematical tools are now available to enable us to apply scientific methods to the study of the decision process itself. We need not look upon human beings as rats or robots in order to study them or to help them.

GENERAL PERSPECTIVES

As suggested in the preceding section, a psychologist preparing himself for practice must consider different perspectives from which to view the whole scene as well as different concepts about particular psychological phenomena. One such difference in perspective has been mentioned in Chapter 2—*the educational versus the medical way of looking at human needs.* Almost unconsciously, as the twentieth century progressed, clinical psychologists shifted from the educational perspective characteristic of Witmer, Binet, and other early leaders, to the medical perspective that dominated the scene in the 1940s and 1950s. We need not go into all the factors involved in this shift. The enormous prestige the medical profession achieved during this period, contrasted with the low regard in which educators were often held, made it natural for psychologists to prefer the "healer" to the "teacher" role. Persons with adjustment difficulties were considered (and considered themselves to be) "sick." The challenge to psychologists was to diagnose the nature of the sickness and provide a cure. The attempt to diagnose produced instruments for personality assessment—both structured inventories and unstructured projective techniques—that were mainly designed to identify special varieties or "syndromes" of maladjustment, such as neurotic and schizophrenic tendencies, rather than to reveal positive personality qualities such as integrity and sense of humor. While many medically oriented psychiatrists attempted to cure by prescribing drugs or brain operations, others, along with medically oriented psychologists, emphasized psychotherapy. The result was a bewildering variety of techniques for conducting therapeutic interviews, rather than efforts to devise new kinds of situations and patterns of relationship designed to produce new habits and skills.

Psychiatrists as well as psychologists have come to see the defects in the *medical model* (Szasz, 1961; Leifer, 1970), and throughout the 1960s and early 1970s heated arguments have been going on in both psychiatric and psycholog-ical circles over the issues. To many of the participants it is a matter of the greatest urgency whether problems of mental health are viewed from a medical or a social-educational perspective. Several considerations are involved in the revolt against the medical model (or *medical perspective*, as we prefer to call it). In the first place, research has discovered few instances of personality disorders resulting from particular physical or physiological causes (the tie between syphilis and paresis has turned out not to be a useful prototype for most psychoses), while the evidence that many maladaptive patterns of behavior are learned has been constantly increasing. In later chapters we shall devote considerable attention to the "behavior therapies," techniques that have essentially nothing to do with medicine. If helping persons who are not functioning well is seen as identifying and changing faulty habits, the traditional psychiatric categories—paranoid schizophrenia, anxiety neurosis, psychopathic personality, and the like—appear to be a useless encumbrance. Time spent in developing and maintaining this structure of concepts about mental illness is time wasted.

In the second place, those who urge that we abandon the medical perspective argue that treatment relationships based on medicine are inappropriate for the psychological helping professions. A person who considers himself to be "sick" can relieve himself of responsibility for his own behavior. A physician is trained to take responsibility for his patients. The combination of sick patient and authoritative physician tends to produce dependence rather than autonomy, conformity rather than initiative in the person being helped. Thus it perpetuates his difficulties instead of relieving them.

The third consideration, expressed with more vehemence than either of the others, is that from the medical perspective one places the locus of personal difficulties in individuals themselves rather than in the society of which they form a part. The medical perspective is thus essentially a conservative point of view. Psychologists along with many other kinds of people have become increasingly concerned during the turbulent 1960s and 1970s about the serious defects in social institutions. They have shifted away from the perspective of medicine to that of social engineering. Instead of attempting to cure patients they would like to redesign the institutions that produce poverty, alienation, and violence.

Finally, there is an ethical consideration that comes out very strongly in some of the attacks on the medical model. Because they were considered to be suffering from mental illness, individuals have been kept in confinement sometimes for years or for a lifetime, losing all their rights as human beings, subjected to indignity or even cruelty. Even benign forms of treatment for mental illness can be used as a means of social control. As evidence has come in that it is the poor who end up in hospitals, receiving only minimal custodial care and drug therapy, while the more privileged classes receive individualized assistance in their home communities, the injustice of the system has become more apparent. Bills to safeguard the civil rights of mental patients have been introduced into a number of state legislatures. More significantly, the advisability of giving professional people the right to control deviant behavior by classifying it as illness, without any of the legal safeguards free societies have evolved to protect the rights of the individual, is being seriously questioned. This questioning is leading to a shift away from the medical perspective.

Although the spirit of the times impels us to turn away from the medical perspective, we should not lose sight of the real values it has held. These values should be maintained in any new system of thinking that emerges. Kindness and consideration for suffering human beings, attitudes inherent in the concept of the good doctor, are important. The medical model was a real improvement on the witchcraft model or the demon-possession model. Let us make sure that the new models now being constructed are advances, not backward steps.

Another change in perspective can also be identified in clinical psychology. Even among those who still view their work from the medical perspective, a shift in the meaning of "mental health" seems to be occurring. Heretofore, what the mental health movement has really been mainly concerned with is mental illness. Little thought has been given to what "health" means, and the tacit assumption has usually been that a person not suffering from one of the known varieties of mental illness can be considered healthy. But as time has passed, more and more effort has been put into attempts to define "positive mental health" as something over and beyond the absence of illness. The core of such definitions is *social competence*, and some psychologists have come to organize their thinking and their activities around it.

Several aspects of the contemporary psychological scene (early 1970s) can be viewed from the social-competence perspective. At least some of the work going on in schools is designed not just to prevent "problems" but to raise the level of social competence in all the children. Research to develop assessment techniques to measure competence is in progress (Goldfried and D'Zurilla, 1969), as is theorizing about competence motivation (White, 1959). Married couples are being trained to achieve sexual competence. Sensitivity groups and encounter groups are set up to increase the competence with which interpersonal relationships are handled, and their appeal is not just to persons in need of therapy, but to the public at large.

SUMMARY

The purpose of this chapter is to sample the rich variety of ideas from which a clinical psychologist's working concepts and perspectives are drawn. Because of the complexity of human nature and the variety of individuals, he must try to understand that the clinician needs to cast his net rather widely. From the laboratory of the experimental psychologist he draws concepts related to learning, perception, and cognition. From the consulting rooms of Freud and his many articulate successors he draws concepts about intrapsychic forces and conflicts, and about the origins of personality patterns in early childhood. He becomes aware of irrational as well as rational ideas, unconscious as well as conscious motives. From the study of groups and society he draws concepts about the impact of interpersonal relationships, social sanctions, and the culture as a whole on individuals. From research on individual differences and their measurement he learns to think in terms of traits and probabilities.

From religion and philosophy he senses different perspectives from which human life can be viewed and shapes his assumptions about determinism and freedom, choice and responsibility.

In two major areas, general perspectives important to psychological work now seem to be in process of change. The dominant medical perspective is being attacked on grounds that it is out of line with research evidence not conducive to the relationships on which personal autonomy and responsibility should rest, not a satisfactory basis for constructive social changes, and potentially dangerous in facilitating systems of authoritarian social control. The dominant orientation toward maladjustments and difficulties is being challenged by those who would work directly for social competence.

SUGGESTED READINGS

Hunt, J. M. Traditional personality theory in the light of recent evidence. *American Scientist*, 1965, *53*, 80 96.

Hunt points out that advancement of scientific thinking about personality can occur when our observations differ from what our theories lead us to expect. He takes five rather common or uncritically held assumptions (e.g., personality traits are the major sources of behavioral variance; painful stimulation in infancy results in sensitivity and proneness to anxiety; emotional factors are more important than cognitive factors in psychological development) and reviews recent evidence. The evidence is incompatible with the assumptions that Hunt then rejects. He argues that experimental and observational evidence must be admitted to test our assumptions and concepts.

Borgatta, E. F. Sidesteps toward a nonspecial theory. *Psychological Review*, 1954, *61*, 343–352.

Borgatta's article is a humorous demonstration of what can happen when theorizing becomes independent of logic and detached from evidence. He pokes fun at theories that explain by merely inventing constructs—his "deumbilification anxiety" has unlimited ability to explain things after the fact.

Koch, S. (ed.). *Psychology, a study of a science*, Vols. 3, 5. New York: McGraw-Hill, 1959 (Vol. 3), 1963 (Vol. 5).

One work that contains articles on a broad variety of psychological perspectives is the famous Koch series. Of the seven volumes, Volume 3, *Formulations of the Person and the Social Context*, and Volume 5, *The Process Areas, the Person and Some Applied Fields: Their Place in Psychology and in Science*, are perhaps most closely allied to the concepts and perspectives discussed in our chapter. The quality of the individual articles is high; they provide excellent systematic and comprehensive discussion of a wide variety of topics, including personality from a cognitive viewpoint, client-centered approaches, psychoanalytic thinking, and several other aspects of personality theory and clinical psychology.

Mowrer, O. H. (ed.). *Morality and mental health*. Chicago: Rand McNally, 1967.

The word "morality" often causes reactions of rejection, the word "ethics" begets a "ho-hum, but it's necessary," while "values" frequently elicits keen attention. Mowrer's collection of seventy-eight papers on the moral-and-ethical-values aspects of mental health discusses a variety of concepts and principles which historically psychologists have paid little attention to, but which increase sharply in importance as we recognize improving the quality of life as a goal of our work, and as we recognize the necessity of communicating with, understanding, and sharing the concepts of other helping networks in the community.

Hall, C. S., and Lindzey, G. *Theories of personality*, 2nd ed. New York: Wiley, 1970.

Many of the useful concepts covered in this chapter are clarified and organized in well written and succinct discussions of thirteen major personality theories of modern times, including the theories of Freud, Lewin, Cottell, Skinner, and Rogers. Hall and Lindzey provide an overall perspective on these theories in introductory and final chapters. They argue that personality cannot really be defined except by the empirical concepts related to the particular observer—theorist. At the end of each chapter on a theory they provide a helpful summary of relevant research methods and evidence and evaluate the theory according to how well it has generated research.

Breger, L. (ed.). *Clinical-cognitive psychology: models and integrations.* Englewood Cliffs, N. J.: Prentice-Hall, 1969.

Breger is deeply concerned with the need to integrate clinical psychology with general psychology, especially as it related to the prime characteristic of man—the ability to symbolize. He is critical of the behaviorist solution. Breger's own research has led him to view dreams as serving "the function of integrating aroused information into existing structures" (p. 223). Among several interesting chapters we would call the reader's attention to Loevinger's presentation of theories of ego development, which is an excellent synthesis and discussion of several points of view.

A further exploration of the relations of cognitive and clinical psychology is in the book edited by Jessor and Feshbach (1967).

Urban, H. B., and Ford, D. H. Some historical and conceptual perspectives on psychotherapy and behavior change. In A. E. Bergin and S. L. Garfield (eds.), *Handbook of psychotherapy and behavior change.* New York: Wiley, 1971, pp. 3—35.

The authors identify, as their preference, a problem-solving model for psychotherapy. They discuss analyzing the problem, selecting the goal, implementing solutions, and subsequent evaluation. They consider the roles of biological, transactional arousal, cognitive, and environmental systems in some detail, and present some implications of their thinking, one of which is that psychotherapy takes its place as but one of a family of helping procedures provided by a range of disciplines.

chapter 4

A Conceptual Framework

Every psychologist, but perhaps most of all the clinical psychologist, carries on a continuing struggle against confusion. The multiplicity of events occurring in any human life must be fitted into some sort of conceptual framework if it is to be comprehended at all. The professional psychologist is dealing simultaneously with at least two streams of experience, his client's and his own, and when the "client" is a family, a working group, or an organization, the complexity is increased many times over. It is on the basis of his conceptions of the nature of man and society, the process of development and change, the causes and symptoms of psychopathology, and many other psychological realities that the psychologist selects from the flux of experience what he will pay attention to. In many cases the conceptual framework remains unverbalized, unrecognized, and unsystematized, but there are distinct advantages in making it explicit—advantages to both psychologist and client. Clarity in communication and agreement about objectives are facilitated by such explicitness.

The first task is to discover the framework within which one is already operating—the process of self-analysis. It begins during training for professional positions but is never really completed. The raw material for this analysis is of three varieties: one's own stream of consciousness, the evaluative feedback by which one senses what others think of him, and one's own behavior products. In his dealings with clients and colleagues, the psychologist notes in passing moments of anxiety, flashes of anger, surges of affectionate feeling. These are indicators of what he responds to in people, and thus indirectly indicators of what he thinks and feels about human personality. He listens to his own recorded interviews, examines reports he has written. What sorts of interpretations has he placed on reported events? Does he use the terminology of Freud, of Skinner, or of Rogers in describing a client? Comparison of his perceptions with those of other people is often illuminating. This is one of the principal values of supervision during training and consultation during professional practice.

Then, difficult as it may seem to be to achieve an integration of what one feels and does with what one knows, the next major task of the psychologist who practices is to bring the abstract concepts of the classroom into alignment with the concrete realities of the consulting room or community. What is required is a theoretical formulation broad enough to accommodate and relate to each other all the concepts and principles that either research or one's experience have demonstrated to be in some sense true or valid. Once such a general framework has been adopted, new research findings, new insights from work experience can be fitted into it. It can be remodeled without being demolished or replaced.

The construction of the basic conceptual framework can be accomplished either by adopting a system that has been elaborated in detail by a major theorist or by selecting building materials from many sources and combining them into one's own, very individual system. As indicated in Chapter 3, adopting an existing system, the first of these techniques, has been by far the more common approach, although there are real advantages in constructing one's own system. Freud has had an enormous influence on clinical psychology as well as on psychiatry, and during the decades of the 1940s and 1950s, probably most clinical psychologists organized their thinking around a psychoanalytic framework. Some would have characterized themselves as neo-Freudian, and they followed systems taken over from Horney or Fromm rather than from Freud himself. Jung, Adler, and Rank also had their followers. After Carl Rogers became highly visible in the early 1940s, the client-centered system of concepts and principles was adopted as a whole by a large number of clinical psychologists. The alternative eclectic approach, in which concepts might be taken over from Kraepelinian psychiatry, from behaviorally oriented learning theory, from anthropology and social psychology, and from whatever other sources the psychologist had access to, has always been less common, but it has many advantages over the more dogmatic approaches, encouraging flexibility and innovative treatments.

What makes most of these frameworks within which clinical psychologists have operated in the past inadequate for the present, however, is their psychopathological orientation. The developed theories, like Freud's, grew out of psychiatry, and psychiatry is a branch of medicine. Freud himself came to view the theory in a much broader way, and applied its generalizations to all aspects of man's life, but as applied in assessment and therapy, it was basically a theory about what goes wrong with human development and how such malfunctioning can be corrected. The eclectic personality theories could have avoided this bias, but in practice usually did not. Concepts derived from learning theory were used to account for the development of neurotic symptoms. Measuring instruments, such as the Minnesota Multiphasic Personality Inventory, were constructed by comparing the responses of deviant groups with the responses of people who were presumably free of psychiatric difficulties. The dominant personality theories have always been linked much more closely to psychopathology than to superior achievement.

The expanding horizons for clinical psychology discussed in the previous chapters, the extension of its range to a wide variety of setting—client—activity combinations, and the questioning of the whole medical perspective, are now creating a serious challenge to the whole orientation represented by most previous theorizing. As long as the central task of clinical psychologists was to diagnose and treat sick or disturbed individuals, theoretical systems were adequate if they generated useful hypotheses about the origins of psychological difficulties and the processes occurring during therapy. This was particularly true for voluntary as contrasted with nonvoluntary patients. They consulted an expert on psychological "sickness" in the same spirit as they consulted a physician specializing in physiological malfunctioning. And while there was increasing discussion of what "positive mental health" might mean, most designated mental health agencies were designed to make an impact on negative conditions, to ameliorate ill health rather than to stimulate good health. The redesigning of community institutions, the transformation of educational systems, the facilitation of rewarding human relationships—these goals require a different kind of theoretical framework. Concepts explaining pathology, the foundation of the "medical model," are not necessarily unsound; they are irrelevant.

THE THEORY OF LIVING SYSTEMS

An organizing theory for the broadly based professional psychology that is replacing the clinical psychology of the past needs to be grounded in biology, psychology, sociology, and philosophy in order to facilitate comprehension of the complex nature of man. Fortunately, during the middle decades of the twentieth century, such an interdisciplinary approach to theorizing has come into existence. The name under which it usually goes, *general systems theory*, is somewhat inaccurate. What we have is not really a single coherent theory but rather a way of looking at phenomena that generates useful theories about them.

It is its comprehensiveness that makes general systems theory useful to clinical psychologists. Many concepts derived from different theories and different disciplines fit into it somewhere. Furthermore, all the diverse kinds of work clinicians find themselves doing, whether mainly assessment, therapy, or consultation and planning, can be analyzed in terms of understanding and modifying systems of some sort. Systems theory can constitute a meeting place for behavior therapists and psychoanalysts, private practitioners, and community psychologists.

The essential characteristic of "systems" thinking is to take as one's unit of observation a delimited set of interacting variables rather than single elements. One simple definition of a system (Allport, 1960) is "a complex of elements in mutual interaction." There must be *relationships between* the parts of a system that are different from the relationships of these parts to things outside it. There must be some sort of distinguishable *boundary*, tangible or intangible.

The distinction between *closed* and *open* systems, first clarified and repeatedly emphasized by Bertalanffy (1968), has been an important one for persons in the biological and social sciences. Physical systems were considered to be *closed*—that is, operating completely within their own boundaries, reacting to external influences only mechanically—whereas living systems were considered to be *open*—that is, actively receiving *inputs* from their environments and discharging outputs into these environments. The sharp distinction between open and closed systems does not appear so obvious now as it once did, but it is apparent that systems differ in degree of openness, and that living systems all belong at the open end of the continuum. All organisms, for example, ingest food and excrete wastes while they maintain the inner relationships that constitute their physiological systems. All task groups are guided by their environments and return their output to it. Every formal organization turns inputs from the environment (e.g., personnel, materials, information) into products and services for external use.

It is not possible or necessary in this brief account of systems theory to cover all the concepts and principles that have been elaborated. Miller's article (1971) is a succinct introductory summary, and Berrien's (1968) book serves as a ready reference for psychologists who wish to explore the ideas in greater depth. What we will do here is to focus on a few aspects we consider to be of particular importance to clinical psychologists.

Inputs—Outputs

The first set of system concepts to which we would call attention includes those having to do with *boundary* phenomena, *inputs* and *outputs*. To many psychologists it may seem that these concepts are no different from those we have been using for years in all branches of psychology, *stimulus* and *response*. However, connotatively, the concepts are not identical, and they lead to somewhat different approaches to research and practice. *Input* refers to everything that gets into the system through the boundary. This may be either less or more than the stimulus the experimental psychologist provides or the verbal interpretation the psychoanalyst makes to a patient. A system boundary acts as a filter, and thus *input* constitutes only a fraction of the stimulation available to an organism. Furthermore, everything surrounding a system is potential input, and even in the most carefully controlled experimental situation the environment of a system consists of more than the stimulus the experimental plan calls for. Similarly, the *output* of a system consists of more than a single response. The psychologist may be counting the number of times a shy child he is trying to help approaches his playmates and speaks to them, but the complex personality system with which he is dealing is also producing various other kinds of outputs. The psychologist using the concepts of general systems theory habitually scans the whole situation for inputs and outputs that are not part of his experimental or treatment plan. In order to stay alive, every person (and every other living system too) inputs and outputs both *matter/energy* and *information*. People get their energy from the food they eat and the air they breathe. But information inputs and outputs—sensations and behavior—are what matter to the clinical psychologist. All social behaviors are learned from past and present information inputs. The systems view reminds the clinician to scan the client's environment for an understanding of why the person behaves as he does, as well as to understand what environmental changes will help him move toward a more desirable state of affairs.

Regulation—Homeostasis

The second set of system concepts that turn out to be very useful as organizing principles includes those concerned with *regulation* within systems. For several decades physiologists have been studying the phenomenon of *homeostasis*, the maintenance of a steady state in the presence of drastic changes in the environment of a living system. The thermometer goes up and down as weather changes, sometimes varying as much as 60 degrees Fahrenheit within a single twenty-four-hour period, but the temperature within the body varies very little from the customary 98.6 degrees. A person eats an unusually large meal, including many complex varieties of proteins, fats, and carbohydrates, but the concentration of sugar and other chemicals in his blood remains relatively constant, as it must if life is not to be threatened.

It is only comparatively recently that we have appreciated what a complex thing this maintenance of steady states within the body is. It requires a very large number of adjustive mechanisms, including delicately coordinated reactions of glands and nervous system, which function automatically without any volition on our part. It is only with the advent of automation and our increasing use of such equipment as thermostats, electronic controls, and high-speed computers that we have been able to imitate such self-regulating processes. Awareness of the near ubiquity of these "field" processes, at least in our corner of the universe, is coming to permeate all scientific thinking.

Psychologists have used the concept of homeostasis a great deal in their theories of human behavior. For one thing, behavior is often a component of the physiological homeostatic processes themselves. The acts of folding one's arms, drawing one's body into a compact ball, or even getting out of bed to find an extra blanket are part of the process by means of which constant temperature is maintained. The idea of homeostasis has figured largely in theories of *motivation*. Psychologists have noted the cyclical nature of hunger and other drives. A tissue need initiates an active period of restless seeking, which leads eventually to eating and cessation of the search. After this reduction of the drive comes a quiescent period, which is followed by another cycle of seeking, consummation, and quiescence. Many theorists have proposed that all drives arise out of some sort of disturbance of inner equilibrium and the need to remove such disturbance. It would appear now that this idea cannot account for all of human motivation. Research evidence is accumulating that human beings seek change and new experience as well as stability. But homeostasis is still an important concept in understanding motivation. It also helps us to make sense of many otherwise puzzling characteristics of perception. Size and shape constancy, for example, can be thought of as homeostatic processes that serve to stabilize the external environment for the person.

Feedback

Out of the study of the complex mathematical—engineering systems that underlie computer technology and automation—the field of *cybernetics*—has come an understanding of processes that enable a system to maintain activity in a constant direction as well as to maintain a steady state. We understand in principle how a person's purposes and goals can influence his behavior, how he can remain "on target," as it were. The essential concept is *feedback*. People, like computers, can be "programmed" in such a way that information about the state of the system fed back to a decision maker will automatically trigger an action that will change this state. Feedback mechanisms, in computers or in people, can be expressed as commands of the "if . . . , then . . ." form. "If the thermometer reads 65°, throw this switch."

Feedback may be either positive or negative. *Positive* feedback would exhilarate the system activities and ultimately be destructive. *Negative* feedback is of greater importance for the governing of system processes. Figure 4-1 illustrates how reversed or negative signals from channel A return to a transmitter also receiving comparison signals. The interaction of these two affects gate-keeping functions in the transmitter and allows feedback to alter the signal in A. This basic mechanism is the fundamental paradigm for governing all controlling functions at all system levels.

Many examples of the operation of feedback mechanisms in living systems readily come to mind. Selye (1956) pointed out years ago the importance of the *general adaptation syndrome* characterizing an organisms's response to *stress*. It involves a series of reactions producing secretions of the pituitary and adrenal

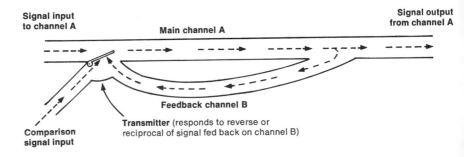

FIGURE 4-1 Negative feedback. (From Miller, 1971, p. 293.)

glands, each delicately coordinated with the others. Tanner (1963) has presented striking examples of what he calls "catch-up growth" in children. These are cases in which some illness markedly reduced food intake for periods of a year or more and thus caused the child to stop growing. After the illness was cured or counteracted, the child grew at several times his former rate until he reached the level he would have attained normally had no illness intervened. Like the automatic pilot on an airplane that changes the direction of flight to keep the plane on course, some automatic feedback mechanism keeps a child moving along his own normal growth curve toward a genetically determined size "target." Although the anatomy of all the detailed feedback mechanisms producing the general adaptation syndrome or catch-up growth is not known, it is clear that they exist, and biologists know how to look for them.

A more specifically psychological example of the operation of feedback is what happens during group therapy. Information about the effect his words, manner, and style have on other people, when fed back immediately to an individual, enables him to "correct" his direction and aim at the kind of interpersonal relationships he is trying to achieve. A consultant with a community agency may observe that previously unexamined admissions policies and waiting lists are resulting in lack of care for certain minority groups; calling this problem to the attention of the head of the agency may result in a review of policies and a change in procedures.

It appears that there are ranges of tolerance in systems for information input. Just as an organism cannot handle too much or too little heat or food, it cannot adequately function (i.e., receive, decode, process, encode, and transmit) with too little or too much information. Milgram (1970) attributes much of the individual alienation stress of living in a city to stimulus overload. Businesses may fail when they do not have the capacity to handle excessive demands. Numerous studies of stimulus deprivation and isolation have shown that subjects in soundproof, dark rooms often develop hallucinations and other forms of maladjustment and demand that they be let out of the experiment.

As external stress increases, the internal strain increases unless the organism can adapt and reestablish the steady state. An organism or group usually follows a predictable course—early shock and decreased adaptation, then energetic efforts to find solutions calling on more of the systems capabilities, and finally either adaptation or collapse. Both in adapting to stress and trying to attain goals, systems ordinarily remove barriers, act to acquire needed supports, or master the problem in some way. However, maladaptive adjustments short of collapse also occur. The ego defense mechanisms pointed out by psychoanalysis are examples—displacement of aggression, rigid compulsions, and denial of the problem.

The Decider and Purposive Behavior

In the information-processing part of a system there are many components, such as input and output transmitters, decoders and encoders of information, associating mechanisms for learning and memory. A component of overriding importance is the *decider*—the executive part of the system, which receives inputs from all subsystems and transmits information back which controls their behavior. "Of these critical subsystems only the decider is essential, in the sense that a system cannot be dependent on another system for its deciding. A living system does not exist if the decider is dispersed upwardly, downwardly, or outwardly" (Miller, 1971, p. 290). Deciders reside in the nervous system of the organism, in leaders of groups, and in executives of organizations. In human groups decision making becomes complex. It is often dispersed throughout subsystems or certain kinds of decisions are made at different levels of organization with the implicit or explicit undertaking of the principal executive.

In the process of growth and learning, living systems develop preferences for one steady state rather than another. Individuals prefer certain environments or select one group association rather than another. Thus a hierarchy of comparison values is built up against which information can be matched in movements toward one situation rather than another. Feedback thus permits *purposive behavior*. "When disturbed this (steady) state is restored by the system by successive approximations, in order to relieve the strain of the disparity recognized internally between the feedback signal and the comparison signal" (Miller, 1971, p. 294). Any system may have multiple purposes at the same time, and there are usually many different paths to attain its goals. Some of these cost more than others, and the decider may weigh the drain on resources against the benefits to arrive at the most efficient course of action.

Hierarchical Order of Systems

A fourth set of system concepts of considerable value to clinical psychologists includes those that have to do with the relationship of systems to one another. Although it is possible for us to single out an individual system for our attention, it does not exist in isolation. The world is made up of systems within systems, organizations of components each of which is organized within its own boundary. It is obvious without any theorizing that a person represents a system at one level, and the family to which he belongs, a system at another. It is also obvious that the person is an organization of many subsystems, and that there are suprasystems in which families constitute components or units. A clinical psychologist often finds that a single neurotic pattern exemplified by a client he is attempting to help has system properties, as when a man drinks heavily to forget his troubles, thus impairing his faculties so that he gets into more trouble, thus maintaining or increasing the need to drink heavily. Such "vicious circles" are familiar to all practicing clinicians, and they have learned how durable such behavioral "steady states" are.

Does the higher-order system control the functioning of the lower-order system or do the parts control the whole? The answer can only be "Both." Suprasystems select from the outputs of their subsystems those they find useful. Other outputs are rejected as waste. Through this action *adaptation* occurs, the

SupraNational System

e.g., Common Market, United
Nations, satellite communications
network

Societal System

e.g., one nation, a large part
of a nation

Organizational System

e.g., industrial concern, social
agency, professional
association

Group System

e.g., family, work team,
recreational group,
animal group

Organismic System

e.g., individual person,
animal or plant

Organ System

e.g., nervous system,
alimentary system

Cell System

e.g., individual cells
within a body

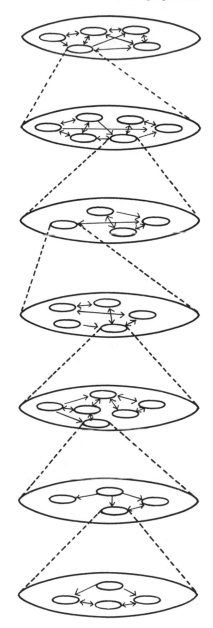

FIGURE 4-2 Levels of living systems.

basic process of evolution. Outputs of a system are somewhat variable, and with
the passage of time the system modifies its behavior in a way that will increase
the outputs. Just as *feedback* is the concept most central to understanding the
stability of systems, *hierarchy* is the concept most central to understanding how
systems change.

Figure 4-2 illustrates the seven levels of living systems described by Miller (1971)—cell, organ, organism, group, organization, society, and supranational system. Each system has its subsystems and suprasystem. Beyond the supranational systems are larger aggregates of mixed living and nonliving forms—planets and solar system. Below the cell are smaller systems such as molecules and atoms. Each living system may enclose and interact with nonliving objects such as chairs, typewriters, computers, or automobiles. When all of the interacting objects and living things within a given physical area are considered together, we may speak of an ecosystem. An example is a pond in a forest with all of the natural processes going on, maintaining a balance between different forms of life and alternating with the seasonal weather. Ecology, as we have noted before, is the study of organisms in relation to their environment. In this book our emphasis will be on human beings, particularly at the organismic (or personal) group and organizational levels, but we will occasionally mention the total environment, including the nonhuman components. We will also be looking at communities, which lie between organizations and societies largely as systems of organization within a geographical area.

Organizing his thinking along the lines of general systems theory and habitually looking at his work in this way enables the clinical psychologist to make choices—to steer a clear course through the confusions and complexities with which he must deal. He can choose, for example, at what *level* to intervene. No longer does he assume that psychotherapy for the individual is always the treatment to be preferred. He may decide to work instead with a family, a sixth grade, a hospital ward, or a community. He can choose also whether to make a direct effort to change the internal structure of a system to which he is directing his attention or simply to manipulate input in order to produce output changes. The psychoanalyst exemplifies the first choice, the specialist in behavior modification the second. Turning to still another example, the psychologist can choose whether to set as his objective an increase in the stability of the system under consideration, or a maximization of changes occurring in it. Too often, especially in recent times, it has been assumed without question that people and institutions must be changed as much as possible. At other periods, stability has been just as uncritically sought. It is part of the clinical psychologist's job to decide in each case what his aim should be.

DEVELOPMENT

Psychologists have studied this process of *patterned change* in individuals in their work on *development*. The word covers a wide range of phenomena. As English and English (1958, p. 148) put it: "Its application ranges from molecular changes in crystals or bones to changes in purposes, ideals, or the structure of society." General systems theory has been formulated to highlight the common features in such diverse processes.

In considering development from a systems point of view, psychologists have been impressed with the transformation of systems over time, producing differentiable *life stages*. The young adult, psychologically and physically, is not just a child grown large. In general as a young system moves to an adult stage it becomes more differentiated in its subsystems, more preferential in its inputs, and more elaborate and patterned in its outputs. The middle-aged woman lives a life whose whole pattern is different form that of a teenaged girl. Aging is not just a slowing down and gradual impairment of function. The pattern and style of life at seventy is different from the pattern and style at thirty-five. A psychologist thinking developmentally in concepts derived from a theory of living systems must take these transformations over time into consideration.

Although there are many ways in which the characteristic features of successive life stages can be characterized, the approach psychologists have found most valuable is that of Erik Erickson (1950), in which he focuses on the developmental crisis that must be resolved. At each stage a new drive and need constellation and a new social environment appear, giving rise to a new pattern of social interaction. The eight stages Erickson delineates are as follows:

1. Infancy: basic trust versus basic mistrust
2. Early childhood: autonomy versus shame and doubt
3. Play age: initiative versus guilt
4. School age: industry versus inferiority
5. Adolescence: identity versus confusion
6. Young adulthood: intimacy versus isolation
7. Adulthood: generativity versus stagnation
8. Old age: integrity versus despair

Erickson's conceptualization provides a framework into which the psychologist can fit the infinitely varied details of individual human lives as they relate to the world around.

POSSIBILITIES, ALTERNATIVES, AND CHOICE

In the section on general systems theory the importance of organization in the psychological life of individuals and groups was highlighted. What we wish to emphasize in this section is the pluralistic nature of psychological reality and the implications of realizing this, particularly in individual human lives. As early as 1890, William James in *Principles of Psychology* called attention to this basic fact, which he was to emphasize again and again in his later writings, but psychologists who have borrowed many ideas from him have usually failed to stress this one as much as he did. Consider, for example, this famous paragraph from the *Principles* (1890, pp. 288–289):

The mind is at every stage a theatre of simultaneous possibilities. Consciousness consists in the comparison of these with each other, the selection of some, and the suppression of the rest by the reinforcing and inhibiting agency of attention. . . . The mind, in short, works on the data it receives very much as the sculptor works on his block of stone. In a sense the statue stood there from eternity. But there were a thousand different ones beside it, and the sculptor alone is to thank for having extricated this one from the rest . . . the world *we* feel and live in will be that which our ancestors and we, by slowly cumulative strokes of choice, have extricated out of this, like sculptors, by simply rejecting certain portions of the stuff. Other sculptors, other statues from the same stone! Other minds, other worlds from the same monotonous and inexpressive chaos.

Psychologists attempting to apply their science to the difficult tasks of improving the functioning of human personalities, groups, and institutions, like the sculptor, have an opportunity to select and to help their clients select from many possible patterns of life the ones that are to be brought into existence. To the theory of living systems sketched above, we now need to add a theory of human possibilities. ("Theory," as before, is used loosely. Organizing concepts rather than tightly organized propositions are what we are considering.)

The fundamentals of such a theory are some biological "givens," so obvious that they are often not noticed at all. The key concept is *multipotentiality*. A living creature possesses infinitely more possibilities for action and for development than can be actualized. When he takes action in a particular situation, he performs one of many possible actions he might have taken. As he grows and develops, the patterns or systems he uses in organizing his experience and behavior represent only a fraction of the organizations possible to him. Psychological possibilities for a human individual, although limited, are multiple.

The limits are set by many factors, beginning with the genetic origins of individuality, but the most important and universal limitation is time. Looking at its short-range aspects, it is clear that only a limited number of experiences or actions can occur simultaneously. From the long-range point of view, only a limited number of traits and characteristics can be developed by an individual during his lifetime. Time's arrow points in one direction, and eventually time runs out. William James (1890, pp. 309–310) expressed this basic fact very cogently, when he wrote:

> With most objects of desire, physical nature restricts our choice to but one of many represented goods, and even so it is here. I am often confronted by the necessity of standing by one of my empirical selves and relinquishing the rest. Not that I would not, if I could, be both handsome and fat and well dressed, and a great athlete, and make a million a year, be a wit, a *bon-vivant*, and a lady-killer, as well as a philosopher; a philanthropist, statesman, warrior, and African explorer, as well as a tone-poet and saint. But the thing is simply impossible. The millionaire's work would run counter to the saint's; the *bon-vivant* and the philanthropist would trip each other up; the philosopher and the lady-killer could not well keep house in the same tenement of clay. Such different

characters may conceivably at the outset of life be alike possible to a man. But to make any one of them actual, the rest must more or less be suppressed. So the seeker of his truest, strongest, deepest self must review the list carefully, and pick out the one on which to stake his salvation. All other selves thereupon become unreal, but the fortunes of this self are real.

The limits James sets on self-development in this passage are perhaps a little more stringent than they need to be. Most of us carry along several somewhat different selves, not completely integrated. But the main point, whether one "stakes his salvation" on only one of his possible selves or not, is that the nature of the situation each human individual faces makes selection necessary. Only a fraction of the developmental possibilities life provides can be utilized.

There are many ways in which this selection can be accomplished. Family situation and cultural environment select for the very young child some sounds and grammatical structures to contain and express his thoughts, some personality qualities to be cultivated, some to be weeded out. The farther along he proceeds in his development, the more this selective process can be accomplished through his own conscious choice. If he is an American middle-class child, he is constrained to learn English during his first year or two, but whether he becomes proficient in French or German or Spanish during his adolescence depends upon his own choice.

However selected, whatever organized systems have already developed out of the matrix of human possibilities are what later organizations must be based on. The child of three cannot be returned to the undifferentiated status of the newborn infant. The man of twenty-one does not have the same freedom as he had when he entered school at six to develop along any one of many different lines. What he has chosen has ruled out alternative choices. If he has not decided much earlier to be a musician or an athlete or a scientist, he will now probably never reach the highest levels of proficiency in these endeavors.

However, at any stage of life, *alternative* systems are always functioning, *alternative* developmental possibilities are always still open. Because of the inconceivable complexity of the human organism, a person is always learning a number of things at the same time. *Personality is plural.* The significance of this fact for the professional psychologist is that in helping a person improve his personality or his relationships with others or to maximize his effectiveness and productivity one need not, in fact cannot, start from "scratch." What one does is to identify and develop one or more of the alternative psychological systems already there. Each of us, even though many possibilities have been ruled out by our experience so far, has more than one habit system, more than one style, more than one set of values. Each of us thus always has a choice about the shape the remainder of his life is to take. When a person says that he has "no choice" about the way he acts or the direction in which he moves, it can be assumed that he simply has not identified and examined the possibilities for change in his own psychological and social situation.

Among the most significant social changes the twentieth century has brought about are the special education and rehabilitation movements. Beginning with Anne Sullivan and Helen Keller, devoted clinicians and teachers have demonstrated for all sorts of people with what would in previous eras have been looked upon as insuperable handicaps the proposition which we are discussing— that there are multiple possibilities for psychological development in human individuals. Persons who are mentally retarded, completely paralyzed, or deeply psychotic have been shown not to be "hopeless cases." For a particular individual, we are justified in assuming that some possibilities for desirable development exist. The task of the clinical psychologist, as of members of the many other "helping professions," is to help him find them and capitalize upon them. The fact that we often fail in this task does not release us from the obligation of attempting it.

We have cast the basic assumptions and principles of a nascent theory of human possibilities in individual terms, but it is applicable also to the many other varieties of systems discussed in the previous section. The system of interpersonal relationships manifested in a family, for example, develops and changes as time passes. The transformation that actually occurs is one among a number that might have occurred, and to some extent conscious or unconscious choices control this selection. A psychologist who accepts a family as his client and attempts to improve its functioning needs to be able to identify alternative patterns of organization and to facilitate the thinking family members do about them. This kind of pluralistic, multiple-alternative thinking can be extended to school systems, communities, professional organizations, even governments. "What is" should always be considered in relation to "what might be."

IMPLICATIONS FOR PRACTICE

The first and most important consequence of casting professional psychological service in the mold of a theory of living systems is that one realizes that plans for treatment or intervention must take into consideration higher-level systems of which the one being modified forms a part. Again and again clinical psychologists, with or without any knowledge of systems theory, have learned from experience that they must do this. A child who makes real progress in developing self-control and skill in communicating with adults in the benign environment of the clinic playroom soon reverts to his former indiscriminate aggressive behavior when he returns to his schoolroom. The model prisoner who leaves the correctional institution with every intention of going straight is picked up three months later for bank robbery because the system of personal associations and societal pressures he becomes a part of functions in the same way that it did before his first incarceration. A stutterer is cured in a behavior-modification laboratory but loses his new-found fluency as soon as he goes home. Thus we are seeing a renewed emphasis on attempts to deal with an individual's interpersonal relationships as a part of any attempt to improve individual personality, from psychoanalysis to rehabilitation.

Also, in one area after another, the creation of a new interpersonal system by persons who use membership in it to bring about changes in themselves is becoming a phenomenon of our times. Alcoholics Anonymous was the first demonstration that such a system could be created by and for its members. Similar associations of drug addicts, former mental hospital patients, and many other categories of people are now functioning. In a way, they are outside the province of clinical psychology, since they are not kinds of treatment or intervention that can be deliberately set up or used by psychologists to benefit the clients they serve. They constitute alternatives to therapy rather than varieties of therapy. But as psychological phenomena to be observed, studied, and understood, they are of the highest importance.

To recapitulate, psychologists have discovered that they must always be aware of two or more system levels as they try to bring about changes in a particular system. One reason, as explained above, is that the tenacity of the patterns of functioning in the higher-level system may negate any changes produced at a lower level. Another reason is that an effective change at the lower level may modify in unpredicted ways the functioning of the higher-level systems. Mr. Lawson, for example, seeks psychotherapy for emotional conflicts that interfere with his work as an investment broker. As therapy proceeds, he notes drastic changes in his relationship with his wife. It is not at all uncommon for "successful" therapy to result in the breakup of a marriage. Or, as another example, when a program of behavior modification succeeds in toning down Jerry's hyperactivity and enabling him to pay attention to what his teacher says, the environment of all the children in Jerry's schoolroom changes significantly. Still another example is what happens when a hospital ward is reorganized to give patients more responsibility. The roles of nurses, aides, and administrators in the hospital of which the ward forms a part may be changed so drastically as to generate widespread opposition to the experimental program even if it is shown to benefit patients. Although such changes at higher system levels are only partly predictable, it is well for a psychologist to be prepared for them by keeping under some surveillance systems upon which he is not focusing his major efforts.

Psychologists have only partially assimilated the concepts growing out of the theory of living systems, but they have made even less progress in coming to terms with the concepts of multiple possibilities. One obstacle has been adherence to rigid deterministic assumptions on scientific grounds, assumptions characteristic of nineteenth-century science rather than the science of the late twentieth century. It was natural for Sigmund Freud to think in this way, although even in the late nineteenth century, as noted above, William James thought differently. Because people are caught up in many systems, only partly overlapping, their behavior is not completely determined by any one of them. Because they have the mental equipment to conceive of alternatives that are not present, to look ahead, to choose, and to plan, they are not completely at the mercy of immediate circumstances.

Acceptance of these basic assumptions about the human situation leads to an increasing emphasis on *choices*, by the psychologist and by his client. Instead of doing "what comes naturally" in attacking a problem presented to him, the psychologist will first canvas alternative plans for proceeding. They are likely to be more numerous and varied than he thinks they are at first. In the case of Billy's behavior problems, alternatives may include the use of a drug to modify his hormonal system and change the pattern of physical growth, working with Billy's parents to change relationships and reinforcement patterns within the family, planning a schedule of reinforcements in Billy's schoolroom to be put into effect by his teacher, transferring Billy to a different schoolroom or to a residential school, and perhaps several other possibilities. As comprehensive community mental health centers replace specialized facilities designed to provide only one sort of treatment, we shall perhaps see more consideration of multiple alternatives for treatment in each individual case.

Clients also have choices, and these should be respected and facilitated. An unhappy housewife may seek psychotherapy from a psychiatrist or a mental health clinic. She may talk to her minister, or join a church if she does not belong to one. She may instead become a participant in an encounter group. She may leave home and family and join a commune. We cannot assume that psychotherapy is for her the best of these alternatives.

Furthermore, choices among alternative ways of proceeding by psychologists and by persons and groups seeking change do not occur solely at the outset of improvement programs. If individual psychotherapy of a particular kind is initiated, there will be repeated opportunities for psychologist and client to consider whether it should be continued, terminated, modified, or supplemented by other kinds of treatment. As the client develops more insight, he sees his alternatives in new ways and may drastically change his own plans for the conduct of his life as he makes choices from among them.

As unitary concepts of adjustment, mental health, and the like are superseded by pluralistic concepts assuming varied ways of adapting to diverse circumstances, we may expect the psychological practice of the future to be far less uniform and stereotyped than psychological practice of the past.

SUMMARY

A psychologist needs a theory, at least a loose one, to enable him to comprehend complex human reality and to allow for his own assumptions as he does so. He can adopt a theory already formulated, such as psychoanalysis, learning theory, or existentialism, or he can be an eclectic, picking up concepts from many sources and combining them into his own theory.

The trouble with most ready-made theories that have dominated the thinking of clinical psychologists in the past is that they have been too exclusively concerned with pathology. As we enlarge the scope of our work to include many new setting–client–activity combinations, we need a theory based not on a medical orientation but on general biosocial and philosophical foundations.

The orientation proposed is one that derives from the burgeoning theory of living systems and an emerging theory of multiple possibilities. General systems theory is made up of concepts applicable at many levels from cell to society, concepts such as boundaries, inputs, outputs, information, and feedback. Research on homeostasis, on stress, and on cybernetics fall into place within this system. Possibilities theory includes such concepts as *multipotentiality, alternatives,* and *choice.*

Adopting this theoretical formulation broadens the scope of concern and increases the diversity in what professional psychologists attempt to do.

SUGGESTED READINGS

Bertalanffy, L. von. *General system theory: foundations, development, applications.* New York: Braziller, 1968.

Bertalanffy, a biologist, was one of the first to propose a general systems theory, and he has continued throughout his long and distinguished career to explore its implications and present it to an ever-widening public. This book constitutes a synthesis of what he has accomplished, bringing together the most important papers he has written on the subject from 1940 through 1967. The emphasis is on living organisms rather than on the mathematical or engineering aspects of systems that constitute an important foundation for modern technology. The concepts that have been discussed in the present chapter are developed in much greater detail in the Bertalanffy book.

Berrien, F. K. *General and social systems.* New Brunswick, N. J.: Rutgers University Press, 1968.

The principal value of this book to the clinical psychologist is that it presents systems theory with a specifically psychological emphasis, thus facilitating one's understanding of the basic ideas. The major focus is on social systems rather than on single organisms. Of particular interest are the later chapters, in which the author discusses the growth of systems, their internal and external adaptations to various kinds of stress, and the nature and consequences of conflicts between systems.

Several others have brought systems theory or similar thinking to bear on psychological and applied social science. Dror (1971) fuses systems analysis with social problem solving. Cooper and Foster (1971) present a theoretical analysis of sociotechnical systems. Schroder, Driver, and Streufert (1967) in their book on human information processing see the process as feedback and mutual adaptation between the person and environment. The earlier work of Miller,

Galanter, and Pribram (1960) posits a system of plans and internal programming in human beings analogous with the computer's program.

Astrachan, B. M. Towards a social systems model of therapeutic groups. *Social Psychiatry*, 1970, *5*, 110–119.

This paper shows how a systems approach can be used to clarify one's thinking about a clinical task and to suggest how the phenomenon in question may be profitably studied. The author distinguishes between three models of therapeutic groups, namely Member to Therapist, Group to Therapist, and Member to Member. He points out the limitations of these models and recommends a conceptualization of group structure, function, and organization based on general systems theory. The aspect he finds most susceptible to study and research is the functioning of the leader as a general regulatory agent in the system. He calls for an examination of variations in the group as they relate to variations in the way this regulatory function is carried out.

Ward, R. F., and Faillace, L. A. The alcoholic and his helpers; a systems view. *Quarterly Journal of Studies of Alcoholism*, 1970, *31*(3).

The authors propose that alcoholism be viewed as a symptom of a complex interactional process, with the behavior of the alcoholic highly dependent on various interactions within the total system. They give several examples of such systems, involving husbands and wives, parents and children, therapists and clients, and police and court dealings with alcoholics. It is suggested that in such situations the education of the alcoholic's "helpers" may be as important as the treatment given the alcoholic himself.

Buckley, W. (ed.). *Modern systems research for the behavioral scientist: a sourcebook*. Chicago: Aldine-Atherton, 1968.

In this one volume we find most of the important papers about general systems theory, along with discussions of the applications of the concepts in a variety of behavioral science areas. For the clinical psychologist, probably the most helpful chapters are the Foreword, by Anatol Rapoport; Chapter 42, The Open System in Personality Theory, by Gordon Allport (described below); Chapter 46, Plans and the Structure of Behavior, by Miller, Galanter, and Pribram; and Chapter 59, Society as a Complex Adaptive System, by Buckley.

Diamond, S., Balvin, R., and Diamond, F. R. *Inhibition and choice*. New York: Harper & Row, 1963.

In this book, the concepts we have discussed having to do with possibilities, alternatives, and choices are placed on a physiological foundation by focusing on neurological inhibition and its implications. Diamond and his co-authors make a good case for defining psychology as *the science of behavioral choice*, rather than as simply the science of behavior. The chapter most relevant to the theoretical thinking we have presented here is Chapter 7, The Spectrum of Choice.

Allport, G. W. The open system in personality theory. *Journal of Abnormal and Social Psychology*, 1960, *21*, 301–311. Reprinted in W. Buckley (ed.), *Modern systems research for the behavioral scientist: a sourcebook.* Chicago: Aldine-Atherton, 1968, pp. 343–350.

One of the most influential American psychologists applies general systems theory to personality and shows how different personality theories have emphasized different aspects of the definition of an open system. Most of the issues that have divided them are related to how open a system personality is assumed to be. Allport argues for a maximum of openness in conceptualization of personality.

Collier (1962) argues in a similar way for an open-systems approach which retains concepts of self and independence.

Tyler, L. E. Towards a workable psychology of individuality. *American Psychologist*, 1959, *14*, 75–81.

This presidential address to the Western Psychological Association represents a first approach to a theory of human possibilities, pointing to two aspects of individual development that it is important to consider, choice and organization.

Tyler, L. E. *The work of the counselor*, 3rd ed. New York: Appleton-Century-Crofts, 1969, chapter 2.

In this chapter the author discusses biological and philosophical bases of a theory of possibilities and the implications of such a theory for counseling.

Peterson, D. R. *The clinical study of social behavior.* New York: Appleton-Century-Crofts, 1968.

In this book, Peterson, without any mention of either systems or possibilities, comes up with an approach to clinical psychology that is very much like ours. The emphasis is on the appraisal of behavior at three levels—the person, the group, and the social system—in ways that will directly facilitate behavior improvement. Because of its brevity, clarity, and straightforwardness, the book may not be recognized as much as it deserves for its implications for clinical psychology. It represents a real break with the past, and sets up a new program for the psychological service professions.

Another very stimulating book relating person and environment and treating psychopathology as a problem of social competence is that of Leslie Phillips, *Human Adaptation and Its Failures* (1968).

chapter 5

The Clinical Psychologist
as a Researcher

Since the days following World War II when massive efforts to shape the profession of clinical psychology began, one central organizing concept, that of the scientist–practitioner, has maintained its ascendancy. Support for the idea has at no time been universal, and often this hybrid species seemed threatened with complete extinction. Opposition to the research requirement has frequently come from graduate students who are frustrated by the insistence of the university that they master statistics and experimental design and devote a major part of their time to the task of acquiring psychological knowledge having little or no relevance to their work with patients and clients. At other times the objections have come from practicing clinicians, who complain that the young psychologists coming to them with fresh Ph.D.s from university training programs have not acquired essential *clinical* knowledge and skills because of the disproportionate emphasis the universities place on research. Still other criticisms of the scientist–practitioner concept have come from eminent psychologists who examine the publication records of practicing clinicians trained in the prevailing manner and conclude that the effort to make researchers of these people has been a colossal waste of time, since the large majority of them never engage in any research after obtaining the Ph.D.

PROFESSIONAL TRAINING AND RESEARCH

There are some very articulate spokesmen for the contention that professional psychologists require a different sort of training from academic psychologists and that the emphasis on research should be decreased. Even though the official policy has been reaffirmed at high-level conferences again and again—starting with the 1949 Boulder conference (Raimy, 1950) and more recently at Chicago in 1965 (APA, 1966a)—that the objective of graduate training programs should be to produce the scientific psychologist who practices rather than the professional man with some background in scientific psychology, new patterns

112

are being tried out. At the University of Illinois, a professional training program leading to the Doctor of Psychology degree is solidly established (Peterson, 1968b, 1971). The California State Psychological Association has set up a special education institution to train clinical psychologists (Pottharst, 1970). Other innovative programs are being proposed.

Whatever develops out of these undertakings, there are still some very sound reasons for continuing to emphasize research in programs designed to prepare clinical psychologists for their work. Prominent among these is the indisputable fact that the accumulated psychological knowledge we now have is not adequate to deal with the complex challenges the practicing psychologist faces. We must increase it and refine it if progress in promoting human psychological welfare is to be made. Clinicians cannot simply apply the knowledge that personality psychologists and social psychologists and physiological psychologists produce. The problems of practice, facing the complexities of real life, are very different from the abstract and specialized concerns of the theorist. Clinicians are attacking problems of a different nature—not just applying the basic scientist's principles. Clinical psychologists must shoulder their share of the responsibility for enlarging a relevant body of knowledge.

Partly what is involved in the foregoing conclusion is the fact that psychology as a whole *needs* the ideas of those who are closest to the concrete manifestations of the human nature that constitutes its subject matter. Medicine with its long history may have moved beyond the stage at which the physician's careful observation of the manifestations of a disease process in individual patients contributes much to scientific knowledge of the disease, although it is doubtful whether even this can be stated with any assurance. But it is certain that psychology has not reached this point. Freud would never have hit upon the theoretical concepts about motivation that have proved so stimulating to several generations of psychologists studying personality had he not been a practitioner. Even the individual clinical psychologist who never designs or publishes another research study after his doctoral dissertation may, through his communication with other psychologists during a staff conference, symposium at a professional meeting, or consulting visit, propose a new idea that will lead to important scientific advances. Scientific psychology needs the contributions of research-oriented clinicians.

There is also another kind of reason to maintain the scientist—practitioner concept in the training of clinicians. It is being increasingly realized that society's attempts to improve mental health and psychological welfare must themselves be subject to research. There should be someone on every mental health team to plan and direct these research efforts, and the psychologist is the team member most likely to be cast in this role. There are, of course, research psychiatrists, research social workers, research-oriented nurses. However, clinical psychologists, because they are Ph.D.s who have taken research courses and written research dissertations, are more likely to be prepared to take on research responsibilities than the other professional workers are. The findings of a study carried on in one hospital, clinic, or agency may never appear in a major journal or monograph, and yet they may be very useful to the organization conducting the study. Research includes the little as well as the big studies, and research skills that contribute to constant improvement in the service offered at a particular place require no further justification.

A final and perhaps most cogent reason for continuing a research emphasis in the training of clinical psychologists is the fact of unremitting change over the years in the ways clinicians think and the things clinicians do. As one studies the history of the profession and surveys the present scene, it becomes clear that it has not been and is not going to be possible for a responsible psychologist to settle down into a comfortable groove and practice for the rest of his life the skills he learned in graduate school. New challenges constantly confront him. Choices and decisions about the directions his own efforts ought to take must repeatedly be made. To respond intelligently to such changes, he needs to keep in constant touch with research findings of others, even if he is not producing any of his own. He must know how to evaluate the significance of research reports, and he must habitually canvas and seek out such information if he is to keep his practice in tune with the times, progressive but not simply "faddish."

A RESEARCH ORIENTATION FOR CLINICAL USE

Underlying much of the controversy over the place of research in clinical psychology and the question of how scientific it is possible for a clinician to be lie differing assumptions about what science is. The strict constructionists insist on the generality of scientific laws, the superiority of experiments over other kinds of observation, the use of rigid controls to rule out the effects of influences other than the one being manipulated, and as much and as accurate quantification of variables as possible. Since much of the research clinical psychologists do on problems growing directly out of their day-to-day activities does not meet these specifications, psychologists who hold a narrow view of science consider it unscientific. In contrast, other psychologists, from William James to the present, have included in their concept of science a much wider range of activities. One can make a good case for the statement that *anything* that adds to humanity's total store of usable knowledge constitutes a contribution to science. The person who in a brilliant flash of insight generates a new idea contributes to the total scientific enterprise along with the person who develops the implications of the idea and devises experiments to test hypotheses based on these implications. The person who makes careful observations of the behavior of people participating in different treatment programs, welfare plans, or teaching and learning situations is a part of the scientific research effort even if he never runs an F test or a chi-square. If we think of scientific research as *an ongoing effort to advance human knowledge*, an effort in which many different kinds of people participate in many different ways, we shall have no difficulty with the scientist—practitioner concept, and individual clinical psychologists can identify for themselves congenial and feasible researcher roles.

What, then, is the best strategy to ensure the rapid development of clinical knowledge? It would certainly seem important to provide the kinds of training and the financial support mentioned above and to break down any social-psychological obstacles that hinder participation in research by clinical staffs. In addition, it would seem very important not to let the development of clinical knowledge become confined to any narrow research sector. In fact, Dittmann (1960) has gone so far as to claim, in reviewing the work of an eminent psychiatrist, that it is questionable whether much progress in ideas in personality and clinical psychology has come from formal research itself. Freud, Piaget, and others who have contributed a great deal to psychological knowledge have concentrated on observing a few individuals closely and in great detail. While it is true that their conclusions have to be treated as hypotheses to be tried out, tested, and varied in many ways on a wider array of human beings, we cannot, *ab initio*, exclude their methods from psychological science. There is a place for *clinical exploration*, the empirically oriented investigation of phenomena. As has been stressed in previous sections, science is not limited to the laboratory or the computing room. The kind of scientist we are talking about does, however, constantly check himself and concedes that his conclusions are open to revision. Darwin, another astute observer and searcher for scientific laws, even kept a notebook in which he entered *negative instances* because he suspected he was more likely to forget these than the instances which, agreeably to him, confirmed his theory. This kind of clinical exploration requires a long period of observation leading to a preliminary statement of principles, then more observation followed by refinement and revision of the principles. It includes the public communication of these ideas and sincere openness to change in the light of new findings, which, perhaps, is rarest of all. This, although not a formal research design, accords with the spirit of science and falls well within the confines of respected inquiry. It is something all clinicians may engage in. Rogers has defended it in these words (1959, p. 189):

It is my opinion that the type of understanding which we call science can begin anywhere, at any level of sophistication. To observe acutely, to think carefully and creatively—these activities, not the accumulation of laboratory instruments, are the beginnings of science. To observe that a given crop grows better on the rocky hill than in the lush bottom land, and to think about this observation, is the start of science. To notice that most sailors get scurvy but not those who have stopped at islands to pick up fresh fruit is a similar start. To recognize that, when a person's views of himself change, his behavior changes accordingly, and to puzzle over this, is again the beginning of both theory and science. I voice this conviction in protest against the attitude, which seems too common in American psychology, that science starts in the laboratory or at the calculating machine.

The foundation of assumptions and attitudes upon which the research done by clinical psychologists rests has been broadened in other ways as well. With the increasing emphasis on humanistic considerations that has come with the widespread interest in existentialist philosophies, some psychologists have transformed the concept of "research subject" into something more like "research partner" or "participant." One cannot really regard the subject in a psychological experiment in the way a chemist regards the substances in the reactions he studies. As psychologists develop more self-confidence so that they no longer feel an urgent necessity to model their research efforts on the "hard" sciences, we can expect this trend to become stronger. (See Argyris, 1968, in Suggested Readings at the end of this chapter.)

Two methodological advances have facilitated varieties of research in which clinicians are especially interested. One is the development of *multidimensional techniques*, such as factor analysis, canonical correlations, and the like. These have been available for many years, but it is only since computers have brought the elaborate computational work they entail within the bounds of practicality that they have been widely used.

The other is the development of techniques for quantitative *research on the single case* (Chassan, 1967; Shapiro, 1966). Whenever we are interested in the effects of intensive treatment of some sort, whether it be drugs or psycho-therapy, the uniqueness of individuals complicates the task of analysis by traditional experimental methods. Because of these individual differences a particular treatment may have opposite effects in two cases. This may produce a *mean* change of zero even though the experimenter knows that both subjects have shown observable effects. Furthermore, attempts to set up control groups have often foundered on this same troublesome rock of individual uniqueness. It is not possible to equate experimental subjects and controls completely, even in the rare instances when these subjects are identical twins. The techniques for single-case analysis arrange for the person being studied to serve as his own control, by setting up appropriate sequences of experimental variable and placebo over time.

To sum up the discussion so far, ideas about what constitutes acceptable psychological research have changed and are changing. Present trends make the scientist–practitioner role for the clinical psychologist more tenable than it has been in some previous periods when research was defined more narrowly than it is today.

THE CLINICIAN'S ESSENTIAL RESEARCH TASKS

Accepting the conceptual framework of general systems theory, as set forth in Chapter 4, enables us to state in an inclusive way what the research efforts of the clinical psychologist should be designed to accomplish. The first of these basic kinds of research objectives is the development of techniques for the *appraisal of ongoing systems*. There are two kinds of research to which clinical psychologists have devoted a great deal of attention in the past that fall under this heading: the assessment of personality, and process research on psychotherapy. In the first instance the individual personality is the system and one takes it apart, as it were, looking at separate traits, motives, and defense mechanisms and analyzing how they fit together to produce the person's characteristic behavior. In the second kind of research effort, the therapist and client together constitute the system, and the complex development of this relationship over time is what needs to be appraised.

As the role of the clinical psychologist has broadened and diversified, this research role has been correspondingly enlarged. Many sorts of *groups* of people are now regarded as systems whose functioning is to be appraised. Group therapy calls for the analysis of a system of relationships more complex than those involved in individual therapy. To counsel a married couple or a family requires some grasp of the way its whole system of interdependent attitudes and behavior works. To manage a therapeutic community, such as a specially designed hospital ward, one must try to understand it as an *organization* into which doctors, nurses, aides, and patients interact as a system.

Because personality assessment has been recognized as the clinical psychologist's responsibility since the beginning of professional work in this field, a large amount of research has already been carried out on tools and techniques to be used in this particular undertaking. The assessment of more inclusive systems—groups and organizations—is a much more recent development and there is as yet no well-established body of knowledge with regard to it. Thus it constitutes a real research challenge. Some of the methods that have proved useful in assessing individuals can be carried over into this new field of endeavor, but new techniques will also have to be invented. Clinical psychologists face intriguing research problems here.

The second major focus of research efforts, important in the past and promising to be even more important in the future, is the *evaluation of change or improvement*. For clinical psychologists in previous periods, what this has meant primarily is *outcome* research on psychotherapy and other methods of treatment, such as drugs. A natural practical question that has turned out to be much more difficult to answer than it appeared to be at first sight is: Does this treatment work? Does it do any good? The complications arise from many sources. As mentioned earlier, different individuals react differently to the same situation or medication. Some persons improve whether they receive any treatment or not. Others improve if they *think* they are receiving treatment—the much discussed *placebo* effect. These are just a few of the difficulties that must be taken into account when planning outcome research.

As in the appraisal research tasks discussed above, the shift to a consideration of more inclusive systems has broadened and complicated the research responsibilities of the clinical psychologist. Outcome research is being absorbed into the larger category of *evaluative* research. We are increasingly concerned with evaluating the effects of *programs* as well as individual treatment effects, and changes in social systems as well as changes in persons. Many of the things psychologists have found out about research designs, such as the use of control groups of various kinds, can be carried over into these different sorts of evaluative task, but there is need for innovative ideas as well.

Before we turn to a more detailed consideration of what research of these two major kinds involves, let us consider briefly the purposes such research serves. Psychology faculties and students tend to think of research mainly in terms of its contribution to psychological knowledge. The final *product* in which they are most interested is a publication—journal paper, monograph, or book. It is clear that this is a desirable outcome of research efforts. As mentioned previously, our present store of knowledge is not adequate to the demands now being placed upon it. However, there is another less generally visible purpose that research efforts can also serve. They can lay the groundwork for *decisions* of many kinds on the part of the agencies and organizations for which researchers work, decisions about patients, about programs, and about policies. For example, the development of instruments and procedures for a continuing appraisal of a mental hospital as a social system is a valuable undertaking even if it never results in a publication or comes to the attention of psychologists elsewhere. The increased benefits to patients resulting from more intelligent decisions about the use of available resources and the improved functioning of the whole complex system are sufficient justification for the research. On a larger scale, the evaluation of several alternative government policies with regard to the training of the hard-core unemployed before any one of them is adopted on a national scale would be a valuable research project in its own right whether or not it contributed to general knowledge in psychology, sociology, or economics.

Research of this second kind—whether one calls it applied research, practical research, administrative research, or policy research—is being increasingly differentiated from theory-oriented or discipline-oriented research. What a decision maker needs to know cannot usually be extracted from the reports of research already accomplished. He requires answers to specific questions related to the particular problem he faces. The research contribution a clinical psychologist can make to the system in which he works may be fully as important as his contribution to psychology.

PROCEDURES AND PROBLEMS IN APPRAISAL RESEARCH

In order to appraise the functioning of any psychological or social system, it is necessary to construct tools or instruments. This has been one of psychology's important tasks. A clinical psychologist must know what techniques are available, how good they are, and what one must be careful about when he uses them. But he must also be able to improvise and to develop new instruments for particular purposes.

Within this broad area of responsibility, the problem on which most efforts so far have been focused is the assessment of individual personality. The considerable success of the intelligence-testing movement, beginning in the latter years of the nineteenth century and continuing during the twentieth, as we have reported in Chapter 2, led psychologists to believe that other significant human characteristics could be conceptualized as *measurable traits*. Work on special aptitudes and talents branched off from intelligence testing. It required a somewhat greater leap of the imagination to think of characteristics such as interests, adjustment, and motives as quantitative rather than simply qualitative things and to attempt to scale and measure them. Psychologists with many kinds of specialization responded to this challenge—educational industrial, military, developmental.

If testing and measurement techniques were to be useful in clinical situations, what were needed were methods of obtaining a comprehensive picture of many characteristics for each individual rather than scales for measuring single characteristics in many people, which is what many of the other kinds of applied psychologists were producing. Out of this distinctively clinical emphasis came personality inventories that could be scored for many traits, such as the very widely used Minnesota Multiphasic Personality Inventory (MMPI). Out of it also came the innumerable projective techniques, such as the Rorschach and the Thematic Apperception Test (TAT), the distinctive feature of which was that free responses of the subject to a standardized stimulus were first obtained and then analyzed quantitatively according to a predetermined system.

Problems of determining how valid and reliable such instruments were turned out to be even more difficult in assessing personality traits than they had been in measuring abilities. The scarcity of unambiguous criteria, the extent to which behavior is determined by situations rather than by inner qualities such as motives or needs, the changeability of moods and attitudes from day to day—these and many other complications to be discussed in more detail later have constituted obstacles to the development of completely satisfactory instruments for the appraisal of personality. But many such instruments are available and can be useful in many situations if one knows their peculiarities and limitations. It is expected that a clinical psychologist will have this sort of special knowledge.

With the extension of the clinician's concern to systems of human interaction, such as families, therapy groups, and the like, it was necessary to develop other sorts of research tools. The first essential is an accurate *record* of what occurs as the members of the group interact. From the first crude phonograph recordings of therapy sessions in the 1930s to the high-fidelity-sound motion pictures and closed-circuit-television techniques of the 1960s, tremendous technological progress occurred. Psychological research accompanied these engineering developments. It was necessary to find out about the effect of the recording procedure on the participants and its influence on the course of the therapy. Ethical considerations are especially important in such research—ensuring that no recording of therapy sessions is ever made without the knowledge of patient and therapist, and safeguarding the confidentiality of the record once it has been made. (In *Methods of Research in Psychotherapy*, edited by L. A. Gottschalk and A. H. Auerbach, 1966, the matter of research on recording is discussed in some detail in Chapters 2–8.)

Obtaining accurate and complete records of the interactions of participants in natural groups, such as families and school classes, presents other research problems. Still different techniques must be worked out for appraising the psychological structure of a mental hospital. Because these systems are greatly extended in time and in space, as compared with psychotherapy systems, complete motion pictures are usually not feasible, and some sort of continuous verbal record of observations, often by several observers simultaneously, is the method of choice.

Whatever is done at this first stage of research to obtain as complete a record as possible, the second stage always involves the analysis of these records according to a set of variables determined by the purpose of the research. This may mean counting the number of occurrences of a particular variety of behavior, or it may mean assigning a rating from 1 to 5 to manifestations of complex psychological variables such as hostility, empathy, or anxiety. The accuracy of such analyses becomes a crucial research issue, and the psychologist directing the research project must set things up so that two or more coders or raters independently carry out each operation on at least a portion of the data so that the extent of the agreement between them can serve as an index of reliability. But more challenging than this problem of reliability is the problem of deciding what aspects of the complex record to attempt to code. A considerable amount of trial and error often occurs in this connection, a sort of research activity quite different from the things one finds in courses on statistical methods and experimental design. A preliminary set of variables to be coded is prepared and tried out on some of the data. Discussion follows, and it becomes apparent that some of these things cannot be rated at all, and others cannot be rated accurately. Still others occur too rarely to be worth bothering with. At this point, someone in the research group is likely to propose a somewhat different model or theory that suggests trying out a different set of coding variables. The two-stage process—data collection followed by data analysis—facilitates this kind of problem-oriented research thinking.

The "cutting edge" of appraisal research, as we move into a period of focusing on systems and the way they work rather than on traits or dimensions of personality, is the effort to deal directly with interactions between components of a system rather than to measure the components separately. Clinical psychologists have always shown some concern with this problem, at least in the practical, applied aspect of their work. In order to produce a meaningful and useful report on a patient, one must do more than give, score, and interpret psychological tests. One considers the relationships of the traits that have been measured to one another. Is a disposition toward a particular kind of defense mechanism keeping the person's level of anxiety within tolerable limits? What would be likely to happen if he were prevented from using defense mechanisms of this sort? One also considers the life situations to which the person is reacting. Is his hostility directed mainly toward authority figures? Under what circumstances does his anxiety increase?

What has been scarce heretofore is *research* on this interactional side of the clinician's activity. Gough (1968a) has worked consistently on procedures for extending the measurement of personality traits so as to determine how various combinations of traits show up in observable aspects of their behavior. In one such study, for example, a regression equation based on the several scores of the California Psychological Inventory was constructed for predicting how successful airline stewardesses would be after their training was completed. By relating the evaluations this equation produced with ratings of the descriptions of the girls obtained by means of a 300-item adjective check list, interesting inferences could be drawn about the overall personality patterns that seem to be involved in adapting to the demands of this particular practical situation.

Another research approach to these problems about how individual personality systems work and how clinicians appraise them has been to try to capture the thinking of the clinician in a natural situation by asking him to "think aloud." Koester (1954) and Parker (1958) used this approach, having clinicians report the thinking underlying responses they had made in their own interviews with clients, using transcribed records of these interviews as stimulus material. It was apparent that a clinician forms fairly quickly a "working image" of the individual with whom he is dealing, and that this may be oversimplified or stereotyped. The point here is that the formation of an impression of a total system is as natural an activity as analysis of system components. The problem of how this impression formation occurs deserves more research than it has had heretofore, because the skill of appraising an acting, changing personality system in all its complexity needs to be taught to new practitioners and sharpened in experienced workers.

Even more urgent and less understood is the appraisal of systems consisting of groups of persons. We can distinguish here between the small groups, in which it is the interactions and attitudinal links between individuals that comprise the system to be analyzed, and the large groups or social organizations, in which the relationships between component subgroups are the important consideration. Until fairly recently, clinical psychologists have not seen research in either of these areas as their responsibility, because their clients were *individuals* attempting to adjust to these social systems rather than the groups making up the systems themselves. With the shift toward community mental health, family therapy, and treatments involving reorganization of whole wards or institutions, research problems formerly delegated to social psychologists and others now challenge clinical psychologists.

An area in which at least a beginning has been made is in *conjoint family assessment.* Bodin (1968) has summarized these efforts to appraise a family as a system rather than describe its members individually. Several ingenious techniques have been tried out, such as giving the family a problem to solve or a choice to make and analyzing the ways in which different families go about the task and the nature of the psychological interaction between family members that characterizes each strategy.

Research on the system properties of other kinds of groups in which clinical psychologists are interested has barely begun. Initial efforts to appraise therapy groups, for example, focused on assessment of individuals making up the group rather than on the nature of the relationships that develop between them or the patterning of the group as a whole. One direction in which progress is now being made is in analyzing a group as a system of *reinforcements* in which the verbal behavior of each participant as he responds to each other participant serves to strengthen some kinds of behavior and to discourage others. Such an analysis is complex enough in the groups of two (e.g., patient and therapist) with which these efforts began, and it becomes intricate indeed in a group of even six or eight persons, but ways are being found to cope with this complexity. On a still larger scale, the methods organization theorists have developed for appraising business organizations furnish leads for the clinical psychologist who attempts research on the system properties of a hospital ward or a community. The role of the clinical psychologist in the assessment of personality and in research designed to improve the assessment process was the first special role assigned to him. To broaden his assessment concern to take in the appraisal of systems larger than individual personality constitutes one of the major challenges he now faces.

PROCEDURES AND PROBLEMS IN RESEARCH ON CHANGE OR IMPROVEMENT

Another major area of research effort is the evaluation of the changes brought about by whatever treatment techniques or programs are employed to improve mental health or human welfare. Clinical psychologists have had several decades of experience with outcome research on psychotherapy, work that has served to make them well aware of the many complexities and pitfalls such research involves. This expertise should be useful in many other kinds of situations in which evaluation research is now being conducted or planned.

There are several major research problems to be taken into consideration in the evaluation of outcomes. The first is the problem of the *criterion.* What shall we use as evidence that psychological improvement of some sort has actually occurred? There are a number of possibilities, including patients' reports of satisfaction or dissatisfaction with treatment received, ratings of behavior by observers or by associates, measurements of psychological traits by means of ability or personality tests, measurements of physiological functions known to be correlated with psychological functioning. In planning research to evaluate the effects of treatment, a decision as to which indicators of change to use is one of the first that must be made. Too often criteria have been chosen on the basis of convenience alone and the utility of the research has been thereby much reduced.

A second kind of difficulty involves measurement problems arising from the use of *change* scores obtained by subtracting initial from final measurements. These include both "unreliability" and "ceiling" effects. Every psychological measurement is to some extent inaccurate; change scores have a double dose of this unreliability. And those who initially score high may be unable to obtain a very large change score no matter how much they improve. Psychologists specializing in measurement have grappled in different ways with these deficiencies in scores purporting to measure how much change has occurred in each individual. In 1962, a symposium set up under the auspices of the Committee on Personality Development in Youth of the Social Science Research Council (C. W. Harris, 1963) brought together fourteen participants who explored a number of possible solutions to the problems. However, Cronbach and Furby (1970) have pointed to statistical defects in many of these procedures. What they recommend in their place is that the researcher at the outset analyze very carefully the *purpose* for which he wishes to use estimates of how much each individual has changed and then adopt a research procedure for the particular purpose that makes it unnecessary to deal with the slippery index one gets by subtracting initial from final scores. The history of this methodological problem in psychological research is instructive as one thinks about what should be included in the training of practitioner—researchers. Although they are not primarily measurement specialists, it is important that they reach a fairly high level of statistical sophistication in order to avoid pitfalls of this sort that are not at all obvious to the nonstatistician.

A third major problem in the appraisal of change usually goes under the label *placebo effects*. The term arose in medical research, which found that patients receiving sugar pills rather than effective medication often improved under this "nontreatment." It came to the attention of psychologists again in industry in what has become a classic report on a research program set up at the Hawthorne Electric Company plant (Roethlisberger and Dickson, 1939). What has come to be called the *Hawthorne effect* simply means that when a group of people is singled out for special attention, they are likely to show improvements in attitude and performance regardless of what particular experimental treatment is being tried out in the situation. Placebo effects or Hawthorne effects must be allowed for in any kind of evaluative research. What the human participants expect to happen is likely to happen, at least to some extent. A change that can be attributed to a special kind of treatment, such as psychotherapy, must be greater than this generalized improvement would be likely to be.

Placebo effects can be distinguished from the effects of the treatment one is evaluating by the use of *controls* of various sorts, but technical problems arise here also. It is not easy to ensure that a control group is equivalent to the treatment group in all respects. In a psychotherapy study, treated patients may be matched with controls on age, sex, social level, intelligence, attitudes, and personality, and still the groups may not be comparable, because the persons undergoing therapy were those who asked for it, thus demonstrating some real though unanalyzed difference from the controls in motivation.

What are called *double-blind designs* help to control placebo effects and motivational differences, when they can be employed. What this procedure means is that subjects available for the study are assigned to treatment and control groups in randomized fashion, each subject is administered something, treatment or placebo, and neither experimenters nor subjects know which group an individual is in until the project ends. To work out such a design in an ethical manner without withholding a treatment of demonstrated value from anyone in urgent need of it, and without deliberate deception of participants, is always difficult, often impossible.

One more major complication facing evaluative researchers is the often-demonstrated fact that individuals react differently—sometimes actually in opposite directions—to the same experimental condition. It now appears possible (Truax and Carkhuff, 1967) that one of the reasons that studies like those of Eysenck (1952, 1966) seemed to demonstrate that persons undergoing psychotherapy showed no improvement, as compared with nontherapy control groups,

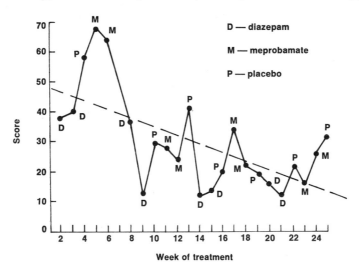

FIGURE 5-1 Drug effects on anxiety. The subject was a patient undergoing analytically oriented psychotherapy. The two drugs Diazepam and Meprobamate were compared with a placebo, the three treatments being administered in random order. Diazepam is most effective. (From Chasson, 1967, p. 199.)

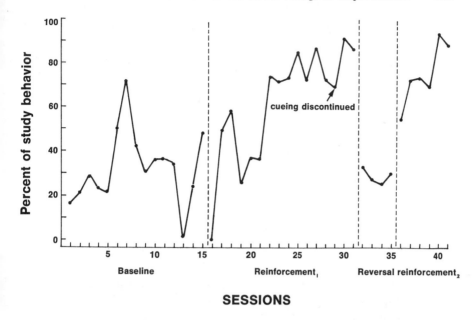

FIGURE 5-2 Record of study behavior for Rose. (From Hall, Lund and Jackson, 1968. p. 4.)

is that some individuals change in a negative direction, thus balancing the positive changes other individuals experience, and producing an average change of zero for the experimental group as a whole. Some therapists tend to produce such negative changes, offsetting positive changes produced by other therapists taking part in the same experiment. Understanding of this complication has led to an accelerated search for experimental designs in which each patient serves as his own control, so that averaging of individual scores becomes unnecessary. Chassan (1967) explains clearly how such one-subject experiments can be set up, and illustrates from studies of the effects of drugs. Figure 5-1 presents a graph of weekly Manifest Anxiety Scale scores produced by a therapy patient taking two different drugs and a placebo over a period of two months. Scores can be statistically checked to see if they are significantly different from the general trend. Mitchell (1969) shows how a similar design can be utilized to evaluate changes occurring during counseling.

Another related problem in studies of change is whether the altered behavior persists after the intervention stops. Psychologists using behavior-modification programs (covered more extensively in Chapters 12 and 14) have developed a technique which they call *reversal*. The treatment, which in this case involves reinforcement, is stopped for a period, and the experimenter sees if the problem behaviors reassert themselves, or the positive behaviors drop to the level measured by the *baseline*, obtained before intervention.

Figure 5-2 illustrates reversal in the case of Rose, a pupil in an elementary school in the most economically deprived area of Kansas City, Kansas. The experimenters (Hall, Lund, and Jackson, 1968) used observers who recorded study behavior and nonstudy behavior. They taught teachers to give reinforcement to children by such behaviors as showing interest, commenting favorably, or giving a pat on the shoulder. After Rose's study had risen to a high level, the teacher stopped her reinforcing behavior for a period. During the reversal period Rose's studying dropped dramatically, but it rose again in another reinforcement period. Thus the research program demonstrates the importance of specific kinds of reinforcement for school children.

With the tremendous interest in social reform generated during the late 1960s, psychologists and other social scientists are challenged as never before to plan and carry out evaluative research on the effects of new programs initiated on an experimental basis. Logically, the task resembles the one clinical psychologists have faced in carrying out research on the effects of therapy. There must be the same concern for criteria, controls, placebo effects, and individual differences. There is, however, one extra factor that greatly complicates this problem—public attitudes affecting political decisions. Whereas a poorly planned or indecisive study on the outcomes of therapy may get little or no attention outside or even inside the agency in which it was done, the results of a similar inadequate research project set up to evaluate a new type of community mental health center may have widespread and long-lasting effects, as measured in taxpayers' dollars or general social progress.

Because of current social trends, techniques for evaluative research, heretofore developed mainly as by-products of research designed primarily to produce increases in basic knowledge, are now being subjected to serious attention. This has led to the addition of several principles to those already discussed. First, it is advisable to have the plan for evaluation incorporated in the design for the program to be evaluated. Unless this is done, it is not likely that criterion information of the kind needed will be obtainable. Second, every attempt should be made to set up a research design that will produce *definitive* results. Too often evaluative research results in a conclusion that differences between groups participating in different kinds of programs are not "statistically significant," but because of insufficient numbers of cases, selective factors in assignment to groups or responses to questionnaires, improper use of statistical techniques, or any one of a variety of other defects, it is not possible to draw any practical conclusion at all from the results. Unfortunately, on the basis of such a totally inadequate research project, legislative bodies may decide not to appropriate funds for any program at all, and the public may conclude that attempts at intervention are hopeless.

Still a third principle should perhaps be added. Since new social programs generally grow out of a developed concern leading to an intensive search for a solution to a problem the public views as urgent, it is advisable to design studies that will compare alternative approaches rather than ask the simple question, Does this program do any good? For example, it became clear to many social scientists, after the report on the evaluation of Head Start programs was issued in 1969 by the Westinghouse Learning Corporation, that the major conclusions of the study—that summer Head Start programs do not produce developmental changes extending into the early elementary school years and that the full-year programs are only marginally effective—put policy makers in an awkward position. Had the study been designed in a manner that would have permitted more detailed comparisons of results from different varieties of educational programs, it could have been much more helpful to policy makers faced with decisions about what the next steps ought to be in using preschool education as a means of stimulating intellectual growth in the disadvantaged.

In spite of the difficulties that have arisen in fully implementing the concept of the clinical psychologist as a research worker, it continues to appeal to psychologists and to those who make use of their services. Knowing that one has added something to man's knowledge about his own nature or helped to develop sharper tools to use in solving his persistent problems is one of the rewards a career in psychology can offer. Current trends in thinking about what constitutes research make it easier than it used to be to combine the research and service roles to achieve an integrated conception of one's own professional identity. It is the responsibility of graduate training programs to help students accomplish this integration.

MISCELLANEOUS RESEARCH ACTIVITIES

By no means all the research activities in which clinical psychologists have engaged or are now carrying on can be classified under the two broad functional headings we have used in the previous discussion and appraisal of ongoing systems and evaluation of change or improvement. The impression one gets in scanning such summaries as *Psychological Abstracts* or *Annual Review of Psychology* is one of great diversity, but several major kinds of studies that show up with considerable regularity in journal publications can be identified.

One such type of study is the *survey*. It is often useful to find out, for example, what kinds of patients are being treated in certain kinds of clinics, what psychological tests are being used most frequently, or what the incidence of mental retardation is in different kinds of communities. The research equipment of the clinical psychologist should make him at least minimally competent to conduct such surveys, with proper attention to sampling problems, the phrasing of interview questions, the design of questionnaires, and the use of appropriate statistical techniques.

Another variety of research that shows up in many specific contexts involves the *comparison of different groups* in the population with regard to some variable or variables. These may be groups carrying different psychiatric diagnoses, such as "schizophrenia" versus "brain damage"; groups differing in age, such as "over sixty" versus "thirty to fifty"; or groups differing in social class, such as "middle class" versus "disadvantaged." There is obviously a large number of other possibilities for such group comparisons. Statistical considerations having to do with the representativeness of samples and the significance of differences are important in the planning and interpretation of such research.

Another common variety of research done by clinical psychologists is the exploration of *personality correlates* of variables in which someone is interested, including the relationship of measured personality variables to one another. Research relating introversion—extraversion, for example, to all sorts of other personality characteristics has a long history. Attempts to identify personality correlates of academic underachievement, continuation in psychotherapy, or participation in campus disturbances have been made. As soon as a new method of measuring some personality characteristics is made available, a "run" of studies involving it typically occurs. For example, in 1954, Whitehorn and Betz found that they could distinguish between therapists who were successful and unsuccessful in treating schizophrenics on the basis of certain items on the Strong Vocational Interest Blank. Since that time, year after year research reports on this A-B variable have been appearing, relating it to a variety of other kinds of behavior and manifestations of personality. (See the research summary at the end of Chapter 11, for example.)

Still another kind of research effort frequently engaged in by clinical psychologists is the *experimental simulation* of a process which it would not be feasible or ethical to subject to experimental manipulation as it occurs naturally. Some of these experiments might be labeled "quasi-therapy." In studying the A-B variable mentioned above, for example, Berzins and Seidman (1969) designed an experiment in which "high A" and "high B" interviewers listened to tapes simulating therapy with a schizoid and a neurotic patient. After each of five segments of each of the tapes, the student quasi-therapists wrote what he would say at this point if he were counseling the patient. Afterward each of them rated his own reactions to each "patient," indicating how satisfied he was with his responses, how uncomfortable or uneasy he felt, and how difficult it was to choose what to say or to think of something helpful to say. The focus of the experiment was on the interaction between patient type and therapist type. Although not many significant differences showed up, there was some evidence that A's listening to the schizoid patient and B's listening to the neurotic patient found it easier to respond and were better satisfied with their responses than under the opposite pairing conditions.

Partly because of the prestige psychologists have attached to experimental research as compared with less rigorous approaches, there have been a great many such attempts to separate out some aspect of a clinical process and study it in the laboratory. One is likely to obtain more clear-cut findings under these conditions; the difficulty has been that they are often not applicable to the natural situation in which the process under investigation normally occurs.

PREPARATION FOR RESEARCH

As suggested by the foregoing section, many kinds of effort are involved in the research clinical psychologists do. Most psychology students do not complete their training programs well equipped to engage in all of them. It would seem desirable that major emphasis be placed on the important research functions discussed first—appraisal of ongoing systems and evaluation of improvement—and that psychologists know enough about sources and authorities so that they can acquire detailed methodological information when they need it. This is not the way in which research is presented to many would-be clinicians. The tendency in many departments is to begin with the most technical material, mathematical statistics and the design of experiments, rather than with the research questions most salient for the professional psychologist.

Ideally, research training should be integrated with field work and practice, so that the student can relate what he learns about research techniques to research questions he can see need to be answered. The logic of the reasoning to be followed should always precede the mathematics. The potential usefulness of new knowledge in important human situations should take precedence over the elegance of the statistical design or the precision of the results. Practical problems of organizing and administering research in a mental hospital, community clinic, or correctional institution need to be dealt with along with problems in analyzing data and reporting results.

Mastery of statistical concepts, basic statistical procedures, and computer usage is at least as necessary for clinical as for academic psychologists. Clinicians need not expect to know sophisticated details of statistics and computer programming; they will often need consultants, but they must be able to think and converse about the fundamental principles. Statistical techniques are indispensable tools in psychological research of all kinds. What the clinical psychologist must always remember, however, is that they are tools, not ends in themselves. It is important for him to keep his eye on the main objective, the understanding and improvement of human functioning.

SUMMARY

The concept of the clinical psychologist as scientist—practitioner has survived repeated challenges. There is still a strong conviction among psychologists that clinicians should enlarge the knowledge base upon which their practice rests if the public is to be well served, and that scientists can benefit from the insights and viewpoints of psychologists who are closely in touch with human problems.

For this conception to work satisfactorily, both scientists and practitioners need to adopt a broad rather than a narrow definition of science and avoid the restrictive fads and fashions that have often limited research horizons. Conceptions of what constitutes research have broadened in recent years to include humanistic attitudes, multidimensional techniques, and experiments on single cases.

There are two main varieties of research tasks most essential for the practicing psychologist. The first is the development and application of techniques for the appraisal of ongoing systems at all levels—individual, group, organization. The second is the evaluation of change or improvement. Each of these kinds of research involves special kinds of problems and difficulties. Appraisal research requires that methods be found to sample and record ongoing behavior, that systems for coding and analyzing it be worked out, and that the reliability and validity of measurements be determined. To their skills in assessing individuals by means of tests, clinicians are now adding skills in assessing behavior in groups. Problems in evaluating change revolve around choice of criteria, ambiguities in difference scores, placebo effects, individual differences, and political and ethical considerations.

In addition to these major research tasks, clinical psychologists conduct various other kinds of research, such as surveys, group comparisons, correlational studies, and experimental simulation of clinical processes.

In preparation for these research roles, students in training should be taught to integrate field work with research training and to view statistical and mathematical techniques as tools rather than ends in themselves.

SUGGESTED READINGS

Chassan, J. B. *Research design in clinical psychology and psychiatry*. New York: Appleton-Century-Crofts, 1967.

The kinds of thinking a researcher in a clinical situation needs to do to obtain results upon which sound conclusions can be based are clearly explained in this book. Statistical methods are introduced by considering the logic on which they are based. Particular attention is given to control procedures and placebo effects. A chapter is devoted to what the author calls "intensive design," a means of carrying out an experiment on a single case. Other topics, such as reliability and validity, are discussed from the vantage point of the person who must deal with the data typically available to clinical researchers.

Another excellent book, broader in scope, is *Research on Human Behavior* by Runkel and McGrath (1972).

Argyris, C. Some unintended consequences of rigorous research. *Psychological Bulletin*, 1968, *70*, 185–197.

The author considers the research situation from the viewpoint of organizational theory (an outgrowth of the general systems theory considered in the previous chapter). He proposes and presents some evidence to indicate that the effect of the psychologist's attempt to be rigorous in his experimental or field research sets up an authoritarian situation such as that characteristic of manager-controlled organizations and that the same unfortunate consequences follow—dependence, passivity, withdrawal, on the part of the subjects resulting in data that are minimally useful or even misleading. A different pattern is recommended for psychological research, in which the subject would be told more about the project so that he would have more influence and more involvement.

Weiss, C. H. (ed.). *Evaluating action programs: readings in social action and education.* Boston: Allyn and Bacon, 1972.

This book is mainly directed to the program-evaluator-in-training. It provides a collection of evaluation strategies from a variety of community programs and identifies areas of consensus about evaluation that have emerged across professional specialties. It also highlights areas that have remained controversial. The Overview chapter is excellent.

Another promising book on evaluation—Guttentag and Struening's *Handbook of Evaluation Research*—is being prepared for publication at present writing. It should appear in 1973. A chapter by Ellsworth on consumer feedback in measuring effectiveness of mental health programs is included.

White, S. H. The national impact study of Head Start. In J. Helmuth (ed.), *Disadvantaged child*, Vol. 3, *Compensatory education: a national debate.* New York: Brunner/Mazel, 1970, pp. 163–184.

The many complexities in the design and conduct of evaluative research were forcibly brought to the attention of social scientists when the study of Head Start carried on jointly by the Westinghouse Learning Corporation and Ohio University was reported in 1969, indicating that summer programs had no significant effect on later school performance, and that the effect of full-year programs was small and varied from place to place. Controversy has continued to revolve around issues related to the method of sampling the matching of experimental and control subjects, the measuring instruments, and other methodological flaws. This chapter provides a convenient account of this controversy and contains valuable lessons for researchers who set out to evaluate any program.

Davidson, P. O., and Costello, C. G. (eds.). *N = 1: experimental studies of single cases.* New York: Van Nostrand Reinhold, 1969.

What this book of readings consists of is fifteen examples of the application of fairly vigorous research methods to the study of single individuals. What this always involves is the making of many separate observations on the one person, so that the N with which one works is the number of measurements rather than the number of persons. It can also involve comparing experimental and control conditions; obtaining data, such as test scores, on a relevant group of persons as a check on whether the subject's behavior is deviant or unusual; repeated administrations of standard procedures, such as Osgood's semantic differential or Kelly's repertory grid; and many other techniques, ready-made and tailor-made.

Thelen, M. H., and Ewing, D. R. Roles, functions, and training in clinical psychology: a survey of academic clinicians. *American Psychologist*, 1970, *25*, 550–554.

This is an example of the sort of survey that psychologists make to obtain information required for planning and policy making. A questionnaire sent to clinical psychologists teaching in university programs approved by the APA showed clear endorsement of the scientist–practitioner model among academic clinicians.

Garmezy, N., Vulnerability research and the issue of primary prevention. *American Journal of Orthopsychiatry*, 1971, *41*, 101–116.

Garmezy asserts that the goal of primary prevention of psychiatric disorder is a worthy one but that it cannot be realized without clear scientific knowledge about etiology. He suggests a strategy for acquiring knowledge about etiology by studying children who are vulnerable to the development of psychopathology in adulthood. In essence, the status of a child as "vulnerable" or "high-risk" is derived from three models, which characterize speculations about the etiology of mental disorder: (1) genetic transmission of predisposition, (2) pathological disorganization in the near environment (the family), or (3) severe disorganization in the molar (sociocultural) environment of the child. A fourth possibility, that of neonatal or prenatal deprivation, is also coming into prominence.

Of additional interest is another paper on research strategies in primary prevention. Flanagan (1971) argues that valid research findings have five requirements: (1) a random or representative sample of sufficient size; (2) a statement of the experimental treatment and the anticipated effect of the treatment; (3) criteria representative of the ultimate objective of reduced incidence rates; (4) a simple, easily understood statistical technique with replication as the best test of significance; and (5) an interpretation that summarizes not only the findings but their practical significance for various situations.

Fairweather, G. W. *Methods for experimental social innovation*. New York: Wiley, 1967.

A clinical psychologist with many years of experience, Fairweather has developed principles for research in practical solutions to social problems. The book discusses steps for planning, implementing, and evaluating new social programs. It does not overlook the administrative and organizational aspects of the research team.

Other sources for learning about applied social and clinical experimentation are a collection of readings by Bachrach (1962), the ideas and methods of Campbell and Stanley (1963) about quasi-experimental designs, and Campbell's article on viewing reforms in organizations and society as experiments (1967).

part **II**

Designing and Implementing Improvement Programs

chapter 6

Information and Decisions

The purpose of the chapters in Part II is to present the heart of the clinical enterprise—*designing, executing, and evaluating improvement programs*. By improvement programs we designate a wide range of clinical efforts aimed at assisting people to change their behavior, attitudes, or relationships or at least to maintain themselves with as much happiness and effectiveness as possible. Improvement programs include individual psychotherapy, family therapy, personal and vocational counseling, rehabilitation programs, changes in schools to eliminate behavior problems, programs on hospital wards for chronic patients, psychological aspects of somatic treatments, group therapy, community efforts to help delinquents—in other words, the many things clinical psychologists do to promote better psychological functioning.

The practicing psychologist himself operates in a *behavioral improvement system*—a system providing service to a certain clientele, having problems or needs concerning their behavior, having a definite setting with support from and communication with certain parts of the community and not others, and performing certain activities internal and external to the system. He is one part of that system; he is likely to have more knowledge and skill than other participants in certain areas (e.g., assessment and research), and he must rely on other people (e.g., court workers, police, ministers, as well as other mental health professionals and paraprofessionals) to provide most of the service. CONSULTANT

The traditional division made in clinical work is between two major activities, *diagnosis* and *therapy*. We are attempting to integrate the two, employing new terms. Our intention is to emphasize the supremacy of improvement efforts in the context or arena of action. The gathering and processing of information (diagnosis) must always be in the service of the improvement program, not an end in itself. The third traditional function of the clinical psychologist, clinical *research*, should also ultimately enhance improvement programs.

Instead of "diagnosis" we will frequently use the words "appraisal" and "assessment" in an attempt to convey a broader and less stereotyped concept of the way clinicians collect information and make judgments. Instead of "psychotherapy" we will often use the words "intervention," "assistance," "modification," "problem solving," or "improvement," again to signify that

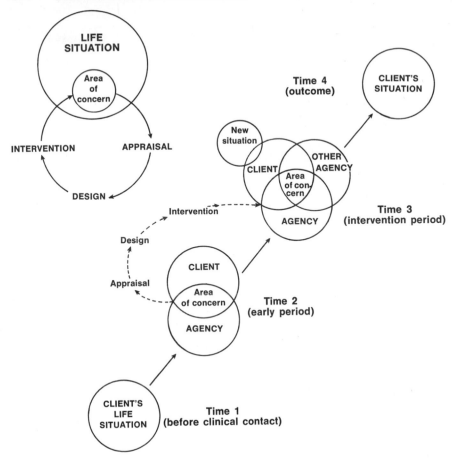

FIGURE 6-1 Contact of a helping agency with a client.

psychological functions are broad indeed and that method is only a means to a needed outcome, not an end in itself. "Diagnosis" and "therapy" are remnants of the medical orientation formerly prominent in clinical psychology; they have served a useful purpose in the past and are still appropriate in some medical settings, but psychology has now moved so far beyond the medical model that it is undesirable to continue to use those restrictive terms. What we are talking about is the involvement or intervention of psychologists in ongoing systems, interacting with them in such a way as to help them function better.

The usual sequence of events is the following: problems of living—appraisal—design—intervention—outcome. Figure 6-1 portrays this process. People come to an agency, are brought there, or are sought out by the organization because they have some problems of living, defined by themselves or by their community. The helping agency then appraises the problems, the client's situation, and the available resources and develops a design for improvement. If this design is acceptable and feasible, the agency becomes involved in treatment, intervention, or consultation. That intervention leads to an outcome—an altered environment, new habits and skills, a changed perspective. This outcome then may become feedback entering into decisions about modifying the intervention plan. The helping agency has thus made an experimental entry into an ongoing system, "unfreezing" or altering some of its interactive patterns and enabling the system to move to a new level of interactive adaptation with its environment.

The process is what all the chapters in Part II are concerned with. Some chapters emphasize assessment methods, others emphasize particular kinds of intervention. Different chapters focus on different system levels, but all have to do with the process of designing, carrying out, and evaluating improvement programs. This chapter serves as a general introduction to the design process as a whole.

Because the shift to this new way of conceptualizing the task of the clinical psychologist is not yet complete, it is easy to slip back into more familiar habits of thinking, to assume that a clinician simply diagnoses and treats psychological malfunctions in individuals. Much of the research clinical psychologists have done has been cast in these old molds. This does not mean that it is valueless, but it does mean that the knowledge it has generated must be reconsidered and translated, as it were, into the new language. We shall attempt this reorientation in this and the succeeding chapters. We recognize that for clinical psychologists the individual personality system is still the most frequent focus of attention, so it is appropriate that it receive more emphasis than the others in a book written for them. But it is desirable to keep other system levels in mind even when designing improvement programs specifically for individuals. And increasingly the group or the organization is itself becoming the focus of the psychologist's efforts.

THE NATURE AND PROCESS OF DESIGN

We have chosen the word "design" to describe the clinician's task for several reasons. The word "design" connotes the use of scientific principles and techniques insofar as possible but recognizes that clinical work is still largely an art. Clinical psychology is in some ways similar to architecture. Like the architect, the clinician tries to develop structures and symbols that will serve his client well and enhance his living. The clinician, like the architect, must deal with environmental realities and adapt his ideal solutions to the habits and preferences of people and to the limited resources available. Like the architect, the clinician is creative and problem-oriented; he contributes to the building of a life or many lives. The task is as great a challenge to imagination and invention as anything can be. Both psychologist and architect deal with the structure of human relations—but the psychologist is often more concerned than the architect with process.

Reduced to simplest terms, the activities involved in designing behavioral-improvement programs are (1) finding out what is what, (2) determining what is desirable, and (3) planning a way to move from (1) to (2).

Let us look at the first of these activities assuming for simplicity's sake that the client is an individual person. "Finding what is what" involves determining the nature of the problem the client reports or others report about him, identifying the significant systems in which the person interacts, and analyzing the resources available to the agency for dealing with such cases. A great deal of narrowing down and choosing must go on just in finding out what a client's situation is; obviously we are not interested in every little thing the client does or every word he utters. The question is to determine what is important for the problem at hand.

The second step—determining what is desirable—also raises difficult questions. What is desirable for whom and from whose standpoint? What are the alternatives and possibilities, the choices the client faces? What are the alternatives from the clinic's standpoint? What would different treatment theories say? Are the goals expressed by the client compatible with those expressed by other important community agents? The question of desirability is a question of values, the question of what is the "good life." The clinical encounter seldom answers such profound questions, although ultimately they lie behind what the psychologist does. In practical work, the question of the desirable is really a search for feasible alternatives of service that can be offered to the client, and reasonable possibilities about his personal decisions and plans to explore with him.

The third step—deciding upon an improvement program—is the most complex of all. At a minimum, it involves comparing the client's present condition with his potential situations, creating a proposal, and "contracting" with the client for the execution of the plan. In the process of arriving at intervention alternatives for this particular individual, the psychologist must call on his knowledge of behavior and behavior change. Because in clinical psychology the "state of the art" is still very imprecise, and because different clinicians have different skills and theoretical biases, one should not expect that they would always agree about what should be done. And even if they agreed, they might be wrong. The proof of improvement programs is in their effectiveness with clients. It requires continuing study of what works or does not work with a variety of clients in a variety of situations to develop better programs.

There are great variations in improvement programs. Some may be short—a 10-minute interview. Others may be long—intensive psychotherapy over years. Some may involve only one person other than the clinician; others will draw upon dozens of community agencies and activities. Some will involve the client very intimately and responsibly in the decision making; such participation must go as far as possible, but in some cases, such as with chronic psychotics or autistic children, most of the planning must be done by the clinical staff. Some designs will be unverbalized; others will be written down and orchestrated in detail.

In all cases, the process of designing will involve two basic processes in the clinician: (1) collecting and organizing information about an ongoing system, and (2) making decisions about how to change it. Both of these processes are bound up in what is often called the assessment, or appraisal, process. It is an important part of the information system every clinical service or agency employs, a system that includes a variety of formal and informal procedures. Appraisal procedures are essential to designing improvement plans for individuals and groups. They also contribute to the research activities on which improvement of the agency's performance and improvement in psychology's knowledge and skill rests.

The word "assessment" itself has a history that contributes to the meaning of the term. The dictionary meaning of the word "assess" is to set or fix the value of property for the purpose of taxation. Probably the first use of the word in the psychological sense was in the book *Assessment of Men* (OSS Staff, 1948), which was a report of the selection of men for special assignments in World War II. The staff of the Office of Strategic Services wanted a word different from "psychodiagnosis" since their goal was not the discerning of pathology but the discovery of the worth of an individual. The OSS staff needed to find the strengths of the person—his ingenuity, leadership, and courage in carrying out difficult and dangerous missions. The word "assessment" with its emphasis on the evaluation of the worth of something seemed like the most appropriate term. We are using "appraisal" in much the same fashion. To function more effectively, the evaluative work of the clinical psychologist needs to turn more and more to the positive and constructive forces in the person. Psychological treatment requires the enhancement of the developmental processes as well as the removal of sources of disorder and disturbance. Like the plant expert, the intervener must not only identify diseases and parasites so as to exterminate them, but concern himself with enriching the conditions to promote growth and blossoming. Assessment or appraisal serves both purposes.

No matter what clinicians do, some assessment or appraisal is always involved, even in instances where the contact is confined to a single interview. The question is not *whether* to appraise or assess but *how* to do it. It is here that disagreement among psychologists is greatest and research unclear. Differences have to do with such questions as these: Should there be a formal assessment through specialized personnel and services? What should the timing of assessment procedures be? Should standardized procedures such as tests be used? Other questions have to do with the effectiveness of various kinds of assessment, such as: Is the gathering of a great deal of behavioral (or historical) data more trouble than it is worth? Does the early use of tests have detrimental effects on intervention? To what extent do each of a variety of assessment procedures increase the value of treatment? Research on these questions will be discussed in later chapters, but it can be said now that the questions are still much bigger than the answers. In the absence of definitive knowledge, it seems important that strategies for assessment be flexible, adapted to particular helping settings. Assessment procedures should never be used for their own sake. One uses tests, behavioral records, and interviews for the welfare of the patient, not for research, teaching, or administrative routine alone. Each clinical psychologist should be prepared to apply whatever assessment procedures will help most in each individual situation.

COLLECTION AND ORGANIZATION OF INFORMATION ABOUT A SYSTEM

Image Making

The working image, or model, is the set of hypotheses about a person and the situations in which he presently or potentially operates. (The concept can be broadened to include groups or organizations, but, as indicated above, we will simplify matters by considering individuals first.) The concept is related to what social psychologists call impression formation. The image is the *hypothetical person*—what the observer sees from his vantage point—be it like the "real" person or not. In clinical appraisal, the psychologist is involved in the making of images for others and for himself.

Hypotheses inevitably develop from contact with a person. They are exemplified in such simple statements as these: "Fred is the sort of person you can depend on when you tell him to do something." "Mary is not sure of herself now; maybe after she's worked at her new job for a while she'll feel more confident." "You never can tell how George will be; some mornings he's as clear as a bell, other times he's hallucinating wildly—it almost seems as if there's some kind of off and on switch in his head." Novelists are experts at describing people in ways that indicate to readers the kind of behavior to be expected from them.

Image making is not peculiar to psychologists. Aides, psychiatrists, social workers, and others develop models of the patients with whom they work—impressions that are more or less accurate and helpful. Some of these are *stereotypes*—relatively rigid and oversimplified conceptions of the nature of people (e.g., the jolliness of a fat person, the vivacity of Latins). In clinical settings staff members may readily jump to the conclusion that a new patient who is a 44-year-old unemployed cook is most likely an alcoholic or that a patient who is a go-go dancer is a psychopath. Some of these stereotypes may be in line with the probabilities, but it is important for the clinician to realize that these are only probabilities. As we will discuss in a later chapter, considerable research has shown the effectiveness of stereotype accuracy in prediction studies; that is, a person knowing only such elementary facts as sex, age, and educational level can predict many things about a person. A psychologist's image of a client should go beyond the simple stereotype.

Psychological case reports and case conferences lead to decisions about the assignment of patients but they do more than that. They disseminate information and establish attitudes that are carried out into the wards and

go-go dancers ?

consulting rooms. A striking illustration is given by Stanton and Schwartz (1954), who describe how improvement was produced in a withdrawn schizophrenic woman in a hospital ward by deliberately changing her reputation with the ward personnel. Some studies have suggested that teachers may behave differently toward children, depending on IQs or test results attributed to them (Rosenthal and Jacobsen, 1968). The image of the client communicated to those who deal with him should help, not hinder.

The words "image" or "model" remind us that always the impression we have of another person is partial, limited. As we develop the image of the patient or client with whom we are working clinically, we need to be aware that we may be overlooking information, overemphasizing the importance of some data, misinterpreting the significance of others.

The use of the word "working" in the term is intended to suggest the concern for the utility of the image and to suggest a parallel with the term "working hypothesis" in a psychological experiment. The clinician can view his situation somewhat as the experimental psychologist views his. At the start the experimenter gets hunches or directional leads about the problem he is investigating. Often he can explicitly state these in the form of working hypotheses. He defines his basic terms in ways that permit him to test his hypotheses. Then he revises his hypotheses in the light of evidence he has gathered while testing them. In a similar manner the clinical psychologist can begin by informally attempting to specify his hypotheses and hunches about a person and his situation and then proceed to check them and revise them as new evidence comes in. The working image is a kind of "hypothetical construct" with an admitted surplus meaning over and beyond the available data (MacCorquodale and Meehl, 1948). It includes more than the recorded report concerning the patient, in that it is shaped by both verbal and nonverbal interactions that have never been caught in the record. The working image is the best approximation a clinician can achieve of a *representation* of the other human being.

The impression-formation process is a rapid one. Meehl (1960) reports that therapists by the second or third interview describe clients very much as they do after many more visits. The image is revised and enlarged somewhat as acquaintance continues. In many ways it can be seen as a creative product similar to an artist's portrait. Major outlines and structures first appear, but further nuances and details are added as the painting progresses. Methods used in research on interpersonal perception, the formation of impressions, and the attribution of characteristics to persons and situations may be adapted to clinical practices to clarify the concept of working image.

We need more research on the influence of these working images on the behavior of the clinician and the other persons whose decisions affect clients of a psychological service. The reason the psychologist writes a report is not to create interesting pictures in others' minds, but to enable staff members to help clients. Because a clinic or agency is made up of human beings whose interaction affects clients or patients, the aim of assessment cannot be decisions or plans alone but also the production of working images that facilitate helpful relationships.

The Process of Interpretation

Once the psychologist has collected appraisal information by interviews, observations, tests, or other methods, how does he "make sense" out of these myriad impressions and measurements? How does he combine the information and move toward an improvement design? How does he interpret observations as he moves along in treatment? A basic assumption, common to all science, is that there is some order in the events of the world. The task is to find the underlying order in the complexity of information about a client and to select and choose which things are important to move the case along.

As we consider this problem, let us keep in mind some background facts, stressed earlier. First, the clinician's perception of his role has an important influence on what he does with the available information. It helps to determine the questions he tries to answer, the alternatives for disposition of the case he considers, and the amount of time he spends analyzing the case and whether he writes a report.

Another important factor in interpretation, discussed in Chapter 3, is the clinician's conceptual framework, the assumptions he makes about the nature of personality, psychopathology, and person–situational interaction—his own "philosophy of life." This framework furnishes the basic ideas, which will be combined with the specific data. Sarbin, Taft, and Bailey (1960) have called this the "postulate system" of the clinician. The postulate system originates from inductive generalizations on his experiences, from the theories he accepts, from analogies with similar situations, and from authoritative statements made by teachers and others. Much of the conceptual framework of the clinician is untested. It would seem likely that the better clinician would be one who is more open to new and more subtle ways of construing his world and more able to perceive both positive and negative evidence.

Each bit of information that has been collected about a person can be viewed in three ways. There are three kinds of questions we can ask ourselves as we attempt to fit it into the total picture. First, what does this mean as a *sample*? Second, with what does it *correlate*? Third, is it a *sign* of an underlying condition? We discuss these ideas as they apply to the task of describing a person, but they can be generalized to other system levels.

A psychologist's observation, the score on a test, or whatever is available is a *sample* of a population of events. All that the psychologist has is his limited record of the patient's history and the notes from the diagnostic study. How generally do these pieces of information characterize the person, or how specific are they to this particular time and place?

The datum can also be viewed as a *correlate* of something else. What would this observation be related to? On the basis of research or clinical experience,

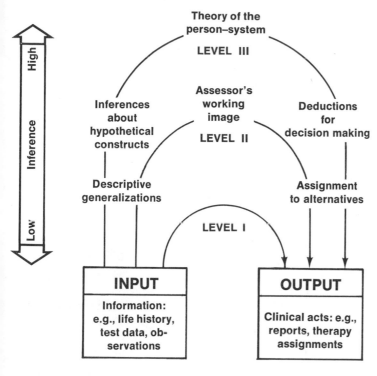

FIGURE 6-2 Levels of interpretation.

what should one expect? As a clinician considers a patient's feelings that others are persecuting him, he looks for feelings of special worth or special powers, since it is common for paranoid people to develop grandiose reasons for the attention others seem to give them.

A datum can also be seen as a *sign* of underlying feelings or causes. Agitation, a flushed face, and changes of the topic of conservation suggest anxiety stemming from internal conflict. What motives, traits, or social pressures account for the agitation? What would psychoanalytic theory or role theory suggest? In combining information from various sources one checks inferences from one kind of data against other kinds of evidence. If a test shows a poor attention span, for example, one looks for evidence of attention difficulties in school work, associated characteristics such as hyperactivity, and background characteristics such as anxiety in the home.

As we think about the "in-between" process linking "input" to "output"—the process we call inference—it will be helpful to distinguish three levels at which it may occur. Figure 6-2 illustrates this idea. Let us look carefully at what the clinician does at each of these levels.

At *Inference Level I* there is a minimum amount of inference. The information about the patient or client is as directly related to resultant action as it can ever be. In nonclinical work this kind of inference occurs frequently. For example, a prospective student applies for entrance to college. He sends in his grade record and takes an entrance examination. The admissions officer accepts him if he is above a certain cutting score, rejects him if he is below it. Similarly, in screening for emotional disturbance in the armed services psychologists used a routine test and a check list, followed perhaps by a five-minute interview. If they detected no gross deviation from normal, they passed the inductee. If they noted some disturbance, they sent him to another interviewer for more intensive evaluation. A well-trained clerk or even a machine can make such inferences. We do not generally think of Level I as being very "clinical"; yet, as Meehl has pointed out (1956), it is potentially an important level for clinicians. It produces standardization and efficiency in the operation of a program. Its main disadvantage is that it provides no way of dealing with exceptions to general trends and unique or idiosyncratic events. If we were content with this level we could dispense with theory.

At *Inference Level II* there are at least two kinds of inference. The first is *descriptive generalization.* Here one attempts to state what is generally true about some observed characteristics. For instance, during an interview with a patient a clinician may observe several instances of slow body movements and long delays in answering questions. The descriptive generalization he uses in interpreting these facts is that at the time of observation the patient was "retarded motorically." If he discovers later that the patient eats and sleeps poorly and says that he is sad and discouraged, the clinician may then use the term "depressed." This term can be thought of as a broader descriptive generalization, or an example of a second kind of inference. a *hypothetical construct*—an inner state—that is more than a pure description of behavior (MacCorquodale and Meehl, 1948). A construct often implies an etiology or causal condition, perhaps physiological. Level II inferences, whether they are descriptive generalizations or hypothetical constructs, permit us to make deductions with regard to the patients needs and treatment. At this level the working image of a person is involved, because impressions are formed through contacts with the person; however, the output of the clinical activity may not be directed to an extensive portrayal of the person.

Inference Level III differs from Level II only in its inclusiveness and integration. Here one attempts to form a consistent overall theory of the person—situation. Such an attempt involves a thoroughgoing exploration of the person's life situation and explanatory speculations about the developmental, social, and physiological underpinnings of his behavior. To be completely successful it requires a coherent integrated theoretical system of hypotheses and deductions. Most clinical work is not pitched at such high level, in part because most of our theories of personality are themselves very difficult to apply consistently to an individual.

At a less pretentious Level III position, we do seem to be using something like a simple "theory of a person" when we form the working image discussed in the previous section. How we put together the bits of information of our initial impressions may depend upon some quite complicated, though unanalyzed, theoretical assumptions about personality.

Behavioral, Psychometric, and Psychodynamic Approaches

Another way of analyzing the complex process by which information about a person is processed and organized is summarized in Table 6-1. The *behavioral* approach confines itself to the actions of an individual in defined situations viewing data as samples. It focuses on behavior change without making inferences about inner states or traits of individuals. In assessment, this approach requires specific observations and record keeping particular to the individual and his living situation. This approach, although appealing in its simplicity, has only recently been utilized to any great extent by clinicians.

In the history of clinical psychology, the *psychometric* approach has been a major one. It takes any given datum and tries to relate it to other data. It particularly emphasizes prediction, making use of tests and formulas. Like the behavioral approach, the level of prediction is kept low, although inferences are sometimes made to traits and inner states. This kind of approach is most useful for what Levy (1963, p. 171) called "bounded" psychodiagnosis (i.e., decisions as to dispositions of persons). It provides answers to questions like "To what psychiatric category does this patient belong?" "Will this client continue in therapy for six months?" or "Is this youngster a potential juvenile delinquent?" Sarbin, Taft, and Bailey (1960) call this way of processing information *taxonomic sorting*.

The psychodynamic approach is the third way of processing information, the one most widely used in the past, and one many clinicians still tend to prefer. Based mainly but not exclusively on psychoanalytic theory, the basic assumptions are *psychic determinism*, that every thought and action, such as dreams and slips of the tongue, has a meaning or psychological cause, and the *projective hypothesis*, that perceptions and reports about ambiguous stimuli are expressions of inner needs, states, and wishes. Following this approach, a psychologist looks at data he collects as signs of intrapsychic, or, less commonly, interpersonal conditions. He tries to build an emergent impression of the "whole person" with emphasis on his inner feelings, conflicts, and motives. The presentation is individually oriented—idiographic. Unlike the psychometric approach, its purpose is not to facilitate particular decisions about a person but to provide a general picture from which many decisions, some unpredicted, may emerge. What it produces is a greatly elaborated working image of the person.

The distinctions have been overdrawn to make the points clearer. Although a psychologist tends to lean in one of the three directions, he is likely to take one of the others on occasion. Often he moves from one approach to the other, dealing with a "bounded" problem by a psychometric method and moving to a

TABLE 6-1 Three Approaches to Processing Information

	Approaches		
	Behavioral	*Psychometric*	*Psychodynamic*
Primary manner in which data are used	As samples	As correlates	As signs
Preferred sources of information	Specific observations, record keeping	Tests, norms, formulas actuarial tables, cookbooks	Case history, projective data, interviews
Preferred methods of interpretation	Levels I and II, at a low level; no use of inner traits or states; emphasis on situations; idiographic	Level I or II; formal, mechanical; emphasis on individual traits; nomothetic; taxonomic sorting	Level III, impressionistic, theoretical, creative holistic, emphasis on intra-psychic and interpersonal states or traits; idiographic; emerging synthesis
Most appropriate applications	Controllable treatment situations	Specified, "bounded" decisions, dispositions	General, "unbounded" development of extensive working image for case management or psychotherapy

more global "unbounded" attempt to describe another case. Cronbach, in writing about the last two approaches, has this to say (1970, pp. 29–30):

> Neither style can be adopted to the exclusion of the other. The measurer must fall back upon judgment whenever he applies score information in teaching, therapy or supervision of employees. The portraitist on the other hand, cannot afford to ignore the accurate facts psychometric instruments provide. The psychometric and impressionistic styles differ with respect to definiteness of tasks employed, control of response, objective recording of basic data, formal numerical scoring and numerical combination of data to reach decisions, and critical validation of interpretations. Most procedures are psychometric in some of these respects and impressionistic in others.

THE PLACE OF CLASSIFICATION AND PREDICTION IN THE CLINICAL APPRAISAL PROCESS

As we have said before, clinical psychology is now in the process of transition. Its tasks and its concepts are changing. If the opponents of the medical model have their way, one major task psychologists have performed in the past may no longer be expected of them the use of tests and assessment procedures to facilitate the assignment of patients to psychiatric categories, such as schizophrenia, depression, or psychopathic personality. In this transition period, however, it must be recognized that the language of medicine is still spoken in the places where many clinicians work, and psychodiagnosis is still considered to be an important part of the whole enterprise.

There is no necessary conflict for psychologists in this situation. What we have been discussing as *appraisal* would fit very comfortably into the concept of *diagnosis* many psychologists hold. Gough (1971b), for example, arguing that clinicians should continue to carry on diagnostic activities, points out that the clinician's descriptions of patients communicate useful information about symptoms, psychopathological processes underlying them, and etiology, whether or not we use these medical designations. Small (1972) also argues forcefully that psychology should not give up diagnosis as a major area for psychological involvement.

We need classifications of some sort to bring order into the chaos of personality malfunctions, and until a better system appears, it is likely that the psychiatric nomenclature will continue to be employed. Research of various kinds is in progress—attempts to set up more useful categories (Thorne, 1967; Phillips, 1968), sophisticated computer procedures for processing assessment data (Gough, 1971b), and perhaps most important, the classification of environments as well as personalities (Craik, 1970; Frederiksen, 1972). Many of the psychologists working in behavior modification have taken steps in the right direction. They are specifying when and where undesired behavior occurs and what conditions promote desired behavior. Their classification system is then in such terms as behaviors, or habits, and reinforcements which are specific to the individual and his situation, rather than in terms of global psychiatric categories or psychological traits. Many humanistic, cognitively oriented psychologists also use a process of studying the individual as he exists and experiences his life here and now, rather than searching for a connection with a disease entity and an etiology. Both the behaviorist and the existentialist are using *processes* rather than static classifications, which is what the medical model has been criticized for. The shift to a process orientation is much more important than is a shift to nonmedical terminology.

The other main medical function to which the assessment efforts of psychologists have contributed in the past is prognosis. This refers to the prediction of the course and outcome of a disease. In the emerging clinical psychology, this is a much less salient feature of the clinician's task than it once was. For one thing, because so much depends upon the client's environment, the prediction of a patient's future behavior from personality data alone cannot be expected to be very accurate. For another, the making of predictions may in itself be a damaging activity, because predictive statements tend to become self-fulfilling prophecies. The clinician's job is now considered to be assisting creatively to develop an improvement design that will move the person toward a more effective and rewarding life rather than to predict his future behavior as accurately as possible.

Accepting this viewpoint enables us to dispose rather summarily of what has been one of the burning issues in clinical psychology, the argument over *clinical versus statistical prediction.* Briefly stated, the question is: Can a clinician, making use of all the skill he has acquired, predict quantitative criteria such as college success, psychiatric classification, and the like, more accurately than they can be predicted mechanically by the use of a regression equation in which items of information such as test scores are weighed according to their demonstrated correlation with the criterion. Starting with Sarbin's study (1943) and spurred on by Meehl's very influential monograph (1954), many research efforts have been directed to this question. The results indicate that in most instances the calculating machine wins out over the clinician.

Because it is not very relevant to the design of improvement programs, we shall not try to summarize this extensive research literature, but simply point out a few implications. First, if what is required is simply the prediction of a quantitative or classificatory criterion from quantitative data, it is a waste of expensive resources to use psychologists to make the predictions. Second, statistical aids, such as norm tables, expectancy tables, prediction formulas, and computer programs—the so-called "cookbooks"—should be used in clinical assessment whenever possible to improve the accuracy of the judgments that enter into the complex process of designing improvement programs. Finally, research to increase the scope and effectiveness of mechanical processing of personality data should be encouraged to free more and more of the time and energy of psychologists for nonmechanical activities.

DECISION MAKING

Designing improvement programs involves decision making as well as the collection and organization of information. Many sorts of decisions are involved at different stages of the process. We shall single out some of these for special attention.

Decisions About Who the Client Is

It is highly important in formulating a treatment plan that the person or group of persons making the decision determine clearly *who* the client is in relation to the objective of treatment. There is often considerable confusion about this, confusion that interferes with the success of any plan adopted. Perhaps mainly because the medical model has predominated for so many years, a psychologist usually sees himself as a professional healer, whose client is the person seeking his services. This assumption about who the client is works very well for the psychotherapist in private practice dealing solely with adults. It is less clearly applicable when the psychologist deals with children, receives his salary from a school district or a hospital, or works as a consultant to business and industrial firms. For a person in one of these more ambiguous situations, the questions about whom one is working for and what one is attempting to accomplish must be decided each time one undertakes a new treatment project.

Take, for example, the school psychologist in a school system consisting of eight elementary schools and two high schools. Referrals come to him mainly from the teachers and administrators of the schools he serves. When Mr. Lawrence, the principal of Franklin Elementary School, asks him to see Billy Anderson, a ten-year-old boy whose disruptive behavior in a fifth-grade classroom is making life intolerable for his teacher, Ms. Hendricks, just where does his responsibility lie? In addition to Mr. Lawrence, Ms. Hendricks, and Billy, each of whom may consider that the psychologist is working for him, Billy's parents also have a stake in the undertaking and must be taken into consideration. The psychologist has several different options but must make all his actions consistent with the one he chooses. He can initiate direct psychotherapy with Billy himself, explaining to all the other people involved that he will *not* be reporting to them directly until the treatment is concluded, and then only in general terms. Or he can work with either the teacher, the principal, or both to modify the school situation in such a way as to control Billy's behavior through rewards and punishments. In this case he may never actually talk to Billy. Or he can make a thorough diagnostic study of the case, attempting to discover the roots of Billy's difficulties by investigating all aspects of his developmental history, and then design a plan for influencing his further development that will counteract whatever the unfavorable factors have been in the past. In this case his primary clients will probably be one or both of Billy's parents, since they are responsible for the boy's continuous development.

Determining who the client is relates to the many complex legal and ethical issues such as the problem of confidentiality. Who should be allowed access to the record the agency keeps for a case? What information should be passed along to others who deal with the person? We shall be discussing ethical issues of this and other sorts in Chapter 20.

Decisions about System Level in Which to Intervene

Another sort of decision toward which appraisal efforts must be directed is the level at which intervention is to occur. Although this might at first glance look like the question discussed in the previous section—Who is the client?—it is not quite the same. To return to a previous example, the school psychologist may decide that his client is Billy, but he may also decide that the best way to help the boy is to bring about a reorganization of Ms. Hendricks' fifth-grade classroom. Many of the subsequent chapters will elaborate on the work of the clinician at different system levels. Here we will briefly illustrate the possibilities and discuss the problem of selecting the appropriate level.

Psychobiological interventions. Considering levels in ascending order of breadth or comprehensiveness, we start with the modification of some physiological system, usually by means of drugs. This is likely to be the treatment preferred, at least at the outset, for seriously disturbed psychotic patients, whether the psychosis appears to be caused by physical impairment or by psychological stress. Changes must be brought about in the functioning of the neural-hormonal systems underlying the mental systems—excitement, depression, or confusion—before the patient is amenable to psychological influence. In the case of some mildly neurotic individuals also, the most economical and immediately helpful form of intervention may be for a physician to prescribe an anxiety-reducing drug. If the physiological treatment is successful, some change in personality and in the social systems in which the person participates will, of course, occur as indirect effects.

Individual interventions. The next level of treatment possibilities is the modification of personal psychological systems. Such interventions may be either verbal or behavioral. A variety of different ways of bringing about personality change is available. Some forms of treatment focus on the self-concept of the individual. Others attempt to alter an individual's behaviors or habits. We shall be considering these and other approaches in more detail in subsequent chapters.

Group interventions. The third level at which intervention can occur involves interpersonal, or small-group, systems. Individual interviews serve the purpose of interpersonal therapy when used to call attention to ways in which the client can improve his relationships with the people who are important to him, although the clinician does not deal directly with those relationships. More obviously social methods of treatment have been gaining in prominence as time has passed, methods in which the clinician conducts meetings of groups of clients instead of interviewing them singly. By creating in the therapy room a miniature social system to be observed, analyzed, and changed, the therapist hopes to modify the functioning of other groups in which his clients participate as well as this one. The therapy group may consist of persons who at the outset constitute a natural social system, such as a family, or it may be made up of persons who are strangers to one another at the time they first meet.

Organizational and community interventions. A fourth level of intervention is that of larger organizations, such as hospital wards, schools, or communities. The task is to analyze and manipulate organizational variables rather than direct person-to-person interactions. Work along these lines has been carried on for some time in business and industry. Generalizations with regard to organizational structures and their effects on participants' attitudes and behavior seem to fit many specific areas of endeavor, including the treatment of psychological difficulties. Fairweather (1967), for example, has demonstrated the feasibility of creating a viable organization of psychotic patients, each of whom would individually not be able to hold his own in the world outside the hospital. Going beyond single organizations, the psychologist, along with others, may become active in altering relations between organizations, community planning, and social policies of a very broad nature. With the growth of community psychology as a field of specialization, increasing emphasis on these kinds of intervention can be anticipated.

Bases for selecting a system level. Selecting the system level at which to intervene is perhaps the most important decision a helping agency makes and one that is seldom explicitly studied. Take, for example, the case of Billy to which we have been referring. His teacher thinks he may be "emotionally disturbed." She is annoyed by Billy's imitations of the way she talks and his frequent wild antics and behavior, which amuse his classmates. Billy's parents have been unhappy with him for some time because he "sasses" them and misbehaves at home, too. The teacher's complaints increase their concern. It is possible to look at Billy's situation from several different levels. A helping agent could, for the reasons given, choose any of the initial plans in Table 6-2. As we see, the choice of system determines the type, or types, of intervention to be undertaken. Techniques are not yet developed for assessing Billy's total situation in a way that will tell us which system level is most promising. Two errors commonly occur: (1) the assumptions practitioners make leave certain systems quite unexamined and untouched, or (2) practitioners fail to link assessment with intervention in any meaningful way. A psychologist who intends to use a *family* therapy approach with Billy has little reason to use a battery of individual tests. Instead he should assess the communication involved in the complaint and the relationships existing among family members.

TABLE 6-2

System Level	Reasons for Selecting	Possible Intervention
Physiological	"It's minimal brain damage."	Secure medication and monitor behavior.
Personal		
Intrapsychic	"He's emotionally disturbed."	Individual play; casework with parents.
Behavioral	"He shows deviant behaviors."	Reprogram behavior contingencies in the home and school.
Family	"His behavior is related to a collapsing marriage."	Intensive family or marital therapy.
Small group	"Need to change his role in the class."	Hold class meetings with teachers and peers.
Organization	"Those teachers get nervous and refer too much."	Group consultation with teachers.
Community	"This involves problems of interagency communication."	Establish new multiservice coordination; hold training workshop.

How many systems should the psychologist pay attention to? Until we have better tools to appraise and select, we suggest that he resort to a system review and a practical ordering procedure to guide his involvement. The psychologist (or others in the agency) should always systematically touch on a wide variety of levels during the early appraisal period. They should select as the primary focus the systems that are most disordered and still most influenceable with the personnel and techniques available. Systems that are adequate or intervention techniques that are too time-consuming or beyond the agency's competence can be put aside. In eventually discussing the complaint with Billy's mother, the psychologist might convey something like the following: "Billy really does seem to have learned ways for making his misbehavior pay off (reflecting the selection of the personal level as the main system of intervention), but I wonder what the family's role has been (reflecting a secondary emphasis on the family). He's had a recent physical, and I know the school situation, although not perfect, is a fairly happy place for him" (reflecting a judgment that the physiological and relevant organizational systems are functioning adequately). A major task for psychologists and members of other helping professions is to make the selection of systems of intervention less arbitrary and more related to beneficial outcomes.

It should always be as we have repeatedly stated—that an improvement plan calling for direct intervention at one system level will produce indirect effects at levels below and above the level chosen. A client who undertakes to bring about constructive modifications in his personality system by means of psychotherapy may at the same time free himself of headaches and indigestion (physiological-system changes) and develop more rewarding relationships with his wife and children (family-system changes). Redesigning the system of organization of a training school for delinquent boys may produce far-reaching changes in the psychological development of each of ten boys participating and also in the larger social system of which the institution forms a part. Recognizing this fact of the interdependence of systems often makes it possible to formulate an improvement plan designed to affect two or more systems simultaneously. A highly anxious patient may receive both drugs and psychotherapy. A school child in difficulties may be scheduled for both tutorial help in school subjects and for group therapy. The good clinician will always be on the lookout for effects, both predictable and unpredictable, at system levels other than those where he is deliberately bringing influence to bear.

Other Factors in Decisions about Improvement Plans ✓

As a helping agent develops a design with a client, several aspects other than system level need to be considered. We shall point out five factors that are important in differentiating between the several kinds of approaches to treatment that will be discussed in later chapters. These factors are not independent of one another, but they can be discussed separately.

Considering the degree of change. First, *how much change* should the psychologist attempt to bring about in whatever system he has decided to work with? Is a major reorganization of a given client's personality required (or *desired* by him), or would a relatively minor change, such as the acquisition of techniques enabling him to improve his social relationships, be a solution to his problem?

In most work with nonpsychotic adults, decisions about how much change is to be attempted are made jointly by psychologist and client, although the matter may never come up for discussion between them. It is probably true that psychologists, unless they consider this factor in deciding about the objective of their efforts in a given case, often tend to aim at more extensive changes than their clients wish for themselves. This can lead to frustration and dissatisfaction on both sides.

Judging the client's commitment. A second and related factor to be considered in designing a plan for improving the client's condition is the amount of commitment the client brings to the undertaking. Most sorts of psychotherapy require some degree of commitment on the part of the client: a decision to participate or at least a willingness to try. But there are degrees of willingness, and these must be taken into consideration.

One of the advantages of the general systems framework is that it provides an approach to designing an improvement program even for a person with no commitment at all to change. In such cases one works with the system of which he forms a part and applies the principles derived from the research on behavior modification in bringing about changes in his *actions* and thus indirectly in his social relationships and attitudes. Examples are to be found in the training of the mentally retarded and chronic psychotics for better social adjustment.

Deciding how much reliance to place on verbal communication. A third factor in planning for the improvement of system functioning at any level is the extent to which verbal communication is to be the medium through which the modification takes place. All varieties of psychotherapy based on interviews rely heavily on the ability of the participants to express in words their feelings, ideas, beliefs, and concepts about personal interrelationships. The utility of such treatments with uneducated people and young children, and their advisability with individuals who use verbal "psychologizing" as a defense mechanism, is clearly limited.

The difference between the quality of the verbalizations of clients who do not benefit from client-centered therapy has been highlighted in research reported by Gendlin et al. (1968). They have developed a scale labeled EXP for measuring the *experiential process*. It is designed to measure the extent to which a subject is able to focus on present concrete feelings, regardless of the content of what he is talking about. "It is the act of paying attention to one's present feelings and coming to a new felt-to-be-meaningful formulation about them which is the essence of focusing" (Gendlin et al., 1968, p. 241). Although clients often increase their ability to think in this way as therapy proceeds, Gendlin's evidence indicates that unless they show some "focusing" during early interviews, they will not improve during interview therapy of the client-centered variety.

Emphasizing integration of subsystems or interaction of the system with environment. Although it is difficult to cover this distinction with any sort of simple label (*internal* versus *external* change comes closest to what is meant), it is often an important consideration. In the case of Billy, whose behavior irritates his teachers and parents, should the objective be to modify the boy's internal state by reducing his feelings of hostility and insecurity, or should it be to change the way he acts, so that he can make more friends and get more help from his teacher and more acceptance from his parents? There should be a decision about this; it should not be ambiguous or uncertain. With the increasing popularity of methods of treatment based on the technology of behavior modification, externally focused treatment procedures are being chosen more and more frequently. They have the advantage that the results can be more reliably assessed than can the results of efforts directed toward internal personality change. In the long run, of course, whichever strategy is adopted, changes of both sorts will be brought about if the plan succeeds. The painfully shy adolescent girl who is taught conversational skills to enable her to reach out toward other people will undergo internal changes as well, increasing her self-confidence and spontaneity. The neurotic housewife who through psychotherapy is freed of her anxiety and guilt will show more sexual responsiveness toward her husband, feed her children better, and be more friendly toward her neighbors.

Determining degree of attention to complaints. The fifth and related consideration entering into the choice of an improvement plan is the question as to whether a direct or an indirect approach to the presenting problems is more likely to be effective—in older terminology, whether to treat the *symptom* or the *cause.* The necessity for making this decision is perhaps most obvious in the case where the client is a young child, but it is also necessary in adult cases where psychotherapy is to be initiated. Is Mr. Lathrop's fear of airplanes the problem, or is it only a symptom providing a clue to what the problem is? Some psychologists believe that it is useless to worry about underlying causes theoretically deduced from symptoms; they would treat the behavior, denying that it is a "symptom" or asserting that it is retrainable. Others think it necessary to get at underlying motivations.

The process of designing a plan for improving the functioning of a psychological system is not usually as clear-cut and rational as the foregoing discussion of factors to be considered suggests that it is. The psychologist's own characteristics and the resources of his agency or office limit the number of possibilities he can consider. If he is a psychotherapist in private practice, his options may be limited to direct interaction with the client who consults him. If he is a staff member of a busy neighborhood clinic, any sort of prolonged psychotherapy with individuals may be out of the question. If his own training has been solely in techniques of modifying behavior through controlling reinforcement schedules, he will not be equipped to attempt to modify internal manifestations of personality through, say, client-centered therapy. A psychologist working in a large city with many special services at his disposal can refer a client to another agency if it appears that his needs can be met more adequately there; a psychologist in a small town in a remote area must do his best to furnish whatever assistance is to be given himself.

However, whether or not circumstances make it possible to design an optimal treatment plan for each client who seeks psychological help, the kind of thinking we have been recommending is not a waste of time. Research and practice in psychology have generated many possibilities for eradicating difficulties and improving the manner in which individuals and groups function. Eventually psychological services should be organized in such a way that all citizens in our society can benefit from these increases in our knowledge. With the growth of community clinics and other forms of group practice, in which professional workers with different skills combine forces, the design of optimal improvement programs for particular individuals, groups, and situations will increasingly become possible. Psychologists who consider alternative strategies, including those which they personally do not have the skills or facilities to employ, are likely to be more useful in such organizations than psychologists with narrower horizons.

THE AGENCY OR ORGANIZATION AS
A DECISION-MAKING SYSTEM

We have been talking mainly about the clinical psychologist's decision-making function. It is important always to keep in mind that he or she does not operate autonomously, especially if he or she is employed by an organization such as a clinic, a hospital, or a social agency. The range of decisions open to the psychologist is limited by the organization to which he belongs. The range of decisions open to this organization is limited by decisions made at community, state, and federal levels.

An agency or institution can be viewed as a system that processes human problems. There is an *input* into the system in the form of new human problems. There is a *throughput or processing stage* in which the input of individuals or groups is involved in various degrees of assessment, disposition, and intervention. Eventually there is an *output* in the form of altered behavior and attitudes of individuals or groups separating from the institution. There are also other outputs or products, such as reports to other agencies, research publications, and training of professionals and nonprofessionals. In a large institution, many subsystems, such as the food service or occupational therapy unit, operate within the overall system. A psychology department may be one of those subsystems, with its own set of inputs, throughputs, and outputs. Each subsystem as well as the total system will have typical sequences of decision making about the problems that come to it. New types of clinical endeavors, such as crisis clinics, street therapy, encounter groups, and in-home family intervention will take different forms, but the basic systems analysis will hold. The psychologist must be aware of the sequence of decisions inherent in the organization to which he belongs. These are of several kinds.

Prior to any specific case, there will have been a number of determinations about institutional policies and rules that have set the stage for later decisions. These relate to the general information abroad in the community about the agency and affect the individual's decision as to whether or not to seek help. The practices of the clinic or agency may involve outreach into the community so that access is very easy. It may even conduct "search and intervene" missions with certain kinds of clients, such as leaders of delinquent gangs or drug pushers. It may conduct open classes on child rearing for parents and teachers. Clinicians often train policemen, ministers, and nurses to handle mental health problems. In any case, the image and regulations of the agency will influence decision making.

The manner of handling cases will depend a great deal on the definition of the service. If the "agency" is a sidewalk worker or an emergency telephone service, there may be no formal intake, virtually nothing in the way of case records, and little or no pause to consider whether to accept or reject. In some clinics and hospitals the processing may be very extensive and formal. Whether the system is simple, fast, and informal, or complex, slow, and technical, there are costs and benefits to each form. Increasingly, new forms seem to be developing that are more prompt, direct, and "natural."

Once the client or patient has come into contact with the helping agency, preliminary decisions are made about the following questions:

1. Will the agency provide service or not? This is the gatekeeping, screening, or, in some cases, such as a drop-in center, a recruiting function. It is often carried out by receptionists, in some cases, such as the newer crisis clinics, specially trained by psychologists. (Chapter 17 discusses this selective function of organizations in more detail.)

2. If the case is not taken on by this agency, how is the person referred to another source of help?

3. If the agency does take the case, what kind of initial information is collected, by means of a routine form or an intake interview, and who collects it?

4. Based on initial information, what does the problem seem to be, and what additional information is then collected, such as school records, medical reports, or parents' statements?

At a later stage, other kinds of organizational factors affect decisions about improvement programs. What alternatives are available? If the charter of the organization covers only specified kinds of services, these limits must be recognized. To what extent will the client enter into the decision making? Some agencies are set up primarily to make decisions about clients, others to make decisions with clients. How and where will the process of intervention occur? Are there limits to the length of time the agency can carry any one case? To whom and how often must reports be made? To what extent does the agency promote feedback to itself for research purposes?

These and many other questions impinge upon the psychologist as he participates in the ongoing sequence of decisions that constitutes an agency's system for dealing with its clients, a system graphically portrayed in Figure 6-3.

DECISIONS AND VALUES

As mentioned earlier, the decisions we make in the course of clinical work are intimately related to *values*—the "conceptions of the desirable that are relevant to selective behavior (Smith, 1963, p. 332)." Whatever system we are dealing with as a client, or whatever system we work in as a clinician, or whatever person serves as observer or recorder of the situation operates by a set of values, many of which have not been formulated in words. Goals of clients, institutions, and clinicians may conflict with each other, sometimes without any of the parties knowing that they have an unresolved difference. For that reason, it is important for the clinician to examine his own purposes and values in his work with his agency and in his relations with a client.

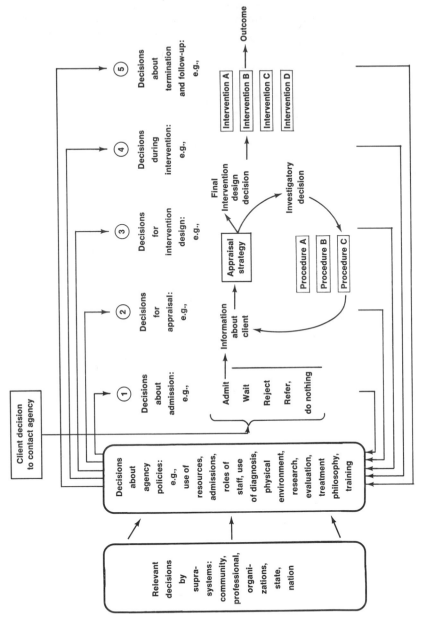

FIGURE 6-3   Clinical decisions regarding a case. (After Cronbach and Gleser, 1965, p. 18.)

Two different orientations characterize the work clinical psychologists do. As indicated in the preceding section, they result in decisions *about* the client and decisions *with* the client. Decisions about the assignment of patients to wards or to different kinds of treatment are similar to decisions about personnel selection in industrial or educational institutions. A mental hospital is interested in operating efficiently so as to produce maximum gains in mental health at a minimum cost to taxpayers. When psychotherapists are limited in number, the patients who may be expected to profit most from treatment have to be selected. Decisions of this first kind are made in the interest of *institutional values*. They are *management decisions* and, for research and practical purposes, need to be related to criteria of outcome, such as cost of services, recidivism, or morale of patients and staff. Much of the research of clinical psychologists can be related in some way to institutional decisions—studies of selection of patients for a new rehabilitation program, studies of assignment to foster homes.

Decisions of the second kind bring in *individual values*. When a person decides to take up an occupation, to undergo training, or to marry, he is, generally speaking, concerned about maximizing his own satisfactions and his own effectiveness and minimizing the "psychological cost." A psychologist can help the individual to assess his special tendencies, interests, abilities, and purposes. Assessment procedures can help the person to identify possibilities for action, to evaluate the appropriateness of various alternatives, and to clarify his own values.

In most clinical assessment, decisions involve both individual values and institutional values. In a mental hospital, a patient cannot be turned away as a job applicant can, because there is nowhere else for him to go. The hospital must usually accept its patients as they come and then try to fit each into a program that will benefit him most. Assessment procedures may also be used to help the institution adapt to individuals. Selection and training of psychiatric aides and nurses can be oriented to the particular needs and characteristics of patients. The effort to maximize both individual and institutional values is a major task for psychological assessment.

STUDYING THE OPERATIONAL EFFECTIVENESS OF CLINICAL INFORMATION SYSTEMS

The hard-headed administrator has the right to ask: "Just what do we gain by having a psychologist do assessment work in our clinic?" The tender-minded humanitarian is justified in asking; "Is assessment contributing to the welfare of each individual client?" At some time every clinical psychologist will ponder: "Is what I am doing really worthwhile? Am I wasting my time interviewing, giving tests, writing reports, and devising treatment plans?" Some psychotherapists have charged that assessment—or at least what they call diagnosis—is injurious, that just going through those procedures may lead the client to be overly dependent on authority and may establish a self-fulfilling categorizing in the mind of the clinician. In a survey of clinical psychologists' opinions and practices, Kelly (1961) found only half considered diagnostic work-ups always, or even usually, essential for therapy.

The position we have taken is that assessment is inevitably part of the whole clinical process. We are concerned with a clinical information system. Once clinicians come face to face with a client, they must make a decision whether or not to accept this client as suited to the kinds of service they can render and, if he is suited, which procedures should be undertaken. Unless they flip a coin, decision making involves some sort of assessment procedure. It also leads to communication of a picture of the client to other persons, giving them impressions that affect their behavior toward him. The question, then, is not whether to have a clinical information system or not, but how to carry it out and what is useful.

Although our main attention is on assessment for clinical treatment of clients, we should keep in mind that clinical psychologists often have other responsibilities which require assessment skills and knowledge. They conduct research on assessment procedures themselves and on psychotherapy and other forms of intervention. They are involved in the selection of psychiatric aides and community mental health workers. Psychologists devise methods for ascertaining effectiveness of training programs. They study the nature of psychosomatic problems, schizophrenia, mental retardation, prevention of disorders, and basic problems of personality and psychopathology. All these kinds of activities involve assessment.

In the clinical function itself, we are impressed with the small amount of work that is done on the understanding, conceptualizing, and researching the clinical processing systems, especially with regard to its basic components—image making and decision making. Cole and Magnussen (1966), in discussing the scarcity of research relating assessment to clinical action, indicate that this is the result of two factors: (1) the traditional compartmentalization of assessment and therapy into two separate areas and roles, and (2) the constricted orientation of assessment to the individual. They urge that assessment be "dispositional," that is, that it concern itself with the usage of information for action and its effects on treatment, the clinic, and possibly the community. Likewise, Levine (1968), in an excellent article on the social context of testing, recommends a decision-and-treatment-oriented approach to assessment. Arthur (1969) reviews several alternatives to the traditional diagnostic model for clinical work and concludes that an operations research model is necessary—an approach that optimizes the total endeavor of the clinic rather than its single decisions or its categorizing (diagnosing) efforts. McReynolds (1971) holds a similar opinion, and Howard and Orlinsky (1972) have developed a useful conceptual framework, described briefly in Suggested Readings at the end of the chapter.

The study of the decision-making process promises to contribute much to future developments in applied psychology. In its rigorous form, decision theory has been applied to economics and related areas. The application closest to clinical psychology is that of Cronbach and Gleser (1965). As yet it is most useful in personnel selection where institutional values predominate, but there are implications for individual orientations. Some general aspects of decision theory are as follows:

1. Emphasis should be on *payoff* or outcomes, not on specific techniques.

2. Questions of the validity of tests or other assessment activities should be considered as problems of *improving on existing procedures* rather than improving on chance.

3. *Strategies of whole sequences of assessment and treatment* should be the object of concern; one asks about the contribution of all procedures to the ultimate outcome.

4. *Examination of values and criteria* is fundamental; decisions are made that will maximize movement toward goals and minimize costs.

In doing research on the effectiveness of assessment in clinical decision making, there are a variety of directions research can take. For one thing, there is the identification of clinical decisions and the alternatives involved. Dailey's study (1953) is one of the few explorations of this question. His study of a VA hospital identified thirty-two questions that might be raised from the time a patient is admitted until he is discharged—from "Should this person be admitted to the psychiatric ward?" to "Should he seek membership in a community AA group?" Dailey obtained these by asking staff members to list the kinds of decisions they had to make frequently. They might also have been obtained by observation or from analyses of case and staff conferences.

Looking into the probability of success in connection with each alternative course of action leads to larger problems. A full study would require a kind of job analysis specifying the abilities and personality characteristics required for success in each of the alternative situations that are open. If the question is one of instituting treatment, we need an *analysis of the functioning of the client in the various kinds of treatment programs that might be designed for him.* What kinds of behaviors does this group require? How much verbal ability does this kind of psychotherapy involve? What sorts of interpersonal characteristics are found in those who comprise an effective group? When a case is going through the clinical decision-making process, the client's characteristics are compared with the requirements of the intervention.

Ultimately, an understanding of a client and the optimum treatment program requires an *analysis of the functioning of the client in daily life.* What sorts of problems do clients commonly run into in the community? What kinds of personal characteristics are required to handle these problems? How much complaining and bizarre behavior can a patient's family tolerate? The effectiveness of an intervention program must be measured against such factors. A view that is particularly helpful in this regard is a concern for the client's competencies, the adaptive assets he possesses already (Phillips, 1968).

If decisional alternatives are known, the nature of the clinic's functioning programs is known, and the major requirements for functioning in daily life are known, the job of assessment procedures is to provide the most useful information possible to come to decisions and to contribute useful working images of clients among the people who work with them. Questions of effectiveness then involve many of the matters already discussed—*optimal combination of assessment procedures, optimal sequencing of assessment to fit decision processes, strategies for combining information for decision making*, and whatever *follow-up and continuation of assessment* is appropriate.

The consideration of the effectiveness of clinical information systems would involve a cost-benefit analysis of the whole clinical enterprise. It would require a close look at the utility of present clinical procedures, many of which may be downright harmful and others of which are simply wasteful. A hard-headed efficiency study of clinical work is not likely to come soon, even if it is desirable. In the meantime we owe it to our clients to study the social context of decision making and impression management, to be concerned with the ultimate criteria in the everyday life of people, and to improve our assessment techniques as best we can.

SUMMARY

This chapter has presented the clinical psychologist as a designer of improvement programs working with others in a behavioral improvement system. In relation to the other functions of the system he is in, the psychologist is involved in analyzing and appraising the client system, determining what possibilities there are for improvement, and deciding on the improvement program. Psychological appraisal, or assessment, involves image making and decision making. Although assessment may be brief and informal, it does occur in some way—impressions are formed and decisions are made—in every case. The images that clinicians develop and convey about clients and their systems seem to be of great importance; research in this area is needed. Psychologists attempt to produce accurate and useful portraits of the persons for whom improvement programs are being designed by collecting information and processing it in several ways involving different levels of inference.

Diagnosis (or classification) and prognosis (or prediction) have been standard features of the psychologist's role in the past and are still important in some medical settings, but the concepts are being broadened to include environments and larger systems than the individual person.

In the decision-making part of the task of designing improvement programs, several varieties of decisions can be distinguished; who the client is, what system level should intervention be directed to, how much change should be attempted, and a number of others. The psychologist's decisions are constrained by the decision-making processes of the larger systems in which he operates. All decisions involve consideration of values, both individual and social. Extensive study of the operations of the clinical information system is needed.

SUGGESTED READINGS

Adinolfi, A. A. Relevance of person perception research to clinical psychology. *Journal of Consulting and Clinical Psychology*, 1971, *37*, 167–176.

In this chapter we have emphasized both the impression-forming and decision-making aspects of psychological appraisal. Much of the basic research on impression formation falls under the rubric of person perception. Adinolfi reviews some of the leading work on such topics as stereotyped accuracy, the study of the perceiver, differential accuracy, perceiver-perceived relations, and labeling. He discusses the possibility of conflicts between orientations toward past events and toward immediate empathic understanding. He notes that the most accuracy in perception is achieved by those who are most similar to the target person or familiar with him and his situation. He mentions the possibility that middle-class white clinicians are likely to have difficulty with perceiving lower-class nonwhite people accurately and thus may try to avoid the incomprehensible. He suggests becoming immersed in expressive works (e.g., poetry, art, film) of other groups in order to understand and empathize better. Adinolfi raises criticisms about the sociobehavioral approach because assumptions are made about the accuracy of observers and about the client's consistency in interpreting rewards and situations.

Mahrer, A. R. (ed.). *New approaches to personality classification.* New York: Columbia University Press, 1970.

Like biology before Linnaeus (1707–1778), psychology is still without an accepted classification for behavior, despite the great influence of Kraepelin (1855–1926) in classifying psychiatric disorders. (See Appendix B for the official American psychiatric diagnostic system, which grew out of Kraepelin's proposals.) In Mahrer's book, ten different proposals for classification systems are presented, some of them extensions of psychiatric nosology, others based on factor analysis, still others emphasizing existentialism and self-actualization. Readers may also wish to refer to the reviews of classification of the behavior disorders by Zubin (1967) and by Phillips and Draguns (1971). The latter has an excellent critique of the latest psychiatric system and some exposition of Phillips's system. Seifert, Draguns, and Caudill (1971) conducted an interesting cross-cultural application of the system developed by Phillips and others. With 412 hospitalized Japanese psychiatric patients they showed significant relations between diagnosis and symptom styles of role orientation (turning against self, turning against others, and avoidance of others) and sphere dominance (thought, affect, and action). Kanfer and Saslow (1965) propose "behavior analysis" as an alternative to diagnosis. Goldberg (1972) demonstrated the value of test data on groups for constructing classification systems.

Arthur, A. Z. Diagnostic testing and the new alternatives. *Psychological Bulletin*, 1969, *72*, 183–192.

Arthur reviews the *diagnostic model*, which has been most prevalent in clinical assessment in its two forms: the psychodynamic or "clinical" method, and the psychometric or statistical method. He points out the limitations of diagnosis as the goal, particularly because it does not relate directly to treatment or disposition. Arthur then examines several alternative assessment models: (1) the *experimental model*, whereby hypotheses about the disturbed behavior are formulated and tested (but he finds it inefficient); (2) the *behavior model*, which aims to find what alters and maintains specific behavior patterns (but he indicates that this approach neglects purely ideational "human" needs); (3) the *decision-making model*, which involves gathering information and determining values of all possible courses of action, including no action; and (4) *operations-research model*, which is an extension of the decision-making model to study the costs and benefits of the treatment endeavor and to upgrade the assessment function through continuous appraisal by expert terms of institutional values, procedures, and efficiency.

Cole and Magnussen (1966) also argue for a "dispositional" orientation to assessment, instead of traditional diagnosis, which has little relation to decisions about treatment or case management. The decision-making and operations approach is also endorsed in a helpful article by Levine (1968) entitled "Why and When to Test: The Social Context of Psychological Testing."

Lanyon (1972) suggests a technology for efficient information gathering and decision making in clinical services.

Meehl, P. E. *Clinical versus statistical prediction.* Minneapolis: University of Minnesota Press, 1954.

This has been one of the most influential books in clinical psychology. The central problem is how to predict a person's behavior. Meehl analyzes methods of inference from class membership. He considers the special powers of the clinician. The main section of the book is Meehl's review of a large number of studies which have contrasted the predictions of clinicians with predictions based on statistical procedures. In none of the studies was the clinician able to improve on the statistical prediction. Meehl says that statistics are indispensable, but he also shows that clinicians do make special contributions, such as providing creative insights. This book touched off a controversy that has been argued in many a symposium and journal article.

For another point of view, see Holt (1970). See also Sawyer (1966) and Goldberg (1968a).

Cronbach, L. J., and Gleser, G. C. *Psychological tests and personnel decisions*, 2nd ed. Urbana: University of Illinois Press, 1965.

Although the title suggests that the ideas in this book might apply only to tests and personnel matters, the potential area of application is much broader. Cronbach and Gleser present ideas that could be used to create extensive changes in methods and research in assessment. Instead of concerning themselves with single measures or tests as traditional test theories do, these authors focus on ultimate outcomes, or "payoffs," and the making of decisions using decision theory, which is defined as rational behavior in the face of unknown states of nature. The psychologist needs to consider combinations and sequences of information input contributing to decisions among alternatives with certain values. Some parts of the book present rather complex statistical details, but the early chapters furnish an easy-to-read overview of decision theory as applied to psychological problems.

For an excellent introduction, see also Raiffa's *Decision Analysis* (1968).

Levy, L. H. *Psychological interpretation.* New York: Holt, Rinehart and Winston, 1963.

Levy's book is one of the few books dealing in both a theoretical and practical way with a most important clinical process—interpretation. Levy points out that interpretive behavior is called for "whenever a state exists that seems refractory to other efforts at mitigation or understanding. In essence it consists of bringing an alternative frame of reference, or language system, to bear upon a set of observations or behaviors, with the end in view of making them more amenable to manipulation" (p. 7). Clinicians believe that a change will be facilitated by viewing a person—situation in a different perspective. Interpretation involves two aspects: (1) the semantic assignment of events to categories, and (2) the propositional assertion of relation between events. (These processes are similar to the coding of observations and the development of generalizations or hypotheses.) Levy distinguishes between two kinds of diagnostic work: (1) the formal approaches, using "cookbook" rules; and (2) the interpretive approach, using higher levels of inference.

For another analysis of the clinician's problem of moving from raw data to a refined inference, see the book by Sarbin, Taft, and Bailey (1960). They assert that clinical inference based on the logician's syllogism is a special form of statistical inference. The process is called *taxonomic sorting.* An inference is a "conclusion which follows from the collocation of a major premise, derived from the clinician's postulate system, and a singular minor premise achieved through observation" (p. 83).

For another comprehensive discussion, see *Clinical and Social Judgment* by Bieri and others (1966), especially Chapter 8 on situational factors. The reader might also like to review a systems-analytic approach to the diagnosis of psychopathology by Nathan and his colleagues (1967, 1968), and Martorano and Nathan (1972). This approach involved laying out the parts of the diagnostic sequence in a flow chart so that the diagnostic cues and their contributions to the final decision are quite clear.

Howard, K. I., and Orlinsky, D. E. Psychotherapeutic processes. In P. Mussen and M. Rosenzweig (eds.), *Annual review of psychology*, Vol. 23. Palo Alto, Calif.: Annual Reviews, 1972, pp. 615—668.

Howard and Orlinsky do more than review the recent publications on therapy. They present an analytic framework that can be used to organize the field and suggest future research. Their rather complex organization breaks down into parameters in three major systems: the social, cultural, and psychological systems. They view the contexts in which people come to therapy and the normative and symbolic value-laden aspects of the systems. Taking a community-wide approach, Howard and Orlinsky look at studies of inputs, processes, and outputs of the therapeutic systems. Ironically they conclude (p. 658) that "the major de facto function of our therapeutic activity system is as a kind of 'higher education' in the development of interpersonal skills and emotional capacities." They recommend studies of the systems for effective communication with many different segments of the patient population.

Wiggins, J. S. *Personality and prediction: principles of personality assessment.* Reading, Mass.: Addison-Wesley, 1972.

This book includes a reorganization and discussion of the research literature in the field of personality assessment. Major topics include the following: the linear prediction model and its applications; moderator variables, higher-order functions, and contingency tables; clinical prediction; personnel decisions in selection and classification; techniques of data collection; models and strategies in personality assessment; historical perspectives; and contemporary personality assessment. The book describes selected tests and procedures as illustrative of broad principles underlying personality assessment. It outlines ways in which assessment ought to be pursued in the future if further progress is to be made.

RESEARCH EXAMPLES

Introductory Note: Here and at the end of most of the following chapters, there are brief reports of research studies selected as illustrations of what clinical psychologists do. The volume of publication is very great, and any selection cannot do justice to the whole movement of research pertinent to the chapter. In most cases we have chosen examples that are directly relevant to clinical work, avoiding the large number of studies found, even in the applied journals, that do not use clinical subjects or deal with clinical problems. Each example should raise questions in the mind of the reader and serve as a stepping stone for further research. Readers are urged to examine the original articles and to consider how to extend and improve the area of study.

Dailey, C. A. The practical utility of the clinical report. *Journal of Consulting Psychology*, 1953, *17*, 297–302.

This study is interesting because it is one of a very few attempts to identify the decisions made about patients in the course of their hospital stay and to study how clinical procedures contribute to these decisions. Dailey's first step was to collect a long list of decisions from the clinical staff members of the VA hospital where the study was made. By eliminating overlap he reduced this list to thirty-two kinds of decisions. Examples on the first list are: Should this patient be admitted to the psychiatric ward? Should he be allowed visitors? Should he have a special diet? If he is to have psychotherapy, should the therapist be male?

In developing the measure of contribution to decision making, Dailey took an important next step. He asked ten clinical psychologists employed on the hospital staff to answer thirty-two decision questions for the average patient in the hospital. This step furnished a baseline against which to measure the amount of *new* information contributed by the psychological report. Then two clinicians read nine psychological reports, without having any other knowledge of the patient, and checked the decision list. Their answers were compared with the baseline answers. The score given each report was the difference between the judges' answers and the baseline answers.

This score was then compared with certain characteristics of the psychological report. It was found that 26 percent of the decisions based on the report were different from the baseline. The number of new contributions was correlated 0.27 with report length, 0.43 with number of technical terms, and 0.32 with personal terms, all these being significantly different from chance.

This study has some limitations. One wonders what the validity of these decisions was. For instance, would there be a correlation between these decisions and the judged success of the actual decisions? There is no report of the correlation of the report-based decisions with actual decisions about the patient. It is not known whether the clinician's baseline answers are actually the base rates on decisions in the hospital. Also, it is likely that one could not readily generalize to other hospitals because of the different possibilities for decisions in different settings. Despite all these shortcomings, the study is interesting and original. It treats of problems calling for much more research. Dailey has studied the behavior of an organization dealing with clinical dispositions. Additional ideas for such studies may come from the growing interest in computer-assisted diagnosis (e.g., Nathan et al., 1968; Spitzer and Endicott, 1969).

Chapman, L. J., and Chapman, J. P. Genesis of popular but erroneous psychodiagnostic observations. *Journal of Abnormal Psychology*, 1967, *72*, 193–204.

Chapman and Chapman report a series of studies that emphatically call attention to the fallibility of clinical thought and the difficulty in training for greater accuracy. The authors used the Draw-A-Person test, which, although frequently used by clinicians, has been shown in many research studies to have very little diagnostic validity. They first asked practicing clinicians to indicate what drawing characteristics would be found in clients who exhibit six symptoms. They found, for instance, that the sixty-seven clinician respondents most frequently believed that patients who worry about their manliness would frequently draw figures with broad shoulders and a muscular manly build, patients who are suspicious would draw atypical eyes, and those who were worried about intelligence would draw large heads.

Hypothesizing that clinicians' errors may be due to *illusory correlations* which many people in the culture hold, they presented forty-five drawings by psychotics and students to 108 undergraduates, who were naïve to the interpretation of drawing. Each drawing was paired randomly with one of the six symptoms mentioned above. Afterward the students were asked to list the characteristics that went with each of the six symptoms. Despite the random experience they had received, their answers were highly systematic, and in every case the most frequent student response was the same as the most frequent clinician response.

In a series of additional studies and variations, Chapman and Chapman produced several other findings. They demonstrated that body parts are frequently associated with symptoms in verbal responses as well as in drawings. For instance, subjects wrote that worries about intelligence would be reflected in emphasis on the head. They found that repeated exposure did not reduce errors, and that the "illusory correlations" were surprisingly resistant to attempts to establish other connections between drawings and symptoms.

The authors conclude that there is strong, widely-shared stereotypic thinking that clinicians seem to be using in interpreting drawings. They are pessimistic about the ability to influence these illusory correlations that clinicians and others use, and they emphasize the need to make use of actuarial methods to avoid the clinician's bias.

Golding and Rorer (1972) found as Chapman and Chapman (1969) had shown, that there are popular, a priori assumptions about signs of homosexuality on the Rorschach (e.g., anal responses). Golding and Rorer used various training procedures in attempts to alter illusory correlations but found that they are very resistant to change.

Goldberg, L. R. Man versus model of man: a rationale, plus some evidence, for a method of improving on clinical inferences. *Psychological Bulletin*, 1970, *73*, 422–432.

Goldberg points out that clinicians are constantly asked to rely on their clinical wisdom to combine fallible cues (predictors) in arriving at decisions, such as assignments to treatment, diagnoses, or prognoses. He mentions the clinical versus statistical controversy and asserts (p. 423) that "when acceptable criterion information is available, the proper role of the human in the decision-making process is that of a scientist: (a) discovering or identifying new cues which will improve predictive accuracy, and (b) constructing new sorts of systematic procedures for combining predictors in increasingly more optimal ways." But, he points out, criterion information is often not available for constructing actuarial decision-making methods, and we have only the judge and his behavior to study. For this purpose, Hoffman (1960) initiated a powerful recommendation—a statistical way for creating "paramorphic" models of the judge. The clinical judge is asked to make a set of judgments from previously quantified cues (e.g., a test profile, a list of background data) for each of a large number of target individuals. The judgments when quantified are used as the dependent variable in a standard linear-regression analysis. The results are a set of regression weights, one for each predictor, which are referred to as his model—a quantified representation of the clinician's behavior in making judgments. In the present article, Goldberg asks the question: How will the models compare with clinicians? Is a formula the clinician created better than the human judge himself?

The judgmental task for this study was the differentiation of psychotics from neurotics on the basis of MMPI profiles. Goldberg used data from an earlier study by Meehl (1959a) on twenty-nine clinicians judging 861 profiles of psychiatric patients. Goldberg (1965) had also used this sample of profiles earlier to develop one actuarial formula, a rather simple linear regression which had proved better than others tried, such as curvilinear or complex pattern formulas.

Goldberg found that the actual judgments of the typical clinician in separating neurotics from psychotics generated a validity coefficient (a term described in Chapter 9) of 0.28; the typical model, 0.30; and the actuarial formula, 0.44. Only in one sample was there a sizable discrepancy favoring the judge over his model, and the model of the most accurate judge was almost as good (0.43) as the actuarial formula. Goldberg concludes that the models of clinical judges can be more accurate diagnostic predictors than are the human beings who are modeled. He urges clinicians to study their judgmental behavior and to substitute actuarial formulas or models for themselves wherever feasible. It appears that the human judge is a fallible instrument when compared with the perfect reliability of a formula. Wiggins and Kohen (1971) found similar results when applying models to predictions of graduate school success. The procedure for creating formulas more effective than the original human judges is called *bootstrapping*.

Such techniques could be applied to a wide variety of judgmental problems. Slovic, Rorer, and Hoffman (1971) did "diagnostic strategy analyses" of physicians judging, from X-rays, malignancy of gastric ulcers.

Broverman, I. K., Broverman, D. M., Clarkson, F. E., Rosenkrantz, P. S., and Vogel, S. R. Sex-role stereotypes and clinical judgments of mental health. *Journal of Consulting and Clinical Psychology*, 1970, *34*, 1–7.

The authors hypothesized that clinicians would share the sex stereotypes of the general culture, displaying a double standard about mentally healthy characteristics of men and women and judging the masculine characteristics to be closer to the ideal of maturity. They tested their hypotheses on seventy-nine psychologists, psychiatrists, and social workers (forty-six men and thirty-three women). Subjects answered a questionnaire under different sets of instructions—one to describe a mature, healthy socially competent adult man; one to describe a similarly competent woman; and one to describe a mature person, sex unspecified. Previously the questionnaire had been given to college students. Results showed few significant differences in the ratings of the clinicians and the college students, and male and female clinicians did not differ in their protrayals of nature men and women. Some of the twenty-seven male-valued items were "aggressiveness," "independence," and "lack of emotionality." Some of the eleven female-valued items were "tactfulness," "gentleness," and "awareness of the feelings of others." Clinicians reported that the mature adult female was likely to have such characteristics as being less independent and more easily influenced. Having confirmed their hypotheses, the authors conclude that clinicians do reflect the sex-role stereotypes prevalent in the society. They upbraid clinicians for accepting these stereotypes and thus helping to perpetuate them.

chapter 7

The Design Process Illustrated:
A Clinic and One of Its Cases

One major difficulty with the sort of presentation made in Chapter 6 is that the reader may get the impression that the work a clinical psychologist does is much more straightforward and logical than it really is—that one first assembles and organizes all necessary information, filling out the details of his initial working image, and then makes decisions about what is to be done in bringing about an improvement in the way the person (or more-inclusive system) functions. To correct such possible misconceptions and provide a "flesh-and-blood" concept of image making and decision making as ongoing processes never completely free of confusion, doubt, and error, we present in this chapter in considerable detail the case of Allen Ward, essentially as it was handled in a mental health center. Names, places, and some identifying events have been changed, of course, to protect the people involved. The comments after each section of the case take up the kinds of questions that were raised in Chapter 6 and that will be considered in more detail in subsequent chapters on parts of the appraisal process.

THE SETTING

Hampton, the American city in which the Hampton Mental Health Center is located, has a population of 100,000. The *catchment area* (the surrounding region for which the Center is responsible) includes a population of 225,000. A major feature of the economy, mainly based on agriculture and light industry, is an army base, Fort Alexander. There are 6,000 soldiers stationed there, many of whom are undergoing basic training. The base has its own small mental health clinic. Hampton mental health resources consist of the Center, a few psychiatrists and clinical psychologists in private practice, and some specialized agencies. The Hampton Mental Health Center includes a small in-patient service connected with a general hospital and an out-patient department located not far from it. The Center also serves to coordinate and provide information about other community resources—counseling programs for families and for community college students, and special services for ex-mental patients, the retarded, the disabled, and dependent and delinquent children. Although these agencies have no administrative connection with the Center, its cases are often referred to them—and vice versa.

In addition to Dr. Thomas, the psychiatrist—director, the staff of the out-patient department consists of two half-time psychiatrists, four full-time social workers, two full-time psychologists, and one half-time psychologist (the rest of whose time is spent in private practice), three student trainees from a distant university, two volunteer therapy aides, two secretaries, and a receptionist. The Center is supported by state, local, and federal funds. Fees to patients are assessed on a sliding scale, so people on welfare and those whose incomes fall below a certain amount pay nothing. The Center has been in operation for over fifteen years and has established good working relations with the community.

FIRST CONTACT

Allen Ward came to the attention of the Center through a telephone call from his commanding officer, Major Pastore, to Dr. Thomas, expressing concern about a soldier in his outfit who had become excessively nervous and jumpy lately and had had some hot arguments with his sergeant. Major Pastore said that he preferred that Corporal Ward go the Mental Health Center rather than the military facility in order to avoid having an army record of psychiatric consultation that might impede the progress of this promising young man. Dr. Thomas replied that such an arrangement was possible. In answer to his inquiry about the nature of the problem, the Major indicated that Ward had been working irregular hours at the installation and had been sleeping very little, keeping himself awake with coffee and antisleep pills. He seemed to be suffering from anxiety and temporary physiological distress. The telephone conversation concluded with an explanation by Dr. Thomas about the Center's new service pattern—psychologists, social workers, and psychiatric nurses were taking turns on intake, combining the old intake and case-load functions—and an agreement that Major Pastore would tell Corporal Ward to telephone for an appointment. Allen's chart was initiated at this time, as it was Center policy to keep records of all contacts.

Image making

Dr. Thomas already had a number of perplexing questions and hypotheses in his mind. From his five years' experience in the Center, he recalled only two or three times when a commanding officer had called about an enlisted man. He wondered what special interest was involved. The brief description Major Pastore had given suggested that Allen Ward was an intelligent, conscientious young man who was going through temporary stress. But if the stress were only temporary, why wasn't the officer doing something to alleviate it himself, perhaps by a change of duty or a transfer? Why did the commander pick this man to be protected from having a military psychiatric record?

Decision making

Dr. Thomas interpreted Center policy as including the army base in its jurisdiction and accepted Allen as a client. These decisions were partly prompted by the "politics" of the situation, a quick judgment that if a commanding officer calls, the case must have some importance, so that the request should be granted if possible. Doing a favor for Major Pastore might make it more likely that the next time the Center identified a military family's need, someone could be counted on to prod the army's machinery into action.

FIRST INTERVIEW WITH DR. GLEESON

Not long afterward Corporal Ward called to make an appointment. When he appeared at the reception desk, Ms. Moody, the person in charge, asked his name and address and filled in some other routine information on his chart. Fee arrangements were agreed upon and Allen proceeded to the waiting room, where Ms. Moody noticed that he paced around, looked at some of the paintings, but did not show any interest in the magazines.

Dr. Ruth Gleeson, the psychologist, met Corporal Ward in the waiting room and asked him to walk back to her office, on the way chatting about the difficulty of finding the clinic. She noticed that he was a handsome, tanned, clean-cut young man of athletic build, wearing well-pressed civilian trousers, a sports shirt, and neatly polished shoes. The one rather jarring contrast to the rest of the picture was his dark glasses on a rainy day (like an "all-American" playing "hood," Dr. Gleeson thought).

During the interview, Allen sat tensely in the easy chair and smoked several cigarettes. His voice and speech were not unusual except for occasional hesitations and some stammering. She started the interview by saying, "I understand you are from Fort Alexander; what do you do there?" Allen responded by telling about his battalion and his job as a clerk, including some information about the extra night work in the office he had been doing during the last month, work that had ended recently.

Dr. Gleeson's next question was: "What brings you to the clinic at this time?" Allen in a defensive and somewhat suspicious way described his restlessness and difficulty in sleeping, and told how he had "lost his cool" with the sergeant. Allen complained that the army was a big machine that seemed to be organized to defeat him. After some probing into his present complaints, Dr. Gleeson asked Allen what had led up to these difficulties. Then, noting that he seemed increasingly willing to talk, even though very tense, she went on to elicit some of the major features of his life, where he grew up, in what kind of family, and how far he went in school. Allen was twenty years old but had not finished high school. She focused the conversation on Allen's usual ways of dealing with stress and how they were working nowadays. Toward the end, a part of the interview went like this:

Dr. G: Almost like everything began to close in at once? . . . The work . . . the barracks . . . you felt. . . .

Allen: Yea, everything, man, I don't know what's going to happen next. I can't make it with that goddam sergeant. *Everything* just went wrong. I'm all goofed. . . .

Dr. G: Things couldn't be worse—or could they?

Allen: No . . . well, maybe.

Dr. G: Lots has gone wrong and you do feel overwhelmed, but look, you've managed OK in quite a few ways. Controlled your temper when you wanted to blow up some of the time, kept up your job, your extra duty . . . it's taken a lot to do that.

Allen: I want to get away. Can't take it anymore.

Dr. G: In a couple of days we'll talk about some changes and we'll talk about your strengths again and things'll get better. But for right now try to stop worrying, stop the worrying, stop the mental thrashing around. You need sleep—let's talk about how you're going to get your sleep tonight.

Allen: Man, even that's hard. But if I trade duty again. . . .

Image making

Allen Ward's behavior would certainly be called anxious but not extremely unusual for new psychiatric patients. He was not grossly disoriented in time, place, or person. The psychologist consciously noted his physical appearance and his neatness, a sign of responsiveness to social expectations. Was he perhaps even overly neat and compulsive? But the dark glasses on a winter afternoon, the suspiciousness, the occasional quick defensiveness—some kind of paranoid problem? alienation? drug reaction? She also noted her own reactions and feeling about Allen, that she liked him and felt sorry that he was so anxious. She found herself feeling that Allen was specially deserving of her help and her affection, a train of thought that rang a warning bell. From her experience she had learned to say to herself, "I feel inclined to 'parent' Allen. He probably affects other people (Major Pastore) that way, too. Dependency and immaturity are possibilities to keep in mind." It appeared to her that Allen had reached a state of crisis; the quick survey of his strengths had suggested that he had few adaptive strategies left and that his capacity to supervise even elementary details of his life had degenerated to either apathy or an energetic but nonproductive "flailing around." Dr. Gleeson realized that she had tried to be supportive of his stengths, and concentrated on helping Allen "postpone" his burdens until he got some proper sleep.

Decision making

Center policy became apparent as a factor in decision making here. In a more traditional clinic, a social worker would have met Allen, obtained information about his present situation and complaints, and then gone on to his view of what caused his problems and his account of his history and background. The philosophy and procedures of the Hampton Mental Health Center's out-patient service stressed flexibility in professional roles, immediate attention rather than waiting lists, active crisis intervention with frequent use of medications, and the objective of stabilizing the client by means of environmental supports. Thus Allen was interviewed as soon as he could come to the Center and again within the next few days. There was no waiting for "staffing" nor a transfer between intake worker and therapist. A quick review of some of the Center's major alternative programs made the decision clear. Had Allen been acutely disturbed in thought and behavior, his physician would have been asked to admit him to the local general hospital, where he would have been given heavy doses of medication with Dr. Thomas' consultation, usually a three- to five-day course of intensive medication treatment resembling "sleep therapy." After that period, the patient would be taken to the Center's Adult Residential Unit, an almost motel-like setting, where the staff stressed readjustment and new ways of coping with life problems. A second way was to refer clients after telephone evulation (or brief interview if they walked in) to the satellite activities within the local Mental Health association, such as the Cooperative Counseling Service or the Council on Alcoholism. Dr. Gleeson's decision to see Allen intensively on an outpatient basis was an example of the third way the Center dealt with many clients.

The preliminary decision was that because Allen was facing a crisis in coping with his circumstances, it was important to bolster his resources quickly. Dr. Gleeson's first design for an improvement program was a strategy of understanding, reassurance, relief from strain, and the structuring of expectations for progress and a favorable outcome. She considered asking Dr. Thomas to prescribe medication, but decided against this, since Allen already had sleeping pills and in the past had not always used chemicals beneficially. Dr. Gleeson's interviewing strategy was not to ask questions that can be answered yes or no; open-ended questions encourage the client to tell his own story.

SECOND INTERVIEW

When Allen came for his interview the next day, his appearance and behavior were somewhat changed. He was dressed in a more casual, rather rumpled, way, and he talked more about himself and blamed others less. He returned to parts of the previous interview and admitted, for instance, that he had indeed been "doing mescaline" until recently. He attributed part of his tension to something he had been taking to keep awake on the extra night work. He recognized that recently his whole life had been getting more and more "screwed up." He mentioned, however, that he did get organized enough to get more sleep the previous night. When he left, he arranged for a third interview.

Image making

Allen's willingness to correct misinformation seemed to indicate some pride in himself, although he still communicated mainly lack of self-acceptance, low self-esteem, and little ego strength. His responsiveness to Dr. Gleeson suggested that trust was developing, increasing the prospects for a resolution of the immediate crisis, and further progress through psychotherapy. Perhaps the improvement program should include the exploration of new styles of coping that would enable him to avoid the kind of "bind" he was now in. With this more optimistic view of the present crisis, Dr. Gleeson was inclined to see his suspiciousness as a sign of the stress, not as a precursor of a large-scale psychotic break.

Decision making

Dr. Gleeson was struck with the progress Allen was making in regaining control over some aspects of his life, such as changes in sleeping schedule, and decreased use of coffee and stimulants. Allen's willingness to make constructive changes, together with his obvious desire to be honest with her, made her decide (1) to obtain more information than she had at first intended, to support the possibility of some longer-range therapy; and (2) to ask Dr. Thomas if he would consider prescribing some medication to help control Allen's anxiety and suspiciousness. Dr. Thomas prescribed a commonly used sedative—a "downer" in Allen's terms.

CONTINUING INTERVIEWS

After three interviews, Dr. Gleeson, with the pharmacological aid contributed by Dr. Thomas, had helped Allen temporarily stabilize his life pattern. She proceeded with the plan to obtain more information, checking into Allen's medical history, asking about diseases, early emotional experiences, early family life, separations from parents, and hospitalizations. Allen had had measles, mumps, and chickenpox but had never been hospitalized with them. "Broken bones, surgical operations?" asked Dr. Gleeson. Allen reported a broken collar bone at perhaps five or six in a fall from a tree and an appendectomy when he was ten, but could recall nothing else. At this stage Allen talked fairly freely about his use of drugs, but always in the past tense. He stated rather unconvincingly that he wasn't using them any more. The history that Dr. Gleeson was able to piece together from details mentioned in somewhat haphazard order in the interview began to present a coherent image or picture.

Allen said that he knew very little about his mother. He understood that she had been the oldest child in her family and that she had given him up to her parents in order to "have more freedom." He had then been raised by his grandparents along with a group of aunts and uncles approximately his own age and various foster children who the grandparents took in from time to time. Allen made good progress at school. He said he could master school work almost in his spare time so that he frequently irritated teachers by the apparently offhand way he achieved good grades. He developed an enduring sense, however, of being somehow of lower status than others in the family, lower even than the foster children because they, after all, were paying guests, while he had been taken in as almost an orphan. His sense of being different was heightened by the curiosity that his adolescent uncles, in the boys' bedroom, would show about Allen's lack of circumcision. Not unkindly, they noted that "Sis was on welfare and they can't afford to 'do' welfare babies." He soon learned to keep himself covered up and inaccessible, not only physically but mentally as well. In his own early adolescence, he masturbated as he had seen his uncles do, but it was from a sense of being compelled or driven, and he experienced shame and disgust at this lonely secret. His uncles proudly shared tales of exploits with girl friends.

When he was just fifteen, a major change occurred. He met a girl who seemed to understand him. He recognized only that through her physical tolerance of his explorations, she conveyed affection and showed that she cared for him. When in the course of this relationship the girl became pregnant, Allen was ready to do what he felt he was called on to do, enter into an "honorable" marriage for the protection of girl and infant. To his surprise and horror, he found out that the girl was not at all interested in this. She was almost pleased at her predicament because of the release from high school that it promised, and she gave no sign of caring at all about the infant-to-be. She rather crassly made plans to have it given up on delivery. Her only concern seemed to be with the pregnancy's upsetting effect on her mother. So this affair ended.

From this time on throughout his adolescence Allen began, however to view himself as a person who could at least attract girls sexually, although he did feel a sense of emptiness about these relationships. He became involved with students who were smoking marijuana and taking other forms of drugs.

The next important relationship in his life was with Jennie, one of the foster girls in his grandparents' house. He and Jennie realized that they meant a great deal to each other and began to make plans for a future life together. They took no contraceptive precautions. "She wasn't that kind of a person; we did it spontaneously," said Allen. When she too became pregnant, Allen felt as he had previously, that he would be prepared to marry this girl and be proud to make the baby his own. Nonetheless, after a great deal of agonizing, the girl decided that she would relinquish the infant. Allen was depressed. When the baby came, under the pretense that he was her brother, Allen made his way to see Jennie in the hospital. After he had visited with her, he went to the nursery, ostensibly to see his sister's new baby. The nurse brought the beautiful, healthy baby boy to the window for him to see.

Brief feelings of pride and fulfillment and love suddenly collapsed as he stood dumbfounded by the realization that he would never see this child again nor ever be known by him. The nurse replaced the infant in its bassinet and Allen stumbled from the hospital in a haze of tears, unable to restrain his grief at seeing his own son put back in his crib nameless, to wait for unknown foster parents. The moments at the nursery window left Allen in almost permanent pain in the grip of a turmoil of feelings about abandonment, isolation, grief, and insecurity—feelings Allen attributed to his young son. So great was his grief and guilt at abandoning the baby that he quit high school and ran away to the nearest big city. There he quickly became submerged in the local drug culture. Years afterward he was still to weep at the memory of this beautiful deserted baby. Even during the interview tears came to his eyes.

Allen told how use of drugs increased in frequency and dosage so that he graduated to more powerful agents, until at last he was confronted with a situation in which an acquaintance offered to give him a shot of heroin. Allen was terrified but nonetheless allowed his acquaintance to administer the injection. The acquaintance said, to his protests that he would only take this one shot, "You'll be back." Nonetheless, the episode seemed to mobilize some forces for change within Allen, and he left the drug subculture at that time and returned home briefly before being drafted for military service. Allen was so relieved at finding that he was not "hooked," and so happy about the fact that he had been able to lift himself out of the drug scene, that the first part of army duty passed fairly uneventfully—except that on army tests he was identified as having "above-normal" potential. He was assigned to a small unit where he was a clerk for the young commanding officer, Major Pastore.

In time he was invited to look after the commanding officer's small children, aged three to five. Allen found a curious enjoyment and singular dedication when he was able to babysit with the children. He would go out of his way to plan exciting or entertaining episodes for them and would save some of his allowance to buy surprises. For him there seemed to be no brighter or more wonderful children in all the world. Predictably, perhaps, Allen's attraction to the young commander's wife began to grow. He saw that she (Elaine) was experiencing some uncertainties in her own life and believed that her interest in him indicated that she was, in fact, falling in love with him. He experienced fantasies about Elaine and her children in which he saw himself supplanting the commanding officer. His anxiety and nervousness increased as his animosity and competition with Major Pastore increased, and he would have an impulse to jump into his car and drive aimlessly around. He started pursuing young girls, many of whom he despised, for sexual relief. He began avoiding his immediate superiors in the Army because of his rather poor performance of duty. He despised his commander for having the place Allen wanted with the wife and the children, at the same time that he admired and worshiped him because of his generosity and gentleness.

It was at about this time that a new man, Sergeant Blair, was assigned to Allen's barracks. Blair had no patience with Allen. When he called Allen in for being late for drill, for which Allen actually had an excuse, Allen lost control. He considered the sergeant's accusations to be insulting and ignorant, and he argued heatedly, pointing out flaws in Blair's argument. As he was leaving, Allen said just under his breath, "This was like taking on an unarmed man in a battle of wits." The sergeant heard him and called him back. To avoid being given a beating or having formal charges pressed, Allen had to accept extra duties in the barracks. It was in trying to keep all of his already excessive commitments along with the extra barracks duty that he came more and more to rely on a wide variety of stimulants to keep him going.

Between appointments Dr. Gleeson had also called Major Pastore (with Allen's permission). Allen's jumpiness, irritability, and poor work had been very apparent to the officer. Both he and his wife noticed that Allen would be "wound up" on some evening visits and completely lethargic on others. It was his talk of suicide and his grossly suspicious outbursts that finally prompted the major to act.

Image making

Dr. Gleeson asked for the life history to get an idea of the ways Allen characteristically reacted, the use he tended to make of situations, and his approach to major decisions in his life. Dr. Gleeson was looking, too, for information about Allen's plans and aspirations so that she might begin to think about counseling and rehabilitation possibilities. There is grist for many an interpreter's mill in the case history, Dr. Gleeson thought. If the Center had been inclined toward psychodynamic interpretations, much would have been made of the confused sexual identification of the young man, castration anxieties, and Oedipal feelings about the commanding officer's wife. The decision would probably have been to devote much more interview time to obtaining life-history information, especially details about the earliest years. Since the Center was oriented strongly toward use of environmental resources and short reality-based therapy, however, the psychologist did not probe for "deep" emotional experiences, although some came out anyway. Dr. Gleeson noticed that some themes recurred again and again—tension and inadequacy, guilt about sex, interest in children, a certain passivity and need for external structure mixed with chronic authority conflict, some ability to respond to guidance, and a general immaturity about life purposes. Allen's inconsistent expressions of autonomy and dependency were producing a great deal of unhappiness. She hypothesized that Major and Ms. Pastore were contributing to Allen's insecurity, each confiding with him about difficulties with the other.

Decision making

Dr. Gleeson now felt that Dr. Thomas, who was the Center's most knowledgeable physician about drugs, should be asked to review Allen's situation—his drug problem and prescribed medication. She asked Allen to see Dr. Thomas before any further plans for psychotherapy were made.

CONSULTATION WITH DR. THOMAS

Allen's next visit to the Center was for a short interview with Dr. Thomas for the purpose of evaluating and perhaps changing the medication. Many of Dr. Thomas' questions, however, were oriented toward eliciting clues of severe drug abuse, despite Allen's statement that he had not been using drugs lately and had had only the one experience with hard drugs. In the short time available for the interview, Dr. Thomas found no evidence of a residual drug problem. He did decrease Allen's prescription even though a good deal of the initial sedation had worn off in the four days he had been taking the medication. Dr. Thomas explained again how necessary it was that he take the medication regularly in order to build up a useful level in the body. They discussed the benefits of sleep and shared some amusement over "the evils of the demon coffee."

Before Drs. Thomas and Gleeson conferred, Allen had seen Dr. Gleeson once more. It was apparent that in the short time since his last visit the florid signs of crisis, the suspiciousness and the bodily abuse with drugs and coffee, had become well controlled. Allen had begun to take pride in catching up on some of his debts and showed a good deal of interest in "picking up the pieces of his life." He reported that he had dissociated himself from the drug scene, and had given away some of his mescaline. But little progress had been made in other departments of his life. Elaine Pastore had told Allen that she had gone alone to a marathon group and talked about him all weekend. Allen often took the Pastore's children for rides. He reported to Dr. Gleeson with all the pride of a young father the happy times they had had. In total, Allen had seen Dr. Gleeson four times and Dr. Thomas once within a nine-day period, and Gleeson and Thomas had conferred once on the case.

Image making

Modifications of the working image came out of the conference in which Dr. Gleeson and Dr. Thomas combined their information and impressions about Allen. They tried to balance Allen's needs with those of other more recent clients and tried to allow for what they knew was their own tendency to offer more to gratifying clients than to nongratifying ones. Both Gleeson and Thomas agreed that Allen's immediate crisis was being resolved. They discussed how appealing Allen seemed to be, and concluded that his dependency offered people an apparent chance to have a bright, sensitive, good-looking son who rewarded them for their attention. The Center's philosophy, combined with this working image of Allen, led to the hypothesis that improvement for Allen could best come through his trying out and succeeding in roles appropriate for him—rather than, say—through finding reasons for his present behavior.

Decision making

Gleeson and Thomas saw their task as, first, to complete the resolution of the present crisis; second, to help Allen take steps that would prevent its recurrence; and third, to explore with him his resources for further life planning. They realized that Allen would be an appealing candidate for workers who believed in "restructuring personality" through long-term verbal therapy. But, consistent with the Center's aims and their personal commitments, they decided that in the long run, it would benefit him more if they could teach him to recognize, develop, and use his own resources. At this point, Dr. Gleeson decided to recommend brief testing designed to provide more information about what these resources were.

UNSCHEDULED VISIT TO THE CENTER

Allen telephoned a few days later asking to see Dr. Gleeson as soon as possible. He arrived in a disheveled state. The various misperceptions the Pastores and Allen had of one another had broken into the open—the confrontation had not been destructive, but it was definite enough so that Allen said a poignant and heroic goodbye to Ms. Pastore, drove around recklessly for a while, and then impulsively called Dr. Gleeson. In her office he was so racked with sobs that he could scarcely speak. Dr. Gleeson noted, however, that he had sought help himself this time and that he had not shown prolonged self-destructive behavior. She encouraged Allen to express his pain in words. At first he had great difficulty in doing this, but after a while his talk became an outpouring of adoration of Ms. Pastore and disparagement of himself as being unworthy, servile, not able to merit love as a husband or father. After much discussion, Allen began to agree with Dr. Gleeson that this break, while painful, freed him to consider more possibilities for his life. He expressed doubt, however, about being able to stand the pain of separation long enough to experience the freedom. He agreed to take some tests that would help him to explore some of these possibilities. A testing session was scheduled.

Image making

What the evidence of Allen's intense pain indicated was the depth of his dependency on Ms. Pastore. This suggested to Dr. Gleeson that she must make sure that he did not transfer this dependency to her. Allen's recognition that the break with Ms. Pastore could be an opportunity was a positive sign. It seemed clear that Allen had felt bad about his restricted role as adorer-without-social-recognition.

Decision making

Dr. Gleeson found herself trying to ignore a feeling of disappointment at what seemed to be a relapse—at the same time she felt fairly certain that the break with Ms. Pastore could be part of a growing-up process. She decided during the session to structure the event for Allen as an opportunity to be exploited for his own growth. She planned the testing as one way for him to become aware that he was trying to grow on his own. She decided because of time limitations to give only part of an intelligence test and then to start Allen on inventories that he could work on by himself—a commonly used personality inventory and interest blank. Thus the testing would help to answer important questions about his general ability, personality, and vocational preferences.

TESTING SESSION AND RESULTS

At the testing session, Dr. Gleeson began with a somewhat abbreviated version of the Wechsler Adult Intelligence Scale. Allen was very interested and cooperative, taking the WAIS problems as challenges. Toward the end of the testing he seemed disappointed when he couldn't finish parts of the performance tests in the time allowed. He stayed two and one-half additional hours and filled out the Strong Vocational Interest Blank and the Minnesota Multiphasic Personality Inventory.

Dr. Gleeson's impression that Allen showed superior ability was confirmed by the WAIS. Based on three parts of the test—Arithmetic, Digit Span, and Vocabulary—Allen's Verbal IQ was 126. His Performance IQ, derived from three parts—Digit Symbol, Block Design, and Picture Arrangement—was 117. The Full-Scale IQ of 124 placed Allen in the upper 10 percent of the people in his age group.

The Minnesota Multiphasic Personality Inventory provides two major kinds of information: (1) self-report answers to a large number of statements like those which patients might give in a psychiatric diagnostic interview, and (2) a profile based on norms obtained by various diagnostic groups. Using a key identifying certain "critical items," Dr. Gleeson's secretary prepared a list of these for her to inspect. Allen reported many unusual things about himself, such as the following:

I am afraid of losing my mind. (True)
I believe I am a condemned person. (True)
I have never indulged in unusual sex practices. (False)
I often feel as if things are not real. (True)

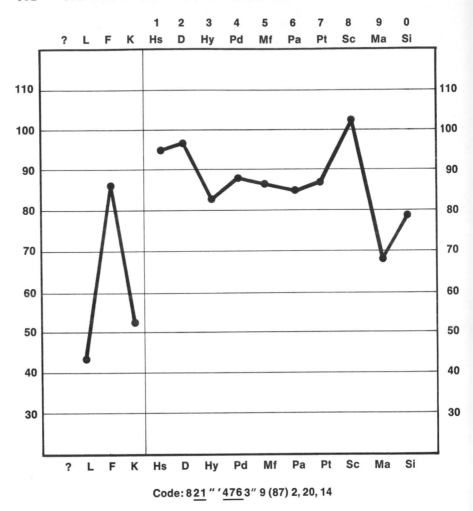

FIGURE 7-1 MMPI profile of Allen Ward.

There were items that Dr. Gleeson would use in the next interview, inquiring of Allen what he was thinking of when he responded to them. The profile, which is shown in Figure 7-1, is very "elevated," pointing to abnormal trends. Most of the scaled scores were more than 80, three standard deviations above the average, which on this scale is 50. The major "peaks" occurred on three scales: Sc (Schizophrenia), D (Depression), and Hs (Hypochondriasis). Such high points are much more commonly found among psychiatric patients than adult normals, but are somewhat more common in college students than in other adults (Hathaway and Meehl, 1951). Among psychiatric samples, the diagnoses most closely associated with these high points are "mixed psychoneurosis," "psychotic depression," and "schizophrenia." Profiles like this are sometimes found with suicidal patients. The profiles of a few young males most similar to Allen's in the MMPI Atlas carried the diagnosis of "behavior disorder" or "paranoid schizophrenia." Dr. Gleeson also looked up the information about profiles with high points like Allen's in two MMPI "cookbooks" (Gilberstadt and Duker, 1965; Marks and Seeman, 1963), to see what symptoms, personality characteristics, diagnoses, and treatments had been found to be associated with such a pattern in other clinical settings. Among the several common codes listed in these books, she did not find any exact parallels with that of Allen, but somewhat similar profiles seemed to reflect combined schizoid and depressive characteristics. The following symptoms were mentioned: high anxiety, somatic complaints, avoidance of close interpersonal relations, resentfulness, tearfulness, inner conflicts about sexuality, suicidal ruminations, and fear of loss of control. Common diagnoses were "depressive reaction, possibly schizo-affective type" or "schizoid personality." In over half of the cases prognosis had been poor, but a sizable percentage made some improvement in psychotherapy. One similar case had responded well to warm, "motherly" relations with a female therapist. Dr. Gleeson wondered how much she should take Allen's drug experience into account in evaluating these reports from these books, since most of the patients had been older and had been studied before the use of drugs had become common. What the "cookbook" survey did give her were some suggestions for further exploration. She asked her secretary to score Allen's MMPI separately for "subtle" and "obvious" items (see Wiener, 1948). It turned out that Allen's answers were predominantly of the obvious kind—that is, anyone looking at them would see that they were blatant complaints about somatic symptoms, distress, and peculiar experiences and behavior. The more subtle complaints often found among psychiatric patients contributed less to Allen's high scores. This suggested that he was, in a sense, trying to look "sick." [Dr. Gleeson later found from an article by Sacks and Kirtley (1972) that she might not be interpreting the subtle and obvious differences correctly.]

The Center was also making a trial practice of sending the MMPI to some computer-based report-writing services. When the reports came back in the mail, they were filed in the chart. (See Appendix C for the reports.) So far the Center's psychologists had not made much use of such reports on their clients because they found that the interpretive language the programmers had used was often too traditional to fit in with the way the Center handled its cases. However, in the case of Allen, Dr. Gleeson found some rather surprising parallels with her own impressions.

Allen's answer sheet on the Strong Vocational Interest Blank was sent away for scoring, as is customary with this blank. The results are reproduced in Figure 7-2. The Strong report consists of three parts. The Basic Interest Scales show how many items of particular sorts the person shows an interest in. The norms are for fifty-two-year-old men (average score, 50; standard deviation, 10). The jagged line in the middle shows the averages for sixteen-year-olds. Allen's scores

NCS PROFILE — STRONG VOCATIONAL INTEREST BLANK FOR MEN — COUNSELOR'S COPY

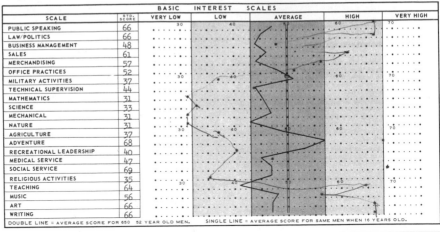

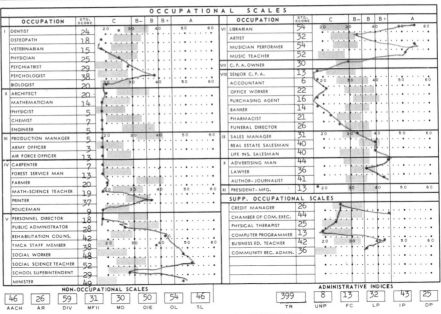

FIGURE 7-2 Strong profile of Allen Ward.

can be compared with those of both age groups. Allen scored high on interest in adventure, but not as high compared with young men as compared with older men. Allen scored very high on Social Service and several other scales as compared with young men. The Occupational Scales enable one to compare his likes and dislikes with those of successful men in particular occupational groups. An A score suggests that one's interests are very much like those of successful men in these occupations. Allen's profile shows A's for Social Worker, Social Science Teacher, Minister, Librarian, Musician, and Music Teacher. The Non-Occupational Scales and Administrative Indices are only for the use of professional counselors and indicate something about other aspects of a person's motivation. The Strong report, unlike the MMPI report, is typically shown to the client. Discussion between client and counselor is mainly based on the Basic Interest scores and the Occupational scores, but the meaning of the other scores is explained if the client asks especially about them.

Image making

The testing session seemed to go well and Dr. Gleeson noted that Allen had participated cooperatively. On the general ability test, the WAIS, he demonstrated a capacity for thinking and handling abstract concepts at the college level. His lower scores on remembering digits and substituting symbols may have reflected anxiety. Although he controlled himself well in carrying out the intellectual tasks, he allowed himself to express very disturbed feelings and perceptions on the MMPI. Dr. Gleeson was somewhat surprised that the profile was "floating" so high; in her experience, such a "cry for help" was more characteristic of a very anxious person when he first comes to the clinic. Clearly Allen was still very upset and wanted to emphasize his psychological pain. The profile peaks suggested feelings of depersonalization and recurrence of strange ideas, depression, heightened awareness of his body, and anger at or conflict with others. The high score on femininity suggested a somewhat passive personality with doubts about masculine potency; the high Mf also is not uncommon among better-educated males who have interests in the arts and dislike sports and competitive activities. The high F (infrequent responses) score and low K (correction for defensiveness) score suggested a tendency to exaggerate symptoms, as did the fact that much of the elevation was due to obvious rather the subtle responses. Though some signs in Allen's makeup indicated serious disturbance, Dr. Gleeson did not feel he was actually undergoing any form of mental collapse. In interviews his thinking was too rational for this. Furthermore, his emotions seemed a reasonable reflection of his life circumstances. She theorized that he had responded less and less constructively to those circumstances, and thus had allowed his controls to slip away, with the result that the problem was making itself worse. Both the bodily awareness and the suspicion in the MMPI could be related to his drug activity. Dr. Gleeson wondered particularly about amphetamines. She speculated further, "Certainly Allen's prolonged feeling of sexual inadequacy could fit in with the suspiciousness—such traits are often seen together—and the alienation and depersonalization could arise from the combination of a grossly irregular life and a lack of any healthy, growth-promoting relationships. He is certainly not getting these in the military, and definitely not with the Pastore family."

The Strong results helped to point to possibilities and directions of a more positive sort. Dr. Gleeson noted that first of all, Allen was much like men in some of the social service fields. This interest direction corresponded to his professed interest in becoming a high school teacher. Second, Allen resembled people in artistic occupations. Here he seemed to be more like those whose medium is music or verbal expression than like graphic artists. More "practical" occupations along this line which his interest profile suggested were Librarian and Advertising Man. A third group of workers, to which his resemblance was a little less close, was the business contact group, Salesman and Chamber of Commerce Executive. Dr. Gleeson was just as much interested in "reject patterns" or unsuitable directions. The lines of work into which Allen would *not* fit comfortably were especially clear—scientific occupations of all kinds, active outdoor jobs like carpenter or farmer, and business detail or clerical work. His pattern of likes and dislikes was very different from that of men in these areas. Dr. Gleeson noted that Allen's present army assignment might contribute to his discontent.

The administrative indices indicated that there was nothing to invalidate or cast doubt on the obtained scores. The scores on nonoccupational scales tended to make the first of the three possible directions that he might go look slightly more promising than the other two. The fact that he scored high on the social service group in spite of the fact that the AR (age-related) scale showed him to be "young" rather than "mature" in his likes and dislikes suggested that the social service interests were genuine, since they typically are not well developed in teenagers. The fact that his managerial orientation (MO) score was low suggested that he might not find the kind of responsibility involved in high-level business contact occupations congenial. His academic achievement score (AACH) was hardly high enough so that one would predict persistence in college to the graduate level. His interests were more "feminine" than those of the average man in our culture, but this is what one expects when artistic or social service interests predominate. It reflected interests, not emotional makeup.

Because there is some tendency for scores on both artistic and social service scales to be spuriously elevated in neurotics, Dr. Gleeson noted that Allen should probably be retested at a later time before career plans were completely crystallized.

Decision making

In general the tests had helped Dr. Gleeson compare Allen with other people in a way that she could only do intuitively by interview and observation. The WAIS gave her assurance that Allen had the ability to compete with others at an advanced educational level, although persistent motivation might be a problem. The Strong gave her an opportunity to discuss with Allen certain directions in which he might well proceed and others he might do well to avoid. The MMPI gave her a check on certain aspects of the working images that she and her colleagues had already built up. Dr. Gleeson had wondered if the MMPI might suggest problems, such as severe psychopathy or decompensation, which should be taken into consideration in planning with Allen. Part of the decision underlying the choice of these tests had involved Dr. Gleeson's past experience. She knew these tests well and "got more" from them than less-experienced people would. She also liked to use tests that stimulated clients' self-exploration in interviews that followed testing sessions. The tests also provided a good framework for discussion with other colleagues when she presented the case to them in a case conference. Dr. Gleeson prepared for the case conference by writing up a brief report. Her working image led to hypotheses around which the discussion could be organized: that the first objective was relief of present stress and the second the formulation of plans for more competent handling of life to avoid future crises. (Such a recipe, thought Dr. Gleeson with a great deal of skepticism, is the same prescription that so many of the nineteen- to twenty-five-year-olds who come to the clinic seem to need these days. The task they face seems to be having to make up for a lifetime of incomplete or inadequate family experience. I must keep working on that grant proposal for helping families cope better.)

CASE CONFERENCE

The next event was a second brief case conference with Dr. Thomas, another Center staff member, and two psychology interns. Drs. Gleeson and Thomas presented their findings. They first considered what diagnostic label they should use to classify the case. At the Hampton out-patient service, staff were required to indicate diagnoses to the agency providing some of the funds and also to their state for records kept on mental health matters. Frustratingly, each agency had a different list of diagnostic labels, neither in accord with the Diagnostic and Statistical Manual of the American Psychiatric Association. Hampton Center had the courage to get rid of diagnostic labels in daily interaction but used them in making the required reports. They agreed on "personality pattern disturbance—passive aggressive" as a poor but possible label for Allen. The major amount of time in the conference was spent on exploring various alternatives for Allen's future. Allen had done very little such planning heretofore. The babysitting with the commanding officer's children had seemed to be an enjoyable aspect of his life, but the staff agreed that Allen should be encouraged to develop relationships with people of his own age. The conference resulted in the decision that Dr. Gleeson would serve as short-term therapist, mainly taking a vocational-counseling role. She would investigate requirements for entrance to college and discuss these with Allen.

SUBSEQUENT SESSIONS AND EVENTS

Three subsequent sessions between the psychologist and Allen allowed time for discussion of his anxieties about sex and drugs, and his relationships with girls, with the disliked sergeant, and with Major and Ms. Pastore. In further discussion of his guilt about adopted babies, Allen came to see that the children might have better homes and upbringing than he would have been able to provide for them. Dr. Gleeson repeatedly would gently lead the discussion into the exploration of plans for the future and immediate actions that might be taken. She discussed the results of the Strong Vocational Interest Blank with Allen. She checked a few of the items on the MMPI with him and asked for further explanations. She interpreted the intelligence test results as evidence that he should be able to master college material well if he could find his interests. The psychologist and Allen together examined various alternatives. Allen began earnestly to outline his dreams of becoming a history teacher, showing for the first time excitement at the prospect of being able to change the course of his life. He planned to enroll at the local community college for night courses which would prepare him for the high school equivalency tests. Passing these would allow him to enter college when his military service ended.

All seemed to be going well when events took an unexpected turn. Allen missed an appointment. The next day two men from the criminal investigation department of the military service presented themselves at the Center with a release-of-information form signed by Allen. They explained that Allen was under arrest on charges of narcotics possession, charges having to do with a period some eighteen months earlier at another army post.

The agents demanded to be able to review the complete chart, but the Center staff noted that the release said "a summary of pertinent treatment and diagnostic information" and refused to give access to the chart itself. Instead, Dr. Gleeson wrote a brief summary. In a telephone call to Major Pastore she found out that Allen had already been taken into custody and sent to another army station, and that he would probably be discharged from the service after the trial.

STAFF DISCUSSION

At the weekly staff meeting, Dr. Gleeson, very frustrated by what had happened, reported with anger and discouragement on the recent developments. Staff members reacted in two ways, some saying, in effect, "A character disorder is a character disorder. What did you hope for—that he'd love you? This is only typical." Others, identifying with Allen and with young people in general, made pronouncements about "the establishment," the harmlessness of marijuana, and the innate rightness of youth in "doing their thing." Dr. Thomas commented that his colleagues' outbursts suggested that aspects of the case had touched many of the staff. Staff members examined their feelings. Someone mentioned that a sense of incompleteness about a case really is very common—one of those things a mental health worker has to live with.

FOLLOW-UP INFORMATION

For a long time Dr. Gleeson felt deeply about the sudden destruction and waste of such potential for growth. She realized that these feelings were probably what made this case stand out above others in her mind. When the Center made its routine telephone follow-up ninety days after the last contact, it was established only that Allen was no longer in the army, according to the enlisted man who answered the barracks telephone. It seemed useless to try to trace him.

However, about two years later a request for information about Allen came through from the Vocational Rehabilitation Division of another state, together with a signed form for release of information. The request did not explain why the information was wanted. Dr. Gleeson knew that such an application could mean anything from Allen's return from prison or a state hospital to his identifying that "Voc Rehab" was something to apply to if you had no job and might be considered to have a social handicap.

Somewhat later, Dr. Gleeson, talking to psychology trainees at the Center, was discussing the case of Allen. They showed a great deal of interest in finding out what had happened in Allen's life. After discussing with them why they were so interested in this particular case, what ethical considerations entered into the follow-up of special cases, and the sheer difficulty of obtaining information, Dr. Gleeson proceeded to call the rehabilitation agency for additional follow-up information. She was referred to a worker in a community college town. He turned out to be a person who knew Allen fairly well and he was not at all hesitant about discussing his impressions. On the positive side, Allen had enrolled in the community college in a study course that satisfied the agency's requirements for early employability yet could provide a foundation for the college degree Allen eventually planned to obtain. Apparently his grades were quite good, especially in some of the liberal arts courses.

The worker confided that Allen was living with a girl who had a child by a previous marriage. The living situation gave the appearance of some stability because the girl was soon to have a child by Allen, who intended to marry her and assume responsibility for both children. The community worker deplored "the way these young people can't see what they're doing to their future by all this marrying and baby-having." He pressed Dr. Gleeson for advice on how he should help Allen. Dr. Gleeson was anxious that the worker not view her as the stereotypical psychologist—expert blessed with some type of mystical knowledge. She indicated that she hoped Allen could achieve a clear picture of his alternatives and that he might be encouraged to make clear, definite commitments. She emphasized how futile authoritarian approaches were likely to be and noted that many people find their own ways in the world, ways that are not ones we would have chosen. She praised the worker's interest in Allen.

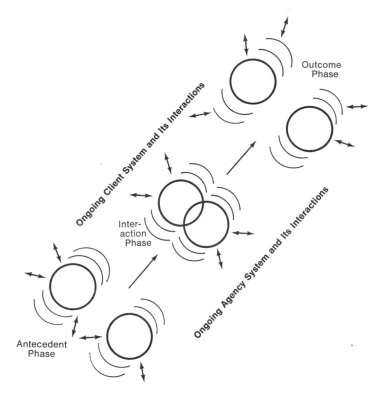

FIGURE 7-3 Phases of relationship between client and helping agency.

The discussion with trainees and staff following Dr. Gleeson's report of the latest information identified two major themes: (1) Somehow—haltingly—Allen was making progress toward the general career goals clarified two years earlier; and (2) the insecurity, the "uncertainty-about-manhood" concerns were probably still present. They might well be a permanent part of Allen's life. There was a good deal of debate, heated at times, about whether or not the Center had served Allen in the best possible way:

"Of course, he should have had dynamic psychotherapy for his inadequacy."

"You say that for everybody—and you'd have called him unmotivated when he wouldn't sit still for it."

"So see the fix he's in now."

"What fix? People experiment with drugs and drop them later. People knock other people up and still live. They also get married in college."

"How do you think he'll make out in the long haul with all that unresolved dependency?"

"Does the past have to rule him?" "You deny its importance?" And so the discussion went on.

CRITICAL ANALYSIS OF THE CASE

Almost as important as service to the client himself is what the agency learns from its analysis of the case. Every experience with a client should challenge the clinician and his colleagues to examine what went on and to apply the knowledge gained to the handling of future cases and to thinking about clinic policy.

Figure 7-3 depicts the ongoing nature of the two major systems involved—that of the client and that of the helping agency—and their interaction. The figure should remind us of the importance of the part of the client's life in which the agency is not involved. During contact with the clinic, the client's 1 hour of 24 in a day, or 1 or 2 hours of 168 in a week, constitutes only a very small part of his life. The influences from other environments, the joining or breaking off of relationships with others, the rewards and discouragements at work or school, and the satisfactions and frustrations from recreation are occurring at the same time as the therapy and also before and after it. Likewise the clinician should remember that the helping agency itself is going through changes and that the interaction with the client is only a small part of its life; some of these other happenings, such as case conferences, training sessions, ups and downs of morale, staff conferences, or secretarial support for processing cases, may affect its relationship with the client during the contact hours and before and after them. Although this "ongoingness" of systems may seem obvious, it is often overlooked as the clinician considers his special and limited interaction with the client.

Another reason for examining the ongoing course of cases served is that this is one of the best sources of research ideas. Each case suggests new hypotheses. Even a small amount of time allocated to such self-scrutiny—say 5 percent—pays off in short-range and long-range improvements in service to clients.

A case can be analyzed in terms of three major questions. What were the outcomes for both client and agency in cost-benefit terms? What was the nature of the processes that occurred in the client, in the agency, and between client and agency? What are the implications for the whole helping system? We shall briefly take up these in turn, as they apply to the case of Allen.

Outcomes for Client and Agency in Cost-Benefit Terms

Looking at it from the client's viewpoint, what did he or she take away from his contact with the agency, and what was the cost to him or her? What was the relative importance of the clinical service in the ongoing experience of the client during that period? How long-lasting were the insights or changed behaviors or sense of relief resulting from the contact with the agency? In the case of Allen, much of the outcome was outside the jurisdiction of the Center. Allen's arrest and incarceration followed the clinic contact, and it would be very difficult to disentangle the two happenings and the other influences that shaped his later life. (Such a profusion of "causes," or influences, in life patterns is not at all uncommon. It is why outcome studies are so difficult.) The costs to Allen, aside from his investment of time and a small fee for services, were not great; he did not seem to suffer or get worse from the contact. He might have made some alternative use of his time, but impressions of what he did before contact with the clinic do not suggest that it would have been more profitable for him than the therapy was. Several beneficial changes occurred for Allen—his vocational planning leading to the later approach to the Vocational Rehabilitation agency, the temporary abatement of anxiety, the establishment of a positive relationship with a therapist, making it easier for him to cooperate with others later. Allen's psychological dependence on drugs may have been decreased through calling attention to the underlying life circumstances that predisposed him to take drugs. As one reviews the case, one of the criticisms that can be made is that client and therapist failed to specify clear goals, the attainment of which could later be evaluated.

We can also look at the costs and benefits from the agency point of view. The time and workloads of Drs. Thomas and Gleeson and some support personnel were involved. Such resources, it might be argued, could have been used for other, more promising cases, if it had been known that Allen was in danger of being arrested. The benefits to the Center included a closer relation to Fort Alexander; increased knowledge about drug problems among young servicemen on the part of Drs. Gleeson and Thomas and the trainees, knowledge that might be useful in later cases; and a meeting of service obligations according to the purposes for which the Center was organized. The Center could also use the case of Allen to help generate hypotheses around which research and program development could be organized, possibly resulting in outside grants or internal program changes.

The Client and Agency Processes

In addition to studying outcomes of case management, one can study ongoing activities and system interactions. This too, worthwhile in its own right, can ultimately lead to improvement of service. For such study one needs to ask "process" questions about change over time, development, growth, interaction, and shifting perceptions. What is analyzed primarily is what went on during the active contact with the case, although relevant data about antecedent personality and situations are not neglected. Different theories suggest different approaches. We might ask: What was Allen's environment and how was it shifting in ways that affected him? How did Allen respond to his environment behaviorally? What were Allen's perceptions, objectives, and "internal programming" and how did this relate to what he did and said? In analyzing the person and the individual—environmental relations in any case, many interpretations are possible, as later chapters will illustrate in more detail. For the time being, we will content ourselves with a few selected process observations about Allen.

Allen's life situation at age 20 presented him with a great many stresses for which he had not learned very effective coping techniques. Late adolescence and early adulthood constitute a period when physical, sexual, and intellectual exploration is at its peak—Erikson's crisis of identity—but individuals arrive at this period with different views of their possibilities and with different skills. Allen was internally programmed to be highly concerned with his sex role. He was still fighting "old fights" with shadows of girls and uncles now gone from his life. The environment of the army and the general environment of television, films, and other media undoubtedly reinforced this concern. These general environments could not easily be changed over a few counseling sessions, but Allen's response to them and his perceptions and controls over his behavior might be. During the period when he was coming to the clinic, Allen revealed his views about his background and looked at some new possibilities for the future. The expression of feeling and the review of his situation with someone else, something he had never done before, was accompanied by a decrease in anxiety.

It is likely that his attitude toward drugs changed somewhat. It could be that the attention Center personnel gave to drugs reinforced his dependence. It is more likely, however, that the shift to prescribed drugs specifically designed for his needs and under the supervision of an authority was a factor leading Allen to question the appropriateness for him of self-administered drugs. (More research is needed on the effect of different kinds of physician contacts with early drug users.) In Allen's case we have no clear data, but it appears that he did improve physically and became less disturbed under the prescribed pharmacological regimen.

The psychological plan for an improvement program included expression of feelings, examination of attitudes and assumptions, and exploration of possible future life plans. Improvement did seem to occur at least on a verbal and emotional level. The Center chose to emphasize the psychological rather than the medical—physiological approach to Allen's drug problem. The Center also chose to concentrate on changing Allen rather than his environment.

Let us now note a few more details about ways in which the activities of the Hampton Mental Health Center in the case of Allen Ward relate to image making and decision making. In this case all the perceptions of people involved were based on information-gathering processes almost exclusively confined to Allen himself. We do not know what the sergeant would have said, or Ms. Pastore, or Allen's barracks mates or girl friends. Dr. Gleeson would have known from previous child guidance work that it is all too easy to blame the parents or the schools and sympathize with the little child who is a client; without balancing information from "the other side" it is difficult to get an objective image or a correct perception of relationships. However, in this case the Center decided that it did not have the time or connections to broaden its information-gathering and treatment program to include the other individuals and groups.

It might be noted that Dr. Gleeson's image of Allen was suffused with a strong liking for him. He was a handsome and cooperative young man. Although to like a client helps in establishing a relationship, there is always the danger of what psychoanalysts call countertransference, which may interfere with a therapist's objectivity. Dr. Gleeson guarded against this danger by obtaining objective evaluations by means of tests and case conferences.

Implications for the Helping System

Finally, each case should provide feedback for examination of agency policies and procedures and of the community service system as a whole. Although Hampton Mental Health Center prided itself on being an innovative, crisis-oriented service, its handling of Allen was actually not far removed from the traditional medical model. It did not produce the traditional involved diagnostic work-up, but it approximated it. Outreach into the natural living situation might have been considered more carefully, but it was not undertaken, for one reason or another.

Evaluated in terms of the basic considerations discussed in Chapter 6, decisions the Hampton Center made in designing an improvement program for Allen were as follows:

1. Level of intervention: focus on the personal system, also some psychobiological intervention through drugs.

2. Degree of change: moderate, with a goal toward exploring real-life choices and reevaluating old emotion-laden areas, such as giving up the baby for adoption; length of therapy to be moderate (probably three intensive weeks with occasional follow-up).

3. Degree of client commitment: based on early evaluation, good client participation, so therapy could be somewhat prolonged.

4. Reliance on verbal interchange: high, in accordance with the client's cooperativeness and high intelligence.

5. Internal versus external emphasis: mostly a concern for helping the client change his own perceptions and consider promising vocational directions, leading to actions in the direction of further self-development. Treatment involved only the client, not outside systems.

6. Directness of attention to symptoms: moderate, with a concern for underlying feelings and perceptions in addition to direct treatment of anxiety by medication; little attempt to change symptoms as such.

Such a list of choices adds up to a rather typical treatment program in a psychiatric clinic, providing that treatment is of moderate length.

One alternative available to the Hampton Center was group therapy for young drug users. It was not used, perhaps because that group had not been functioning very well. Another possibility might have been an interview with the Pastores or with the sergeant; these were not explored because Drs. Gleeson and Thomas had concluded that Allen needed self-development rather than a mitigation of trouble-causing situations. Another possibility that might have been considered is referral to a drug treatment center, such as a Synanon group in a nearby city. This was not considered seriously because the clinicians did not think Allen's drug problem was that salient.

The case of Allen did, however, stimulate the Hampton Center to think more seriously about the establishment of ties with the Army base, and to get a mixture of Army and community people involved in therapy groups. Community college people were also interested. Another indirect outcome was the realization that some research needs to be done on how career planning is done by people of this age. It was apparent that many people of this age, both civilian and military, needed such services, and that they were not available except in the community college. Ultimately some research in cooperation with counseling psychologists in the college was undertaken that could lead to the establishment of such services.

SUMMARY

The case of Allen Ward has been presented in considerable detail—not simply as a report on a client, but also as a rather intimate portrayal of how a clinic goes about developing its services to a client. The setting for the Hampton Mental Health Center was described as well as many of the policies and procedures it uses in handling cases. With each clinic contact, the processes of image making and decision making were reported. Finally, the case was critically evaluated as to costs and benefits to the client and clinic, the processes, and the policies of the helping system.

SUGGESTED READINGS

Burton, A., and Harris, R. E. (eds.). *Clinical studies of personality*. New York: Harper & Row, 1955.

The case histories have been prepared by clinicians with a wide variety of backgrounds. The diversity of theories and approaches both to therapy and assessment techniques of the mid-1950s is well illustrated. Most of these approaches would still be in use, but the reader should recognize that there have been shifts in emphasis and that new procedures have been developed.
Allison, Blatt, and Zimet (1968), in presenting their approach to test interpretation, illustrate extensively from a case.

Aronow, E., and Reznikoff, M. Application of projective tests to psychotherapy. *Journal of Personality Assessment*, 1971, *35*, 379–393.

This reading will help supply the reader with examples of assessment devices not used in the case of Allen Ward. Aronow and Reznikoff argue for the use of projective techniques both for estimating the extent of pathology before and after therapy and in therapy itself. They illustrate the use of the WAIS, Rorschach, and TAT with a 19-year-old student presenting feelings of irreality and paranoid inclinations.

Manning, H. M. Programmed interpretation of the MMPI. *Journal of Personality Assessment*, 1971, *35*, 162—176.

Manning presents a well-organized overview of developments following Meehl's address entitled "Wanted—A Good Cookbook" (1956). The results of his submission of the same MMPI profile to two automated interpretation systems are given. Manning also raises critical questions about the ethics and public reactions to programmed reports on personality.

For a discussion of the application of automation to a variety of assessment procedures, including the interview and projective techniques, see Klett and Pumroy (1971). Elwood and Griffin (1972) have reported high reliability for an automated method of administering the WAIS.

Dailey, C. A. *Assessment of lives.* San Francisco: Jossey-Bass, 1971.

Dailey, who has had experience as a clinical and industrial psychologist, presents a plea for a more humanistic approach to human beings than he has found in modern institutions. He urges that the person be understood as a unique individual with a personal history. Of particular interest are the series of programmed case studies in the latter part of the book, which can be used for understanding and developing one's empathy for cases.

RESEARCH EXAMPLES

Gauron, E. G., and Dickinson, J. K. Diagnostic decision making in psychiatry. *Archives of General Psychiatry*, 1966, *14*, 225—232.

This study illustrates a method that might be used for the study of case-history information in a broader sense than just psychiatric diagnosis. The authors chose three cases from the files of a psychiatric hospital, which provided case-history data on forty categories of information. Their categories were such as age, sex, marital status, medical history, and different parts of the psychiatrist's mental-status examination (a common, semistandard interview covering content of thought; orientation for time, place, and person and level of intellectual thinking; emotional tone; stream of speech; insight; and attitude, appearance, and manner). They presented each of twelve psychiatrists with the randomized list of categories with the instructions that he could ask for one item of information at a time and he should verbalize his diagnostic impressions as he received the information. After the psychiatrist reached his final diagnosis, he was asked to choose the five items of information that were most useful.

The results showed that the average number of information categories requested was twenty-three of the forty. The first five items requested most commonly were age, sex, reason for referral, race, and site of residence. The clinical laboratory results and the psychological test results were very late in the list. The five items perceived as most important were reason for referral, previous personality, age, mental status—content of thought, and mental status—stream of thought. So the major tool in reaching the diagnosis was the clinical impression reported from the mental-status examination originally given the patient. The authors indicated that psychiatrists often could not verbalize how they arrived at their conclusions.

In an article immediately following this one, Gauron and Dickinson hypothesized that there were six methods or styles the psychiatrists used in approaching the diagnostic problem—the intuitive-adversary approach, diagnosis by exclusion, the overinclusive-indecisive approach, the textbook approach, the bibliography approach, and the flexible adaptive approach. Without describing these in detail, one can understand that what the authors are trying to do is to develop theoretical understanding of the cognitive styles of clinicians, a large undertaking of considerable interest to psychologists. Another more statistically sophisticated approach to determining the weight clinical judges put on various items on information was mentioned in Chapter 6—that of L. R. Goldberg (1970, 1971).

Scherer, S. E., Ettinger, R. F., and Mudrick, N. J. Need for social approval and drug use. *Journal of Consulting and Clinical Psychology*, 1972, *38*, 118—121.

The author's basic design was the correlation of reported use of drugs with a self-report of need for social approval (the Crowne—Marlowe Social Desirability Scale). The subjects were sixty-six undergraduates, who indicated anonymously whether they had not used illicit drugs at all, used soft drugs only (marijuana or hashish), or used hard drugs (LSD, barbiturates, amphetamines). The results were in line with what the authors hypothesized: hard-drug users scored highest on the measure of need for social approval. Soft-drug users scored the lowest. They pointed to the importance of peer pressure on drug usage and to the clinical descriptions of hard-drug users as immature and unable to endure deprivation or frustration. The study is not a very definitive one; the sample is small and limited to college students, and data depend on honesty of report. Further research is needed to test this hypothesized relationship in greater refinement.

Kostlan, A. A method for the empirical study of psychodiagnosis. *Journal of Consulting Psychology*, 1954, *18*, 83—88.

Kostlan (as part of a doctoral dissertation) addressed himself to the following problem: "Which of several sources of cues permits the clinician to make the most valid inferences when he uses them in certain combinations?" (p. 83). In this research, four sources of information often used in a clinic were employed: the social case history, the MMPI, the Stein Sentence Completion Test, and the Rorschach examination. Test scores and social histories were obtained from five VA outpatients. These materials were presented to the judges under five different conditions: four of them with one source of information missing (an example would be the MMPI, SSCT, and social history minus the Rorschach) and a fifth with identifying (face sheet) information only.

The judges were twenty clinical psychologists with at least two years of diagnostic experience. Each judge was systematically assigned records of five patients, one set from each of the five conditions. Judges were told to study the information available as in a typical diagnostic study. Their task was to fill out a specially devised 283-item true—false check list of psychological inferences about the patient systematically derived from sentences in psychological reports. The criteria were two: an "internal" criterion consisting of check-list items agreed on by six of eight criterion judges using all four sources of information, and an "external" criterion was based on the progress reports of the patient's therapists.

The results of this latin-square analysis of variance design led to the following conclusions (p. 86): (1) Minimal data (the identifying data alone) permitted inferences which were better than chance; (2) without social case histories, the clinicians were no more accurate in their inferences than they were on the basis of minimal data; (3) the batteries that included both the MMPI and the social case history were superior to the others; (4) there are large differences in the accuracy with which particular patients can be diagnosed; and (5) clinicians differ in diagnostic skill.

For additional confirmation of many of these findings, the reader would do well to consult the study by Soskin (1959). The criterion was different. Soskin required clinicians to predict the subject's characteristic behavior in defined situations. The kinds of data given the clinicians were different (observation of role playing, the Rorschach protocol, or a battery of tests) and the particular kind of data given each clinician was in addition to the basic biographical data which they all received. However, the major results of Soskin's study were similar to Kostlan's. None of the sources of information produced improvement over predictions from basic data alone. In addition, Soskin found that giving the Rorschach to the clinicians changed their judgments toward inaccurate estimates of maladjustment. He also found that student nurses could predict as well as clinicians using basic biographical data. These two studies and others similar to them in some respects constitute a serious challenge to researchers to discover just what kinds of information are most useful in clinical assessment.

chapter **8**

Appraisal of Individuals in Situations: Observing, Interviewing, Using Records

In the Chapters 6 and 7 we have explained and illustrated the complex undertaking of designing improvement programs. Clinical psychologists play an increasingly important part in this effort at all system levels, but the task for which they are best prepared by inclination and by training is the appraisal of individual clients in life situations. In this and the next chapter, we shall give specific attention to the primary methods clinical psychologists use in appraising clients and their situations—observation, interviewing, and testing. In this chapter we deal with the two most basic and universally used procedures—observing and interviewing. In clinical psychology as in ordinary life, when we want to learn something about other persons, we "watch 'em" or "ask 'em." In addition, toward the end of the chapter we will briefly mention another common source of information—personal and social records.

Because of the enormous complexity of human life, only a small fraction of what is going on with even a single person can be assessed through observations or interviews. Barker, Schoggen, and Barker (1955), for example, found that 8-year-old Mary Ennis, in the course of only one day of her life, interacted 1,882 times with 571 people and things, and Pittenger, Hockett, and Danehy (1960) spent years in the detailed analysis of only the first 5 minutes of a recorded psychiatric interview. In deciding what aspects of the client's life to focus on, a psychologist makes use of his knowledge and his common sense, keeping clearly in mind the purposes his appraisal activities are intended to serve. As explained in Chapter 6, he is engaged in constructing an image upon which sound decisions about improvement programs can be based. He will select a role and a procedure, keeping in mind alternative possibilities and decisions and formulate a flexible plan that will allow him to be responsive to what he finds out as he goes along.

The most basic question is: *Why* is the appraisal being made? In addition there are other questions that enter into the formulation of a plan. *Who* should be interviewed or observed—just the client or other informants? Also, *who* should do the observing or interviewing? *What* should the clinician look for? *Where* should the observations or interviews take place? *When* should they be conducted—only at the beginning, during the intervention process, at the end, and also in a follow-up session? *How* should the procedures be conducted; for example, should there be certain standardized ways of recording observations? He should also ask himself what his personal involvement in the process will be? Will he be a participant in a group to which the client belongs, a detached observer, or a combination of the two?

OBSERVATION AS A CLINICAL TOOL

For discussion purposes we shall take up observation and interviewing separately, although they often occur together in practice. Observation generally refers to nonverbal behavior—the person's actions rather than the content of what he says, but the sensitive clinician listening to this content will at the same time observe many of these nonverbal behaviors, "looking with a third eye" as he "listens with the third ear." In addition, much observation goes on in noninterview situations.

The most important *where* distinction is between *contrived and natural settings*. Keeping in mind that the purpose of the appraisal is the improvement in the behavior of persons in their own living situations, observation in an office where interviews occur, a group therapy meeting where clients interact with one another, or an institutional setting such as a hospital ward ought perhaps to be supplemented more frequently than it usually is by field observation. Although some ingenious ways have been devised for field assessment for research purposes (Webb et al., 1969; Sommer, 1969) and a few developments will be reported on observations in homes and schools, the great bulk of clinical work still takes place in contrived settings. The surprising thing is that clinicians have paid so little attention to the effect of their environments on clients, a hidden assumption being that the behavior—environment interaction is of rather small importance. This assumption is being challenged now in many quarters with the increased concern for ecology of behavior, systems theory, and systematized behavior change. Even if field observation is not possible, the clinician can at least take special pains to obtain information like this: What are the major arenas in which the client's activities take place? In which of these situations is the client most effective and most disturbed? What are the characteristics of these settings, such as presence or absence of people, and the timing of problem behavior, and what events seem to change behavior? We shall return to these considerations later.

The *who* questions are about potential observers who may be able to contribute to the appraisal of a client. In hospitals, nurses and aides are often asked to carry out this task. In dealing with disturbed children, teachers or parents may be in the best position to observe. Self-observation is encouraged in some adult clients. The person may be asked to observe and report the occurrence of dreams, of disturbing behaviors or thoughts, and of daily mood changes. In fact, one of the by-products of a clinical contact is increased self-observation; sometimes this has a therapeutic effect in itself, helping to give the client some perspective about disturbing problems. The clinician's observation of his own feelings and reactions to a patient or client is also a very useful information. If he feels himself becoming angry and impatient, or loving and sympathetic, he should take notice of what is going on in the interaction and incorporate this evidence into his image of the client—and of himself.

Several major categories can be differentiated in answer to the question of *what* is to be observed. In psychiatric clinics, the psychologist may be looking primarily for *pathognomic signs*, especially in situations where differential diagnoses must be made. Inappropriate emotional behavior and actions that seem to be in response to hearing voices suggest schizophrenia. Inability to use an arm or leg, in the absence of physical disorder, suggests conversion hysteria. Psychiatric diagnosis is based on patterns of disorder rather than any one sign, but several signs that are associated with a certain disorder add to the probability of its acceptance as the diagnosis. This concept of pathognomic signs has been extended to test results, such as Rorschach indices. Clients may be observed for *personality characteristics and style*, their individual ways of coping with problems and expressing themselves. One patient may be very talkative, another very quiet. One client may be expansive in his movements, another constricted. One person may have "nervous habits" such as chewing on his fingernails, another may avoid looking the observer in the eye. The observer notes the frequency of such behaviors and relevance to the situation in which they occur. Observation may be directed to *group interaction* and the roles different individuals play—initiator of new topics, provider of emotional support, the moderator of the discussion, and so on. For such determinations, observations are made of verbal as well as nonverbal interaction. One may also observe the group as a whole, looking at the level of activity, productivity, or anxiety that seems to characterize it, and how these shift over time. Sometimes observers look only for *specified behaviors* in the persons for whom improvement programs are to be designed. This approach is typical of those doing behavior modification. The behavior in question is usually the symptom or complaint reported by the client, such as a nervous tic or hyperactivity. The behavior is defined as precisely as possible and the psychologist develops a system for conveniently coding and recording observations. The client himself or a member of the family or a clinician may serve as observer. Typically observations are taken during a baseline period before treatment begins, from time to time during the treatment, and afterward. This approach to changing behavior will be discussed in more detail in Chapter 12.

In addition to the *where, who,* and *what* aspects of observation, one needs to include in his plan some attention to *how* the observational data are to be recorded. Here the distinction made in Chapter 6 between samples and signs is relevant. If one is observing *samples*, as in behavior modification, one simply counts the number of instances of the behaviors in which one is interested that occur within a specified time period, perhaps using a check list to make sure each instance is noted.

If one is viewing behavior as a *sign*, as when a hospital patient's furtive glances are interpreted to mean paranoid suspiciousness, or slumping, downward-looking posture interpreted as depression, the observer's impressions of underlying characteristics may be recorded on *rating scales*. One special technique especially useful when a considerable number of observations is to be used to evaluate simultaneously a considerable number of personality traits is the Q-sort. The observer sorts into piles a set of cards with descriptive words or sentences printed on them, according to how characteristic each description is of the person observed. A Q-sort provides a quantitative description of personality that may be especially useful for research purposes. Q-sort items may be devised to record *phenotypical data*, that is, observable characteristics such as symptoms; or *genotypical data*, that is, inferences about underlying conditions or causes (see Block, 1961).

There are hazards of various sorts in using observations in the image-making process, such as the selectivity and biases of the observer and the possibility of subjective distortion of events as they are recorded. When data are collected from two observers at the same time, one may find that observations are not very reliable, and when they are viewed as signs, they may not be valid. (Validity and reliability will be discussed in more detail in Chapter 9.) Furthermore, there are definite limits to the use of observation by working clinical psychologists. There is often neither time nor personnel available to do anything other than the informal observations that occur during interviews or in a waiting room. Furthermore, the behavior of concern may not be easily observable—delinquent acts or sexual problems. Even if one could monitor behavior continuously, some behaviors are so infrequent that an enormous and impractical amount of material would have to be gathered. As a supplement to observation and for purposes for which observation cannot be used, interviewing is an appropriate and very versatile technique.

PERSPECTIVES ON THE CLINICAL INTERVIEW

Relationship, Communication, and Structure

In considering what makes clinical interviews productive, attention must be given to three principal aspects of the interview situation—the *relationship* between the participants, the nature and quality of the *communication* that takes place, and the *structure* or underlying form of the interview. At the beginning, all three aspects are important.

The initial aim of the interview is to establish *rapport*—that is, *a mutuality of purpose within a comfortable relationship.* Typically, it helps if the clinician assists in providing a transition from the client's previous situation, thus establishing some suggestion of empathy at the start and providing a few checks on commonality of perception. Remarks to the newcomer about the weather or whether he had difficulty in finding the office serve such a function. Cultural customs, such as a handshake (or a bow in some countries) and offering a lady a chair, help the client feel that he is "received" and respected. Both the clinician and the client will come to the interview with purposes and understandings of their own about the intent of the interview. Nearly always an early part of the interview will involve an examination or explanation of these purposes. Every interview is different, and the sensitive clinician realizes that each client is an individual with whom he is entering a special kind of relation involving an exchange of information. Much important information will remain locked up by the client's anxieties unless the clinician can help the client feel free to relax and trust him.

The early part of an interview will be influenced by the way in which it was arranged—whether it is client-initiated or clinician-initiated. If the client initiated it, he is likely to come with some form of introductory expression of purpose. It may be a personal problem or complaint. The initial statement should be recognized as important, but the clinician should also know that it may be only a superficial "ticket" designed simply to admit the person to counseling or psychiatric attention, a reflection of the person's understanding of what the agency is supposed to do. It may be very difficult for a person to express some really important underlying purposes. A girl comes ostensibly to discuss a recent onset of painful headaches and in the course of her discussion reveals that she is afraid that she is pregnant. A father comes in to seek advice about his teenager's drug problem, and it soon becomes apparent that the drug problem is less significant than his own fear of losing his wife. In any case, the clinician's task is to help the person express the concerns and purposes that brought him to the encounter.

If the interview is initiated by the clinician, his responsibility is to tell the person about the purpose very early in the interview. This exposition should not be long and complicated, and should provide ample opportunity for the client to react and question. The clinician may explain that he is a psychologist with the hospital, and he has asked the patient to come in in order to get acquainted with him and to give him some psychological tests. The clinician may say to another person that he was asked by the court to talk with the prisoner about his side of the story. With a child, he may explain that school records indicate that the child may have some troubles, which he would like to understand.

Whether client-initiated or clinician-initiated, there are almost always some differences in expectations about what each will do for the other. A patient coming to a medical center may expect a magical cure through pills. A client may desperately want sympathy, reassurance, and love, but the interviewer, having in mind the larger goal of the client's development and maturity, must discourage such dependency and not give the gratification the client longs for. An agency asking for a consultation may expect more service than the clinic can provide. A psychologist may expect more interest in his tests than the client exhibits. Throughout a series of interviews occasions often arise when the clinician must again help straighten out understandings of purposes.

Let us consider in a little more detail the relationship between interviewer and client. It is important to recognize that this involves their interpersonal *feelings*—the emotional closeness or distance between them, their liking or disliking for each other. Each new interview undoubtedly to some degree echoes earlier relationships with similar persons who have at some time entered the participants' lives. When one of us meets a person for the first time it commonly happens that we start comparing the person with someone already familiar; or we rack our memories in vain to discover who it is that the new acquaintance resembles. When this relationship goes further and the client starts acting toward the interviewer as if the latter were his father or mother, we have what the psychoanalysts call *transference*. If, on the other hand, the interviewer gets overly involved with the client, the relationship is said to involve *countertransference*. When this happens, the participant's own emotional needs have entered so strongly into the relationship that there may be interference with the process of helping the client. Transference and countertransference are more likely to occur in the interviews of more sustained and intensive therapy rather than in assessment interviews, although elements of them may enter into that relationship also. During a first interview a psychologist will do well to take note of his feelings of liking or disliking as these intrude upon the accurate empathy and nonpossessive warmth that is usually considered ideal.

Looking more closely at *communication* as it occurs in the interview, we can see it as a process of sending and receiving messages. Each message—from client to psychologist or from psychologist to client—has a source and a destination. In between is a medium or channel of communication (such as spoken or written words or nonverbal movements) in which varying amounts of "noise" accompany the message. The person who is the source of the communication must *encode* the message by putting it into signs that are comprehensible to the other, and the person receiving the message must *decode* it in order to understand it. Errors and disturbances can happen at any point along the way. This analysis of the process of communication as it applies to interviewing helps us understand what may go wrong when we engage in it. For instance, a patient may decode a statement in a very different manner from that in which the interviewer encoded it because he does not share the same signs or "language." When Bill says that he "made out" with a girl, what he means depends upon the region in which he lives. In one part of the country it may mean he has had intercourse with the girl; in another it means simply that he arranged a meeting with her. Another useful term communication experts use is *feedback*. We have mentioned in Chapter 4 this process by which servomechanisms govern and control their own activities. In interviewing, the clinician is constantly receiving feedback from the client, and he in turn is reacting to the client's communications in ways the client may be quick to detect and respond to; in this way feedback enables each of the persons to govern or modify his behavior during the interview. When there is some disturbance in this feedback system, communication is impaired or altered.

Our modern emphasis on words, which extends to the typical subculture of clinics and colleges, may make us forget that communication is *nonverbal as well as verbal.* One reason that the face-to-face interview is usually much preferred to correspondence or telephone calls as a medium of communication is that it provides an opportunity for nonverbal forms of communication and observation. Nonverbal communication is likely to be less under conscious control because we are less aware of it. We cannot always discern the meaning of gestures, actions, marks, signs, objects, sounds, smells, touch, and so on, but they do communicate. Almost certainly some of the disturbances of communication are nonverbal in origin.

Communication brings about *interactive learning.* Inevitably during the interview, some modification (which may be fleeting) of each participant's behavior will occur. Although the aim of an appraisal interview may not be to produce a change in the client's behavior, research on verbal reinforcement indicates that definite modifications of verbal behavior do, in fact, occur during such interviews (Matarazzo, 1965a). The assessment interviewer should be aware of the way in which he is affecting the client. If the client says, "Every now and then I have a dream about going into a deep, dark cave," and the clinician says, "Yes, tell me more," and leans forward eagerly, the client is likely to respond by telling more dreams. If the clinician perks up whenever sex is mentioned, more sexual content is likely to appear in the interview. Intentionally or not, the interviewer is engaged all the time in encouraging or discouraging certain kinds of responses, and the client is learning to behave in certain ways and not others. The behavior of the interviewer is also "shaped" to some extent by the client, although because the interviewer is more in control of the situation, he will probably tend to adhere more steadily to the pattern he intended to follow.

As we look at the structure of an interview, we see first that it can be divided into *developmental stages*—a beginning, a middle, and an end. As indicated earlier, the beginning stage consists of mutual exchange about previous happenings and the purposes of this meeting. Whether it is the first contact or not, a client often reveals something quite significant at this early point—by an air of nervousness, an off-hand remark, or a general optimism or pessimism regarding any opening subject. He is telling the interviewer "how to take him" today. The middle of the interview usually involves an exploration and elaboration of the stated purposes. The clinician conducting an assessment interview must be particularly careful at this stage not to interfere with the client's account of his own view of things. If the clinician turns the situation into a question-and-answer game, little will be revealed about the client's personal feelings or perceptions. Obviously the clinician must be very aware of time limitations, but he needs to realize also that he cannot understand the client without allowing him to tell his own story in his own way. As the interview hour nears its end, the clinician has the responsibility of bringing it into its closing phase. He may have certain questions he has to cover and will explain to the client that time is short, but that certain things must be done. The closing phase also involves summarizing what has occurred and making arrangements for next steps. If there are to be additional appraisal interviews, times must be set. As they end the interview, clinician and client should have a feeling of accomplishment and an interest in meeting again if there is more to be accomplished.

What gives each interview its individual structure is the *purpose* it is intended to serve. Some are designed for the taking of a case history, others for the making of a psychiatric diagnosis. Where general appraisal is the aim, specific purposes might be stated in such ways as these: "to explore Mr. DeSilva's relations with his family, expecially his wife and eldest son, and to get a picture of his ability to plan realistically for a job"; "to discuss with Ms. Grant her somatic symptoms, which have been shown to have no organic basis, and then to explore intensively the possibility that tensions over relations with her husband may lie behind them"; or more generally, "to understand the client's reason for coming to the clinic, to examine his complaints in detail, and to obtain a social, medical, and educational history."

Interviews vary a great deal in the degree to which their *structure* is apparent. Bordin's research (1959) has made it clear that the interviewer may vary the degree of ambiguity of goals, content, or relationship. Structuring may vary all the way from very general (such broad questions as "What brings you here?" to very specific (the exact-answer questions of a survey interview or a police interrogation into minute details of a crime). In thinking about the structure of an interview, it is useful to distinguish between *scanning* and *focusing*. It is usually a good plan to start an interview by scanning (i.e., sweeping broadly over important areas of living: "Tell me something about what brought you to the clinic?" "What is your family like?" and "How have things been going with your work?"). Then from time to time when the clinician believes he sees as opening that may lead to closer understanding (and if the relationship is good), he may focus on a topic in some detail: "Tell me exactly what happened the morning you first noticed the pain," or "Why is it that your neighbor seems to be watching you?"

Above everything, the interviewer needs to keep in mind the effect of the structure of the interview on the client. In order to encourage him to tell his own story, the direction must be left open enough to permit him to select what he thinks is most important, especially at the beginning of an interview. Some clients, however, find an extremely unstructured situation unsettling and anxiety-producing. Thus it may be desirable that the clinician at the beginning of the interview give an anxious client a clear explanation of what is wanted. There are occasions when a clinician must conduct a more forceful interrogation.

Occasionally a surly delinquent or a catatonic schizophrenic may refuse to speak at all. In that case observation may be the only method available. There is no substitute for the psychologist's sensitivity to the feelings of the person he is dealing with.

BEHAVIOR-ORIENTED INTERVIEWING

Appendix D presents a guideline for an extensive history-taking interview. A briefer form of interviewing which focuses on the behavior of the client is used in many instances of clinical work. It is particularly important when the treatment being considered is to emphasize behavior modification or "here-and-now" counseling concerning activities in the client's living situation. Such a focus is also appropriate as part of a more extensive exploration. Peterson (1968a, pp. 121–122) presents an outline for such a behavior-oriented interview, as follows:

A. Definition of problem behavior
   1. Nature of the problem as defined by client
      As I understand it, you came here because . . . (discuss reasons for contact as stated by referral agency or other source of information).
      I would like you to tell me more about this. What is the problem as you see it? (Probe as needed to determine client's view of his own problem behavior, i.e., what he is doing, or failing to do, which he or somebody else defines as a problem.)
   2. Severity of the problem
      a. *How serious a problem is this as far as you are concerned?* (Probe to determine perceived severity of problem.)
      b. *How often do you* . . . (exhibit problem behavior if a disorder of commission, or have occasion to exhibit desired behavior if a problem of omission. The goal is to obtain information regarding frequency of response.)
   3. Generality of the problem
      a. Duration
      How long has this been going on?
      b. Extent
      Where does the problem usually come up? (Probe to determine situations in which problem behavior occurs, e.g., Do you feel that way at work? How about at home?)
B. Determinants of problem behavior
   1. Conditions that intensify problem behavior
      Now I want you to think about the times when . . . (the problem) *is worst. What sort of things are going on then?*
   2. Conditions that alleviate problem behavior
      What about the times when . . . (the problem) *gets better? What sorts of things are going on then?*

3. Perceived origins
   What do you think is causing . . . (the problem)?
4. Specific antecedents
   Think back to the last time . . . (the problem occurred). *What was going on at that time?*
   As needed:
   a. Social influences
      Were any other people around? Who? What were they doing?
   b. Personal influences
      What were you thinking about at the time? How did you feel?
5. Specific consequences
   What happened after . . . (the problem behavior occurred)?
   As needed:
   a. Social consequences
      What did . . . (significant others identified above) *do?*
   b. Personal consequences
      How did that make you feel?
6. Suggested changes
   You have thought a lot about . . . (the problem). *What do you think might be done to* . . . (improve the situation)?
7. Suggested leads for further inquiry
   What else do you think I should find out about to help you with this problem?

Any clinical interview reveals something about the goals and assumptions of the interviewer. Peterson's guideline emphasizes problem behavior and the conditions surrounding its occurrence. His purpose is to gather information for a behavioral intervention. An interview for the purposes of client-centered Adlerian or psychoanalytic therapy would be very different. Most traditional psychotherapists would aim to arrive at the client's feelings and perceptions of his life, some particularly probing for early childhood experiences. They would tend to describe clients in terms of traits and personality characteristics. Mischel (1968, p. 280) summarizes the differences between a behavioral learning perspective and traditional therapy very well: "In behavioral analysis the emphasis is on what a person *does* in situations rather than on inferences about what attributes he *has*. . . . Social behavior assessments seek behavioral referents for the client's complaints; thereafter they identify the precise conditions that seem to be maintaining and influencing these problems so that appropriate rearrangements can be designed to achieve more advantageous outcomes."

CRISIS INTERVIEWING

The human service innovations of recent years are obliterating old distinctions between assessment and therapy and between appointments in the office and "house calls." Thus storefront clinics and paraprofessionals mingling in bars and streets with disturbed people and delinquents will not note whether they are conducting therapy or "just getting information." The important thing is to find common purposes and assist the person to move toward constructive behavior. Interviewing along with all kinds of other activities—playing ball or checkers, organizing group sings, or helping take care of children—is part of the *modus operandi*.

The telephone is a natural means of communication in a mass society, making it possible for strangers to find help. In most large cities in America there are crisis centers or suicide centers which advertise in the yellow pages of telephone books. Below is an example that is similar to verbatim transcripts of telephone interviews used on NIMH training tapes. The worker (a specially trained nonprofessional) collects some of the same information as is obtained in a full-blown interview, but in very abbreviated form. The caller "becomes a person" to the worker as a few facts emerge. The interviewer, a woman, immediately tries to give a sense of purpose, reception of feeling, encouragement, and action in the present situation. She has two purposes—to evaluate the lethality (likelihood of death) and to reduce the chances of suicide.

Caller: . . . Is this the . . . (unclear) (Sounds of sobbing)

Worker: Yes, I'd like to talk with you.

C: I feel so horrible . . . (more sobs) I just don't know what to do any more. (pause)

W: Tell me a little bit about yourself. How old are you?

C: I'm thirty.

W: Are you married? Or living alone?

C: I am . . . I was married. I'm divorced . . . living all alone. I'm so lonesome, I can't stand it. I'm sorry to bother you.

W: That's all right. I want to talk with you. You're feeling upset, and very low?

C: I just haven't, I haven't cried for so long. Now I can't stop, I just . . . I just want to get out of it all. I just don't know what to do, you know. I feel like what the hell's the use. I mean I can sit here and cry all day or . . . And for a simple, simple little thing, it is a simple little thing in a person's life to be rejected and be alone, I guess, but I just can't seem to stand it any more. I've been alone too long now. I don't have any purpose any more. I guess I'll just get out.

W: You say you are thinking of getting out. What do you mean? Do you have some ideas about ending it all?

C: If I didn't, I wouldn't have called you.

W: Yeah, I know.

C: I don't like that . . . I don't like that idea. I don't like it at all, but I just don't care.

W: What sort of thoughts do you have about suicide?

C: I just want to put a bullet in my head and forget about it, you know.

W: Do you have a gun?

C: Yes, I do.

W: You do. Have you ever tried anything in the past? Have you ever made any suicide attempts in the past?

C: I beat my head against the wall a few times. Played a little Russian roulette, I guess. I won. Unfortunately.

W: Uhha. Well, that's a terribly serious game. Have you ever talked with anyone before about these ideas?

The worker continued to pursue the idea of talking it over with someone. The caller was persuaded to come in person to the suicide prevention center and to bring his gun, unloaded, with him.

(For another illustration, see Atkinson, 1970, or refer to issues of the *Bulletin of Suicidology* or *Life-Threatening Behavior.* Litman, 1971, discusses evaluation of telephone interactions.)

LIFE-HISTORY INTERVIEWING

One particular purpose for which interviews are used in clinical situations is salient enough to deserve some lengthy consideration. Life is a process in time, a lifelong process of change and adjustment. Common sense and a great deal of research indicate that it is important to know something about the life history of a person one is attempting to help. Whether the clinical psychologist is seeing someone briefly in order to make a decision about whether he should be placed on a particular hospital ward or working for years with a client in intensive psychotherapy, he needs to see the contact as an excerpt from a larger, longer pattern—the life history of the person. This life history will combine both personal and situational variables. It will include a picture of a person's choices and developmental tasks as they relate to present assessment goals.

As explained before, the specific assessment goals in an individual case will determine the extent to which the life history is studied. The object of clinical work is not to write a biography nor to conduct a personality research project. The extent of a particular study will be limited by the nature of the task—deciding whether Fred Pearson should be committed to an institution or not, or developing a working image of Ms. Antonio, whose psychological conflicts underlie her painful migraine headaches. But knowing something of a client's life history throws light on present problems and suggests future plans.

A central feature of the assessment of life history is the study of the person's *choice patterns.* Information will usually be obtained by interviewing the patient and other informants.[1] First one identifies the major periods of shift in a

[1] One of the authors of this book (Tyler et al., 1968) with her colleagues has developed an assessment technique for studying choice patterns of individuals. The stimulus materials consist of one large set of cards, on each of which the title of an occupation appears, and another set, each of which has on it a common leisure-time activity. Working with one set at a time, the subject first separates these into liked and disliked groups. Then he sorts the items into

person's life: perhaps marriage, leaving to go to college, shifts in occupation, onset of symptoms. Then one inquires into the circumstances of the person at these periods of change (and most probably stress) looking for evidence about the way decisions were consciously or unconsciously made. Did the individual take an active stand, or did he let things happen to him? Did he consider long-range effects of possible courses of action, or was he influenced mainly by considerations of benefits in the present and immediate future? Various other aspects of these "times of change" can also be considered.

In examining choice patterns one needs to keep in mind the developmental tasks characteristic of various periods of life. If the client does not mention his adjustment to his developing sexuality in adolescence, the clinician wonders why. If the occasion seems appropriate, he inquires in some subtle way about this area of life. In order to make use of the developmental-task notion, the clinician must have some knowledge of normal development and "subjective norms" about expected averages and deviations.

A picture of the role development of the person begins to emerge. The clinician sees what kind of role the person has tended to assume in family and other groups. As he explores the life history of a client, he should pay particular attention to the role implications of the client's memories of early events. These earliest recollections seem to reflect the client's perceptions of his place in relation to significant persons in his life and his prototypes of mothering or other roles. If there is a consistent thread running through these recollections, one may hypothesize (along with the Adlerian theorist) that they serve as "guiding fictions" in his present activities.

There are many other aspects of life history—physical functioning, births and deaths in the family, economic problems. To help him organize and interrelate all the information, the clinician may wish to prepare a chronological chart. Adolph Meyer early advocated such longitudinal outlines, and many others have also used them. (For illustrations, the reader is referred to Richards, 1946; Cobb, 1953; and Burton, 1959, pp. 164 165, 195). Figure 8-1 shows one possible life-history chart. This chart can be used in taking notes on major events, choice points, and disturbances of a person's life, as one reads over a case history. In preparing to write a case study or psychological report, such a chart can be very useful as a source of hypotheses about conditions that have influenced the development of the person and stresses that may have led to his symptoms. It helps organize the confusing details of a case history. One may see, for example,

---

[1] *continued*

whatever categories he wishes, being instructed to group things which seem to him to go together. This freedom of procedure allows the subject himself to tell how he conceptualizes an area of life. The assessor interviews him extensively to uncover his modes of thinking. Norms for the quantitative aspects of performance—number of positive and negative items, number of positive and negative categories, and the like—can be developed. The actual content of the categories the person uses, however, is idiosyncratic.

Client's name _____ Age _____ Sex _____

Date of interview _____ Interviewer _____ Address _____

Family constellation (names of brothers and sisters and number of years older or younger than patient):

Father (occupation, education, and age at time of client's birth):

Mother (occupation, education, and age at time of client's birth):

Major childhood community (kind of neighborhood, friends, activities):

Client's earliest recollections:

Marital family (family of procreation) (names of wife and children):

Year	Age	Major Events in Life Situation	Physical and Medical Events	Psychological Functioning
19____	Birth	(For each year describe major events, e.g., who cared for client at birth, births of siblings, deaths, school problems)	Describe onset, cessation, and changes in severity of symptoms, illnesses, injuries, etc.)	(Onset, cessation, and changes in any psychopathological symptoms—also periods of greatest effectiveness, productivity, and satisfaction)
19____	1			
19____	2			
	etc.			

FIGURE 8-1 Life-history chart.

how a child's psychosomatic disorders started when a younger sibling was born or how a man's income and productivity improved when he was working under supervision rather than independently. Gaps and holes in the history also become apparent as we study such a chart.

For several reasons it has been difficult to work out exact ways of studying life history. In the first place, what is a life history? What the person tells you himself may be a gross distortion of the facts, whether through lapse of memory, unconscious distortion, or intentional omission. The histories we obtain from other informants, such as wives or parents, are also subject to distortion. Furthermore, to delimit the area to be studied as life history is difficult, because the broad scope of life makes it impossible really to know what is important and what is not. Finally, the history of each individual is so different from that of another that it is difficult to develop comparable procedures. Although there is no real solution to these problems of distortion, delimitation, and individual differences, we can set up specific definitions for specific research purposes. Some beginnings of research on life history have been made.

One practical research question is whether the inferences clinicians typically make from case-history data are warranted. We usually assume that certain events in a person's life are particularly meaningful, but we have not really checked these assumptions in a systematic way. Some discrepancy between the beliefs clinicians hold and the facts is demonstrated in a research project by Hovey (1959). He asked six psychiatrists and psychologists working daily with neuropsychiatric patients to check a long list of history items indicating whether they are significantly associated with neuropsychiatric conditions. He then compared these answers with a list derived from actual case histories of psychiatric patients and veterans. Hovey found that the clinicians were right about the predictive value of 73 percent of the items. But there were many errors. Among the items erroneously predicted to be indicative of mental illness were the following: "From time to time I had nightmares as a boy; I used to stammer or stutter; My home was broken by separation or divorce of my parents by the time I was twelve years old." In a study of an entirely different sort, Barron (1954) reports that many successful and mentally healthy graduate students have had incidents in their backgrounds which would be considered traumatic or pathological. Schofield and Balian (1959) in a study of schizophrenics and normals (presented in an expanded form at the end of this chapter) found "traumatic histories" in one-fourth of their normal subjects. The authors caution against oversimplified ideas that any single event or deprivation necessarily leads toward schizophrenia, and they urge that more intensive studies of case histories be made in order to detect "suppressor" of "immunizing" factors in the lives of those normal people who do not succumb to mental illnesses.

DEVELOPING SKILLS IN INTERVIEWING

There are no easy formulas for conducting good interviews or for selecting good interviewers or observers. Richardson, Dohrenwend, and Klein (1965, p. 2) after many years of research conclude "there is no one correct way to interview" and "no one optimal set of interviewer characteristics." Yet these conclusions do not mean that one cannot develop skill and knowledge about the basic clinical operations. Quite the contrary. Interviewing and observation are such flexible methods and the differences among clients and differences among interviewers are so great that no single prescription for performance can be given. For instance, it takes a very different kind of interview to evaluate the psychotic thinking of a manic murderer in prison than to obtain answers from housewives in a door-to-door canvas of attitudes toward mental illness. Any research project using interview or observation methods entails training of observers or interviewers. The person who is to become skilled in clinical work needs to expect to spend a great deal of time becoming adept. Clinicians will also find themselves training others to interview—paraprofessionals, nurses, aides, students.

In learning to interview, one should observe others, study phonographic and televised records of his own interviews, and obtain extensive supervision. Different varieties of improvement programs require different specialized interviewing skills. Particular interview techniques have been established in connection with particular theories, such as free association with Freudian psychoanalysis, participant observation with Sullivanian interpersonal therapy and reflection or clarification of feeling with Rogerian counseling, and relaxation and suggestion with hypnotic therapies. Other specialized techniques have been developed in connection with nonclinical uses of the interview for survey research, selling, or military interrogation. Gradually since 1942, when Carl Rogers published the first verbatim recorded interviews, techniques have become more clearly identified, although a comprehensive theory of interviewing practice has yet to emerge.

Although there are no formulas, there are a few directions that might be mentioned. One is the importance of *learning how to listen actively.* In interviewing, major purposes are to understand the client's view of the world and to obtain information from him, including information about feelings. The interviewer's attitude must be different from that of people in everyday conversation, in which intense listening seldom occurs. Many listen only enough to be polite and to provide an opening to vent their own expressions. Even in lectures it has been reported that only a small percentage of the college student audience is listening at a given time.

A related problem for beginning interviewers is the *handling of silences.* In Western cultures, as nature abhors a vacuum, everyday conversation abhors silence. The expected norm is that there will be continuous chatter. Consequently, it often seems awkward in an interview if a silence occurs. The experienced interviewer generally avoids breaking into a silence, especially if he sees that the client is wrestling with a problem or is deep in a reverie. Matarazzo (1965a) summarized studies indicating that interviewees usually break the silence after some time anyway. If the silence goes on too long, the interviewer may find it useful to remark about the fact that there was a silence after a certain subject was brought up or to indicate that it may be difficult to talk about certain things. In the case of silences with resistive or psychotic persons, the problem for the interviewer may be to find nonverbal techniques for interaction and evaluation or to postpone the interview until a later time.

Another problem for beginning interviewers is *how to deal with personal questions that clients ask.* In the writers' experience, patients or other clients have asked the following: "Do you believe in Christ?" "You're a psychologist; tell me what you would do if you were me." "I would like to talk with you some more; let me buy you a drink at the bar down the street." Psychotic patients or psychopaths may make direct sexual advances. In situations like this, the psychologist must be clear in his own mind about his role and the purpose of the interview. Generally, he will need to mention the client's concern for the topic, e.g., "Religion concerns you a great deal?" or "You want to feel closer to me as a person?" Sometimes it is necessary to explain the purpose of the meeting and to indicate that the focus of the discussion is on the client, not on the interviewer. On some occasions it is useful for the interviewer to report his own feelings to the client in the immediate context of the interview, e.g., "What you said just now makes me feel uncomfortable; I get the impression that you are trying to make me take responsibility for your life. Does that seem understandable?" Clinicians will vary a great deal with regard to how much they let their own personal feelings enter into interviews; some therapeutic approaches advocate highly personal intervention at proper points, but this should be done only with proper professional training and with due regard to ethical questions that might arise.

Another concern for the interviewer is *how to communicate with someone with a different ethnic or cultural background.* When it is quite apparent that basic communication channels do not exist, as with people from other countries that do not speak English, special efforts must be made to get someone else to conduct the interview or serve as interpreter. There are also psychological tests and procedures for which instructions can be given in pantomine. Drawings and observations of activities can be used. We all recognize gross language differences. A major problem comes in interviewing members of ethnic minorities and subcultural groupings. The language of the black ghetto is far from the language of the typical white middle-class psychologist; the relations that ghetto residences have with whites in the past will often be detrimental for establishing rapport between black clients and white clinicians. Ledvinka (1971) found that white interviewers elicited less information from black interviewees than black interviewers did. Similarly, minority psychologists may run into initial difficulties in relating to white clients, and nearly all psychologists will have problems communicating with people who have little education and poorly developed verbal skills. The topic is too complex to deal with here; psychologists need special training in work with different cultural groups, and they need to learn to make use of assistants from those cultures and to train others to work directly in ghettos, skid rows, migrant-worker camps, remote rural areas, and other nontypical places. The beginning psychologist can, however, do two things: first, he can learn as much as possible about the language and customs of the special group. For instance, he should not be surprised that a young black man mentions getting angry about being called "boy." He should get to know the special argot for sexual activities, drugs, and other topics that may be mentioned in interviews. Second, the psychologist will profit greatly by observations in the environment of clients he is working with. If he is to deal with people from American Indian background, he should visit Indian schools and reservations and see how Indians live in the city. If he is to work with poor people, his training should include, if possible, living with a poor family and getting to know their problems and way of life. Many of the techniques for training for the Peace Corps and VISTA could be profitably applied to the training of clinical psychologists. Before leaving this topic, we should note that different cultures may not be the only impediment to communication. Many professionals speak in a *jargon* clients cannot understand, as Korsch and Negrete (1972) demonstrated with physicians.

Finally, we should call attention to *how to check one's perceptions and understandings*. During the course of the interview, the clinician should in some way see if he can put into words important feelings and information the client has been expressing. One technique for this is called *paraphrasing*—the interviewer's attempt to state a parallel expression of what the interviewee has just been saying. For instance, if the client says "Things seem to be piling up on me; I have so much work to do, my wife is nagging me to get a better job, and I worry about the kids," the interviewer might respond, "You seem to be saying that everything is pressing in on you." *Reflection of feeling*, which is emphasized by the Rogerian client-centered approach, is a special case of paraphrasing, in which only the feeling aspects of a client's remarks are clarified and given back to the client. Paraphrasing is useful for checking on content as well as feeling. In assessment interviews, questions also naturally fit into this framework—"Do you mean that _____ ?" or "Am I right that you feel such and such?" The client then has a chance to see if your perception is the same as his. Asking the client to summarize at the end is another way to have him tell you again what has been important; for example, "It might be helpful if we would go over the main things we've talked about this hour; would you tell me what stands out in your mind?" Again the writers would like to state that there are no magic techniques for interviewing. A clear understanding of purposes and context and a deep interest in the client help the clinician a great deal.

USING PERSONAL AND SOCIAL RECORDS

Along with observation and interviewing, the psychologist seeking information about individuals or situations uses documents. These may be either personal records or records of a social organization. Some are taken from existing files;

others are elicited for particular assessment purposes. Tests, which we will take up in Chapter 9, are a form of elicited records.

Personal documents include letters, diaries, artwork, school papers, and even family albums of photographs. Clients or patients sometimes offer to bring these to interviews. When this happens, they often provide a sense of the living situations of the client and his personal world that one can hardly obtain from discussions alone. Organizational records the clinician often uses are hospital charts or school reports.

The clinician may ask the client to produce some written records. As mentioned before, behavior therapists often request the parent of a problem child or an adult client himself to keep records of the occurrence of symptoms. A client may also be asked to write down positive experiences he remembers; this gives the behavior therapist an idea about the kind and amount of reinforcements the client is obtaining in his daily life. A daily activity record (called a "time budget" in sociological research) is another procedure that helps the clinician understand the client's living situation. Some therapists make "homework assignments." Any of these personal records may be quantified by simple frequency counts, by ratings, or in some other way if a quantitative record is needed.

Documents and records play an important part in the appraisal of systems larger than individuals or small groups. To understand an agency or community, one needs at least a minimal knowledge of its history, organization, power structure, and communication network. Often the public media are helpful— newspapers, television, and radio. The town's Chamber of Commerce or the library may have information about organizations and community activities. Schools, hospitals, and governmental offices keep their own records. Some communities have an interagency record-keeping system, a clearing house of information about services provided to individuals or families throughout the locality. Another source of community information is the yellow-page section of the telephone directory. We will have more to say in later chapters about the work clinical psychologists do in organizations and communities.

SUMMARY

In carrying out his appraisal function the clinical psychologist uses observations, interviews, and records. What information he seeks and how he obtains it depend upon the purpose the appraisal serves in designing an improvement program for a particular client.

Observations may be made in either natural situations, such as schools or street corners, or in contrived situations, such as offices or group therapy meetings. Others besides the psychologist may be asked to make some of these observations, and others besides the client himself may be observed as they relate to him. Observations may focus on pathognomic signs, personality characteristics and style, group interactions, or specified categories of behavior, such as tics or temper tantrums. There are various ways of quantifying observational data.

Interviewing involves attention to relationships, communication, and structure. From the first contact on, the interviewer attempts to establish a warm and constructive relationship with the client. He uses his knowledge of communication processes and his skill in active listening to maximize his understanding of the meaning the client is trying to convey, noting nonverbal aspects as well as words. Each interview has a temporal structure, and the psychologist adapts himself to the differences between beginning, middle, and ending stages. The structure depends to a large extent on the purpose the interview serves. A psychologist should have some particular skill in conducting life-history interviews.

Certain kinds of interview skills must be developed by clinicians—attentive listening, dealing with silences, dealing with personal questions, communicating with persons from different ethnic and cultural backgrounds, and paraphrasing what clients have said.

As a part of the appraisal process one makes use of personal records, such as letters, diaries, and so on, and of organizational records, such as hospital charts. Clients are sometimes asked to keep special records themselves to contribute to the appraisal process. The use of records and documents is especially important in the appraisal of more-inclusive systems, such as communities.

SUGGESTED READINGS

Weick, K. E. Systematic observational methods. In G. Lindzey and E. Aronson (eds.), *The handbook of social psychology*, Vol. 2, 2nd ed. Reading, Mass.: Addison-Wesley, 1968, pp. 357–451.

Weick has provided an excellent overview of a wide variety of problems and methods related to observation, incorporating material from approximately 300 references. The purpose is largely for assistance of researchers, but clinicians will find many items that may help them understand observation better. Weick (p. 360) defines the observational method as the "selection, provocation, recording, and encoding of that set of behaviors and settings concerning organisms 'in situ' which is consistent with empirical aims." The use of the word "provocation" in the definition reflects Weick's suggestion that observers introduce subtle changes in natural settings which will increase clarity without destroying the setting.

Kahn, R. L., and Cannell, C. F. *The dynamics of interviewing: theory, technique and cases.* New York: Wiley, 1957.

This book, although primarily based on the experience of the University of Michigan Survey Research Center with the interview as it is used in surveys, goes far beyond this. The authors, who have been influenced by the theories of Lewin and Rogers, are interested in the clinical aspects and psychodynamics of the two-person interpersonal situation. The transcripts of interviews from a variety of professional settings are valuable for study and discussion. The same authors (Cannell and Kahn, 1968) have presented an extensive review of the interview as a research instrument.

Benjamin, A. *The helping interview*. Boston: Houghton Mifflin, 1969.

This little book is a useful introduction to interviewing; it is practical and has many sensible illustrations. It is the kind of book that might be useful for training nonpsychologists in interviewing.

Another small book also useful for training is *Problem-Solving Interviews* by Beveridge (1968).

See also Morgan and Cogger (1972), *The Interviewer's Manual*, a clear guide for a variety of interviews.

Banaka, W. H. *Training in depth interviewing*. New York: Harper & Row, 1971.

This short training manual emphasizes interpersonal communications theory adapted from Bales and from Schutz. It provides a detailed system of evaluating interviews from audio or video tape with emphasis on interviewer self-evaluation.

Pittenger, R. E., Hockett, C. F. and Danehy, J. J. *The first five minutes, a sample of microscopic interview analysis*. Ithaca, N. Y.: Paul Martineau, 1960.

This book of 264 pages is a detailed analysis of 5 minutes of an initial interview with a psychiatric out-patient. The phonographically recorded sequence begins with the therapist saying "Will you sit there? What brings you here?" and the patient, a thirty-one-year-old nurse, saying "I get so irritable, tense, depressed. Just everything and everybody gets on my nerves." In an unusual split Dutch-door page, the authors present the transcription in the upper half and the linguistic and psychiatric commentary in the lower half. The analysis of the therapist's second question calls it his opening gambit and indicates how open it is, allowing the patient to choose and define its meaning very freely. The stress, pitch, and vocal quality of the words are analyzed, and alternative possibilities with their meanings are discussed. The authors point out how the patient's responses show unmistakable signs of being rehearsed. The whole *tour de force* demonstrates the complexity and richness of human communication.

Matarazzo, J. D. The interview. In B. B. Wolman (ed.), *Handbook of clinical psychology*. New York: McGraw-Hill, 1965, pp. 403–450.

This chapter is an excellent review and commentary on theories and research by a psychologist who, with his colleagues, has probably done more research on the interview than anyone else in the history of the method. Matarazzo relates techniques to the leading personality theories, analyzes the findings in the use of the interview for psychiatric diagnosis, reviews social science research usage, and summarizes studies of the form and structure of the interview. The overall tenor of the review is positive and suggests that behavioral laws are on the way toward specification in this very flexible interaction of the interview.

Matarazzo and Wiens (1972) have more recently published an excellent review and report on research on the structure of interviews.

Webb, E. J., Campbell, D. T., Schwartz, R. D., and Sechrest, L. *Unobtrusive measures: nonreactive research in the social science.* Chicago: Rand McNally, 1969.

This delightfully written little book is a survey of ways of obtaining nonreactive data (i.e., data not dependent on the stimuli supplied by the researcher, such as that of interviews and questionnaires). The authors review an odd collection of physical measures that reveal something about human behavior, such as the amount of wear in front of various exhibits in a museum, governmental actuarial records, sales records, and a variety of data-gathering methods from observations. Among the observations they mention is that suggested by a waitress's song, "My Lover Was a Logger" (p. 141):

> I can tell that you're a logger
> And not just a common bum,
> 'Cause nobody but a logger
> Stirs his coffee with his thumb.

Allport, G. W. *Letters from Jenny.* New York: Harcourt Brace, 1965.

Jenny Masterson, unknowingly, left for psychologists a valuable record of her personal life in a series of 301 letters to a young married couple who had been friends of her only child. The correspondence covering Jenny's life from age fifty-eight to seventy when she died (over the years 1926 to 1937) was a vivid portrayal of her loneliness, resentments, jealousies, strivings, and defeats, particularly in relation to her son. The famous personality theorist Gordon Allport used these letters to illustrate how personal documents may be used in the study of an individual. He interprets her character neurosis from several standpoints, both with objectivity and sympathy. He also summarizes a content analysis of her letters.

For an intensive discussion of content analysis, see Holsti (1968).

Rich, J. *Interviewing children and adolescents.* New York: St. Martin's Press, 1968.

Communication between young people and adults is an art that is sometimes difficult for clinicians to master. This is a practical book by a worker experienced with emotionally disturbed and delinquent youngsters. At the end there are several hypothetical interviews and commentaries.

Kaswan, J. W., Love, L. R., and Rodnick, E. H. Information feedback as a method of clinical intervention and consultation. In C. D. Spielberger (ed.). *Current topics in clinical and community psychology*, Vol. 3. New York: Academic Press, 1971, pp. 123–161.

Kaswan, Love, and Rodnick make use of a wide variety of observation and rating techniques in working with children, parents, and teachers. This chapter, which illustrates one of the recent developments, provides a high degree of blending of information gathering and treatment, with the clients fully aware and involved in the process of both generating and using (interpreting) the immediate data. The children and their parents observe themselves interacting through television feedback and they record behavior on check lists. The authors found in preliminary analyses that the information feedback method was more effective than parent counseling alone. Implications for consulting in the school are discussed.

RESEARCH EXAMPLES

Speer, D. C. Behavior problem checklist (Peterson–Quay): baseline data from parents of child guidance and nonclinic children. *Journal of Consulting and Clinical Psychology*, 1971, *36*, 221–228.

Psychological instruments of any kind need to be questioned on a great many technical points raised in Chapter 9. This study is an illustration of the need to get normative information from different groups and to break down the data obtained by sex and age and other attributes of the population being considered. Over six months Speer asked all parents applying for assistance from a child guidance clinic to fill out the Peterson–Quay Behavior Problem Checklist for both the problem child and its siblings. He also sent the same check list to parents in a representative sample of school districts asking them to fill out the form for school-age children and their siblings. He accumulated responses from parents on 173 clinic patients, 357 siblings of patients, and 445 nonclinic children. Behavior Problem Checklist provided scores for Conduct Disorder, Personality Disorder, Inadequacy-Immaturity, and Social Delinquency. The ratings on the children were sorted out by clinic status, sex, and an analysis of variance was performed.

The results clearly showed that parents differentiate child patients from their siblings and from nonclinic children on the first three of the four scores from the check list. As is commonly found, boys received higher ratings than girls. The authors were surprised to find that the nonclinic children were reported to have more symptoms than the siblings of clinic patients; they conjure that their sample of nonclinic parents returning the forms may be more willing to volunteer problems than those not responding; they were particularly concerned about "social delinquency"—a condition that did not seem to be bringing children to the clinic as much as other problems—thus reflecting the public image of that clinic. The author also points to the problem of disagreement over problematic behavior of a particular child and calls for a recognition in research and clinical practice of the situation-specific and role-specific nature of observations. Baseline data such as this can be used for evaluating new cases and for studying changes in relation to treatment. Another check list of deviant behavior for school children has been studied by Miller (1972).

Rappaport, J., and Chinsky, J. M. Behavior ratings of chronic hospitalized patients: cross-situational and cross-rater agreement. *Journal of Consulting and Clinical Psychology*, 1970, *34*, 394–397.

The authors' purpose was to compare behavior ratings of the same patients made by two different kinds of raters in two different situations. The patients met in groups of eight with thirty undergraduate students from a nearby college who made ratings based on group behavior. The final patient *N* was 150, 86 males and 64 females. Twenty-six ward attendants also made ratings based on their observations on the ward. The procedure for recording observations was the Ellsworth MACC Behavioral Adjustment Scale (Ellsworth, 1962), which consists of four scales: mood, cooperation, communication, and social contact. Raters check sixteen items using five-point scales. Ratings were done twice, 5.5 months apart.

The correlations of the two groups for the four Ellsworth scales and the total adjustment scale ranged from 0.19 for mood to 0.56 for social contact; all were significantly different from zero. The second set of ratings after 5.5 months were higher than the first. The authors conclude that there is some cross-situational and cross-rater generality of behavior, which should be investigated further; they suggest the usefulness of the scale for evaluation of hospital treatment programs.

This study is illustrative of only one of many methods of recording observations of patients (Lyerly and Abbott, 1966). Another widely used procedure for similar patients is the Hospital Adjustment Scale. Lentz, Paul, and Calhoun (1971) report on the reliability and validity of three measures of functioning of chronic patients.

Boucher, M. L. Effect of seating distance on interpersonal attraction in an interview situation. *Journal of Consulting and Clinical Psychology*, 1972, *38*, 15–19.

The anthropologist, Hall, has coined the term *proxemics* to refer to the study of man's use of space as a means of nonverbal communication (1966). He has identified the typical activities and meanings attached to different distances between people—the intimate, the personal, the social, and the public. Boucher used a room for a brief structured interview in which the chairs were fixed to the floor at varying distances—12 inches (intimate), 39 inches (personal), and 9 feet (social). Forty-two schizophrenic patients and forty-two alcoholic patients were brought to the room in turn for the interview, the chair distances being randomly varied. Afterward two dependent variables were obtained—a rating of attraction to the interviewer and a clever "unobtrusive measure"—the closeness to the interviewer when the patient brought up a chair in a later interview. As predicted, schizophrenics were less attracted to the interviewer at the intimate distance; alcoholics did not show that difference. When the patients could move their chairs freely they tended to shy away from the interviewer after the intimate-distance interview. The authors concluded that the nonverbal qualities of seating distance can affect the interviewer–interviewee relationship. For an extensive discourse on personal space, see Sommer (1969). The way people use the physical area around them is a proper subject for clinical observation.

Persons, R. W., and Marks, P. A. Self-disclosure with recidivists: optimum interviewer—interviewee matching. *Journal of Abnormal Psychology.* 1970, 76, 387—391.

Jourard (1964) has explored the meanings of self-disclosure and has indicated that willingness to communicate personal information and be intimate is related to ability to maintain interpersonal relations. One of the kinds of personality most resistant to psychotherapy has been the psychopath. In this study Persons and Marks investigated the possibility that interviewers with certain character-istics and training might be able to establish self-disclosing interactions with prisoners who have a strong psychopathic character structure. The interviewees were 78 male prison inmates having high scores on the Psychopathic Deviate Scale. (For those familiar with the MMPI coding system, the most frequent high-point MMPI codes were 4-2, 4-8, and 4-9). Three of the interviewers were college students with similar codes, and three were other prison inmates with similar codes. After training for self-disclosing interviews, each interviewer met with twelve inmates, equally divided among the code types. Selected topics of discussion intended to elicit personal content were presented, and the half-hour interviews were taped. The major dependent variable was ratings by two judges as to how revealing the inmate actually was.

The results showed that inmate and student interviewers were equally able to elicit disclosure. A three-way analysis of variance showed no significant differences except for an interaction between personality measures and interviewer class. Five of the six interviewers obtained the greatest intimacy from subjects of the same MMPI code type. The subjects became significantly more self-disclosing over time. The results suggest the potential value of matching people on personality characteristics, at least for the start of a relationship; the effectiveness of counseling or therapy was not investigated here.

In a similar study, Berzins, Ross, and Cohen (1970) studied the interpersonal and situational determinants of self-disclosure with another kind of "un-promising" client—the drug addict. Forty psychiatric aides interviewed forty hospitalized addicts for about twenty minutes each. Interview dyads were paired so as to represent either high or low scores on the A-B scale, a short interest inventory which has been shown to differentiate between therapists who work well with schizophrenics versus neurotics. Patients were also given two different sets toward the interviewer—one to emphasize the hostile and manipulative quality of the aide—interviewer and the other friendly helpfulness of the aide. Thus a 2 x 2 x 2 factorial design was set up with five dyads in each cell. As predicted, A-type aides with patients given the hostile set and B-type aides with patients given the helpful set obtained better self-disclosure than those oppositely paired. Addicts who thought the aides would be hostile and manipulative were more self-disclosing than those who thought they would be helpful, perhaps because they expected the first type were more tough and could not be "conned." For further reporting on the A-B variable, see one of the research summaries at the end of Chapter 11. Both of these studies investigate what kinds of people work best with each other and with what kind of training and expectations are involved. As yet a general theory bringing these studies together has yet to emerge.

Wirt, R. D., and Briggs, P. F. Personality and environmental factors in the development of delinquency. *Psychological Monographs*, 1959, *73*, No. 15, 1–47 (Whole No. 485).

This study relates personality characteristics and case-history factors in a long follow-up study of delinquents. In 1948 all ninth-graders in the Minneapolis schools had been administered the MMPI, a total sample of about 4,000. Hathaway and Monachesi (1953) reported the results of an extensive analysis of these data and identified certain codes as being related to subsequent delinquency. In particular a 489 code (the Psychopathic Deviancy scale highest followed by the Schizophrenic scale and Hypomania scale) was frequently associated with delinquency in boys and a 025 code (the Social Introversion scale highest followed by Depression and Femininity) was seldom associated with delinquency in boys. Wirt and Briggs conducted a follow-up in 1956. The authors were interested in comparing nondelinquents and delinquents representing each of the code types. They located 71 to 73 boys from each of the four possible combinations—*delinquency-prone* personality with and without a history of delinquency and *delinquency suppressor* personality with and without a history of delinquency. The environmental data were gathered from records of social agencies; also there were interviews with the subjects, a Q-sort by the interviewer, and a standard history questionnaire from the mother. Data from the four different groups are compared.

Some of the numerous results are as follows: Certain profiles on the MMPI and the fact of the family having had contact with a social agency taken together successfully differentiated boys with delinquency records. Forty-two percent of the boys with 489 codes whose families had agency contact had become delinquent, whereas only 11 percent of boys with 025 codes who had become delinquent were extremely deviant. Among boys with delinquency-prone personalities (489 codes), the greatest differences between those who became delinquent and those who did not centered around family sufficiency and occupational–educational level. The delinquent group came from worse homes with poor family ties; there were records of disease, poverty, dissocial behavior in the family, absent mothers, and disparity of views between mothers and sons.

This study is of value not only for what it contributes to our knowledge about delinquency and the information it gives us about MMPI patterns, but also as a demonstration of a method for combining personological and sociological data. An additional study, using the same ninth-grade MMPI pool, exemplified another kind of design and a sophisticated statistical technique. Rempel (1958) applied a multivariate statistical analysis to MMPIs and school records of a large number of delinquents and nondelinquents. By a combination of the two kinds of data he was able to correctly identify 74 percent of the nondelinquents and 67 percent of the delinquent boys.

Both these studies, as well as the book on delinquents by Hathaway and Monachesi (1953) and the 10-year follow-up of high school dropouts by Hathaway, Reynolds, and Monachesi (1969), exemplify the research possibilities in a well-planned collection of data from a large population in a community or region. This approach makes it possible to do true prediction studies. Measurements are made *before* delinquency or mental illness occurs. Later follow-up in social agency files locates the deviant or disturbed groups. Then the research worker can go back to the data and check which measures actually relate to later events.

In a somewhat related study, Cowden and Pacht (1967) studied the prediction of institutional and postrelease adjustment of delinquent boys. With 152 boys in a correctional school, they found that a global prognosis based primarily on personality factors best predicted institutional adjustment, but a global prognosis based primarily on family background factors best predicted post-release adjustment.

Schofield, W., and Balian, L. A comparative study of the personal histories of schizophrenic and nonpsychiatric patients. *Journal of Abnormal and Social Psychology*, 1959, *59*, 216–225.

The authors do a test of the currently popular view that the seeds of mental illness are to be found in life experiences, especially in critical periods of childhood. In a survey of over 300 studies of life histories of psychiatric patients, they found fewer than 10 which included data from a reasonably comparable control group. The purposes of this study were to examine the life histories of "normal" persons for evidence of psychiatric problems and to compare the histories of these people with histories of schizophrenics.

The schizophrenic sample consisted of 178 hospitalized patients on which there were comprehensive personal history statistics. The "normal" sample was mainly composed of medical patients coming to the same hospital who showed no evidence of present or previous psychiatric disorder. The selection of the nonpsychiatric sample was dictated by an attempt to match on age, sex, and marital status. The life histories of the 150 normals were collected by a comprehensive clinical interview. After the interview the interviewer immediately recorded data on a standard schedule for recording developmental, personal, social, and medical history, the same schedule which had been used with the schizophrenic sample. MMPIs were also available on the normal sample.

The single most impressive feature of the statistical comparison was the sizable overlap of the normal and schizophrenic samples on distributions for personal history variables. Of 35 major aspects of early history and adjustment, 37 percent failed to show a significant difference, and on an additional 14 percent it was the normals who showed a significantly greater frequency of undesirable or "pathogenic" characteristics. Specific items that were higher for normals than for schizophrenics were: frequency of poverty and invalidism in their childhood homes, poorer heterosexual adjustment and adequacy of sexual outlet, and a greater incidence of an intellectualized or ritualized orientation toward religion. Divorce in the childhood home approached significance.

The schizophrenics showed a significantly high incidence of unfavorable history items having to do with withdrawal and poor relationships with others: poor relations with parents, unfavorable attitudes toward school, less occupational success, more social withdrawal, lack of poise, narrow interests, limited aspirations, vague life plans, and lack of initiative. However, the extent to which these same characteristics were found in normals argues strongly for caution in interpreting any single event as traumatic or pathognomonic. Schofield and

Balian judged that nearly one-fourth of the normal subjects had "traumatic" histories, but their MMPIs did not indicate that they were very different from the rest.

The authors concluded that many theories about the etiology of mental disease in early experience need to be carefully checked. Patterns of life events rather than single events should be studied. They suggest that research might identify "suppressor" experiences or psychological processes that immunize normals with deleterious early experiences against psychological breakdowns. (For a brief discussion of a hypothetical X factor, an ability to resist psychological stress, see Pascal, 1951).

Later studies have focused on parts of the case history. For instance, Turner, Dopkeen, and Labreche (1970) confirmed the frequent finding that schizophrenics who had been married had a better prognosis. However, when socioeconomic status was controlled, the differences disappeared. Overall (1971) found that patients with multiple marriages showed less pathology than those with one marriage; he hypothesized that the first marriage is a screen for schizoid withdrawal, while a second marriage cuts out depressive tendencies. Peskin (1972) in a longitudinal study found early predictors of adult psychological health. Rahe, Mahan, and Arthur (1970) have demonstrated the relation between life changes and physical illness using the Social Readjustment Rating Scale (1967).

Braginsky, B. M., and Braginsky, D. D. Schizophrenic patients in the psychiatric interview: an experimental study of their effectiveness at manipulation. *Journal of Consulting Psychology*, 1967, *31*, 543–547.

The authors pose the question: "Can schizophrenic patients effectively control the impressions (impression management, Goffman, 1959) they make on the professional hospital staff?" They allow that clinical observers might expect schizophrenics to be responsive to social situations and to show some manipulative characteristics, but assert that formal theories of schizophrenia consider schizophrenics incapable of successful manipulation of other people.

A sample of thirty male schizophrenics (median length of hospitalization, 10 years) was randomly selected from ward rosters. Two days prior to the experiment, the patients were told that they were scheduled for an interview with a staff psychologist. Patients were interviewed individually. As the patient was escorted to the interview, an assistant casually informed the patient in a tone of confidentiality about the purpose of the interview (preinterview induction). Patients were randomly assigned—without the interviewer's knowledge—to one of three induction conditions. The three conditions were *discharge* ("I think the person you are going to see is examining patients to see if they are ready for discharge"), *open ward* (" . . . examining patients to see if they should be on open or closed wards"), and *mental status* (" . . . interested in how you are feeling and getting along in the hospital").

The interview, recorded and terminated after two minutes, included the questions "How are you feeling mentally?" and "How are you feeling physically?" Three staff psychiatrists without knowledge of the experiment each rated the recorded interviews on three dimensions: (1) the patient's degree of psychopathology, (2) the amount of hospital control a patient needed, and (3) the structural or qualitative aspects of the patient's speech.

If long-term patients are motivated both to live in open wards and to stay in the hospital, and if they effectively engage in impression management, then the authors predicted mental status—usually associated with discharge—and discharge interviews would both be rated as "sick" and in need of hospital control because patients were trying to decrease the probability of discharge. They also predicted that patients in the open-ward condition would be rated significantly less mentally ill and significantly less in need of hospital control than the patients in the other two conditions, in order to maximize their chances of staying on an open ward. The psychiatrists' ratings confirmed the predictions.

In order to investigate the way in which the different impressions were conveyed, the authors examined (1) the number of positive statements patients made about themselves, (2) the number of negative statements they made about themselves, and (3) normality of speech characteristics, that is, how normal they sounded, independent of what they actually said. The greater the frequency of positive statements made by a patient, the less ill he was perceived and the less in need of hospital control. Conversely, the greater the frequency of negative statements, the more ill and the more in need of hospital control.

Going beyond frequency of negative statements, the authors examined the number of reports of hallucinations or bizarre delusions. None of the open-ward patients made such references, while nine patients in the other two conditions did.

The psychiatrists rated 80 percent of the patients as having relatively normal speech characteristics. Thus psychiatrists' judgments of psychopathology were based primarily on the symptoms patients reported rather than on symptoms patients showed.

The authors argue that the patients changed the impression they gave of themselves to maximize the chances of fulfilling their self-interests and goals. Schizophrenics, like normal people, are goal-oriented and are able to control the outcomes of their social encounters in a way that satisfies their goals.

Watt, N. F., Stolorow, R. D., Lubensky, A. W., and McClelland, D. C. School adjustment and behavior of children hospitalized for schizophrenia as adults. *American Journal of Orthopsychiatry*, 1970, *40*, 637–657.

In order to refine their concepts of psychopathology, psychologists must study the various classes and entities that are proposed. But in his practice the clinician often has to assign time and resources to some clients while withholding them from others. The question "Who is most at risk for psychological difficulties?" requires that the clinician have an understanding of which signs look potentially serious and which do not. The Watt paper is a good example of retrospective life-history investigation designed to illustrate specific premorbid differences.

One of the most firmly established findings from research in schizophrenia is that prognosis for recovery depends upon the quality of social adjustment before breakdown. This means, say the authors, that accurate prediction of psychiatric outcome requires longitudinal investigation of life histories with emphasis on childhood and adolescence, because early adulthood is the most common period for schizophrenic breakdown. Previous studies using this approach, typically follow-up studies of child guidance clients, have been limited in several ways: overrepresenting males and lower social classes, limiting Ss to children so maladjusted as to require psychiatric referral in childhood, and underrepresenting normal children in the controls.

A computer listing was obtained from the state giving names of every patient 15 to 34 years old who was first admitted to any state mental hospital during the period from 1958 through 1965. There were 15,811 diagnosed as having functional psychiatric disorder at first admission. They were checked against the files of Maybury (a fictitious name disguising a Boston suburb) High School from which 162 school records were obtained. The authors report on the cumulative school records of 30 patients first diagnosed as schizophrenic. Three matched control records were randomly selected from the files for each preschizophrenic record.

The comparisons are based on two types of measure derived from the records: (1) a six-factor coding system to analyze the content of the annual comments written by the teachers, and (2) impressionistic clinical ratings on conformity, social participation, facial appearance, and emotional stability.

The authors comment carefully about ethical concerns such as invasion of privacy. Their outline of the steps needed to ensure safeguards for the hospital's and the Maybury school's clients typifies concerned good practice on all sides. Confidentiality was respected and anonymity preserved wherever possible within appropriate formal agreements with the agencies involved, including the university research ethics committee.

The results showed that

1. A substantial portion of children destined to be schizophrenic as adults can be identified by their behavior in public school before they break down. Possibly a majority of the preschizophrenic boys and a substantial minority of the preschizophrenic girls could be picked out by appropriate screening techniques.

2. The patterns of maladjustment of preschizophrenic boys and girls are quite different. The boys show primary evidence of unsocialized aggression and secondary evidence of internal conflict or overinhibition, with a substantial component of emotional depression. The preschizophrenic girls are primarily overinhibited, with the strongest evidence of sensitiveness, conformity, and introversion.

3. Family background and parental social class, in particular, seem to be implicated as important causes of these patterns of maladjustment.

4. No behavioral evidence of sex-role reversal or sex-role alienation was found in the preschizophrenic children. Their patterns of maladjustment were expressed in the culturally prescribed modes: aggressiveness for boys and expressiveness for girls. The results for boys could be interpreted to mean that in circumstances where aggression is tolerated (e.g., in lower social class families), aggression will be found as an expression of maladjustment, but where aggression is strongly prohibited (e.g., in some middle- and upper-class families), pathology will be manifested in internal conflict and social inhibition.

chapter 9

Using Tools of Appraisal:
Tests and Reports

Ask a person to free associate to the word *psychologist* and the chances are that before many words are out he will mention *tests*. The use of psychological tests in the United States is very widespread, especially in education, government, and large industries, where most testing is on a mass or routine basis. The wave of testing in America and Western Europe, now spreading to other countries, aroused vehement opposition in the 1960s and caused many people to take a second look at the side effects of testing. Two frequent criticisms are that testing has led to discrimination against minority groups and constituted a serious invasion of privacy for everybody. Some congressmen have denounced tests and testers and some restrictive legislation has been passed. Most of the critics are concerned about mass testing rather than the clinical use of tests, but many psychologists themselves have become very critical of clinical assessment. They can point to research findings that justify considerable skepticism. Thus the present situation is one of ferment, controversy, and reevaluation. However, it is highly likely that clinical psychologists will continue to use tests in some form, and it is incumbent upon students to be thoroughly familiar with their strengths and weaknesses.

This chapter will provide an overview of tests—their major characteristics and ways of evaluating them. It will also relate tests and alternative assessment procedures to reports and overall strategies for the design of improvement programs, the image making and decision making we have discussed in Chapter 6.

TESTS AND ALTERNATIVE TECHNIQUES
IN CLINICAL PRACTICE

In spite of the criticism and skepticism about testing, in the situations where clinical psychologists serve the public, the use of tests goes on much as it did before. Lubin, Wallis, and Paine (1971) have reported on a 1969 survey involving

251 clinical agencies and hospitals to ascertain what tests were being used. At least half reported using the following thirteen tests, which are listed in order of frequency of usage:

1. Wechsler Adult Intelligence Scale
2. Rorschach
3. Bender Visual-Motor Gestalt Test
4. Thematic Apperception Test
5. Machover Draw-A-Person Test
6. Minnesota Multiphasic Personality Inventory
7. Wechsler Intelligence Scale for Children
8. Stanford-Binet Intelligence Scale
9. House-Tree-Person Projective Technique
10. Rotter Incomplete Sentence Blank
11. Vineland Social Maturity Scale
12. Memory-for-Designs Test
13. Peabody Picture Vocabulary Test

Results from this survey corresponded quite closely to those Sundberg (1961) obtained a decade earlier. Clinical psychologists are still evaluating intelligence and personality traits, using both objective and projective methods. The meaning of these terms will be discussed in more detail later in this chapter, and descriptions of the tests themselves can be found in Appendix E.

Which tests any given psychologist prefers to use depends upon his own personal background, training, and theoretical preferences and also upon the role he plays in his agency or community. Some psychologists specialize in a single test and develop unusual skill in extracting meaning from that one manner of sampling behavior. Some psychologists use batteries of tests; others use alternative procedures such as those discussed in Chapter 8. Let us look at two examples.

Pope and Scott (1967) in their book entitled *Psychological Diagnosis in Clinical Practice* devote several chapters to the use of assessment procedures. They present a number of referral questions, mostly from psychiatrists, which psychologists translated into psychological terms and attempted to answer. A sample of the referral problems and the tests used to answer them follows (pp. 203–311):

> "Is there a thought disorder present?"
> The patient was a 35 year old woman. To differentiate between neurotic depression and an underlying psychotic process, the psychologist used the Rorschach.
> "Is there evidence of suicidal risk?"
> The patient was a 24 year old student of engineering, who later committed suicide. At the time of testing the psychologist examined the TAT and Rorschach for evidence of suicidal ideation, a depressive lack of relatedness, agitation and self-destructive impulsiveness, and failure to make the usual value distinctions between life and death.

"Is the patient's psychosis functionally or organically based?"

The psychologists sought evidence of cognitive impairment, disruptive disturbances of perception and thinking, and symptoms that might be compensatory for organic problems. In dealing with this diagnostic problem in a 27 year old woman who had been earlier diagnosed as schizophrenic, the psychologist used the WAIS, Bender Gestalt, Draw-A-Person, and Rorschach.

"How refractory are this patient's neurotic problems? How susceptible is he to psychotherapeutic influence?"

With a 32 year old man suffering migraine headaches and marital troubles, the psychologist used the Rorschach, WAIS, and TAT to look for verbal fluency, capacity to tolerate anxiety, effective functioning in life situations, social relatedness, and an active orientation to treatment.

"Is this patient's psychological pathology a reaction to his physical illness?"

The referral was a 28 year old laborer who had developed paranoid delusions while in the hospital for a broken leg. The psychologist used the TAT and Rorschach to answer the question.

"What is the evidence for psychological impairment and how severe is it?"

The referral was a 51 year old male out-patient who seemed to be suffering a mild involutional depression and was doing less well than before in his watchmaking job. The psychologist looked for such things as perceptual distortions, confusion, and memory loss on the WAIS, Bender, and Rorschach.

On nearly all these illustrative assessment tasks the psychologists used the Rorschach, and on some they used the WAIS, TAT, and Bender Gestalt. Other psychologists with different backgrounds and competencies might have used other tests, such as the MMPI, tests for brain damage, sentence completions, or observations on the ward. Others might have redefined the referral questions differently. But all these illustrations are examples of the clinical psychologist operating as an associate, generally with a psychiatrist, helping to develop a diagnosis and assisting in decision making about the patient.

As explained in previous chapters, this concept of the psychologist's role—as a member of a psychiatric team contributing to medical diagnoses and decisions— is precisely what is now being called into question. Those who view diagnosis as outmoded or even pernicious are likely to use tests much less frequently, basing their appraisals to a large extent on the techniques discussed in the previous chapter, interviewing and observation. At the forefront of this movement in psychological assessment are some of the experts in behavior modification as a way of dealing with problem behavior. This will be discussed in detail in Chapter 13, but let us consider at this point what Bijou and Peterson (1971) have to say about the assessment techniques psychologists who work with children should use. The approach can be used for adults as well. What they propose is a functional analysis of behavior. Instead of personality traits, thought of as internal conditions or processes, they would concentrate only on behavior relevant to the treatment program. They consider assessment very important, but not to produce psychiatric diagnoses. Bijou and Peterson classify the complaints children present into three categories—behavioral excesses, such as hyperactivity; behavioral deficits, such as poor achievement or withdrawal; and inappropriate stimulus control, such as bed-wetting. For assessment, they recommend that the parent fill out a check list of behavior problems (e.g., Peterson, 1961, or Quay, 1966) and that the informant be interviewed about the child's history and living situation, devoting particular attention to the way he behaves in relation to objects, people, and situations. To interpret this information about behavior, the psychologist needs information about norms of development. As one plans an improvement program for a person, it is usually essential to conduct observations in the home and/or the school in order to assess the conditions under which the problem behavior occurs. One also needs to assess behavioral skills, to consider behaviors that might replace the problem behavior, and to order the things to be learned in a sequence. One assesses also what rewards would serve as effective reinforcers for learning for this particular child in this particular learning situation. A list of such reinforcers is based on the reports of parents, teachers, and perhaps the child himself. The psychologist's task is to develop the assessment instruments needed for these purposes— check sheets and recording devices for baseline data, age norms (including range as well as central tendency) for the behaviors involved, and forms for monitoring progress in the treatment program. Assessment techniques provide feedback information to the parents, teachers, researchers, and often the child himself. After the treatment phase is completed, follow-up assessment determines whether the behavior change is lasting or whether other treatment is needed. Bijou and Peterson state (1971, p. 77) that functional assessment "*describes how the patient behaves in relation to the events in his life*, and the *how* is stated in objective terms. Information on the functional meaning of the environment is obtained only from observations of actual interactions of the person with people in the home, school or job, and in his recreational and avocational activities. On the basis of such information, one can determine which situations are primarily supportive, neutral and aversive for him." They point out that no current assessment techniques, such as paper and pencil personality tests, thematic stories, peer ratings, ability tests, or interviews, can yield definitive information on how the person functions in his environment.

The assessment tests and tasks in the two illustrations are vastly different. The psychologist oriented toward psychiatric diagnosis uses tests and other assessment techniques mainly to compare patients or clients with norms based on groups of previous patients who represent particular pathological types and processes. He is a member of a psychiatric team with a medical approach to psychological problems. The tests developed by clinical psychologists have largely been constructed with this role and this framework in mind.

In contrast, many of the assessment devices advocated by Bijou and Peterson have to be newly constructed. Although comparisons with age norms are still needed to identify the magnitude of the individual's problem and set goals for treatment the major concern is with the individual's situation, which seldom is very comparable with that of others, and the orientation is toward desirable behaviors, not just problematic or pathological behaviors. The psychologist does not think of himself as a member of a psychiatric team but assumes that he is responsible for the whole process, from the inception to the conclusion of an improvement program. The orientation of these programs is educational not medical. Most existing tests do not fit very well into this framework.

Certain principles and ideas, however, hold for both, and it is these that we will try to emphasize. Questions of reliability and validity should be raised whether the assessment instrument is well established or brand new. Any sort of instrument used for appraisal—interviews, observations, ratings, check lists, and coding systems as well as tests—must deal with questions such as these: To what does this finding relate? What does it mean? How generalizable is the finding to other times and places?

TEST-TAKING ATTITUDES

Whatever the assessment instrument, one task the psychologist faces in interpreting its results is to evaluate what the testing situation meant to the client—how he felt about it and what he tried to communicate about himself. A number of questions may occur to the psychologist who is trying to make sense of a test protocol.

1. Were the test instructions and items clear to the client? Did he seem to have any trouble understanding the meaning of words of the intent of the task?

2. Does the client come from a cultural background that would make the test inappropriate or would suggest a cautious interpretation?

3. Did the client show a positive interest in taking the test, or was he uninterested or hostile? How hard did he try on difficult tasks? How did his attitude show on various parts of the test? Did he seem to be trying to fake answers?

4. What was his manner of taking the test—confident or hesitant? Constricted or expansive? Attentive or lackadaisical? Careful or impulsive? How anxious did he appear to be?

5. Were there any problems of physical functioning that seemed to affect the test, such as fatigue, handicaps, or the effects of drugs?

6. How did the client respond to the testing environment? Was he distracted by anything in the situation? Did his attention fluctuate?

7. Had he taken this test before, or ones very similar? Was there evidence of effects of practice?

8. In giving the test, did the examiner depart from the standard administration sufficiently to affect the client's responses?

Such questions will help the psychologist understand the particular meaning that the test had with a given client. With reasonable allowance for possible distorting influences of this sort, one can make use of the normative and correlational information from a test in drawing inferences about the person tested, since in clinical work such inferences constitute hypotheses to be checked against other sorts of evidence.

There has been a considerable amount of research on general *response sets* or *response styles* in the testing situation, particularly *social desirability*, or the attempt to give answers considered normal or acceptable in one's culture, and *acquiescence*, the tendency to say "Yes" rather than "No" to any question one is asked about oneself. It was thought that such sets might constitute serious sources of bias when scores on personality tests were interpreted at face value. The psychologist using tests as appraisal techniques should be aware of the possibility of such effects in individual cases, making a client appear more "normal" or "abnormal" than he really is. With some tests special scales have been developed to use in correcting for such biases. However, the conclusion one can draw from the most penetrating research on the problem is that response sets are not an important source of error in most cases (Block, 1965; Rorer, 1965).

Let us turn now to some of the more technical aspects of psychological testing.

THE DEFINITION AND NATURE OF TESTS

Cronbach in the 1970 edition of his influential book, *Essentials of Psychological Testing*, defined a test as follows: "*A test is a systematic procedure for observing a person, a person's behavior and describing it with the aid of a numerical scale or a category-system*" (p. 26). He indicates that the test can be applied to a group as well as a person, as in studies of leadership which involve responses from a set of group members. Behavior includes vocalized or written responses, checks on paper-and-pencil forms, movements of the body, physiologic responses like a rise in blood pressure, and performances using many sorts of apparatus. (In this book we are using the word *test* in a broad sense; some psychologists would confine the word to highly standardized measurements and would call projective devices *techniques* and paper-and-pencil personality tests *inventories* or *questionnaires*.)

"A *standardized test* is one in which the procedure, apparatus and scoring have been fixed so that precisely the same testing procedures can be followed at different times and places" (Cronbach, 1970, p. 27). Tests vary a great deal in the extent to which they are standardized. One of the great advantages of tests over other approaches derives from good standardization, which allows persons to be compared with considerable exactness. Such comparisons of persons are needed for purposes of selection, classification, or evaluation of change. Well-standardized tests also have *norms*, or tables showing the distribution of scores made by individuals in defined samples of populations. In an earlier edition of his book, Cronbach highlighted this characteristic in his definition of a test—"a systematic procedure for comparing the behavior of two or more persons" (Cronbach, 1960, p. 21). One of the reasons for the change in his definition was that we now recognize that tests may be used for studying one person by repeated measurements. We realize the value of such *idiographic* procedures, which compare different aspects of an individual's behavior with one another or compare his responses at different times. Behavior modification programs often use idiographic devices.

For a test to be standardized it is desirable that the test be *objective*. When one looks at what psychologists have written about this characteristic, however, it is apparent that they are defining the term in different ways. What we will take it to mean is the quality that makes it possible for testers, scorers, observers, or judges to report in precisely the same way about an observation. Tests are called objective when the subjects select from a definite set of response possibilities (true–false, check list, a set of buttons to push). Scoring keys can be applied, and if there are no clerical errors, scoring agreement will be perfect. The opposite of objective is subjective. An example of a subjective procedure is the use of free drawings to be judged for personality implications. A test can be objective in scoring and subjective in interpretation, and vice versa.

Complete objectivity is not possible or even desirable in clinical appraisal. Different clients require different approaches; some require a much longer time to get acquainted and to establish a cooperative relationship than others; some need much more explanation of instructions than others. Schafer (1954, p. 6) in a book on Rorschach testing has expressed the problem very well:

> The clinical testing situation has a complex psychological structure. It is not an impersonal getting-together of two people in order that one, with the help of a little "rapport" may obtain some "objective" test responses from the other. The psychiatric patient is in some acute or chronic life crisis. He cannot but bring many hopes, fears, assumptions, demands and expectations into the test situation. He cannot but respond intensely to certain real as well as fantasied attributes of that situation. Being human and having to make a living—facts often ignored—the tester too brings hopes, fears, assumptions, demands and expectations into the test situation. He too responds personally and often intensely to what goes on—in reality and in fantasy—in that situation, however well he may conceal his personal response from the patient, from himself, and from his colleagues.

It is probably a mistake to think of objectivity as a quality inherent in testing instruments themselves, since they represent only a part of the complex testing situations. What we can talk about is differences between tests in degree of *structuredness of the task* and degree of *ambiguity of the stimuli*. Differences arise from both the physical stimuli and the instructions the subject is given. The task of telling what you see in an inkblot or an assignment to compare and contrast three people you know presents much less restriction or direction to the subject than does the task of identifying objects in a photograph of a street scene or multiplying 79 by 13. Even on an inkblot, if the subject is told to trace the edge of the blot or to point out a certain color, the task becomes much more clear and structured. A test is highly structured when all subjects interpret the task in the same way. A test is unambiguous when all subjects report similar perceptions of the stimuli.

In clinical work, because it is highly individualized and objective procedures are seldom available, there must be great reliance on the psychologist to judge many aspects of the person's behavior. As indicated in Chapter 8, observation is an important source of information even when an objective test such as the WAIS or MMPI is being administered. The psychologist is continually evaluating the degree of disturbance a testee manifests, his test-taking attitude, and whether or not the test is appropriate for this person whose background is different from that of the groups used in standardizing the test.

MAJOR VARIETIES OF TESTS

Cronbach distinguishes between two broad classes of tests, according to whether they assess maximum performance and typical performance. In *maximum performance,* or *ability tests*, subjects are instructed to do the best they can. This classification would include tests of general mental ability, such as intelligence tests; tests of specific abilities, such as measurements of mechanical or musical ability; proficiency or achievement tests; and aptitude tests. In clinical practice the clinician frequently has a need to use intelligence tests, frequently the Stanford-Binet or Wechsler tests. In a neurological ward or a general medical hospital, he may make use of tests of intellectual deficit, such as the Reitan tests Some recent thinking has emphasized an approach to thinking of personality as ability (Wallace, 1966), but most personality tests are not based on this assumption.

The *typical,* or *characteristic performance tests* attempt to find out what a person usually does in various life situations. Qualities such as honesty and optimism are not abilities. Most people know how to be honest, but they may not typically act that way. Tests of this sort usually have no right or wrong answers, although the way they are scored may reflect implicit values. A low degree of abnormality, for example, or a high degree of ego strength, are usually considered desirable. Tests in this category include personality inventories, such as the Minnesota Multiphasic Personality Inventory; a great variety of projective techniques, such as the Rorschach and the Thematic Apperception Test; interest inventories such as the Strong Vocational Interest Blank and the Kuder Preference Record, measures of values and attitudes; behavior observations; and a variety of other tests and techniques.

In the 1960s psychologists began to make another important distinction between psychological variables measured by these typical performance tests—namely, the trait versus state distinction. The usual personality test attempts to measure *traits*—considered to be enduring predispositions to think or behave in a certain way, things such as introversion and extroversion, neuroticism and psychoticism, orality and anality, hostility, depression, hysteria, need for heterosexuality, and so on. In contrast, a number of psychologists (e.g., Johnson and Spielberger, 1968; McReynolds, 1968; Zuckerman et al., 1967) are now recognizing the importance of measuring *states*—thought of as more momentary and situation-oriented personality characteristics. A student is anxious before an examination, but this anxiety may have passed completely an hour later. A housewife is depressed after her husband scolds her about a poor meal; she is elated when he brings her flowers the next evening. Attempts are now being made to measure states as well as traits, and a number of new measurement problems are appearing. Because most existing tests are designed for trait measurement, most of our discussion focuses on them.

Combinations of tests are often used to study individuals. Sometimes a hospital or clinic administers a routine test battery to all new patients. In Appendix E we describe briefly thirty tests frequently used in clinical practice. The student of psychological assessment should have at least some knowledge of all these tests and should be able to find out more about them if necessary. Even more important than knowing specific tests is a knowledge of how to evaluate them. Many clinical psychologists are also involved in developing new tests for special clinical needs or for research. In the past it has been thought to be essential for a clinical psychologist to know thoroughly three or four of the widely used tests, such as MMPI, TAT, Rorschach, or Strong Vocational Interest Blank and to be able to evaluate the others competently; at present an alternative for some psychologists is to be able to develop and use assessment instruments for special purposes in connection with improvement programs, as Bijou and Peterson (1971) recommend in the paper discussed earlier in this chapter.

EVALUATION OF TESTS

In evaluating published tests, one may turn to several sources of information—test manuals, specimen sets, textbooks on testing (such as Anastasi, 1968, or Cronbach, 1970), and, most importantly, descriptions and reviews in the Buros *Mental Measurements Yearbooks* (especially those of 1959, 1965, and 1972). Tests that have not been published are harder to evaluate, but a book by Johnson and Bommarito (1971) provides information about unpublished children's tests. In the absence of such general sources, or as a supplement to them, one turns to research reports in journals and books. There are widely used tests such as the F-scale for authoritarianism that have never been issued in published form, although they appear in hundreds of articles. Finally, the person wishing to learn about a test may write for information to the author or to others who have used it.

In becoming acquainted with a test, it is usually a good idea to try it out on oneself while one is still as naïve as possible. The procedure will help one to get a "client's-eye view" and to raise questions about administration and interpretation. It is also wise to try the test out on a variety of people one knows, interviewing them about it afterward.

The process of becoming acquainted with a good test never ceases. As our familiarity increases, we usually see more and more in it. Thus older tests may be more valuable to the clinical psychologist than new ones—because he has built up his own dependable internalized methods of using them. Experienced Rorschachers, "MMPI'ers," or Wechsler specialists can somehow extract much more from a protocol or profile than the published reports claim for it. At the same time, we must remember that this kind of experience and clinical know-how has its dangers. One danger is that a clinician may become so "overly sold" on a test that he loses his objectivity and willingness to criticize it. He can no longer see its limitations. The antidote for such hardening of the testing arteries is to keep abreast on studies going on elsewhere and to conduct research checking on how the test is actually working out in one's own situation. Another danger is that habits of using old tests may prevent the clinician from perceiving assumptions underlying them and from trying new tests.

There are various practical considerations that enter into the evaluation of a particular test. What does a given testing procedure *cost in materials, training, time, and effort*? Is its contribution to decision making about the client worth the cost? Every test requires certain amounts of time from the patient, the examiner, the scorer, and the interpreter, but some are much more time-consuming than others. Paper-and-pencil tests such as the MMPI, CPI, and some intelligence tests require very little of the psychologist's time to administer them. They do require that the patient be free to spend perhaps an hour with the test blank, but time may not be much of a problem for persons on a hospital ward or in an out-patient clinic, where the patient has to do a good deal of waiting anyway. Another consideration is how much *interest* the test is likely to have for the individual tested. This is especially important with children. The items in such tests as the Stanford-Binet have been selected especially with this in mind. Another practical matter is the availability of *equivalent forms* if it is going to be necessary to repeat the test.

A psychologist in a particular clinic or hospital also needs to evaluate how well a test will fit into the general framework of local clinical procedures. He must be satisfied that a test being introduced will "pay off" in supplying answers and generating hypotheses that meet both his own needs and those of the institution for which he works. If such a test does not at first have *acceptability* to the clinician's colleagues, he may either drop it or convince them that it is worthwhile.

Last, and most important, the psychologist must evaluate the *technical adequacy* of a test he is considering for use. The American Psychological Association has published a useful reference, *Standards for Educational and Psychological Tests and Manuals* (APA, 1966b). Unfortunately, publishers of tests do not always furnish as much technical information as is needed for such an evaluation. Also, since each clinical situation is unique in some ways, what information they do give may not be relevant because of lack of correspondence between the situation from which studies have been reported and the situation for which the test is being considered. In evaluating the technical adequacy of tests, one must adopt a research attitude—a concern for evidence both positive and negative, a detached willingness to "test the test." Convincing sales talks or testimonials are no substitutes for statistical evidence.

Evaluation of technical adequacy involve questions about validity, reliability, objectivity of scoring, norms, and aids to interpretation. *Validity* is most important, here is the "meaning" of the test. We shall devote the next sections of the chapter to validity and reliability. Scoring objectivity is a problem only when judgment enters, where numbers must be assigned or the responses be classified by categories. Evidence for scoring objectivity or lack of it is often discussed under the term *inter-rater reliability*, the degree of similarity between the quantitative judgments made by several persons. *Test norms* permit us to know how a patient's performance compares with that of other persons with whom he may be appropriately compared. Test publishers often furnish norms for a number of different classes of subjects so that the appropriate comparisons can be made. Some research workers are beginning to stress the desirability of additional *aids to test interpretation*. For instance, test users can be supplied with a "cookbook," such as a list of adjectives or descriptive statements that have been shown to characterize high and low scorers. Some tests, such as the MMPI, have been adapted to automated computer programs that provide printouts of personality descriptions and reports on how past patients with such profiles have responded to treatment. (See Appendix C and Klett and Pumroy, 1971.) Undoubtedly there will be many additional developments along this line.

VALIDITY

Put in simplest terms, evidence about a test's validity answers such questions as: What does the test result mean? What is the test good for? What can be accomplished with it? Validity information provides evidence as to whether the test works or not. Cronbach (1970, p. 121) "Validity is high if a test gives the information the decision maker needs." Validity reaches out to something other than the test itself. One cannot simply ask: How valid is test X? The question should be: How valid is test X *for* differentiating between depression and schizophrenia, or *for* predicting whether a particular kind of therapy will be effective?

How does one make the connection between the test and the variable we would like to be describing or predicting? Sometimes we run across the term *face validity*. This term refers to the logical or apparent worth of the test. Common sense tells us when a questionnaire relates to health or to mathematical ability, and whether it appears to have good questions or not. The Rorschach inkblots are on the low end of the dimension of face validity; to most laymen, they appear to have no relation to diagnosing mental illness or judging intellectual processes. Face validity sometimes is important to get the acceptance of patients or one's colleagues, but one should not confuse apparent relevance with demonstrated validity. A behavioral check list used by ward attendants to get at the social adequacy of patients may have good face validity; the aide checks whether a patient dresses himself, whether he gets in fights, and so forth. Such a check list provides a good record of the patient's behavior. But when the psychologist attempts to generalize from this scale to likelihood of adjustment outside, he must demonstrate, for instance, that patients who rate high on the scale do better on trial visits than those rating low. Such demonstrations provide *empirical validity*.

There are four types of empirical validity: content, predictive, concurrent, and construct validity. *Content validity*, which is most like face validity, answers the test-user's question: How well does this test sample the behavior domain that I am interested in? Answers to this question are clearest with such tests as school achievement tests; the items of a geography test can be compared with a standard text to determine the percentage of major concepts and facts represented and the degree to which the test gives well-balanced coverage of topics. Even in personality inventories, a domain of items must be defined originally when the test is developed, and questions can be raised about the adequacy of representation of that domain. But when we come to projective techniques, it is much less clear what content validity means. Here we look not simply at the stimulus material, such as inkblots, but also at the content recorded and scored by the tester; do these results cover the content we wish to be covered? The same argument would apply to subtle items on a personality inventory (Wiener, 1948). In some instances, the process of clinical interpretation is very dependent on the psychologist; so content validity becomes a difficult and complex question.

The kind of validity most important for practical purposes is *predictive validity*. The question is how well the test results relate to future performance. To answer that question the researcher must correlate test findings with follow-up data employing a *criterion*, or a set of criteria, some measure of outcome that we are interested in. What proportion of boys obtaining an X score on a delinquency test actually come into trouble with the law? What are the chances that a given brain-function test will pick the locality in which a tumor, or other lesion, is found? What is the correlation between mothers' reports of effectiveness of reinforcements and the findings of clinicians carrying out a treatment program? The judgments about criteria and the measurement of them are sometimes very difficult. Psychiatric diagnoses have often been used as criteria; yet they may be more unreliable than the test itself. Other ratings of individuals by psychiatrists, psychologists, and other observers are frequently used as criteria, but their own validity is open to question.

The only difference between predictive and *concurrent validity* is time. Concurrent studies use criteria that exist at the time of the test. For instance, it might be useful to know that a life-history inventory could produce the same results as a lengthy interview. Also the psychologist will frequently want to know if a new intelligence test correlates well with an old, familiar one.

Construct validity answers the test-user's question: How well does this test reflect some trait, quality, or construct presumed to underlie performance on the test? The interest is not in direct sampling of behavior and its correlates, but in measuring a hypothesized or theoretical state, such as anxiety, ego strength, or intelligence. Anxiety cannot be measured directly, although the inference that one is "getting at" anxiety is justified if test performance can be shown to be related to such indicators as the tension reported by the patient, psychiatrists' ratings of anxiety, amount of palmar sweat, or other physiological indications. The term *indicator* is more appropriate in speaking of construct validity than the term *criterion* (Meehl, 1959b). Cronbach and Meehl (1955) speak of a set of interconnected indicators, the relevant conceptual framework, or model, as a *nomological net*. Both a logical and an empirical attack are required to develop a nomological net, and the procedure may be deductive or inductive. Deductively, the psychologist armed with his theory predicts that a particular sort of variation from person to person or from occasion to occasion will occur if he uses this test, and then he gathers data to discover how well his predictions are confirmed. Inductively, when he observes, for example, that on scale X, persons of some kinds score high, his hunch is that this is because they possess a hypothetical something he calls, let us say, "independence of judgment." From this inference he makes some predictions deductively and then proceeds to check them. It is ordinarily necessary to have many measures to establish the construct validity of a test. The evaluation of construct validity usually is associated with theoretical research. As valuable as that is, we need to remember that overemphasis on it may lead us to forget the practical side of psychological testing. Little (1959) has pointed out that construct validity is all right for theoretical psychology, but clinics and hospitals need answers to such questions as: Is this patient likely to attempt suicide? Will psychotherapy help enough to be worth diverting our limited staff? He emphasized the importance of "effective validity"—the making of predictive statements for practical use.

The correlation of test scores with a criterion is called a *coefficient of validity*. The size of validity coefficients is seldom very high, and we must be satisfied with different levels in different areas of testing. Ability tests, including intelligence (or general ability) tests, usually produce higher validity coefficients than do personality tests. In well-designed studies, the correlation between intelligence test scores and indexes of success in school or college generally fall between 0.40 and 0.60. Ghiselli (1955) has summarized hundreds of validity coefficients in research published between 1919 and 1955 on personnel selection and placement. The highest validity coefficient for intelligence tests was 0.61, and one test of mechanical comprehension gave a coefficient of 0.66. The average for all intelligence tests was 0.38, against criteria of successful outcomes of training programs but only 0.19 against criteria of success on the job. What correlated most highly with criteria of job success were indices from biographical data blanks—providing an average coefficient of 0.41. The importance of such life-history data will show up in several places in our discussion of assessment.

The many influences between the test measurement and the measurement of the criterion are well illustrated in Figure 9-1. It compares three types of personnel (or clinical) evaluation: one using inferences based on dynamic interpretation (a high level of inference, as mentioned in Chapter 6), another involving direct impressionistic evaluation from behavior samples, and another using psychometric prediction (the lowest level of inference, arrived at by a "cookbook"). The predictions are numbered 6a, 6b, and 6c on the figure, respectively. The three prediction situations clearly vary in the number of intervening stages and the corresponding chances for error. Simply because of

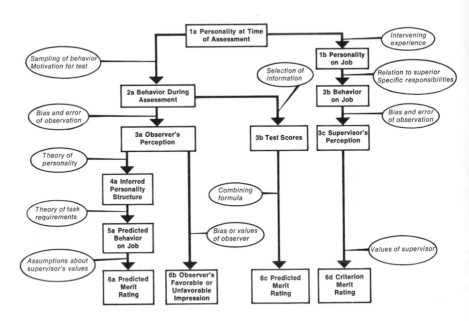

FIGURE 9-1 Stages in assessment and in criterion development. (After a figure from Cronbach, 1960, p. 591. Used with permission of Harper & Brothers.)

the greater number of intervening links (and more opportunity for "slippage"), the use of intervening theoretical models and clinical impressions is more hazardous than when straightforward psychometric and statistical methods are employed. The criterion labeled 6d is also affected by intervening stages, including not only a person's actual performance but also the supervisor's sampling of observations and his biases. Small wonder, then, that high-validity coefficients are hard to come by.

In order to judge whether a validity coefficient is high enough to warrant using a test, we can only judge in relation to its intended context. The basic question is whether or not the test provides an improvement over whatever alternative methods one has available. Furthermore, one should keep in mind that the most valid tests we have seldom account for more than half of the variation among individuals that we are interested in predicting. However, one may be satisfied to improve the accuracy of prediction even slightly if the test is easy to give or the decision is an extremely important one. Finally, making use of a validity coefficient, the test interpreter must determine if the group on which it is obtained is similar to the group he is predicting to and whether the client fits conditions under which the original group was tested.

RELIABILITY

Reliability refers to the consistency, reproducibility, generalizability, or accuracy of test results. To measure the consistency of a measuring device such as a test, it is necessary to take more than one measurement of the same variable, using the same subjects. If these supposedly parallel scores vary widely, the test cannot be relied upon, for its results are inconsistent. The larger the variability due to chance (by which we mean any factors irrelevant to test purposes), the less faith we can put in any score obtained from it. In interpreting test results we should think of a test score, such as a child's IQ of 115, not as a point, but as a sample with a range of scores. The child's "true" IQ probably falls somewhere between 110 and 120, assuming that the test is highly reliable. The less reliable the test, the wider the range within which the true score might fall. In order to use tests for individual prediction, reliability coefficients should be as high as possible, preferably about 0.90, based on a group similar in its range of scores to the kinds of people one is testing. The more the reported reliability coefficient falls below this figure, the more guarded one should be in statements one makes about individuals on the basis of their scores.

There are two major ways of measuring reliability. Repeating the same test after an interval and correlating the two sets of scores produces a *stability* coefficient. Administering two parallel forms on the same occasion, or scoring separately two parallel halves of a single form, makes it possible to compute an *equivalence* coefficient. Stability coefficients are more appropriate for some kinds of tests, equivalence coefficients for others. Since they reflect somewhat different aspects of reliability, it is desirable when possible to have both kinds of evidence.

It is in relation to reliability that the distinction between states and traits of personality becomes important. For state measures we do not expect or want high coefficients of stability. Using the Multiple Affect Adjective Check List (Zuckerman and Lubin, 1965), Zuckerman (1971) and colleagues asked subjects to describe themselves as they feel generally and as they feel at various moments by repeated testings. They demonstrated that equivalence reliability is high for both trait and state descriptions but that stability coefficients are high for trait conditions, low for state conditions.

Peak (1953) has elaborated on the equivalence concept using the term *functional unity*, pointing out that it is basic to measurement that we find "something that holds together" in the ongoing stream of behavior and interaction. To measure this unity operationally, such methods as item analysis, intertest correlations, and factor analysis may be used.

These basic concepts we have been discussing apply very broadly in assessment work. The relation between the concepts of reliability and validity can be seen if one thinks in terms of internal and external relations of the test—or for that matter not only tests but test batteries or a clinical team—any assessment system. Reliability deals with internal relations—the consistency within the system and its parts. Validity is concerned with external relations of a system with higher and lower systems—the relation of a test to other tests or to future outcomes. One can stop at any level or organization in the hierarchy of assessment and speak of these two concepts—the reliability and validity of items, of tests, of batteries of tests, of the clinician—battery system, of the psychiatric team.

INCREMENTAL VALUE OF ASSESSMENT TECHNIQUES

When a clinical decision is to be reached, the contribution each bit of information can make to the total picture has to be considered. How much, we wish to discover does any given assessment procedure add to the prediction obtainable from other sources of information? This is the question of *incremental utility*, or *incremental validity*, as Meehl (1959b) and Sechrest (1963) have termed it.

The first important question is: *Does an individual test or other assessment technique add anything to prediction over what we already know from the base rates for the appropriate population?* Meehl and Rosen (1955) mention a study (Hanvik, 1949) in which a scale was developed for differentiating between psychogenic and organic low-back pain. It was found that 70 percent of the psychogenic cases scored above a certain cutting score and 70 percent of the organic cases below. If this test is used in a neurology service where 90 percent of the patients are in fact organic, testing everyone to detect the psychogenic cases would yield a great many "false positives," people who were labeled psychogenic but were actually organic. However, such a situation would not be typical. More commonly the neurologist refers only questionable cases to the psychologist for testing. Thus the *base rates* (the statistics on incidence of the disorder) in which we are interested are those of the select group referred. If records of such past referrals or of patients with minimal signs show that 90 percent are ultimately diagnosed as psychogenic, a person achieving a high score on the test can be diagnosed as psychogenic, but low scores are difficult to interpret because the records indicate that *most* low-scoring patients also turn out to be psychogenic. Where the base rate is 90 percent in either direction, the test is of little value because knowledge of the base rates alone provides such high accuracy of classification. It is in situations where the base rates are closer to a 50–50 split that the tests are more likely to improve prediction. However, if a certain kind of decision is very important, such as in the detection of brain tumor or suicidal tendencies, the hospital may be willing to consider many "false positives" in order to catch the few "true positive" cases. In such a situation, even a test of low validity with adverse base rates may be useful.

Another problem of incremental validity arises when we ask *whether a given assessment procedure adds information beyond that available from necessary or routine techniques.* The most common question is whether a test contributes useful information beyond what is obtainable from the interview or case history discussed in Chapter 8. Winch and More (1956) have compared ratings given by judges using only interview information, only the case history, or only the TAT. These ratings were compared with criterion ratings derived from a panel of five experts who used all three kinds of information. Winch and More found that the interview and case-history data together correlated more highly with the criterion than either alone but that the TAT made no statistically additional contribution. Sechrest (1963) also concluded that biographical and interview data carry most of the validity in an assessment battery. The question can also be asked in reverse—whether the interview contributes anything beyond what a simpler and less time-consuming test can give. Several studies have shown that clinicians using interviews could not improve on the prediction of academic success made on the basis of ability tests alone (Sarbin, 1943; McClelland, 1942; Kelly and Fiske, 1951). On the other hand, Sines (1959) found that the interview coming early in an assessment series did contribute to the prediction of the personality picture that psychotherapists developed later. When we put all this evidence together, it points to the need for constant questioning on the part of the psychologist in any particular situation about how to carry out his appraisal tasks most effectively and economically. He cannot simply rely on a standard set of procedures that has been found useful in other situations.

ORGANIZING AND COMMUNICATING THE RESULTS OF APPRAISALS

Obviously the work of the psychologist is all for naught if his findings are not put to use. One link in the information chain that is sometimes left weak or dangling is the reporting of assessment results. The knowledgeable psychologist takes into consideration the needs of the recipient of information and the responsibility he has to assist in image making and decision making. He has analyzed the referral question and developed a picture of how his assessment findings may fit most effectively into the ongoing agency system.

Setting aside the direct reporting of findings to the client, which is discussed and illustrated elsewhere, the psychologist is usually involved in oral and written reports to the *primary recipient* or in written reports to a *secondary recipient*. (This distinction parallels the terms of Hammond and Allen, 1953, concerning primary and secondary readers of written reports.) The primary recipient is the person to whom the report originally goes—usually another professional person, such as a psychiatrist, educator, or worker in a social agency. The secondary recipient is a person who does not work directly with the client but administers programs or conducts research involving the client. Sometimes two different reports will be necessary; we shall concentrate here on the primary recipient, since it is he who is most important for client welfare. Also we will emphasize in what follows the production of written reports, although the reader must understand that effective communication usually requires oral and written interchange, both in defining the original purposes of appraisal and in transmitting the results.

Organizing Material for a Case Report

What does a psychologist do when he is sitting at his desk with all the information he has collected spread before him? There are the test records, the patient's chart, and statistical comparisons and predictions. He has already started making inferences and interpretations of the case, and is now beginning to organize and select from among these many impressions. Sometimes it is necessary to read through case material many times before themes begin to emerge and conclusions become clear. He checks whatever statistical data are available. As groupings of notable data grow from the case itself, he begins to get ideas and hypotheses about basic themes in this person's life. He checks these hypotheses against other data and develops subjective impressions of the probabilities attached to each of these hypotheses.

As he organizes the material into a report, the clinician asks himself the questions this report is to answer. If his purpose is differential diagnosis, he will be seeking evidence both for and against each of various possible diagnoses. If decisions involving court action or school placement are to be made, he looks for evidence in the record that would predict good or poor adjustment in specific situations.

There are certain kinds of evidence he pays particular attention to. *Congruencies* between several tests, or between repetitions of a test, are good clues. When evidence for schizophrenic behavior and ways of thinking is found in the MMPI, the Rorschach, and from his own observation, the clinician will be more certain of his diagnosis. *Discrepancies* among various tests or observations may be equally significant, although they may raise more difficulties. *Deviant behavior* of any sort is of unusual interest. After considerable experience in a given working situation, the clinician develops more or less explicit expectations of what his clients or patients are going to do when confronted with certain tests, certain turns in interviews, and the like. *Typical behavior* must also be noted, for it is the usual, the typical, conduct of a person with which unusual acts are compared and which will figure heavily in any decisions and planning with regard to him. Every psychologist needs to bear in mind the dangers of "overpathologizing" people. One of the greatest advantages of standardized procedures is that they provide norms against which to check clinical judgments that might otherwise run to extremes.

Improving Communication in Reports

The most important thing to keep asking oneself as one writes a report is: What are the main points that emerge from this particular psychological work-up and how am I to make sure the reader will understand them? Unfortunately there is no one clear, simple outline for every report. As Tallent (1960, p. 5), after years of research on writing reports, has stated, "The conclusion is overpowering that there is no best way or correct way to carry out this duty." It makes a big difference if the report is to be read by a teacher in a class for retarded children, a counselor in a high school, a social worker in a welfare agency, a pediatrician in a remote town, or a psychiatrist working in the next office. The level of language used, the length of the report, and the kinds of things reported will be determined by the interests and responsibilities of the reader vis-à-vis the patient and by the reader's sophistication in psychological matters.

In what kind of language should the report be written? Since most of us are prone to assume that other people understand what we say and write better than they usually do, misjudging the reader's ability to understand our language is a frequent cause of poor report writing. Klopfer has asserted, "If the clinical psychologist really comprehends what he is attempting to communicate, a technical language level is really unnecessary" (1960, p. 58). He urges clinicians to write in a basic English that any reasonably intelligent layman can understand. He illustrates his recommendation with several "translations" from psychological and psychoanalytic jargon. For instance, a patient's "great desire for affiliation" becomes the patient "would very much like to have friends"; and "personality dynamics" becomes "interesting characteristics of this person" (1960, pp. 59–61). As a check on the communication value of a report not intended for fellow professionals, it is often a good idea to have a secretary or other nonprofessional person read it over and tell you what seems vague, obscure, or meaningless.

How detailed should the report be? Should the psychologist report the IQ? Should he quote a client's remarks verbatim? Should he only report general conclusions? Again the role and interests of the reader should be kept in mind. A vocational counselor might wish to have exact details on a person's intellectual level and tested vocational interests that a psychiatrist would want to know about only in a general way. Many psychologists have experienced instances in which readers such as physicians and teachers have handed psychological reports directly over to the patient's or client's relatives to read. If there can be the slightest question of this happening without prior planning, a report should be boldly marked "confidential."

On the other hand, a report with no detail, along with a barrage of abstract generalities, is hopelessly vague and not likely to be convincing or persuasive. Some evidence and a concrete example or two, at least, have a place in every psychological report. In fact, one study of criticisms of psychological reports by psychiatrists revealed a good number of complaints over their lack of raw data and their wordiness (Tallent and Reiss, 1959). There is a distinction between *psychometric detail* and *behavioral illustration*. Statements such as "the Rorschach F plus is 69 percent" or "Block Design on the Wechsler is the highest of the Performance subtests" communicate very little. However, illustrative statements made by the patient or samples of his behavior may clarify a more formal description a great deal. For instance, a patient's bizarre definitions on the Wechsler might well illustrate schizoid tendencies, or a patient's particular words in completing a sentence might be cited to throw light on his attitudes toward his family. Such direct quotations and reports of behavior illustrating salient features of the client's behavior may be as important as anything that comes up in an early interview or in therapy.

How long should a report be? Probably most psychological reports tend to be too long. Foster (1951) states that it is a rare report that needs to be longer than one page, but few psychologists would agree to such a rigid rule. The needs of readers and the complexities of cases vary too widely to make a definite limitation. The most important thing is that the report communicate clearly just what it is intended to say. Occasionally an involved case intensively studied will require several pages, but such a report should always contain a summary planned to save reading time when the reader is in a hurry, and often, in addition to this, a covering letter should call attention to outstanding points.

In a number of publications over the last few years, psychologists have denounced "pseudo-reporting," a kind of writing that substitutes generalities, trivialities, and ambiguities for specific, clear, and practical communication. Meehl (1956) has coined the term *Barnum effect* to stigmatize spurious descriptions composed of a mixture of stereotypes and evasion. Tallent (1958) has labeled another kind of report an *Aunt Fanny report* because it contains mostly information that would be true of anybody's "Aunt Fanny." Klopfer (1960) has condemned reports that seem subtly designed to play up to a psychiatrist or to sell points like merchandise as *Madison Avenue reports.*

The problem of individualizing a psychological report is not an easy one. As Forer (1949), Sundberg (1955), and O'Dell (1972) have shown in research studies with college students attempting to identify their own personality descriptions, it is extremely difficult to differentiate fake "universally valid" statements from bona fide attempts at interpretation. Indeed, both the students and their friends were unable to do so. Tallent (1958) has made several suggestions for individualizing the psychological reports. They include recommendations to indicate the individual's special characteristics as exactly as possible by illustrating how a trait is manifested, or by describing the situations in which such behavior becomes overt or important, and to avoid "shotgun" listing of all possible findings, "wastebasket" classifications, and vague generalities; in addition, one should make an honest statement of the circumstances of his testing and observation and the limitations of his procedures. Appendix F has illustrations of several psychological reports to assist the reader in development of this important art.

MISCELLANEOUS RECOMMENDATIONS ON ASSESSMENT

In the last few chapters we have covered a great deal of territory. We have not gone into detail about assessment techniques; that is done in special courses and through the supervised practical experiences of students. What we have tried to present is a point of view. Summarizing a number of points and adding others, we would call the following to the reader's attention:

1. All assessment is part of an ongoing clinical process. It is typically an interpersonal event and it is within a social context. As such, it must be interpreted in that context.

2. Of primary importance is the clarification of the assessment questions. The psychologist should always study a referral problem to ascertain what the referring person needs and what the alternatives for disposition are.

3. Interviewing and observation are basic tools of the clinician, requiring much skill and training.

4. As a measuring instrument, interviewing leaves much to be desired. Studies of interviewer bias and of the reliability of psychiatric diagnoses (Matarazzo, 1965a) give mixed results. In general the broader the categories in which people are to be placed and the more clearly structured the interview is, the higher the reliability. Brief interviews (Wittson and Hunt, 1951) have been found to be valid for gross screening for psychiatric disability in the military

service. Interviews are not just measuring devices; they are means for establishing a relationship and they provide what most people want if they are to work together—face-to-face observation; nothing else seems as convincing.

5. Interviews and some check lists and projective techniques are often useful for quick scanning purposes. In Cronbach's terms (1970), they may not have high *fidelity* (high reliability and validity), but they do have a wide *bandwidth*. They provide an opportunity to explore a variety of topics and obtain many small samples of the client's functioning. Initially, such a scanning operation is almost always necessary in clinical work.

6. After broad scanning identifies problems or opportunities for improvement, most assessment requires more detailed probing of specific areas. The clinician needs to develop a battery of procedures for going into depth in the particular kinds of problems coming to his clinic. The more detailed procedures may be interviews, tests, experimental tryouts of treatment, home observations, and so on.

7. The clinician should know the advantages and disadvantages of tests in order to combine and use them flexibly. He should remember that the value of tests depends on the competence of the interpreter. He should avoid becoming overly dependent on tests as an "easy way out" to cover up lack of analysis of the case, lack of other assessment skills, or a fear of becoming personally involved.

8. The clinician should be on the lookout for cultural, social, and ethnic differences. These will undoubtedly affect many of the assessment procedures he uses.

9. Wherever possible and appropriate to the problem, the clinician should use "hard" procedures, such as standardized tests and statistical prediction methods. There is ample evidence of the limitations of even the well-trained clinician in processing information when compared against tested psychometric methods. Still the clinician has an important place in the whole clinical operation, only a small part of which is now covered by statistical procedures.

10. The clinician should develop local base rates, expectancy tables, norms, and reliability and validity evidence. Experience tables based on cases handled in a clinic or other agency are fairly easy to develop and will pay off in improvements in the helping organization or agency over time.

11. In collecting new information, restrict attention to a limited amount of information. Strange as it at first seems, it may not be helpful to have a lot of information. The fact that the successful statistical procedures make use of only a few variables (usually no more than three or four) suggests that the clinician may be trying to take in too many things at once. Goldberg (1968b, 1971) has produced evidence that when a person is asked to judge any trait in others, he uses only a few items of information, even though many more are available; so far research suggests that items are most effectively combined in a linear fashion rather than by more complex patterning. The masses of information on their cases which clinics typically collect may actually increase confusion rather than

accuracy. The heart of the undertaking consists not in increasing the amount of data, but in getting the right kind.

12. Be especially careful about making predictions concerning "low probability" events. The lesson from a knowledge of base rates is that the probabilities are increasingly against the clinician as he makes predictions of events very different from those that usually occur. It is very tempting to show original and dramatic clinical insights, but these need to be checked very carefully against the probabilities.

13. Do not jump to an overly high inference level. It is possible to get too far away from one's data. A clinician faces two dangers: (a) being overly simple and thus missing the latent and unconscious meanings of things, or (b) being overly abstract and subtle and thus missing the obvious meanings of things. At the present time the second type of error appears to be more common (Soskin, 1954, 1959). This warning against high-level theorizing applies to practical problems only. For research and theorizing, let us leave the doors open to any kind of speculation.

14. When interpreting data be very skeptical of principles and premises that are not tested empirically. The largest difficulty for the clinician according to Sarbin, Taft, and Bailey (1960) is the failure to use major premises that are empirically supported. The clinician in his search for certainty and desire to see patients helped is lured to consider theoretical and authoritative assertions that have not been tested, such as: "Psychotherapy can succeed only in cases where the patient's ego strength is adequate." Whether the clinician should or should not use such additional considerations in any given case is open to debate, but is is clear that he should not let them lead him to disregard empirical evidence that is available.

15. Become thoroughly acquainted with the facts of the situation you are trying to predict. This may be the most important counsel of all. The outcome you are trying to predict determines what information you need to collect as relevant to the situation. In clinical work we often have too vague a notion of the possible alternative courses of action, such as various treatments that might prove beneficial to a given patient. If we are going to predict whether or not he will have to return to the hospital, we need to know what his home and job are like. If we are predicting his response to group therapy, we need to know the kinds of groups in which he might be placed.

16. Whenever possible, make use of judges other than yourself—especially those similar in background to the person being studied. Studies (e.g., Chowdry and Newcomb, 1952) have shown that one predicts best for people similar to oneself. Working-class people can predict most accurately what other working-class people are likely to do. Religious people can predict best the responses of religious people. Part of one's ability to predict comes from the mere fact of similarity. Being unlike the person you are trying to understand constitutes a difficult handicap and the clinician needs to recognize his limitations.

17. Keep a record of your own "batting average." Every clinician has his special strengths and weaknesses, but many do not recognize what these are. It should be possible for any clinician to develop a form for recording predictions in some exact fashion at the time he writes his assessment report. Then he could follow up on these predictions regularly and see with what kinds of patients and problems he judges well and where his difficulties occur.

18. Remember that the utility of assessment depends on effective communication, both oral and written. Reports require careful study of the findings in relation to the users of the results, using appropriate language and detail. As indicated in examples at the end of the chapter, studies show a varying effectiveness of psychological reports (Garfield, Heine, and Leventhal, 1954; Mintz, 1968; Smyth and Reznikoff, 1971), one indicating that psychiatrists made use of the reports only 20 percent of the time (Moore et al., 1968). Differences in interpretations of terms in reports contribute to the communication problem (Cuadra and Albaugh, 1956). Checking on how well he is communicating is another assignment for the alert psychologist.

SUMMARY

Considerable rethinking of the place of tests in psychological practice has been going on in recent years, but a recent survey indicates that some tests are still being very widely used. In the present transition period, many psychologists are still serving as members of clinical teams, contributing their special skills to the solution of diagnostic and therapeutic problems, but others are faced with the task of developing new appraisal procedures for particular purposes. Basic psychometric and interpretive concepts are applicable in both areas.

It is important for the psychologist to consider the whole testing situation as it appeared to the client and make allowances for any aspect of it that may have influenced the results obtained.

A standardized test is one in which testing procedures are specified precisely and norms are provided so that an individual's score can be compared with the scores others in a specified population have made. It can be considered objective if responses are in a form facilitating agreement between scorers. Clinical procedures are never completely objective. Tests can be classified as indicators of maximum performance or typical performance.

In evaluating tests one considers many questions, especially those concerning its technical adequacy. One always looks for evidence about the test's validity (What is it measuring?) and reliability (How accurately or consistently does it measure this?). There are several different kinds of evidence bearing on validity and reliability. Beyond the validity of single assessment techniques, it is important to consider incremental utility as well—the question of how much this technique adds to the others being used in the appraisal process. The process of communicating results is another part of the evaluation of a psychologist's effectiveness in appraisal.

SUGGESTED READINGS

General introductions to tests and assessment devices

A large number of books provide general introductions to testing and assessment. Tyler (1971) furnishes elementary principles and examples of testing. Cronbach (1970) and Anastasi (1968) present more comprehensive introductions. Some books deal with broad problems of personality measurement, for example, Fiske (1971), Kleinmuntz (1967), Jackson and Messick (1967), and Wiggins (1972). Mischel's book (1968) is a strong statement against trait psychology and in favor of behavioral and situational approaches Megargee (1966) has an excellent collection of research articles on clinical assessment.

Some books present specialized coverage, for example, Palmer (1970) and Johnson and Bommarito (1971) on assessment of children; Mittler (1970) on mental and physical handicaps; Rapaport, Gill, and Schafer (edited by Holt, 1968) on diagnostic testing; Murstein (1965) and Rabin (1968) on projective techniques; and Bass and Berg (1959) on objective personality assessment. The March 1969 *American Psychologist* was a special issue on instrumentation in psychology; several articles cover such topics as computers in behavior therapy, use of film, automation of testing, and electronic data collection in the field. Klett and Pumroy (1971) discuss use of computers in processing personality information.

Buros presents reviews of published tests and techniques in his several *Mental Measurements Yearbooks*, of which the most important are those of 1959, 1965, and 1972 and *Personality Tests and Reviews* (1970). From time to time the *Annual Review of Psychology* reviews pertinent topics, for example, Fiske and Pearson (1970) on theory and techniques of personality measurement, and Molish (1972) on projective techniques. McReynolds in *Advances in Psychological Assessment* (1968, 1971) has published many useful reports related to clinical assessment.

In Appendix E of this book the reader will find thirty commonly used psychological tests and techniques together with brief descriptions and additional references.

Masling, J. The influence of situational and interpersonal variables in projective testing. *Psychological Bulletin*, 1960, *57*, 65–85.

This review is applicable to all assessment procedures, not just projective techniques. Masling reports research findings on the effects of different instructions in taking projective tests; effects of special influences upon the situation, such as stress, drugs, or hypnosis; examiner influence; and influence of the subject on the examiner. The bulk of the studies do indeed indicate that changes occur as a result of such influences, but the extent of these influences and the interrelationships among them are still to be discovered. Also see Masling (1966).

Goldman, L. *Using tests in counseling*, 2nd ed. New York: Appleton-Century-Crofts, 1971.

Goldman covers the selection, administration, interpreting, and reporting of tests with an emphasis on educational–vocational purposes, but with a sensitivity to "clinical" needs. Of particular value to the reader would be the sections on statistical aids to interpretation and the case illustrations. The cases illustrate both statistical and clinical interpretations, with such problems as deciding on vocational plans, planning about about military service, and considering whether to marry or have a career.

Meehl, P. E., and Rosen, A. Antecedent probability and the efficiency of psychometric signs, patterns, or cutting scores. *Psychological Bulletin*, 1955, *52*, 194–216.

This is an important article describing base rates and their relationship to psychological assessment. The authors point out many of the errors that are likely to be made in clinical research. They show that the practical value of any psychometric score depends jointly on its intrinsic validity and the distribution of the criterion variable in the clinical population. Information on base rates of patients' characteristics can be readily obtained by file research. They show how test development should ordinarily be concentrated on characteristics having base rates near a 50–50 split. Dawes (1962) explicates the problem further, saying that the crucial problem is what proportion of a group representative of the general population would be allocated to the criterion groups by the test—a question seldom asked in research.

Levy, M. R. Issues in the personality assessment of lower class patients. *Journal of Projective Techniques and Personality Assessment*, 1970, *34*, 6–9.

Most of the concern expressed in the 1960s about testing of the poor and minority groups revolved around intelligence evaluation. Levy points out that there are also dangers of bias in personality testing. He reviews several research reports of socioeconomic differences on results of both projective and objective tests. Factors involved in projective techniques include differences between examiner and client in language used, unfamiliarity with the testing situation, verbal expressiveness of different classes, and the middle-class backgrounds of interpreters. Adler (1971) found that figure drawings show differences related more to socioeconomic status than ethnicity of patients. Trachtman (1971) demonstrated that clinicians informed that Rorschachs came from alleged lower- or middle-class clients showed a class-related diagnostic bias. However, the backgrounds of the clinicians themselves did not seem to be related to bias.

Klopfer, W. G. *The psychological report: use and communication of psychological findings*. New York: Grune & Stratton, 1960.

This is an excellent book on report writing, based on a great deal of practical experience in varied settings. It discusses the purpose, focus, style, language, and organization of the psychological report. It describes an excellent method for organizing the multiplicity of assessment material in preparation for writing a report. It contains numerous extracts from reports and one complete case. For another reference on report writing, which pays particular attention to the language and construction of reports, see Hammond and Allen (1953). The book by Huber (1961) also provides some very helpful suggestions and illustrations concerning report writing.

Davidson, in a readable series in *Mental Hospitals* (1957–1958), considers the common (and not so common) descriptive words which are the basic palette for the descriptive canvas of a psychological report. He pays careful attention to feeling tones and to etymology. For instance, he says, "See the wilderness in 'bewildered.' A wilderness is a waste, a trackless, pathless waste. When you are in a wilderness you don't know where to turn . . . Bewildered then means 'lost in a wilderness.' By contrast, examine the word 'distracted' . . . Its Latin forebear *trahere* means to pull or draw; distracted means 'pulled apart.' " Davidson helps with the understanding and the selection of the most appropriate descriptive terms.

Holtzman, W. H. The changing world of mental measurement and its social significance. *American Psychologist*, 1971, *26*, 546–553.

In a presidential address to the APA Division on Evaluation and Measurement, Holtzman reviewed the criticisms of testing, including the growing meritocracy that has been built around traditional schools and jobs. He calls for recognition of linguistic and cultural variability and for ways of valuing competencies such as social leadership, self-awareness, regard for human rights, and social responsibility, which have not been important in traditional academic pursuits.

Other papers taking new looks at assessment and social problems include Greenspoon and Gersten (1967) and Anastasi (1967). The APA (1970) issued a statement on psychological assessment and public policy with the following points about policy implications: Individuals should be protected from unwarranted inferences from poorly equipped assessors; the person should be protected against unfavorable evaluation based on obsolete information; he must be protected against unnecessary intrusions into his privacy; and conditions should facilitate research on new and improved assessment procedures.

RESEARCH EXAMPLES

Scott, W. A., and Johnson, R. C. Comparative validities of direct and indirect personality tests. *Journal of Consulting and Clinical Psychology*, 1972, *38*, 301–318.

One of the fundamental questions about assessment is whether it is better to conduct measurements by direct self-reports or by indirect methods, such as used in projective techniques or physiological procedures. Self-report is more common because of its convenience and the theoretical argument that self-observation and verbal behavior are important. Indirect measures are used because of the presumed nonobjectivity of clients and their inability to describe themselves. Scott and Johnson point out that there are very few studies comparing the two approaches, despite the practical and theoretical importance of the dilemma.

In a series of three studies, Scott and Johnson asked subjects (college students or prison inmates) to take both direct and indirect tests; then they compared the results with criteria of validity, such as friends' ratings or expert judgment. The content consisted of the following: (1) political and social attitudes, either directly or indirectly expressed in a task of judging effectiveness of arguments; (2) personal motives, such as needs for achievement or affiliation, either expressed directly, as on the Edwards Personal Preference Schedule, or expressed indirectly, as with stories told about the TAT; and (3) three questionnaires related to prisoners' attitudes, evaluations of others' attitudes, and choices of outcomes for imaginary situations.

Scott and Johnson found that correlations of criteria with direct self-report measures were superior to those with indirect measures for the college student groups. The reliability of the measures for the prisoners was low; indirect measures were not superior to direct self-reports, although the authors expected considerable defensiveness or deception on the self-reports. Scott and Johnson conclude that the direct measures show an overall superiority.

Mischel (1972) and McClelland (1972) present reactions immediately following the article by Scott and Johnson. Both point out the limitations of the instruments used, most of which were new. Mischel indicates that the issue of direct versus indirect personality assessment is a significant one. He argues that the relation between observed behaviors and inferred states is a very tenuous one that presents many problems for indirect measurement with its high reliance on clinical judgment. He concludes that the findings in this study support the utility of direct measures. Mischel advocates treating behaviors as samples rather than signs of underlying states or traits.

McClelland takes a contrary point of view, revealed by the title of his article, "Opinions predict opinions: so what else is new?" He says the predictor and criterion measures used by Scott and Johnson both rely on similar processes of coding thoughts, so that friends' or judges' opinions are likely to be similar to the subject's. McClelland, who has done a great deal of research using TAT-like methods to measure achievement and other personality needs, says he wishes to get behind the common coding processes to the raw behavior they represent. Scott and Johnson in a rejoinder (1972b) recognize some of the criticisms but point out possible directions to go; they indicate the great difficulty in getting criteria from natural situations.

This series of papers would provide many ideas and references for those who wish to pursue this important line of inquiry. The issue of direct versus indirect personality assessment could be as generative of research as clinical versus statistical prediction was in the 1950s and 1960s. Those interested in such an endeavor might well note Allport's belief that direct, conscious report of self about personality was especially valuable with normal as distinguished from maladjusted subjects. Davids (1955), in a study of direct and indirect measures, also points out that the test-taking attitude affects responses, too—especially depending on the subject's idea about what the results will be used for. Another important consideration in further research is the need to find ways of interrelating different "levels" of personality or, more properly, different forms of reports about persons. Leary (1957) was one of the few psychologists who developed a system for measuring unconscious expressions, self-report, and observations of others on the same dimensions. Cattell also has done extensive research on different methods of personality investigation and description (e.g., see Cattell and Warburton, 1967).

Demming, J. A., and Pressey, S. L. Tests "indigenous" to the adult and older years. *Journal of Counseling Psychology*, 1957, *4*, 144–148.

The authors argue that most intelligence tests are constructed to fit the interests and problems of children or young adults. The decline in the curve of intellectual ability beyond middle age may appear greater than it is, owing to lack of items appropriate for the older persons. In order to develop a test with suitable content, the authors attempted to select items related to the everyday life of older adults. They developed three objective tests covering (1) use of the yellow pages of a telephone directory, (2) common legal terms, and (3) information on people who perform services needed in everyday life.

The authors administered these three new tests to a sample of inmates of a state penitentiary aged twenty to fifty years, most of whom were in their thirties, and to elderly persons in evening school classes and Golden Age Clubs. In addition to the new tests they also gave these subjects the Army Beta, the Otis Self-Scoring test, the Minnesota Paper Formboard, and the Bennett Mechanical Comprehension test.

The results, shown in tables, indicate a progressive decline on the four "traditional" tests with age and increases on the three new tests. The authors conclude that the tests they developed might have value in assessing the practical information of older people who are to be returned from institutions to the community.

This study, although limited in many ways and certainly in need of repetition, does suggest a very interesting and important point for the study of elderly persons. Just as it would be inappropriate to expect a young child to be interested in purchasing real estate or qualified for driving a car, so it seems inappropriate to expect elderly people to be proficient in childish activities. With a rapidly increasing number of elderly people in our population, psychologists are going to be faced more and more with the problem of discovering what older people can successfully do and at the same time are really motivated to do in daily living. For further information on the problem of geriatrics and aging, see the review by Inglis (1958) of methods of assessing cognitive deficit in elderly psychiatric patients, also the appropriate chapters in Birren (1959).

Baughman, E. E. An experimental analysis of the relationship between stimulus structure and behavior on the Rorschach. *Journal of Projective Techniques*, 1959, *23*, 134–183.

In an excellent review made by Baughman earlier (1958b), he had reported that he found a remarkably small number of studies out of the thousands on the Rorschach in which stimulus properties had been systematically varied. The purpose of this study was to study how Rorschach responses changed in a normal population as a function of several stimulus properties of the inkblots.

The subjects were 648 employees of an insurance company. The subjects were divided into eight groups equated for age, sex, IQ, and education. Two of the eight groups were given the standard Rorschach; the rest were given specially modified forms of the test in which the modifications were made in the color, shading, and figure-ground contrast of the blots, while their basic form was kept the same.

The resulting data are presented in detail so that students and users of the Rorschach can make use of the tables as basic references in their work. The major point, supported by his statistical analysis, is that the properties of inkblots other than form do affect the responses of subjects in contrast to what had been found in some earlier, more limited studies. In discussing the results, Baughman states, however, that the effect of structure upon content is fundamental. It can be seen that some scores (such as for Movement, Animal percent, and Populars) are related directly to content, but other scores not directly related to content (such as scores for Detail and Space) are also linked to form. Baughman concludes that it is difficult to generalize regarding color and shading effects and the context of each individual card must be considered. This study is interesting for its experimental variation of Rorschach stimuli, and its norms are valuable because the number of subjects is large. The study does not contribute anything directly to the question of the validity of the test. Baughman does have something to say about examiner reliability.

In other articles (1958a, 1959a) he has presented a standardized method of inquiry for the Rorschach. (In administering the Rorschach the subject is first asked to free associate to the inkblots; subsequently he is asked to explain where and why he saw what he reported; this latter part of the administration is called inquiry.) Baughman argues that the usual approach in inquiry leaves too much room for variation among examiners and is one of the reasons for the disagreements among different Rorschach studies.

Gough, H. G. Theory and measurement of socialization. *Journal of Consulting Psychology*, 1960, *24*, 23–30.

This article presents the theory and development of the Socialization scale of the CPI (Gough, 1957). The author points out the similarity of his theoretical position with that of G. H. Mead: socialized behavior is behavior based on a proper viewing of oneself as a social object. Gough's major point is that a scale measuring such a theoretical dimension should not just separate delinquents from nondelinquents but should differentiate along the whole range of the socialization continuum.

In the main body of the article means and standard deviations for the So (Socialization scale) are reported on forty-one research samples, totaling 1,294 male delinquents and criminals and 9,001 male nondelinquents, 784 female delinquents, and 9,776 female nondelinquents. A rank ordering of the various samples on the So scale, which is a psychological measure, agrees closely with the way they would be ranked sociologically, according to their actual adjustment to the standards of society. Those nominated as "best citizens" in high school are at the top of the list, followed by applicants for medical school and banking executives. At the bottom of the list are inmates of federal reformatories. Several studies by other investigators demonstrate the validity of the scale over the whole socialization continuum.

This article is a demonstration of the theoretical foundaiton of an empirically developed scale. The CPI was mainly developed by selecting from an item pool those items which statistically differentiated between normal and deviant groups. In the development of the So scale, items were selected to differentiate also between gradations of behavioral deviation. The CPI aims to measure "folk concepts" of interpersonal dimensions. Those dimensions, such as socialization, responsibility, and dominance, are presumed to be transcultural (not peculiar to the culture in the United States).

Gough has reported evidence that the validity of the So scale holds in several other countries (Gough, 1960a; Gough and Sandhu, 1964; Mizushima and DeVos, 1967). In other studies Gough has developed an index of *social maturity*, which is not the same as *socialization*. (For instance, an oversocialized person may act in an immature or inappropriate way in certain situations.) In a research study, Gough (1971a) found with a set of occupational groups that his social maturity index correlated highly with rated levels of social maturity. He illustrates with two cases of men scoring high on social maturity who show rational independence, acceptance of self and others, and openness to innovation. Those wishing to read extensively about the CPI should see Megargee (1972).

McClelland, J. N., and Rhodes, F. Prediction of job success for hospital aides and orderlies from MMPI scores and personal history data. *Journal of Applied Psychology*, 1969, *53*, 49–54.

This study is an example of what some clinical psychologists might do to improve the functioning of their institution. Selection of the best kind of nurses' aides and hospital orderlies is important both for the institution and the patients. The authors used eighteen MMPI scores and ten biographical information items from application blanks as predictors and ten ratings of performance by supervisors (such as quality of work, absences, resourcefulness) as criterion measures. Records of over fifty aides and fifty orderlies working in a general hospital were available, the numbers varying somewhat in different analyses.

Correlations between single predictors and single criteria were small, but a corrected multiple correlation coefficient of 0.48 was obtained between each weighted composite criterion and combined MMPI and biographic predictors. The background data, such as marital status, were relatively more important as predictors. In general the findings were similar to other studies. The study was based on those employed, not unselected applicants.

Kulik, J. A., Stein, K. B., and Sarbin, T. R. Dimensions and patterns of adolescent antisocial behavior. *Journal of Consulting and Clinical Psychology*, 1968, *32*, 375–382.

In this and a follow-up study (Stein, Sarbin, and Kulik, 1971) these authors considered the broad area of adolescent antisocial behavior and undertook what was in effect an attempt to identify patterns of delinquent behavior and to establish the beginning of a sound classification scheme. Methodological problems, such as inadequate population sampling, narrow range of considered antisocial behaviors, and the confounding of dimensions of conduct with types of persons—a shortcoming that follows from a search for pure types of delinquent—have weakened much previous work in this area.

The authors proceeded to identify four dimensions of antisocial behavior using a cluster-analysis procedure to examine Delinquency Checklist data from three separate samples of boys: 100 incarcerated delinquents plus 100 high school boys, 100 incarcerated delinquents, and 505 high school boys. The separate analyses determined the stability across samples of the four dimensions, which were (1) Delinquent Role, (2) Drug Usage, (3) Parental Defiance, and (4) Assaultiveness. The validity of these dimensions was demonstrated by significant mean differences in dimension scores between matched delinquent and nondelinquent samples.

The authors' next step is analogous to asking: What characteristic profiles occur on these four dimensions? An inverse cluster analysis was performed on DCL data from all 391 delinquents. Seven patterns of antisocial behavior were identified through which 346 of the 391 boys could be classified. These seven pattern types were named (I) Mild, (II) Parentally defiant mild, (III) Average, (IV) Non-parentally defiant, (V) Assaultive gang, (VI) Drug using, and (VII) Parentally defiant. For example, taking a mean of 50 and a sigma of 10, the profile for Type I, Mild, was Delinquent role 35, Drug usage 43, Parental defiance 38, and Assaultiveness 43. For Type VI, Drug using, elevations were 55, 66, 46, and 40, respectively.

Of the classical conflict—criminal—retreatist divisions of delinquency, the dimensions and pattern types established in the analysis generally support the notion of a retreatist or drug orientation (dimension 2) and a conflict orientation (dimensions 1 and 4). The authors note, however, that their data do not support the existence of a preprofessional criminal at this age.

The analysis points to the importance of conflict with the parents as a part of antisocial behavior itself, although it showed differences on the dimension between Negro and white delinquents, conflict with parents being nearly absent in largely Negro delinquent patterns (types I, IV). Negro delinquency seems much less centered around the home than does delinquency of Caucasian boys.

In their three-year follow-up the authors found that both membership in type and magnitude of scores needed to be combined to achieve the best recidivism predictions. Neither type of membership nor possession of high-dimension scores predicted as well alone. They suggested—since Type I has many redeeming features and potentials for prosocial behavior and an overrepresentation of Negroes—that a racial bias in institutionalizing may account for Type I's merely average recidivism rate. Similarly, Type IV, the other type that is predominantly Negro, has a pattern score falling distinctly below average on several of the dimensions, yet the proportion of members reinstitutionalized is above the average of the sample.

The authors see their results as supporting the utility of a self-report check list of antisocial behavior for establishing types of persons. They present a way of distinguishing among the undifferentiated mass of "delinquent boys." The next step seems to be to see if different approaches to intervention will do better with the different types; for example, the methods and emphases may be different from those types where parental defiance is the focal problem and for those where it is not. Those who identify with the delinquent role may have to be reached and treated by methods different from boys not accepting the role. Assaultive and drug-using delinquents might also require specialized forms of treatment.

Little, K. B., and Shneidman, E. S. Congruencies among interpretations of psychological test and anamnestic data. *Psychological Monographs*, 1959, *73*, No. 6, 1–42 (Whole No. 476).

The primary purpose of this study was to investigate the agreements, or congruencies, among personality descriptions when such descriptions are based on different sources of information. Congruencies were examined for different subjects, different assessment instruments, and different interpretive tasks. The forty-eight clinical psychologists who served as test judges were experts in the tests used; twelve each interpreted the Rorschach, TAT, MAPS, and MMPI. The tests were obtained from twelve male subjects of normal intelligence; three from each of the following categories: normal neurotic, psychophysiological, and psychotic. In addition to the test data a comprehensive psychiatric case history was submitted. The typed case histories (the anamnestic materials) were judged by twenty-three psychiatrists and one psychologist, half of them psycho-analytically oriented.

Each judge, using the test or anamnestic materials assigned him, made five kinds of interpretive judgments: diagnostic label, rating of degree of maladjust-ment, a 76-item Q-sort of social behavior and adjustment items, a 117-item true–false questionnaire with items like those on psychological reports, and a 100-item true–false questionnaire of a factual nature about the subjects' past and present life. (The procedures and cases are described in such detail in the monograph that the study could be repeated by other researchers.)

The bulky data were analyzed by correlation analysis of the various methods. The monograph presents the findings in detail. In general the results are disheartening to anyone hoping to find that these common assessment procedures have high validity. Even though the judges were experts in their particular tests, the best they could do amounted to only a small increase over chance variation. This small increase might be considered useful for screening purposes by anyone who overlooks the fact that the tests, especially the projective techniques, are as time-consuming as they are. The MMPI fared slightly better in the outcome, and it also has the practical advantage of requiring less time. There were certain limitations in the procedure, such as the fact that only blind interpretations were used. This study certainly raises questions about the value of having merely the results of a test, without additional information. No attempt was made to go into the validity of a test if there is added material. The use of psychiatrists' consensus of judgment based upon the anamnestic material as a criterion of validity of the tests can also be questioned; the psychiatrists were not given the full facts about each subject and did not interview him.

Little and Shneidman's study makes an interesting comparison with the somewhat similar study by Silverman (1959) in the monograph that follows it in the series. Silverman studied the validity of projective-technique interpretations by thirty clinical psychologists with varying amounts of experience. The interpreters' Q-sorts were correlated with the Q-sorts by psychiatrists after 35 or more therapy sessions. The patients taking the tests (Rorschach, TAT, HTP, and Most Unpleasant Concept) were ten young adult males beginning treatment in a clinic. The results indicated significant agreement of interpretations with the criteria. There was no significant difference connected with less or greater experience among the psychologists. Psychologists who had undergone analysis did significantly better. However, it needs to be remembered that the criterion was the judgment of psychiatrists who were analytically oriented. Inter-psychologist agreement on the cases was significant, although the correlation was only 0.34. Whether the projective techniques really added significantly to evaluation is not clear from this study, but the author is more optimistic than Little and Shneidman.

In another study, Datel and Gengerelli (1956) collected blind interpretations of Rorschachs on eighteen neuropsychiatric patients from twenty-seven clinical psychologists. The psychologists were then asked to match the Rorschach interpretations of other psychologists. In general, they were successful in matching to a particular patient the interpretations made by different psychologists. Success was facilitated by the diversity of the patient group. The authors concluded that there would have been less success in a more homogeneous group and that, even as it was, some psychologists were not above chance in their matching and that many of the Rorschach reports had little communication value.

Ladd, C. E. Record-keeping and research in psychiatric and psychological clinics. *Journal of Counseling Psychology*, 1967, *14*, 361—367.

In the chapter we emphasized the writing of psychological reports—writings that are typically sent by the psychologist to a recipient. Another aspect of the psychologist's writings which deserves study and care is the client record or chart, a true and honored record of all an agency's dealings with a client.

Ladd examined the record-keeping procedures of ninety-two training clinics and surveyed the publications of forty-nine of the same clinics over a three-year period. He found that records on psychotherapy patients were typically verbal and lengthy (5—6 pages). Psychological clinics used tape recordings and tests more often than psychiatric clinics did, but neither systematically collected the sort of quantitative data that could lend itself to empirical research.

Ladd found that relatively few attempts were made to assess objectively changes that occurred in the patient during teratment, and that even fewer systematic follow-ups were carried out. Publications using patient data in any way were produced at the rate of one for every ten years of professional staff time. Ladd argues that clinical records should become more quantified and that service and research should be integrated and undertaken simultaneously.

He points out that there are reasons besides client service (or patient care) and research which underlie the elaborate keeping of records by psychologists. Some training activities require detailed records, for instance, and certain elements of a record may furnish legal protection. On the other hand, a record can be a source of prejudice and bias. The same basic caution must apply to records as to psychological reports: Writing needs a clearly understood purpose and methods deliberately designed to achieve that purpose.

Affleck, D. C., and Strider, F. O. Contribution of psychological reports to patient management. *Journal of Consulting and Clinical Psychology*, 1971, *37*, 177–179.

The writers point out that a functional examination of psychological reports (e.g., to what extent they supply significant information or modify decisions) is a relatively neglected area. They investigated two samples of reports, totaling 340, in response to written referrals in a large psychiatric institute in Nebraska. The frequency of kinds of information requested, ranked from highest to lowest, were appraisal of intelligence, personality, diagnostic impression, organic brain damage, psychotherapeutic potential, and vocational–educational possibilities. The referral source (usually psychiatric residents) regarded the reports as generally very valuable, giving confirmation of suspected conditions in about half the cases and adding new and significant information in an additional fifth of the cases. Furthermore, Affleck and Strider found that the referral sources when interviewed about the specific cases indicated that 52 percent of the reports had altered management of the cases in some way and only 22 percent had no effect; 2 percent were viewed as detrimental. These differing findings suggest that reports are useful in relation to specific clinical settings, clients, and psychological reporters.

The authors state that future work should consider other settings (e.g., private practitioners and recipients with more sophistication than mainly psychiatric residents). Another direction is the content of the report; if only one report in two makes a contribution, what are the predictors for contribution?

Other studies of global impressions of the usefulness of reports vary in their results. Mintz (1968) found that student therapists rate psychological diagnostic reports as moderately valuable but actually do not give much weight to specific aspects of reports. Smyth and Reznikoff (1971) did a questionnaire study of fifty-seven psychiatrists in New York, asking their reactions to a variety of questions about the usefulness of typical psychological reports. The results were more favorable than those of Mintz. Smyth and Reznikoff (p. 286) conclude that these psychiatrists of various backgrounds who had referred patients for testing "felt that diagnostics were most helpful in adding to the psychiatrist's knowledge of patient's dynamics, degree of pathology, and strengths which could be used in treatment." Moore, Bobbitt, and Wildman (1968) in a survey in the Southeast found that psychiatrists made use of psychological reports only 20 percent of the time.

Garfield, Heine, and Leventhal (1954) compared ratings of the value of reports made by several judges representing different mental health professions. Social workers rated the value of the reports higher than did members of the other professions, and they were less critical.

chapter 10

Psychobiological Systems: Appraisal and Treatment

While clinical psychologists are not primarily concerned with the person as a biological system, they do make contact with these levels of human systems in a variety of ways. This chapter is intended to give an overview. For a more detailed discussion of biological aspects of psychological work, readers should turn to various specialized texts in abnormal psychology, neurology, and testing for organic disorders.

IMPORTANCE OF THE BIOLOGICAL SYSTEM

The psychologist may have many reasons to be concerned about the bodily system of a client or patient.[1] We have grouped these concerns into three general categories of involvement. First, *somatic changes often affect personal and social systems*; that is, they influence personality, skills, and roles in family or community. Most dramatic are cerebral hemorrhages or heart attacks, but the common cold causes more man-days of lost work than any other disease.

Any one of many bodily problems or bodily conditions or processes may influence the behavior the clinician sees. How much of old Ms. Jones's difficulty with a test is because her arteries are hardening and her brain no longer has a full blood supply? Does Ms. Buckingham's rather nervous, irritable behavior stem from psychological or social factors in her life, from premenstrual tension, or is it because she is drinking too much coffee and not eating enough breakfast or getting enough sleep? Alcohol or hallucinogens in the blood stream, or very high

---

[1] As we mentioned in Chapter 1, we generally incline to the term "client" because of its broad applicability and nonmedical connotation. Matarazzo (1965b) however, points out that if we see an individual in a hospital, or other medical context, "patient" is the common and logical term, just as "student" or "prisoner" may be in other special contexts.

fever, may have their own distinct effects upon behavior, sometimes leaving a residual of changed brain tissue. The psychologist needs to know the characteristic ways in which behavior and thinking are altered by such damage.

Second, headaches, ulcers, low-back pain, and certain paralyses are examples of how *some somatic problems signify distress in personal or other systems*. It is estimated that one-half to two-thirds of the patients coming to physicians with physical complaints are primarily suffering from psychological disorder. Clients who have such psychosomatic problems as skin eruptions, ulcers, or other physical complaints which cannot be positively diagnosed often turn out to have problems in their personal or family lives. In such instances, the bodily dysfunction is a signal pointing to distress or trouble in family relations (e.g., divorce), organizational commitments (e.g., job), or community systems (e.g., discrimination). Later we will also take up drug effects, alcoholism, and suicidal behavior under the heading of somatic "self-assaults" signaling psychological distress.

Finally, *somatic treatment may affect psychological problems*. The psychologist, for example, often plays a part in decisions about the use of psychoactive medication. He may recommend its use, monitor its effectiveness, and advise about dosage changes. For instance, the acutely disturbed schizophrenic, who shrinks from the sinister horrors that pursue him, probably obtains maximum relief in minimum time through medication. The clinician must be sensitive to psychological conditions requiring medical intervention, such as the psychoses or acute grief or anxiety, so that he may make timely and effective referrals.

Where intervention in biological systems is called for, the psychologist makes a referral to a licensed physician. Obviously we would all recognize that no psychologist would perform surgery, but we need to recognize less obvious boundaries between professions. To a friend we may say, "Take an aspirin for that symptom," but to clients we must avoid even this much advice, because it implies knowledge and experience about the management of physical conditions. Clearly, the safest course is to call upon a physician—or recommend a visit to one—when there is any doubt about a client's physical state, even if the doubt occurs to the psychologist rather than to the client.

The manner in which we refer a client to a physician has as much to do with his response to our request as the physician's style of referral does with our response. A letter or a phone call giving some background and making our concerns and expectations clear often ensures a smooth transaction. Furthermore, such efforts to communicate clearly can lead to later referrals from physician to psychologist and thus facilitate good working relationships.

Clinics must often decide what their policy about physical examinations is to be. For instance, if there is no physician on the staff of a psychology clinic, for the protection of both client and psychologist it may be advisable to require that every client have a physical examination if he has not had one recently.

ILLUSTRATIONS OF
PSYCHOLOGISTS' APPRAISAL ACTIVITIES

Twenty-five-year-old Joe Woods was referred to a mental health clinic by his physican, who thought that perhaps Joe had emotional problems that were causing him to shake a great deal. Dr. Wrightman, the psychologist, reviewed the referral letter and felt that Mr. Woods was probably responding to situational stress. He was a marginally successful graduate student in art whose marriage was on the verge of breaking up and whose career prospects looked rather poor. He had undergone a complete neurological examination three years before without significant findings. But when they met for the first interview, Dr. Wrightman immediately noticed that the shaking was sometimes regular and extreme. Mr. Woods didn't shake much when sitting, but when he tried to do anything like writing or standing up, he shook grossly. Dr. Wrightman immediately suspected a form of brain disease. He noticed that Mr. Woods' handwriting was tortuous and that he had difficulty enunciating some words. On the Trail Making Test and on the Graham and Kendall Memory-for-Designs Test, Joe showed the slowness and types of errors common to many brain-damaged patients. In conferring with the clinic psychiatrist, Dr. Wrightman speculated that the cerebellum, a lower part of the brain, might be involved. He contacted Joe's physician and suggested a thorough neurological work-up.

Another illustration is the case of Mary Bain. Her frequent headaches became worse, and recurrent nausea and vomiting finally brought her to her physician, who saw changes within her eyeballs which are characteristic of increased pressure within the head. Further examination quickly established that she had an intracranial neoplasm—a brain tumor. Surgery successfully removed the slow-growing benign tumor, but, as is frequently the case, it left Mary unable to remember things and with difficulty recognizing familiar people or objects. Her short-term memory and her recognition improved within two weeks; after a few months she seemed virtually unimpaired. But was she? Did Mary have a permanent impairment, and if so, what? Would she be able to return to her job as a typist-receptionist? Dr. Newton, a psychologist, was asked to assess Mary's functioning and answer those questions. He administered the Halstead Aphasic Test (for assessing speech problems), the Wechsler memory scale, the WAIS, the Benton Visual Retention, and the Rey Auditory Memory tests. In Mary's case, rehabilitation services, speech therapy, or counseling about a different job all appeared unnecessary because none of her functioning showed notable decrement. Two years later, though, the psychologist heard informally from the neurologist that Mary had begun to have minor seizures—apparently because of the buildup of scar tissue. Antiseizure medications were working effectively, but the neurologist said if a second operation became necessary, he would refer Mary for a preoperative evaluation.

Freddie Norton, a nine-year-old, was referred to the child guidance clinic. He was obviously slow in school work. He could read only a few simple words. He usually played with younger children or by himself. On the recommendation of the teacher, and because the school had no psychologist to test him, the family brought Freddie to the clinic. After an intake interview with the mother, the clinic staff immediately decided to evaluate Freddie's level of intellectual functioning and body coordination in addition to interviewing and observing him. The staff wanted information about his potential for going on with the regular school routine and about any additional reasons there might be for his school difficulties, such as, for example, eye trouble. His mother had mentioned that he was slow to "get going" after delivery, raising the possibility of brain damage caused by oxygen deficiency. Freddie had had high fevers as a child, a symptom that also suggested possible brain damage. Was he insufficiently motivated to do well in school because of fears, anxieties, or other emotional problems? Among the various aspects of intellectual functioning, did he do better on some than others? If so, how could these facts be used to help the teacher in her program for teaching Freddie to read? All these questions, and doubtless others, occurred to the psychologist as he was planning his appointment with Freddie. He chose to give the boy the Stanford-Binet because this well-standardized and developed test provides for testing lower mental age levels than can be evaluated with the other major test he might have used. He chose also to administer the Gray Oral Reading Test in order to get a quick indication of Freddie's reading ability. He decided to keep in reserve other possibilities, such as the Bender-Gestalt Test or a story-telling test, until he could see how well Freddie did with the other tests and how much his attention wandered.

George B was a seventeen-year-old who, although bright, had compiled a poor high school record. His physican told Dr. Cann that he'd been treating George for many years. His most recent involvement had been when friends had brought George into the emergency room of the local hospital on a "bad trip," apparently from an LSD episode. This was the third such episode for George, and his recovery was proceeding slowly. He was under a Thorazine-Stelazine regimen of the "major tranquillizers" (phenothiazines), which did seem to be clarifying his thinking. "But," said the physician, "he can't go on like this . . . Do you think a counseling relationship could help him? He doesn't seem to know where he's going in life and I always felt he had great potential. I'm not sure in my mind if there's any permanent change from this LSD stuff—it's so hard to know what it is they get." Dr. Cann said that he could see George and that he was trying a group approach to counseling people like George, helping the group score and interpret various tests to provide information on which future plans could be based. Rather than to test for difficulties or defects, he tried to focus on awakening the group members' interest in themselves and resume the interrupted process of self-development.

SOMATIC PHENOMENA AFFECTING PERSONAL OR OTHER SYSTEMS

To some extent, nearly all bodily problems influence one's personal or family system. Many of us stay away from work during the acute stage of a cold, for example. Sometimes such a break is welcome, but sometimes even a minor somatic problem makes the sufferer face the need for a change in identity and role, or the need to maintain motivation to keep trying even for what appear to be limited or unattractive goals.

The Body and Life Cycles

Cycles characterize all of life. Our daily cycle involves waking hours, eating and sleeping, and a diurnal rhythm of bodily temperature changes. Each individual life constitutes a comprehensive cycle from birth to death—with definite phases and landmarks along the way.

Every cycle involves characteristic behaviors which *in context of the cycle* may be quite normal or natural. It is easy for us to understand that our client is sleepy because he has had too big a lunch, and our patient in her mid-forties is distraught because she is at the menopause. We should also understand that sleepiness and alertness vary with the daily blood sugar cycle, and a woman's state of mind may vary with her cycle of fertility.

When bodily cycles become disarranged, the resulting behavior may easily be misinterpreted by the unwary. Behavior and thought patterns similar to those characterizing some psychotic states may appear. Sleep deserves major emphasis in this connection. Sleep researchers (and college students) have demonstrated that thought processes may be markedly changed as a result of prolonged sleep deprivation. If the psychologist suspects such a condition he may inquire about natural cycles. "When are you eating?" "How well are you sleeping?" "At what time do you go to bed at night?" Many aspects of the "crisis" on the basis of which a patient is admitted to inpatient or out-patient services seem to moderate as normal sleeping and eating patterns are restored. The menstrual cycle is important because of the depression and tension that sometimes occur. Other cycles with psychologically crucial concomitants are the onset of puberty, with its problems of identity and role; the period after delivery of an infant, when the mother may experience unanticipated depression; or approaching death, which may bring sharp concern over meaning and separation.

Illness, Accidents, and Aging

The strains of temporary incapacity, of perhaps not knowing the outcome, of fearing loss of some capacity—each of these may underlie a request for hospitalization or out-patient consultation. It has been frequently observed that serious hospitalization will evoke dependent, frightened reactions in even normally strong, independent people. Persons observing this phenomenon from different theoretical viewpoints interpret it differently, but it is one that must be faced. The psychologist who communicates honestly with the patient, who strives to keep the patient's relations with family and friends intact, and who makes clear what some expectations of patienthood in crisis are ("stop all fruitless struggle immediately . . . you *should* feel overwhelmed just now . . . It's all right to be that way for now . . . ") builds a good foundation for a helping relationship.

Not all somatic problems affecting other parts of our lives stem from sickness or accident. The birth of a new child sends "shock waves" through the organized structure of the family, necessitating sudden and rather complete change on the part of all its members. Most problems arising from this course, as when a sibling begins to behave like a younger child, can be resolved by helping the parents to be supportive yet clear in the new diversion of attention. Another natural nontraumatic change has to do with aging and adjusting to a less active life and to the segregation that we impose on our aged.

Ultimately, of course, the bodily system ceases to function, and the life cycle ends in *death*. Here psychologists have two concerns: (1) counseling the dying person, and linking this counsel to other life supports the person has previously had or can use, and (2) promoting a perspective on death which can help us all handle it more openly and more constructively, so that as a society we need not live as if death were some type of final obscenity. Often a minister, priest, or rabbi will be very important in planning for making a person's last days as meaningful as possible. An increasing number of writers are addressing themselves to the psychological aspects of death. Kubler-Ross (1969) speaks of a five-stage process which a person goes through as he faces death. The first stage is *denial and isolation*, a temporary defense. This is soon replaced by the second stage, *anger, rage, envy, or resentment*. She writes: "If our first reaction to catastrophic news is 'No, it's not true, no, it cannot involve me,' this has to give way to a new reaction, when it finally dawns on us: 'Oh, yes, it is me, it was not a mistake.' Fortunately or unfortunately very few patients are able to maintain a make-believe world in which they are well and healthy until they die." The third stage brings various attempts to *bargain* or in some way alter or modify the fate. It is followed by the fourth stage, *depression*, a preparatory grief in preparation for final separation. Usually such depression is accompanied by early morning awakening, loss of appetite, and psychomotor retardation. She suggests that our efforts to cheer a person out of such depression may reflect our own vulnerability to such feelings rather than the dying person's needs. The fifth stage is *acceptance*, in which death, although not welcomed, is at least tolerated.

Genetics

One aspect of bodily structure with which a psychologist needs to be familiar is the genetic aspect. If a condition should be found to be genetically transmitted, the psychologist must often focus on amelioration and adaptation rather than cure. He must understand how biological and social factors interact in the development of the individual and realize that genetic endowment determines the range of each person's potential. He must keep abreast of advances in research on behavior genetics, so that he recognizes conditions and behavior patterns that may be genetically transmitted and is ready to promote strategies for training and adaptation as the best way to help with such problems, and genetic counseling as the best way to prevent their occurrence in the future.

"If it is true," says Rosenthal (1970) "that genes influence behavior (in the sense that they are the instrumentalities that lead to differences in the organization, structure, and chemistry of all systems in the body that mediate behavior), it is equally likely that they influence much behavior we call abnormal" (p. 7). The current listing of psychodiagnostic categories by the American Psychiatric Association may eventually have to incorporate separate genetically based categories if the research findings become decisive. Even at present it is clear that certain diseases are genetically transmitted. One of these is Huntington's chorea, a progressive, fatal illness characterized by spasmodic twitching. The choreiform (dancelike) movements appear in an affected individual about fifteen years before death, generally after he is old enough to marry and transmit the pathological gene. Emotional disturbance (usually first identified as neurosis or psychosis) precedes the emergence of the choreic movements. A number of other genetic conditions, such as Down's syndrome (or mongolism), Turner's and Kleinfelter's syndromes (conditions involving the sex chromosomes), and diabetes mellitus (abnormality of sugar metabolism), involve behavioral difficulties.

It is especially important for the clinical psychologist to understand the part that genetics plays in the etiology of schizophrenia. Although there was little good evidence a decade ago, it has now accumulated in such quantities that Lindzey et al. (1971) state: "The presence of genetic predisposition to schizophrenia-like disorders may now be regarded as firmly established." The predisposition is often referred to as the *diathesis*. However, it is clear that the predisposition does not always become manifest in clinical schizophrenia, a fact that is generally accounted for by postulating that symptoms are precipitated by some stress. The assumption that a particular stress can bring on schizophrenic symptoms in people with the genetic predisposition is called the diathesis–stress hypothesis.

This hypothesis has important implications for clinical psychologists. If data continue to support the position that a genetic predisposition is involved in such conditions, then they must face new challenges. As mentioned before, environmental causation and cure become less pressing issues; amelioration of the condition, investigation and decrease of stresses that precipitate it, genetic counseling—all these become more salient activities for practitioners. Major goals for the clinician will increasingly be things like teaching schizophrenics to live in

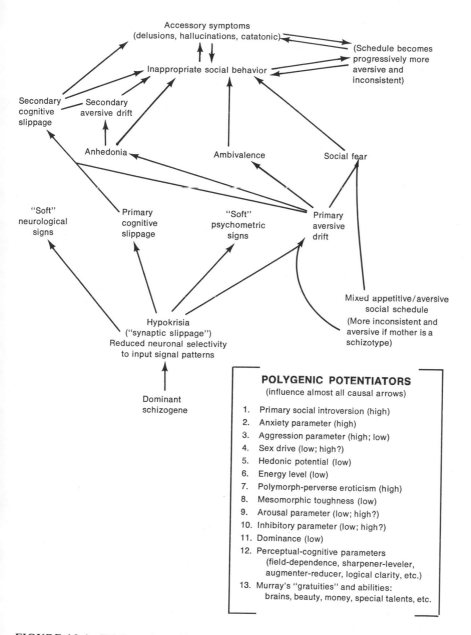

ORGANISM   ENVIRONMENT

Accessory symptoms
(delusions, hallucinations, catatonic)

(Schedule becomes
progressively more
aversive and
inconsistent)

Inappropriate social behavior

Secondary
cognitive
slippage

Secondary
aversive drift

Anhedonia   Ambivalence   Social fear

"Soft"
neurological
signs

Primary
cognitive
slippage

"Soft"
psychometric
signs

Primary
aversive
drift

Mixed appetitive/aversive
social schedule
(More inconsistent and
aversive if mother is a
schizotype)

Hypokrisia
("synaptic slippage")
Reduced neuronal selectivity
to input signal patterns

Dominant
schizogene

POLYGENIC POTENTIATORS
(influence almost all causal arrows)

1. Primary social introversion (high)
2. Anxiety parameter (high)
3. Aggression parameter (high; low)
4. Sex drive (low; high?)
5. Hedonic potential (low)
6. Energy level (low)
7. Polymorph-perverse eroticism (high)
8. Mesomorphic toughness (low)
9. Arousal parameter (low; high?)
10. Inhibitory parameter (low; high?)
11. Dominance (low)
12. Perceptual-cognitive parameters
(field-dependence, sharpener-leveler,
augmenter-reducer, logical clarity, etc.)
13. Murray's "gratuities" and abilities:
brains, beauty, money, special talents, etc.

FIGURE 10-1 Etiology in schizophrenia. (From Meehl, 1972, p. 16.)

the community, establishing halfway houses where necessary support will be provided while the patient is helped to use his skills, and other activities that concentrate on expanding and upgrading skills and creating situations in which human dignity is safeguarded. Such approaches are very different from those based on assumptions that schizophrenia originated in the family or in the psyche, and that it could be "cured" by psychotherapy. Meehl (1972) has summarized a conception of the complex interplay of genetic and sociopsychodynamic etiology in Figure 10–1.

Sexuality

In its broadest form, sexuality affects virtually all aspects of an individual's makeup. Readers will note that each succeeding chapter contains some reflection of its importance, perhaps in shaping what a person thinks of himself, perhaps in defining the kind of role to be played in a group. There are, however, specific aspects of sexuality that lead to bodily conditions that impair psychological functioning.

The psychologist will, for example, often see youngsters whose very early or very delayed puberty has set them apart from other children. This causes acute personal worries as well as uncomfortable interpersonal relationships. Breast development, male voice changes, and other hormone-related changes can be matters of intense importance to adolescents. Of longer duration are the psychological effects of enduring abnormalities or inadequacies of sexual endowment or function. Recent work of Masters and Johnson (1970) and of Money (1970) makes use of physical treatment and even surgery in addition to the more usual psychological therapies.

The psychologist is likely to be confronted with the problem of an unwanted pregnancy and conflicts about abortion. Although he may have strong views of his own, his duty to the client who is considering an abortion is to help her clarify her own feelings and desires and to separate her concerns from those of other people or other institutions.

Abnormalities of Form and Function

Certain individuals are born defective; others become defective through disease or accident. They may then have considerable difficulty when they try to adjust to the world and to compete within it. Even fairly normal biological conditions can give rise to psychological concerns. A man may feel that he is too short; a teenager may worry about his facial acne. These and many other ideas people may have about the structure of their bodies are referred to as "body image."

The clinician must also be alert for perceptual deficits. Deafness or blindness, for instance, make interviewing a patient difficult. They also suggest that the client may be short of certain types of experience for which his input system has been defective. A child, for instance, may have exceptionally poor vision which only the alertness of the clinician who requests an examination will discover, because the child himself may be quite unaware of what good vision "looks like."

Central Nervous System Defects

One major task of psychologists in some settings is to examine patients who are specifically referred for the evaluation of central-nervous system defects. Even in other settings, however, and in cases not referred specifically for this reason, it is well to be aware of the possibility of organicity in problem behavior. What particular types of signs might suggest central-nervous-system problems in a client?

Observing a patient's behavior on a test or in other situations is usually not sufficient to allow us to determine with certainty that particular behavior patterns arise from organic impairment rather than from purely psychological sources. Perseveration, echolalia, or bizarre thinking, for instance, may stem from either cause. Nonetheless, there are broad classes of signs that might make us suspect organicity. These signs might include a reduced capacity for information processing (i.e., reduced speed with which problems can be solved or reduced complexity of problems that can be solved), difficulty in dealing with novel and unfamiliar problems, memory loss, perseverating (i.e., inappropriately continuing to repeat a response), or impaired perceptual motor skills, such as poor copying of a figure or drawing of a line through a maze. The more gross the damage, the more it may become obvious in such symptoms as paralysis, speech problems, and blindness.

Both neurologists and psychologists are concerned with central-nervous-system defects. Generalizing, we might say that the neurologist looks for attributes of the *intactness of the brain*, its blood vessels, pressure, and so on. Besides the grosser reflex-type tests, neurologists have highly sophisticated techniques, such as radioisotope scanning, pneumoencephalography, X-ray, and so on. The psychologist's tools allow him to look at a person's *behavior* with some skill. The two types of information, neurological and psychological, supplement each other because they do not necessarily correlate (a patient may have extensive physical damage and yet not show much psychological deficit, and vice versa). The psychologist may look for behavior patterns often associated with brain damage, or in a person with known brain damage he may be concerned with measuring deficits of functioning or with recommending rehabilitative measures and evaluating recovery of function.

What are the signs the psychologist is most likely to be the first professional to see? One classic sign is deficit in memory. When less severe, the deficit is likely to involve memory for more immediate or more recent happenings. Certain disorders of speech, for instance "knowing what word it is you want but not being able to say it," should turn attention toward organic problems. Rigidity or perseveration in the interview, when, for instance, a patient may be unable to let go of a particular phrase which keeps returning whether appropriate or not, should also alert us to the possibility or organicity. Sometimes peculiar gaps in ability will come to the clinician's attention: "Joe operates the machine fine, but he can't copy the drawings." "Mike can tell you he wants to get dressed but he doesn't seem able to begin—he just stands there and says 'ok, ok' until you tell him each little step." One characteristic of some organically impaired persons is a lowered tolerance for the frustration of being unable to complete a simple task. An organic patient may become quite vocal, perhaps suddenly weeping, in the midst of a routine task such as the arithmetic subtest of the WAIS.

If a psychologist suspects brain damage, what steps should he take, keeping in mind that he is inferring through behavioral signs a physical condition? In the event of severe signs—gross headaches, convulsions, blackout spells, losses of sensation or movement, problems of vision, progressive worsening of complaint—immediate neurological referral is necesary for the patient's safety. In cases where suspicion of organicity is vague, where the signs show up mainly in psychological functioning, then the psychologist should suggest evaluation with psychological measures. His findings should always be communicated to the client's physican even in cases where permanent damage is apparently benign because of the possibility of medical procedures being indicated (e.g., surgical intervention, vasodilating medications) or because the report may provide valuable diagnostic data in case of the onset of later symptoms such as seizures.

APPRAISAL TECHNIQUES

Appraisal of Organicity

Tests for organicity (more correctly, tests for behavioral characteristics of central-nervous-system impairment) fall into two principal groups: *multiphasic measures*, such as the Halstead-Indiana Battery of Neuropsychological Tests, which sample several diverse areas of functioning, and the *single-phase tests*, which sample only one area, usually visuomotor performance, memory, or conceptual ability. Typically, one test will be administered as a screening device. Among these tests are the Bender-Gestalt, the Benton Test of Visual Retention, the Trail Making Test, and the Graham and Kendall Memory-for-Designs Test. Such measures must show themselves worthwhile against some three criteria in addition to the usual validity/reliability requirements. First, they must show that they can do better than chance—and Goldberg (1959) has shown for the Bender-Gestalt that ordinary clinicians and secretaries have an undistinguished "hit rate." Second, such tests are of little use if they make accurate discrimination between categories of clients who are quite obviously different. Their value lies in differentiating among clients who are clearly diagnostic problems—and, in general, this is precisely where they are weakest. Finally, their major difficulty lies in trying to capture all types of brain dysfunction on their single axis by sampling a very limited range of behavior in a single situation. (For some of the methology used in prediction of brain damage, see Wheeler, 1963, 1964.)

Nonetheless, interest in tests designed to screen the organicity continues strong, probably because some discriminative power is better than none. Besides the tests mentioned, which emphasize visual motor skills and to a lesser extent memory and thinking, there is one pure memory measure (Wechsler Memory Scale) and there are several tests of conceptualization, made up of object sorting and classifying problems (Vigotsky Test, Goldstein-Scherer Tests of abstract and concrete thinking).

Midway toward a multiphasic test are the Wechsler Intelligence Scales, the profiles of which can be "read" for allegedly characteristic patterns of organicity. Significantly low points on Digit Symbol (a figure-copying task) and on Block Design (a task of building patterns with colored blocks) have often been considered indicative of organic damage. Parsons (1970) has assembled several findings which experimentally relate WAIS profiles to organic conditions. He offers sets of WAIS signs associated with left hemisphere and right hemisphere damage (for example one of the six profile signs associated with left hand damage is vocabulary > comprehension). His chapter is a most useful summary of clinical neuropsychology.

In general, then, the clinician will go through a sequence of signs—tests—decisions—outcome. On the basis of the test outcome he should validate or not validate his hypothesis based on signs. The clinician should keep in mind that physiological confirmation of suspicions based on psychological testing, while difficult, is increasingly available using newer techniques such as the brain-scan procedure. If his referral results in the use of such a procedure, there is a chance for him to obtain futher validation data about the testing procedures he employs.

Miscellaneous Appraisal Techniques

There are several special techniques for evaluating the functioning of psychobiological systems with which the psychologist should be familiar, although administration and interpretation of the techniques frequently are the responsibility of other members of a therapeutic team. The *electroencephalogram* (EEG) measures the pattern of electrical activity in the brain and thus contributes to the diagnosis of epilepsy, brain tumors, and various other neurological conditions with psychological concomitants. The *galvanic skin response* (GSR) is a sensitive indicator of autonomic responses to emotional stimuli and situations. Sensory defects may need to be explored through the use of the *audiometer* or equipment to analyze visual responses to stimuli. The list of such techniques, marginal for psychologists, essential for somebody, could be extended almost indefinitely. The general rule that can be formulated is that a psychologist familiarize himself with whatever diagnostic techniques are important to the clients he serves.

SOMATIC PROBLEMS THAT SIGNAL DISTRESS IN PERSONAL OR OTHER SYSTEMS

Psychosomatic illnesses ("The doctor says it's emotional but I know I have an ulcer/diarrhea/vomiting/headaches/numbness . . . ") have been widely studied. The prevailing view is that disorders in the personality system are expressed as bodily symptoms. Freud originally explored the possibility that certain anethesias or paralyses might serve the function of disabling the sufferer in such a way that he need no longer do that which was frightening to him. These notions are of great theoretical interest, but not of great relevance, to Americans, who seldom manifest the hysterical conversion symptoms Freud encountered in Viennese clientele of his day. There are, however, many conditions, for example ulcers, when psychologists look into emotional factors such as day-to-day pressures, anger, or poor expressive ability. Exploration and intervention in personal and family systems, and treatment by relaxation and desensitization, have seemed to be useful approaches to such psychosomatic problems.

Biofeedback

Until quite recently it was thought that bodily functions controlled by the autonomic nervous system were beyond the influence of operant (Skinnerian or instrumental) conditioning. Progress with psychosomatic problems has taken a major leap with the discovery (N. E. Miller, 1969) that autonomically controlled functions such as heart rate are responsive to conditioning using electric shock or stimulation of "pleasure centers" in the brain. Among the functions that have been altered in animals are heart rate, intestinal contraction or relaxation, increase or decrease of urine formation in the kidney, and increased blood flow in the rat's tail.

The significance of these discoveries is that a whole new mechanism of etiology of psychosomatic conditions may have been identified. The gastric hyperfunction associated with stomach ulcers, for instance, may be a conditioned response to, say, certain stimuli of one's job or even certain thoughts. Such an etiological mechanism suggests treatment strategies consisting of carefully planned and monitored conditioning programs to modify a wide variety of psychosomatic conditions.

In work such as this, information from the muscles or brain, amplified and presented as audio tones or visual displays, forms a key part of the procedure. Only in comparatively recent times has there been instrumentation able to detect, amplify, and present to us the minute electrical, thermal, or pressure changes within the body which we are unable to detect proprioceptively with our own sense organs. The types of display typically presented to the subject are patterns of lights which change according to input level or a tone which rises in frequency as, say, the level of electrical activity in a muscle increases with contraction. *Biofeedback* has become the shortened title for work using such feedback of bioelectric information.

Two theoretical viewpoints have become associated with research on biofeedback: *conditioning*, as we have mentioned above, and *cybernetics*. Brown (1970, 1971), noting that alpha brain waves are usually associated with feelings of calmness or floating, demonstrated that people could increase their percentages of alpha rhythm merely by trying to, once they were given feedback on their amplified alpha activity. She maintains that the link between the biofeedback and the biological change of alpha rhythm appears to be more the providing of feedback (cybernetic) information than a process of conditioning.

Workers in the biofeedback area fall generally into two camps: those who seek to change body states to relieve body problems (e.g., presenting patients with information about their muscle potentials to promote fullest relaxation), and those who seek to change body states to produce altered states of consciousness (e.g., the work on alpha-rhythm work mentioned above).

The demonstration that with biofeedback people can, within limits, control several of their own internal functions suggests possibilities for self-regulation and self-control. There is the clear possibility that new types of "patient-operated" therapies may come into being in the future, in which patients provided with particular biofeedback information may work unassisted to normalize or regularize particular functions. Similar kinds of phenomena seem to be manifested in subjects doing transcendental meditation (Wallace and Benson, 1972) and other exercises related to yoga or Zen. Psychologists must pay careful attention to this burgeoning new area of research, which opens up a new frontier in psychosomatic treatments, altered states of consciousness, self-control and self-regulation.

Sexual aberrations are not properly classed as psychosomatic problems, but some of the same ideas apply. Males who expose themselves are likely to have psychologically painful problems of impotence or inadequacy. Psychologists often look for inadvertent vicious cycles in the personal sphere ("I feel bad about myself; having sex with John will prove my femininity," "I feel undesirable, I need to have sex with Bill to prove . . .") or for stress in the family, which makes sexual behavior seem to be a solution.

Another bodily condition sometimes reflective of discomfort in the personal system is obesity. All weight problems are not psychologically caused, of course, with genetics now entering the list of other possible causes. But it is true that eating may serve as a diversion from psychological discomfort. Furthermore, the condition of being obese carries with it an entirely different and usually less demanding set of social expectations. Food, of course, is just one of several substances that may be involved in problems of abuse or overreliance.

Drug Abuse and Alcoholism

The intake of chemicals under this heading confronts the clinician with the task of distinguishing the effect of drugs from psychologically caused states that resemble them and making medical referral if needed. We must remember that the use of drugs involves strong social components. Smoking "hash" or drinking alcohol may occur largely because the person wants to be identified with a particular group; overdosing on LSD may occur because this is an accepted way of indicating distress in a particular subculture or group of friends. Whether or not psychoactive medication is prescribed for a patient may also depend on the psychiatrist's training or ideological allegiances.

The clinical psychologist should be able to recognize the effects of several classes of nonprescribed or often-abused drugs. Manifestations may range in intensity from those constituting a hospital emergency, through routine need for detoxification or talking down, to conduct within an interview context giving rise to a suspicion that the interviewee may be under the influence of a particular chemical agent.

The effects of various drugs on the behavior of different persons differ widely. We have noted that different friends act differently when "under the influence." Because of these individual variations, it is difficult to attribute particular signs or symptoms unambiguously to particular drugs. Two major additional facts make it difficult to identify characteristic patterns of behavior produced by intoxication. The first is, as Beecher (1956) observed, that expectations play a large part in production of the effects, so that what happens reflects some of the properties of the subculture in which the drugs are used, as well as characteristics of the ingested drugs themselves. The second and equally important reason for the variability of effects is that the drug user seldom knows the exact chemical composition of the substance he ingests—especially in the case of illegally manufactured material.

Chronic abuse of some nonprescribed drugs has characteristic effects on the biological system which the clinician should recognize. With alcohol, the changes in skin pallor, liver physiology, and central-nervous-system tissues are fairly well known. Chronic alcoholics show the effects of cerebral damage in their performance on intelligence tests and tests of organicity. Cerebellar damage often shows up in gross tremors of the hands and excessive lifting of the feet when walking.

But far too little is known about the long-term effects of many other substances. There have been suggestions that LSD usage over a long time may result in chromosomal damage; some clinical cases have been reported showing paranoid reactions after prolonged use of amphetamines. Although we must add our voices to the clamor for outcome research on these drugs, we must point out that even if the *biological* effects of a particular substance such as marijuana are found to be minimal over a long time period, the clinician must still consider what has happened at other system levels. For instance, what effect on the developing self-concept does the prolonged use of marijuana and other drugs have?

The psychologist will also encounter problems of *addiction*. Addiction has been subdivided into the physiological and psychological varieties. The first is a genuine property of the biological system. The body adapts to, then later requires, the presence of the drug. Withdrawal reactions make "kicking the habit" a supremely difficult task. Eddy et al. (1965) define drug dependence, and review dependency patterns for several classes of drugs. Physiological dependency patterns can arise from the use of opiates, barbiturates, and alcohol. Patterns of dependency involving marijuana, amphetamines, and hallucinogens are psychological rather than physiological (as indicated by a definite withdrawal syndrome), although withdrawal from amphetamines is followed by a state of mental and physical depression.

Psychological addiction is really a property of the personal, rather than the biological, system. A psychological addiction (or psychological dependency) arises because the drug plays a vital part in the particular organization of a personal system. A client may have organized his life in such a way that putting himself under the influence of the drug may be the only way he can avoid or handle painful relationships or ideas about himself. Psychological intervention and management is called for. The term "dependency" suggests to us the general direction such intervention should take. People can be helped to outgrow their dependency in a variety of ways, including several types of psychotherapy. More recent notions that "for drugs, substitute people," lead to programs in which drug-dependent people are taught to enjoy interpersonal pleasures in a variety of settings not requiring the altered state of consciousness.

People abusing alcohol form an exceedingly large and needy group. It is a rare psychologist who never sees effects of alcholism in the people he serves. But, despite the size of the problem, controversy about the nature of alcoholism, whether it should be considered a moral weakness, a learned behavior pattern, or a disease, has largely prevented a systematic or coordinated approach. Until recently some states refused alcoholics admission to state hospitals. As public awareness of the size of the problem grows and as support for research and intervention increases, psychologists are challenged to increase their contributions to the solution of a problem with clear national impact. Although some respected authorities (e.g., Jellinek, 1960) have endorsed the disease concept of alcoholism, several more recent ones advance a learning etiology (e.g., Keehn, 1970; Blizard, 1971; Verden and Shatterly, 1971). Psychologists participate in a wide variety of treatment settings for alcoholism, but they are most likely to be involved in those that emphasize counterconditioning or group therapy.

Detoxification, drying out, and talking down. Psychologists may participate in such activities and refer cases to agencies that specialize in them, but more important perhaps is work that coordinates or organizes networks of volunteers to serve those in immediate need.

Abuse of drugs signals to the psychologist that personal and family systems—and perhaps relations with an employer—may not be functioning properly. There seems to be little doubt that the rapport and confidence which can be established by someone who "has been there before" is likely to exceed that which most professionals can establish at a time of crisis. The psychologist's main responsibility is to plan and evaluate. What happens to alcoholics on binges or to people on a bad trip or overdose in this community? How do the gatekeepers, such as physicians or persons in the hospital emergency room, quickly mobilize community resources? Has the actual frequency of need been evaluated? Is our network, be it Alcoholics Anonymous or an independently organized group, as responsive as it could be, and is it doing the best job it can? All these questions bear on ways the psychologist can help evaluate and meet needs caused by acute phases of alcoholism and the abuse of other drugs.

Forms of Self-Assault

Just as drinking or taking drugs may represent an escape from personal discomfort or from the pain of a family or employment situation, some persons find that they can demonstrate their discomfort by inflicting damage on themselves having "accidents," planning or gesturing or attempting suicide, and so on. We recognize, of course, that a person may be aware or unaware of what he is doing, may be in contact with reality or quite disoriented. The phenomenon of *suicide* has attracted a great deal of study in recent years. (In other cases the problem is assault on others rather than the self. We briefly take up the problem of child abuse in Chapter 14.)

SOMATIC TREATMENTS THAT AFFECT PROBLEMS IN OTHER SYSTEMS

Treating the body in order to cure psychological problems has taken a variety of forms in psychiatry. Many procedures, including surgery or mutilation of the brain, have been tried. However, lobotomies or lobectomies, operations for altering the central nervous system surgically, have largely been abandoned as ineffective as well as difficult to justify. Psychologists in mental hospitals will still find somatic procedures in use; they include passing electric current through the temples.

Sophisticated administrations of electroconvulsive therapy (or "shock," usually referred to as ECT or ECS) is preceded by a drug-induced relaxation or paralysis of all muscle systems so that major spasms with their possible injury do not occur when the shock passes. Many practitioners believe that ECT is especially effective in cases of psychotic depression. An older and now out-of-fashion approach was insulin shock treatment. Other procedures, such as wrapping potentially violent patients in layers of dry, hot, wet, or cold bedsheets ("packing"), and strenuous needle showers, whirlpool baths, and exercise, are also still employed occasionally.

Sometimes professionals infer that a person's self-concept—and perhaps his range of skills—may be so impaired by a physical condition that corrective surgery or plastic surgery is likely to have a beneficial effect on many areas of his life. A psychologist may encounter candidates for vocational training, for instance, whose fears of interpersonal ridicule may seem closely related to bizarre tooth malformation or odd facial characteristics of scars. He must evaluate the potential psychological gain to the client of changed appearance or improved function.

Chemical Input—Prescribed Medication

One of the first comprehensive clinical texts in psychopharmacology is *Diagnosis and Drug Treatment of Psychiatric Disorders* by Kelin and Davis (1969). In reviewing a great deal of literature dealing with the psychological effects of drugs, the authors leave no doubt that the chemical input to the biological system can be of great importance in dealing with psychopathology.

In the last ten or fifteen years, the spectrum of available medications that will influence thought patterns, mood, or level of activity has become broad indeed. These medications have played a significant (although probably not single-handed) role in helping begin the trend away from large mental hospitals, enabling patients to stay in their homes and communities. Although the medication approach has often been considered the inferior one by "talk" therapists, medicating therapists disagree. For the latter it is not at all certain that the recipient of "talk" therapy is generally better off than the recipient of medication.

The effectiveness of medication in the treatment of hospitalized persons has been documented by May (1968) in an extensive study comparing treatment methods usually accorded to hospitalized schizophrenics. Psychologists and psychiatrists of psychoanalytic persuasion have sometimes found it difficult to accept approaches based on medication, a fact that leads May to observe rather wryly that ". . . psychoanalytic terminology may be used by the resident as an intellectualizing defense against a deeper understanding of the dynamics of drug response." Even though the psychologist does not administer medications, his understanding of basic facts about them enable him to give greater service to the mental health team and to his client.

First, there is a diversity of agents. Klein and Davis present four major categories: (1) antipsychotic agents, (2) mood-active drugs, (3) nonbarbiturate minor tranquilizers and sedatives, and (4) nonbarbiturate hypnotics.

The antipsychotic agents—sometimes called "major tranquilizers"—have common thought-clarifying properties, but they vary widely in the degree of activation or sedation they produce and in the degree to which they suppress anger or anxiety. The thought-clarifying effect takes time, sometimes seven to ten days, because it depends on a sufficient level being built up in the body. A useful analogy for explaining to patients the necessity of taking their medication steadily in order to build up the proper level is: "It's like trying to make and keep a bathtub half full of water with the drain open." The analogy makes clear why patients may experience "success" at quitting their medications for several days before symptoms return.

The mood-active group of agents has three major subgroups: (1) the tricyclic antidepressants; (2) the MAO inhibitors, generally less effective as antidepressants and quite dangerous with certain other compounds; and (3) the stimulants, of which amphetamines are representative. Klein and Davis's third and fourth groups contain milder agents more commonly seen in treating more "neurotic" symptoms, such as anxiety, tension, and sleeplessness.

The list of available drugs is very long, and a sophisticated psychiatrist can design a regimen for a patient taking into account several factors, such as type of presenting symptoms, level of agitation, and sleep patterns. He may combine three or more agents, some to be built up in the body, and others to be taken at particular times of day for particular shorter-term effect. But few drugs are without *side effects*, unwanted effects that are produced along with the beneficial changes. Typical side effects of high doses of antipsychotic agents is a drying of the mouth and pseudo-parkinsonism, or minor tremor of the extremities. In general, when this happens dosages can be reduced and anti-parkinsonism agents administered, so that such side effects need not be a serious problem.

In working with patients on a medication regimen, the psychologist's role is to understand something of the process, help structure the patient's expectations, help them take the dosage prescribed, and communicate necessary feedback about main effects or side effects to the physician. For example, 16-year-old John's physician called the local mental health clinic. John was in a florid psychotic condition. He was talking rapidly about wanting to play football as soon as school began, needing pressure to make him perform his best, and saying over and over, "Man, I gotta face life, man!" He confided that he had "hangups, hangups, hangups" and that he had to work his emotions off on the football field. From time to time John would jump up and throw imaginary footballs. The psychiatrist advised that John be given an injection of an antipsychotic agent with sedative properties and that he be brought to the clinic the next morning. The psychiatrist and psychologist talked with John and his parents next morning, primarily to decide where John should be cared for—the local general hospital, his home, a nonmedical halfway house, or the distant state hospital. John's level of sedation and his parents' willingness to look after him made the team suggest that he be kept at home even during the acute phase. The psychiatrist carefully outlined the medication regimen for John, while the psychologist made plans for short-term intensive therapy after John had recovered sufficiently, this to be followed by brief family therapy to deal with the parents' overly high expectations of the boy. Although the plan had been carefully outlined by the psychiatrist, the psychologist found himself having to explain and reexplain to the distraught parents what the effects of the medication were likely to be, that a great deal of sleep was desirable at this time, and that John must take his medication as prescribed. Because of the good working relationships, the psychologist became a major part of the psychiatrist's monitoring system, reporting John's condition and facilitating changes in prescription as John progressed.

Klein and Davis take an approach to psychiatric treatment which is essentially "make a diagnosis, then administer the medication found to be most useful." But in a hypothetical "middle-of-the-road" setting, signs frequently suggesting that medications be considered are the psychotic conditions, severe depression, acute anxiety, and hyperactivity in children. The control of seizures by medication deserves special mention. In general, good control can be obtained with Dilantin (often given with phenobarbitol) or Mysolene in perhaps 85 percent of patients who suffer recurrent seizures.

PREVENTIVE POSSIBILITIES

Although medicine, in particular as practiced by the public health agencies, is the profession charged with preventing problems involving the biological system, there are some essential contributions to be made here by psychologists. Psychologists should be aware of the increasingly clear deleterious effects on central-nervous-system function of maternal malnutrition and early malnutrition of the children themselves (e.g., Eisenberg, 1969; Scrimshaw, 1969). From a professional as well as a humanitarian standpoint, improving early nutrition qualifies as a worthwhile preventive measure, and psychologists can help clients understand and apply what we know about it.

Programs aimed at the reduction of alcoholism and drug abuse can also use the psychologist's skills. Suicide prevention, in which the most effective approaches use emergency contact networks with supporting organizations within the community—for example, the renowned Suicide Prevention Center in Los Angeles—is another challenge which psychologists have met, even though attempts to predict suicidal behavior using psychological tests have not been very successful (Lester, 1970).

The area of human reproduction seems to have greatest potential payoff for many phases of psychological prevention work involving biological systems. Problems of having too many offspring for a family to support materially or psychologically are only beginning to be studied seriously. Clausen (1966) in reviewing family structure, socialization, and personality has noted that children from small families tend to make higher scores on intelligence tests than children from large families, even when social class is held constant. Family size is only one of many important variables in this area. Unwanted pregnancy, single-parent families, very young parents, overcrowding, and so on, all involve psychological concerns and are often related to aspects of reproduction. The psychologist's efforts would seem to be best directed to disseminating knowledge, facilitating choice, and helping design systems for family supplementation. Other specialized tasks, such as promoting the use of prenatal care, educating about adequate nutrition, and counseling about genetic conditions, are preventive activities that will become easier to carry out if we continually help individuals, families, and communities to reexamine, define, and work toward having families of the desired size.

SUMMARY

Biological systems are important to the practicing psychologist for three broad reasons: (1) bodily problems may have an effect on personal or other systems; (2) some bodily problems signify distress in other systems; and (3) some bodily treatments may help relieve certain psychological conditions. In the first place, illness, accidents, aging, and impending death are problems having inevitable effects on the personal system. Also into this first category falls central-nervous-system dysfunction, or brain damage. Genetic factors now require the attention of psychologists because of the mounting evidence that genetic linkages are present with some psychological abnormalities. In the second category, "psychosomatic" illnesses and the abuse of prescribed or nonprescribed drugs are perhaps the most obvious examples of bodily problems signifying distress in personal systems. The third category, bodily treatment for psychological problems, is primarily restricted to medication, although a variety of procedures, ranging from electroshock to exercise to vitamin therapy, are sometimes used. Psychologists may help prevent bodily related problems by providing their skills for activities such as designing adequate nutrition programs for very young children and expectant mothers, and family planning activities.

SUGGESTED READINGS

Rosenthal, D. *Genetic theory and abnormal behavior.* New York: McGraw-Hill, 1970.

Rosenthal's book is one of several current efforts to summarize progress in behavior genetics. It forcefully invites psychologists to consider genetic factors in abnormal behavior, especially in schizophrenia and manic-depressive psychosis, on which the book primarily focuses. Rosenthal, perhaps knowing that eager readers may be underprepared in genetics, begins the work with excellent review chapters. Although they are necessarily short, the sections on genetic studies of psychopathy and criminality, and on neurosis, homosexuality, and alcoholism, are useful summaries of work in those areas.

Lennard, H. L., Epstein, L. J., Bernstein, A., and Ransom, D. C. *Mystification and drug misuse.* San Francisco: Jossey-Bass, 1971.

Lennard and co-authors use the subtitle "Hazards in using psychoactive medication" in building a case criticizing the poorly thought-out use of legally obtained psychoactive agents. They accuse commercial and professional interests of building a climate of mystification through which everyday human problems can be redefined as medical problems for which the taking of drugs is an answer. Another useful book for discussions of personal experiences with hallucinogenic drugs and their relation to society, religion, and therapy is *Psychedelics* edited by Aaronson and Osmond (1970). Smart and Jones (1970), studying illicit LSD users, found a much higher incidence of psychopathology than in controls.

Pohlman, E. *The psychology of birth planning.* Cambridge, Mass.: Schenkman, 1969.

Pohlman's work is a landmark in the growing interest psychologists are showing in birth planning and reproductive behavior.

Abt, L. E., and Reiss, B. F. (eds.). *Progress in clinical psychology, Vol. 8.* New York: Grune & Stratton, 1969.

This volume is devoted, save for one article on suggestability, to articles on sleep and dreams. One of the four on the topic of sleep is about sleep disorders in children; of the five on dreaming, one is on drugs and dreaming and another on clinical implications of recent dream research.

Reiterman, C. (ed.). *Abortion and the unwanted child.* New York: Springer, 1971.

Abortion dilemmas confront many psychologists. Reiterman's book is a useful introduction to an area about which little systematic knowledge exists. The book includes a twenty-one-year follow-up study of 121 children born after abortion requests were refused.

Shneidman, E. S., Farberow, N. L., and Litman, R. E. *The psychology of suicide.* New York: Science House, 1970.

A comprehensive statement about suicide by some of the most noted pioneers in the area, arising from their work at the famous Suicide Prevention Center in Los Angeles. Its broad organization makes one of the best single sources on suicide. Feifel's discussion (1969) of attitudes toward death and society's suppression of considerations of death would also be relevant. Scott and Brewer (1971) have edited a book of readings used for a class and workshop on confrontation of dying.   Kastenbaum and Aisenberg's (1972) *Psychology of Death* is an excellent compendium.

Wender, P. H. *Minimal brain dysfunction in children.* New York: Wiley, 1971.

Wender's book takes a careful look at a difficult problem: why (or why not) say that hyperactive or hyperkinetic behavior is due to a disorder of the brain so minor as to be unverifiable? The topic is important for psychologists working with children because of the frequency with which parents, teachers, and other child-care workers raise questions about hyperactivity and the apparent polarity of the "train them" and the "medicate them" camps.

Luria, A. R. *Higher cortical functions in man.* New York: Basic Books, 1966.

Luria's book is a very comprehensive and readable statement of brain-behavior relationships. It is also very useful clinically.

Russell, E. W., Neuringer, C., and Goldstein, G. *Assessment of brain damage.* New York: Wiley, 1970.

The subtitle, A Neuropsychological Key Approach, indicates that the authors have approached the assessment of brain damage using detailed neuropsychological examination procedures, for example measurement of tapping speed right and left, measurement of grip strength right and left, and a host of other measures, instead of the more common but poorly validated single test with statistical cutoff procedure. The Halstead neuropsychological battery as modified by Reitan is basic to the authors' approach.

Talland (1965) has an excellent book on abnormalities of memory. Parsons (1970) also gives an excellent introduction to recent research on clinical neuropsychology. Readers may also wish to consult the "classic" book by Halstead, *Brain and Intelligence* (1947).

Barber, T. X., DiCara, L. V., Kamiya, J., Miller, N. E., Shapiro, D., and Stoyva, J. (eds.). *Biofeedback and self control, 1970.* Chicago: Aldine-Atherton, 1971; and Kamiya, J., Barber, T. X., DiCara, L. V., Miller, N. E., Shapiro, D., and Stoyva, J. (eds.). *Biofeedback and self control.* Chicago, Aldine-Atherton, 1971.

These two books are a unique compilation of the broad core of research and writing in biofeedback. They form a sequence, the first dealing with work up to 1970 and the second with subsequent contributions.

RESEARCH EXAMPLES

Kaspar, J. C., Millichamp, J. G., and Backus, R., Child, D., and Schulman, J. L. A study of the relationship between neurological evidence of brain damage in children and activity and distractibility. *Journal of Consulting and Clinical Psychology*, 1971, *36*, 329–337.

Nowhere is the area of brain-behavior relationships of more topical importance to the psychologist than in the area of brain damage as it affects child behavior. Some workers, generally not psychologists, have chosen to name certain hyperactive and distractible behavior in children "minimal brain damage." Other workers argue hotly that no physical damage has been demonstrated for this group, so a label that infers organic damage is probably wrong and misleading. The general area is ripe for research contributions.

Kaspar et al. note that the presence of brain injury is typically assessed through the use of three techniques: neurological examination, EEG, and psychometric examination. The relationship between the various methods is hazy, and understandably so, they feel, because the three methods assess quite different domains of functioning. In a separate review (Kaspar and Schulman, 1971) they concluded that the research literature does not support the contention that the brain-damage syndrome exists as a convergent syndrome in the sense that the behaviors purported to follow brain injury inevitably do follow it. They also concluded that distractibility, difficulties in control of activity levels, and possibly emotional lability may be parallel consequences of brain injury shown by some children and not by others.

This study attempted to test the existence of a relationship between brain injury and behavioral measures of activity and distractibility in a group of children who were diagnosed as brain-damaged by neurological examination. A central assumption was that "hyperactivity" or "distractibility" are socially defined labels that are bestowed when a child is unable to modify his level of attention or activity in accordance with demands being placed on him. From this point of view, the investigators felt it unlikely that brain-damaged children would be more active than normal children in a free situation; differences would be expected, however, in a structured situation.

The subjects were forty-eight males and twenty-four females between five and eight, half of whom (Es) had been diagnosed by neurological examination as showing signs of brain damage. E and C groups were matched for sex, but Cs were found to have significantly higher IQ scores on the Peabody Picture Vocabulary Test, although both groups fell in the normal range.

In a structured situation, Es were more active than control Ss. In three of four distractibility tasks employed, more Es than Cs were found to be distractible. Both of these findings point to a deficiency in control mechanisms, a deficiency that has its primary and most consistent effect in restrictive situations. In the free situation, an interaction between sex and damage was found. Correlational analysis suggested a two-part explanation of all the findings: brain-damaged children tend to be distractible, and when this is true, being brighter leads to being less distractible. On the basis of their total findings, the authors conclude that brain injury does not lead to difficulties in modulating activity level and to distractibility in response to *all* stimuli but to some forms of hyperactivity in certain children and to other forms of distractibility in others. Although the picture is complicated, they feel the data indicate that brain injury affects the child's capacity to control his immediate exchanges with his environment in terms of activity level and attention.

Sprague, R. L., Barnes, K. R., and Werry, J. S. Methylphenidate and thioridazine: learning, reaction time, activity, and classroom behavior in disturbed children. *American Journal of Orthopsychiatry*, 1970, *40*, 615–627.

Using drugs to calm hyperactive children is a procedure surrounded with a variety of conviction and insufficient information. These authors undertook a three-factor study: (1) methylphenidate, (2) thioridazine, and (3) placebo. Number (1) is a stimulant, Ritalin; (2) is a tranquilizer, Thorazine; and (3) is an inert substance. Three dependent variables, learning, reaction time, and activity level, were measured in a highly structured laboratory situation. The subjects were 12 boys from three research classes for emotionally disturbed children in a school district. They had a mean age of 9.42 months, a mean IQ of 98.6, and had been placed in special classes for antisocial, distractible, and hyperactive behavior, although 3 Ss were shy and withdrawn. Academically, all were underachievers. Ss served as their own control in a design featuring two dosage levels for each drug and a counterbalanced sequence of drugs.

Methylphenidate significantly increased correct responding, decreased reaction times and hyperactivity, and significantly increased attention and cooperative behavior in the classroom. In discussing the often-noted inverse correlation between activity level and learning, the authors note that methylphenidate may improve some aspects of learning, thus reducing motor overflow, or it may reduce activity, thus reducing distractibility, or affect a central process, with both motor activity and learning changing as a result. The authors also discuss the disquieting finding from other studies that drug-facilitated learning may be less durable.

Reitan, R. M., and Fitzhugh, K. B. Behavioral deficits in groups with cerebral vascular lesions. *Journal of Consulting and Clinical Psychology*, 1971, *37*, 215–223.

Reitan and Fitzhugh, long associated with work in brain-behavior relationships, underscore the point that "brain damage" is too gross a category to be meaningfully investigated. Type of lesion is a principal neurological variable. Three groups of patients with cerebrovascular disease (right hemisphere, left hemisphere, or generalized involvement) were identified and matched for age, sex, education, and duration of the disease. Comparisons within the group and between the three groups were made on measures including IQ, motor strength, and speed psychomotor performance and sensory functions.

Significant differences were found between groups with the lateralized lesions, with the generalized involvement group occupying an intermediate position. The group with left cerebral damage had significantly lower verbal IQ than performance, whereas the relationship was reversed in the group with right cerebral damage. Motor, psychomotor, and sensory functions were consistently impaired on the side opposite the damaged hemisphere for the groups with lateralized lesions.

Reitan and his co-workers plan a sequence of studies of the psychological correlates of cerebral vascular, neoplastic (e.g., tumors), and traumatic lesions.

Satz, P., Fennell, E., and Reilly, C. Predictive validity of six neurodiagnostic tests: a decision theory analysis. *Journal of Consulting and Clinical Psychology*, 1970, *34*, 375–381.

The authors used cases in the files of a medical school hospital which were classified as brain-injured by an extensive work-up or functional. The two groups were compared to obtain validity estimates for five neurological tests (the electroencephalogram, skull X-ray, and others) and one neuropsychological test (the Block Rotation Test). Each test's prediction could be either true positive for detecting brain damage or false positive. The best, the EEG, showed a very high percentage of valid positives (83 percent) but also the highest percentage of false positive errors (29 percent). The Block Rotation Test demonstrated a moderately high percentage of true positives (60 percent) and a low false positive rate (20 percent). The authors compared the tests against various base rates (i.e., numbers of actual brain-damaged patients found in given hospital populations). The results of their analysis showed that all the tests would be useful, compared with a base rate giving a 50-50 chance of being brain-damaged or not. They point out that there would be dollar cost savings through using the tests. Another consideration, as Meehl and Rosen (1955) point out, is that the discovery of brain damage may be so important that any simply administered test that will sort out likely cases, even though there may be many false positives, would be worthwhile.

Rudestam, K. E. Stockholm and Los Angeles. a cross-cultural study of the communication of suicidal intent. *Journal of Consulting and Clinical Psychology*, 1971, *36*, 82–90.

Rudestam studied fifty cases of recent suicides selected from the coroners' records in Stockholm, Sweden, and Los Angeles, California (using whites only). Stockholm has a high suicide rate, 23.6 suicides annually per 100,000 people, but Los Angeles County's frequency is also high, 17.9 per 100,000, as compared with the national rate of about 11.0 per 100,000. The sex ratio found in Los Angeles (27 men to 23 women) was also used to select Swedish cases. Rudestam's method was called a "psychological autopsy"—an interview with a near relative or a close friend covering specific topics such as details of the suicidal act, motivations and intentions, and the medical, occupational, and social condition of the deceased person.

Among the important findings were the fact that it was rather common in both countries for victims to communicate their suicidal intent directly to significant others—56 percent in Los Angeles and 66 percent in Stockholm. In addition, many communicated intent in more subtle forms. Contrary to expectations, men communicated intentions as frequently as women.

The methods of suicide varied cross-culturally; 50 percent of the Swedish suicides were by drug overdose, compared with 34 percent in Los Angeles; 42 percent of the American deaths were due to firearms, but only 4 percent of the suicides in Stockholm, where there are strict gun-control laws. There were 16 percent deaths by domestic gas in Sweden, where the gas is more lethal than in this country. The predominant method for women was drugs, and death by firearms was almost entirely confined to men.

Rudestam discussed responses to suicidal communication at some length. Many of the people around the to-be suicide victim were either insensitive or maladaptive in their responses. He detected some cross-cultural differences in handling suicidal possibilities. Greater concern for the victim was verbalized by respondents in Stockholm. In only one-third of the cases in each city was a professional person consulted. Rudestam suggests improved services for potential suicides and training of significant others to handle situations in which a person has expressed an intent to commit suicide.

Further cross-cultural study was done by Krauss and Tesser (1971) in testing the thwarting disorientation theory of suicide. The theory postulates that suicide occurs when a person's social ties are threatened and also that certain social conditions make such threats more likely. Using records on fifty-eight societies, Krauss and Tesser studied seven societal situations in relation to suicide rates. Two conditions successfully predicted higher suicide rates—social conditions permitting men to divorce their wives without grounds or approval of others and presence of homicide in defiance of society. The actual suicides were sometimes not by the people directly involved. The authors see their findings as partial confirmation of the theory being tested.

chapter 11

Personal Systems:
Individual Psychotherapy

If we were to measure the importance of a concept by the number of words that had been spoken and written about it, or the number of conferences and symposiums devoted to it, surely psychotherapy would receive a very high rating. A large fraction of clinical psychologists spend most of their time in this activity. Others whose jobs require that they do other things or who are assigned to a nontherapy role on a mental health team struggle to achieve the right to be psychotherapists. Counselors and social workers in schools and social agencies tend to look upon therapy as their real business; the other tasks for which they are responsible are seen as less significant and challenging. And a whole series of movies, novels, and television programs has brought the message to the general public that psychotherapy is the way to get rid of psychological handicaps and find the path to a more rewarding life.

As time has passed, however, it has become apparent that individual psychotherapy is not the universal solvent for stubborn human ills that its enthusiastic practitioners and clients had thought it was going to be. Although the number of psychotherapists and the number of clients seeking therapy continued to increase in recent decades, many psychologists began to work out alternative improvement strategies and direct special attention to groups in the population for whom psychotherapy had not proved to be very helpful. The practice of psychotherapy is becoming a field of specialization within clinical psychology rather than a skill that all clinical psychologists practice. It is one among many ways of helping people who need help.

Viewed from the vantage point of general systems theory, what distinguishes psychotherapy from the other strategies is that it is an attempt to change the *personality system* of the individual so that it functions better. Although it does not assume that the larger social systems of which this individual human being is a part have no control over him or can be ignored, it does not attempt to deal directly with the wider systems but focuses attention on the pattern of feelings, assumptions, concepts, motives, and habits through which the impact of the world outside the person is screened and processed. Its objective is not just to make the person feel better or behave better but to extend his control over both feelings and behavior.

In this and the following chapters we will consider some of the ideas and procedures drawn upon in this endeavor, in the kinds of treatment that go on in interviews between "doctor" and "patient," designed to help the latter to achieve an understanding of himself that he can use in reorganizing his own life. Because it is primarily a verbal process (although research has shown significant nonverbal components) it works best with clients who are fairly intelligent and articulate. Because it can be long-drawn-out and discouraging, it requires from client and therapist more commitment and willingness to persist in the face of difficulties than most other psychological improvement strategies do. Because it is a self-study procedure, persons who find introspection natural or congenial react more favorably to it than do those whose whole orientation is outward-rather than inward-looking. For these reasons it is usually *voluntary*. The person experiencing personality difficulties seeks out someone he hopes can help him overcome them and enters into a sort of working agreement with him.

As explained in Chapter 1, this distinction between voluntary and nonvoluntary arrangements has not always been made as clearly as it deserves to be. When a zealous psychologist or psychiatrist undertakes to provide psychotherapy to mental hospital patients who have not asked for it or to inmates of a correctional institution who may be resisting this or any other kind of effort to change their personalities, the psychological situation created in the interview room is vastly different from the voluntary situation, similar as the physical arrangements may appear. The difference did not really become apparent during the period when only the well-to-do presented themselves for psychological therapy. Increasingly, in the decades since World War II, efforts have been made to provide more than just custodial care for persons with psychological problems at all levels of the population, and the plans that have worked best have not been based on the psychotherapy model of the 1930s and 1940s.

Even though it is limited to certain kinds of people under certain circumstances, however, psychotherapy is a very important variety of human activity. The number of people who seek it out, or would seek it out if they knew it was available, is very large. The development of this branch of knowledge and professional practice following upon Freud's initial ideas and procedures can be considered a significant achievement of modern man.

THEORIES AND GOALS

There are almost as many theories about psychotherapy as there are psychotherapists. The dominant theory has always been Freudian psychoanalysis, but the impact of the views of Adler and Jung, Horney and Sullivan, Rogers, Mowrer, Frankel, Glasser, Ellis—to name just a few of the many who could be listed—is considerable.

We shall not discuss these different theories and the practices growing out of them one by one because such an approach would be both time consuming and confusing. One source of confusion is that the ideas of every theorist undergo continual modification as he lives and works. The concepts Freud stressed in 1910 are not identical with those upon which he rested his theoretical structure in 1935. Rogers's second book on psychotherapy differs markedly from his first. Thus it is difficult to write for the beginning student of clinical psychology an account of one of these comprehensive theories that includes *all* the concepts, early and late, actually incorporated in the thinking of some of its adherents.

Another reason for confusion in the theories therapists have produced about therapy is that they overlap. If such theories are taken up one by one, the student is confronted with the task of judging for himself how great this overlapping is. This is especially difficult for an inexperienced person because much of the common ground is found in practice rather than in conceptualization. Psychologists and psychiatrists, when writing about their work, are most likely to stress the aspects they consider to be unique or original, while they slight the aspects that fit in with many other theoretical orientations. Thus the student trying to find a way of approaching his own professional tasks is likely to assume that the differences between theories are sharper than they actually are, and he may conclude that he is required to identify himself with one and only one of the theorists and to repudiate the others. The richness of his own theoretical formulation and the range of his helpfulness to others may be diminished by such a decision.

Therefore, instead of outlining the different complex approaches to therapy connected with the names of Freud, Rogers, Sullivan, and the other founders of systems or schools, we shall discuss first the principal purposes therapy has been thought to accomplish by some influential thinker at some stage of his development. We shall then look for common threads and basic issues and attempt to put the separate pieces together in a new way.

The first of these major purposes basic to some kinds of therapy might be labeled *strengthening the client's motivation to do the right things.* It is the oldest of the aims we shall discuss. Suggestion in all its forms, ranging from gentle advice to the use of hypnosis to produce tendencies to act in specified ways, is one kind of procedure through which this purpose is carried out. Encouragement and inspiration, whether administered through informal praise and appreciation or through books and sermons, are intended to serve this purpose. Long before there were any professional specialties like psychology, this kind of treatment was constantly attempted. In our own time, therapeutic organizations such as Alcoholics Anonymous attribute most of their success to this kind of influence.

A second purpose of therapy that has often been stated is to *reduce emotional pressure by facilitating the expression of feeling*, the process called *catharsis*. When the average layman thinks about therapy, it is probably this meaning that he is most likely to connect with it. Dozens of motion pictures have given dramatic portrayals of a sudden relief from neurotic symptoms and anxiety following a flood of emotional expression touched off when contact is made with some repressed memory. Like suggestion and inspiration, the use of this process of emotional expression covers a wide range of depth and intensity, from the common "blowing off steam" at work or at home to the use of drugs or hypnosis to enable a patient to relive a traumatic experience.

A third way of formulating the purpose of therapy makes use of concepts from the psychology of development. Therapy aims to *release the potential for growth*. A basic growth tendency in every person is postulated, a tendency toward maturity and integration. Unfortunate circumstances or adverse influences can block or temporarily reverse this process, but cannot destroy it completely. What therapy aims to do is to remove these obstacles, whatever they are, and allow the person to start growing again along the lines of his own unique pattern. The psychotherapist should not be thought of as a mechanic, locating and repairing defects in a piece of equipment, but as more like a gardener, removing weeds, providing light, nutrients, and moisture to stimulate a plant intrinsically disposed to grow. Two aspects of developmental theory may be distinguished. One calls for the analysis of each life stage in childhood to ascertain what kinds of neurotic symptoms and faulty character structures may have arisen from failure to negotiate it successfully. The discussions by psychoanalysts of symptoms arising through arrested development at the oral, anal, phallic, or latency period have this focus. The emphasis psychoanalysts place on the necessity for transference, a term signifying the process of projecting childish attitudes onto the therapist, comes from the conviction that early periods must in some sense be relived emotionally if personality reorganization is to occur. The other aspect of developmental theory, expressed more clearly by Jung and by Rogers than by Freud, places the emphasis on development as a process that continues throughout life, whatever the early handicaps have been. A person is so complex that many avenues of growth and creativity are open to him if they can only be recognized and encouraged. Whether the emphasis is on unraveling the tangled strands of childhood or on opening up new vistas for the future, developmental theories have in common the assumption that therapy means discovering ways of facilitating a natural process rather than undertaking the construction of something new.

A fourth purpose of therapy, in some ways related to the preceding one, is the *modification of the cognitive structure of the person*, by which is meant the interrelated set of concepts and fixed ideas that determine his perceptions of the world around him, of other persons, and of himself. Theorists who approach the problems of therapy from this direction have surmised that the roots of a person's difficulties lie in his basic misconceptions about the nature of things, mistaken ideas he acquired at a former period of his life. He is likely to be quite unaware of these cognitive structures. The conclusions to which they lead him are axioms, taken for granted. An early theorist, Alfred Adler, discussed the effects of this phenomenon under the graphic term *life style*. More recently, Kelly, in his *The Psychology of Personal Constructs* (1955), presented not only a coherent theoretical statement of this point of view, but also a number of ingenious methods for identifying the basic cognitive structures in an individual and for helping him to modify them if they need changing. The theoretical formulations of Carl Rogers have emphasized the importance of clear, finely differentiated perceptions of self and the world as a basis for effective living. As many clinical psychologists see their task today, the aim of therapeutic activity is to make a client aware of his basic cognitive structures and enable him to produce a change in the pattern. Change will often come automatically once the person becomes aware that one of his "personal constructs" is inconsistent with other aspects of his personality.

A fifth stated purpose of therapy is *self-knowledge*, broadly defined. This can be an extremely inclusive concept. It is basic to most counseling and rehabilitation activities. The client is given aptitude and interest tests and helped to examine his own capacities, attitudes, needs, background, and opportunities. Self-knowledge is also prominent among the goals of psychoanalysis. The attempt to bring unconscious material into consciousness where the ego of the person can cope with it is so basic in therapeutic procedure that for many theorists this growth in self-knowledge *is* therapy. The word that has been much used as a label for the process of attaining self-knowledge is *insight*. As a theoretical concept, insight is not being stressed as much at present as it was in previous periods. There has come the recognition that an intellectual awareness of all the recesses of one's personality does not necessarily make for psychological health. There must be some emotional quality to insight if it is to be effective, and it has proved to be very difficult to state how the word is to be defined in these emotional terms. Furthermore, striking improvements occurring in the absence of any manifestation of insight whatever have seriously challenged those who would use self-knowledge as a central therapeutic concept. In short, it seems that insight is neither a necessary nor a sufficient factor in therapy. Nevertheless, it still has its place as an important organizing concept, and the procedures most commonly used in therapy perhaps serve this purpose better than any other.

A sixth way of stating the purpose of therapy is *habit change*. Neurosis or maladjustment are viewed as the end result of a learning process in which undesirable or ineffective habits have been formed. For many reasons these may be difficult to get rid of once the person is saddled with them. The task of the therapist, then, is to arrange learning situations in which the patient can modify such undesirable habits or replace them by others. There was real excitement among psychologists when J. B. Watson reported in 1920 that an irrational fear of furry animals had been experimentally produced in a child using conditioned-response methods and when M. C. Jones reported a few years later that conditioning could also be used to remove such fears from children's experience. These experiments seemed to point the way to a rational, scientific kind of therapy free from mystery and uncertainty. The years since the 1920s sobered hopes for simple methods of "emotional reeducation," as many irrational fears proved to be impervious to such treatment. But straightforward conditioned-response methods were still used quite widely in the treatment of behavior patterns such as enuresis and alcoholism, and the modification of social habits such as shyness and tactlessness was often attempted through planned learning situations. During the 1960s there was a tremendous resurgence of interest in this approach to therapy, based on Wolpe's (1958) techniques applying conditioning principles and Skinner's (1938) research on altering responses by their reinforcements. The difference between the thinking on which this kind of improvement strategy, generally called *behavior modification*, is based, and the thinking underlying the first five purposes we have listed, is far wider than the differences between each of these five and the others. We shall consider in a separate chapter this kind of strategy for improvement.

Still another type of theory emphasizes *interpersonal relationships*. According to such a theory, we must look for the sources of all psychological ills in the person's relationships to the "significant others" in his life. Here, too, some therapists place the emphasis on the very earliest periods of life as the time when the patterns for future relationships are laid down. They hope, by understanding what occurred then, to find ways of modifying these patterns so that they will no longer exert unhealthy influences on present relationships. Other workers pay more attention to their client's current relationships to spouse, children, friends, and colleagues. They hope to find relationships that may be changed for better rather than to identify the remote childhood origins of the difficulties. One major source inherent in all types of therapy for producing change in interpersonal relationships is the fact that the client is at the time experiencing a new relationship, without the defects of those previously formed—his relationship to the therapist. A strong emphasis on *communication* distinguishes the interpersonal theories of therapy. Isolation and estrangement are involved in much psychological disturbance. One way to combat them is to improve communication.

Furthermore, the possibilities for therapeutic intervention are not limited to the things that can happen between just two individuals. The unique advantage of *group therapy* is that it allows the participants to establish new relationships, observe and study them, and modify them in constructive ways. Patients can make emotional contact with others as individuals; they can also practice the different *roles* they must play in dealing with other people—whether children, bosses, co-workers, or strangers.

From the perspective of general systems theory, formulating therapy goals in terms of interpersonal relationships involves shifting attention to a new system level. Actually moving more than one step up in the system hierarchy may be necessary. The family or marriage counselor, for example, deals with the complex system that the husband, wife, and children make up in their close, although perhaps troubled, relationships to one another. But the psychologist who sets himself the task of transforming a mental hospital into a genuine therapeutic community is dealing with an *organization* rather than with simply a group of interacting individuals, and the relevant system characteristics may be quite different. Because of these differences in the system to which attention must be directed, these kinds of effort are discussed in separate chapters rather than included among the varieties of psychotherapy considered in this chapter.

COMMON FEATURES

Writers who explain what psychotherapy is all about, and to an even greater extent practicing psychotherapists themselves, recognize more than one of these purposes, weighting them differently and finding different kinds of links between them. Rogers, for instance, has stressed the ideas of catharsis, self-knowledge, perceptual shifts, and creative growth. His publications over the years show that he has emphasized catharsis less and creative growth more as time has passed. Freud's early formulations centered on catharsis and self-knowledge, but he later shifted the focal point to development and interpersonal relationships in infancy and childhood. Adlerian therapists devote a good deal of attention to perceptual and cognitive structures and social relationships, but use suggestion and advice to promote self-knowledge and habit change. One of the reasons for the many controversies in the field of psychotherapy may be that there are so many ways in which complex theories can be contrasted with one another!

The procedures actually used show much common ground. In the first place, all methods of personal therapy must concentrate on bringing about *a sufficient lowering of the patient's level of anxiety so that he will be able to permit himself to explore the painful areas of his experience.* An interview where the person is guaranteed privacy, freedom from interruptions, and complete confidentiality has the effect of making him feel at least a little safer than he does at other times in other places. Special group situations may also produce this relaxed attitude. More important is the whole attitude of the therapist and the feeling he communicates to the patient in many subtle ways that he is no longer *alone* with his troubles. The strength of another person has been added to his own.

Dealing with anxiety is one of the basic skills that a psychotherapist must acquire, and it can never be learned from books or lectures. It is not accomplished by simple kinds of verbal reassurance, no matter how earnest. Furthermore, the goal can never be to eliminate anxiety completely, because anxiety constitutes the principal motivation for undertaking therapy as well as the chief reason for resisting it. Some therapists approach the problem of reducing anxiety by combining tranquilizing drugs with psychotherapy in the treatment of severely disturbed cases. To calm a person enough so that he can face all kinds of potentially threatening inner feelings and outer situations and cope with them may be a valuable treatment maneuver. But to carry this so far thas he no longer cares what happens to him or no longer sees the sharp outlines of unyielding facts is not therapy. One of the reasons alcoholics have responded less well to psychotherapy than many other types of neurotic patients is that drinking has become a habitual way of reducing their anxieties—too much.

The second thing that all varieties of therapy attempt to do is to create *a strong personal relationship that can be used as a vehicle for constructive change*. In individual therapy this is a relationship between patient and therapist; in group methods the ties between group members may be the important ones. Research by Fiedler (1950a, 1950b) has suggested that the nature of this relationship may be very similar for kinds of therapy that are differently labeled. It is a significant fact that many theoretical writers, as their experience increases, come to place much more emphasis on this variable. At first, Freud insisted most on the necessity of achieving *insight*; as time passed, *transference* took its place as his central concept, and he turned his attention to the way in which the patient relates himself to his doctor during the different stages of treatment. More recently in psychoanalytic writings there has been a strong emphasis on *countertransference*, or the way in which the doctor relates himself to the patient. Other theorists also talk about the therapeutic interaction—what the situation means to the therapist as well as to the client.

The important idea arising from all this discussion is one that beginning students sometimes miss—that it is necessary for the therapist himself to participate on a deep emotional level in the psychological process that constitutes therapy. Verbal techniques and skills are no substitute for this emotional participation. There are hazards for the psychologist as well as for the client in launching out upon the deep waters the two of them must traverse together. Learning to deal with such hazards is a far more difficult thing than learning to say something appropriate in response to a client's remark.

Another common feature in many diverse systems of thinking about psychotherapy is an emphasis on *communication as a way of enabling the patient to establish connections with his own inner and outer worlds*. Obviously, any talking involves communication to some degree. It might be maintained with some plausibility that all psychological disorders are essentially communication problems and that treatment consists in repairing or installing lines of communication so that they will connect the patient with the complex human world in which he must function and assist him in articulating his thoughts and feelings, thus making them more accessible. At any rate, some of the most essential of the therapist's skills are the ways he has of facilitating free expression in the client with whom he is working. This, like the emotional participation discussed above, is not just a matter of knowing what to say. It consists rather in a sensitive awareness of the way the other person feels, a general perceptiveness that makes it possible for him to pick up faint clues and to grasp meanings in confused and halting attempts to say something—or even in silence, for that matter. A sense of being understood acts as a powerful motivating force for a troubled client, encouraging him to try to communicate more of his experience. To provide this understanding requires great effort as well as extreme sensitivity. One must listen to the other person with a kind of concentrated yet relaxed attention that one seldom brings to the other situations of life. It may even be that it is this *interested attention* rather than the understanding itself that promotes further effort on the part of the client, since occasional failure to grasp a particular meaning seems not to impede therapeutic progress. However, needless to say, if the therapist, well meaning though he may be, never quite understands what the client is trying to say, the therapeutic process is hardly likely to continue for long.

WHAT PSYCHOTHERAPISTS DO

Let us look a little more closely at what it is about the psychotherapist's behavior that produces the effects we have been discussing, the reduction of anxiety, the establishment of a constructive personal relationship, and the facilitation of expression of subtle and complex thoughts and feelings. The qualities in therapists that distinguish the successful (those whose clients improve) from the unsuccessful (those whose clients may actually get worse) have been intensively studied by Truax and Carkhuff (1967). There are three that appear to be most essential. They label them *accurate empathy, nonpossessive warmth,* and *genuineness,* although they have been called by various other names in the writings upon which Truax and Carkhuff have drawn. Rogers, for example, in the analysis of the "necessary and sufficient conditions of therapeutic personality change" out of which this whole line of research has grown (Rogers, 1957), called the same characteristics *empathic understanding, unconditional positive regard,* and *self-congruence.*

Qualities of the Good Therapist

Accurate empathy covers not only sensitivity to feelings and meanings a client is expressing, putting oneself in his place and seeing the rest of the world from his vantage point, but also skill in communicating to the client that one does understand. Truax and Carkhuff have presented evidence that therapists differ with regard to this characteristic, that it can be accurately rated from tape-recorded samples of their interviews, and that such ratings are related to whether or not clients improve as a result of the therapy experience.

The second essential characteristic, possibly better described by a term of Rogers, *unconditional positive regard,* than by the Truax and Carkhuff term *nonpossessive warmth,* is the therapist's capacity to accept the client's experience without evaluating or criticizing it and to communicate to him by words, expression, and gesture that he likes and respects him as a person. What is often not realized by persons not trained as psychotherapists is that refraining from evaluations or expressions of disapproval does not mean that one endorses or approves of the kinds of conduct and experience a client has been talking about. Indeed, to refrain from reinforcing undesirable attitudes by showing special interest in them is one aspect of skill in therapy. After a sound relationship has been established, disapproval of particular activities, and reinforcement of constructive attitudes and plans, is quite compatible with a high level of unconditional positive regard. What the good psychotherapist makes clear from the beginning is that he does not reject, dislike, or disapprove of the person himself and that he wholeheartedly wishes him well. This quality, too, can be rated with satisfactory accuracy, and is significantly related to client improvement.

What the third essential, *genuineness* or *self-congruence*, means is that whatever the therapist says and does should be sincere rather than phony. He must not hide behind a professional facade, saying the right things, going through the right motions, but not really experiencing anything himself. This does not mean that he must always express everything he himself feels and thinks. Checking impulses to launch into accounts of one's own experience is part of therapy skill. But what he does say and do must reflect a real person, not some sort of professional robot. To smile when one is genuinely angry, to choose one's words to make them sound like a model of the good psychotherapist rather than to make them spontaneous responses to what the client has said, to express warm friendliness when one is really distracted and eager to get out of the interview situation—these are negative examples of what genuineness means. It is difficult to give positive examples, since a high level of this quality cannot be identified just from words that can be put down in black and white.

One might conclude from the foregoing discussion of essential qualities that good psychotherapists are born and not made. This, however, is not true. Although there are many people who lack aptitude for this sort of professional specialization, a considerable proportion of the human race probably possesses it to some degree. Like other talents, we can expect that this one is developed through training, and expertness grows with experience.

What Therapists Say

The actual words the psychotherapist uses in response to what the client says and does in the interview depend partly on the theoretical orientation of the school or institute in which he receives his training. But this is more a matter of degree or proportion of responses in one category or another than the person who knows therapy only from reading theoretical descriptions might think. Mainly, the content of what the psychotherapist says can be classified as *reflection, interpretation,* or *teaching.*

Psychologists and others whose theoretical roots are grounded in Rogers's theory of client-centered therapy, especially its early versions, try to say something that will accurately reflect the meaning of what the client has been struggling to say, and clarify its feeling components so as to advance him a little further along the road to self-understanding and self-acceptance. Psychologists and others who follow psychoanalytic theories, including those of Adler, Jung, and others who left the Freudian fold to set up analytic schools of their own, as well as others who call themselves cognitive, rational, or existential therapists, place more emphasis on insight and are more likely to attempt an *interpretation* of what the client has said. This involves going beyond the meaning he has expressed to suggest reasons why he feels as he does or relationships between the expressed feeling and something else, such as a childhood experience or an area of his life he has been reluctant to examine. The psychologists Albert Ellis and Hobart Mowrer and the psychiatrist William Glasser, who are convinced that the client must be willing to embark upon a course of right actions before he can straighten out his tangled feelings, are more likely than those of other orientations to try to *teach* the client what he ought to do and to use their influence to weight the scales in favor of right action. However, it is difficult to draw sharp lines between these classes of verbalization. Reflection of feeling shades over into interpretation; some interpretive comments may have an exhortatory ring about them. The overall set a skilled psychotherapist holds is to say something that advances or facilitates the process of change going on in the client rather than to say something prescribed by the theory he holds.

The nature of what is said during therapy sessions is likely to change over time. Like all human undertakings, psychotherapy with a particular client has a beginning, a middle, and an end. At the beginning, when the participants are feeling their way toward an understanding of what they wish to accomplish, reflection is the predominant kind of response the therapist makes. Toward the end, when the client is getting ready to live his life without the support of the therapy relationship, teaching may occupy more of the time.

Decisions During Therapy

Besides manifesting consistently the characteristics of empathy, warmth, and genuineness, and responding verbally to what the client says in interviews, the psychotherapist has one other important duty—to make *decisions*. Considerable knowledge as well as skill is involved in these. At the outset, in order to decide whether to take on a new client for individual psychotherapy, to refer him for some other kind of help, or to recommend no action at all, the psychologist should be familiar with the research that has shown what kinds of people do not improve with the common kinds of psychotherapy but may actually get worse (see Gendlin et al., 1968), and with research that has demonstrated the utility of other kinds of improvement programs. During the course of therapy, if for a number of sessions progress seems slow or nonexistent, the psychotherapist must decide whether to continue the relationship or to bring it to a close; and to do this he should be able to draw on the experience of others as well as his own in distinguishing between a temporary obstacle and a permanent impasse. In cases where therapy goes well, a decision must still be made as to when and how the relationship should be terminated. It is true that the client also plays a part in these discussions, but it is the psychotherapist who, as a professional person, must take the major responsibility for ensuring that they are made as wisely as possible.

EXAMPLES

For a reader who has not participated in individual psychotherapy sessions himself, some examples taken from recorded interview hours may help him understand what the process is like.

Client-centered therapy. The first is an excerpt Truax and Carkhuff (1967, pp. 56–57) give as an example of a high level of accurate empathy. These writers have their roots in Rogerian client-centered theory, and clarification or reflection of feeling is the principal mode of response, but many of the responses shade over into *interpretation*. C stands for client, T for therapist. (The authors do not provide information about the participants, but it appears from the context that both client and therapist are male.)

> *C:* . . . uh–I've always been–so afraid–uh–to show just how I–how I felt– (*T:* Mhm)–and I–and I–think. . .
> *T:* (Interrupting) Showing feeling is–weak or–something. (Gently, fading into near inaudibility)
> *C:* Yeah–that's how it seems to me. (Lengthy pause) I know I–I've been in the TV room–and I–all of a sudden–had the feeling that–I was going to start crying. (Almost tearfully)
> *T:* Mhm.
> *C:* . . . and–uh–I knew then that I'd have to leave and go somewhere . . .
> *T:* Mhm.
> *C:* . . . where nobody was, so in case I did start crying that nobody'd see me. (Bashfully)
> *T:* Mhm–it'd just be–terrible to stand if you–if you ever did show this much feeling. (Sorrowfully) (Long pause)
> *C:* The thing is–that–I'm–I'm afraid of–well–I'd be so embarrassed afterward. (Ashamedly)
> *T:* Mhm–this would be–just–terrible–uh–a man wouldn't cry, a grownup wouldn't cry. (Almost tearfully)
> *C:* Yeah.
> *T:* . . . or at least. . . . (leaves thought suspended)
> *C:* (Filling in for T) At least without an apparent reason.
> *T:* Mhm.
> *C:* (Long pause) An'–uh–an'–I–I don't have–an apparent reason. (Emphatically)
> *T:* . . . it wouldn't only be weak, but–be crazy or something. (Very gently)
> *C:* (Chiming in) Yeah. (Very positively)

The adverbs in parentheses make it clear that what the therapist is attempting to do here is to understand how the client feels and to show that he really does understand by his expression and tone of voice as well as by his words.

Brief psychoanalytically-oriented therapy.   The second example is presented by Wolberg (1954, p. 461), whose general approach shows the influence of Freudian thinking. It is an interview with a man who had, after three months of treatment, gone back to his wife and three children, whom he had left in order to live with a prostitute. The therapist's comments on the case, in brackets, show how he was attempting to use interpretation to help this man come closer to understanding his own emotional reactions.

C: I know I shouldn't want Marie [the prostitute] as bad as she is. The whole thing is silly, the kind of person she is, I mean.

T: But you do seem to want her in spite of her faults. [Reflecting underlying attitudes.]

C: I know she is bad for me; Rita [his wife] is so much more of a real person. But I can't get Marie off my mind. I don't want to go back to her, though, because the same mess will happen all over again. I would like to think about Rita all the time, to be thrilled by her. But I can work better now and would like to help Rita get the art training she wants. (Long pause)

T: I see. (Pause) What are you thinking about?

C: A flash came to me, a fantasy of my standing on a subway platform. A person in front of me. As the subway approaches, I imagined myself pushing this man off.

T: What kind of a person is this?

C: Unidentified. I couldn't identify the man. I seem to see him with a blue suit. He seems sinister for some reason. Sometimes when I stand on the platform of a subway, I have a fear I may jump off, or that someone may push me off.

T: But in your fantasy you push this man off. You're angry with him?

C: Oh no, I don't feel . . . I didn't feel anything. Just felt like pushing him off. (Yawns) I'm kind of tired today. I had a hard day at the office, all kinds of pressures. I thought of canceling my appointment today, because my secretary had forgotten to make it and I forgot it, and I was supposed to talk to one of the out-of-town advertising people. [This sounds like resistance.]

T: How do you feel about coming here? Do you feel it's an inconvenience to you? [Handling his mention of wanting to cancel his appointment.]

C: (Laughs) It is. I come because I think it's necessary, not because I want it. There isn't anything enjoyable in it.

T: So maybe you resent coming here. [A tentative interpretation.]

C: No, I don't think I resent it, because I know I *should* come. [He rejects the interpretation.]

T: Mm hmm mm.

C: But it is a lot of work to get here; it does take time. It isn't anything I would do for fun. And then I feel that I have the responsibility to my family to get this thing straightened out.

T: But how do you feel about doing it for yourself?

C: Frankly I'm doing it for my family. Indirectly, I suppose, I benefit from it.

T: You know, I get the feeling that you really resent coming here. [An authoritative interpretation.] Let's take that fantasy. Here in fantasy you do an aggressive thing to someone in a blue suit.

C: Yes.

T: What kind of a suit do I have on?

C: (Startled) Why *your* suit is blue! [The patient seems astonished.]

T: Maybe I'm the man in the fantasy and you want to get *me* out of the way. If so, you do seem to resent me. [Tentative interpretation.]

C: Oh, I almost forgot. [Reaches in his pocket and pulls out a check.] I've been carying this around for two weeks and always forget to give it to you when I'm here.

T: There must be a reason for that.

C: You mean I might not have wanted to pay you?

T: That's possible. (Pause)

C: But I did have the intention to pay you. I just forgot.

T: People forget for definite reasons very often. Could you possibly not have given me the check because you felt critical of me? [A tentative interpretation.] If that's the case, then your giving me the check now is making up with me for being critical.

C: (Laughs) Well, I'll tell you, I have been annoyed having to come here. I've even resented your good intentions. Not that you've ever told me to stay away from Marie, but I've been ashamed to go on the way I did. I've even wanted you to tell me Rita was better than Marie for me. But, damn it, the pull is there, the excitement. I can't go back, but I can't seem to push myself forward either.

T: You see, there is a contradiction in some of your strivings. Your present stalemate is a result of being wedged in between your desire for Marie and your guilt and sense of responsibility to the family. You want me to make the choice for you and you are angry if I don't. [Authoritative interpretations.]

C: Yes, I can see that, and I know that, attractive as Marie is, life with her would be poison for me. I don't need you to build up Rita because she's a person with quality.

T: Now, were I to make the choice for you, you'd have trouble. For instance, if I told you to give up Marie, I'd become the repressing authority you've been fighting all your life. As a matter of fact, you may find Marie attractive and want to kick over the traces to defy this authority and to do as you please. Then our relationship would get bad, because you'd probably want to defy me. On the other hand, if I encouraged you to give up Rita and to yield to your desires, you would be contemptuous of me. And if you went back to Marie, you'd blame me for exposing you to something from which you got pleasure, but which was very destructive to you. [More interpretations.]

What is evident in this excerpt is the therapist's constant effort to delve into the hidden meaning of what the client has just said. One notices also how he focuses on the patient's relationship to him, attempting to uncover the negative attitudes that constitute resistance.

Rational-emotive therapy. The third example is one given by Ellis (1962, p. 126) to show the active, teaching approach that characterizes his system of *rational-emotive psychotherapy*. It is a dialogue Ellis carried on with a client who had reported unhappiness over the fact that a group of men with whom he had played golf had not liked him.

T: You think you were unhappy because these men didn't like you?

C: I certainly was!

T: But you weren't unhappy for the reason you think you were.

C: I wasn't? But I was!

T: No, I insist: you only think you were unhappy for that reason.

C: Well, why was I unhappy then?

T: It's very simple—as simple as A, B, C, I might say. A, in this case, is the fact that these men didn't like you. Let's assume that you observed their attitude correctly and were not merely imagining they didn't like you.

C: I assure you that they didn't. I could see that very clearly.

T: Very well, let's assume they didn't like you and call that A. Now, C is your unhappiness—which we'll definitely have to assume is a fact, since you felt it.

C: Damn right I did!

T: All right, then: A is the fact that the men didn't like you, C is your unhappiness. You see A and C and you assume that A, their not liking you, caused your unhappiness, C. But it didn't.

C: It didn't? What did, then?

T: B did.

C: What's B?

T: B is *what you said to yourself* while you were playing golf with those men.

C: What I said to myself? But I didn't say anything.

T: You did. You couldn't possibly be unhappy if you didn't. The only thing that could possibly make you unhappy that occurs from without is a brick falling on your head, or some such equivalent. But no brick fell. Obviously, therefore, you must have told *yourself* something to make you unhappy.

The foregoing excerpt is probably not a complete, word-for-word account of the interaction. Ellis explains early in his book (1962) that the excerpts he uses as examples have been slightly abridged and grammatically organized, as well as cleared of all identifying data. What Ellis considers to be the major feature of rational-emotive therapy is very evident. The therapist challenges the client's conclusions, exhorts him to think along other lines, and assigns him a task to be accomplished between sessions.

APPRAISAL AND THERAPY

There are two major functions served by systematic efforts to collect and organize information about individual clients participating in the kinds of improvement programs considered in this chapter, although the amount of emphasis on individual assessment and the uses to which information is put vary from one theoretical school to another, from one therapist to another, and from one situation to another.

Assessment for Therapy Planning

The first of these purposes is to contribute to planning about what sort of psychotherapy is most appropriate for the person applying for it and which therapist (if several are available) should work with him. This function is somewhat similar to medical diagnosis—to analyze what is wrong with the patient and predict how he is likely to react to each of the available ways of treating his condition. Although the medical model predominated as a framework for organizing psychologists' thinking, clinical organizations usually provided for this kind of activity, but even before the general decline in the popularity of the medical model, serious doubts had been expressed about the usefulness of assessment procedures for individuals to be treated by means of psychotherapy. Writers representing the Rogerian, client-centered school were most explicit about this. In the first place, they found no evidence in their research that the kinds of diagnostic classifications psychologists in other settings were trying to make, such as neurosis versus psychosis, hysteria, psychopathic personality, anxiety state, and the like, were related in any way to the process or outcomes of therapy. But a more important reason than this for not making a thorough personality study before initiating therapy was their conviction that an evaluative, judgmental attitude actually interfers with the empathic, accepting attitude upon which the success of the therapy depends. To some extent this difficulty can be bypassed by having another psychologist, who is not to serve as the individual's therapist, carry out the assessment. But even if this is done, the pattern is wrong from the *client's* point of view. He first encounters evaluation rather than acceptance.

In places where the psychoanalytic orientation prevails, assessment by means of projective tests such as the Rorschach, the Thematic Apperception Test, and the Draw-A-Person has commonly been a standard step in the procedure for handling new cases. Ability tests such as the Wechsler Adult Intelligence Scale, and personality inventories such as the Minnesota Multiphasic Personality Inventory are sometimes included in the study of the prospective client's personality. In such situations it is the psychologist's task to put together background information from the person's file, if there is one, material brought out in intake interviews, and results of the specialized testing procedures. He must attempt to organize all these varied kinds of evidence into a coherent picture and then write a report. The report is used both to determine whether or not the person is suitable for insight-oriented therapy and to provide clues as to how he is likely to respond to various aspects of it—how readily he will form a transference relationship, for example, or how strong his resistance to unwelcome interpretations will be. The report may include material that will aid the therapist in getting interpretations over to the client, such as evidence about his reactions to authority or his relationships with his parents.

In clinical situations where the emphasis is on cognitive change, such as Adlerian therapy or Ellis's rational-emotive therapy, assessment procedures are not commonly employed. What the therapist considers most important are the client's constructs or assumptions about himself and the world, and while some assessment procedures have been especially designed to get at such constructs— George Kelly's Role Construct Repertory Test, for example—they have not been used very much in clinical settings. In rational-emotive therapy, assessment goes on along with the therapy itself rather than as preparation for it. Many practicing clinicians make combinations of the various therapeutic and assessment procedures, of course.

Assessment in Research

The second function systematic information about clients serves in connection with psychotherapy of all varieties is to contribute to knowledge about what it accomplishes and how. As the diagnostic function we have been considering in the preceding pages has declined in importance, this research function has been increasing. A psychologist cannot practice psychotherapy for very long without being confronted with innumerable questions about this highly complex process, from the broadest, most basic one of all: Is all this effort to help people really doing any good? To such specific things as: What characteristics in clients, therapists, or client–therapist combinations lead to favorable outcomes? What kinds of personality change are most likely to occur? How lasting are personality improvements produced by psychotherapy? The psychologist is more likely than the representatives of the other professions involved in improvement programs, such as psychiatrists and social workers, to be assigned major responsibilities in this area. As we have explained earlier, fusion of research and practice is one of the unique features of clinical psychology as a professional field. Research techniques are not stressed to nearly the same extent in the training of people in the other "helping professions."

If he is to be prepared to use assessment techniques skillfully for varied research purposes, the clinical psychologist must know a great deal more than how to give and interpret a Rorschach test or an MMPI. He must understand the principles upon which psychological assessment procedures are based. He must have a broad familiarity with all sorts of testing procedures and realize what information about them he must have in order to decide whether or not to employ them. He must on occasion be able to invent special techniques for special purposes and be aware of the limitations of what he concludes from them.

In summary, the research function of assessment related to individual psychotherapy is a part of a larger undertaking, evaluative research on programs for human improvement. Such research is central to the role clinical psychologists should be prepared to assume.

CRITICAL EVALUATION

The major question with regard to all the effort that has gone on in individual psychotherapy is the question of how much good it does. Eysenck (1952) assembled all the evaluative research he could locate in the literature and came to the conclusion that the proportion of clients who improved as a result of therapy was no larger than the proportion who improved spontaneously without treatment. His updating of the evidence (Eysenck, 1966) did not lead to a change in the conclusion.

Meltzoff and Kornreich (1970), after a much more thorough survey than Eysenck had made, concluded that the outcome research had clearly demonstrated the positive effects of psychotherapy. Of the 101 investigations they located, 80 percent reported positive results, and the percentage was even higher if only adequately designed studies were considered.

Looking at the matter in another way the great popularity of psychotherapy seems to indicate that it serves a social function. As long as it is voluntary, it seems perfectly legitimate for clients who desire it to purchase the experience for themselves. Perhaps insight is a desirable thing whether it improves the functioning of one's personality or not.

What does not seem to be warranted by the evidence is making individual psychotherapy the treatment of choice for persons society decides to try to change, in other words, nonvoluntary clients. Thus it is natural that, as social programs to rehabilitate the psychotic and the delinquent and to improve the status of the disadvantaged take on increasing prominence, psychologists should extend their range to cover other sorts of designs for improvement quite different from individual psychotherapy.

SUMMARY

Individual psychotherapy came into prominence during the middle decades of the twentieth century and became tremendously popular. Many varieties and theories were elaborated. The goals emphasized by the various schools can be summarized under seven headings: (1) strengthening the client's motivation to do the right things, (2) reducing emotional pressure and anxiety, (3) releasing growth potential, (4) modifying cognitive structure, (5) increasing self-knowledge, (6) changing habits, and (7) improving interpersonal relationships.

All varieties of individual psychotherapy have several common features.

Therapists of different schools all attempt (1) to lower the client's anxiety level, (2) to establish a strong personal relationship, and (3) to facilitate communication. What therapists say to clients during interviews can mainly be classified as reflection of feeling, interpretation, or teaching, and the proportions of each vary somewhat from one theoretical school to another. Therapists also must make decisions at several stages of the process.

Systematic appraisal of the person serves two purposes in psychotherapy—to facilitate decisions and plans about whether and how a client is to be served, and to carry out research on process and outcome.

It is now clear that there is evidence for positive changes brought about by psychotherapy. Furthermore, the history of the movement demonstrates that individuals seek the experience and are willing to pay for it. Thus it is continuing to flourish for voluntary clients but is being superseded by other approaches to problems that society is attempting to ameliorate.

SUGGESTED READINGS

Meltzoff, J., and Kornreich, M. *Research in psychotherapy*. Chicago: Aldine-Atherton, 1970.

This is one of the most important reference works a therapist or therapy student should have, if he is interested in what research has shown. The analysis of problems in the design of research in this area is exceptionally thorough and complete. The synthesis of what outcome studies have shown, referred to in the text, is definitive. Subsequent chapters cover research on more specialized questions—the effects of therapeutic method, client and therapist characteristics, temporal variables on outcomes, and the findings of the many investigations of the therapeutic process.

For other important reviews and reports on research in psychotherapy, see the important *Handbook*, edited by Bergin and Garfield (1971), which is summarized elsewhere in this book. Also from time to time the American Psychological Association, with the cooperation of the National Institute of Mental Health, has sponsored invitational conferences on psychotherapy research. The publications following the three conferences (Rubinstein and Parloff, 1959; Strupp and Luborsky, 1962; and Shlein, 1968) are among some of the best sources we have of ideas about the special technical problems involved in such research, the important long-range projects under way, and the findings that appear to be most significant.

Truax, C. B., and Carkhuff, R. R. *Toward effective counseling and psychotherapy*. Chicago: Aldine-Atherton, 1967.

The authors clarify by explanation and example what they mean by *accurate empathy*, *nonpossessive warmth*, and *genuineness*. They then present empirical evidence from their own research and that of other investigators to demonstrate the effectiveness of therapy based on these principles in a variety of situations and to indicate how persons with varying amounts of background and education have been trained so as to develop these characteristics and facilitate their expression.

Ellis, A. *Reason and emotion in psychotherapy.* New York: Lyle Stuart, 1962.

In this book Ellis brings together several previously published papers, supplementing them with new material to produce a clear, readable statement about the theory and practice of rational-emotive psychotherapy. The point of view is one that has been increasingly influential in the years since the book came out. It might almost be called "commonsense" therapy. The essence of the theory on which Ellis operates is that because man is a thinking animal prone to irrational ideas, the major source of the psychological difficulties that lead a person to therapy is not frustrating circumstances or unfortunate happenings in his past life but statements he uses in talking to himself about these troubles. What the therapist then should attempt to do is to persuade him to change his irrational assumptions. This may involve suggestion, argument, homework assignments, and many other special techniques. Numerous examples are given in the book, showing how the method can be applied to sexual difficulties, some kinds of psychotic conditions, psychopathic behavior, and other intransigent personality disorders.

Trexler and Karst (1972) found in a careful study that rational-emotive therapy was more helpful in relieving speaking anxiety than methods used to control groups.

Perls, F. S. *Gestalt therapy verbatim.* Lafayette, Calif.: Real People Press, 1969.

For those interested in Gestalt therapy, this book presents direct records, mostly from audiotapes at weekend "dreamwork seminars" at the Esalen Institute.

Schofield, W. *Psychotherapy: the purchase of friendship.* Englewood Cliffs, N. J.: Prentice-Hall, 1964.

With one of the most telling book titles in the field, Schofield explores the history, the appeal, and the practice of psychotherapy. He urges a more realistic public attitude and a relief for overburdened professionals by the development of trained "therapeutic conversationists."

Gordon, J. E. (ed.) *Handbook of clinical and experimental hypnosis.* New York: Macmillan, 1966.

This collection of articles by leading experts on hypnosis is an advanced work. For those seriously interested in the very important phenomena of suggestion and hypnosis, this book will provide a very useful source of theoretical and practical knowledge.

Razin, A. M. A-B variable in therapy: a critical review, *Psychological Bulletin*, 1971, *75*, 1–21; and Chartier, G. M. A-B therapist variable: real or imagined? *Psychological Bulletin*, 1971, *75*, 22–33.

Whitehorn and Betz (1954) reported that two kinds of therapists could be distinguished on the basis of scores on the Strong Vocational Interest Blank, the

As, with high scores on Lawyer and CPA scales, and the Bs, with high scores on Printer and Mathematics and Science Teacher scales, and that the As were more successful than the Bs in treating schizophrenics. In the years following this report, a large number of studies of this A-B variable and its interaction with personality types in clients seeking therapy have been reported.

In these reviews about fifty of these reports up through the middle of 1969 have been brought together in considering (1) the differential effects obtained by A and B therapists, (2) the relationships of the A-B variable to other therapist personality variables, and (3) analog studies, not involving actual therapy but a simulation of it.

Bergin, A. E., and Strupp, H. H. New directions in psychotherapy research. *Journal of Abnormal Psychology*, 1970, *76*, 13–26.

At several of the national conferences on psychotherapy, it was proposed that arrangements be worked out to facilitate large scale, collaborative research. Bergin and Strupp undertook a study of the feasibility of such a step. After a thorough investigation including a review of past research, interviews with expert consultants, attempts to formulate suitable research designs, and a number of other activities, they concluded that studies of the kind they had envisaged were not going to be feasible. Instead, they recommend discontinuing most of the kinds of research carried out heretofore and trying a variety of new approaches, such as the analysis of spontaneous change processes, case studies, analog studies, research on cognition and cognitive change, and biologically oriented efforts. This important paper may represent a turning point in psychological research on psychotherapy.

Luborsky, L., Chandler, M., Auerbach, A. H., Cohen, J., and Bachrach, H. M. Factors influencing the outcome of psychotherapy: a review of quantitative research. *Psychological Bulletin*, 1971, *75*, 145–185.

In this comprehensive review all quantitative studies that have been reported from 1946 through 1969 of the factors related to outcome in individual psychotherapy for adult patients were examined. There were 166 studies in all. The most numerous variety were concerned with variables in the patient. They showed that indicators of psychological health and adequacy tended to predict favorable outcomes. Therapist factors pointing to favorable outcomes are experience, empathy, and certain interest patterns. Similarity between therapist and patient, especially with regard to interests and values, makes for success. The treatment variable most clearly related to successful outcome is the number of sessions.

The appendix, which lists individual studies, is a very useful reference for clinicians and investigators.

RESEARCH EXAMPLES

Berzins, J. I., and Seidman, E. Differential therapeutic responding of A and B quasi-therapists to schizoid and neurotic communications. *Journal of Consulting and Clinical Psychology*, 1969, *33*, 279–286.

Increasingly, process research on psychotherapy has been concerned with the interactive system set up when a particular kind of therapist and a particular kind of client interact rather than with therapist characteristics or client characteristics alone. One such interaction much studied during the 1960s made use of the A-B classification of therapists proposed by Whitehorn and Betz (1954) (See Suggested Readings.) Whitehorn, Betz, and others produced considerable evidence that A therapists, identified by their pattern of scores on the Strong Vocational Interest Blank, were more successful in treating schizophrenics than were B therapists, identified by a different pattern of Strong scores. Subsequently, McNair, Callahan, and Lorr (1962) and others obtained results indicating that A therapists were not more successful than Bs with neurotic patients. This set the pattern for studies of the interactions: A—schizoid versus B—neurotic.

The experiment reported here is an example of research that simulates some aspects of therapy in a controlled laboratory situation. The subjects were 72 college students, classified on the basis of A-B scale responses into A, B, and intermediate categories. The procedure was to have each of them listen to five recorded communications expressing psychological difficulties of a schizoid type and five expressing difficulties of a neurotic type. The subject's task was to write down a helpful response at each pause in the recorded communication. These responses were analyzed by psychologists using several standard techniques to identify differences between "compatible" and "noncompatible" pairs.

Statistical significance tests indicated that in "compatible" pairs, the quasi-therapists gave longer responses, more declarative rather than questioning responses, and showed more positive and fewer negative social-emotional reactions. Persons in the intermediate A-B category did not react differentially to the two types of patient communication.

The experiment thus furnishes support for the conclusions proposed on the basis of analysis of actual therapy cases and suggests that it would be advisable to pay some attention in clinical situations to the assignment of clients to clinicians.

Fiedler, F. E. A comparison of therapeutic relations in psychoanalysis, nondirective, and Adlerian therapy. *Journal of Consulting Psychology*, 1950, *14*, 436–445.

In this frequently quoted study, Fiedler's purpose was to investigate differences between three major schools of psychotherapy and between beginning and expert practitioners. He collected ten recorded therapy interviews from ten psychotherapists. The therapists included from each school at least one expert who enjoyed a national reputation and one therapist who was a novice. There were some specifications as to the choice of the patient in therapy, and the recorded session came sometime between the sixth and seventeenth interview.

Four judges listened to the recordings. They made their judgments by sorting a Q-sort deck made up of seventy-five statements about the nature of the therapist's communication, emotional distance, and status relative to the patient. Each Q-sort was then intercorrelated with each of the others and with an Ideal Therapeutic Relationship sort obtained in a previous study by the author.

The results led to the following conclusions: (1) Expert psychotherapists create a relationship closer to the ideal relationship than novices; (2) the therapeutic relationships created by experts resemble those of other experts more closely than they resemble those of nonexperts in the same school; (3) differences between experts and nonexperts were greatest with respect to communication; and (4) differences between schools were most apparent on status items, with Adlerian and some psychoanalytically oriented therapists adopting a more tutorial role.

This important study does not say anything about the effectiveness of the three schools, of course. It does provide a method of describing the nature of the relationship, the Q-sort, which is very usable in research. In another study (1950b) reported earlier in the same journal, Fiedler found that therapists of different schools do not differ in their concept of the ideal therapeutic relationship and that nontherapists describe it in about the same way. He concluded that the ideal therapeutic relationship is but a variation of good interpersonal relationships in general.

For additional studies exploring the orientations of psychotherapists, see Sundland and Barker (1962) and Spilken et al. (1969).

Mintz, J., Luborsky, L., and Auerbach, A. H. Dimensions of psychotherapy: a factor-analytic study of ratings of psychotherapy sessions. *Journal of Consulting and Clinical Psychology*, 1971, *36*, 106–120.

The technique most frequently employed in multivariate research is factor analysis. This involves a mathematical process in which a large number of correlations between variables is reduced to a smaller number of factors on the basis of which it is possible to account for the relationships.

In the present large-scale study, three raters independently rated tape recordings of sixty sessions of psychoanalytically oriented therapy on 110 process variables, some of them indicative of therapist qualities and attitudes, such as "Therapist Empathy," some indicative of client qualities and attitudes, such as "Patient Anxiety."

The factors that emerged from the analysis were as follows: (I) *Optimal Empathic Relationship*, a dimension representing therapist ratings for warmth, empathy, perceptiveness, likability, and so on: (II) *Directive Mode*, a dimension representing therapist ratings for directiveness, activity, intrusiveness, and so on; (III) *Patient Health versus Distress*, a dimension representing a client's position on a health-sickness rating scale, and negative ratings on anxiety, guilt and shame, depression, and so on; (IV) *Interpretive Mode with Receptive Patient*, representing both therapist variables, such as the giving of psychoanalytic interpretations, and client variables, such as receptiveness and responsiveness.

The investigators then analyzed the relationship of scores on these factors to the outcome of treatment. The therapists' judgments of the amount of improvement in their clients could not be predicted from any of the factors, singly or in combination. The therapist's evaluation of client satisfaction with the treatment was most clearly related to factor III, Patient Health versus Distress, and to the sex of the patient. Female patients and those less maladjusted at the outset tended to be most satisfied.

Howard, K. I., Orlinsky, D. E., and Hill, J. A. Content of dialogue in psychotherapy. *Journal of Counseling Psychology*, 1969, *16*, 396—404.

The purpose of this investigation was to find out what topics clients and therapists are most likely to discuss in therapy sessions. The subjects in this large-scale study were 118 female patients at a Chicago mental health clinic who reported on 2,318 interviews, and 27 therapists who reported on 1,091 interviews. There were 45 cases in which both patient and therapist reported on at least five of the same sessions. The vehicle for reports was a structured questionnaire covering nineteen topics. Total scores for each of these were correlated and factor-analyzed separately for patients and therapists.

Seven factors were obtained in both factor analyses: (I) Parental Family, (II) Conjugal Family, (III) Fantasy, (IV) Work or Education, (V) Therapy and Therapist, (VI) Religion, and (VII) Opposite Sex. The largest individual differences were on factors II and IV, with some patients expressing more fantasy, others more concern with the actual life situation. There was considerable variation. There was considerable variation from session to session. In the cases reported on by both patient and therapist, agreement was fairly high.

This is a descriptive rather than a definitive study. Its greatest value is probably that it provides factual data that may be useful when further research is planned.

chapter 12

Personal Systems: Behavior Change

Although they differ in detail, the varieties of psychotherapy considered in Chapter 11 are all based on the assumption that it is the whole personality that must be considered and that particular difficulties that a client reports are in some sense *symptoms* of a more pervasive malfunctioning. Generally speaking, psychotherapists who carry on conversational or interview therapy do not aim to treat particular symptoms or habits but think of them as expressions of motives and conflicts involving the total personality. Thus if a woman complains of a persistent phobia of railroad trains, they do not attempt to rid her of this one special fear but rather to help her understand and get rid of the general anxiety of which this phobia is presumably one crystallization, or otherwise to modify her personality sufficiently so that she can cope with her anxiety in a constructive way.

There is, however, another current of thinking about how one helps people. Its course is nearly as long as that of the main stream, but it was only with the decline of the medical model and the resurgence of interest in applying learning principles to therapy, a major trend of the 1960s, that it became highly visible. It derives mainly from Pavlov, Hull, and Skinner rather than from Freud. Its central thought is that all the things psychologists had been viewing as unsatisfactory *mental health* are actually unsatisfactory *behavior*, bad habits acquired under special circumstances and generalized to many other life situations. Looking at his task from this vantage point, the psychologist is not primarily interested in ferreting out the *origins* of the behavior deviations, as psychoanalysts do, but rather in setting up learning situations in which the undesirable behavior patterns will be modified. His ideas about how to accomplish this come from the experimental work on the learning process that has been carried on in psychological laboratories. However, it has become apparent that it is never possible simply to apply learning principles in a mechanical way, because the detailed circumstances vary in complex ways from person to person. A kind of reward that works well for Edna may have no effect on Ruth; Henry may be quick to imitate the behavior of a friendly adult, while

Stuart chooses his models entirely from boys his own age. There are innumerable ways of applying learning principles. The challenge to the therapist is to design an individual program to fit each case.

EARLY EFFORTS

Every student in a course in general psychology knows of J. B. Watson's experiments with little Albert, briefly mentioned in the last chapter. He was a healthy child in his first year who showed no initial fear of a white rat. After a series of learning experiences in which an iron bar behind him was struck loudly just as he began to reach for the animal, the boy began to show the same reaction to the rat that he had naturally made to the noise—starting violently, drawing back, and screaming. Watson was also able to show that these fear responses had generalized to a number of stimuli similar in one way or another to the white rat. Albert had learned to fear all kinds of furry or fuzzy objects—cotton wool, a fur coat, a Santa Claus mask.

Perhaps even more important for therapy than Watson's early experiments were some attempts to eliminate such experimentally induced fears by conditioned-response methods. Jones (1925) succeeded in overcoming a child's fear of a furry animal (in this case a rabbit) by presenting the animal to him at a time when he was reacting positively to food. If the experimenter was careful at first to keep the animal far enough away so that the strength of the fear tendency did not overbalance the strength of the positive food-taking tendency, she found that eventually the sight of the animal itself was enough to initiate pleasant rather than fearful feelings.

Down through the years this kind of model has often been used in the treatment of particular fears. Meyer (1957), for example, cured a woman of a crippling fear of going out by herself by first establishing in her a strong positive feeling toward her therapist and then conditioning this feeling to the outside world. First she walked with him for a little while in the hospital roof garden. Afterward they extended the range of their walks, first to the hospital grounds, then to back streets, then to main thoroughfares. As the patient came to feel more positively toward these formerly feared situations, she was able to behave normally in them even without the therapist's presence.

Progressive Relaxation

Other workers have devoted efforts to devising ways of training patients in habits that would counteract every sort of neurotic manifestation. The most widely known of these endeavors produced the progressive-relaxation technique of Jacobson (1929). One behavioral component of the neuroses, including their psychosomatic accompaniments, is undesirable muscular tension. It seemed to

Jacobson that if a person could train his perceptions to recognize initial signs of the buildup of excessive muscular tension and then train his muscles to relax voluntarily, he would have in his own hands a powerful tool for combating neurotic difficulties, whatever their sources. The Jacobson relaxation techniques form a system of therapy that can be applied by general medical practitioners, physical therapists, and teachers of physical education as well as by psychiatrists and psychologists.

Conditioned-Reflex Therapy

Another attempt to build a general habit to eliminate all kinds of neurotic responses was Salter's method of conditioned-reflex therapy (1949). Salter's basic model was the classical Pavlovian conditioning experiment. The only one of Pavlov's specific ideas that he used extensively, however, was the concept of a conflict between inhibitory and excitatory processes in the brain. The neurotic, whatever his symptoms, Salter said, is a person too much in the grip of inhibitory processes. The thing he needs most is to have his general level of excitation raised. To accomplish this, Salter trained his patients to express their feelings even when they were hostile or sad, to assert themselves on all occasions, to use the word *I* as much as possible, to act on impulse instead of planning ahead. Through such *re*conditioning he tried to overcome the *mal*conditioning of the past.

Salter, along with various other workers who thought of therapy as habit change, used hypnosis or waking suggestion as an accessory technique. The most difficult part of this kind of habit molding is often to create a situation in which the new response will actually occur. Posthypnotic suggestion may accomplish this. For example, if a singer is crippled by stage fright, some way must be found of making her sing with confidence in front of a crowd so that confident singing may be reinforced. If she is hypnotizable, appropriate suggestions can be given that she will feel strong and secure when she comes on stage for a certain concert. Once this happens, the applause of the audience will serve to reinforce the kind of habits she is seeking to strengthen and she is started on the road toward the elimination of the stage fright. The procedure will doubtless have to be repeated over a period of time if steady progress is to be made.

Enuresis

Another application of laboratory research on conditioned responses that began early and has continued down through the years is the treatment of nocturnal enuresis in children. Since the 1930s, equipment has been available that is designed to associate bladder distention with waking up. The child lies on a pad constructed in such a way that as soon as any moisture touches its metal parts, an electrical circuit is closed and a bell rings. The bell is, of course, a natural stimulus for awakening. Conditioned-response principles would lead us to predict that the sensations from bladder distention immediately preceding the sound of the bell would soon be sufficient in themselves to wake the patient up. Several outcome studies have reported about 70 percent success in curing enuresis by these methods. In one of the most complete, that of Baller and Schalock (1956), of fifty-five patients treated, 90 percent showed marked improvement immediately following a few weeks of treatment, and a two-year follow-up indicated that in 65 to 70 percent of the cases, results were still good. An interesting sidelight is that twenty-four of the twenty-five cases interviewed to secure more than the minimum information about the effects of the treatment reported favorable personality changes in addition to the elimination of the enuresis. Both social relationships and general "disposition" were said to have improved.

Alcoholism

Still another special variety of treatment for a particular kind of problem that has been used for several decades is the therapy for alcoholics that uses an alcoholic drink as a conditioned stimulus, combining it with an emetic drug. The vomiting, or at least the nausea, produced by the drug becomes associated with the taste of the alcoholic beverage so that the patient is no longer able to drink it. Voegtlin and Lemere (1950), reporting on 4,096 cases they had treated over a thirteen-year period, indicated that 60 percent had abstained from drinking for one year or longer, 51 percent for two years or longer, 38 percent for five years or longer, and 23 percent for ten years or longer. Reports from other institutions using these techniques vary. Some show a high percentage of cures, others low.

SOME MAJOR CONTRIBUTORS

Eysenck

An influential spokesman for the behavior therapies during the 1950s and 1960s was H. J. Eysenck. After his challenge to psychoanalysts and other "conversational" therapists in 1952, bringing together the available outcome studies and pointing out that there was no evidence that psychotherapists were producing any more improvement in patients than would naturally occur without therapy, he developed therapy techniques based mainly on the learning theory of Hull (1943). He also brought together and disseminated information about what other behavior therapists were doing. His book of readings, *Behaviour Therapy and the Neuroses*, published in 1960, constituted a valuable source book for psychologists who wished to try these methods.

Probably the two most influential sources of ideas for behavior therapy, however, have been the work of Wolpe (1958), who proposed a new way of applying Pavlovian conditioning principles in eliminating neurotic handicaps of long standing, and Skinner (1953), out of whose research on *operant conditioning* a comprehensive technology of behavior modification has grown. We shall consider these major lines of development in the next section.

Wolpe—Reciprocal Inhibition

Wolpe (1958) began by formulating a coherent theory about what *neurosis* is and how the condition gets started. "Neurotic behavior is any persistent habit of unadaptive behavior acquired by learning in a physiologically normal organism." Almost every word in this definition is important—*persistent, unadaptive, learning, physiologically normal*—and each can be pinned down to a fairly precise meaning. The central idea is that neurotic behavior has been *learned* and can be *unlearned* or replaced by more adaptive kinds of behavior if the right stimulating situation can be set up.

Anxiety, an important concept in almost all theories of neurosis, is important here, too. But as Wolpe uses the word, it is synonymous with fear. It may be more pervasive and occur as a response to many more kinds of stimuli, but it is, like any fear, a response to a stimulus. All its well-known physiological concomitants, such as rapid pulse rate, raised blood pressure, or sweating, are part of the total fear response.

How does Wolpe think human neurotic behavior is acquired? First, there are predisposing conditions in the makeup of some persons, based either on hereditary physiological idiosyncrasies or on the previous development of anxiety through learning. Second, the person is exposed to a stress situation, which may be one of several types. It may be very intense, painful stimulation such as the prisoner in a concentration camp might undergo. It may be a severe threat or conflict from within the personality. It may be a summation of a number of experiences, no one of them intense enough by itself to produce a neurotic response. Third, there are two kinds of responses, either one or both of which can be conditioned to all stimuli present in the stress situation. The first kind are high-intensity anxiety responses; the second kind are derived responses such as hysterical responses and some kinds of obsessional behavior. Last, secondary anxiety-relieving activities may be learned. These include physical avoidance of stimuli, displacement of attention, drug-taking, and anxiety-relieving obsessions.

This formulation of the origin of neuroses suggest the kinds of therapeutic intervention Wolpe thinks are most likely to succeed in overcoming them. To *extinguish* or abolish the unadaptive habits would appear to be almost impossible because of the pervasiveness of anxiety responses and their attachment to innumerable stimuli. Furthermore, the person's unwillingness to encounter situations that increase his anxiety make it extremely unlikely that he will ever undergo enough unreinforced trials to produce extinction. What seems a more promising approach is to design a situation in such a way that a response incompatible with the neurotic responses will occur. When this happens the strength of the neurotic response decreases through "reciprocal inhibition." Tersely stated, the principle is as follows: *If a response antagonistic to anxiety can be made to occur in the presence of anxiety-evoking stimuli so that it is accompanied by a complete or partial suppression of the anxiety responses, the bond between these stimuli and the anxiety responses will be weakened* (Wolpe, 1958, p. 71).

The last half of Wolpe's book explains in detail the procedures he uses to put these principles into effect. The first step is to arrange one or more interviews designed to obtain as clear a picture as possible of the nature of the patient's anxiety reactions—what they are like and under what circumstances they occur. A life history is taken, but the emphasis is on the present rather than the past. During this phase, the therapist maintains an objective, nonjudgmental attitude. As part of this diagnostic interviewing he administers a brief personality inventory to assess the amount of neurotic anxiety that is present.

The second step is to explain the model and the plan of attack to the patient. The therapist makes a brief statement in which he shows with down-to-earth examples how a neurosis gets started. He then points out what the pattern seems to have been in the patient's particular case and explains that the task is one of weakening the neurotic habits by strengthening some responses antagonistic to them.

The kinds of responses Wolpe has identified that may be expected to have such inhibitory effects on anxiety are (1) assertive responses, (2) sexual responses, (3) relaxation responses, (4) respiratory responses, (5) "anxiety-relief" responses, (6) competitively conditioned motor responses, (7) pleasant responses in the life situation (with drug enhancement), and (8a) interview-induced emotional responses and (b) abreaction (Wolpe, 1958, p. 113). The last two kinds may occur spontaneously; the first six must be planned by the therapist so that they occur in some strength in situations where the cues for anxiety are present. Which kind of response he decides to use depends to a considerable extent on what the patient is anxious about.

In some cases the patient is trained to produce the positive response in life situations. A shy, timid person, for example, may be schooled in giving assertive responses. Role playing may be used as a part of such training. A man suffering from impotence may be shown how, with the cooperation of his sexual partner, he can set up a situation in which the positive sexual response will become strong enough to inhibit his anxiety. Relaxation is used a great deal in connection with those strategies. As Jacobson has shown, a person who knows how to produce relaxation responses in himself can gain control of various situations that would otherwise cripple him.

Perhaps the most interesting special technique that Wolpe describes is what he calls "systematic desensitization based on relaxation." Before putting this into effect, the therapist has drawn up a list of anxiety-producing situations, arranged in order of severity, based on what he has learned from his patient during his interviews. Such a hierarchy will range from situations the patient finds almost intolerable, through those he finds moderately disturbing, down to those that bother him only slightly. He then trains the patient in the Jacobson relaxation techniques. At the first of the special desensitization sessions he hypnotizes him and tells him to relax deeply. At this point he asks him to imagine a certain scene very vividly, raising his hand if he feels disturbed. The therapist uses first a scene from the low end of the patient's list of anxiety-producing situations. Usually this produces no disturbance because it is too weak to counteract the general relaxation. After about two or three seconds of this he moves up to the next situation in the list, asking the patient to imagine it as vividly as possible. If he signals any disturbance the procedure is discontinued, and in any event it is stopped for the day after several such scenes have been reacted upon. The patient is then roused from the hypnotic state and questioned about how he felt while it was going on.

Over a series of sessions, therapist and client gradually work themselves up to the top of the anxiety hierarchy. As the anxiety response becomes weaker, the person can tolerate a more intense stimulus. If all goes well, he finds after a number of such sessions that things that used to throw him into a panic no longer trouble him at all.

Skinner—Reinforcement Contingencies

The second major source of ideas for the burgeoning work on behavior therapy is B. F. Skinner. In an extremely influential book, *The Behavior of Organisms*, first published in 1938, and in a series of later books and research reports Skinner elaborated the concept of *operant behavior*, behavior that is controlled by its *consequences* rather than its origins. Whereas Pavlov and the learning theorists who based their work on the conditioned-response principles he proposed emphasized the way in which a particular *stimuli* became able to touch off a response, the central concept in research involving operants has been *reinforcement*. It is assumed that all living organisms, man included, engage in a large amount of random activity for which it would be difficult or impossible to identify specific stimuli. What then happens is that the actions followed by favorable consequences are strengthened; those not reinforced in this way drop out of the behavior repertoire. The objective in operant conditioning and in the behavior technologies based on it—for teaching, for acquisition of skills, and for therapy—is to increase the frequency with which certain kinds of responses occur and to decrease the frequency with which other responses occur by managing reinforcement contingencies intelligently.

This approach to problems of learning and teaching is of course similar to the commonsense use of reward and punishment in child rearing and schoolroom management. But the extent of the similarity should not be overemphasized. When one actually analyzes reinforcement situations in homes, schools, correctional institutions, mental hospitals, and many other places, as behavior technologists have done, it is often quite apparent that the incentives, rewards, and punishments ordinarily used are administered in such a way that they are completely ineffective or that they even work in the wrong direction, so as to strengthen and maintain the very actions that are classified as "behavior problems." The ways in which parents, brothers, sisters, and playmates reward and punish a child who throws temper tantrums, for example, often serve to produce bigger and better tantrums as the weeks and months pass. The contingencies of reinforcement in a training school for juvenile delinquents are often arranged in such a way that antisocial rather than law-abiding behavior is what is actually learned in the situation.

This one central idea—that increasing or decreasing the incidence of particular kinds of behavior can be accomplished through differential reinforcement—generates a large number of subsidiary principles and variations to be tried out in clinical work. It is important that the reinforcement be clearly *contingent* upon the occurrence of the behavior to be strengthened or weakened. The thing that is wrong with many life situations in which commonsense notions of reward and punishment are put into operation is that it is not at all clear what behavior a person is being rewarded or punished for. Time relationships are very significant. The more promptly the reinforcement follows the act, the more effective it is in strengthening it, especially for young children. Provision must be made in an improvement plan for ensuring the *generalization* of the habit that has been strengthened in a particular situation to the many other real-life situations in which the person needs to use it. It is quite possible, for example, to train a stutterer to speak fluently in the psychologist's office but find that he stutters as badly as before in school. In other instances, *discriminations* must be developed in the course of the training program. A very shy, fearful adolescent, trained to make self-assertive remarks, may find himself very unpopular if he goes around insulting people indiscriminately. Schedules of reinforcement must provide for the *maintenance* as well as the acquisition of new habits; otherwise they are likely to be *extinguished* as soon as the improvement program is ended.

One of the most useful ideas coming out of the research on operant behavior has been the notion of *shaping* responses through the reinforcement of successive approximations to the finished product at which one is coming. A pigeon that is to be trained to peck at a circular spot whenever a light flashes is very unlikely to do just this spontaneously. What the experimenter does with a "naive" pigeon is first to watch for a time when he approaches the corner of the cage where the target is located and reward him for this movement. Attention to the target itself is then rewarded, and little by little the pigeon's behavior is shaped to the purpose of the experiment. In an analogous clinical application of the technique, a "back ward" patient in a state hospital who spends the whole day sitting in a chair in the corner looking at the floor may first be rewarded for getting up and moving in the direction of some other person, patient or staff member. The next step may be to reward him for saying something to another person. Showing any sign of interest in something going on, such as a card game or a work project, may be rewarded next. By such gradual steps the patient may advance to a level of functioning at which he is taking part in therapeutic activities and working toward the kind of changed behavior that will enable him to leave the hospital. In order to strengthen good behavior through reinforcement, one must first make it occur. Shaping is one of the strategies available for doing this.

Bandura—Modeling

A third major source of ideas for behavior therapy is of particular importance in planning for the production of new responses, but it is useful for other purposes as well. It is the work of Bandura (1969) and his associates on *modeling*. The research carried on by this group of investigators has shown that for human subjects one of the quickest, most efficient ways to get a person to do something is to have him watch someone else do it, either "live" or on a film. They have demonstrated that the principal concepts from previous research on learning—reinforcement, generalization, discrimination—are useful in analyzing the effects on the learner's behavior of what happens to the model as well as what happens to him. If a child sees a model getting a piece of candy when he says "Please," he will be more likely to say "Please" himself in this particular situation and, through generalization processes, in other situations as well.

Like the other concepts we have discussed, research on the modeling concept has pointed to innumerable variations. In some studies, live and filmed models have been compared; their influence on the watchers' behavior turned out to be similar. In other research the effects of material and social rewards given to the model were compared; here some kinds of watchers react more favorably to the former than to the latter, others do not. The prestige of the model makes a difference in some situations; in others it is desirable to match models and observers in age, sex, and other characteristics, to facilitate the imitative process. The research is much too extensive and detailed to summarize here, but Bandura's (1969) book makes it readily available.

For the behavior therapist, the possibility of stimulating his client to do something new that he has never done before and would not be likely to do spontaneously is the most valuable aspect of the concept of modeling. But the technique can be used for two other purposes as well: (a) to strengthen or weaken inhibitory responses, and (b) to elicit previously learned responses that match those of the model. An overly aggressive child can be shown a boy refraining from hitting his little brother and receiving a piece of candy or an appreciative comment from his mother when he does so. A mute hospital patient can view someone like him saying "Good Morning" and being rewarded in some way for this. When reinforcement for the desired behavior as carried out by the model is combined with reinforcement for the observer when he imitates, behavior change may be rapid and encouraging to both psychologist and client.

Patterson—Training Natural Caretakers

A fourth main line of research on behavior modification that opens up a large number of possibilities for designing improvement programs is the work of Patterson et al. (1972), which focuses on the training of children's natural caretakers, especially parents and teachers, to set up and maintain situations in which the behavior of problem children is transformed into socially acceptable activity. A more detailed account of the procedures used will be presented in Chapter 14. First the parents learn to think in terms of reinforcement contingencies and to analyze what these actually are in a particular problem situation. Then the psychologist helps them work out a detailed plan for changing the reinforcement pattern. Records are kept from day to day of the frequency with which the "bad" behavior and the "good" behavior occur. As progress is made, the original plan may be revised.

In projects of this sort, the psychologist really becomes a consultant and teacher rather than a therapist. This shift in his role seems to represent a trend that is likely to become increasingly important as time passes. It is conceivable that the whole concept of "therapy" is a passing phase in the development of new kinds of social controls, new patterns of mutual helpfulness.

In line with this trend is the extension of the same concepts we have been considering as a means of correcting malfunctions to schools and other educational institutions. Reinforcement, modeling, discrimination, generalization, extinction, and other basic concepts growing out of research on learning are being applied in programmed instruction, with or without the assistance of computers, in presenting material to be learned in an optimum sequence, at an optimum rate, with adequate reinforcement contingent upon correct responses. Individualized programmed instruction may well be adopted by most school systems before many years have passed. Such efforts are clearly a part of *educational* rather than *clinical* psychology, but to the extent that they prevent "learning problems" they render unnecessary a kind of therapeutic effort that has in the past taken up a great deal of clinician time.

An educational effort even closer to what has been considered the special province of clinical psychology is the setting up of "token economies" in institutions to train inmates to behave differently. One demonstration that has attracted much attention (Cohen, 1968) was a system in a training institution for young offenders. Immediate rewards in the form of tokens were given when the boys did the "right" things. These tokens could then be exchanged for privileges such as private rooms, weekend leaves, and so on. The main objective was to get these boys, for whom the ordinary public-school situation had not worked, to educate themselves to a level that would permit them to get into the main stream of life in a complex modern society once they left the institution. Encouraged by the impressive gains in educational level this project produced, psychologists in many other correctional institutions and mental hospitals have set up "token reward" plans designed especially for their particular patients and objectives.

SALIENT FEATURES OF
THE EMERGING TECHNOLOGY

Creative Aspects

What seems to be taking shape is a real *technology* of behavior change, not just another theory or "school" of psychotherapy. The psychologist faced with the task of coming up with a plan for producing improvement in an *intra*personal or *inter*personal system (individual personality or relationships between persons) has at his command a broad range of techniques to consider. Some of these, such as modeling and shaping, are designed to produce new kinds of behavior different from those the client (person or group) spontaneously carried out. Others, based on variations in the kind, amount, and timing of reinforcements, are designed to increase the frequency with which a desired response occurs and to extinguish unwanted kinds of behavior. Still others are available for analyzing the complex environments through which particular kinds of behavior are being maintained, and then producing beneficial changes in these controlling situations. Behavior modification is not just a set of rules to be applied; each client constitutes a new challenge to the psychologist's ingenuity.

As this creative aspect of the behavior therapies has become more and more salient, the misgivings held by many thoughtful psychologists about its manipulative orientation have to some extent subsided. Many of the most successful improvement programs to be reported in the late 1960s and early 1970s, such as Goldiamond's (1966) work with stutterers, and Patterson et al.'s (1972) work with the parents of children with behavior problems, involve the active *collaboration* of client and psychologist. Together they decide on the objective to be accomplished. Together they work out ways of analyzing reinforcement contingencies and assessing initial status and progress. The psychologist is a consultant who helps the client apply sound principles derived from experimental work on learning to attain his own freely chosen goals. This active participation in the behavior-modification process of the persons whose behavior is being modified is less apparent in projects carried on in correctional institutions and mental hospitals, but it is not entirely lacking even under such circumstances. Such projects are more likely to succeed if the patients or prisoners are told what is going on and how the rewards and punishments are to be applied than if the psychologist attempts to manipulate them without their awareness (Ayllon and Azrin, 1964). Thus, as time has passed, the arguments once waged with considerable heat between "behaviorists" and "humanists" have lost much of their force. The distinction is becoming blurred, although Skinner himself, in his 1971 book *Beyond Freedom and Dignity* still considers it important.

Rapprochements

There appears to be a fairly large area of overlap between the behavioral therapies and the more traditional forms of psychotherapy discussed in Chapter 11. As early as 1950, Dollard and Miller attempted to translate psychoanalytic procedures into terms of learning theory. Looking at interview therapy based on the theory of either Freud or Rogers in the light of what behavior therapists have discovered, we can now recognize that both reinforcement and modeling may play a prominent part in behavior changes produced through such interviews. By his comments and his silences, his expressions of interest or of boredom, the psychotherapist influences the course his client's verbalization, and thus his thinking, takes. By what the therapist reveals of his own orientation toward life, he provides a model the client may imitate, whether he realizes it or not.

Proceeding from the other direction, many behavior therapists have come to recognize that a *relationship* much like the one on which interview therapy is based facilitates the creative collaboration between client and therapist we discussed earlier. Some specialists in behavior modification still hope that eventually the whole process can be programmed for computers so that it can be used to correct most kinds of deviant behavior without any sort of personal therapeutic involvement. But others see a warm, genuine human relationship as essential, even in cases where a computer does most of the work of presenting stimuli and dispensing rewards. Collaborative efforts to improve human situations work best when the participants like and trust one another.

Furthermore, it now appears that cognitive and affective factors may be involved in behavior change, even when the original plan for accomplishing it did not recognize them. It was Greenspoon (1955) who first demonstrated that if an interviewer said "Uh huh" every time an interviewee used a plural noun, the frequency of plurals could be significantly increased, ostensibly without the client's awareness of any change. The "Greenspoon effect" was demonstrated again and again in subsequent experiments on the shaping of verbal behavior. With more penetrating efforts to find out just what was being learned in such interview situations, however, it became more and more apparent that most subjects did form concepts and react accordingly rather than simply change their verbalizations automatically. There may be some "learning without awareness" in therapy situations. However, it is fairly clear on the basis of research that "learning with awareness" is much more efficient.

The rapprochement between different approaches to behavior change is particularly evident in the work of Kanfer and Phillips (1966, 1970). Their techniques for developing *self-regulation* may serve to bridge the gap between behaviorist and cognitive varieties of therapy. By training clients in skills of self-observation, self-evaluation, environmental modification, and self-reinforcement (Kanfer, 1970), these clinician-scientists restore to the individual the control over his own behavior that the new technology has been criticized for undermining.

Some approaches to psychotherapy that would not ordinarily be classified under behavior modification at all, approaches such as Glasser's *Reality therapy*

(1965), can readily be reconciled with it. Their objective is to transform irresponsible behavior into responsible behavior. They attempt to do this, however, not by modeling or reinforcing particular actions but by assisting the client to change his own concepts about how one should act and strengthening his determination to act in these ways. During the first phase of reality therapy, Glasser's objective is to bring about involvement on the part of the client, using the interview time to discuss not his symptoms or past life but rather his present interests, fears, aspirations, and values. The client learns that he can trust the therapist and at the same time gains more respect for himself as he becomes convinced that someone really cares about him and is interested in him. After this involvement occurs, the therapist begins pointing out to the client how he could fulfill his needs by acting more responsibly, emphasizing his strong points and constructive resources. When he fails or falls short, he is required to take the consequences of his lapses, as when a girl with whom Dr. Glasser was working at the Ventura School would be sent to the discipline cottage for failure to meet the standards for behavior at the institution. But the therapist would continue to encourage her to meet the next challenge in a more responsible way. Glasser's procedure, while superficially similar to "talk" therapies, really belongs with the varieties discussed in this chapter in that its objective is to change behavior. Mowrer (1967b) has developed a somewhat similar procedure for assisting clients to act responsibly, a procedure he calls *integrity therapy*. Ellis's *rational-emotive therapy*, discussed in Chapter 11, could also fit well into this one.

New Concepts

Thus with the passage of time the distinction between the behavior therapies and the more "humanistic" therapies based on psychoanalysis, existentialism, or various other philosophies and theories of personality has become somewhat irrelevant. With the broader perspective that has emerged, it is possible to see that the behavioral orientation has added not only techniques but valuable new concepts to our thinking about how to be psychologically helpful. Patterson and Reid (1970) have emphasized two such useful shifts in our thinking. In the first place, the fact that troublesome behavior patterns may be shaped *inadvertently* makes it unnecessary for people to blame themselves or each other for them. A mother need not feel guilty because her little boy throws temper tantrums. If she and the psychologist she has consulted are able to analyze just what she and others are doing to maintain this behavior pattern through the nature and timing reinforcements, they will probably find that it was what she was doing unintentionally that was wrong; this she can now deliberately correct. Viewing problems in this way should serve to make psychological consultation less threatening and thus more palatable to many people who need it.

A second conceptual shift Patterson has emphasized arises from the idea of *reciprocity*. Both parties to a behavioral transaction are shaped by its contingencies of reinforcement. In the case of the child with temper tantrums, he repeatedly creates a stormy scene because he gets whatever he is demanding when he does this. His mother and other family members give him what he demands because the cessation of the disturbance he is making serves as a potent reinforcer of the yielding behavior. It is these symbiotic reinforcement arrangements that perpetuate much unsatisfactory behavior. Identifying and changing them becomes the central task of the behavior technologist.

One other useful conceptual shift should perhaps be added to the list, the increasing tendency to think in terms of positive, desirable behavior rather than difficulties and symptoms. While the concept of *reinforcement* covers both reward and punishment, and in some particular kinds of cases carefully planned negative reinforcement is a crucial part of an improvement program, it has generally been shown that establishing and maintaining desirable responses through some sort of positive reinforcement is a more effective way of controlling behavior, one's own or other people's. Down through the centuries this has not been the prevailing view, especially in schools and in legal and correctional institutions, where it has been assumed that what keeps people in line is punishment or the threat of punishment. If a sizable proportion of society's caretakers were to make this conceptual shift from punishment to reward, the effects might be considerable.

EXAMPLE OF BEHAVIOR MODIFICATION

One of the most impressive aspects of the behavior modification movement is that it has provided a method of approach to persons so seriously disturbed that it seemed impossible to help them by any therapeutic techniques commonly employed. An outstanding example of an extended program of treatment and research on such heretofore almost hopeless cases is the work of Lovaas (1968) on schizophrenic or autistic children. The condition covered by this psychiatric label is still something of a mystery. It may arise from neurological or biochemical deficits in the first place, but regardless of its origins, Lovaas has shown that the behavior itself can be changed through a carefully planned combination of techniques taken from the technology we have been considering in this chapter.

The nature of the deviant behavior is graphically described by Lovaas (1968, p. 109):

> At the behavioral level they all have this in common: they show gross deficiencies in behavioral development and a virtual absence of response to social stimuli . . . Thus, they were so oblivious to their surroundings that they behaved as if they were blind and deaf. They were incontinent. They were completely engrossed in self-stimulating behaviors, such as twirling, rocking, spinning objects, flapping of the arms at the wrists, etc. In six of the children, speech was essentially restricted to occasional vowel productions, with no communicative intent. They evidenced no imitative

behavior of any kind, neither did they respond to speech. Four of the 10 children had echolalic speech, and two of these children evidenced some appropriate play. With these two exceptions, the children did not engage in appropriate play behavior. About half of the children engaged in tantrum behaviors, which included smearing of feces, biting attending adults, and self-mutilation.

The aim of the program Lovaas and his associates carried out went far beyond the elimination of grossly deviant behavior. It was to make the children responsive to social stimuli, so that they could learn as more normal children do. The first step in the improvement program is the one that has attracted the most public attention and criticism, because it involved inflicting pain in order that its termination might acquire reinforcing properties. They electrified the floor and terminated the shock when the subject sought the company of the attending adults. Lovaas justifies the use of this extreme measure by citing its results. Children who before had been impervious to any influence began to show some responsiveness. This made it possible to employ modeling as a means of getting the children to engage in new behaviors, and especially to train them to imitate speech and thus learn to use language. In practice, the whole long process becomes very complicated because arrangements must be made to teach meanings as well as verbalizations and to ensure that behavior established in the laboratory generalizes to the world outside it. Reinforcement contingencies must be carefully programmed, and the farther from the laboratory one moves, the more difficult it is to do this. Fortunately, a variety of reinforcers become effective as the child builds more and more verbal and nonverbal bridges between himself and his fellows. Some kinds of behaviors, once learned, can serve as reinforcers for other kinds, as Premack (1965) has pointed out. Once the child has learned some sort of play behavior, the opportunity to play becomes a reward that can be given for doing less preferred things, such as learning language.

It will be some years before we will know how normal the later development of children undergoing this program of behavior therapy turns out to be. But whether they are "cured" or not, results reported so far make it clear that drastic changes did occur. There is now some hope for heretofore hopeless cases.

APPRAISAL, THERAPY, AND RESEARCH

Psychologists working in the ways described in this chapter have made considerable progress in integrating the three roles clinicians have customarily played—assessment, therapy, and research. In fact, the three kinds of activity are so completely welded together in major programs of work like those of Lovaas, Bandura, and Patterson that it is impossible really to separate them. In combining the components, however, it has been necessary to change them rather drastically from the form they have assumed in other situations in which clinical psychologists work.

In place of assessing general aspects of personality by means of tests and projective techniques, what a person initiating a program of behavior modification will do is to make a detailed appraisal of the behavior to be "worked on" and the situations in which the behavior occurs. Techniques for accomplishing this are varied and ingenious. Workers whose approach is based on Skinner's concepts about operant conditioning typically use controlled observation and counting techniques to obtain accurate records of the frequency with which problem behaviors occur under various conditions of reinforcement. How many temper tantrums does a five-year-old show during the hours when he is at home alone with his mother? When his father is home? When he is at kindergarten? (See examples in Chapter 14.) Workers who derive their basic approach from

TABLE 12-1   Mixed Desensitization Hierarchy for Test Anxiety

Fear Ratings	*Hiearchy Items*
0	Beginning a new course
15	Hearing an instructor announce a small quiz two weeks hence
20	Having a professor urge you personally to do well on an exam
35	Trying to decide how to study for an exam
40	Reviewing the material I know should be studied—listing study to do
60	Hearing an instructor remind the class of a quiz one week hence
60	Hearing an instructor announce a major exam in three weeks and its importance
75	Hearing an instructor announce a major exam in one week
80	Standing alone in the hall before an exam
80	Getting an exam back in class
80	Anticipating getting back a graded exam later that day
80	Talking to several students about an exam right before taking it
85	Thinking about being scared and anxious regarding a specific exam
90	Studying with fellow students several days before an exam
90	Hearing some "pearls" from another student which you doubt you'll remember, while studying in a group
90	Cramming while alone in the library right before an exam
90	Thinking about not keeping up in other subjects while preparing for an exam
95	Thinking about being anxious over school work in general
95	Talking with several students about an exam immediately after
100	Thinking about being generally inadequately prepared
100	Thinking about not being adequately prepared for a particular exam
100	Studying the night before a big exam

Source: Kanfer F. H., and Phillips, J. S. *Learning foundations of behavior therapy*. New York: Wiley, 1970. © 1970 John Wiley & Sons, Inc.

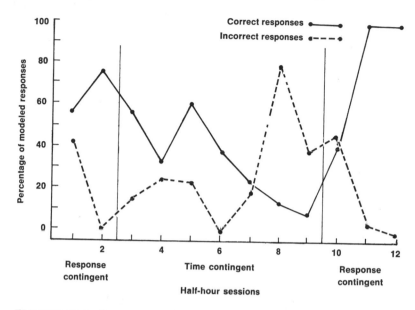

FIGURE 12-1 Percentage of responses correctly and incorrectly reproduced by an autistic child during periods when rewards were made contingent on imitating the adult's speech (response contingent), or the elapsing of a certain amount of time (time contingent). (From Lovaas, 1968.)

Wolpe appraise the behavior to be changed by using interviews in which they ask clients to think about the situations in which the difficulties occur and arrange them in order from least to most serious. In preparation for desensitization therapy, for instance, Lang uses what he calls a fear thermometer. Table 12-1 shows ratings by a student starting treatment for anxiety about taking tests. Ratings run from 0 (totally relaxed) to 100 (as tense as you ever are). The objective in either case is to get a fairly detailed and specific picture of just what needs to be modified through a learning process. As the treatment proceeds, its effects can be evaluated using the same individualized assessment procedures.

The merging of clinical assessment and treatment with research is a salient feature of the work of the operant conditioners. Each case in a sense becomes a separate experiment. After the preliminary assessment has given the psychologist some basis for a hypothesis about the nature of the reinforcement contingencies controlling a particular kind of behavior, he sets up a three-stage plan, called a *reversal*, to test this hypothesis. As mentioned in Chapter 5, it consists of a period in which the experimental factor, a change in the reinforcement contingencies, is present, a following period in which the experimental factor is discontinued, and a third period in which it is reinstated. If his hypothesis is sound, the hypothesized behavior change should occur during the first period, undergo extinction during the second, and occur again during the third. In the Lovaas work with autistic children discussed above, Figure 12-1 illustrates the way in which such an experiment on a single subject works. Results such as these provide guidance to the psychologist about how to proceed with the improvement plan for the individual he is attempting to help and also contribute to general theoretical understanding of behavior modification. This graph illustrates a principle for which considerable support has accumulated: that reinforcement designed to increase the frequency of a certain kind of behavior be given only after the behavior occurs.

It is fairly obvious that important theoretical issues cannot be completely resolved by an experiment in which N equals 1, and research designs in which experimental groups are compared with control groups are still necessary. But, as explained in Chapter 5, the experiment on a single subject, varying the treatment over time so that the subject during one of the periods serves as his own control, constitutes a valuable addition to the research resources of the clinical psychologist.

Symptom Substitution

One particular theoretical issue generated a considerable amount of research at an earlier time when behavior therapists were struggling for a place in a domain dominated by psychoanalytic practitioners, the question of whether or not *symptom substitution* would occur. Psychoanalytic theory would lead one to predict that since neurotic symptoms express unconscious motivational conflicts, the removal of a symptom would simply lead to the development of some other symptom, perhaps more troublesome than the first. From the theoretical vantage point of the behavior therapists, the symptom *is* the neurosis, so that they would not expect such substitution to occur. Most of the research directed to this issue indicated that symptom substitution does not tend to be a problem (Grossberg, 1964) but that, in fact, the by-products or indirect effects of behavior therapy are likely to be beneficial to the persons treated.

The whole problem is now being viewed in a broader context, however. It is increasingly clear that what happens after a planned program of behavior modification ends will depend upon the reinforcement contingencies in the life situation the person faces. If nothing has changed from the situation in which he was enmeshed before the treatment began, it is quite likely that he will relapse into his former habits. If no arrangements have been built into the improvement plan to ensure that the client learns constructive new ways of coping with his problems to replace the bad habits that have been rooted out, it is quite likely that some form of response substitution will occur that can be seen as simply substituting one symptom for another. Thinking of this sort leads into the vast problem of designing human environments that will facilitate and maintain desirable behavior. This is perhaps the most challenging task of our time. We shall consider what is being done along these lines in later chapters.

When the client is an adult, much can be done to change the system in which he must function after therapy has ended by enabling him to change his own concepts and attitudes, and thus the nature of his interactions with other people.

He can make choices with regard to situations, voluntarily placing himself where the consequences of the kind of behavior he wishes to develop will be rewarding, not punishing. The fact that behavior-modification techniques were employed to rid him of a stubborn handicap does not preclude the use of other therapeutic approaches, of the various kinds mentioned in the preceding and following chapters, to help him reorganize his life.

CRITICAL EVALUATION

It is to the credit of the behavior-modification movement that its practitioners have carried on outcome research systematically as they treated patients or clients in the ways that have been discussed in this chapter. Wolpe, for example, in his first book on reciprocal inhibition (1958) specified his criteria for effectiveness and then cited figures indicating that of 210 cases treated, 39 percent were apparently cured, 50.5 percent much improved, 7.2 percent slightly or moderately improved, and only 3.3 percent unimproved. Follow-up information on 45 of the patients in the two top groups showed that 44 of them had held their own or gained ground over a period of two years. Similar favorable outcomes have been reported by many of the other leaders in the movement.

Furthermore, in instances where some form of behavioral therapy is compared with a more traditional kind of interview treatment, the evidence seems to favor the former. (See a brief account of the study by Paul, 1967, in the Research Summaries at the end of the chapter.)

It is not feasible at this point to examine all this evidence in detail. Impressive as it is, it does not warrant a conclusion that we have at last discovered how to cure all human ills as some messianic interpreters of the behavioral therapy movement have suggested. For one thing, the difficulties of research on change discussed in Chapter 5 all show up here—criterion problems, measurement problems, problems of controls. For another, more long-term follow-up studies will be required before we can be confident that changes in behavior are lasting. Lazarus (1971), who has done some of the most outstanding work on the treatment of neuroses by desensitization methods, is much less enthusiastic than he once was about the results because of follow-up studies pointing to a high number of relapses in subjects who were apparently "cured." He emphasizes the importance of a process similar to what was discussed in Chapter 11 under the heading of rational-emotive therapy—that in addition to changing specific habits or responses, a person needs to develop a new philosophy of life, greater self-esteem, and a broader range of interpersonal and behavioral skills if improved functioning is to be maintained.

In spite of such reservations, the conclusion is still warranted that the development of a technology of behavior change has greatly enlarged society's resources for dealing with individual problems, unsatisfactory interpersonal relationships, and malfunctioning groups and organizations, as well as for teaching cognitive and social skills that prevent the occurrence of deviations and malfunctions. We can anticipate continued progress along the paths that have been charted.

SUMMARY

Methods of psychological treatment based on the application of principles derived from research on learning were elaborated several decades ago but were not extensively applied until the decades of the 1950s and 1960s. Some major contributors whose work stimulated widespread efforts to deal with many intransigent psychological problems were Wolpe, who described a technique for eliminating neurotic symptoms by reciprocal inhibition; Skinner and his colleagues, who systematically explored the uses of reinforcement in controlling operant responses; Bandura, who showed how modeling could be used to establish new responses and increase the probability that existing ones would occur; and Patterson, who showed that the persons in a client's natural environment could be taught to play the major role in modifying his behavior and maintaining the improvements made.

The result of these and many other concurrent efforts by others is that a useful technology of behavior change is emerging. A resourceful technician can design an individualized plan for each individual to be served. Often the client himself participates actively in such planning, and concern over the manipulative aspects of behavior therapy has somewhat diminished. The technology now includes cognitive as well as behavioral concepts. The line between behaviorists and humanists is becoming blurred.

Appraisal plays an important part in programs for modifying behavior, but it rests on quantified observations of what individuals do in particular situations rather than on the more general psychological methods such as ratings and tests. A research component is built into most projects with the subject serving as his own control during phases when the independent variable is discontinued. Because of the variety of special techniques now available, studies comparing one treatment plan with another are feasible, and specially designed individual plans for special categories of people can be evaluated.

Evaluative research has generally shown that treatment by behavior-modification works and, where comparisons have been made, that it works better than alternative ways of dealing with the problems. The main doubt remaining is with regard to how lasting its effects are. While symptom substitution has not turned out to be a very serious by-product, there is a tendency for the old habits to return when the experimental program ends. This finding points to the need for more attention to the larger systems in which individuals normally function.

SUGGESTED READINGS

Bandura, A. *Principles of behavior modification.* New York: Holt, Rinehart and Winston, 1969.

Several comprehensive textbooks covering the area discussed in this chapter are now available. This one by Bandura is one of the best, providing a balanced account of a considerable number of approaches and techniques. The book is also a convenient source of information about the research Bandura himself has done, such as the important series of experiments on modeling.

Lazarus, A. A. *Behavior therapy and beyond.* New York: McGraw-Hill, 1971.

As indicated in the chapter, Lazarus concluded from his analysis of the later progress of persons he had treated twelve years before that the techniques he and Wolpe had been using to eradicate neurotic symptoms did not always produce lasting improvements in patients. He presents the results of this follow-up study in the book, but most of its emphasis, as the title suggests, is on a variety of techniques that may be useful in helping particular kinds of individuals reorganize their lives rather than simply eliminate their anxieties and fears. It is an eclectic book, with a practical rather than a theoretical focus, a book for practicing therapists.

Neuringer, C., and Michael, J. L. (eds.). *Behavior modification in clinical psychology.* New York: Appleton-Century-Crofts, 1970.

The book is an outgrowth of an institute held in 1967 at the University of Kansas. The emphasis is on research rather than practice, and the authors of the separate chapters, outstanding contributors to research on behavior modification, have their eyes on the future rather than the past. One finds here some new ways of thinking that can be expected to generate innovative approaches to stubborn psychological difficulties.

Watson, D. L., and Tharp, R. G. *Self-directed behavior: self-modification for personal adjustment.* Monterey, Calif.: Brooks/Cole, 1972.

Based on behavioral learning theory, this book is a clear presentation of principles and methods for self-improvement intended for students, or clients, or the general public. There are many case examples, such as that of a college student who wishes to improve his relationship with his parents. The book advocates a selection of specific behaviors the person wishes to change, a period of self-observation during which the person keeps baseline records of his behavior, and several different ways by which the individual intervenes in his behavior and alters his environment to establish new action patterns. For a more advanced discussion of theory and research related to self-control of behavior, see Kanfer and Phillips (1970).

Weiss, R. L. Operant conditioning techniques in psychological assessment. In P. McReynolds (ed.), *Advances in psychological assessment*, Vol. 1. Palo Alto, Calif.: Science & Behavior Books, 1968, pp. 169–190.

Weiss reviews the operant-conditioning literature from the standpoint of its usefulness in providing indicators of individual differences. He notes that the basic idea of the contingency—the "if—then" statement—embodies the need to measure a variety of individual characteristics (e.g., a person's preferences for reinforcers, differences in ways subjects respond to reinforcers, and appraisal of a person's response repertoire). He reviews studies with responsiveness to reinforcement as a dependent variable and as a predictor variable. Weiss reports on his imaginative procedures for studying emitted reinforcing behavior (or reinforcing skill) in social situations.

Krasner, L., and Ullman, L. P. (eds.). *Research in behavior modification*. New York: Holt, Rinehart and Winston, 1966.

Each chapter in this collection opens up new possibilities for using behavior-modification techniques in therapy. Several of the persons mentioned in this chapter describe in some detail the kinds of work they have been doing.

RESEARCH SUMMARIES

Ayllon, T., and Azrin, N. H. Reinforcement and instruction with mental patients. *Journal for the Experimental Analysis of Behavior*, 1964, 7, 327–331.

The purpose of the experiment was to study the effectiveness of instructions and reinforcement, singly and in combination. In Experiment I the subjects were eighteen female patients of forty-three on a mental hospital ward selected because they failed to pick up utensils when obtaining food from the counter. In Experiment II, twenty female patients participated. During a baseline period, patients were observed and the behavior recorded. During a reinforcement period, the patient was offered a choice of reward (candy, cigarette, coffee, milk) if she picked up utensils but was given no explanation. During an instruction period she was asked to pick them up and given the reward if she did so.

Experiment I:
Results: Baseline—less than 10 percent responded correctly
            Reinforcement—only very slight rise
            Instructions—by twelfth meal, 12 of 18 patients responded correctly

Experiment II:
Results: Baseline—0 percent responded correctly
            Instructions only—25 percent-60 percent responded correctly
            Instructions plus reinforcement—80-100 percent responded correctly

Paul, G. L. Insight versus desensitization in psychotherapy two years after termination. *Journal of Consulting Psychology*, 1967, *31*, 333–348.

In the original study, Paul (1966) compared three experimental groups with a control group and with each other. Each experimental group consisted of fifteen students in a public-speaking course who volunteered for treatment for performance anxiety. One group received systematic desensitization, another insight-oriented therapy, and the third simply interested attention (placebo). The control group was made up of forty-four students from the same population who were given no treatment of any kind. Anxiety before and after treatment was assessed in several different ways, including a speech performance. The results immediately after the five-session treatment period and in a follow-up six weeks later showed that all three treatment groups had improved significantly as compared with the control group, and that the effect of the desensitization was significantly greater than that of the other techniques.

This follow-up two years later, in which data were obtained from 100 percent of the treated subjects and 70 percent of the controls, showed that the improvement had continued and that the desensitization group was still significantly superior to the others.

chapter 13

Utilizing Personal and Environmental Systems: Counseling and Rehabilitation

As explained earlier, one important consideration in deciding upon a plan for helping a client is the extent to which personal and situational resources already available to him can be used without attempting to bring about changes of any magnitude in his personality. Psychologists have been engaged in efforts of this sort for a long time, but most of them would not have considered themselves to be *clinical* psychologists. They would be more likely to identify with counseling or rehabilitation, and they probably would not call their task psychotherapy. However, as time has passed, it has become more and more difficult to draw sharp lines between the psychological specialties, and there seems to be less and less reason for doing so.

HISTORY AND PHILOSOPHY OF COUNSELING

One of the historical sources of counseling and rehabilitation psychology is the vocational guidance movement. The first decade of the twentieth century was a period of unusual importance in the history of American psychology. At about the same time that Freud's ideas were being introduced to a skeptical but fascinated public and Binet's tests were opening up the whole vast field of mental measurement, Parsons published a little book called *Choosing a Vocation* (1906). His ideas caught on immediately, and within just a few years a flourishing vocational guidance movement was under way. To start with, it had little to do with psychology, but psychologists soon saw the significance of the movement and began to make contributions to it, devising tests for the assessment of vocational aptitudes, working out occupational classification systems that made psychological sense, and refining interview techniques.

The aim of guidance is to help a person arrive at sound decisions and thus to set his course in the direction he wishes to go. It has nothing to do with neurosis

338

or psychosis, and concepts of illness and cure are foreign to it. Thus its principal beneficiaries have been high school and college students, although there have always been some other agencies designed to serve adults at times when they face vocational decisions.

As time passed, psychologists began to realize that the two areas, clinical and counseling, were not so unrelated as they had at first appeared to be. Uncertainties about occupational choices and other important life decisions contribute to the anxiety underlying various psychiatric symptoms. Personality problems are common causes of vocational maladjustment and must be considered when vocational plans are being made. On the positive side, it has become more and more apparent that work is one of the great stabilizing forces in human life. Even Freud, when asked what was most important in life, responded *Liebe und Arbeit* (love and work). Many psychotherapists, realizing this fact, have turned their attention to this aspect of their patients' problems and in doing so contributed to the development of a kind of therapy resting primarily on the exploration of individual resources.

During the 1950s there was a tremendous upsurge of interest in the rehabilitation of the handicapped. A movement that in the 1920s appeared to be a minor offshoot of the general vocational guidance movement joined forces with those branches of medicine that are especially concerned with the restoration of function to the disabled. At first only physical handicaps arising from illness and accident were considered, but gradually rehabilitative work was extended to patients in mental hospitals and to the mentally retarded. All these efforts have contributed to the ideas about improvement programs we shall review in this chapter. It has become apparent that because of the rich resources the process of development has built into a human personality, it is often possible to disregard a person's weaknesses and handicaps almost completely and instead help him build his future on his strengths or assets.

Fortunately, this was not an all-or-none distinction. Typically, therapist and client weigh and consider both assets and liabilities and work out appropriate ways of dealing with them. What distinguishes counseling and rehabilitation from other treatments we shall be considering is that, instead of attempting to bring about as *much* change as possible in a client's personality, its aim is to help him utilize as much as possible of the structure that already exists. An attempt is made to discover an unblocked path along which the person can move forward, develop his unique individuality, and thus transcend, rather than penetrate into, the anxieties and conflicts in which he is enmeshed.

A psychologist embarking upon a plan of this sort with a client tends to think of the change to be brought about in the person as primarily a change of *direction*. That a person is encountering difficulties may be a sign that he is headed toward goals that are wrong for him or that at a former time he has made a turn leading into a blind alley. The therapist's first aim is to create a situation in which the client can see what shifts in direction are possible for him, and second, to give him confidence that someone will see him through the initial uncertainties that arise because he does change his course.

Although this kind of assistance to clients owes much to the vocational guidance movement, its applicability extends far beyond vocational adjustment. In any kind of situation where a person's forward movement is blocked for one reason or another, these concepts may be useful. Examples could be multiplied. Perhaps it is a husband and wife who have come to realize that their marriage has become intensely frustrating to both of them, and they cannot seem to surmount or get around the obstacles that are preventing the continued development of their relationship. Or a bright young high school girl wishes to get married immediately to the classmate with whom she is deeply in love, but hesitates to cut herself off from the possibility of the career in science she had looked forward to. A young man brought up in a devout Catholic family finds that his beliefs are being undermined by his associations with faculty and fellow students in college.

In all these situations and in countless others, the common feature is that some choice or decision faces the client. He may not see it this way. The situation may be so confused at the outset that it is not at all clear what decisions are possible. And he himself may be so anxious and upset that he is in no condition to make important decisions. The therapist's responsibility is to create a special kind of environment in which difficulties can be faced and overcome. The client must be protected at least partially and for a time from outside pressures. He must be helped to obtain the information he needs and to attack doubt and confusion at their source. He must have his confidence in himself strengthened so that he can take the action necessary to establish the new direction and can accept the consequences of the action he takes. The psychologist in this case resembles not so much a physican who cures psychological ills as he does the proprietor of a service station who furnishes road information, supplies fuel, and helps get stalled vehicles moving in the direction their drivers wish to go.

Because of its origins in vocational counseling rather than in psychotherapy, we shall call this kind of technique *counseling* as we proceed with the chapter. The word *counseling*, to be sure, is even more ambiguous than most of the other terms we use in psychological practice. But for want of a better word we shall use it to refer to the kind of intervention we have been describing, where the emphasis is put on assets rather than liabilities, on small modifications of direction rather than large changes, either quantitative or qualitative, and on decisions made by the client rather than influences brought to bear by the psychologist. Similarly, for the purposes of this chapter as of several others, we shall refer to the recipient of the service as a *client* rather than a "patient." It is fundamental to this approach that even though he may be a chronic schizophrenic with twenty years of hospitalization behind him, rehabilitative efforts must start with the assumption that he is a client making use of a service offered him rather than a patient hoping to be cured.

Plans for the utilization of the client's resources can often be combined in constructive ways with other sorts of therapy. For example, a patient admitted to a mental hospital in an acute psychotic state may first undergo a period of drug therapy, then participate in individual or group psychotherapy designed to help him develop self-understanding. At this point, a plan for his reinstatement in the world outside the hospital, based on an analysis of his abilities and interests and of the opportunities available to him, will be worked out. Counseling is often the last phase of an improvement program that extends over a considerable period of time.

EXPLORATION OF POSSIBILITIES

Like all psychotherapy, counseling requires that a secure, dependable relationship be established. The client must have confidence in the counselor. The counselor must be genuinely interested in the client. They must like one another as persons.

What has not always been fully recognized, however, is that interest and goodwill, while necessary, are not *sufficient* to ensure that the kind of thinking out of which good decisions come as actually done. If such thinking is to be accomplished, the client must first survey the possibilities open to him. Psychologists responsible for helping clients "find themselves" must know how to facilitate such surveys. This means examining the psychological resources the client himself possesses and the alternative opportunities his situation provides, and arriving at criteria for assigning relative weights to the alternative courses of action that are identified. It is a complex task, one for which the clinical psychologist is often not adequately prepared but for which, unfortunately, he often does not realize that he lacks preparation.

Surveying the Client's Characteristics

As far as the possibilities within the client himself are concerned, the major sources of data are case records, interviews, and tests. Going through a case folder with this purpose in mind is different from reading it in order to diagnose the particular kind of pathology manifested or to change maladaptive behavior. What the psychologist looks for is evidence about experience the person has had that may have produced at least the beginnings of a usable skill, interests he has shown at some period of his life, abilities as demonstrated in school or at work, motives and attitudes expressed in his past actions. It is important to notice where, how, and why the client has failed, but it is even more important to consider periods and areas in which he has succeeded.

Whether a scrutiny of the records available for a particular client turns up any possibilities or not, interviews are major sources of ideas. Interviews designed to serve the purpose of identifying alternative possibilities are somewhat more focused than the usual therapeutic interview, but they cannot be just question-and-answer sessions, and there is no standard formula to be followed. One interview may begin with a question about the nature of a job the client has held in the past; another may clarify what he really wants from life. Hopes and fears are expressed and recognized. No attempt is made to gloss over negative attitudes or argue the person out of them, but the general atmosphere is constructive and forward-looking. The interview takes the shape of a search carried on jointly by counselor and client for unblocked paths into the future.

Tests and assessment techniques are also useful in identifying possibilities the client might not think of without them. Psychologists often do not think of assessment in this way, even when they have had a great deal of experience in the use of tests for diagnostic evaluation. It is not personality tests of either the structured or the nonstructured variety that are employed for this purpose so much as aptitude, achievement, and interest tests. These are available in considerable variety. There are intelligence or scholastic aptitude tests suitable for all ages and levels for preschool children to graduate students. Because many plans for the future involve further education it is often important to forecast as accurately as possible how well an individual is likely to get along in a program he is considering. A general intelligence test such as the WAIS or the WISC provides some information on this point, but not nearly so much as a more specific test such as the Scholastic Aptitude Test of the College Entrance Examination Board or the Graduate Record Examination for prospective graduate students.

Special aptitude tests for a large number of occupations have also been developed. For exploring vocational possibilities, the General Aptitude Test Battery (GATB), which can be taken at most public employment offices, is often very helpful (see Figure 13-1). A person may discover that there are twenty different kinds of work he has never even thought of doing for which he has the requisite abilities. Most of these may be of no interest to him at all, but one of them may set off a whole new train of thinking about his future.

The assessment technique most specifically designed for this particular purpose—helping a client explore possibilities for future development—is the vocational interest inventory. The best of these instruments, such as the Strong Vocational Interest Blank (illustrated in Chapter 7), indicate to an individual how much his general orientation toward life and work resembles that of successful people in various specialized fields. Thus he is able to arrive at a forecast of how he is likely to react to being an architect, school superintendent, or certified public accountant, whether he would feel at home with his colleagues, and whether he would be content to stay with this kind of work year after year.

In order to play his part in helping a client survey his own resources, the psychologist needs to know how to select tests intelligently on the basis of dependable information about their validity, reliability, norms, and other technical matters mentioned in Chapter 9. He also needs to be able to translate test scores into meaningful statements about assets and limitations, and to

Name JONES, MARY J.   Date 9-4-70
(Last name) (First name) (Middle initial)

	S'	S'

COMMENTS: _____

Adult ☑   B-1001 ☐
Grade 9 ☐   B-1002 ☑
Grade 10 ☐ Form: Ⓐ B C D

G A T B
INDIVIDUAL APTITUDE PROFILE

Part B-1002	B-1001	Raw Score	G	V	N	S	P	O	K	F	M
1	B	54						108			
2	D	25				82					
3	H	16	16			101					
4	J	26	63	111							
5	A	37					65				
6	I	8	19		14						
7	L	29					51				
8	K	71							103		
9	M	90									23
10	N	103									79
11	O	27								36	
12	P	34								69	
Aptitude Scores			98	111	96	101	116	108	103	105	102

FIGURE 13-1 Report form showing scores on the GATB made by one individual. Combinations of these scores can be matched with ability profiles for a large number of occupations to identify kinds of work for which Mary would qualify. (From U. S. Department of Labor, 1970, p. 122.)

communicate to the client what his performance does and does not mean. Research on what people learn and remember of the information they receive about their own test scores has shown that such communication is a complex and difficult task. (See Research Summaries at the end of the chapter.) Often almost nothing of what a person is told about his own abilities and interests seems to register with him, and thus the time that has been spent in assessment procedures is largely wasted as far as his self-knowledge is concerned. Skill in communication is important to the clinical psychologist here as in almost everything else he does. It is more a matter of listening than of talking, of sensing what the other person is hearing rather than what is actually being said.

Surveying Situations

Surveying a client's possibilities involves looking at his situation as well as his personality. The system with which the psychologist is dealing in such cases is an organism-environment system. As in the case of the personal characteristics we have been discussing, the psychologist gets some of his information about the client's situation from case records and interviews. But because he is looking for possibilities rather than just present circumstances, it is desirable for him to cast his net more widely. He should know something about the whole world of occupations, for example, and be familiar with the sources from which dependable information about particular occupational fields can be obtained. He should be familiar with specialized social agencies set up to deal with particular kinds of problems and with new programs provided for by legislative enactments. Sociological research has shown that the development of individuals has often been limited by a severely restricted opportunity structure. However, national programs like the American "war on poverty" do make changes, and opportunities exist now that did not exist at an earlier time. It is a part of the psychologist's responsibility to ensure that changes are incorporated into the thinking that goes on when a person's future possibilities are being surveyed.

It is apparent that in order to provide the kind of service to clients we are talking about in this chapter, a psychologist must have breadth as well as depth, and some familiarity with many situations and kinds of information that would not ordinarily be classified as psychology at all. Not all clinical psychologists enjoy working in this way. Many of them prefer to focus their attention exclusively on intrapsychic systems. There is no reason that they should not do so if they wish, and there is no dearth of patients who desire psychotherapy and are willing to pay for it. The only point to be made about breadth of view is that *if* the plan for work with a client involves locating promising situations in which he can utilize his present resources without undergoing any major personality change, *then* the psychologist who participates in this plan should be a person with this broader knowledge and outlook. Experience with "deeper" varieties of psychotherapy does not constitute adequate preparation for dealing with "person–situation systems."

FACILITATING CHOICES AND DECISIONS

Assuming that several possible plans of action have been identified in the sort of exploratory activities we have been discussing, how can the psychologist help the client decide which of them he wants to follow? Can he glean from the extensive research that has been done on models of rational decision making any concepts or principles that can be applied in the clinical situation?

Factors in Decisions

The models with which decision researchers have worked have two major components, *utility* (the chooser's values, desires, wishes, etc.) and *expectation* (the probability the chooser sees of attaining each of the alternative goals). If some way of accurately measuring each of these components can be devised, such models lead to a prediction of what a person will choose. By inducing changes in either or both of the variables, utility and expectation, changes in choice behavior can be brought about. Like other lines of research, this one has led to all sorts of complexities as work progressed. The decisions people actually make often do not correspond closely to those they would be predicted to make from measurements of their utility and expectation variables. In other words, people are not completely rational. Some individuals are willing to take much greater risks than others. People vary in the degree to which they are motivated by fear of failure and by hope of success. Furthermore, to obtain precise quantitative indices of any of these motives or expectations in the clinical situation is usually impossible. Thus the psychologist cannot actually apply any of the available decision models to the client's problem, but the general formulation coming out of such research provides clues as to the sort of thinking that needs to be done in decision-making interviews.

Clarifying "Utilities"

Although the client may never be able to specify in exact quantitative terms the "utility" to him of each of the alternative futures that have been identified, he can in interviews with the psychologist clarify his motives and values and arrange the things he wants from life in some sort of priority order. The psychologist contributes to this process in various ways. He may suggest that the client take an inventory of values or needs, such as the Allport-Vernon-Lindzey *Study of Values* or the *Edwards Personal Preference Schedule*, and then discuss with him what the results seem to show about his motivation. He may focus attention on choices the client has made in the past, encouraging him to introspect about the reasons he made these choices as he did. It is obviously impossible for a counselor to force a person to carry on serious thinking he does not wish to do, but if the timing and preparation are right, the responses the counselor makes to what the client says in an interview—expressing approval, asking for more information, raising general questions, or remaining silent—influence the shape the interview takes. If the purpose of a particular session is to facilitate responsible decision making, it is well during this hour to discourage conversation about the trivial or irrelevant and to encourage serious thinking about long-range goals. An important part of the psychologist's skill is the ability to sense whether or not the time is ripe for such thinking.

Objectifying Probabilities

A psychologist's knowledge and skill can also add clarity and definition to the thinking carried on about the other component, the *probability* of a desired outcome that the client sees for each of the alternative courses of action. Some objective probabilities may actually be available in quantitative form in the shape of *expectancy tables*. What such tables as 13-1 and 13-2 show are the relative numbers of successes and failures, and in some cases the relative numbers at each of several success levels, in a particular sort of situation, among persons

TABLE 13-1 Expectancy Table Showing Relations Between Scores on College Qualifying Test (CQT) and College Grade-Point Average for 1,340 Men

CQT total	Grade-point average			
	D and F	C	A and B	
High	16	45	39	100
Middle	43	50	7	100
Low	80	19	1	100

Source: Test Service Bulletin, Psychological Corporation, May 1966, No. 56, p. 3.

TABLE 13-2 Expectancy Table Showing Relation Between Scores on College Qualifying Test (CQT) and College Grade-Point Average for 1,053 Women

CQT total	Grade-point average			
	D and F	C	A and B	
High	6	43	51	100
Middle	25	60	15	100
Low	57	41	2	100

Source: Test Service Bulletin, Psychological Corporation, May 1966, No. 56, p. 3.

with particular combinations of defined characteristics. An expectancy chart worked out by a rehabilitation agency for predicting the success of mentally retarded individuals of different levels of measured intelligence in repetitive jobs in a local industry may show, for example, that for persons with IQs of 60 to 70, trained before they entered upon their jobs, 83 percent remained on the job for six months or more, and seventeen quit or were fired. For later clients of an agency serving the retarded, these figures can be translated into a probability statement that the chances of success for a person with an IQ of 67 who make this choice are five out of six. Interesting research is going on aimed at programming computers to produce probability estimates of this sort for complex information. It may eventually be possible for the client of a rehabilitation agency to feed into the computer all the relevant facts about himself, such as the nature of his disabilities, his test scores, his previous occupations, and various other data, and ask it to give him an estimate of his probability of success in each of the occupations he is considering.

Assessing Subjective Probabilities

Most often, however, objective estimates of the probability of a favorable outcome are not readily available, and even when they are, the client's *subjective* probabilities may be the most important determiners of his decision. If, for example, Sally Sherman, a divorcee with an eight-year-old child, is trying to make up her mind whether (1) to marry a man who lives in a small town in another state, giving up her secure, well-paying position in a department store in order to do so, (2) to begin part-time college work at the local community college, or (3) to continue her present pattern of life without change, the probabilities to be considered are complex and involved. In order to assess the likelihood that the new marriage would be rewarding, she may have to examine her feelings about the prospective husband, consider what went wrong with her first marriage, and analyze her attitudes toward the kind of small town to which this move would take her, as well as to give some thought to the effect the change is likely to have upon her daughter. Outcome probabilities for the other alternatives in this case can be formulated more precisely. She has a fairly clear idea where her present life is leading, and the college prospects depend upon readily identifiable aspects of her own personality and the college situation. However, it is unlikely that a computer could ever be programmed to deliver quantitative probability estimates for Sally's whole decision problem.

As mentioned earlier, the experimental investigations of models of rational decision making are useful to clinical, counseling, or rehabilitation psychologists chiefly in providing a general framework for constructive thinking about an individual's alternative futures. The psychologist's task is to help the client clarify his utilities and probabilities and combine them in such a way that a decision he is satisfied to live with emerges.

PLANNING FOR DEVELOPMENT OF SKILLS

The psychologist with the objective we have been discussing in this chapter—to help a client use his resources productively—has still another role to play. The client's decision about what he wishes to do is likely to necessitate detailed *planning*. The occupational choice he makes will probably require that the person undergo some kind of training program. In some cases this may be provided on the job; more frequently schooling is called for.

Unless a psychologist makes a special effort to broaden his horizons he may not realize just how varied the possibilities are in our society for training in specialized skills. His own educational experience has made him familiar with the channels leading from high school through college to graduate or professional school, and he may never have thought about the alternative channels that are available—apprenticeships, trade schools, two-year colleges, volunteer work overseas, and many others. He needs to become familiar with all these training resources.

But occupational skills are not the only ones that individual clients may need to develop in order to function productively in society. A psychologist working in a rehabilitation agency that serves clients with serious disabilities works with other members of the rehabilitation team, such as physical and occupational therapists, in planning a sequence of experiences designed to equip the person for the ordinary business of living—eating, moving around, and the like. A psychologist in an agency serving the retarded helps to plan programs of training in basic skills such as reading and performing simple arithmetical computations, as well as more general social skills such as listening to what people are saying and getting to work on time.

Cooperating in Planning

Planning is often a cooperative effort involving several staff members rather than a single psychologist and his client. The special contribution that a psychologist should be able to make to the undertaking comes from his understanding of the learning process. His professional training has included courses and perhaps research activities designed to produce such an understanding, and thus he should be able to analyze motivational situations, reinforcement contingencies, and cognitive structures as they affect the individuals for whom and with whom plans are being made. Learning is the one human characteristic that psychology has investigated most extensively and accumulated most knowledge about. It is important, in this and other contexts, that clinical psychologists acquire a thorough knowledge of what research has shown and develop skill in applying it to particular individuals and situations. It is as important in the work we are considering in this chapter as in the behavior therapies discussed in Chapter 12.

Coordinating Services

In agencies where much of the effort is focused on utilizing present psychological and societal resources rather than on changing personality, the psychologist is quite likely also to be a coordinator as well as an interviewer, tester, and planner. Several persons and agencies may be involved with each client, but some one staff member must be responsible for organizing their activities and monitoring the client's progress. Thus he needs to know as much as possible about many aspects of social psychology. It is not easy to establish and maintain organizational arrangements involving the cooperation of specialized workers from different professions and different social agencies. Each group tends to be jealous of its own prerogatives. The nurses may not trust the social workers; the psychologists may resent the psychiatrists; school counselors and employment service personnel may doubt each other's competence. As the attention of the public and of clinical psychologists themselves has shifted from an exclusive emphasis on psychotherapy to an emphasis on community psychology, social psychology has taken on increasing importance in graduate training programs.

AN EXAMPLE OF POSITIVE APPRAISAL AND COUNSELING

Sandron (1971) has cited an interesting case that illustrates the approach we have been discussing. The twenty-six-year-old patient, Mr. Smith, had been hospitalized for twenty-two months, and his record showed that there had been a prior hospitalization for a "mental disorder." On the first occasion he had been given a psychiatric diagnosis of "schizophrenic reaction, acute undifferentiated type," and on the second occasion the diagnosis was "schizophrenic reaction, paranoid type." An evaluation based on the MMPI read as follows (p. 83):

Symptoms and Personality Characteristics
   The profile indicates a severe disturbance. Tension, worrying, self-doubts, and multiple fears and anxieties appear severe if not over-whelming. In some related cases such symptoms as the blunting of affect, concreteness of thinking, morbid ruminations, and ideas of reference suggested schizoid trends or a chronic undifferentiated schizophrenic reaction. Suicidal preoccupations, phobias, and feelings of despondency, hopelessness and guilt are suggested. A pervasive loss of interest along with ambivalence and indecisiveness is also suggested. Shy and withdrawn, he appears markedly uncomfortable socially, keeping others at a distance and fearing close involvement.

There was some evidence that Mr. Smith had defined his own role as that of a mental patient and thus set up a "self-fulfilling prophecy" of continued psychiatric difficulties—a *working image* likely to be used by readers to Smith's disadvantage. Dr. Sandron therefore defined his task as one of breaking the existing pattern of failure and "substituting a self-fulfilling prophecy of positive achievement and growth." The first step was to reorganize his own perception to Mr. Smith, defining him not as a patient but as a person.
   There were a total of five testing and counseling sessions with Mr. Smith. The emphasis was on appraisal of his strengths and weaknesses and on involving him in decisions about what he wished to do with his life. The psychological report that resulted from this effort was strikingly different from the previous psychological reports in Mr. Smith's file (Sandron, 1971, p. 83).

Evaluation of Educational and Occupational
Strengths and Limitations of Mr. Jim Smith

I.   *Occupational Assets*
   (a) Mr. Smith is a tall, pleasant, and personable individual who is well mannered. He expresses himself well and can make a favorable impression on a prospective employer.
   (b) He has a good command of the English language and communicates effectively via the written word. His spelling is excellent, and he has

a good command of verbal concepts, which he uses appropriately
and in good context.

(c) He has superior intellectual potential, which is especially evident in
his ability for abstract verbal thinking, which is one of the "higher
human processes."

(d) He has significant work experience and marketable work skills in
clerical and office fields.

II. *Limitations and/or Detriments to Fulfillment of His Potentials*

(a) Lack of formulation of worthwhile goals in life, which is closely
related to lack of self-esteem and fear of failure, also a preoccupation with immediate needs and avoidance of looking toward the
future.

(b) Feelings of inertia, which are related to a prolonged pattern of
dependency on an "institutionalized" pattern of living.

(c) Too much emphasis on negative factors; feelings of not being a
worthwhile human being (this is closely related to items a and b),
focusing on past failures in lieu of utilizing current strengths and
assets in a positive and gratifying way.

At the time of his final interview, Dr. Sandron gave Mr. Smith a copy of this
report. Several days later Mr. Smith, on his own, made an appointment to take a
Civil Service examination for a clerical position. He passed the written
examination and when he appeared before a panel of interviewers for an oral
examination, he submitted to them a copy of the psychological evaluation Dr.
Sandron had written. He was hired for the job, and at the time of a follow-up
fifteen months later, he reported that he had passed an examination and received
a promotion. Sandron concluded (1971, p. 87):

It is the central thesis of this paper that counseling psychology should
reaffirm its dedication to positive working models and reject the
pathological, medical illness model, not simply because counseling
psychology has been historically rooted in positive models, but because
they are more fruitful and more compatible with a democratic humanistic
philosophy of man. Positive models also appear to be more conducive to
the realization of desirable self-fulfilling prophecies, as illustrated by the
case study that has been presented.

EVALUATIVE RESEARCH

A survey of the research activities of counseling and rehabilitation psychologists
would undoubtedly turn up projects of all the sorts we have considered and will
be considering in later chapters—process and outcome studies, analyses of
prognoses for clients of different types, and research on counselor characteristics
and on appraisal techniques.

Perhaps the most significant contribution that has been made in the course of these attempts to help individuals find situations in which they can function well is the contribution to evaluative research made by systematic follow-up studies. All the general problems and difficulties discussed in Chapter 5 have complicated outcome studies in this area, but some of these are easier to deal with in this than in other kinds of improvement programs.

With regard to the all-important criterion problem, because we are not primarily interested in personality change but rather in the use clients make of the personalities they now have, difficulties inherent in personality measurement can be circumvented. What is needed as a criterion variable is an objective index of how well the client is "getting along" before and after participating in the program for improving his status. Often there is an obvious way of obtaining such an index—grade-point average or dropout rate for students receiving vocational or educational counseling, incidence of self-support among clients served by a rehabilitation program, discharge and readmission rates for mental hospital patients. All these criteria have obvious flaws which the sophisticated research planner must counteract or allow for, but they are available and relevant.

The problem of experimental controls is far more vexing and has often not been adequately taken into consideration. When a rehabilitation agency reports that 78 percent of its clients obtained full-time jobs and held them for at least a year, this sounds like an excellent record of accomplishment. But there is a supplementary question, and a very important one. How many of these clients would have succeeded in this way without the services of the agency that claims to have rehabilitated them? It is not too difficult to put together a control group similar to the agency clientele in ability, social status, and medical diagnosis. But if this group consists of people living in the same community who were eligible for rehabilitation services but did not make use of them, there is a possibility that the controls differ from the experimental subjects on some crucial motivational variable that has not been measured. Researchers have dealt with this problem in various ways. The one most obvious solution—to provide service to half the applicants, leaving the other half as an untreated control group—is usually ruled out by ethical or legal considerations. A helping agency cannot withhold help from people who need it. It is sometimes possible to *defer* service to some of the applicants and compare the progress made by the counseled and the deferred groups during a limited period of time. It is also sometimes possible to compare the progress of two groups for which different kinds of service are provided. For example, one group of amputees can be fitted with prostheses and placed in suitable employment, whereas another group can participate in a series of counseling sessions in addition to the other basic services. It is important that psychologists engaging in evaluative research and people making use of the results in setting policy be aware of the special problem experimental controls pose in research of this sort. As provision for evaluative research is made in connection with all sorts of new programs designed for the betterment of society, as increasingly is being done, such understanding should become much more widespread than it has been in the past.

A respectable body of evidence has accumulated (see Research Summaries for examples) that counseling does help clients to handle their lives somewhat better than they would have done without it. Students in counseled groups average slightly but significantly higher in scholarship and are more likely to finish their courses and graduate. Vocational counseling leads to slightly but significantly improved vocational adjustment. Attempts to measure changes in personality characteristics as a result of the counseling experience have not shown that such changes occur with any regularity, although there is a shift in self-concepts, as reflected in Q-sorts. As after more extended therapy efforts, clients tend to bring their concepts of real and ideal selves into closer alignment with one another (Williams, 1962). There has been much wasted effort in this as in other kinds of efforts to help people, but it has been clearly demonstrated that in many cases present resources for improving a person's life circumstances can be found and utilized.

SUMMARY

One useful means for improving the functioning of a person in his environment is to focus on personal and situational resources already available to him rather than to attempt to bring about major changes in his personality. Although such efforts have usually been called counseling or rehabilitation, they are clearly relevant to clinical psychology. Often the objective is a workable vocational plan.

The first step is the exploration of possibilities in the person and in his situation. Case records, interviews, and tests of abilities and interests are useful techniques for identifying possibilities in the client himself. Knowledge of occupations, educational institutions, training programs, social agencies, and legislation contributes to the identification of situational possibilities.

The psychologist also helps clients to choose and decide. To make a good decision one must consider two kinds of data, relating to utility (the chooser's values and desires) and expectation (the probability of success he attaches to alternative goals). Such evidence should be brought into the interview in which decisions are to be made.

Planning and the carrying out of plans involve the psychologist in relationships with various representatives of other professions and community agencies and organizations. Thus he must be something of a social psychologist as well as a clinician.

Appraisal plays a very large part in counseling and rehabilitation. The tests used are more commonly ability, achievement, and interest tests than person-ality-assessment instruments. An important skill is that of communicating in plain language to the client just what his test results mean. All information generated by the appraisal process is for the benefit of the client.

The greatest research contribution coming out of this psychological specialty has been ways of dealing with the troublesome problems that arise in carrying out follow-up studies of outcomes. Such studies have shown that although counseling does not produce demonstrable personality changes in clients, it does lead to more successful functioning than occurs in control groups without the service.

SUGGESTED READINGS

Tyler, L. E. *The work of the counselor,* 3rd ed. New York: Appleton-Century-Crofts, 1969.

This book introduces professional people and students with various backgrounds to counseling. In addition to a greater elaboration of counseling principles, use of tests, and so on, than this chapter affords, it reviews research in the field.more extensively.

Macht, L. B., Scherl, D. J., and English, J. T. Not as a patient: psychological development in a job training program. *American Journal of Orthopsychiatry,* 1970, *40,* 142–150.

The authors argue for the value of a service of the sort we have discussed in this chapter and provide some good suggestions about how it is set up.

Lofquist, L. H., and Davis, R. V. *Adjustment to work: a psychological view of man's problems in a work-oriented society.* New York: Appleton-Century-Crofts, 1969.

Over a period of two decades, psychologists in a research group at the University of Minnesota have been developing a comprehensive theory of work adjustment that would be serviceable to rehabilitation counselors and many other kinds of professional people. This short book distills the essence of what has appeared in a large number of research reports. Although the theory is complex enough to take all aspects of work adjustment into account, the basic assumptions and concepts are relatively simple. In the appendix, copies of the instruments designed to measure the essential variables are shown.

Glasscote, R. M., Cumming, E., Rutman, I. D., Sussex, J. N., and Glassman, S. M. *Rehabilitating the mentally ill in the community.* Washington, D. C.: Joint Information Service of the American Psychiatric Association and the National Association for Mental Health, *1971.*

This book, short and simply written, constitutes an excellent overview of contributions that can be made to the lives of persons diagnosed as mentally ill through a rehabilitative, as contrasted with a therapeutic, orientation. The early chapters present the essential concepts of rehabilitation and the history of the movement for the rehabilitation of the disabled in the United States. Following this are detailed descriptions of six programs in different parts of the country and a discussion of what has been learned from them to facilitate planning for the future.

RESEARCH EXAMPLES

Campbell, D. P. *The results of counseling: twenty-five years later.* Philadelphia: Saunders, 1965.

The monograph by Campbell represents the most recent chapter in an effort to evaluate the effects of counseling, an effort that began in the 1930s with a large-scale investigation by Williamson and Bordin (1940) in which 405 freshman counselees were followed up a year after counseling and compared with a matched control group on several indices of adjustment and achievement. Control subjects were individually paired with subjects in the experimental group on the basis of college class, age, sex, size and type of high school, grades, and college-entrance-examination scores. Significant differences in favor of the counseled group were found for both adjustment and scholarship.

What Campbell did was to locate 99 percent of these persons who had been in the experimental and control groups twenty-five years later. He persuaded 90 percent of them to provide information about their lives and careers during the twenty-five year period. He found that the counseled group had continued to be at least slightly superior to the noncounseled on all measures of academic success, such as grades, graduation from college, honors, graduate work, and participation in campus activities. The counseled males also received significantly higher ratings for life success, although the females did not. On indicators of "mental health," however, counseled subjects placed slightly lower than noncounseled. They rated themselves a little more anxious and worried and they expressed more willingness to consult a psychiatrist or psychologist. This difference perhaps reflects original differences in motivation between the two groups, so carefully matched in other ways. But in another analysis Campbell (1963) showed that motivational differences were not the only factor involved in the achievement differences. He identified sixty-two students who as freshman were members of the control group but who later sought counseling at the university. Before counseling, their adjustment ratings were similar to those of the other control subjects rather than those of the counselees. After counseling, their achievement, judged by the one criterion of percentage graduating from college, was like that of the counselees rather than that of the controls. This whole lengthy research undertaking seems to indicate that if students are provided with assistance in utilizing personal resources, the probability that they will use such resources well is increased.

Williams, J. E. Changes in self and other perceptions following brief educational-vocational counseling. *Journal of Counseling Psychology*, 1962, *9*, 18–28.

One of the criteria often used to evaluate the effects of counseling and psychotherapy is change in the client's self-concept. The most common technique for assessing self-concept is the Q-sort, in which the individual classifies descriptive statements about personality into categories indicating the degree to which they apply to him. It has also been a common procedure to have him sort them also according to his concept of his ideal self and his concept of what an ordinary person is like. Measurements of the congruence of actual with ideal self can be derived from such sorts, as well as measurements of the level of personality adjustment indicated by the placement of positive and negative statements. Considerable evidence has accumulated that psychotherapy tends to improve adjustment as measured by Q-sorts.

In this experiment, the subjects were 121 undergraduate students who sought educational-vocational counseling, not psychotherapy. The 45 clients in Group I were counseled immediately, with the Self-Ideal-Ordinary Q-sort administered preceding and following the counseling experience, which typically consisted of an initial interview, some aptitude and interest tests, and a second interview in which test results were interpreted and occupational possibilities explored. The 46 clients in Group II were placed on a waiting list and assessed before and after the wait period, which was approximately the same length as the counseling period for Group I. This was to see whether motivation for counseling, by itself, was sufficient to bring about change. Group III consisted of 30 students in introductory psychology, who had not asked for or received counseling. They were also assessed twice, with the same interval.

The results clearly showed that while scores on the Q-sort improved for all three groups, indicating a practice effect of some sort, the change was strikingly greater in the case of the counseled group. In fact, these subjects had increased their adjustment scores about as much as clients in previous studies had done following much longer periods of intensive psychotherapy (Dymond, 1954). A follow-up of counseled clients more than 18 weeks later showed that the gain had been maintained.

A later study in this series (Hills and Williams, 1965) showed that the improvement in self-concept did not occur as the result of having test information communicated to clients without the opportunity for a second interview with the counselor. The whole sequence—preliminary interview, tests, final interview—seems to be required to bring about the self-concept change.

Tipton, R. M. Relative effectiveness of two methods of interpreting ability test scores. *Journal of Counseling Psychology*, 1969, *16*, 75–80.

The use of tests to provide information for a client about his own talents and limitations is not as straightforward a technique as it would appear to be at first glance. It is often difficult for a person to accept information not in harmony with his image of himself. Thus one research problem upon which a number of psychologists have worked involves comparisons of different ways of presenting such information.

In this investigation, the subjects were 193 college freshmen who had taken one of the tests published by Educational Testing Service, the SCAT (a test of college aptitude) and the MCET (a test of achievement in English). Out of this group the 100 who at the outset had overestimated their college ability by two deciles or more were randomly assigned to two experimental groups and a control group.

Members of the first experimental group had their test scores interpreted to them by a skilled counselor. Members of the second experimental group received the test information from a computer specially programmed to provide it. The control group received no interpretation.

The criterion was change in concepts about the self measured by means of the Semantic Differential, a method for assessing attitudes. These ratings were made before the test interpretation, immediately following it, and four weeks later. The immediate assessment indicated that students in both experimental groups had changed their attitudes about themselves significantly more than the controls had but that there was no difference between the two experimental groups. In the later assessment, however, counselor-interpretation subjects had increased the amount of change, computer-interpretation groups slipped back.

Massimo, J. L., and Shore, M. F. The effectiveness of a comprehensive, vocationally oriented psychotherapeutic program for adolescent delinquent boys. *American Journal of Orthopsychiatry*, 1963, *33*, 634–642.

Juvenile delinquency is a major problem in modern society, and the kinds of psychotherapy and personal counseling provided for persons with other sorts of problems have not been very successful in dealing with it. (For instance, see Sowles and Gill, 1970.) This experiment involved only a very small number of subjects (ten in experimental group, ten in control group), but the careful evaluation of results and the later follow-ups make it impressive.

Boys were selected for the research and randomly assigned to experimental or control groups who (1) were between fifteen and seventeen (2) had IQs between 85 and 110, (3) had a history of antisocial behavior, (4) had been suspended from school or dropped out, (5) showed no gross psychotic behavior, and (6) had not been involved in previous psychotherapy.

Evaluation of changes involved tests of school knowledge and attitudes related to delinquency and observation of overt behavior—employment, legal difficulties, and other indicators of social adjustment.

The treatment was initiated at a crisis point in the boy's life and began with an offer to help him get a job. Flexibility, motility, and action were its keynotes. The therapist had no central office and operated completely independently of schools, courts, and social agencies. He helped each boy discover his aptitudes and interests and locate a job in keeping with them, and arranged for some kind of remedial education if the boy needed and wished it.

Results after ten months on all indicators, both tests and overt behavior, showed striking differences between experimental and control groups. The adjustment of control boys had worsened, whereas nine of the ten in the experimental group had made steady progress. Follow-up studies two years later (Massimo and Shore, 1966) and five years later (Shore and Massimo, 1969) indicated a widening gap between the two groups. At the time of the second follow-up, eight of the ten treated subjects were employed, and seven had obtained some formal schooling. The arrest record showed that seven had had no arrests, as compared with only two in the untreated group. Three of these controls had been incarcerated in adult criminal institutions on major charges, as compared with none of the experimental subjects. Qualitative aspects of the employment record showed clear differences for the two groups.

Pallone, N. J., Rickard, F. S., and Hurley, R. B. Key influencers of occupational preference among black youth. *Journal of Counseling Psychology*, 1970, *17*, 498–501.

Pallone, Rickard, and Hurley review Super's analysis of the importance of key figures in influencing vocational development and note that Moynihan's influential report had contended that lowerclass black families lack effective role models for male youths. The purpose of the study was to determine the key figures influencing vocational preferences as reported by black youths and to compare results with whites.

The subjects were 161 black and 218 white high school youths (eleventh and twelfth grades) of both sexes in four New York State communities. They came from working-class backgrounds. As part of a larger study, Pallone, Rickard, and Hurley asked subjects to supply their occupational preferences and to indicate from a list of persons (e.g., mother, father, neighbor, teacher) the ones that had the first, second, and third greatest influence on his selection of occupational preferences. The first one was taken to be the key influence.

The results showed similarities occurred across race and sex—persons holding the preferred occupation being uniformly high—but there were some differences. Rank-difference correlations were 0.82 between black and white males, 0.68 between black males and females, 0.59 between black and white females, and 0.48 between white males and females.

In general, the most potent influencers of occupational preference were people who held the preferred job. The next strongest influence reported was the parent of the same sex. The influence of the parent of the opposite sex is high only among the black males. Teachers and counselors rank moderately low, but no lower among blacks than whites. The authors conclude that school counselors should recognize that they will exercise little direct influence over vocational choice and should concentrate on "influencing the influencers" in whatever impact needs to be made. A similar admonition could be applied to clinical and community psychologists.

Gregory, C. C., and Downie, N. M. Work history of schizophrenics and alcoholics. *Rehabilitation Counseling Bulletin*, 1970, *13*, 355–363.

The subjects in this study were 308 alcoholics and 297 schizophrenics, all service veterans. The purpose was to find out which diagnostic group was most likely to be helped by vocational rehabilitation counseling, and what background variables were related to success or failure. The variables were age, number of hospitalizations, financial resources, educational level, number of jobs previously held, quality of jobs, and the longest time spent on the same job.

The work history of alcoholics turned out to be significantly more favorable than that of schizophrenics on all variables. The authors concluded that an alcoholic who has held a job more than five years is a good employment risk, and that schizoprhenics may need a progressive, sheltered workshop situation and help after placement if they are to be rehabilitated.

Stotsky, B. A., Daston, D. G., and Vardack, C. N. An evaluation of the counseling of chronic schizophrenics. *Journal of Counseling Psychology*, 1955, *2*, 248–255.

This is a report on a program of the Vocational Counseling Service with long-term regressed patients in the "continued treatment service" of a VA hospital. The counseling program was part of a very intensive attempt to activate these "back ward" schizophrenics. Experimental and control groups of fourteen patients each were selected randomly. The experimental group received the following services from the counselor: weekly group meetings, individual counseling sessions twice a week, and informal visits to the ward. Before and after the eight weeks' period these data were collected: Q-sorts, group Rorschachs, Hospital Adjustment Scale ratings, and some other ratings of work behavior and symptoms.

The results indicated that though the two groups remained homogeneous with respect to psychiatric symptoms, ward adjustment, and Rorschach measures, they showed significant differences on four of the five work variables, on Q-sort self-descriptions, and on number of trial visits outside the hospital. The authors concluded that such a counseling program was of definite value.

Another counseling psychologist, C. H. Patterson, in his comments at the end of the article calls this is a very significant report because it shows the importance of the counseling approach with even very disturbed patients long before they are being considered for discharge. It also demonstrates and evaluates counseling techniques such as group counseling. The mixture of techniques in the whole program makes interpretation of the effects of any single method difficult. Also, it is likely that it was not this counseling approach per se that proved efficacious. Any kinds of attention and personal interest shown these unfortunate back ward cases is likely to have effects. Results from such approaches over a longer term need to be studied. Does the patient soon regress to his former state? What length should a special program be (this one was only eight weeks) to produce the maximum recovery rate?

Another study of chronic patients by Meyer (1960) is of interest. This is a follow-up study of fifty-seven VA neuropsychiatric patients who had been hospitalized for eight or more years and who were referred to the counseling psychologist with a view to planning for discharge. Counseling with such persons involving fairly concrete vocational planning and counseling was continued after the patients were returned to the community, along with the development of work skills and the resolution of family problems. The author concluded that the rehabilitation potential of these patients was surprisingly high. A significant number of the patients in this study were able to rise from unskilled to skilled work.

chapter **14**

Small-Group Systems:
Working with Families

Most people live in families of some type or other, and their personality difficulties are family affairs. It seemed to take the helping professions a long time to recognize this obvious fact and to begin to focus their efforts on families as units rather than just on individuals. Of recent years, the practice of working with whole families has expanded in several directions. In this chapter we shall take up the principal approaches to assessment and intervention in family systems, approaches that differ in techniques and supporting theories.

The same factors that affect personal systems, such as life cycles, crises, and external influences, also affect families. Births, illnesses, puberties, departures, or emancipations change the family structure. Roles change as families reach the post-childbearing stage. Conflicts may develop between husband and wife or between parent and child. The bizarre behavior of one of the children may have complex effects on all the others. All these things and many others may strain family units to the point where they fail to perform family functions effectively. In such cases, clinical psychologists may be asked to help.

Unfortunately, the number of families seeking assistance from the mental health professions, for whom the voluntary, cooperative techniques we use are appropriate, constitutes only a small fraction of the families that are not functioning well. Some of those who do not seek assistance pose a difficult ethical question: "How much can society allow a parent, just because he or she is a parent, to harm a child?" Historically children have been seen as little better than the family's chattels; only in comparatively recent times has official interest in the well-being of children advanced to the point of recognizing the need for child advocacy, the representation of the child's interests by a competent independent authority. Psychologists and other professional mental health workers have had so little to say about working with families who are not voluntary clients that in this book, as in others, the problem gets less attention than it deserves. The last section of this chapter (on use of community resources) is primarily concerned with families who are nonvoluntary clients. Until then, our concern will be with cooperative, voluntary intervention.

The *methods* agencies use seem to fall into three broad categories. Workers coming from psychoanalytic and other psychotherapeutic persuasions have tended to develop styles of family intervention which are principally *evocative*, that is, styles in which the family members are led to explore their own feelings, motivations, and interrelationships so that they may achieve more productive relationships. The evocative methods emphasize the importance of a warm, safe relationship with the therapist as a basis for the exploration. The trouble with such approaches is that they may lose their focus on the family as a system because they deal purely with personal system concepts. Workers who come from "newer" therapeutic schools, and to some extent those from social work, are more likely to use techniques that are *communication-clarifying*, focusing on the way in which family members respond to each other. A majority of current efforts to help families would probably fall in this category. Some communication approaches emphasize "getting the messages straight"; others are concerned also with examining the roles family members play and the effect this role structure has on the flow of messages. Techniques involving confrontation can be classified as specialized communication techniques. Finally, there are signs that some workers, among them psychologists with an experimental orientation, are doing family intervention that is distinctly *learning-focused*. In general, such workers feel that the trouble with a disturbed family is that members have learned to deal with one another in ways that provoke or maintain difficulties, so that it is necessary to teach them more adaptive kinds of responses. Naturally in actual clinical work the evocative, communication-clarifying, and learning-focused or teaching approaches are often combined. We shall consider first how the three approaches are used with couples in marriage counseling, and second how they are used in families with children. Finally, as mentioned above, we shall comment on how the psychologist may use community resources in his efforts to help families who do not, at least initially, want to be involved.

MARRIAGE COUNSELING

When marriage counseling began it was thought of as a branch of individual psychotherapy. Therapists assumed that if individuals were helped to overcome their own personality difficulties, this would have a beneficial effect on their marriages. This approach now seems to have fallen from favor. As might have been predicted from systems theory, Hurvitz (1967) notes that marriage counseling is more difficult after one spouse has been in individual psychotherapy. Most marriage counselors now prefer to see husband and wife together, or in a group made up of married couples.

Although communication-clarifying and learning-focused methods predominate and learning-focused approaches have received the majority of systematic attention, some evocative, relationship-based work is carried on. We shall not consider here the approaches that are essentially simply individual psychotherapy for husband and wife rather than attempts to treat the family as a system.

Evocative Methods

Goodwin and Mudd (1969) provide a good introduction to evocative counseling, emphasizing feelings and relationships. In their explanation of the meaning of family homeostasis, they say (pp. 94–95): "One of the basic concepts that determine both theoretical formulation and methods of working with marriage partners is related to balance within the reciprocal marital interaction. So long as there is an adequate dove-tailing of each partner's needs and acceptable patterns of reciprocity in meeting them, the union seems to remain stable. . . ." They also draw attention to residues of the past in a relationship. Partners may carry into adulthood a number of needs unresolved in childhood. In attempting to get the spouse to satisfy these needs, they may make it impossible to achieve a harmonious emotional "give-and-take" balance. A counselor must recognize that each couple is unique in its individual needs and desires, concepts of marital roles, methods of communication, reciprocity in the sharing of responsibility, and degree of commitment to the union. The difference between marriage counseling and individual counseling, as Goodwin and Mudd see it, is that the focus is on the marital relationship and the circular interaction *between* the partners rather than on specific intrapsychic forces *within* the partners. The goals of marriage counseling, then, are to help the troubled partners come to some understanding of the interlocking and intermeshing nature of their problems, and also, perhaps, to help them come to terms with the realities of adult life, accepting the satisfaction that is realistically possible within the specific existential situation of their marriage. "Through a compassionate and empathic relationship with a marriage counselor, the partners are helped to some awareness of the ways in which their own feelings, attitudes, demands, expectations, patterns of relating, and responses affect this circular 'interaction' " (Goodwin and Mudd, 1969, p. 96). As in individual therapy, a warm relationship to the therapist is considered to be the basic vehicle for experiences that move clients toward awareness and growth.

Communication-Clarifying Approaches

Workers using communication-clarifying approaches assume that symptoms and behaviors are messages or communications of some sort. Much of the thinking underlying this movement came out of a group in Palo Alto working under the leadership of the late D. D. Jackson. Jay Haley and Virginia Satir are the most prominent spokesmen.

For Haley (1963) marriages are patterns of communication occurring in several modes at once, including verbal (content), verbal (tone), facial expression, body posture, and body activity. Communication expresses not only content, but also aspects of power and control. A wife may say to her husband "I feel tired" and lie down on the couch. In this case both her words and her actions are congruent. But, looking at symptoms as messages, some noncongruence is apparent when a hypochondriacal wife says to her husband "I do so want to go out with you, but I can't. My back is killing me." Haley emphasizes that such tactics produce control over others. A special variant of control tactics arises from impossible instructions, which Haley calls *double binds*. An example of a double bind is a wife's superficially passive attitude, inviting dominance (e.g., "You decide where we should go for dinner, dear," said in a hostile tone that means the opposite). If the husband does make decisions and dominates his wife, he is complying with the order and is under the wife's control. If he declines to comply, she "wins" by "having a right" to get angry at him. In "double-bind" situations, the person is giving two conflicting messages—usually verbally saying one thing and nonverbally saying something else.

The process of working out a satisfactory marital relationship is seen as a process of arriving at shared agreements and definitions. Marital conflict is likely to show itself in (1) disagreements about the rules for living together, (2) disagreements about who is to set those rules, and (3) attempts to enforce rules that are incompatible with one another. It is these conflicts the counselor must help husband and wife to resolve.

Simple stability in a marriage relationship is not enough. Couples may reach agreed definitions ("He's the leader; I'm the follower") or they may agree not to define certain aspects of the relationship ("We can't talk about that because of her nerves"), and in so doing create stable systems in which problems persist. Haley holds that the central task of marriage therapy is to modify that stability so that the marriage can be altered and restabilized in more comfortable or productive patterns.

In trying to change a system of marital communication, Haley focuses on actions that will amend the balance of power and change the means for gaining control. [He says (1963, p. 149), "Provoke a change in the ways that the couple keep the marital system stable."] For example, he might request that a couple continue to behave in their usual way; this makes him the rule setter. If they wish to deny him control, the couple must alter their behavior. In the same way, in the case of a woman who controls her husband by self-sacrificing tactics (because he cannot criticize behavior that is "for the good of others"), the therapist provokes a change by encouraging the "self-sacrificing behavior." To avoid being controlled by the therapist she must change to a different type of behavior. Or, in another case, the therapist might redefine a wife's insomnia, long an "unavoidable" control on the couple, as actually too much sleep and advise that she not increase her sleep at all. He thus makes regaining of the wife's control contingent on his defeat, which in this case requires her to commence sleeping more appropriately at night.

Haley (1970) contrasts the family-system-oriented therapist with the individually-oriented therapist who deals with families. The former does not try to adapt families to one therapeutic theory or technique, nor does he concentrate on case history. He does not believe that one brings about change by interpreting feelings and attitudes. His objective is not to reveal underlying hostility but to resolve the difficulties in the relationship which cause the hostility. He attempts to come up with a tactical plan to persuade family members to behave differently.

Learning-Focused Approaches

There are two potential advantages to learning-focused methods of marriage counseling. First, if the process of marriage counseling involves teaching, it may be feasible to train nonprofessionals or lower-salaried staff members to do it. Second, teaching methods readily lend themselves to group presentations. Several theoretical positions are compatible with a didactic orientation.

George Bach's methods are based on the assumption that conflict is inevitable. He believes that training in constructive styles of conflict—"fight training"—leads to stable and productive patterns of interaction. According to Bach, aggressive feelings cannot be avoided in a marriage; some frustration inevitably accompanies each partner's discovery that the marriage thwarts and interfers with his or her goals and desires. The aggressive feelings produce verbal conflict, covert conflict, or "gunnysacking" (suppressing) feelings. Verbal conflict can be more constructive and desirable than the other alternatives. Bach's system, "fight training," endeavors to bring inevitable conflicts into the open where they may have outcomes. Bach teaches couples to *manage* inevitable intimate aggression. Management requires continual stocktaking or "book balancing." "The payoff of a truly intimate fight . . . is not to chalk up a win or a loss for one partner or the other. Only a joint win or loss is possible; either the partnership gains and emerges in an improved state as a result of an aggressive encounter, or the unit loses and its relationship deteriorates." Couples are taught to analyze their interaction (scoring the fight) along nine dimensions: reality, injury, involvement, responsibility, humor, expression, communication, directness, and specificity. Each partner rates each "fight" for instance, on the reality dimension, analyzing whether it was authentic and realistic (the positive direction) or about imaginary issues (negative). On the humor dimension, was there laughter of relief (positive), or ridicule, clowning, or laughing at (negative)? The importance of Bach's procedure appears to be the way it emphasizes that in each dimension a positive or bonding style of encounter (Bach uses the phrase "style of aggression") is an alternative to a negative or alienating style. His emphasis here is on helping partners convey to one another what the effects of each communication were. In brief, Bach attempts to teach a different style of interaction, one that marriage partners can practice on their own and use to overcome future problems in living. In the following excerpt (Bach and Wyden, 1969, pp. 220–222), the authors emphasize that the fight's content is important for what it says about the state and progress of the marital relationship rather than for the psychological interpretations that can be made about the individuals involved in it.

The transition from courtship images to post-courtship realities tends to be not only painful but downright puzzling, as the following case shows. Jack Marks felt cheated because after three years of marriage his wife no longer behaved as she did in the first flush of their romance.

> *Jack* (exasperated): Whenever I want her, I can't have her, so I have to take her the way she wants to give herself to me.
>
> *Helen* (self-righteous): What's the matter with that? Ask the doctor here: that's the way women love. You can't make them love you. It has to come from within, doesn't it, Doctor?
>
> *Dr. Bach:* Love has many faces and styles. You two have the problem of calibrating, fitting your style of loving to one another. (Toward Helen) You need not quote to yourself or to him generalities about love and loving to defend your particular way. Let's hear more from you two.
>
> (At this point, Jack, who had been sitting on a couch, was offered a comfortable swivel chair and wheeled, with him in it, right in front of his wife for better eyeball-to-eyeball contact. Helen was already seated in the same kind of chair.)
>
> *Dr. B:* Now, just face each other and level with one another. Leave me out of it for a while. Let me listen. I'd like to hear and see how you talk to each other about this.
>
> *Jack* (disgusted): Oh, Doc, we've been all over this so many times and we always wind up nowhere. It's a vicious circle. She's heard it all before and I've heard it all before.
>
> *Helen:* He's right. We've nothing to say to each other because we'll get into the same old hassle like a broken record. I'm tired of it, just plain old tired!
>
> *Jack* (getting angry and rolling closer toward Helen in his chair): You're tired! I'm disgusted! It's driving me nuts! I've told you a thousand times I resent that it's me that has to come to you everytime I want to make love, every time! You used to be so affectionate before we got married and during the first two years. Now you never come to me any more.
>
> *Helen* (controlled and not moving her chair): Never? Well, hardly ever, I guess. It's difficult for me to be sexually aggressive. But I always respond to you when you make the advances.
>
> (Silence. Jack sat angry and sullen, his facial expression saying: "See, Doc, she's not even trying to make me happy.")
>
> *Dr. B:* How do you feel about each other right here and now?
>
> *Jack:* Lousy. We're deadlocked again.
>
> (Another long silence.)
>
> *Helen:* Why are you so depressed about a good thing?
>
> *Jack:* What's good about it?
>
> *Helen* (reasonable): We have a good marriage, that's what's good. I really don't know what we're doing here except you always seem to be so dissatisfied with everything: not just me, the kids, your work, our income,

nothing is ever enough! And speaking of premarital times, sure I was affectionate and maybe even seductive! I felt it. There was nothing phony about it. I wanted you for my husband and still do. And you played differently then, too. You were enthusiastic and stimulating, nothing like you are now.

Jack (heatedly): I felt that way then because *you* (pointing strongly) loved *me*. All I had to do was respond, and I lapped it up. I love to be loved! Now—nothing!

Dr. B: Well, I can see you're stuck like a broken record that keeps saying, "Oh, where are those exciting courtship days?" They're over and you should be going through the reality-testing phase. But you're fighting it and this creates a crisis . . .

Helen (shocked and moving her chair slightly toward the left): Crisis? We're in no crisis! That sounds awful!

Dr. B: Yes, you're in a crisis because a decisive *change* for better or worse is imminent. The burial of the courtship phase has been long overdue. Both of you have hung onto expectations that are no longer appropriate.

Helen (toward Dr. B): "Crisis" sounds so dangerous and foreboding. (Toward Jack) I don't feel our marriage is that bad, do you, darling?

Jack (decisive): What the doctor means is that there have to be some *changes* made. Isn't that right?

Dr. B: Yes. A marriage crisis is an unbalanced state of affairs. If it's not straightened out there'll be stress to a point of intolerance. The imbalance requires decisive change. You can't persist in your present mood. The main problem is to channel the change into a constructive new direction. In marriage you can never go backward. The romantic doll-playing days are over. Now the question is, "Are you happy?" You no longer have to confuse what you really are with the way you want each other to be. People are so eager to mate that they instinctively behave—and even feel—like the kind of man or woman whom the lover wants! But in intimacy old phases are not renewable or relivable. It's no use dwelling on the romantic past of your relationship. The real questions are: Where do you want to go from here? What can you do with—and for—each other except to have regrets?"

(Dumbfounded silence.)

The interview continued for several more minutes before the therapist summarized (Bach and Wyden, 1969, pp. 223–224).

Dr. B: You're just starting to become intimates! You see, intimacy starts where romanticism leaves off. And true intimacy starts with realistic appreciation of your differences. Never mind your similarities! They don't count because they're so comfortable. It's your differences that stimulate and present a challenge. The problem of how to fuse two people into one close relationship is not for little girls and dream boys. It's an adult problem. Try to feel each other's nature. Things will be different. You will experience the same situations very differently when you share your differences openly. It'll bring you closer together.

Jack: How's that?

Dr. B: Because when you appreciate differences you're showing empathy. And respecting differences earns and deepens intimacy and gains responsive respect. We'll work on this next time, when you report to me that you've found out about how different you are and in what respect, besides your style of sexuality.

Jack and Helen wound up sitting in dumbfounded silence. They had become so accustomed to their impasse that it required two more sessions with the counselor before they could act on the notion that a new orientations was possible for them, even though intellectually they accepted this at the first meeting.

From a different theoretical viewpoint, Stuart (1969) is exploring direct use of operant conditioning in the modification of marital problems. (See Chapter 12 for an explanation of operant conditioning.) He begins by making explicit three assumptions. First, the exact pattern of interaction that takes place between spouses at any time is the most rewarding of all the available alternatives—the clear implication being, for instance, that when a husband spends more time with his friends than with his wife, his friends are offering greater relative rewards than his wife. Second, most married adults expect to enjoy reciprocal relations with their partners; that is, they expect that the role of each will involve rights and duties by means of which social reinforcement for the other is dispensed. Jackson (1965) calls this reciprocal arrangement that underlies successful marriage "something for something." Third, in order to modify an unsuccessful marital interaction, it is necessary to develop the power of each partner to provide rewards for the other. In unsuccessful marriages either or both of two unsatisfactory patterns of behavioral control, *coercion* and *withdrawal*, are likely to be in evidence. In the coercion pattern, one member tries to gain positive reinforcement from the other in exchange for stopping negative reinforcement. Stuart's example (1969, p. 676) is clear: " . . . a husband might wish his wife to express greater affection; following the failure of his advances, he might become abusive, accusing his wife of anything from indifference to fridigity, abating his criticism when he receives the desired effect." Coercion is obviously a "blind-alley" strategy. The withdrawal strategy has the advantage that the other partner is forced to continue to be active or assertive. Thus the withdrawer's risk is low and the condition may easily stabilize, for, as Stuart notes (1969, p. 676): if "the husband is withdrawn from his wife . . . he may find other social and nonsocial reinforcers in his cronies, mistress or can of beer."

The operant interpersonal method of counseling based on these considerations consists of teaching the couple two premises—(1) that the impressions which each forms of the other are based on the behavior of the other; and (2) that in order to change interaction in a marriage, each partner must assume the initiative for changing his own behavior before changes can be expected in the spouse. From this point, couples are asked to list three behaviors which each would like the other to do more frequently. Here, as usual, clients at first tend to use global terms rather than observable kinds of behavior and find it easier to list behavior they object to than behavior they would like to see. These tendencies must be overcome. Next, the behaviors to be accelerated (increasing in frequency) are posted in the house in order to record "baseline" rates. Finally, a series of exchanges is negotiated. Stuart views the typical complaint couples make about "lack of communication" as an euphemism for the failure of a couple to reinforce each other. Tokens are used to systematize the exchanges of reinforcement. For instance, the husband may earn tokens for conversing with his wife. Each couple thus produces its own improvement plan and proceeds to work on it. Stuart reports that this approach works with couples varying widely in age, education, and length of time married.

Adherents of rational-emotive psychotherapy have formulated another learning-focused approach to marriage counseling. Because illogical or irrational beliefs are viewed as the cause of difficulties, couples are taught to correct them. Asserting that irrational, traditional, or stupid patterns of thinking about life, the self, or a spouse are the chief blocks to more effective functioning, Harper (1960) advocates challenging such thinking directly. The method Ellis (1958) uses consists largely of showing each partner (1) that he has some basic irrational assumptions; (2) precisely what these assumptions are; (3) how they originally arose; (4) how they are correctly being sustained by continual unconscious self-indoctrination; and (5) how they can be replaced by much more rational, less self-defeating philosophies. In mounting this direct attack on the irrational beliefs and supplanting them with rational productive beliefs, the therapist stresses the fundamental importance of the process of facing and handling problems, of love, and of humor. He suggests effective alternatives in thought and action to the irrational patterns.

How Effective Is Marriage Counseling?

Outcome research here involves the same problems as outcome research in individual psychotherapy and also the additional complications that marital interaction introduces. Thus it is perhaps not strange that not much research on the effectiveness of marriage counseling has been reported. Another research question has to do with how acceptable marital counseling services are to potential clients in different social contexts. This is important when we are considering their extension to social strata which traditionally have received little or no service. Does the service "make sense?" Is the jargon difficult—or facilitative? Is it socially degrading or socially enhancing to seek out and participate in such services? How useful marital counseling services are to society depends not only on how favorable the clinical outcomes are for clients who actually participate, but on the way potential clients answer such questions about them.

Appraisal in marriage counseling is an ongoing activity used to direct the course of intervention. Haley, for instance, when he sees a couple or a family behave in a particular way, deduces that more effort should go into resolving a communication problem. Bach views a struggle he watches as a sign that the couple needs more emphasis on some aspect of handling conflict.

Systematized appraisal that proceeds separately from the intervention (comparable to testing in personal systems) has had only limited development. Some workers have assessed couples by means of standard tools such as the Interpersonal Checklist (Leary, 1957), comparing self-descriptions with descriptions of mate, ideal self, and ideal mate. There are several tests directed specifically at marital assessment, for example, Shostrom's (1971) very promising Pair Attraction Inventory and Schultz's (1966) Marriage Personality Inventory. The Blazier-Goosman (1966) Marriage Analysis Checklist emphasizes more history and background. Manson and Lerner (1962) use sentence-completion methods to assess a marital system.

Systematic marriage-assessment devices might serve as good global screening devices directing the counselor's attention to significant differences between couples in history, attitude, or style. Perhaps they may become useful in training nonpsychologists such as ministers or even in prompting self-examination and growth in the husbands and wives who take them. Such benefits at present are potential rather than actual. There has been only slight progress toward getting clear and useful pictures of marital interaction from self-report inventories, probably because significant dimensions of marital interaction are so difficult to identify.

FAMILY INTERACTION

Work with families is generally undertaken when a deviant child is presented to a therapist to be "cured." Here as in marital situations traditional analysts, child-guidance workers and behavior modifiers have discovered, apparently independently, the crucial "system" aspects of the family and proceeded to modify their techniques accordingly.

A recent summary of reports from 520 family therapists (GAP, 1970) points to much diversity in methods employed and many influential theorists. The major distinction is between therapists whose focus is on the personal system, the individual, who use family data to help them understand and help individuals, and therapists whose focus is on the family system itself. In this section we shall emphasize family concepts and not concepts that are essentially individual therapy transplanted to families.

One of the first to focus on the family system itself was Ackerman (1958). In *The Psychodynamics of Family Life*, he shows over and over again the interdependence of the individual, his family, and the society of which he is a part. No patient can be adequately understood in isolation from his family. Ackerman says that the first member of the family to consult the clinic, "the primary patient," is an emissary in disguise of an emotionally warped family group (p. 104). This concept of *family homeostasis*—that is, of the family as a system that has the capacity to achieve and maintain certain forms of stability—looms large in the thinking of many family theorists, who stresses the necessity for viewing the symptoms of the identified patient within the total family interaction. The work of a psychoanalytically trained group will be discussed first.

Evocative Methods

Boszormenyi-Nagy and Framo (1965) begin with the assumption that symptoms serve to balance forces within the family as well as within the individual personality. Deep, unconscious multiperson motivational structure is assumed to exist in every family. A person's behavior is not entirely the product of his own psychic forces but is determined in part by the motive systems of important others who can gratify or frustrate him. In such an interlocking homeostatic system, if one family member gets better, another one has to get sick in order to balance the system. As is typical of orthodox psychoanalysts, long-term family therapy (one or more years) predominates in this group. During the early stages, two therapists (often a man and a woman) encourage each of the family members in turn to talk about their experiences so that central themes may emerge rather indirectly and without threat ("John, I had no idea you've felt this way all these years"). The therapists believe that significant themes will eventually emerge, and if seemingly "lost" for a time, will reemerge later. They expect reactions of attempted withdrawal, or of attempted changes of focus ("Now just a minute, Doc, it's our daughter who's the sick one"), sudden outpourings of unmet needs, and/or expressions of disappointment or frustration to occur.

In the middle phase (Framo, 1965) families find themselves working toward "the real core of family therapy," understanding and working through, often through transference to each other and to the therapists, the attitudes and feelings with deep roots in the past. Parents can see and experience how difficulties manifested in the present system have emerged from their unconscious attempts to perpetuate or master old conflicts arising from their families of origin. They realize that they tend to impose the same acts of unfairness and overburdening on their children that their own parents imposed on them. Framo emphasizes how difficult the understanding is, noting, however, that after several years of such therapy the family shows deepened confidence and an increase in spontaneous behavior. At its termination, handling dependency may be difficult. Although this procedure is too long and involved to be used in most clinical settings, there are some useful ideas in the Framo chapter. One is the use of a visiting or substitute therapist to provide fresh perspective. Another is to handle dominating, aggressive mothers who react to direct interpretation with cutting, belittling rejoiners and involve the therapists in protecting each other, by focusing on what they have missed in life rather than on what they have done. In that fashion their controlling defenses can slacken and they can ultimately speak of their feelings of weakness.

In general, evocative approaches have a somewhat traditional character. Accounts are full of rich clinical lore, but the process itself seems to be too ponderous and time-consuming to be used extensively.

Communication-Clarifying Methods

The GAP (Group for Advancement of Psychiatry) report (1970) on family therapy shows that the communication-clarifying approach is the dominant viewpoint. Virginia Satir, one of the most influential therapists, has evolved what is called *conjoint family therapy*. Her volume by that title (2nd ed., 1967) is a clear exposition in outline form of the family approach developed at the Mental Research Unit in Palo Alto, where she was associated with D. D. Jackson, Bateson, Weakland, and Haley, in work on interpersonal communications and "double binds." Satir's focus is on the family unit—on its pain and its patterns of communication. She views the family unit as an entity, accepting in general the idea that families tend to stabilize themselves, their members acting in various ways to preserve or restore the stability of "family homeostasis."

She assumes that enhancement of self-esteem—not sexual gratification—is the basic force motivating individuals. The parents, the architects of the family in the sense that they set the tone of interactions, have overt or covert agendas and expectations when they select each other; for instance, George marries pretty, vivacious Jennifer to help make up for his own social inadequacy and to improve his self-esteem. Unavoidably, both discover after marriage that there is more "different-ness" than they had expected. In the dysfunctional family, different-ness develops into disagreement; trust is difficult to maintain. The marriage fails to make up for defective self-esteem of the partners. Satir (1967, p. 28):

> The marital relationship between Mary and Joe is dysfunctional. Mary and Joe are low in self-esteem. They looked to each other to enhance self-esteem. But because each saw the other as an extension of self, each failed to give to the other as well as get from the other. So their relationship only increased low feelings of self-esteem. They both became disillusioned and disappointed.

The next step is for children to become implicated in the interaction, perhaps being asked to be allies of one of the parents, or being used as a sign of the family's worth ("he's the best reader in his class"). The dysfunctional marriage subtly shapes the child, who becomes the family member likely to exhibit his discomfort in symptoms and thus show up as the identified patient. It is important for us to note here that the explanation of symptomatic behavior rests primarily on *marital* interaction. The child is induced to behave as a patient through prolonged exposure to particular conditions of conflicting communications, often where the behavioral"message" conflicts with the spoken "message." Satir's examples (p. 37):

> A father says his son shouldn't defy him. Yet he also complains that his son doesn't stand up to him like a man. A mother and father urge their daughter to stay away from wild parties, yet they allow her to go to such parties. Then, when she calls her father to ask him to bring her home, mother and father kid her about "being scared" in a provoking, demeaning tone.

She also states what would make for the stability of the system (p. 37):

> Ways of acting which would not make sense outside of the family, like the behavior of a problem child, may be eminently functional within the family, because it allows the marital partners to keep the focus on the child as troublemaker and divert suspicion from the real troublemaker which is their own conflicted relationship.

In conducting family therapy, Ms. Satir brings in *both* parents together and sets up the idea of working *as a family*. The therapist emphasizes the importance of having the perspective of *both* parents for a complete picture of the situation. The parents usually respond to questions about the pain in their own family by giving details about the identified patient, to which the therapist listens only *briefly*. She or he decreases the threat of blame and emphasizes the idea of good intentions ("This must have puzzled you, that you did all these things and still nothing seemed to turn out as you had hoped") and moves to consider the family as a unit. In taking a chronology from each parent, the therapist is alert to ways in which the family unit functions, such as (p. 110):

> Who speaks for whom? Who makes the family rules? Who makes the plans? Who carries them out? How clearly are the plans communicated? Who speaks the most? Who speaks the least? What is the general pacing and tone of family communication? How clear and direct is family communication? How does the family respond to crises? In what area of behavior is the symptom manifested (I.Q., body, emotions, social)? What were the circumstances surrounding the onset of the symptom? What gap existed between onset and labeling of symptom? Who (or what) has been blamed for the existence of the symptom (neighbors, teachers, God, heredity)? What purpose does the symptom serve in the family?

Taking a family life chronology, talking about it, engaging in role playing, and making it come to life are thus useful ways of *assessing* the family unit. The assessment process has three functions: (1) it provides a history of the people involved; (2) more important, it gives the therapist the opportunity to see the family interact and thus evaluate communication styles and role patterns; and

(3) the process provides the therapist with the framework for the *active* role he needs to take. Early sessions may stimulate some hope and communicate confidence. They serve to shift the focus in a nonthreatening way from the identified patient to the family. If there are discrepancies in the pictures given by the parents, the therapist tries to clarify them. He begins to introduce the couple to the notion that there are ways to correct misunderstandings. ("What happens when either of you sees that each of you somehow has not gotten the other's message? *This of course happens to everyone. Everyone needs techniques to handle this.*") In similar vein, the therapist explores how each partner handles different-ness, a loaded area in a dysfunctional family. He moves to explore the similarity of styles of partner and partner's parents and to comment on the way the person uses these styles (the same way parents did, as if your wife were your mother, and so on). Other ideas are introduced—people do disagree and still live together; people have pain and *can* talk about it; people can have fun and talk about that, too. The therapist explores what each partner expected of marriage and how the experience has turned out to be in reality. Moreover, it is important to understand how, if at all, the partners can communicate their expectations, hopes, or fears to each other.

Children are present from the beginning, although not always central to the discussion. Focus on the children typically occurs after the chronology of the married partners is completed and after the therapist has some idea of marital functioning. In general, Satir always sees the whole family, including the young siblings of the "patient," in order to watch them interact together, although the very young do not attend all the time. Parents are expected to look after the children's requests and behavior. Gentle matter-of-fact questioning of and listening to the child begins the process of intergrating him into the group. The process of interacting with the child serves as a model of healthy styles of clear communication and mutual respect for both child and parents. In brief, the course of the therapy involves (1) helping the parents separate themselves from their own parents, (2) helping strengthen the marital relationship, (3) helping equalize parental responsibilities, (4) helping strengthen same-sex parent-child relationships, (5) questioning overdeveloped relationships between opposite-sexed child-parent pairs, and (6) helping mates attend more to each other and less to the children.

Conjoint family therapy is considered a growth (rather than, say, a curing or an atoning) experience. The assumption is that people can be taught to be congruent, to speak directly and clearly, and to communicate their feelings, thoughts, and desires accurately, in order to be able to deal with reality. The goal is to establish those behaviors. Flexibility, enthusiasm, and a natural style are necessary to the process. The therapist's guiding principle is: "Be a model of good, clear, unambiguous communication."

Learning-Focused Approaches

Learning-focused approaches to family intervention are not as diversified as were the didactic applications to marital problems, but some promising efforts are being made, especially in the behavior-modification tradition. Accepting its basic premises, "behavior is learned," "behavior that is reinforced tends to occur more often," therapists look for ways in which a child's deviant behavior has been shaped by and is being reinforced by the environment, usually by his parents or peers. Detailed analysis of behavior reveals *who* is training *whom*, and with *what* reinforcers. For example, if Johnny shouts to his mother in the supermarket, "I want an ice cream bar," he is emitting a coercive behavior which Patterson calls a *coercive mand*. If the mother does not comply, she is punished by increases in rate or volume. On the other hand, if she does, the reinforcer for the child demanding the cone is both the cone *and* the mother's compliant behavior. The reinforcement for the mother's compliance is the turning off of the mands and the avoidance of a supermarket "scene." Crudely, then, the mother is teaching Johnny coercive behavior using ice cream and compliance as reinforcers, while Johnny is teaching his mother compliant behavior using "turning off noxious behavior" as a reinforcer.

Treatment requires changing the social reinforcement contingencies which impinge on the child, in effect reprogramming the social environment (Patterson et al., 1967). Patterson selected families with aggressive males between the ages of eight and eleven as a target population, because of evidence (Roff, 1961; Robins, 1966) showing that this group produces a wide variety of serious maladjustments, both psychiatric and criminal. His work involves several stages. First, the parents are "taught" social learning theory. Second, they are trained to observe the rate of occurrence of various behaviors and reinforcing contingencies. Finally, the experimenters and members of the family design intervention programs which the experimenters model and turn over to the parents.

Basic assessment, direct observation of family interaction in the home, is carried on first to provide initial levels, or baselines. The assessment techniques themselves deserve comment. Many schemes for making an orderly record out of the continuous stream of interactive behavior have been attempted. A system such as the one in Table 14-1, which is similar to that of Patterson et al. (1968), permits behavior to be recorded in interactive sequences (e.g., mother-child-mother or child-mother) and time sampled (e.g., a fifteen-second block every two minutes).

An observer watching the following episode would enter the codes as shown:

Mother: Please put your sweater on.   CM
John: (Walks into next room, begins to play with toy)   NC, PL

Mo: (Ignores John's noncompliance)		IG
J: (John continues to play)		PL
Mo: Please, John, put on your sweater. You've just had a cold.		CM
J: So what?		NC, NE
Mo: You're the rudest little boy—how you hurt your mother!		DI
J: Darn bitch.		HU
Mo: (Strikes at John)		PN
J: (Yells vigorously)		YE

Actual entries on the code sheet show the sequences:

CM-NC, PL-IG
PL-CM-NC, NE
DI-HU
PN-YE

We recognize the first sequence as one that is likely to increase John's rate of noncompliance. Further, the repetition of the Command-Noncompliance sequence following a period of ignoring previous noncompliance appears to lead quickly to escalated conflict. The mother must be taught to recognize noncompliance when it occurs, to use an effective consequence, and not to be a part of the destructive CM-NC sequences. At present she is rewarding noncompliance. In the typical behavioral-improvement training programs, she would be taught not to make DI comments that indicate he has really "gotten to her."

In this manner assessors seek answers to three questions. First, what about the *specific behavior and rates*? What is happening and how frequently? Perhaps the mother brought Suzanne to the clinic complaining that she doesn't do what she's told. However, home observations show that such noncompliance occurs infrequently but that Suzanne hits her young brother eight times during an observation hour. Second, what kinds of *consequences* are used? A parent may

TABLE 14-1 A Code for Observing Parent-Child Interaction

AP	Approval	DS	Destructivenss	NR	No Response	SS	Self-Stimulation
AT	Attention	HR	High Rate	PL	Play	TA	Talk
CM	Command	HU	Humiliate	PN	Negative contact, Physical	TE	Tease
CN	Command (Negative)	IG	Ignore	PP	Positive contact, Physical	TH	Touching, Handing
CO	Compliance	LA	Laugh	PX	Proximity	WH	Whine
CR	Cry	NC	Noncompliance	RC	Receive	WK	Work
DI	Disapproval	NE	Negativism			YE	Yell
DP	Dependency	NO	Normative				

attend to noxious behavior by stopping what she is doing and saying with resignation: "I have to tell you a hundred times a day not to do that." Or the parent may simply ignore or fail to pay attention to the behavior. Third, what *sequences* or *chains* keep occurring? It is important to find out how the deviant behavior is being inadvertently maintained. For example, one coded sequence may indicate that a parent indulges a child by doing for him something he can do for himself, thereby promoting dependent behavior on the child's part.

AN ILLUSTRATION OF LEARNING-FOCUSED FAMILY INTERVENTION

In designing intervention programs, parents are helped to specify what *positive* behaviors of their child they wish to accelerate. They often find this difficult, for various reasons, as the following paraphrased case from Patterson, Cobb, and Ray (1972) illustrates.

Fred's mother, Ms. F, was an ebullient, attractive, divorced, middle-aged woman; she preferred to be a friend to her children rather than a mother. As such, it was difficult to set rules, limits, and contingencies. However, she believed that if she could be warm and loving enough, the children would mature. Unfortunate y, most, or all, of the children were out of control; and she was finding it commensurately more difficult to be "loving." Fred was eleven, a middle child in a family of five children. He presented the general picture of a sullen, unhappy boy whose out-of-control behavior was becoming increasingly dangerous. He frequently attacked the other members of the family. At age eleven he had come to be identified at school as an extreme problem. The mother said, "We have already 'had' behavior modification, and he was too smart for it."

Observational data were collected for twelve days in the home. The entire family exhibited deviant behaviors at the rate of 1.89 per person per minute. This was the highest rate for any of the twenty families with which Patterson and his team had worked. The observation teams reported that the noise level in the home was similar to what one might find in a machine shop.

The data showed that the youngest children had the highest rate of out-of-control behavior. It was decided to start the training by teaching Ms. F how to handle their behaviors first. She began her training by responding to the programmed textbook *Living with Children* (Patterson and Gullion, 1971). This reading convinced her that the ideas presented were *not* applicable to her family. As a matter of policy, however, arguments were avoided, and she was encouraged instead to begin observing and collecting data and let the attitudes and theories take care of themselves.

Ms. F first recorded each "noncompliance" response for a period of two days for both of the younger children. A behavior was counted as "noncompliance" on each occasion that the mother presented a clear request, or command, which was followed either by an argument, refusal, or an acquiescent verbal response not accompanied by actual compliance. Daily telephone calls revealed that she was having no difficulty in collecting data; noncompliance occurred at the rate of about 0.009 response per minute for both of the children.

Following the mother's baseline observations she entered the parent group to design and discuss her intervention program. The intervention program for the two children included "Time Out"[1] for each occasion when noncompliance occurred. If they had less than two noncompliances for the day, the children "earned their mother," and she spent some time reading to them. Follow-up telephone calls indicated that the initial program was effective in controlling their behavior. It was gradually altered, to add the possibility of a Saturday afternoon in the park with mother.

Reinforced by these rapid changes, Ms. F felt that she was now ready to take on more difficult problems. After counting Fred's rate of "hitting," she initiated a program to reduce it. If he did not hit anyone, he was allowed to stay up an extra half-hour to watch television. If he did hit someone, he was to be placed in Time Out. The first night of the program he "tested the contingencies." After hearing his program described, he went to his younger brother and gave him a sharp punch on the arm. Mrs. F told him to go to Time Out (TO), whereupon he hit him a dozen or more times. In this fashion he earned seventy-five minutes of TO. The next day was a replication of the first day, his disruptive behavior in TO earned forty minutes total time. Following this high point, the rate of hitting steadily decreased and was no longer a problem. Both the mother's and the observers' data indicated that the program had produced a rapid decrease in hitting behavior, in fact a 100 percent decrease from baseline. The behavior remained under good control during the follow-up.

The next program for Fred involved "noncompliance." Ms. F began to ask him to do various tasks around the house, requests that she had *never made before*! The first time she asked him to take out the garbage he refused. She placed him in Time Out. His reentry to the world was met with a repeat of the former request. He refused; she asked him again and he refused. He reentered Time Out. When he was released, she again repeated her request; this time he complied by taking out the garbage, but left the container in the trash can. She placed him in Time Out. Following this, he took the container out of the trash can and returned it to the house, and *earned points for compliance*. The backup reinforcers varied from the daily permission to watch television to going on picnics with the family, football games, scout trips, and acquiring a pair of ski boots. By the close of intervention, social reinforcement was the primary means of maintaining the changes in his behavior. The mother's data for noncompliance reflected a rapid decrease of 94 percent within a week's period of time.

---

[1] "Time out" simply means removing the individual from the situation and placing him in a room by himself for the designated period of time.

Once Fred and the two younger siblings were under reasonable control a program was instituted for the older brother and for the fourteen-year-old daughter. Another program on which data were not collected, but which was reported by the mother to be effective, was aimed at increasing the number of positive statements each family member made to another member. Training sessions occurred during dinnertime; for each positive statement that a person made, he received a penny. There was a game atmosphere to the sessions and the children learned to provide more positive reinforcement for each other.

In the fall Fred was assigned to a male teacher who placed clear limits on his behavior. Periodically the school was contacted to check on his academic as well as behavioral progress. His general academic improvement was reflected in his scores on the Gray's Oral Reading Test. In six months he went from grade 2.7 to grade 5.0.

Following the third month of follow-up Ms. F returned for a "booster shot." First she collected data on all the behaviors that she had altered during the intervention phase. Again, she practiced reinforcing the children socially for their adaptive behaviors and used Time Out for the inappropriate behaviors.

The total cost of the program in terms of professional time was 13.9 hours, including intake interview, staff conference, group meetings, and telephone contacts.

Although behavior modification for families is a relatively young approach, its effectiveness can be easily examined because of its close relationship to observables and to data. Its acceptability to parents appears high because its concepts seem close to the level of common sense. Additionally, it appears that workers can be trained to give this type of service without involved professional preparation. Learning-focused approaches to family intervention lend themselves to a group format and thus appear to offer a practical approach to prevention and educational efforts.

USING COMMUNITY RESOURCES

We turn briefly to the problem of working with families who do not seek help or who are initially uncooperative, in short, families who do not "play the game" according to the rules agencies and psychotherapists accept and follow. Psychologists should be concerned about such families for two reasons: (1) they are very numerous, and (2) their problems can be serious or even grave.

When families decline to act on their own behalf—or on their children's—law and regulations become important. In dealing with such families we must be concerned with legal matters—the family's rights and responsibilities and the helping agency's obligations. Although each state varies in specifics, there are common themes. In the case of child abuse, for example, states generally either require or encourage professionals to report incidents of child abuse. Various agencies, such as child welfare, children's protective services, and the juvenile courts, have responsibilities for action in certain types of family problems and frequently have legal relationships with a family where, say, delinquency or incest has occurred. They may refer these families for therapy as if they were no different from families that seek help voluntarily. Frequently such families can become cooperative if the clinician approaches them honestly, blending respect and compassion with a clear perception of reality and the childrens' needs. Insofar as families can agree to cooperate with the psychologist, the preceding sections of the chapter can apply. But many families and family fragments are too disorganized or too distraught to participate voluntarily and can only respond with irrational defenses or withdrawal. Instead of abandoning them as "unmotivated," the psychologist can coordinate or invoke existing community and legal resources for help or protection.

The clinician dealing with families must be thoroughly familiar with the basic obligations of law and the capability and functions of the various relevant agencies. Exactly what are the paths to mental illness and correctional institutions? If the Youth Authority removes a child from home temporarily, what plans do they have for helping the family reintegrate afterward? If a client is committed, what service is he likely to receive while in the institution, and how will his return to the community be arranged? Will it be preplanned so that he has a place to live, a job/school situation, and alerted caretakers, or will he be just "discharged?" What community help is available for *that* family? What legal safeguards for *this* child? Although there are no research-based guidelines for action, the practicing psychologist does not have to be passive; he may be able to help his client family by taking an active coordinative or facilitative role. In extreme cases he may need to assume the role of advocate. The following examples illustrate these kinds of service.

Gina, a sixteen-year-old high school girl, called Dr. B, a psychologist who had seen her brother after a hunting accident. After two apparently aimless interviews (which her mother knew of) she revealed that she was caught in an incestuous relationship with her father, who was threatening to maim her if she should tell anyone. Dr. B immediately telephoned the local Juvenile Court and Child Protective Agency office, asking for their counsel. He was told in this case that CPA could provide foster care, physical protection, and so on, on order from the court. The court said it could only act if the girl (Dr. B was scrupulously protective of Gina's identity) herself would personally appear to execute a complaint. Besides providing his own support, while Gina wrestled with the question of reporting her father, Dr. B encouraged her to talk with her minister. As soon as she did, the minister wanted to place Gina informally with a family in the parish. Dr. B had enough information to be able to point out the dangers of such courses of action and the necessity of involving the court. The minister prematurely and awkwardly confronted the parents but became protective of the father, who was highly placed in his church. At length, Gina contacted the court. Although there was no trial, the resulting separation from home was aided by all the community resources: court orders, foster placement, and CPA caseworker. But for the psychologist's "case manager" function, Gina might not have fared as well. Gina's father and mother totally rejected her and all authorities except the minister. The father was righteously indignant while the mother (with the characteristic passivity so often seen in such incest mothers) said "*I* had to submit to *my* father. Gina shouldn't have made trouble."

Patrick was twelve. His parents had sought help from the local child-guidance organization because Patrick was allegedly obstreperous at home. The parents had seen a social worker for about eight months without any apparent result. Patrick's mother demanded that he be put in a foster home. Hoping to avoid placement, the social worker consulted Dr. L, a psychologist, about using a behavior-modification approach. Ultimately, Patrick's mother said that all this, too, was "hogwash" and Patrick should be put in foster placement. It appeared that Patrick's father was quietly driving his wife to desperation by passive nonsupportive behavior and the mother was striking back by trying to eject her husband's favorite child from the family. When this whole question came up, the family broke off treatment. Some nine months later, Dr. L. was contacted by the court to consult about Patrick, now a thirteen-year-old who seemed bound for group home placement or for commitment to the state youth authority because of breaking into a neighbor's house, but whose objective-test protocols showed relatively little disturbance. Noting the name, Dr. L suggested a thorough check with all the helping agencies. Their material substantiated his previous observation—that marital troubles were severe and that treatment was usually broken off when the marital topic came up. Because of his previous experience with the case, Dr. L suggested that the family be required to try counseling before Patrick could be sent to a foster home. The resultant progress kept the family (including Patrick) together for two years before the parents separated. Was this worthwhile? If so, for whom? Patrick? The father? The mother? The taxpayers? Outcomes like this are especially difficult to evaluate.

Not infrequently a family hides its problems and refuses to become engaged with helping agents until some form of pressure is brought to bear, such as the prospect of public exposure or, in the case of child abuse, prosecution. Although the extent of child abuse is still poorly documented, Steele and co-workers estimate that some 40,000 children are seriously injured by their parents each year, and that about one-third of these are under age three. Steele and Pollock (1968) reported on the characteristics of 60 parents who attacked children, injuring them seriously. They found that, in general, there was little obvious difference between their sample and the general public. Contrary to earlier studies, they found no significantly greater incidence of poverty, alcoholism, broken marriages, or prominence of certain racial groups. But they say "From direct observation of parents with children and the descriptions given by them of how they deal with their offspring, it is obvious that they expect and demand a great deal from infants and children. Not only is the demand for performance great, but it is premature, clearly beyond the ability of the infant to comprehend what is wanted and to respond appropriately" (p. 109). For the child beater, the infants and children seem to exist primarily to satisfy the parent's needs: children's and infants' needs are unimportant and can be disregarded; children who do not fulfill the parents' requirements deserve punishment. Steele and Pollock outline the difficulties of reaching out to immature and threatened parents who are likely to construe many approaches as evidence of their own inadequacy, taking away their parental rights, and so on. Steele (1970) elaborates a sensitive neoanalytic approach to treating such people, which avoids condoning or punishing the parental violence but which attempts to show consideration to the parents in a nonjudgmental fashion. Once the engagement with helping agents is brought about—even if it is through some "legal clout"—the suffering family unit may become accessible to intervention, resulting in beneficial outcomes.

Psychologists may also be concerned with improving community services for families. Although we take this up at greater length in "working with communities," providing family services somewhere in the community appears to be of vital importance because of the sheer number of families in need of some type of assistance. A program of augmentation of family function might include setting up a network of housewife volunteers to fill in needed domestic or transportation functions in emergency times, such as hospitalization of a parent, the provision of small group homes in the community to take children in between foster homes and the state institutions, and the training of both group home and foster home parents in dealing with the natural family. There are, of course, a vast group of services aimed at helping family units. Some are of the self-help variety, such as the Parents Without Partners organization; others depend on external corporations, organizations, or grants. "Drop-in" centers can have services designed to help restore parent-child communication, communities can establish donation-funded cooperative family counseling services, and family counseling or behavior-modification training can be set up in conjunction with school psychologists or with Head Start centers. Many other examples might be given. Funds may be secured for some kinds of family services by the psychologist, who is skilled at "grantsmanship." The psychologist confronted with problems in many of the community's basic units, including families, should consider where his effort should be expended. Before he commits his time to single-family units, perhaps he should ask which community units might be helped to handle this *class* of problems effectively?

SUMMARY

As psychologists have become interested in systems larger than the individual, the family system has received more and more attention. They have worked mainly with problem families who voluntarily apply for help, although the much larger challenge of families who need help but do not seek it is now receiving some consideration.

There are three principal approaches to family counseling– the *evocative*, the *communication-clarifying*, and the *learning-focused*. In marriage counseling, where only the husband-wife system is dealt with, evocative therapists encourage the marriage partners to express their feelings in the security of a good therapeutic relationship and to use the insight they achieve to help them strengthen the marriage relationship. Communication-clarifying counselors help the marriage partners to work out shared agreements and definitions, using a variety of maneuvers to unsettle the existing stable but unsatisfactory system of communication and control in order to facilitate its reorganization. Learning-focused therapists teach marriage partners how to manage conflicts, to change behavior in such a manner as to provide mutual reinforcement, or to replace irrational with rational beliefs and expectations.

The same three approaches can be distinguished in work with children and parents in families. In these cases therapy is often initiated when a deviant child is referred for treatment and it becomes evident that the family system must be modified in order to change the child.

In dealing with involuntary cases, psychologists are likely to make use of community resources rather than to intervene personally. One important aspect of the psychologist's responsibility is to know what resources are available in his community and to help organize new ones as the need for them becomes apparent.

SUGGESTED READINGS

Patterson, G. R., and Gullion, M. E. *Living with children, new methods for parents and teachers,* rev. ed. Champaign, Ill.: Research Press, 1971.

This paperback and that of Becker (1971) on behavior management of children are in programmed-instruction format. They are excellent for step-by-step instruction of parents, singly or in groups. Becker contains more elaborated examples and situations; Patterson is perhaps the easier source, for parents with weak reading skills or concentration, for the acquisition of a working knowledge of behavior-management principles.

For an interesting comparison with historical trends in the popular literature on "good" child-rearing, see Bigner, 1972.

Langsley, D. G., and Kaplan, D. M. *The treatment of families in crisis.* New York: Grune & Stratton, 1968.

Langsley and Kaplan describe the work of a family-treatment unit in a hospital. Their extension of crisis concepts to family work is clear and lucid. They provide some excellent descriptions of various types of family crises they have handled, along with sufficient interview transcripts to make clear how the crisis-intervention goals differ from longer-term psychotherapy goals—for example, discouragement of regression, encouragement of competence rather than encouragement of regression.

For the special problems of poor and disadvantaged, see *Families of the Slums* (Minuchin et al., 1967).

Patterson, G. R. *Families: Applications of social learning to family life.* Champaign, Ill.: Research Press, 1971.

A clear and straightforward elaboration of the interactive patterns of family systems from a social learning perspective.

A more detailed presentation of this point of view as applied to families of aggressive boys is Patterson, Cobb, and Ray (1972).

Bodin, A. M. Conjoint family assessment: an evolving field. In P. McReynolds (ed.), *Advances in psychological assessment*, Vol. 1. Palo Alto, Calif.: Science & Behavior Books, 1968, pp. 223—243.

Bodin reviews a variety of approaches to assessing family systems. He classifies approaches to such work as Individual, Conjoint, and Combined, and reviews the latter two categories using divisions of subjective techniques and objective techniques. He gives references to prior reviews and useful commentary on the issues impeding progress in assessing family units.

Gardner, R. A. *The boys and girls book about divorce.* New York: Science House, 1970.

A volume with humorous illustrations, written to speak directly to children involved in divorce. Its clear, candid style gives some explanations and perhaps more important, some "how-to" material, including pointers on how to avoid getting caught between the warring parents. Like many other books mentioned here, it may be useful in working with parents.

Ard, B. N., Jr., and Ard, C. C. (eds.). *Handbook of marriage counseling.* Palo Alto, Calif.: Science & Behavior Books, 1969.

Ard and Ard present 50 articles forming a broad introduction to marriage counseling and therapy.

Lederer, W. J., and Jackson, D. D. *The mirages of marriage.* New York: Norton, 1968.

Lederer and Jackson write about marriage from the communications perspective for which Jackson and co-workers (e.g., Haley, Satir) are noted. The authors begin with a series of myths about marriage and discuss marital structure and destructive elements in marriage. They provide sections on ways to make marriage work and on seeking professional help. The book is highly readable and well provided with examples.

Haley, J. *Changing families.* New York: Grune & Stratton, 1971.

Haley presents a collection of recent papers on family therapy, including some of the evolutionary developments that are essentially changing the focus of intervention from the family system to the community system.

Olson, D. H. Marital and family therapy: integrative review and critique. *Journal of marriage and the family*, 1970, *32*, 501–538.

This survey of the fields of marital and family therapy covers developments in research, theory, and clinical practice. Olson presents a system for categorizing various approaches and summarizes a number of approaches he feels to be exemplary.

Winter, W. D. Family therapy: research and theory. In C. C. Spielberger (ed.), *Current topics in clinical and community psychology*, Vol. 3. New York: Academic Press, 1971, pp. 95–122.

Winter's chapter takes family therapy in its broadest sense—working with families—and thus contains a variety of perspectives not often found together. Winter discusses research on family therapy and reviews process variables such as therapist characteristics and examines reported outcome research. He concludes with a discussion of who should do family therapy.

Constantine, L. L., Constantine, J. M., and Edelman, S. K. Counseling implications of comarital and multimarital relations. *The Family Coordinator*, 1972, *21*, 267–273.

This article discusses the experimentations with altered forms of marriage going on in America in recent years, and the ways counselors might better understand and deal with these relationships. A comarital relationship is defined as an intimate involvement which is an adjunct to a dyadic marriage, open and shared by the spouses. Mate swapping ("swinging") is sometimes a secondary phenomenon. A multilateral marriage is a voluntary family group of three or more persons who regard all participants as being "married" to each other. The authors indicate that it is important for the counselor to thoroughly examine his or her attitudes concerning such relations; they view illegality as insufficient to justify counselor condemnation. In counseling, the authors recommend a "growth orientation," striving for openness and authentic self-disclosure. As an assistance in the counseling discussions, they use the Edwards Personal Preference Schedule, followed by ratings of self and other group members to reveal perceptions of their personal needs.

RESEARCH EXAMPLES

Bernal, M. E., Duryee, J. S., Pruett, H. L., and Burns, B. J. Behavior modification and the brat syndrome. *Journal of Consulting and Clinical Psychology*, 1968, *32*, 447–455.

This paper resembles many studies which show beneficial changes in the behavior as one subject brought about by the use of behavior-modification techniques. But, in this report, Bernal and co-workers did not do the actual behavior modification themselves. Instead, they reprogrammed the mother, in effect teaching her to be the agent of positive change in her child's behavior.

The subject was an 8.5-year-old boy, referred to an outpatient psychiatric clinic because he frequently had temper tantrums and physically attacked his mother, teacher, and peers, and showed a variety of deviant behaviors.

After preliminary observations by the investigator, the first step in training was to teach the mother to reduce her verbal output and to selectively ignore Jeff's abusive behaviors so that she could better make decisions about her own behavior. Step two was to establish a set of conditioned negative reinforcers (ignore, frown, use angry tone, say "don't," finally spank) which should assume control functions when produced contingent on bad behavior.

In step three, the mother was to identify acceptable behaviors as they occurred, positively reinforce them by responding warmly, and praising Jeff, specifying which of his behaviors were acceptable.

Maternal control was established within twenty-five weeks, as verified by the time-sampling data from the videotapes. The authors note that components of success probably included (1) the mother's cooperativeness and continuous effort, and (2) the continuous feedback she received from the procedures and from relatives, friends, and also from Jeff. Furthermore, that mother and Jeff lived alone probably made change simpler to implement.

Bee, H. L., Van Egeren, L. F., Streissguth, A. P., Nyman, B. A., and Leckie, M. S. Social class differences in maternal teaching strategies and speech patterns. *Developmental Psychology*, 1969, *1*, 726–734.

The Bee study does not concern identified patients or help seekers but it does involve a population to whom a psychologist may easily be expected to give service, namely Head Start students and their mothers. The investigators examined and compared child-interaction styles of lower-class mothers to identify factors that might affect the child's cognitive development. The subjects were 76 lower-class children and mothers (37 boys and 39 girls), and 38 middle-class children and mothers (22 boys and 14 girls). Each mother and child was seen for approximately ninety minutes: (1) ten minutes of their "waiting room behavior" was observed and recorded; (2) the mother was interviewed while the child was given 13 brief tests of cognitive and motivational behavior; and (3) mother and child were reunited for a series of problem-solving interactions in which the mother's teaching strategies were observed and recorded. Only the interactional and interview behavior were reported.

The results of the waiting-room comparison showed that middle-class mothers were less controlling and less disapproving than lower-class mothers and gave more information to their children. Middle-class mothers also gave their children more attention. Middle-class children were lower in acceptance of controls and questions and higher in spontaneous information statements than were lower-class children.

In the problem-solving comparison, middle-class mothers and children spent more time on the assigned "build a house of blocks" task than did lower-class mothers. Middle-class mothers tended to give more suggestions in the form of questions. Finally, middle-class mothers tended to tell their children what they were doing correctly rather than what they were doing wrong. Middle-class and lower-class children did not differ in their reactions to or requests for help.

In the interview, middle-class mothers used more words, longer sentences, greater syntactic complexity, a higher adjective-verb quotient, and a lower percentage of personal pronouns.

The investigators conclude that the findings provide evidence of impoverished language and ineffectual teaching strategies experienced by the lower-class child.

Anderson, L. M. Personality characteristics of parents of neurotic, aggressive and normal preadolescent boys. *Journal of Consulting and Clinical Psychology,* 1969, *33,* 575–581.

Anderson was interested in patterns of parent personality which are associated with particular behavior problems in children, a field of research that is increasingly important as diagnosticians and therapists focus on the whole family unit. A major problem in whole family research is that of classifying Ss in a meaningful way.

Experimental Ss were parents of 9- to 11-year-old Caucasian boys who had been seen at four psychiatric facilities. Surveys of available files enabled them to select 29 boys who fit experimental class A (aggressive) and 23 pairs who fit experimental class N (neurotic), and to obtain information about their parents. The control group consisted of 50 boys from a local school and their parents. Anderson found that N boys tended to be first-born and A boys middle children. On the MMPI, a number of significant differences appeared between experimental groups and controls, and between A and N groups.

In her discussion, Anderson points to the greater deviance of the A fathers as the most striking finding. Their scores suggest that they tend to be persons with poor impulse control and an inability to tolerate meaningful close relationships: persons who are cold, distant, hostile, and unpredictable. (In terms of MMPI scales, the findings were an elevation on the Pd scale and some elevation on the Sc scale.)

Mothers of boys in the three groups differed relatively little from each other in configuration. This suggests that the mothers were not as important in influencing the development of characteristic pathology in their sons as were the fathers. The most important clinical implication of the study is the need to include the father in assessment and treatment of boys, particularly aggressive boys.

Hurley, J. R. Parental malevolence and children's intelligence. *Journal of Consulting and Clinical Psychology,* 1967, *31,* 199–204.

Hurley's study shows how characteristics prevalent within the family system influence parts of the personal system of the family's children. We must be careful, however, about inferring more causation than has been demonstrated.

The sample consisted of 206 girls and 245 boys and their mothers and fathers. All the parent-behavior indexes used were taken from an objective 286-item precoded interview schedule administered separately to each parent. The interview resulted in scores on scales for Punishment, Judgment of Punishment, Aggression, and Rejection. Parent education and SES levels were also rated at the time of the interview. The intelligence of the children was assessed using the California Test of Mental Maturity (CTMM), a group intelligence test.

Childrens' IQ's were correlated with each of the four parental malevolence indicators (Pun, JP, Agg, and Rej). Significant relationships were found for the Pun and Agg variables. Daughters' IQs were apparently more closely linked with parental malevolence than were sons'. IQs were also related to parental educational and socioeconomic level, and correlations between IQ and malevolence scores were higher in less well educated families.

The correlational results are, of course, compatible with various causal interpretations, but Hurley suggests that the view of parental malevolence or rejection as an important cause of low intelligence in children deserves careful attention. It is clear that the problem is difficult to investigate "cleanly." Critics might be concerned about the problems of social class and their accompanying subcultural norms. Others would, of course, find a group intelligence test inadequate and would wish to know about differences in thinking styles or strategies, and differences in characteristics of the child's stored information.

chapter 15

Small-Group Systems:
Group Therapy and Related Methods

Clinical psychologists work with groups—many kinds of groups under a wide variety of conditions. The only thing they have in common is that the members of the groups come together with the aim of individual improvement. There are, of course, other groups that come together to carry out a task—for example, to make a product with machines, to manage a jail, or to operate a welfare agency or a city, but the clinician's main responsibility is with groups designed for therapy or personal development.

In earlier discussions, we have made a distinction between voluntary and nonvoluntary patients. This distinction is an important one in working with groups. A group of involuntary patients, for instance, those on a certain ward in a mental hospital, requires additional safeguards of procedures designed to restore autonomy and liberty, whereas persons who have voluntarily chosen one particular experience rather than another, already have this liberty and autonomy. The picture is not a simple one, but we must again underscore the belief that procedures performed with involuntary patients and procedures undertaken at public expense must be designed in such a way as to enhance fully functioning citizenship. Our consideration of groups, then, will deal with the work of psychologists doing "therapy" for psychologically impaired people, those using groups to promote better role performance in members of organizations, and those promoting personal growth and interpersonal encounter in essentially healthy people.

Having been broadly inclusive of group-improvement patterns, we find that the range of settings in which they occur is also broad: out-patient settings, hospitals, new centers, and institutes devoted to growth and encounter; client-administered institutions such as Alcoholics Anonymous; and addict institutions such as Synanon. At the edge of our area of consideration are those workers who offer group services in the clients' place of work.

EVOLVING CONCEPTS AND TRENDS

Although "therapeutic" or improvement experiences in groups have apparently been rather common throughout history (such as some experiences in theaters and religious meetings), the development of group intervention, originally labeled group therapy, followed the practice of individual therapy. The rationale of "doctor treating patients" was used by early workers who applied the ideas of individual psychotherapy—usually Freudian—to the group situation. Their objective was for each patient in the group to undergo changes in intrapsychic organization; procedures used were those that would facilitate examining defenses, accepting interpretations, and working through transferences Foulkes and Anthony (1965) present a step-by-step comparison of the group-analytic approach with individual psychoanalysis, comparing, for example, the nature of the therapeutic (transference) relationship in group analysis (regression not encouraged by situation, relatively realistic role by group analyst and interaction with others, transference neurosis not fully established, less-dependency problem) with the conventional one-to-one psychoanalysis (regression encouraged by situation, relative anonymity and passivity of the psychoanalyst, transference neurosis fully established, problem of dependence and fixation on psychoanalyst). Similar translations from individual to group approaches were made by many of the followers of neo-Freudian schools.

Examination of phenomena of transference led to a focus on the importance of the relationships with other people in the group as well as the therapist. That, in turn, led some workers to view the group as an entity, a system, having its own attributes, such as a group temperament, a group mood, a collective level of anxiety, and so on. They came to emphasize the effect the participants had on each other. Group leaders began to focus on the individual's overall experience within the group at the hands of other group members, who were seen as agents of change for each other. In the proliferation of methods and applications of group work, some leaders introduced structured activities in an attempt to ensure that all members would have a type of experience that would produce particular kinds of change.

Interest in group interaction was stimulated by other kinds of work psychologists were doing—research on attitude change, training programs for employees, attempts to improve school programs. Persons variously designated as consultants, group workers, and mental health professionals functioned in a diversity of settings from churches to correctional institutions, from industry to police units. Older taxonomies of "group therapies" seem restrictive in this age of proliferation of styles, goals, and locations of the group activity. In an attempt to convey some of the extent of group phenomena now faced by the psychologist, we have arbitrarily divided general practice into five areas whose boundaries overlap. Readers will, of course, recognize that some characteristics of each are to be found in many of our common gatherings, such as church services or cocktail parties, PTAs, or rap sessions.

First are the *traditional group psychotherapies*. Usually there is a personality theory implicit or explicit within such activity, a theory out of which come guidelines as to how large the group should be, how often it should meet, and what the goals for individuals should be. Its purpose is to correct patients' psychological disorders (rather than, say, a behavior or conduct disorder or illegal activity).

Second are *psychodrama and role playing*, in which the concepts involved are distinctly social rather than intropsychic. The procedures, as their names suggest, use the vehicle of drama and the flexibility of roles to explore personal problems. This type of work has been applied to other than treatment situations, for instance, in helping teachers explore their interaction with students.

Third, a series of group techniques that qualify as therapies because "they have turned out to be helpful to people"—although they did not begin as therapy—is the *therapeutic use of environmental conditions*. With their rationale in social psychology, these techniques focus on how people can be helped by new role definitions in a social climate especially designed to encourage or force the person to take on the rights and obligations of an adaptive role. The work of Maxwell Jones on therapeutic communities is best known here, although when we become sensitized to see the constraints that tight social systems (from the traditional British boarding school to the cloister of a monastery) can put on behavior, we realize that a great many situations can be included under this heading. In Chapters 16 and 17, which deal with organizations and communities, we develop further this concept of the therapeutic use of environmental conditions.

The fourth kind is *organization development*, OD. In this approach "trainers" assist representatives of institutions, managers, or parts of organizations to improve their interactions. The groups are often called *T groups* (for training). What distinguishes the fourth category from the fifth is that the focus of OD is on tasks, on *working* together, rather than on personal growth and social interaction. Of course the two approaches overlap.

The fifth area of practice in groups we may call *personal development groups*. Such groups also receive such labels as *encounter, marathan, confrontation, growth,* or *sensitivity groups*. Often *T groups* are oriented toward personal growth, too. In general, adults who are not formally identified as patients seek experiences within a group setting with the purpose of "developing understanding of others," "dropping falseness," "trusting others " "being accepted by the group," and "confronting one's self as one really is." This is a rather new area, distinguished by a great deal of fervor both for and against, and a variable set of practices and procedures.

TRADITIONAL GROUP THERAPIES

The psychologist who expects fo find applications of technical or systematic knowledge—such as assessment procedures or outcome studies—in the reports about group procedures will be disappointed. Few of the accounts of group activities state their processes and goals in such a way that the assessment procedures we normally use—tests, ratings, and so on—are applicable, and the variables of group process are usually not defined clearly enough to permit quantitative evaluation.

Members of groups are not generally assigned to this sort of treatment on the basis of formal assessment, but in many cases a sort of assessment-like judgment does play a part in the assignment. Hospital or clinic patients for whom group therapy is considered appropriate are those whose problems will not overwhelm other patients, who are accessible to interaction with others, and for whom experiences of "feedback" from others or relationships with others seem likely to be beneficial. It is regrettable that group therapy is often initiated only because the caseload in one-to-one psychotherapy has become excessive. No evidence suggests that group therapy and individual therapy do the same thing or have the same outcomes.

Let us look first at some descriptive accounts of what group therapy is like. A small interaction group most frequently consists of five to ten patients. The seating arrangement is often circular so that each person can see and talk readily with any other. The therapist's responsibility is to encourage discussion and to structure it so that the flow of interaction will be therapeutic rather than damaging, but the main responsibility for the content and manner of interaction usually remains with the clients themselves. One of the things a new group therapist finds difficult is to focus his attention on the group interaction rather than on the problems and dynamics of individuals, as these become evident. He must accustom himself to thinking in terms of such things as kinds of interaction and roles clients take within the group instead of allowing himself to be diverted by individual feelings and reactions. As mentioned before, the selection of clients for group therapy can become a rather complicated undertaking. In order that the group may go actively to work on problems, it is advisable not to have its members too similar, but there must be enough common ground between them so that it is possible for them to pull together for a good part of the time.

Some illustrations of how group therapy may work follow. They are selections from an introductory book by Hinckley and Hermann (1951). Their practice, a modified psychoanalytic one, is fairly common, although it is but one among a wide variety of possible ones. Hinckley and Hermann see the group-therapy experience as primarily emotional, though with some rational elements in it. The therapist is expected to assume a kindly parental role in the group, remaining relatively quiet and permissive, but directing the group function in a broad general way. The first excerpt from a transcript of a group meeting, together with comments by the authors, demonstrates the effects of a minimum amount of activity by the therapist in the opening session (Hinckley and Hermann, 1951, pp. 22—24):

Therapist (enters after men assemble): Hello men. (Members respond with various greetings.) Let's introduce ourselves first of all, and then perhaps talk a bit about ourselves. Jack, would you like to begin?

Jack: We introduced ourselves, Doc, before you got here. So I guess that's taken care of. (Pause) Well—my problem is asthma. I've had it since I was four and no one knows what it's all about. It left me once when I was given some shots, and I thought that was it. But when I was in the Army I really began to have attacks. I got in school here and finally wound up in the Clinic. There are emotional factors, I guess. One damned thing, though, I'm far from being an emotionally adjusted person!

Albert: What do you mean—who is well adjusted? And how do you know he is?

Jack: Well—you fellows all look well adjusted, and it seems kind of foolish to shoot the bull this way! (At this point regarding the therapist with evident resentment.)

Oliver: You guys call me Oliver in here. My name is Jack, but the other Jack spoke first. (To Jack) I'd really like to correct you. I don't think this is shooting the bull or that being able to talk even is well adjusted. I think that's my problem—that I talk too easily and too much. I think it's worse than your problem. With me it's an attention-getting device, and I do it because I'm anxious.

Jack: (To Albert) What do you think about this?

Albert: I don't think either of you is right. Why is Oliver so easy and free, and why are you at the opposite end of the chain? What is normal?

Oliver: I'm not happy unless I'm getting attention. You sounded kind of disgusted there, Al. Well, I dream of suicide every night and of an obituary, and I have no intention of doing it. It's just attention-getting.

Jack: I still say this is just bull!

Therapist: A few moments ago when you said that, you seemed resentful toward me.

Jack (laughingly): Yeah—I guess maybe I was. I don't know why, though. (Although up to this point the therapist has been mostly silent, one does not feel he maintains this quiet arbitrarily or punitively. After the introductory remarks, the patients pursue their own patterns. They mention some of their symptoms, disagree with each other, and one dares to show some hostility by glancing at the therapist resentfully. Yet, when this display first happens, the therapist accepts it without comment. Later, rather casually, he suggests the possibility of resentment. When Jack's tension is released a little by laughter, the therapist again lapses into silence. Nor does he suggest a cause for Jack's angry feeling or offer any explanation at all. Jack, as a matter of fact, arrives at interpretation indirectly somewhat later during the same session.)

Joel: You can call me Red—everyone does. Say, are all you guys maladjusted? One thing worries me—you fellows are all so darned normal!

Oliver: Another thing that is really my problem is that I'm accident-prone I get into accidents about once a year—really serious ones.

Jack: You're farther along the scale, maybe, than I am, but in the Army I used to have problems too, very much like that.

Mark: I guess I'm afraid of people. My object is never to be the big wheel. I suppose they found out I had high blood pressure, and that's why they sent me here to the Clinic. I don't know just why I have it, though. In the Navy I was in the Personnel Bureau. I was a conference reporter in one of the "red rooms."

Jack (laughingly): We're in the wrong room, boys. Let's move.

(The patients compare notes and see their resemblances and their differences. This spontaneous contrast and clarification results in group identity, a feeling one for the other in the permissive presence of the therapist. A less mature therapist easily could seize upon Oliver's admission of being accident—prone for interpretation, could point it up as a possible indication of a need to be self-punishing; or he could use Mark's comments in regard to his war assignment to show need for status. Instead, although undoubtedly aware of the inferential possibilities, the therapist permits the patients to explore further their self-directiveness.)

There is often a beginning period in which patients work through their discomforts, establish trust in the group and the therapist, and develop a readiness to accept help and participate in the group. As group feeling grows in the early sessions, Hinckley and Hermann see the therapist as encouraging catharsis of feelings and greater freedom of association while supporting the equilibrium of any patient who appears to be under stress and keeping the group reminded of reality, of problems they have in common. The patients also support each other and are active contributors to the therapy of each other. Transference, or strong emotional feelings toward each other, develops in the group, but not as intensely as in individual therapy. Groups also show resistance to therapy through such behavior as talkativeness, denying certain implications of their symptoms, hostile attempts to break up the group, "flight into health," displacement, and other defenses. The therapist's interpretations may take the form of reflections of feelings, questions, suggestions, or explanations of motives. The following excerpt from an advanced session with another group shows not only the therapist's way of approaching interpretation, but also the interpretations that other patients may give in helping each other (Hinckley and Hermann, 1951, pp. 83–84):

Therapist: Will you review for us what happened last time, Alice?

Alice: I was scared. I didn't like getting together with people I hardly knew. Telling things about myself was awful.

June: Well, I felt just the opposite. I loved it. I suppose the lesson of the session was that by listening to others and helping them, we learn about ourselves.

Ellen: I'm having a bad day. Someone bumped my car, and I've been fuming. I'm not sure I can contribute much today at all.

June: Now that I think about it, I don't know where to start in regard to my problems. I'm too fat. I know it's from eating too much, but there must be some reason behind it, I know. Why do I pick at food all the time?

Therapist: Tell us something more about your background, if you will.

June: Well, everybody in our family have beautiful figures. They all disapprove of my overeating.

Sara: You mean you have to fight it? You don't look overweight to me.

June (in great surprise): Won't you all come home with me?

Alice: Are you hungry all the time? Are you hungry when you're happy and satisfied?

June: No, I guess not. I was with a fellow over the weekend and had a wonderful time, and I wasn't hungry at all.

Therapist: Sounds psychological. Perhaps you know something of the psychology of overeating.

Alice: My little niece has the same sort of trouble.

June: Well, I suppose when you keep on eating all the time and never really get satisfied, it can't be food you want at all. (Silence) Maybe—maybe—the eating is a substitute for something else that is lacking.

Therapist: You feel something else is lacking?

Alice: She is right. Something else probably is lacking. She wants something, but it's not food. She feels OK—at least not hungry—when she is with her boy friend. (Laughing) Maybe it's love she is looking for.

June (surprised): Why, yes, that could be, couldn't it? How reasonable that seems! But why should I need to look for love?

Alice: Guess I can't help there. I don't know.

June: There must be something wrong in the family—something lacking. Can it be love there, too? Oh, I'm getting confused.

Sara:, No, I think you are on the right track. I've got trouble along that line, too, but I don't try to solve mine by eating. I do it in other ways.

Karen: Well, what is this trouble at home? I've got troubles with my boy friend, and I never can get along at home. My mother nags if I don't jump when she wants me to. My boy friend used to take my part, but since my father died, he sides with my mother when he knows about our arguments. My mother ends up crying all the time. Something is wrong.

Therapist: Conflict with parents sometimes does cause painful behavior symptoms.

Such discussions suggest many research questions but provide few answers. What has been done is summarized in a chapter by Bednar and Lawlis (1971), who review 38 outcome studies in tabular form. They report that research on the outcome of group therapy still usually involves an undifferentiated and poorly specified treatment variable, "group therapy." Group therapy should be viewed as a two-edged sword, they say, one that can both help or hinder client adjustment. They make a plea that therapists find out how effective they usually are, the type of client with whom they are most and least successful, and begin a system of placing clients in groups based on therapist and client characteristics.

The rather favorable outcomes reported by Bednar and Lawlis must be tempered by their warning that without an attempt to transfer treatment effects to community living, there is considerable risk that the gains reported immediately after treatment will dissipate.

In discussing process research in group psychotherapy, Bednar and Lawlis point to the virtual absence of studies linking group process to therapeutic outcome, but they deduce that group cohesion is an important curative agent. In considering the question of when group therapy should be recommended, and when individual therapy, they conclude that only nonpsychotic patients benefit from the standard group experience. For severely psychotic patients, physical activity, group tasks, or the use of drugs may be helpful in setting up special kinds of groups from which they can benefit.

In their section on pretherapy considerations, Bednar and Lawlis recommended that, since composition of the group is a powerful determinant of group behavior and group adjustment, clinicians should place patients to facilitate (1) warm responsive interactions between some group members, (2) sufficient courage to discuss the unpleasant, (3) sufficient compatibility to increase personal attraction, and (4) sufficiently adequate adjustment to provide models for more effective ways of coping with stress. Preparing patients pays off: client role expectations should be clear and clients should have a framework to help them anticipate and understand the process. Finally, although leaderless groups have been useful in some settings, leaderless groups with psychiatric patients are found to be more potentially dangerous than professionally led groups.

PSYCHODRAMA AND ROLE PLAYING

J. L. Moreno, who has been especially prominent in the development of social approaches to treatment, started his work as a young physician in 1921 by founding the *Stegreiftheater*[1] (the Theater of Spontaneity) in Vienna. Moreno's strong motivation and originality came in part from his reaction against the Freudian psychoanalytic movement which had become dominant in Vienna at that time. Moreno became convinced of the therapeutic importance of acting out personality problems on the stage when he observed changes in people as a result of their spontaneous performances. Over the years, he contributed a number of ideas that greatly influenced social psychology and sociology, as well as psychiatry and clinical psychology. The beginnings of sociometric approaches can be credited to him. Although he was a pioneer in the development of group psychotherapy, he is best known for his work with psychodrama.

Psychodrama takes place upon a stage, often a specially designed one, in front of an audience. The chief participants are the protagonist (the client), the

[1] The word *Stegrief* itself is interesting. It means "stirrup." To speak "from the stirrup" is to speak extemporaneously.

director (the chief therapist), the auxiliary egos (assistant therapists or other patients), and the group making up the audience. The therapist-director gets the psychodrama going by asking the client to act out a scene spontaneously. Auxiliary egos take parts that will support the action and help bring out the problems and conflicts of the client. The techniques for developing the production are many and varied (Moreno, 1959). The director encourages the client to achieve catharsis in order to liberate himself from his problems. The goal is to produce a spontaneous, creative person. One of the interesting by-products of the psychodrama is its importance to the client-audience. In one mental hospital a patient about to be discharged was asked what had helped him most in the hospital. He replied that the psychologists' psychodrama sessions had given him the most help. This was a patient who had never actively participated in the psychodrama, but as a member of the audience, he believed that he had profited greatly, presumably by working through the problems vicariously.

On a level less elaborate than psychodrama, many therapists use *role playing*. It can become the primary technique in therapy or remain an auxiliary method resorted to occasionally. Some situation that has arisen quite naturally in group therapy may be taken as a starting point. A client tells of his mother's harsh treatment when he started going out with girls in high school. The therapist asks the client to describe a particular time when he came home from an evening with a girl. Members of the group are assigned to play the mother and other significant persons involved. Roles may be switched around and much discussion results. Another occasion for the use of role playing is in preparing clients for job interviews or future stressful situations. Ossorio and Fine (1960), aiming to benefit chronic patients, have used role playing and psychodrama as techniques for changing the social atmosphere in hospital wards and especially for increasing communication. There are many other possibilities.

THE THERAPEUTIC USE OF ENVIRONMENTAL CONDITIONS

It is commonly recognized that a person's environment has a great deal to do with how well he feels and how much satisfaction he takes in life. The advice of a friend or a physician to go on a vacation when you are under tension or "worn out" is often good advice, even if it is not a cure-all. Sometimes a change of jobs will revitalize a person. Social workers know the importance of the proper kind of foster home for a neglected or disturbed child. The sheltered workshop, the day hospital and the night hospital for mental patients, and the rest home for the aged are examples of environments especially developed to provide the necessary support for persons who are only marginally adequate to the demands of life. The psychologist's techniques of assessment and therapy need to be extended so that they cover the adjustment of patients and environments to each other. Here is a great challenge, indeed. We will discuss environmental matters extensively in Chapter 17, but a number of ideas and examples should be mentioned now to alert the reader to the importance of the environment in group efforts.

Sometimes interpersonal therapeutic techniques can be applied in the natural environment itself. Redl (1959) has proposed what he calls the *life space interview*, an on-the-spot handling of emotional problems Suppose, for instance, in a residential treatment home, that most of the boys suddenly turn on one of their number, tease him unmercifully, and reduce him to angry tears and wild fighting. When the melee is over, the psychologist who was on the scene may be able to use this immediate moment as an opportunity to give "emotional first aid" to the boy. Perhaps he might even be able to conduct a brief and informal therapy session, skillfully helping the boy to see the situation more realistically and to detect what it is about his own behavior that may have helped elicit the teasing. Such impromptu therapy may have greater possibilities for effectiveness than if the boy has to wait until the next therapy hour to discuss a matter that is already cold or perhaps repressed, pushed out of mind. In a similar manner in recent years, "aggressive" social workers have been working directly with delinquent gangs on the streets. This kind of "therapy *in situ*" raises problems for the selection and training of personnel.

Institutions such as mental hospitals, schools for mental defectives, and prisons are beginning to understand the rehabilitative effects that the right kinds of environmental conditions and institutional personnel can have. Mental hospitals are trying to become more therapeutic and less custodial, and there is a definite movement to leave patients in their own community as much as possible. As long as it was thought that mental illness was a dangerous "disease" that must be treated by isolating and imposing special restraints on the patient, everything that was done to or for him was dehumanized; and little attention was paid to the possibly ameliorating effects that might be produced by the right social influences. Occasionally, reformers would plead for more humane treatment. The newly awakened interest in the therapeutic effects of the environment is reminiscent of the "moral treatment" that emerged at the end of the eighteenth century with Pinel's breaking of the mental patient's chains (Carlson and Dain, 1960). Later in the nineteenth century, the harsh and cruel treatment of patients returned to full force. One exception has been the long history of the town of Gheel, Belgium, where chronically ill mental patients have led nearly normal and useful lives in foster homes in the community. Only a few require conventional hospitalization, even though most of them have been classed as incurable and have failed to respond to treatment in public institutions (Amrine, 1960). Thus we see the treatment of mental illness and deviant behavior in general is related to public and professional attitudes.

The work of Fairweather (1964; Fairweather et al., 1970) represents pioneering efforts to design a social-psychological milieu for the treatment of mental illness. Fairweather worked first within hospital settings and later in a halfway house, formerly a motel. There, the milieu for group living, both the internal aspects of participating in decisions and operations of the living group and the external aspects of operating a neighborhood janitorial service, was shown to have a therapeutic impact. Later developments have involved teams of patients as active competitive bidders, performing large-scale refurbishing and rebuilding of repossessed homes. Ellsworth's (1968) work using nonprofessionals as key personnel in a psychiatric hospital is another example of the therapeutic use of environmental conditions.

Recently therapeutic environments designed to help drug abusers and alcoholics have come into being. Some are spontaneous creations of the participants themselves, others have been built into the regular structure of mental health services, along with the more traditional treatment by professionals. Among the most interesting examples are the Synanon and Daytop homes for addicts, groups that are outside the domain of publicly supported mental health services. They are thus somewhat more free to construct their internal environment as they find it useful, and they may restrict their membership as they wish. Basically, they make an applicant demonstrate a great deal of desire before they will accept him, and then force him to take a very menial place in a demanding hierarchy. The new member is confronted and challenged in a systematic fashion until, apparently, without the outside world to sustain his former perception of himself, he gradually assimilates the redefinition furnished by his associates. They customarily "strip away" the former notions of self by denying the individual's former worth. He is reduced to low self-esteem and allowed approval only for behavior in conformity with the group ideals and practices. Some who have noted the apparent harshness of the confrontation have also emphasized the eventual support given to the resident by his peers.

Alcoholics Anonymous uses some of the same techniques (such as public confession of subjugation "to a power greater than I"), although it is basically a nonresidential organization. Its methods of assigning newcomers to older "graduates" and the provision of phone contacts, places to go when needy, and sometimes even "rescue squads" are a therapeutic use of environmental conditions within the community.

However, in general, the potential for the therapeutic use of environmental conditions appears as yet poorly developed. We have several provisionally successful models, each one of which requires systematic investigation. They have shown us that old-style institutions inadvertently taught a great deal of sick or criminal behavior and that they should be restructured. But changes designed to cope with one problem may beget others. For example, a new institution for young delinquents, well staffed and beautifully appointed, began to suspect that teaching ghetto children not to retaliate with violence could be harmful to the children when they were returned to the ghetto. The staff found also that several children were so impressed with institutional life that they had no wish to return to their communities. One special advantage in the therapeutic use of environmental conditions as a means of treatment is the fact that these techniques do not require much specialized manpower. They constitute a new resource for promoting effective community living for substantial numbers of people.

USE OF GROUPS IN ORGANIZATION DEVELOPMENT

Growing out of earlier interests in "group dynamics," encounter groups, T groups, and a variety of forms of human relations training have come into common use during the 1960s and 1970s. In organizing our thinking about these variants of group process, we should first recognize two basically different objectives. One application of group process, which we will call *organization development*, or *applied human relations training* after Birnbaum (1969), is designed to improve the task-oriented interpersonal functioning of individuals who control, manage, or participate in various bureaucratic structures. The other application of group process aims to provide a quasi-psychotherapeutic experience for its members, or a form of social-emotional learning. We shall discuss it below under *Personal Development.*

Applied human relations training (covering laboratory training group dynamics, and T groups) originated in the National Training Laboratory, whose founders were originally interested in applying group processes to institutional change. The T-groups they recommended usually contained ten to sixteen persons, who meet periodically in a residential setting (the laboratory) for about two weeks. Birnbaum says "the objectives of the T-group are to help individual participants become aware of why they and others behave as they do in groups . . . [that is, to] become aware of the underlying behavior dynamics of the group" (Birnbaum, 1969, p. 83). To accomplish this task, a trainer creates an atmosphere in which motivations for typical behavior often unclear to the individuals concerned are brought out in exaggerated form of discussion and analysis. Each participant asks himself: "How do I affect the group—and why?" Birnbaum makes the point that although this training has a clear emotional component, it is not therapy. There is a difference between therapy focused on the problems of emotionally disturbed people and training that aims to help normal people improve their human-relations skills and their effectiveness in organizations.

In this unstructured, face-to-face collection of ten to fifteen people, the trainer rejects the traditional expectation that he be the *leading* person. The leadership void produced by the trainer's refusal to provide structure provides an opportunity for behavior from which group members can learn about themselves. With a focus on the "here and now," the participants discuss themselves and the way they portray themselves in the group, as shown in the following example (Tannenbaum, Wecshler, and Massarik, 1961, p. 123):

At the fifth meeting the group's feelings about its own progress became the initial focus of discussion. The "talkers" participated as usual, conversation shifting rapidly from one point to another. Dissatisfaction was mounting, expressed through loud, snide remarks by some and through apathy by others.

George Franklin appeared particularly disturbed. Finally pounding the table, he exclaimed, "I don't know what is going on here! I should be paid for listening to this drivel? I'm getting just a bit sick of wasting my time here. If the profs don't put out—I quit!" George was pleased; he was angry, and he had said so. As he sat back in his chair, he felt he had the group behind him. He felt he had the guts to say what most of the others were thinking! Some members of the group applauded loudly, but others showed obvious disapproval. They wondered why George was excited over so insignificant an issue, why he hadn't done something constructive rather than just sounding off as usual. Why, they wondered, did he say their comments were "drivel"?

George Franklin became the focus of discussion. "What do you mean, George, by saying this nonsense?" "What do you expect, a neat set of rules to meet all your problems?" George was getting uncomfortable. These were questions difficult for him to answer. Gradually he began to realize that a large part of the group disagreed with him; then he began to wonder why. He was learning something about people he hadn't known before. " . . . How does it feel, George, to have people disagree with you when you thought you had them behind you? . . ."

Bob White was first annoyed with George and now with the discussion. He was getting tense, a bit shaky perhaps. Bob didn't like anybody to get a raw deal, and he felt that George was getting it. At first Bob tried to minimize George's outburst, and then he suggested that the group get on to the real issues; but the group continued to focus on George. Finally Bob said: "Why don't you leave George alone and stop picking on him. We're not getting anywhere this way."

With the help of the leaders, the group focused on Bob. "What do you mean, 'picking' on him?" "Why, Bob, have you tried to change the discussion?" "Why are you so protective of George?" Bob began to realize that the group wanted to focus on George; he also saw that George didn't think he was being picked on, but felt he was learning something about himself and how others reacted to him. "Why do I always get upset," Bob began to wonder, "when people start to look at each other? Why do I feel sort of sick when people get angry at each other?" . . . Now Bob was learning something about how people saw him, while gaining some insight into his own behavior.

Plainly, *feedback* is the primary component of the learning experience. Participants not only learn about their original behavior but also about their ways of giving feedback (feedback on feedback). Campbell and Dunnette (1968) identify two additional elements which they believed to be necessary: *anxiety* or *tension* and *psychological safety* (Schein and Bennis, 1965) or *permissiveness*

(Bradford, Gibb, and Benne, 1964). The anxiety serves to shake up the participant and jar him loose from his preconceived notions and his habitual forms of interaction so that feedback can have its maximum effect. Psychological safety or permissiveness—a generally supportive and nonevaluative attitude in the groups—serves to make participants willing to try out new ways of interacting. Another aspect of group experience is *modeling*. Rogers (1970) recommends that the group leader model exactly the behavior he wishes participants to acquire. If they are led by example into certain responses, they are likely to use such techniques on others.

In a review of the effectiveness of T-group experiences for managerial personnel, Campbell and Dunnette (1968) have synthesized a list of common goals: (1) increased self-insight and self-awareness concerning one's behavior and its meaning in a social context; (2) increased sensitivity to the behavior of others, a goal akin to increasing empathy; (3) increased awareness and understanding of the types and processes that facilitate or inhibit group functioning and the interactions between different groups (e.g., why do factions that oppose each other often form?); (4) heightened diagnostic skill in social, interpersonal, and intergroup situations; (5) increased skill in intervening in inter- or intragroup situations so as to increase member satisfactions, effectiveness, or output; and (6) increased skill in analyzing one's interpersonal behavior for the purpose of achieving more effective and satisfying interpersonal relationships.

Campbell and Dunnette distinguish two main types of criteria that may be used to evaluate the effectiveness of T groups. Internal criteria are measures that are linked directly to the content and the processes of the training program but not to actual job behavior or organizational goals. *External criteria*, on the other hand, are linked directly to job behavior, such as ratings by others in the work situation or the amount of work produced by a section.

In their recommendations for more and better research, Campbell and Dunnette suggest that the desired behavioral outcomes should be specified in advance so as to avoid post hoc assertions that the particular results obtained, regardless of what they were, constitute evidence for the efficacy of the method. Investigators must deal with the question: For what kinds of people are particular effects found? They must also examine the interaction among organizational characteristics, leadership climates, organizational goals, and training outcomes and effects. The question of whether there are alternative methods that might be more effective and cheaper should be considered. Differences among trainers, techniques, and varieties of preparatory experience need to be explored.

Phares and Campbell (1971), in a chapter on sensitivity training in industry, continue the review of relevant studies and issues. They support Gomberg's (1966) criticism that such human relations programs in industry have a serious shortcoming: They fail to come to grips with the fundamental problem of the locus of power in industrial structure. The question seems to be: What is the place or role of a democratic or pseudo-democratic sensitivity group in a structure where, outside the group, lines of authority are clear and no pretense of democracy exists? In many instances it is clear that the relative risks involved in potential system disruption have not been responsibly weighed.

Another serious ethical matter raised by Phares and Campbell has to do with the difference between voluntary and involuntary clients, an issue we have raised in other connections. They suggest three general criteria to be used in selecting a participant from a business firm—and presumably from other organizations like schools and mental health clinics as well—to attend a T group:

1. He or she should really want to go and not be under direct or implied coercion to attend.

2. The person should be assessed to determine whether he is likely to learn from the program.

3. He or she should be evaluated to determine whether there is a probability of psychological injury or psychiatric disorder from attending the T group (p. 181).

Condition 1 is sometimes met, they say, but 2 and 3 are rarely considered.

Phares and Campbell conclude their review of history, issues, and empirical studies in sensitivity training in industry with these points:

1. There does not exist, to date, a single successful demonstration based on objective measures of positive or negative outcomes showing individual or group changes external to the training process. Such evidence is needed.

2. Dunnette's (1969) study of the development of empathy and Hall and Williams's (1970) study of improvements in decision making indicate that individual and group changes internal to the training process do occur.

3. The outcome studies based on criteria *internal* to the training situation, even though separately open to criticism, collectively constitute compelling evidence pointing to beneficial outcomes of sensitivity training.

4. There are documented cases of harmful outcomes from variants to sensitivity training. (These are few, and often stem from encounter-group experiences).

5. Closer attention must be given to the screening of participants and organizations and to the competence of trainers. Argyris (1964) has provided minimal criteria for screening individuals. Bennis has proposed criteria for the introduction of laboratory training into organizations.

GROWTH OR SENSITIVITY GROUPS: PERSONAL DEVELOPMENT

In the more than twenty years since the founding of the National Training Laboratory, group work has become diversified in duration, technique, location, and aim. Many people have become interested in the activity until growth groups have become a massive social movement. Those who wish to concentrate on the paratherapeutic aspects, that is, on stimulating personal growth in a variety of ways, have promoted *basic encounter groups, confrontation sessions, marathon sessions,* and *nonverbal exercises.* Some growth group leaders deny that the groups are "clinical" or "therapeutic" and treat them as "educational" or "entertaining." Rather than "therapists," they often call themselves "trainers" or "facilitators." These differences are more than changes in labels; they have serious implications for applications of professional ethics and training, which we will discuss later.

The goals of such groups typically include openness, honesty, and breaking through ordinary defenses in order to relate to others on more authentic levels. The groups vary in the amount of "pressure" used: Rogers's (1970) basic encounter groups, for instance, tend to elicit the exploration of feelings, motivations, and styles. Like Rogers, Satir's marathon groups use confrontation only occasionally, perhaps when a member is frustrated. But some other groups, such as Synanon, mentioned earlier, emphasize confrontation, taking active steps to encourage harsh attacks in the belief that only unremitting pressure from a group will cause the target person (or subgroup, as in groups made up of blacks and white officials) to feel the intensity and seriousness of the others' perspective.

Diversity in approach, method, and theoretical underpinnings characterize the movement. For example, in the book edited by Burton (1970) the contributors supply a number of interesting—and quite divergent—viewpoints:

1. Modern life dissociates the individual and forces him to feel shame, guilt, and anxiety. He becomes ultimately fearful of his own expectations, and settles for little. Encounter forces the client to experience himself totally, to verbalize his expectations, and to listen to his self-condemnations against the background of group response.

2. Institutional approaches to healing have ossified and are related to power struggles in society. Effective treatment must demonstrate care and concern on the part of the therapist, and contact must involve increased emphasis on authenticity, congruence with one's feelings, and confrontation.

3. Most of those who commit themselves to the venture can experience highly rewarding states of being. The essential attitude is attending or letting be and possessing a trust in the nature of things. The facilitator must develop the courage to be and to allow himself to be known by others. Given the right environment, spontaneous growth appears through the two experiences of nurturance and challenge—growth toward the goal of each person's finding answers within himself rather than looking outward for the answers.

4. Rational encounter groups contain core rational-emotive concepts and should emphasize that universal ideas of perfection—that one should be loved by all, that people are wicked, that things always have to go right—are irrational concepts. The encounter group can help its members to change such mythologies. However, certain marathon groups teach their participants that they *are* worthwhile people, other members of the group exchange bear hugs and

expressions of affection. The rational encounter weekend is designed to show members what their specific self-defeating philosophies are.

One important additional perspective is *Gestalt therapy*, which was associated with Perls, Hefferline, and Goodman (1965; Perls, 1969). Gestalt therapists typically work with one person at a time, using the groups as a backdrop, but the basic goal of personal growth through awareness is the same as for other approaches. The group leader therapeutically frustrates or encourages the member who is "working" (in the "hot seat") helping him give up self-avoidance ploys and become more aware of presently existing unfinished situations. Gestaltists assert that increasing awareness of one's total being, "getting it all together," is a step toward self-regulation, and hence a step toward taking more responsibility for the self and shedding unhealthy responsibility for others.

Perhaps the following excerpts can convey some of the feeling tones—the empathy and the warm enthusiasm—many "encounterers" convey:

Interpersonal learning in a college teaching situation
(Thomas, 1970, pp. 69, 70)

I am seated in front of a group of students in a college classroom. "Is it possible to deal with some things that really matter to us?" I ask. We will be together for only an hour and fifteen minutes since I am substituting for a colleague who is ill. "Let me hear what you are most interested in right at this minute. What you can put into words I shall write on the board." A young man asks, "How can we break down the barriers between people?" A young woman chimes in, "How do we communicate better with each other?" There is a long pause. No one else responds. I ask myself, "What now?" Shall we talk about the topic of communication? No, let's act instead. "Are you game to experiment a bit?" I ask. There are a few tentative nods from some of the students. "O.K., push the chairs aside, mill around the room and pick out a person you don't know but would like to know better. This may sound a little crazy, but sit on the floor back to back with your partner and carry on a conversation for a few minutes." After a short period of time I ask the pairs to turn around face to face and share their feelings. Next, the pairs face each other and each person takes a turn at mirroring the actions of his partner. We then form groups of eight and share our experiences. After the period of sharing, each member of the group in turn is asked to close his eyes and allow himself to be passed around by the other members, who are standing in a circle. People are now experiencing how much they are willing to let go and trust others to support them. Soon the entire group is standing in a large circle with arms entwined and people are looking at and experiencing each other in a very different way than they were at the beginning of the session. Several express surprise at how much closer they feel to others in the group. During that hour and fifteen minutes, in a very real sense, we dealt with the initial questions of the students regarding interpersonal barriers.

Sensitivity training for staff members
(Thomas, 1970, pp. 70, 71)

A university counseling center staff of about fifteen has invited me to spend the day with them in a sensitivity-training session. The stated purpose is to deal with interpersonal problems in the hope of improving staff effectiveness. This is a relatively sophisticated group with a variety of experiences in individual and group therapy, sensitivity training, sensory awareness and related activities. Seemingly little of significance has happened throughout the day as the group struggles for authenticity. With little more than an hour remaining I reveal my own feelings of frustration to the group and ask, "What does one do at times like these?" I feel as though I have nothing to offer. An attractive young woman turns to me, eyes flashing in anger, "Well, if *you* don't know, then who does? I had heard a lot about you, and I'm really disappointed. I came here expecting you to turn us on, and you haven't done a damn thing! Where's your act?" I can only reply, "This *is* my act." I have no suggestions to make, I can only be what I am. Soon she begins to weep and, looking at me and then at her supervisor, with whom she had had great difficulty relating, she exclaims with intense emotion, "Now I really understand. You are people, too! Here I've had you up on high pedestals, fearing you, both admiring and hating you, but I couldn't get close to you. I also expected you to have the answers for me." Looking at others in the room she exlaims, "My God, we're all just human beings and that's great!" This seems to produce an electrifying effect on the group which is no longer stuck on dead center. Persons are communicating with persons rather than roles talking to other roles.

Sharing feelings in a T group
(Cahn, 1970, pp. 98, 99)

What happened was that Stu Atkins and I agreed to ask our T-groups to cluster and observe each other for an hour or so.

When our groups met—his already seated in the inner circle—there was instant drama for all of us. Without any hesitant preliminaries, a dark-haired young lady named Beth explained that she had been reviewing the group's feedback since the afternoon session—"your horrendous feedback"—and going through some careful and rather painful introspection. The group listened in eager silence. I felt quickly involved. The feeling was thick and contagious. Her shaking voice, her commanding hold on our attention, and her words—"it struck me in my soul"—pointed out that her circumstance was far more compelling than the possible embarrassment of appearing in front of a new and strange group of people.

I was particularly interested in Stu's behavior, too. One of my strong motivations for joining our two groups was to see if I could catch some sense of his style. He was about three or four seats from her, his body in a strange tilt in her direction. When someone else spoke, he settled back slightly and turned toward the speaker. But soon again his body leaned forward and then swiftly he took an empty chair near Beth. In a moment, she was sobbing on his shoulder. It happened quickly and movingly. She sobbed deeply and unevenly; none of us knew when she would sob again, or if she might say something cheerful between the tears. People came up with Kleenex; Stu whispered to her as though none of us were present. He was with her all the way. It was a rather beautiful and intimate experience.

This event dominated the entire session—first, Stu holding her and really being with her through the tearful episode; then others commenting about this intimacy.

The diversity of encounter techniques is very great and growing: warm-up exercises, teaching of paraphrasing, role playing, games, all-night sessions, screaming, body massage, meetings in swimming pools, and many other approaches. "Nude marathons" have attracted a great deal of publicity but constitute a very small percentage of encounter groups.

Rogers (1970) describes the common threads of encounter groups (pp. 6–7):

A facilitator can develop, in a group which meets intensively, a psychological climate of safety in which freedom of expression and reduction of defensiveness gradually occur.

In such a psychological climate many of the immediate feeling reactions of each member toward others, and of each member toward himself, tend to be expressed.

A climate of mutual trust develops out of this mutual freedom to express real feelings, positive and negative. Each member moves toward greater acceptance of his total being—emotional, intellectual, and physical—as it *is*, including its potential.

With individuals less inhibited by defensive rigidity, the possibility of change in personal attitudes and behavior, in professional methods, in administrative procedures and relationships, becomes less threatening.

With the reduction of defensive rigidity, individuals can hear each other, can learn from each other, to a greater extent.

There is a development of feedback from one person to another, such that each individual learns how he appears to others and what impact he has in interpersonal relationships.

With this greater freedom and improved communication, new ideas, new concepts, new directions emerge. Innovation can become a desirable rather than a threatening possibility.

These learnings in the group experience tend to carry over, temporarily or more permanently, into the relationships with spouse, children, students, subordinates, peers, and even superiors following the group experience.

While this description of basic aspects of the experience would probably fit a majority of groups, it would be less applicable in such situations as

Gestalt therapy and other groups where the leader is much more in charge and much more manipulative.

Rogers's description of the process shows that it involves a number of patterns or stages which form a rough, approximate sequence: milling around, recognizing the lack of structure; resistance to personal expression or exploration; description of past feelings; expression of negative feelings, the beginning of revealing current personal feeling; expression and exploration of personally meaningful material; the development of a "healing" or "growth" capacity in the group; self-acceptance and the beginning of change; the cracking of facades; the individual receives feedback; confrontation, the helping relationship of members by others outside group sessions; the basic encounter—fully open, authentic exchanges; behavior changes in the groups. Rogers's discussion, besides emphasizing the potential of groups and their positive aspects, pays careful attention to pitfalls, drawbacks, and difficulties, such as "old pro" facilitators who impose their "rules of the game," thus stifling spontaneity and free exploration of feeling.

Rogers (1970) presents a chapter on the research that has been done on encounter groups. He relies heavily on Gibb's (1971) review for the more quantitative section. Gibb argues that it is not true that research is lacking. He was able to find some 229 studies, of which he analyzed 106. In addition, several doctoral dissertations are now being produced on encounter topics. Taking Gibb's review, a lengthy process study, and an extensive outcome survey, Rogers puts together a spirited and appealing case for the effectiveness and worth of encounter groups. Many of the research issues raised in the previous section apply here. Although we may recognize that research is in progress, the classic questions have not been answered: For whom are these procedures suitable? What criteria of outcome should be used, experiential or behavioral? It is difficult to deal with such questions because of the immense variation in things like facilitators' backgrounds and methods, and members' reasons for participating. Rogers's concern for client well being and ethical practices leads him to set high standards for group facilitators. While he asserts that encounter groups are the best instrument for healing the loneliness that so many human beings are experiencing, he recognizes that the movement is vulnerable to faddists and manipulators.

Recognizing this danger Birnbaum says, "The most serious threat to sensitivity training comes first from its enthusiastic but frequently unsophisticated supporters, and second from a host of newly hatched trainers, long on enthusiasm or entrepreneurial expertise, but short on professional experience, skill, and wisdom" (p. 84). Shostrom (1969) gives clear cautions to prospective group members about injudicious "shopping" without knowing the qualifications of the leader and the nature of the processes; "Let the buyer beware" he says. All these things must be taken into consideration in evaluating the encounter-group movement.

Lakin (1969) has discussed ethical issues raised by sensitivity training. The core problem, as he sees it, is that the new participant cannot really know what he is letting himself in for even though he forms the group voluntarily. Thus the trainer bears full responsibility for the psychological soundness and ethical defensibility of the procedures used. Lakin considers ethical problems related to inadequately trained trainers; pseudo-democratic group processes; widely divergent goals and expectations of groups; the casual selection of members, some of whom may not profit from the experience, or even be harmed by it; the self-gratification trainers seek and obtain; and general lack of followup. Clark (1970), in an interesting response to Lakin, proposes that a vulnerable public be safeguarded not by requiring more training and certification, but directly, by "flooding the public with information." As one example, Clark suggests making available to a group leader's potential clients computer-digested feedback from all the participants in previous groups he has led. Better evaluative research is needed if we are to deal with the ethical problems Lakin (1969) has pointed out. Was the actual activity chosen appropriate for the task?

Evidence as to whether people have been harmed by the group experience is as scarce and unsatisfactory as other kinds of evaluative evidence. Verplank (1970) made a brief survey of psychology departments. Out of the 157 departments responding, 19 reported "incidents" arising out of sensitivity training, ranging from "few" to a "disturbing number" and from "minor" to "serious." Among these respondents 77 thought that the activity should be systematically investigated. Yalom and Lieberman (1971) studied 16 "casualties" among 209 undergraduates in 18 encounter groups. They concluded that the best indicator of a casualty was the opinions of other group members, not the leaders; that the most vulnerable individuals were those with a low self-concept and high expectations; and that the highest-risk leadership type was characterized by aggressiveness, charisma, and an individualistic focus.

Because of growing demand for group experiences and the shortage of trained leaders, lay persons of varying backgrounds are entering the ranks of group leaders (or facilitators, as Rogers prefers to call them). This means that the situation is likely to get worse rather than better. Thus, from the perspective of the helping professions, it appears that there are problems in the "group" movement: open advertising, insubstantiated claims, and untrained leaders—at least on the fringes of the movement. But because ordinarily no law or statute is violated if such words as psychologist, psychotherapy, and treatment are avoided, it is difficult to do anything about such problems. The movement has attracted ideological enemies, too, who feel that the collective accord and understanding most groups try to reach constitutes loss of respect for individuality. The eminent psychologist Sigmund Koch (1971) calls the encounter process a shallow, ritualized kind of game, weak on theory and contrary to the character of the humanities that "humanistic psychology" seems to support. Disagreeing with Carl Rogers, who called the encounter group movement the most important social invention of the century, Koch (1971, p. 112) stated:

> Within the lexicon of its concepts and methods, openness becomes transparency; love, caring and sharing become a barter of "reinforcements" or perhaps mutual ego-titillation; aesthetic receptivity or immediacy becomes "sensory-awareness." It can provide only a grotesque simulactrum of every noble quality it courts. It provides, in effect, a convenient psychic whorehouse for the purchase of a gamut of well-advertised existential "goodies": authenticity, freedom, wholeness, flexibility, community, love, joy. One enters for such liberating consummations but inevitably settles for a psychic strip-tease.

Although the whole T-growth-encounter group movement may indeed be able to help some persons to greater openness or authenticity and some organizations to better functioning, we must, if we think of human personality as a system, keep in mind two important generalizations. First, it is true that a system may be damaged by the clogging of input and output channels, a condition that may be corrected through group process, but it is also true that input and output channels cannot be enlarged without limit—in the interest of greater authenticity or openness—without producing other sorts of damage to the system. Second, the kinds of experience sensitivity groups offer to their members can also be obtained in naturally occurring groups. Confrontation, interpersonal accord, sharing of personal information, demonstration of feelings toward one another, the touching of bodies, all are found to varying degrees in natural groups. When we think of the rock festivals of young people as an example of a group with a good deal of body contact in their collective behavior, we may overlook the fact that many churches have long promoted expressions of involvement. It would seem that while sensitivity groups have their own structure, time, frame, and goals, their essential processes are a particular blending of universal human group experiences, perhaps providing for rootless verbal middle-class men and women some of the experiences others find in rock festivals or glossolalia (the speaking with tongues found in some religious groups). Kavanaugh (1971) has underscored such thinking in his article "The New Salvationists." Similarly, the sociologist Schwartz (1971) describes encounter groups and the like as a new fanatacism—a new way to salvation—"a magical experience . . . in which the corruptions of civilization are transcended. He notes that both "buyers" and "sellers" of therapy seem to be moving from dyads to groups.

Although no definitive study of sensitivity-group consumers has appeared, it appears that in general they are like clients in individual psychotherapy, predominantly from verbal, middle-class, liberal backgrounds. As some observers have stated, many may be following a currently popular "fad"; others are *retreaters* . . . avoiding all environments except, at most, a communal "roll your own" or a weekend bash at Esalen; some long for a "peak experience" or "instant nirvana," hoping to beat out reality and consequence (Birnbaum, 1969, p. 96).

In summary, because of the scarcity of real knowledge about the sensitivity-group movement, its customers and its effects, we should exercise caution about promoting it, especially within the domain of publicly supported services.

CRITICAL COMMENT

Because of the diversity of the material discussed in this chapter, we have introduced evaluative comments at various points rather than at the end. However, something needs to be said about this diversity itself, which gives to the collection of procedures included in this chapter an unsatisfying "miscellaneous" quality. Some can be considered a form of therapy; others cannot. Some belong at this supraindividual level in our general plan of classification by the nature of the system change sought; others would probably fit better into the section on individual therapy, since their objective is clearly to improve the functioning of members as individuals rather than the group as a whole. Some are derived from the medical model; others have essentially nothing to do with sickness and health. Not all of them can even be considered to be the concern of professional psychology or any of the other helping professions, since they are organized by their members for their members and repudiate specialized "leaders."

The burgeoning interest in what might be labeled "groups of strangers" is a prominent feature of the American cultural scene in the early 1970s, when this book is being written. Whatever this cultural phenomenon means, psychologists are very much involved in it. Whatever his theoretical orientation—behaviorist, existentialist, Freudian, eclectic—the psychologist can make perhaps his greatest contribution if he draws upon his background of knowlege and research skills to bring some clarity and order to this confusing realm. What do people desire from group experience? To what extent are particular kinds of people obtaining the desired results in particular kinds of groups? How widely and to what other kinds of situations do changes produced in individuals and personal relationships generalize? Dozens of other research questions could be formulated. To answer them, new assessment techniques, new observational methods, new experimental designs may need to be devised. For clinical psychologists who consider themselves scientist-practitioners, the situation constitutes an exciting challenge.

SUMMARY

Psychologists work with many kinds of face-to-face groups organized to bring about some sort of improvement in the members. One basic distinction that must be kept in mind is the one discussed earlier between voluntary and involuntary participation.

Beginning with group therapy in which the objectives were much like those of individual therapy, emphasis shifted as time passed to more attention to interpersonal relationships and behavior as manifested in the group situation itself.

Five main streams can be separately considered, although they merge to some extent. In the first, traditional group therapy, participants are helped to understand their motivations as these are revealed in the group communications. Insight is the general objective. In the second, psychodrama and role playing, psychological problems are acted out, with actors and audience participating in the search for a solution. In the third, the therapeutic use of environmental conditions, hospital wards, correctional institutions, or other environments to which individuals have been committed or assigned are reorganized so as to provide support for the development of new habits and attitudes. The fourth, the organizational development group, is being widely used in business and industry to improve managerial and organizational effectiveness. The fifth, personal development groups, appears in a variety of forms—such as encounter, confrontation, sensitivity, and marathon—groups whose objective is to promote personal growth. These are being sought out by individuals in many walks of life who are willing to pay to participate. As yet very little research shows what these groups accomplish.

Research has not kept pace with the development of the group movement, and many questions remain unanswered. Evaluation is needed if important ethical and policy issues are to be resolved.

SUGGESTED READINGS

Cashdan, S. Sensitivity groups—problems and promise. *Professional Psychology*, 1970, *1*, 217–224.

In this concise review, Cashdan traces the beginnings of sensitivity training to a workshop in Bethel, Maine, in 1946, from which the Basic Skills Training Groups (T groups) evolved. In the years shortly after that, the programs split into human relations training and organization skills training; these separations have maintained various degrees of difference or integration. Cashdan also discusses training the trainer, the use of groups in reducing racism, and the dangers, such as individual stress for disturbed individuals and reeducation that is itself culturally deviant. Other useful discussions can be found in the 1970 issue (Vol. 2, No. 2) of *The Counseling Psychologist*, which is on encounter groups.

Goldberg, C. Group sensitivity training. In J. Aronson (ed.), *International Journal of Psychiatry*, Vol. 9, New York: Science House, 1970, pp. 165–192.

Goldberg's article, typical of the style of the *International Journal of Psychiatry*, is followed by five invited comments. A main value of the series lies in the extreme diversity of viewpoints: what is important for one is irrelevant for another, what is a virtual certainty for one is completely unproved to another. Such diversity illustrates the lack of even basic agreements about sensitivity-related work. Not surprisingly, protagonists are very keen to emphasize the differences and the uniqueness of sensitivity training, whereas more systematic reviewers look for historical perspective and similarities with other methods as well.

Yalom, I. D. *The theory and practice of group psychotherapy.* New York: Basic Books, 1970.

Yalom takes a comprehensive approach to group therapy, separating what he calls "front" from "core" of the many schools of therapy. His treatment of group therapy is reminiscent of Ford and Urban's (1963) analysis of psychotherapy, although simpler and more practically oriented. Many of his chapters, such as that on specialized formats and procedural aids, are useful summaries.

Rogers, C. R. *Carl Rogers on encounter groups.* New York: Harper & Row, 1970.

This warm and personal account by one of the elder statesmen of humanistic approaches in psychology conveys a good deal of Rogers's own commitment to the development of persons who are more effective in their interpersonal relationships. The emphasis on acceptance and on empathic understanding suggests the Rogers tradition, but he adds the use of his own feelings as a basis for operating within the group—for facilitating it. He stresses the importance of attempting to carry change over from group to daily-life setting and differs sharply with manipulative, interpretive, highly specialized expertise, and avoids the group exercises and games "which have become such a large bag of tricks for many group leaders."
Burton (1969) has edited a useful introductory collection of papers bringing varying perspectives to group experiences.

Gibb, J. R. The effects of human relations training. In A. E. Bergin and S. L. Garfield (eds.), *Handbook of psychotherapy and behavior change.* New York: Wiley, 1971, pp. 839–862.

Gibb's chapter defines the area of human-relations training with respect to what it focuses on and its differences from educational activities. He identifies its most frequently cited objectives from the training literature, sensitivity, managing feelings, managing motivation, functional attitudes toward self, functional attitudes toward others, and interdependent behavior, and he examines research findings relevant to each one. The middle section is a glossary of various kinds of groups. The chapter concludes with a discussion of implications, one of which is that the reputed dangers of sensitivity training are greatly exaggerated.

Harrison, R., Research on human relations training: design and interpretation, *Journal of Applied Behavioral Science,* 1971, 7, 771–785.

Harrison discusses difficulties in the selection of criteria in human-relations training research. So many observers are interested in global outcome that even though it is so difficult to measure, it must in some way be reported on. He reviews methodological problems with the hope that administrators who may have to make decisions about human-relations training can fairly quickly grasp some of the major issues necessary for intelligent decisions about it.

Hall and Williams (1971) have developed a means of measuring group encounter style and personality preferences.

RESEARCH EXAMPLES

Bolman, L., Some effects of trainers on their T-groups. *Journal of Applied Behavioral Science*, 1971, *7*, 309–325.

In a dissertation study, Bolman investigated relationships among certain dimensions of T-group trainer behavior, members reactions to the trainer, group climate, and participant learning. He used questionnaires administered to 118 participants and 20 trainers in a human relations lab held at Bethel, Maine. The training was of two weeks' duration held with ten participants for two trainers: one experienced trainer and one trainer intern. Data were collected by questionnaires to trainers before the program and to the participants three times during the lab. The participants' questionnaire asked about the behavior of the trainer, the participants' reactions, the group climate, and the amount of learning the participant felt he and other members were achieving. In addition, participants completed peer ratings that ranked members of each group by their learning and their influence on the group. Trainers responded to twenty-eight items, measuring affections, conditionality, empathy, openness, persuasion, security, and amount of conceptual input.

As expected, trainer empathy and security related to liking for the trainer and to perceived member learning. Trainer affection was related to participants liking the trainer but not to learning measures. Trainer tendencies to reward and punish were related to discomfort and tension but not to learning. Unexpectedly, trainer openness showed little relationship to participant learning.

In discussing the implications of the findings for the characteristics of affective change agents, Bolman suggests that a change agent is likely to be effective to the extent that certain conditions hold: (1) he is personally secure and nondefensive in the change situation; (2) he is in touch with the concerns and feelings of his clients; (3) he is congruent in the sense that what he says is consistent with what he is actually thinking and feeling; and (4) he possesses a "cognitive map," a theoretical set of concepts that makes reasonable sense to the change situation and suggests strategies compatible with his personality.

Bolman notes that, as in Fiedler's (1950a, 1950b, 1951) classic studies of psychotherapists, specific theoretical orientation of a practitioner seemed less important than the way he relates to his clients.

Truax, C. B., Shapiro, J. G., and Wargo, D. G. The effects of alternate sessions and vicarious therapy pre-training of group psychotherapy. *International Journal of Group Psychotherapy*, 1968, *18*, 186–198.

The authors addressed the manpower problem in psychotherapy by trying two ways of enhancing the effectiveness of group psychotherapy and thus presumably cutting the time invested by professionals. Accepting the usefulness of self-exploration is often a difficult task for patients. Truax proposed to overcome the problem by showing the clients specifically what was expected of them through a one-session vicarious pretraining experience, in which clients listened to taped segments of actual therapy. The second variable investigated was the provision of extra, alternate sessions without a therapist present.

Eight groups of ten patients were used, half hospitalized mental patients and half institutionalized juvenile delinquents, in a balanced factorial design. All subjects were administered Q-sort self and ideal-self concept measures before and after therapy. Groups met twice weekly for one-hour sessions for twenty-four sessions. The therapist-absent sessions started after the tenth regular session, adding 14 regular sessions for that group.

The pre and post measures suggested that the alternate sessions had a retarding effect on patients' self-concepts. The alternate sessions appeared not to be useful. Vicarious therapy pretraining, on the other hand, had positive effects, especially on patients' ideal self-concepts, although results were not clear-cut. The basic strategy of this study, to test the effectiveness of innovations to procedure, is one that holds a good deal of promise, because even negative results have implication for the direction of future modifications to therapy procedures.

chapter 16

Consulting and Working
with Organizations

Psychologists trying to improve the quality of life for clients face the problem that their own resources are limited, their manpower short, and the problems staggering. Some have turned naturally to the idea that if they can influence an organization positively, they can provide improved conditions for all the people it serves. With or without such intentions, psychologists are involved with organizations in many ways. Early in the history of psychology, around the turn of the century, Munsterberg and Gilberts began to work with industry and business. Scientific management, time-and-motion studies, and personnel selection procedures developed early. But those kinds of psychological work were oriented more toward the efficiency of the organization than toward such goals as the mental health and social competence in its members. In this chapter we are concerned with clinical, counseling, and community psychologists who deal with organizations as a part of their efforts to improve conditions for individuals.

Psychologists approach organizations with different goals, and there is little agreement as yet about methods or ways of measuring outcomes. Our chapter, then, must be considered a rough survey of a new area—an area that is rather like a shanty town. There is much feverish construction, using almost any available idea, but systematic planning and solid building will have to come later. There is no doubt about the vitality of the settlement, but there is great question about which of its neighbors should annex it—should it belong to community psychology, to clinical psychology, to social work, to applied sociology, to organizational psychology—or should it incorporate on its own?

In accordance with our systems theme, we may see an organization as another form of a living system. It has boundaries, internal activities, input, output, and throughput. Working with organizations usually has one of two general objectives. The first is to change the orientation or role of this organization in the matrix of other organizations, much as one might change a ship's course. The second is to improve its internal functioning, much as one might overhaul the

414

boilers or feed the crew. Working with organizations comprises a very wide range of activities, many of which, unfortunately, are called "consultation." For clarity in our discussion we shall try to focus on what psychologists do. First we shall review the organizations he should be familiar with.

RELEVANT ORGANIZATIONS

Traditional Members of the Network

The number of individual organizations the practicing psychologist may come in contact with is far too great to attempt a comprehensive listing. We can, however, consider certain main categories which include most of them. They range from large public organizations supported by various levels of government, to small private organizations such as the office of a physician. There may be an "organization's organization" where a consultant's contribution could achieve wide effects. Most communities will have organizations to deal with problems of mental health, public assistance, delinquency and crime, employment, special educational problems, housing, health services, and legal services. Readers will be aware of examples of organizations that are prominent in their areas of the country. Everyone interested in approaching human betterment through work with organizations should take the time to become acquainted with those in his community—a necessary guide in considering where consultative efforts should be directed.

New Kinds of Community Organizations

In the last few years several newcomers to the network of community helping organizations have sprung up. The increase in drug usage, the emergence of a "counterculture," together with the apparent inability of existing organizations to address the new problems, has brought a variety of new organizations into being. Raphouses, detoxification centers, drop-in centers, stations offering medical and legal aid to youth, agencies to help runaways—these are only some of the wide variety of organizations appearing on the scene in the late 1960s and early 1970s.

A caution. All too often, as disenchantment with the power of psychotherapy to help masses of people becomes widespread, mental health professionals have sought other forms and structures. In the late 1960s naïve thinking and the availability of federal grants seduced professionals into many proposed "innovations"—some of which were reinventions of organizations tried before and found wanting. In the first place, without the artificial stimulus of federal grants, ability to create organizations at will is limited, and most of those we do set up are not very durable. In the second place, organizations created to solve particular human problems may have unfavorable effects on related systems. If, for instance, the (hypothetical) Central Grief Agency were to send a physician with a syringe of medication to give all newly bereaved persons a "shot," the effects on personal, family, and community (neighborhood support and mourning) systems would probably be harmful. Finally, organizations once firmly established tend to cling tenaciously to life even when their usefulness has long since passed or when, as in the case of many social agencies, alternative organizations could probably do the job better. Working with organizations, then, has important limitations and pitfalls.

ROLES OF PSYCHOLOGISTS WITH ORGANIZATIONS

Consultation may take many forms, ranging from emphasis on the individual case with minimal attention to organization variables, to emphasis on the organization as client with little or perhaps no attention to individuals in need of service. A consultation about an individual case does not really constitute working with an organization but such consultation with a resource person is one of the most frequent ways in which work with organizations is initiated. How the psychologist moves from the case consultation is likely to determine whether or not there will be continuing work with the organization. He may ask himself such questions as: What is the general set of needs which this case exemplifies? What is there in my preferred solution which could be taught others, especially nonprofessionals? What could be done to prevent this class of problems? As he examines questions like these, he puts himself in a position to go beyond the case consultation and to attempt to influence the organization itself.

Psychologists may provide many kinds of service such as the following:

Psychological help for staff. The psychologist consulting in a school may suspect that Ms. Berk, the teacher, is having trouble with pubescent Sally because Sally is reawakening in Ms. Berk memories of unresolved conflicts from her own adolescence. He may delicately explore with her how she was handled similiar problems in the past, and what her own feelings were, in an effort to release Ms. Berk's potential for handling Sally as capably as she does her other students.

Knowledge and advice about groups of cases. A psychologist was consulted by the caseworker at a local child welfare office for advice on how to evaluate applications for foster placement. What aspects of this undertaking are really psychological? Where is psychological help useful? Another psychologist was asked by the local juvenile court to recommend a screening procedure for their inmates to determine which boys might best qualify for a new community treatment program.

Knowledge and skill about program change. Dr. Black was called by a caseworker at the local department of public assistance to help in a case where foster parents, the Ws, were having a difficult time with Steven, a nine-year-old foster child. Steven himself behaved well when he was alone with the Ws, but he acted up after visits from his natural parents, who were in the process of divorcing after a painful, unsatisfactory marriage. Dr. Black began consultation and found that the natural mother and father, Mr. and Ms. D, were seeking to vindicate themselves and trying to make someone else—Steven, the Ws, or the caseworker—appear to be the villain. Dr. Black noted that Steven wasn't the only child of the Ds; two others were also in foster care. He saw that the sort of help he had to offer was also needed by the other foster parents, none of whom had received any preparation for their rather difficult role. So he talked to the caseworker and his supervisor about the goal of giving all foster parents some understanding of family systems so that they could be more realistic about their role, not resenting the foster child's tie to his natural parents and not needing so much to be loved by the foster child. Dr. Black and the caseworker put together a short training syllabus to serve as a basis for discussion with foster parents. They taught a social worker to provide this service.

Help in designing, creating, and funding new organizations. Dr. Mayhew had noticed that in his community there was no help available for families with teenagers who were "acting out" their problems. There was a busy family counseling service, but its clients were mostly middle-class families with younger children. The community inadvertently put families with predelinquent children in a difficult position. Either the family "took care of" the problem almost on their own (only scanty probation officer visits were offered), or they would be broken up by having their child sent away to a correctional institution. Dr. Mayhew presented his observation to the local mental health board of the county, eliciting interest from some members. Together, they looked into the possibility of a grant-funded demonstration project that would use the techniques of behavior modification to eliminate the predelinquent behavior while keeping the child at home. Together Dr. Mayhew and the staff of the mental health board wrote the grant application. Since the project was to be affiliated with the local mental health center, the staff from the center was involved from the beginning in the planning.

In another community, Dr. Shapiro decided to attempt to do something about the problems of alcoholism. He had noticed that the laws of his state excluded alcoholics from treatment in state hospitals and that local resources were quite overburdened. He gathered together a number of concerned citizens, and founded a nonprofit citizens' council on alcoholism, carefully choosing a board of directors from high posts in local administrative, judiciary, governmental, and business circles. The council became affiliated with the local (private) mental health association and sought funds from the county mental health board. It functioned as a clearinghouse and referral center while it was applying for a federal grant for the staffing of a treatment center. The new agency adopted a broad-spectrum approach, placing initial emphasis on preventive education through alcohol and drug seminars, often cosponsored by the local community college. Besides its value for prevention, this educational campaign helped to produce the community awareness that was a key to acceptance and support for the remainder of the program. Dr. Shapiro found that his painstaking early coordination with the local Alcoholics Anonymous group, neighboring residential alcoholic treatment facilities,. local physicians, and the mental health center had the effect of making the addition of a new agency and a new set of services neither threatening nor upsetting to people involved in existing services in the community.

"Troubleshooting" and improving existing organizations. The Centerville Community Action Association was plagued with frequent turnover of personnel, low morale, and a great amount of difficulty in furnishing the services expected of it. At last the director was forced by action of his board to call in a psychologist to evaluate the situation. (In general, an organizational psychologist would be involved in such a job, but in this case, a clinical psychologist known to the board chairman was invited.) The psychologist did not find any "maladjusted troublemakers" as the director alleged, but he did find a number of practices within the organization which made people uncomfortable and less productive. For example, the director liked to "help people with their problems," a behavior that workers saw as an invasion of their privacy, making them personally vulnerable to the boss. Also, the director regularly turned down reasonable requests for mileage and expenses on the grounds that he must not show "favoritism." People in the organization felt free to reveal these problems to the outside consultant. The psychologist was able to bring about an organizational change in this case by tactfully suggesting changes in the behavior of the director.

Although the foregoing examples constitute only a small sample of the ways in which psychologists relate to organizations, they emphasize the diversity of consultative activities and show how desirable it is to specify in each case what the purpose of the consultation is. With the growing frequency of grant-funded organizations and suborganizations, and publicly or privately supported organizations such as youth homes, cooperative counseling services, and so on, it is increasingly likely that psychologists will need to be sensitive to variables of organizational functioning, productivity, and morale. In work with organizations we must remember that many other health and social service practitioners' efforts closely resemble our own in many ways. Many professionals have expertise only at one system level; people with sensitivity and skill in several systems are sorely needed.

EXTENDED ILLUSTRATION

In a small city, the County Juvenile Court Detention facility, an old inadequate house next to the County Courthouse, was intended to provide services for children who had come to the attention of the court because of delinquency or dependency—having no proper supports in the community. Overcrowding was severe. At length, a bond issue was passed so that a new facility with adequate space—even including a school activity area—was built. During the transition from one building to another, senior probation staff realized that staff training would be useful for shifting the emphasis from custody to treatment.

A clinical psychologist and a social worker were asked to "come over and teach us how to understand child behavior and development and that behavior-modification stuff." This team first looked at the records about some training that had been given some three years before by a panel of experts. There had been a series of formal presentations followed by feedback from the audience. The probation officers had responded positively, but the detention staff indicated that the training had been of little assistance to them in their jobs. Both groups had rated the most showman-like presentations highest.

On the basis of this information, the psychologist and social worker planned a different approach. First, they would avoid putting together a series of lectures by experts. Second, they would attempt to be sensitive to organizational variables. For instance they would look at procedures, commmunication patterns among the staff, how they shared knowledge, and how decisions were made. Third, and perhaps most important, they would try to put into practice the notion that the best programs are produced by people who are involved in generating them.

The meetings began with enthusiasm. The team asked "What are some of your concerns?" The staff first bemoaned their lack of psychological knowledge and soon complained about lack of structure, standard procedures, and communication channels. It was apparent that the brand new, apparently comfortable building had done away with many of the old meeting places and ways of doing things. In particular, in the shiny, sprawling structure, the central meeting place, the old coffee pot, had disappeared. (The team was tempted at first to blame the chief probation officer for the lack of structure. Later they realized that the lack of an imposed structure was an advantage if the staff was to generate its own structure to fit the new situation.)

Enthusiasm for the meetings decreased as time passed. Because the chief probation officer could not authorize overtime or compensatory time for the meetings, the upper-level probation officers did not return, and the enthusiasm of the lower-level detention staff was somewhat dampened. Detention staff members frequently communicated a sense of frustration about their roles. "Are we first-class turnkeys or third-class therapists?" was the way one staff member put it, adding, "I'm not qualified like you people to be a real therapist." The team continually emphasized that "treatment" consists of many varied activities and that the staff's brand of care, concern, and consistency in helping the children act in a dignified and age-appropriate way was a contribution that simply could not be achieved by people in offices. But it was not easy to bolster the staff's sense of worth. They were constantly attempting an impossible task of "making over" the attractive, dependent, manipulative children, and were inclined to dismiss the hostile, bitter ones as hopeless.

As the team inquired about how staff members treated the children, complaints about inconsistency were voiced. Some staff members, they said, *thought* carefully about what they did while others "shot from the hip." There was general agreement that consistency and definite objectives were desirable. It turned out that there were only two basic program parts: (1) an unstructured situation of liberty in which a detainee could be out of his cell and participate in group meals, television, sports, and schoolwork, or (2) solitary confinement. The team pressed the staff, saying, "Should there be only these two conditions? If there ought to be more, what should they be?" At this point, staff members became somewhat resistive and complained that the team was not supplying enough answers. It seemed for a time as if the consultation was unsuccessful. The senior official responsible for it pointedly suggested that there should be more teaching about abnormal behavior and emotional development. The team resisted the temptation to follow this recommendation, convinced that worthwhile change could arise only from within the staff itself, through decisions made and ideas tried out.

Two of the young staff members, in response to the question "Which children may do what and when?" designed a pegboard using colored pegs to record the privileges of detainees. The approval of the consultation team served to reinforce the staff members for such initiative. Other staff members also said that the pegboard was useful as an information device enabling them to keep track of exactly what was happening with each child. The pegboard represented an important turning point. It gave the beginnings of an orderly and consistent way of managing detainees, based on behavior rather than on popularity or whim. At the same time it helped give the detention staff a feeling of having the beginning of a coherent program of their own and a sense of worth growing out of their treatment responsibilities.

By this time several of the questions about procedure had become fairly specific. The team helped the staff invite representatives of the court and the health department to answer the legal and medical questions. During three such sessions a number of anxiety-laden topics were covered, such as "How can we protect ourselves from the VD these children carry?", "Is it likely that if I take a couple of girls down to the swimming pool they can charge me with rape even though I don't touch them?" As the anxiety subsided, the team began to challenge the staff, suggesting that some of their reluctance to design appropriate procedures arose from a desire to maintain their power to be a little bit arbitrary or unaccountable for what they did.

Some staff members expressed the concern they felt when some children— apparently "repentent" ones—were committed to the state correctional system. The team found that few of the staff knew anything at all about the state diagnostic center, to which all committed children were sent first. A program of visits was arranged, followed by a discussion of what might be done to prepare children better for such commitments.

The consultation team tackled the problem of actually generating a coherent program by encouraging the staff to write a brochure for new detainees. That task pressed the staff to discuss and agree on the major elements of the program. They had to specify the relationship between the probation officer and the detention staff and specify in what ways detainees would be handled and by what criteria. The result was that many of the issues that could not be directly tackled before were brought up in the course of the attempt to make the program clear for detainees.

At about this time, some major changes took place. The chief administrative officer of the service took a new job. Administrative reassignment of the psychologist and a change of duties for the social worker brought the weekly meetings to a sudden and unforeseen end after the twentieth meeting, some twenty-five weeks after the first meeting. Hastily constructed opinion questionnaires showed that the staff had seen the consultants' work as generally positive, although it was plain that the field trip and the general information provided were overtly more popular than the consultants' efforts to stimulate program clarification and internal change.

Follow-up three months later showed that the brochure and the pegboard had become integral elements in a more defined and purposeful program. Not all staff liked the accountability and the need to be consistent. The detention supervisor had elaborated the program and the pegboard system to the point where the neighboring county wanted to hire him on a federally funded demonstration project. Follow-up ten months later showed that the pegboard was still in use and that still other elaborations of the program—ways to earn and spend points—had been developed. The brochure for detainees had captured the staff's attention as a vehicle for formalizing and summarizing objectives, relationships, and expectations. It was in its second edition and used routinely.

THE CONSULTATION PROCESS—THREE ESSENTIALS

Establishing a Sound Relationship

The first difficulty a psychologist experiences when he undertakes to work with organizations is a lack of awareness of what he has to offer. He cannot assume that his efforts to help will be welcomed. He must make himself known in such a way that he will be invited—and invited back—as a consultant. This calls for more than a simple passive announcement of availability. An active out-reach program to make contact with organizations whose goals and methods do not always coincide with his must be planned.

It may be necessary to overcome negative feelings that have arisen from previous contacts with mental health "experts." Because in the past, mental health consultants, especially psychiatrists, were expected to provide instant answers to serious human problems, it was inevitable that disappointments occurred. Community leaders became disillusioned about intrapsychic approaches and turned to what they considered more realistic ways of dealing with problems. An officer of the Juvenile Court, for example, may say, "I've got four fatherless fourteen-year-olds in a cell big enough for two—I already know that it would be nice if they could all have a deep meaningful relationship with a mature father figure. It's not worth spending money for psychologicals. What can we *do* that will change their behavior in the community?" The head of public assistance may say, "It's no use sending low income families over to the clinic. None of the young children from First Street dares cooperate in the doll play because they'd be laughed out of existence in the neighborhood—and if a twelve-year-old ever stopped long enough to say to the sixteen-year-old who's taking his bicycle, "You must have some deep feelings about this,' he might get killed."

Although psychologists must actively seek to be involved in consultation, they should remember that the persons carrying on the work of the organization have skills and experience different from theirs and operate under pressures with which psychologists are unfamiliar. The court officer, for instance, may be handling contacts with angry juveniles, angry parents, the police, the judges, and the caseworkers under a pressure many people would find intolerable. The psychologist's contributions will be enriched by his appreciation of the strength and skills of the people he works with. It is particularly important in work with organizations that the consultant check his expectations with those of the people with whom he is consulting.

Getting these expectations straight often requires candid, open discussion of such questions as: "Ideally, what would you like to see us be able to do together?" Note that the question suggests that something less than ideal may happen and also that consultant and consultee will work together as peers. It is important that the situation be structured in such a way that it does not produce dependency on outside experts. The agreement between consultant and organization may be modified as time passes. Getting to understand one another is a continuing process.

Involving Others in Decision Making

The degree to which others are involved in decision making frequently determines the degree of commitment, involvement, and loyalty which they will show about an activity. The psychologist who goes to a local park to organize recreation among neighborhood children, and to learn about the grassroots needs of the families there, soon has to ask himself what he expects of the parents. Even though he could develop a program more rapidly and smoothly by ignoring the children's parents, it would be unwise in the long run for him to cut himself off from parent involvement and support. In order to interest the parents and involve them actively he must let them participate in the basic decisions about what is to be done. Our extended illustration earlier showed some of the difficulties and advantages of involving others in decisions. In another kind of setting Ellsworth and co-workers (1971), who examined nineteen treatment units in five Veterans Administration Hospitals, found that the effective programs were characterized by active participant roles for both nursing staff and patients.

Paying Attention to Outcome

Consulting rarely has a textbook completeness about it, as our extended example tried to convey. Classic cases where the consultation leads to clear changes in procedures which bring about clear improvements in clients are rare. It is the consultant's responsibility, however, to evaluate the outcomes. It is not easy to find appropriate criteria. In his brief but important article on choosing criteria for evaluating consultation, Barry (1970) says that the criteria for evaluating consultation should state the ultimate goal to be achieved, frequently a goal set by the consultee or his organization. One gross but practical indicator of effectiveness is whether or not the consultee again seeks consultation, although repeated invitations may, of course, reflect only the dependency one wishes to avoid. While the controlled research approach is too ponderous to be practical, some procedure for analyzing what happened to clients as a result of the consultation should be adopted. The extent to which the consultee understood, accepted, and applied the information provided should be assessed. It is sometimes appropriate to break the consultation process into parts and evaluate them separately. Gibb (1959), for instance, has identified eight steps: (1) entry into the relationship, (2) diagnosis or evaluation of the problems, (3) data collection, (4) establishing a relationship, (5) defining the limits of consultation, (6) developing resources needed to solve the problem, (7) decision making, and (8) termination.

Barry stressed the need for new research procedures to evaluate the effectiveness of consultation. However, even in the absence of formal measures and designs, consultants should specify criteria and arrange for an after-the-fact review of the degree to which the criteria were met.

APPRAISAL OF ORGANIZATIONS AS ONGOING SYSTEMS

As explained in earlier chapters, designing improvement programs involves, first, appraisal of the way the client is now functioning. When the client is an organization, the task is somewhat different from the task of assessing an individual or a small group. The consultation team in our extended illustration assessed the juvenile court's organization system in informal ways. They examined aspects of the organization's history, its divisions of labor or role patterns, the communication patterns among staff and between staff and detainees, and analyzed how these had changed in the new building. Clinical psychologists are often not familiar with the techniques organizational psychologists have developed for such assessments. Some knowledge, at least of the basic concepts, is helpful.

Organizational Theory Applied to Schools

Schmuck and co-workers (1972) have furnished a useful amalgamation of general systems theory and organizational theory in their plan for producing organizational changes in schools. It rests on four postulates about schools as systems and subsystems: (1) schools are composed of basic units referred to as components (e.g., people, curriculum); (2) as living systems, schools are goal-directed, (3) schools as systems are open and adaptable; and (4) the subsystems that constitute a school contain many resources that at any time are not being used. Such a repertoire of resources is referred to as a *variety pool*.

The four postulates lead to conclusions about intervention:

1. Interventions will be more efficient if they deal with subsystems and not just randomly selected components. (As an interesting example, the authors cite that training a principal in new skills of interpersonal relations will not necessarily affect the organizational patterns of his staff when he returns to his school, whereas training a group of interacting teachers may.)

2. Interventions should confront the school with discrepancies between the goals it strives for and actual goal achievement.

3. Interventions should be aimed at making every subsystem in the school district more open to other subsystems.

4. Interventions should (a) help the school define its variety pool by identifying system-wide resources, and (b) help the school to build communication connections between components and subsystems.

Adaptability, the primary characteristic organizational intervention seeks to increase, depends on the openness of a school district to its environment, on its responsiveness (and on the way it selects what to respond to), and on the use it makes of the variety pool. Resources in the variety pool include innovative ideas and the skills of specially trained teachers. What must be fostered if the variety pool is to be utilized are attitudes that question established patterns and foster creative risk-taking.

As they look at internal features of school districts, Schmuck and co-workers apply concepts from organizational theory, as presented by Lorsch and Lawrence (1970). *Differentiation and integration* have four subdivisions: (1) structural formality (relative degree of reliance on formal rules and procedures and tight control), (2) goal orientation, (3) time orientation, and (4) interpersonal orientations (concerns for task accomplishment versus relationships with others). Effective organization requires that subsystems have a degree of actual differentiation consistent with the degree of differentiation required by the environment.

Norms within the school district give it structure and coherence. Members of the staff behave in patterned, predictable ways because their behaviors are guided by common expectations, attitudes, and understandings. Norms define organizational climates. *Roles*, sets of working activities, accomplish differentiation and integration within subsystems. Consistent with the suggestion elsewhere in the chapter that looking for pathology in employees creates problems rather than solves problems, Schmuck and his colleages state (1972, p. 13): "Since role-taking always involves interactions, the focus of organizational training should *not* be placed on the internal dynamics of any one participant, but rather on the behavior patterns which link two or more role reciprocators."

In their comments on patterns of motivation and emotion, the authors note that people invest emotion in at least three domains: achievement, affiliation, and power. Power concerns, or problems of authority, occupy a prominent place in this era of American society, they state.

Applying these ideas, what the consultant tries to help his client organization accomplish is to clarify communication, establish objectives, uncover conflicts and interdependencies, improve group procedure, solve problems, make decisions, and assess change.

Students should note that a future agenda for clinical psychologists working with organizations is to develop or adapt theoretical perspectives and approaches in their inventions. Sociological theories, such as that of Parsons (Black, 1961), need further refinement before they can be applied in practical situations with the same effect that personality theories have for individuals.

One problematic aspect of working with organizations is the almost inevitable conflict between individual and institutional values and needs. The bureaucracy prospers by subordinating personal interests. Fullest development of the personal system may occur with either a high degree of self-interest or an emphasis on dedication and sacrifice to organizational goals. In assessing an organization, a psychologist may find that workers are required to ignore their own interests in favor of the organization's.

No clear resolutions to these basic dilemmas appear to be forthcoming. Some consultants speculate that good organizational management may involve moving slowly back and forth between the poles. Perhaps, as when sleeping in bed, no one position suffices and we must change positions from time to time, not because any are bad, but because we eventually tire of them.

In our appraisal of organizations, clinical psychologists need to be especially concerned about prematurely invoking ideas of personal psychopathology. If people feel bad and act unconstructively in organizations, it may not be that they have anything wrong within the realm of their personal system, such as maladjustment or psychopathology. Imposed solutions to the dilemmas of social relations may be at fault. Blatant disregard of individual feelings or individual achievements may be causing pain. Equally possibly, unfairness or inequality may be involved.

EVALUATION OF RESULTS
IN APPRAISING ORGANIZATIONS

In an appraisal of an organization, attention must be paid to its output. What is it accomplishing? How effective is it? These questions may involve the consultant in assessment at lower system levels than that of the organization itself. Every organization has effects on biologic systems (even by failing to provide a hot lunch), personal systems, families, other organizations, and the community. When we ask about effectiveness, then, we must specify the system we are concerned with, and must recall that other systems are affected, too.

Fifteen-year-old Georgie N and her mother had been outpatients of a mental health center for about a year. The mother, who had complained of Georgie's insolence and poor study habits, had been involved in weekly casework. The contacts were terminated because the psychiatric resident who had seen Georgie was being reassigned, and her problems seemed not to be severe enough to justify including her on the next year's waiting list. During the year the mother had developed a great deal more understanding about herself and her family. Georgie had formed an intense relationship with the young resident. She had become less overtly insolent according to her mother, who said her school work was "a bit better." How effective had the work of the mental health center been?

There was some difference of opinion among staff members about this. The psychiatric resident who had been seeing Georgie was impressed with the personality changes he observed in her, but a psychology intern argued that one would need evidence from personality tests or ratings before and after treatment in order to draw this conclusion. The social worker criticized the psychiatrist and the psychologist for paying attention to just one person, and pointed to beneficial changes in the way Georgie got on with her peers and in the way family members interacted with one another. The psychologist insisted that these changes also ought to be measured objectively. Thus there was no clear verdict as to whether the clinic had been effective at the personal system level.

How effective had the clinic been in producing desirable changes at the organizational level? Georgie's school was pleased with her progress, and her principal chalked up one more "successful liaison" for his annual report. The mental health center itself had "done its thing"—one more resident trained, one more chart for the vault. But the school was not changed in structure or function by this experience, and the community was no better able than before to handle the problems of poverty, housing, employment, drugs, and illegitimacy with which it was struggling. Judged by its organizational impact, the clinic's service to Georgie N seemed only minimally effective.

At what system level should an organization like the mental health center be accountable for demonstrating favorable outcome if we assume that proof of effectiveness is mandatory for publicly supported organizations? There is little agreement in the mental health movement on the question of which kinds of systems should be examined for change. Are changes in personal indices such as self-report or observational data more valuable than changes in the community divorce rate? Are changes in a family's interaction patterns more valuable than changes in the way a school teaches about mental health and community living? The selection of the system level for evaluating mental health organization is difficult. For mental hospitals, legal requirements and the presence of florid signs of deviancy make the choice of the personal system a good deal more obvious. A good example of such evaluation is the work of Ellsworth et al. (1968), which we summarize at the end of the chapter.

Evaluation of Cost-Effectiveness

Increasingly organizations are being required to produce evidence about the costs of the services they provide, together with evidence of their effectiveness. This is because helping services compete for public funds, and there is never enough money to finance all worthy projects and organizations. Officials who make budgetary decisions require certain kinds of accounting and cost-control practices. Psychologists in a mental health center, for example, may be asked to account for their time each day to the nearest fifteen minutes, and calculate quarterly the cost per interview.

Although this is an extreme and easily questioned sort of cost accounting, mental health organizations are learning to live with the idea that good professional work and sound business practices can coexist. Macleod (1971) describes a system used at the famous South Shore Mental Health Center in Massachusetts. Basically the new system divided services into five main categories—clinical service, community service, retardation and rehabilitation service, training, and research—each of which was subdivided into specific programs. Under clinical service, for instance, five programs were listed—child, adult, aftercare, disturbed children's nursery, and court-requested evaluations. In all twenty-six programs were identified. Next, the director obtained periodic estimates from the staff as to the percentage of their time given to each of the twenty-six programs. From those figures, with overhead costs added in proportion, a crude cost per program was derived. Macleod noted (1971, p. 52): "Even a rough idea of the cost of a program is so useful that arguments about precision are reduced to the level of quibbles."

Such a cost-accounting system in an organization provides useful information to professional workers as well as to accountants at budget time. Macleod cites, for example, that by making a 5 percent cut in the children's program, funds for doubling the work with police could be obtained. Although such information does not make the ethical decisions about the relative worth of different kinds of services, it does give the psychologist-administrator a way to respond to the demands for business practices and to explain what funds are being used for and why. It may serve to protect the organization from arbitrary budget cuts and unjustified criticism.

THE PSYCHOLOGIST IN ADMINISTRATION

As suggested by the foregoing discussion, the management of organizations is of crucial importance. With increasing frequency the psychologist finds himself taking on administrative duties. Feinberg (1971) reminds us that the administrator's job is to plan, organize, assemble resources, direct, and control. To do this well calls for specific administrative skills and training. Does the psychologist's training and experience help or hinder him in these efforts? Feinberg asked the opinion of a number of adminstrators, psychologists, and others. The advantages they saw were things like sensitivity to individual differences, awareness of social and psychological forces, objectivity and skill in communication, selection, and evaluation. But they considered that the psychologist-administrator also faced certain special difficulties, such as a tendency to overanalyze workers, conflicts between helping and controlling roles, an overemphasis on empirical data as a basis for decisions, and the lack of certain essential management skills.

Peter Drucker, responding as an outside management expert to Feinberg's opinion survey, summarized the advantages and disadvantages of psychologist training (Feinberg, 1971, p. 113):

> If the administrator becomes concerned with the clinical understanding of human behavior, he, almost at once, loses sight of the purpose of the effectiveness of the organization, of the objective results which are its only reason for existence. But in a different sense, I think the ability to understand human behavior helps the administrator not in understanding the people who work under him, but, I believe, in understanding himself. A good manager is always conscious of his own weakness and limitations. For the first, the clinical approach is a real handicap. For the second, it is probably invaluable.

Decisions about Objectives and Priorities

Every organization needs to know "where it's going." It needs a clear understanding of its responsibilities, goals, and service priorities. Some settings in which psychologists work, such as state hospitals, have rather clear mandates, while others, such as community mental health centers, are continually struggling with questions of how to be more effective with a greater number of clients.

One common problem faced by many out-patient clinics is how to restrict the flow of direct service cases (therapy, evaluation, etc.) so that staff members have the time necessary to carry on the kinds of consultation we have been discussing in this chapter. They find it difficult to change their patterns of activity because of their concern for "the people we have to turn away." In one child guidance clinic, the chief psychologist began the process of reorganizing the agency's patterns of activity by writing down some ideas for the staff to think about and discuss. Dr. Ormiston's memorandum to the staff included the following:

These notes are written in an attempt to distinguish the problem of giving service to the vast number of people who need it from the problem of having too big a direct service intake.

Many need service

If we grant that our catchment area has roughly some 200,000 inhabitants and perhaps some 45,000 children, then we could imagine that between 10–15,000 children are in need of mental health assistance of some kind. Enlarging the area in question to the whole city gives a figure of roughly 30,000 children and I couldn't face generating the figure for the county.

Few apply

These figures suggest that the intake or service request population is very special population and that our caseload which stems from the intake group is equally special. I have tried to list some possible factors which make for the reduction from 10,000 to the 400 that we see in a year.

Possible reduction factors

Assignment of a priority to certain types of cases that we may decide to see.

The client's area of residence.

The use of a waiting list as a caseload limiting or client discouragement device.

The restriction of time given to outpatient cases. (Historically, the restriction has been on the basis of the work week but it may of course be shorter than that.)

The behavior of referral sources—e.g. frequency and types of people they send.

The public's awareness of our service pattern.

The way the public and the referral sources define some behaviors as problems.

The way we provide alternative service to direct caseload services.

The way in which and the rate at which we refer clients elsewhere.

The ways in which we have strengthened or failed to strengthen existing services in the community.

The degree to which we are unknown or misconstrued.

The degree to which we are unapproachable or incompatible with potential clients.

The degree to which a clinic or center might have a bad reputation.

Conclusions

This list should be studied and refined.

As a staff we should give attention to each of these elements so that our caseload can be controlled in a planned way with the most effective outcome for the large number of clients who need service.

Whatever we decide upon as a way of limiting direct service cases should be made overt and generally published rather than being covert.

Our guilt feelings about rejecting applicants for direct service should be balanced by guilt feelings that a vastly greater number of people in serious need have been customarily ignored by mental health.

Dr. Ormiston's notes were amended by other staff members who offered additional reasons for the particular intake situation. Each reason was then examined and the staff began the long process of trying to establish desired and realistic controls on the direct service load by generating new priorities and by actively regulating client contacts. The process of sharing ideas openly and motivating the staff by involving them in decisions is an especially important one for psychologists in administrative positions.

Improving Internal Functioning

Bringing about change in an organization is difficult. Tradition and economic restraints play a large part, but often the greatest opposition comes from a group with a vested interest, whose present status or equilibrium appears threatened. It is not uncommon, for instance, for the psychology service in a mental hospital to meet opposition to new program proposals from other services, such as psychiatry, nursing, or even housekeeping. Sometimes such opposition is reasoned and most responsible. On many occasions, however, preservation of status, power, and equilibrium are the main reasons for opposition. Similarly, the psychologists in a hospital sometimes oppose responsible innovation by other services. Change may be threatening to any of these professional workers since it often involves having one's effectiveness or usefulness measured and compared with that of others.

There seem to be few guidelines for successful induction of change. As far as possible, people like to be involved in decision making about their own roles and futures. They need a clear set of expectations about the new roles and to have access to channels of communication and feedback so they may continue to feel themselves to be a contributing part of the process. Reward or reinforcement comes from an increased sense of worth and the satisfaction one gets from seeing clients benefit from the changes. It is often easier to involve aides and attendants in an innovative program than to involve professional workers.

ORGANIZATIONAL INNOVATION: AN EXAMPLE

Making a go of a new organization, no matter how dedicated its staff is, requires a great deal of leadership. Not only must the organization relate productively to segments of the community (and "productively" generally means that besides good will, money must be forthcoming) but it must perform its function to the benefit of both clients and staff. In the example which follows, the prime movers were a local physician and two graduate students in counseling psychology. The setting is a university town. The three leaders, having decided together that they wanted to do something relevant to the widespread alienation of young people, undertook a study of local, state, and national aspects of the problem of alienation. Using the resulting understandings, they began a six-month planning effort, which included making and maintaining contact with all agencies in any way involved in service to youth. They were particularly attentive to the establishment of good relations with the police system, since policemen often are involved in drug-abuse incidents. The leaders studied current drug information and research and the political processes of the local community. They drew up alternative models and selected among them.

For the White Bird Socio-Medical Clinic, as it came to be called, five maxims stood the test of time and appeared fruitful.

1. Gain community support, confidence, and awareness before initiating the service.

2. Attempt to keep the financial base small and keep support at the local level (city, donations, fund raising, etc.).

3. Use a staff consisting of 90 percent volunteers from all areas of the community, with strong support from various professional groups.

4. Maintain effort and accountability with growth.

5. Gradually expand the facility, depending and relying upon other groups' involvement and help (e.g., the medical laboratory was designed and staffed by local lab technicians).

The threefold purpose of the clinic became (1) to provide medical, dental, and psychological services to alienated youth and individuals with drug problems, (2) to serve as a middle ground, where people from different segments of the community could meet—to be a "neutral" setting; and (3) to serve as a central informational resource center providing valid, reliable, unbiased data on drug use and abuse, and to attempt to correct prevalent misinformation. The Clinic incorporated as a nonprofit corporation with a board of 20 directors and a staff of over 300 volunteer workers and 11 "core" members (paid nominal salaries).

After six months of operation the clinic closed for a week to reorganize its internal structure. It changed from a horizontal "everybody doing everything" operation to a standard vertical or bureaucratic organizational hierarchy. Intensive review of the year's experience with the vertical system revealed that service had been better than it previously was, but discussion also showed that paying the staff different "nominal" salaries for the same amount of effort helped create a competitive, alienating atmosphere. The majority of the paid staff became overworked and tired; motivation declined. The vertical arrangement created subgroups (e.g., the counselors, the receptionists), each close within itself but giving rise to ethnocentrism and alienation between groups. Finally, the vertical arrangement showed that the Peter Principle (people rise in a bureaucracy to their level of incompetence) could appear even in this unorthodox clinic.

After many hours of considering the results of the vertical year, the staff decided to make another pair of major changes. First, the clinic was divided into two major functions separated geographically, treatment and rehabilitation going into one old house, and prevention and education into another. The second change entailed beginning a "horizontal/lateral" organization for the paid staff. With the exception of the clinic director and the clinic physician, all paid positions were designed to carry equal responsibilities and hence were paid the same salary. The clinic staff was convinced of the advantages of eliminating status differentiation and providing easy lateral transfer (presumably after training). Their report forthrightly noted, however, that if that system failed to serve clients and staff well, it would be changed.

This final illustration points to an observation about organizations. (For other observations of free clinics, see Freudenberger, 1971.) Any chosen pattern may be imperfect and every pattern may need to be changed from time to time or abandoned. The test of an organization is its ability to remain open and adaptive enough to respond to its changing internal subsystems and external ecology—to keep sufficient structure to maintain itself if that seems desirable and sufficient flexibility to redirect itself when that is needed.

SUMMARY

Working with organizations enables psychologists to increase their outreach and promote the well-being of larger numbers of clients. Attempts to improve the way organizations function are particularly important when the organizations are doing an inadequate job or actively detracting from the quality of life. It is difficult, however, to change organizations and still more difficult to create new ones. We must remember also that organizations may actually weaken or undercut existing adaptive mechanisms in community or family systems.

Psychologists differ in the degree to which they see the individual as client or the organization as client. Organizations relevant to human well-being form a complicated network in the community, a network it is well to become familiar with.

Consultation with organizations often grows out of discussion of an individual client. If the discussion is to move to consideration of program, the consultant must show a nonpassive respectful openness to the consultee's strengths, involve others in the decision-making process, and pay attention to outcomes.

Techniques for assessing the structure and internal functioning of organizations are not highly developed. Such skills are mainly the province of
organizational psychologists and applied sociologists. Some concepts from
organizational theory are useful to clinical psychologists.

Assessing output characteristics of organizations, notably mental health
organizations, becomes increasingly important as the practice of management by
objectives spreads. Psychologists will do well to become familiar with evaluation
techniques for programs and organizations because (1) there is increasing
likelihood psychologists may enter administrative positions, (2) evaluation skills
may be one of the psychologist's most important assets, and (3) increasingly,
funds will depend on effective evaluation. Psychologists going into administrative positions have certain advantages over other administrators but must acquire
some additional skills.

SUGGESTED READINGS

Argyris, C. *Intervention, theory and method: a behavioral science view.* Reading,
    Mass.: Addison-Wesley, 1970.

Three broad approaches to modifying organizations have been advanced:
changing structure, changing technology, and changing interpersonal relationships. Argyris is one of the leading proponents of the interpersonal approach. His
book suggests roles and functions for an internal agent "interventionist" who
functions as an organizational catalyst.

American Institutes for Research. *Evaluative research: strategies and methods.*
    Pittsburgh: American Institutes for Research, 1970.

This book is the report of a seminar by the same title. It contains eight papers
each with a comment by one of two discussants. Carver's paper on the special
problems of measuring change with psychometric devices gives support to using
criterion reference measures rather than norm-referenced tests in evaluating;
Gold's illustrations of evaluating a complex social program and Flanagan and
Jung's illustration of evaluating a comprehensive educational system provide
concrete introductions to the enormity, complexity, and necessity of the
evaluation process. The papers' references give a good sampling of the evaluation
literature and the book's summary, a précis of the papers' main ideas. Another
resource is Suchman's *Evaluative Research: Principles and Practice in Public
Service and Social Action Programs* (1967).

Koontz, H., and O'Donnell, C. *Principles of management: an analysis of
    managerial functions,* 5th ed. New York: McGraw-Hill, 1972.

The psychologist or the would-be psychologist who is confronted by the need
for managerial skills must do more than read books. But skimming such a book
as the highly regarded introductory text by Koontz and O'Donnell is useful in
obtaining an understanding of the scope and the basic concepts and processes in

managing organizations. Some of the ideas from business and public administration may prove useful in human service operations. For those interested in PPB (Planning-Programming-Budgeting), the book edited by Lyden and Miller (1972) will be useful. A similar systematic approach with a different title is *Management by Objectives* (Association for Systems Management, 1971). Drucker (1967) and Odiorne (1969) would also prove useful. Squire (1970) presents several reports of the application of administrative practices to psychiatric services; the reader should also see Pratt's critical review of Squire's book (1971).

March, J. G. (ed.). *Handbook of organizations.* Chicago: Rand McNally, 1965.

This large book is a collection of excellent articles on almost every topic related to organizations—individual decision making and problem solving (by Donald Taylor), organizational decision making (by Feldman and Kanter), and the interaction of small groups with organizations (by Golembiewski and by Shepard). Another helpful reference would be Katz and Kahn, *The Social Psychology of Organizations* (1966). Two good books on organizational development are an introductory one by Bennis (1969) and a book on process consultation by Schein (1969). Schmidt's book (1970) discusses organizations from the standpoint of the need to change them to be more consistent with human values. Levinson (1972) presents the clinical psychologist as an "organizational diagnostician."

Schulman, J. *Remaking an organization: innovation in a specialized psychiatric hospital.* Albany, N. Y.: State University of New York, 1969.

This is one of a few books in recent years that have tried to analyze changes in psychiatric and mental health organizations. A sociologist acting as a participant observer, Schulman studied over a hundred innovations in a New York psychiatric setting. Among many rather complicated findings, Schulman shows that higher-ranking persons are much more likely to get their innovations adopted. Other interesting studies of mental health organizations include Ullman's (1967) comparison of thirty VA psychiatric hospitals, Graziano's report (1969) on the resistance of the mental health power structure to change in a community. Kahana and Kahana (1970) demonstrated that changing elderly patients from an age-segregated to an age-intergrated ward improved their mental status and responsiveness. Although it pertains to an industrial organization, the twenty-year history of counseling in the Western Electric Company, growing out of the famous Hawthorne studies, would be of interest to students of clinical work; Bromer (1968) reviews the book by Dickson and Roethlisberger (1966) and adds observations of his own to explain the failure of this counseling as an agent of change; this work also has relevance to the use of nonprofessionals in community mental health work.

Terreberry, S. The evolution of organizational environments. *Administrative Science Quarterly*, 1968, *12*, 590–613.

Bringing together a general systems viewpoint and the perspective of evolution, Terreberry points to the importance of looking at the environment in which an organization is developing. Her review of the literature gives evidence of the decreasing autonomy and increasing interdependence of organizations. The implication is that the consultant to an organization must assess not only the internal dynamics but also the input of information and support (e.g., budgetary influences) for the organization and its responsiveness and adaptability in return. Terreberry's thesis is that "the selective advance of one intra- or inter-organizational configuration over another cannot be assessed apart from an understanding of the dynamics of the environment itself. It is the environment which exerts selective pressure. 'Survival of the fittest' is a function of the fitness of the environment. The dinosaurs *were* impressive creatures, in their day" (p. 613).

RESEARCH EXAMPLES

Goodwin, D. L., Garvey, W. P., and Barclay, J. R. Microconsultation and behavior analysis: a method of training psychologists as behavioral consultants. *Journal of Consulting and Clinical Psychology*, 1971, *37*, 355–363.

Microconsultation is a method of training modeled after the microteaching format of Bush and Allen (1964). Both procedures consist of a series of brief face-to-face practice sessions designed to give the trainee an opportunity to acquire specific skills in a naturalistic setting. The microconsultation procedure (1) identified the skills to be learned, (2) showed trainees a model performing the skills, and (3) gave the trainees videotaped practice in using the techniques until criterion levels were attained. The purpose was to train school psychologists to apply behavior-modification techniques in the classroom. The behavioral-analysis procedure consisted of four main steps: (1) selecting a target behavior for change, (2) identifying environmental events sustaining the target behaviors, (3) planning a strategy for change, and (4) evaluating the program for change.

The authors assert that the approach shows exactly what needs to be changed, and leads, therefore, to the development of a strategy—a radical difference from traditional assessment procedures. Also, they say, it is important to note that what is eventually changed is the environment itself.

Groups of thirty school psychologists comprised the experimental, control A, and control B groups. The experimental group received pretest, eight-week microconsultation institute, posttest, and field observation. Control B had the same activities except that video training only was substituted for microconsultation. Control A was an inactive control, receiving only the field observation, which took place two months after the institute, in Ss home school district. Scores on pretest, posttest, and field observations consisted of ratings of twenty categories (e.g., structures interview, identifies reinforcers, suggests dynamic interpretation, reviews behavioral data) relevant to the sequence of a school psychologist's engagement with a problem.

The microconsultation group showed marked and lasting changes in interview techniques associated with microconsultation training. The authors feel that the microconsultation format shows a great deal of potential because of the brief

8-week involvement used in the change of behavior of traditionally trained and traditionally functioning school psychologists. They imply that analogous techniques hold promise for helping clients systematically modify their own behavior.

From the working with organizations perspective, this project is an excellent example of clarity in definition, delivery, and measurement. Next steps might be to assess the program's impact on the organization: How well were the psychologists—with their new behavioral patterns—reintegrated into their school system? How did the organization handle any reactions to the loss of the familiar traditional perspectives—for instance, was a service needed to help teachers understand, accept, or use the new resources?

Frankel (1971) evaluated the effects of videotape modeling and videotape feedback on the counseling behavior of undergraduate trainees learning microcounseling. Judges found that both techniques increased the frequency but not the accuracy of focus on client feeling.

Robins, L. N. *Deviant children grown up.* Baltimore: Williams & Wilkins, 1966.

Robins' book, a longitudinal study of children seen at a child-guidance clinic, is, in effect, a study of the effectiveness of an organization. Although it is written from a rather medical perspective—emphasis on diagnostic categories and on the notion of sociopathy as a disease—the study deserves serious consideration because of its careful execution, large scale, and notable findings.

Robins investigated the adult status of 524 former child-guidance patients. She used 100 controls matched for age, sex, race, intelligence, and neighborhood origin. Extensive structured interviewing constituted the major data source, along with the clinic's and other records.

Serious antisocial behavior in childhood was a particularly ominous childhood pattern. It appeared that the clinic had virtually failed to affect the course of the antisocial or sociopathic child. The study was not able to investigate the environmental teaching of antisocial behavior, though it did establish that antisocial behavior in the father was associated with similar behavior in the offspring, both when young and when mature.

Any organization dealing with antisocial children needs to ask itself if its program is influencing their behavior—and if it isn't, why continue.

Ellsworth, R. B., Foster, L., Childers, B., Arthur, G., and Kroeker, D. Hospital and community adjustment as perceived by psychiatric patients, their families, and staff. *Journal of Consulting and Clinical Psychology Monographs*, 1968, *32*, No. 5, Part 2, 1—41.

In a significant and careful study, Ellsworth and co-workers attempted to evaluate the outcomes of psychiatric hospitalization as perceived by staff, patients, and their relatives. They point out that although most professionals want to know something about the effectiveness or treatment procedure, there is doubt about the best data source (patient, relatives, or professionals) doubt about reliabilities and validities, and uncertainty about which kinds of adjustment and functioning to measure. Their subjects were 178 male veterans, diagnosed as schizophrenic, who met a number of criteria, such as being in the community at least 100 days prior to admission, being under 60 years of age, and having an identifiable informant who could be visited by the team social workers.

Twenty dimensions of adjustment were scored from five different rating scales, yielding a variety of behavioral adjustment data, including patient's behavior (1–9), community adjustment (10–15), social-work scale (16–19), and patient self-rating scale (20). Data collection was scheduled at four times: at admission, two months postadmission, three weeks after release, and three months after release. The authors divided their study into four main sections:

1. Comparing the validity and reliability of staff, patient, and family ratings of patients' hospital and community adjustment. The results indicated that all three rating sources—patients, staff, and families—were acceptably reliable. Patients' self-ratings had no predictive validity for length of hospitalization, which family and staff ratings predicted equally well. Staff ratings were slightly higher in their relationship to rehospitalization than family ratings, but not significantly so.

2. Adjustments following hospitalization showed that symptom areas of adjustment were significantly and pointedly affected by hospitalization as viewed by all raters (family, staff, and patient). Instrumental performance and social behavior were less affected, with employment showing a slight posthospital decline. Conforming behavior was higher in the hospital than in the community, and community improvement was typically maintained between the third and twelfth posthospital week. The authors suggest that "if a patient's primary problem is an area of role functioning (i.e., work and/or social involvement), psychiatric hospital programs may not be especially relevant" (p. 23).

3. Congruence between community and hospital adjustment and behavior showed that no overall congruence was found between patients' initial hospital adjustment and their preadmission community behavior. Similarly, no overall relationship was found between hospital adjustment at release and posthospital adjustment. The writers found that behavioral consistency was greatest across time when rater, scale, and situation were held constant. They concluded that behavior and adjustment are greatly affected by situational changes, suggesting that behavioral determinants are more situationally than personally related phenomena. Based on these findings, the writers ask interesting questions about the utility or relevance of certain traditional procedures. It may be an error, they suggest, to try to identify a patient's relevant problems through psychiatric interview at the time of admission. An appreciable amount of his symptomatology may be a function of being in the hospital setting. Similarly, they point out that if the patient's adjustment and functioning in the hospital does not predict his community functioning, it becomes hard to see how the hospital staff can make decisions about readiness for release on the basis of the patient's hospital behavior.

4. Assessment of treatment outcome used community informants—usually relatives of the patient—to provide relevant and economical outcome data without investment of substantial professional time. The writers emphasize the importance of using the residual score method of handling before and after scores to avoid effects due to level of initial score. They found no relationship

between hospital and community improvement, noting that the patient showing improvement in the hospital is not necessarily a community-improved patient. The before and after community adjustment profiles have been used first, to give the ward treatment team a picture of the areas of adjustment that represent problems in community functioning for the particular patient. Later, after discharge the same system is used to provide the ward team with information on their patient's level of posthospital functioning in the community. The writers discuss the impact that such knowledge of results can have on treatment teams, both for identifying strengths and weaknesses of their own programs and for examining the effectiveness of innovations.

chapter 17

Working with Communities and Society

In Chapter 16 we examined the part psychologists play in agencies and organizations. Complicated as these systems are, they are themselves subsystems of the community and society as a whole. Increasingly psychologists are directing their efforts to these more-inclusive systems, these systems of systems. There is much confusion still about how this can best be done, but community psychology is being practiced and is giving rise to new programs and new ideas about human betterment. We shall consider these efforts in this chapter.

While the establishment of community psychology as a separate field is a development of the 1960s, stimulated by the legislation setting up community mental health centers and the Boston conference (Bennett et al., 1966), and given official status when a Division of Community Psychology within the American Psychological Association was set up in 1966, psychologists have been concerned with community problems for a much longer time. Lightner Witmer reached out to homes and schools in his clinical work. John Dewey in 1899 entitled his presidential address to the American Psychological Association "Psychology and Social Practice." Freud's book *Civilization and Its Discontents* was published in 1930. Kurt Lewin, in the 1930s and 1940s, stimulated a great deal of interest in action research, carried on by participating members of community organizations. What is occurring now is the professionalization of this area of psychology, making it possible for practitioners to focus their efforts on community improvement.

It is often difficult to establish clear boundaries between community psychology and other professions with similar objectives. Social workers, for example, have been involved in community efforts for a long time. Economists, political scientists, urban planners, and public administrators are all engaged in attempts to improve communities, and it is not always clear where psychology ends and political science, for example, begins. But such "jurisdictional disputes" need not trouble us. There are challenging tasks enough for all.

Working with communities is so different from what we often considered to be the typical roles a clinical psychologist plays that some might question whether he or she belongs in this field at all. When we look more closely, however, at the central purpose to be served by community work, we see that it is, in fact, the same as that which has always characterized clinical psychology— to understand and improve the functioning of the *person in context*. Community psychology is continuous with clinical psychology. What it does is to expand the range of interventions that can be attempted in order to bring about better functioning of individuals by considering more aspects of the context, more system levels, in the designing of improvement programs. The psychologist's general orientation and special training enables him to keep the basic purpose of community efforts at any level constantly in mind.

THE MEANING OF COMMUNITY

The word "community" is related to the words "common," "communion," and "communication." It expresses the idea of human relatedness and of common sharing—a body of people living in the same place under the same laws and regulations, as one dictionary says.

There are several ways of conceptualizing a community. One way is to emphasize *common interests and strivings of individuals*. This sense of the common identity and cooperation is exemplified by Klein (1968, p. 11): "The community ... may be defined as *patterned interactions within a domain of individuals seeking to achieve security and physical safety, to derive support at times of stress and to gain selfhood and significance throughout the life cycle.*" This kind of definition, which might be applied to other groups as well, emphasizes the social-psychological benefits of working together.

Klein's definition reminds us of the wide-ranging functions of the community. It is responsible for meeting human needs over the whole hierarchy described by Abraham Maslow (1954, 1968, 1971): the fundamental physiological needs for food, air, and other basic life support; the safety needs; needs for belongingness and love, needs for recognition and esteem; and needs for self-actualization, knowledge, and beauty. Maslow indicates that if a lower need, such as safety, is sufficiently satisfied, then the satisfaction of other higher needs, such as recognition and self-actualization, will be sought. In an analogous way, human beings in communities can move to the common attainment of higher satisfactions if basic needs are taken care of. In times of internal stress and polarization, the social body may slip from a concern for enhancement of positive aspects of life, such as education and culture, to a concern for "law and order." As reading of newspapers makes clear, a wide diversity of human needs is being expressed and promoted in communities at any one time.

Another way to conceptualize community is to define it as a *sociogeographical* locality—a town, a neighborhood, that is, a cluster of people in a bounded area interchanging goods and services and recognizing a common place name. Place identity is fostered by the interactions of parents and children affiliated with a particular elementary school or by the excitement of a small-town high school football team. Common geographical and architectural experiences aid in defining community identity. A hill or high steeple often serves as a landmark not only orienting the inhabitant's physical movements, but also in providing a common perception, unique to their town. In a similar way people may share common events—storms, fairs, reports of crimes—and so build up experiences of geographical and social sharing which help generate and maintain common concerns and awareness. Like persons and agencies, localities also have life histories. As we study communities we can find themes in their development, often influenced by geography and by early events. We can detect choice points in a city's career. The sensitive psychologist thus gets to understand his "community client" and to assist in his development.

Still another way to conceptualize community is in terms of *communicating networks* of people wherever they are. Professional organizations often foster this kind of network. A molecular biologist in southern California may have more of a sense of relationship and more actual communication with another molecular biologist in New York, or even in England or India, than with his next-door neighbor. Families, although scattered over thousands of miles, perceive themselves as having a basic identity. People who have once lived in San Francisco, Kyoto, or Paris may become "partial citizens" of those cities, feeling a kinship and concern that will cause them to show interests and take actions when their favorite places are in trouble. To some extent such identities lead to conflict. University psychologists, like many other academic people, often have a national orientation; their professional advancement partially depends on recognition outside their own area, and they often move from college to college. They may give more time and attention to furthering their "cosmopolitan" connections than their "local" ones. This may also be true for business and industrial executives whose organizations are owned by national chains. In studies of communities, a fruitful key to understanding behavior may be to distinguish between *cosmopolites* or *localites*.

Another way to look at a community is in terms of its *organizational structure and interaction*. Roland Warren (quoted in Cox et al., 1970, p. 59) defines a community as "that combination of social units and systems which perform the major social functions having locality relevance. This is another way of saying that by 'community' we mean the organization of social activities to afford people daily local access to those broad areas of activity which are necessary in day-to-day living." Cox and his colleagues note that the community can be viewed as a "system of systems" or an "ecology of games" and that unlike formal organizations, a community is not centrally directed, but its parts run themselves conflicting, competing, and exchanging resources in unplanned ways. The system of community organizations and its often flimsy interconnections is very important for a community psychologist to grasp in the locale in which he works. Figure 17-1 shows the many human-care organizations to be found in a city. The exit doors show how communities extrude cases they seem unable to handle.

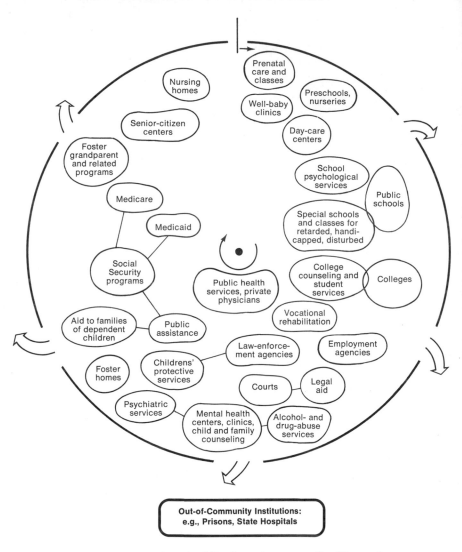

FIGURE 17-1 "Community clock" of services over the life cycle.

Cox and his coauthors state (1970, p. 59) that "community organization practice may be defined as the deliberate effort of a practitioner to influence the ties that bind individuals into small groups, relate two or more groups, connect two or more formal organizations, such as social agencies or businesses." Cox and his colleagues were mainly speaking to social workers, but the line between social work and other professions is difficult to draw when we come to matters of community organization and development.

Let us then define the word *community* as *a locality recognized as having a separate identity by most of the people in it and nearby, having comprehensive services and provisions to meet most human needs, and consisting of a loosely organized set of groups and organizations.* Generally communities will be towns, clearly labeled rural districts, or neighborhoods in large cities.

ROLES OF PSYCHOLOGISTS IN COMMUNITIES

In discussing community psychology as a professional field, we cannot be bound by any clear-cut definition of community. A great many kinds of projects are being undertaken. In their concern for persons in contexts, psychologists play many roles. Anyone who requires standard position descriptions will search in vain; one of the qualities that a community psychologist must have is a certain tolerance—or even enthusiasm—for variety and diversity. Some of the work going on clearly fits the definition of community given above, some does not. What distinguishes it from traditional clinical psychology is that the psychologist is helping other people to carry out the activities through which the quality of their life together is to be improved, rather than working with individuals or groups on their own improvement. Community efforts bring together people with interests in the physical environment, the social environment, politics, economic development, people of all ages, diverse ethnic groups, leisure-time activities, legal systems, and many other areas of human activity. At a meeting with planners in the morning, the community psychologist may be confronting the problem of the effect of a new freeway on the poor and elderly population it would displace; in the afternoon he may be teaching interviewing to Mexican-American housewives who are conducting a survey of behavior problems in their section of the city.

In other words, the community psychologist provides *indirect* assistance to people, as distinguished from the *direct* assistance of face-to-face clinical work with clients and patients. The psychologist interacts with representatives or organizations or community groups, or he helps citizens to develop their own services. There are three basic roles: consultant, program director, and participant-organizer or facilitator.

The *consultant* role, discussed in Chapter 16, is a familiar one to psychologists. They have served for many years as consultants to schools, industry, mental hospitals, and clinics. For instance, a psychologist may work with a school teacher to improve his or her interaction with students; he may lead a workshop in a school or business designed to improve organizational functioning; he may consult on the establishment of a program for introducing a token economy into the environment of patients, inmates, or clients. A consultant in a community may work with a wide variety of community groups and institutions. He advises, evaluates, leads group discussions, helps plan programs, and in some cases provides an opportunity for individuals in an organization to vent some of their feelings to a nonthreatening outsider. As Kelly (1970b) points out, community consultation should be a radiating process that improves the functioning of the person or group participating, who may in turn improve others' functioning. Good assistance to a school teacher will benefit the children she teaches and the colleagues with whom she associates and will help the teacher solve future problems as they arise.

The role of *program director* in a community is somewhat rare for a psychologist but is coming to be more common. Such positions involve administering a service, training program, or research program aimed at community betterment. One example is organizing and administering a family counseling service. Another is developing a program for training mental health workers in a community; for instance, members of a ghetto neighborhood might be trained to provide psychological services in a local halfway house or clinic. Planning such programs demands careful consideration of the general community climate, because their success depends on the cooperation or endorsement of what might be called "significant groups," just as an individual client's improvement may depend on the environment provided by "significant others."

The third role is that of *participant organizer or facilitator* of community efforts—the "change agent" role. The psychologist serves as a direct participant in ongoing community decision making in regard to local development, social planning, or social action. He may take a leadership role, or a catalytic, facilitating role to marshall resources and encourage leadership in others. Because of his background and training, it is likely that he will often be able to assist in analyzing the psychological needs of the community members and to suggest techniques for social organization.

To all these roles, the psychologist brings specialized knowledge in research and assessment and specialized skills in getting people to express themselves and work together. He will be expected to utilize his knowledge and skills. Sometimes more expertise than he possesses is expected of him.

Sometimes community decisions about service patterns, funding, and priorities become exceptionally complicated. Recently, a psychologist from a private child and family agency became involved with six separate planning groups in one year, each of whom had assembled a substantial number of persons in various child and family services:

1. State officials charged with mental health services, who control state mental health funds.

2. State officials charged with providing services to children, who control federally augmented funds for child care.

3. The coordinator for the county mental health/mental retardation board, who was charged with overall planning for the county.

4. The chief of the county juvenile court, who sought to present a comprehensive child treatment/crime suppression plan to a city and county authority that had recently been awarded a large grant by the Law Enforcement Assistance Administration.

5. A group planning to write a staffing grant for a comprehensive mental health center.

6. A local group of child mental health and court workers, who sought to found a nonprofit corporation to obtain grants and to lobby for adequate attention to children's bills in the state legislature.

Ironically, each of these groups was planning aspects of services to children and families. All the participants attended out of a desire for improved and better coordinated services and out of a need to please the various sources of funding and power. None, the psychologist included, had the power or the vision needed to press for global consolidation or articulation of the health, welfare, mental health, criminal justice, and so on, efforts as they were represented in local, county, state, and federal activities.

The psychologist should recognize that in many instances he will be acting as a citizen and not as an expert. Like other members of the community, he will have strong feelings in favor of and against certain programs. Recently it was a surprise to many people in a university community to encounter objections to a halfway house for mental patients; some well-trained professional people thought a halfway house was a good idea—if only it would be located next to other people's houses and families, not theirs.

The psychologist cannot expect to know a great deal about many areas of community functioning unless he has made a study of the particular areas. His opinion may be no better than that of any other citizen and in many cases, e.g., in a low-income area of town where he has never lived, it may be worth considerably less. Recently, for example, the governor of a state appointed a committee to plan a mass-transit system. None of the people he appointed had ridden the bus for twenty years; it is hard to imagine how these people can have much natural understanding of the daily problems of the aged, the poor, and the young, many of whom have no other means of transportation. If psychologists are in positions to advise governors or mayors, it would seem to be their special responsibility to help them realize that the citizens most affected by decisions should participate in the decision making.

Kelly (1971) has identified seven qualities for the community psychologist:

1. A clearly identified competence, so that the psychologist enters the community with some skills, skills that give him some value to the community and at the same time provide him with some occupational independence.

2. A community eco-identity, an identification with its interrelated geosocial ecology and its subcommunities.

3. Tolerance for diversity and encouragement of many options in the locality.

4. An ability to adapt his efforts to varied and limited resources, especially to identify and encourage the development of talents and skills needed in the community.

5. A commitment to risk taking, and a willingness to advocate and work

persistently for a worthy cause, particularly when it relates to sectors of the community that are low in status and politically weak.

6. An ability to balance patience and zeal, mobilizing energies when necessary and laying back at other times.

7. A disposition to "give away the byline"—to be rewarded by the consequences of his work, not by personal glorification.

This prescription for the ideal community psychologist is not an easy one to fill. It requires a deep caring for the locality, which Kelly has passionately expressed in making comparisons with biological ecologists, as follows (1970a, p. 524):

> If all of the stimulating ideas from biology are distilled into a single theme, it is a fondness, a commitment, a love, if you will, of the very community where you live and work; an involvement that engulfs your attention and draws your curiosity to make an adventure out of knowing all there is to know of its heritage, its conflicts, its people, its political forces, and its efforts to launch campaigns for social goods, as well as its failures when the status is quo. Few of us have been trained to cathect to a locale. I am confident that few psychologists have been taught to work about our communities, and still fewer of us have given our time to see the promotion of a civic cause fulfilled.

In brief, the clinical psychologist in the community puts the skills he has acquired from his training in other aspects of clinical work at the service of the community, assisting with problem clarification, appraisal, design, intervention, and evaluation, as he does at other levels of organization. Just where a psychologist will fit into the community organization varies from situation to situation. Glasscote and Gudeman (1969), in an extensive study of eight comprehensive mental health centers in the United States, found that psychologists and other mental health workers functioned in a wide variety of assignments. In some centers roles were blurred and interchangeable except for special functions such as the prescription of drugs by physicians. In other centers distinct services were provided by small teams. Frequently separate teams were organized in different geographical regions of a community. The traditional out-patient mental health team, where the psychologist does mainly testing, was not found among the eight centers visited.

One inference that can be drawn from such studies as this is that mental health centers—as important as they are to communities—are not really doing much community work. The majority of staff's activities reported by Glasscote and Gudeman (1969, p. 165) were related to direct care of patients (57 percent). Only 5 percent of their time was spent in consultation outside the center. More time (16 percent) was consumed in staff meetings within the center than in work with the community. It looks as if those comprehensive mental health centers were doing very little work toward the prevention of disorders or the amelioration of conditions in the community which produce distress and deviance. Future psychologists, we hope, will help move the community toward a larger scale, more effective solution of community problems than has been developed by comprehensive mental health centers.

ILLUSTRATIONS OF COMMUNITY PROGRAMS

In the wide variety of programs to be briefly presented, psychologists have assumed the different roles we have discussed—consultants, program directors, or participant-organizers. These illustrations are only a few out of a great many that could be mentioned; they give one a sense of the experimental, growing vitality of the work community psychologists are doing.

Organizing and expanding mental health services in a community. In the 1950s it became apparent that packing mental patients away into large and distant hospitals was not doing much to solve the problem of mental illness. Experiments were carried out in which patients were kept in their communities or were returned to them as soon as possible. A classic study in West Sussex, England (Carse, 1958), demonstrated that providing facilities for screening and brief treatment could dramatically alter the hospitalization picture. In the Worthing district simply by requiring all patients to see a psychiatrist in the community before being admitted to a hospital, the number of admissions was reduced by 56 percent. Similar results were found when the plan was applied in other districts. Later, Pasamanick, Scarpitti, and Dinitz (1967), in a well-designed study in Ohio, showed that periods of hospitalization could be remarkably reduced with schizophrenics whose families were willing to keep them at home if they received some assistance from a public health nurse. The well-known Project Re-Ed (Hobbs, 1966; Lewis, 1967) initiated at George Peabody College in Nashville, demonstrated the feasibility of a brief residential treatment program for emotionally disturbed children, reinforced by a mobilization of resources in the child's natural environment. It involved the training and use of teacher-counselors, social workers, liaison-teachers visiting the home, and mental health consultants. The emphasis was on competence and self-fulfillment rather than on illness and pathology.

The organization of a comprehensive mental health center, several hundred of which now exist in the United States, requires that many community services be provided. For instance, the Westside Community Mental Health Center in San Francisco is composed of 16 organizations tied together by written agreements (Feldman, 1971). The legislation specified that in order to receive federal grants, communities must demonstrate that they would provide coordinated services for both in-patients and out-patients and that they were prepared to follow through on patients discharged from the state mental hospitals. In the preparation of state plans for such centers in the mid-1960s some 25,000 individuals throughout the nation participated (Roen, 1971). Relations between different community services and agencies had to be examined and redefined. New services had to be developed to fill in the gaps. The organization of an urban mental health program is described by Whittington (1969) and a rural program by Kiesler (1969).

Although the operation of the centers, as previously mentioned, has been somewhat disappointing in the amount of community work carried on, they represent a real advance over previous mental health services.

Dealing with special problems of disorder and deviance in the community. Community psychology is not concerned exclusively with mental illness and health. Other kinds of community problems come in for consideration. For instance, the impetus for the development of the White Bird Socio-Medical Clinic mentioned in Chapter 16 was the concern a number of university students, physicians, nurses, teachers, and psychologists felt about drug problems among high school and college youth; they saw this as a facet of a wider problem of alienation in the community, a problem with physiological, psychological, and social aspects. In the process of organizing the clinic that we have described, they also organized the community. Police policies and programs had to be coordinated with the clinic in order that "stoned" youngsters could be reached by "bummer squads" rather than be arrested and thrown in jail. Organizations had to be set up to find temporary housing for runaways and to provide abortion counseling for girls who asked for it. Financial support had to be obtained from the Community Chest and from general solicitations. The effort to assist alienated youth was broad and community-wide.

Some communities have set up innovative treatment programs for delinquent boys (Shore and Massimo, 1969, summarized at the end of Chapter 14), in which cooperative agreements were reached among the schools, employers, the police, and the counselor-therapists. Others have organized suicide-prevention centers and other crisis clinics designed to deal with emergencies. Still others have developed programs for early detection of behavioral problems in the schools (Zax and Cowen, 1969).

Some community programs are set up on a time-limited basis, as for example, when a music festival or a youth fair is held in the vicinity. In such cases, counseling and drug-assistance programs lasting only a few days are organized. It seems extremely important in such programs to have the "helping persons" live with the temporary community and move about through it with as little strangeness as possible, keeping communication open. The lore of contact centers seems to hold rather clearly that helpers must be "co-cultural" with those in need and that helpers need to have "been there" themselves. For instance, someone with LSD experience is usually selected to "talk down" a user on a bad trip; a mystical religious "freak" is believed more ready to enter the personal world of an agitated person who was similar to him; a "straight" medical-type helper might best reassure a straight high school student on a first trip with a drug. The general hypothesis behind this treatment plan is that a similar personal experience is desirable, if not necessary, to give effective empathy and support. Such a hypothesis needs testing.

In each of these examples the community psychologist focuses on a problem and cooperates with others, to define and solve it using community resources.

Working to improve the position of economically disadvantaged groups. The previous two sets of illustrations focused on services designed to deal with problems. A community psychologist may also identify certain groups, such as the poor or a suppressed minority, and work with them to improve their status and power. (These various categories overlap a great deal, of course poor people may be mentally ill, for instance, or alienated.) His manner of working with such groups may take many forms. He may make city government aware of their needs and demands, he may help them organize for social action through militant protests or he may help them set up self-help projects. A psychologist may find himself helping, studying, or implementing a community action agency—the organizing structure for the community's antipoverty programs (Zurcher, 1969). He may serve as a consultant for an organization designed to provide health and educational programs for migrant workers. He may help schools and businesses define new jobs and career lines to allow people with limited education access to career ladders (Pearl and Riessman, 1965; MacLennon, 1969). He may help organize poor neighborhoods against exploitation by slum landlords. The Economic Opportunity Act of 1964 initiated a wide variety of programs aimed at amelioration of the plight of the poor. These programs have gone through many changes as the political climate has shifted. But the problem of poverty remains and deserves the attention of psychologists because it is related to so many other aspects of functioning in society. The discerning psychologist who follows the causes of stress in the lives of people in communities will often find economic factors to be major components. In general, psychologists have been poorly trained for dealing with economic matters. Coming mostly from the middle class, they have a great deal to learn from low-income people, who must themselves be involved in planning and implementing poverty programs.

Assisting in community planning. When a community becomes interested in where it is going, psychologists have an opportunity to bring behavioral considerations into the planning. City and regional planning has mainly been concerned with the physical environment—utilities, sewers, transportation, land usage. But in recent years social planning has become more prominent, especially as federal money has become available for planning of health services. The psychologist's skills in measurement and evaluation can be very useful here. The development of behavioral ecology and environmental psychology (Barker, 1968; Craik, 1971; Proshansky, Ittelson, and Rivlin, 1970; Wohlwill, 1970) promises to bring much greater understanding of the ways in which physical and psychological aspects of the environment interact.

Psychologists may contribute to community planning by serving on advisory boards or as consultant-participants in urban renewal projects (Lemkau, 1969). Psychologists are needed in the designing of new communities. (The psychiatrist Lemkau reported in 1969 on the planning of Columbia, Maryland.) In discussions with urban planners, psychologists can bring to their attention the needs and activity patterns of the wide variety of people who would be inhabiting the area—the aged, the children, the adolescents—and to suggest ways in which stresses might be reduced by the physical layout. Psychologists are interested in community plans for services, recreation, and activities. The goal is the development of a humane environment for people at all stages of the life cycle.

Principles of Design, Development, and Intervention in Community Programs

New as it is, community psychology is still in the process of formulating a coherent conceptual framework. Those who practice it make use of ideas drawn from general systems theory, epidemiology, ecology (Roen, 1971; Kelly, 1970a), and role theory (Sarbin, 1970). A new theoretical formulation that has been particularly useful in community psychology is *crisis theory*. The theory grew out of Lindemann's (1944) analysis of grief reactions to the 1942 Coconut Grove dancehall fire and was elaborated in the book by Caplan (1964) on preventive psychiatry. What "crisis" means is a sudden disruption of a person's or group's equilibrium that occurs in the natural environment and results in changed behavior based on feelings of helplessness and tension. Severe accidents, threats to life, loss of a loved one, or sudden shifts in the surrounding culture or environment are common causes. Crisis theory maintains that interventions at such times are especially helpful to the person because the crisis forces a restructuring of the person's life. Taplin (1971) has argued that crisis can be viewed as the overload of a person's coping skills; crisis prevention, then, can be approached by large-scale training or teaching of coping skills and community reduction of the stress of overload.

On a larger scale, disasters such as earthquakes, floods, war, or a change in government may bring openings for constructive change in social systems. Kelly (1970b, p. 184) quotes Laotse's aphorism, "In every crisis, there is opportunity as well as danger." These concepts fit well into an overall framework based on general systems theory, especially the aspect having to do with how systems react to stress. Crisis and traumatic experiences are not, of course, the only situations producing rapid "unfreezing" of attitudes and behavior. Sudden good fortune, training in new skills, or therapeutic programs may also stimulate rapid change. In communities such changes may also occur when a federal grant program makes it possible to attack a community problem. Any sudden change in a situation creates an opportunity for constructive change.

With or without a comprehensive theory, community psychologists have accumulated some practical knowledge about what to do and not to do. Some of it can be summarized as guidelines.

1. *Focus on the living environment of the people involved.* In developing community-improvement programs a major concern is to avoid placing blame on

individuals or diagnosing personal pathology. Dörken (1971, p. 79) says "The major faults of society lie not in its people but in its systems, and this premise is basic" to community psychology. Look for the causes of disorder in the homes, work places, parks, schools; look for dehumanizing aspects of institutions, ignorance, feelings of alienation, the teaching of antisocial behavior on the mass media. Also look at the constructive and rewarding community processes.

2. *Limit the role of the psychologist to encouraging participation and assisting in the clarification of concerns and the setting of priorities.* The community psychologist usually cannot know the community as well as its inhabitants do, and the success of a program depends upon the mobilized energies of the people of the community. It is important for the "expert" to prove that he can be trusted and that he has a legitimate interest in the community and its projects.

3. *Seek out resources–financial, human, and organizational.* In most communities, new projects have trouble getting financial backing. Federal grants may be available, but someone must put a great deal of effort into writing the application. The Community Chest may provide support, but the project must be demonstrated first to be workable. Volunteers willing to donate time may make up for a lack of financial resources. Someone must help fit individuals, paid or unpaid, into the roles the project calls for. Organizational resources in communities must be analyzed to see what they have to contribute to a new program. Questions arise, such as: Is a present agency capable of doing the job, or should a new one be created? With what organizations will the program most need to coordinate its efforts? In seeking financial support, one must analyze what the support may cost in terms of altering the program; the old adage is often true, "He who pays the piper calls the tune."

4. *Consider both crises and the development of competence to prevent crises in initiating programs.* Communities need to be prepared for emergencies–large-scale calamities such as power failures or severe snowstorms. They also should be prepared to handle individual or small-group emergencies–such as automobile accidents, marital fights, muggings, drug freak-outs, or suicides. Community psychologists are concerned with programs to handle such crises and with the training and support of people who are normally "on the front line," dealing with human breakdown. The police are especially important; so are the people who man emergency rooms in hospitals, ministers, and teachers

Communities should be prepared to deal with stresses characteristic of different periods in the life cycle. Leighton, Leighton, and Armstrong (1964) found in an epidemiological survey of "nervous" problems that peaks occurred for men in their thirties, for women in their forties, and for both sexes in their sixties. The birth of the first baby may bring disruption as well as joy, so new parents often need help. Women in their forties and fifties face the menopause and the loss of meaningful activity as their children leave home; community programs may assist them to recover their self-esteem. People in old age have their special problems. Intelligent community programs can help people undergoing stress while preventing such difficulties in others.

5. *Make use of both conflict and problem-solving strategies.* The strategies for change in communities are many and varied, but two distinct models stand out. One is the conflict model typically used by some labor unions and by revolutionaries. It is based on the assumption that management or government does not change quickly enough to alter people's distress; major changes come through conflict. The forces brought into the conflict can range from Gandhi's truth force (Satyagraha), or nonviolent civil disobedience, to sabotage and guerrilla warfare. Labor has often used the strike or threat of a strike.

The other approach is to develop shared concerns and engage in community interaction designed to achieve cooperative problem solving. When differences arise, the parties involved sit down together, often in the presence of a third party, and identify objectives on which they can work together. In the process of exploring desirable conditions, shared values and goals often arise. Needless to say, such a process is not easy once strong polarities have developed. The participation of a third party respected by both sides is often essential to its success. Whether a conflict or a consensual approach is appropriate depends partly on the situation and partly on the personal predilection of the change agents. Most psychologists prefer the consensual method, but more evidence is required before we can say that it always works.

6. *Look beyond the immediate change to a new level of stability that provides for continuity of problem solving.* As in psychotherapy, the community clinician aims not only to help the client through the current crisis but also to increase his skill in solving similar problems in the future. As Klein (1968) indicates, community change involves "unfreezing" a situation, producing changes in it, and "re-freezing" it with a new and improved pattern. Because people cannot live in chaos for long, communities always have structure. Restructurings should provide for continued evolution through input from ordinary citizens and experts. A structure that a new program has brought into existence should provide for periodic review to facilitate orderly change in personnel and ideas.

7. *Be accountable to the community.* The public which supports and develops a program is entitled to feedback about it. Too often, psychologists, physicians, and other professionals accustomed to individual practice fail to realize this. Accountability means describing the nature of programs, studying their effectiveness, responding sensitively to community questions and complaints, and disseminating the results to relevant audiences and consumers. Accountability also involves wider humanitarian goals and sharing insights with other communities.

THE APPRAISAL FUNCTION IN COMMUNITY PSYCHOLOGY

In the process of planning, executing, and evaluating an intervention in a community, there are many occasions for gathering and using information about communities. The clinical psychologist's background of assessment and research is very helpful in many ways, but, in addition, community work will need an understanding of methods used by social psychologists, sociologists, and other social scientists. Some information gathering is just a matter of good common sense; there are many sources of information in communities which are there for the looking or asking. Observations made on the street, in shops, on playgrounds, and in public places are very useful to a community worker.

One of the first tasks of appraisal is the defining of a target area for a particular investigation. In view of the enormous amounts of data that could be collected, the community psychologist has to set limits and boundaries—geographical limits, such as a section of a city, a whole city, or a region, or a state; time limits, how far back in records or interviews to make investigations; and content limits, what data really bear on the problems to be attacked and the purposes for which the data are to be used. The community psychologist may need to obtain facts and figures about the physical environment, the economic structure, communication media, organizations, leaders, or history in appraising the system into which the improvement program is to be introduced. What he wishes to clarify is the way the community system works—its input and output, its controls and decision mechanisms, its traditions and expectations.

If, as is often the case, a *survey* seems to be in order, one task he faces is the selection of a sample to be surveyed that will adequately represent the population. An alternative to the survey is open hearings, at which anyone who wishes to voice an opinion is given the opportunity. Still another appraisal technique is to use informants as anthropologists do in investigating a new culture. *Records* of community activities (e.g., court records, hospital records, and census reports) are often useful. As mentioned earlier, observation of an informal sort often serves to round out the appraisal of a community. Controlled observation is more expensive than other methods in time and manpower. Psychological tests as appraisal techniques also tend to be impractical unless they are group tests routinely administered to school children.

As in the case of organizations discussed in Chapter 16, a principal purpose of appraisal activity is to evaluate programs. Even more than most other research, evaluation studies deal with sensitive areas. Decisions about budgets, future personnel assignments, and program change are likely to hinge on outcomes. People are often so ego-involved in programs that outcomes cannot be discussed dispassionately. It is especially important in evaluation research that an atmosphere of interest and trust surround the work and that the results be presented as ways of improving services rather than as criticisms of what people have done. Often it is possible to design the research to include alternatives for improvement programs so that the results will lead to decisions about what to do next rather than simple acceptance or rejection of a program.

In his discussion of program evaluation, especially as it applies to community mental health, Roen (1971, pp. 804–806) makes fifteen recommendations under three major headings—planning, program, and dissemination:

1. *The planning phase.* (a) "The beginning of evaluation is working with a sincere program based in a dedicated center"; the investigator should test mutual commitments by thoroughly expressing himself. (b) Even though overall goals may be global and inspiring, specific objectives must be stated which are practical and attainable. (c) The investigator must analyze and chart the whole system, conceptually reflecting different levels of input, programs, and outputs. (d) Several evaluative designs should be thought through and options kept open for some time before the program solidifies. (e) Explorations or "dry runs" should be made in the natural setting before the program starts.

2. *The program phase.* (a) When a particular researchable problem is chosen, a model should be developed and, if possible, a simulation run to detect deficiencies. (b) Questions should be formulated that are answerable, relevant, and important to the sponsoring agency; outside consultants are often of help at this stage. (c) On the basis of questions, specific research designs should be formulated, related to hypotheses and ways to prove or disprove them; principles of research design should be used, such as control groups, baseline data, retrospective cohort analysis, or before-and-after measures. (d) Instrumentation of data gathering should be developed. (e) Data have to be carefully collected and provisions made for follow-up to check on lost cases and other problems that might be encountered. (f) The criteria for success or confirmation of hypotheses must be designated; usually several criteria are needed and consideration must be given to the practical, clinical uses to which the results may be put.

3. *The dissemination phase:* (a) The analysis of the data should relate clearly to the kind of information one wants to impart to others. (b) Although one cannot study everything, whenever possible some extra information should be obtained, as this sometimes leads to unexpected conclusions and new ideas. (c) Consider staging the reports as sections are completed; it is often useful to have the ultimate writer designated as historian from the beginning of the project. (d) Dissemination of the findings should be planned so as to have appropriate impact—through press releases, informal reports to participants, formal journal articles and books; unless people are well informed, especially decision makers, the work may have little influence.

One of the unsatisfactory aspects of evaluative research is that often the evaluators are brought in almost as an afterthought after the project starts and then only because the grant specifies that there must be evaluation. In general, far too little money is spent on research activities, especially development and evaluation. The report of the Joint Commission on Mental Illness and Health (1961) recommended that 2.5 percent of the patient service budget be given to research on mental health. Smith and Hobbs (1966) recommended that community mental health centers allocate between 5 and 10 percent for program evaluation and other kinds of research.

A second disappointing aspect is that psychologists have not compared mental health or psychological projects with other projects, institutions, or systems that try to improve the quality of life. Evaluation designs rarely look at such questions as: How does the Salvation Army's outreach program compare with mental health centers? How does our availability compare with the policeman's? Do church-sponsored youth groups have greater or lesser impact than the mental health industry when it comes to prevention? Lennard and Bernstein (1969) have given attention to the question of what attributes psychotherapy contexts share with other human interaction systems which make them either beneficial or harmful to the functioning or well-being of the members of such systems.

In community mental health projects, high cost factors, modest effectiveness, and failure to be relevant to some of the most behaviorally handicapped—such as "skid row" people—require that psychologists working for community better-ment respect and evaluate the contributions of a wide variety of "lay" or nonprofessional efforts.

A city council may say to a psychologist "We have enough money for outpatient mental health services for 200 children *or* for expanding the Interfaith Council's organized recreation program to serve the whole town's children." How should this psychologist proceed in advising the council? He knows that people are helped by varieties of informal or nonprofessional contacts. But the attention of community psychologists has not sufficiently turned to such a question as: What are the social learning, psychological developmental, or preventive mental health aspects of a recreation program, a club, or a rehabilitation program likely to be? The development of concepts of comparative effectiveness or comparative impact is sorely needed.

Besides comparing the effects different programs have on people, community psychologists must examine what different programs or systems do to each other. Is the mental health program teaching dependency and helping other community problem-solving mechanisms and systems close down? Is the X agency's program wasting effort competing with the Y agency? Is the Alternative School breeding frustration and cynicism in hundreds of potential students because it can serve only fifteen?

Lennard and Bernstein (1971), writing about mental-health-program evalua-tion from a community perspective, underscore the problem of choosing criteria for evaluation. They suggest that the first major task is to understand what is happening in society as well as in the mental health movement. They emphasize the need for looking at unintended consequences of effects of our programs; for example, we need to concern ourselves, they suggest, with the ends being served by labeling with its consequences (p. 309):

> Labeling has implications in many areas: (a) *Manpower*: the more persons are defined as "mentally ill," the more manpower is needed in the mental health field . . . . (b) *Social*: to the extent that the problem is defined differently by other forces in the society (the courts, political groups etc.), the labeling of new groups . . . leads to competition for the management of these persons; for example, who will serve them; to whom do they "belong." (c) *Personal*: labeling, while sometimes functional, is

often dysfunctional. It transforms persons into patients. Difficult children, when defined as disturbed, are given tranquillizers. What does this do to the role of a mental health professional? He is often called on to help manage and control, for example, and thus serves as an agent for the establishment and the status quo.

Among similar issues they present is the question: If we give lip service to the idea that parts of the social context cause dysfunction, why do we continue, principally, to intervene with individuals?

Assessing the impact of different programs and activities on the community may move from being impossible to being merely exceptionally difficult if investigators agree on criteria relevant to the community system, for example the ability to derive benefit from the community and ability to contribute to its functioning. Community psychologists face a major challenge but one that should eventually throw a good deal of light on resource allocations for improving the quality of life in the community.

NEW IDEAS ABOUT COMMUNITY MANPOWER

In the decade of the 1960s several ideas coalesced to chart new directions for community development. For one thing, it had become very apparent that there would never be enough of the traditional clinical services to meet the needs for psychological and psychiatric assistance. Other fields also, such as health and education, faced manpower problems. For another thing, certain sectors of society—minority groups, youth, students, the aged, and the poor—were expressing more and more dissatisfaction with the professional services they were receiving. The sociologists Cloward and Ohlin (1960) proposed what is called *opportunity theory*—the theory that delinquency is caused largely by the exclusion of large sectors of society from its money and prestige reward systems. Because of lack of opportunity for employment, the delinquents had not been able to participate in normal society. The result was alienation and the development of antisocial subcultures. This theory also applied to other social problems. Putting together vast needs for service and large unused pools of manpower points to an apparently simple solution of social problems—to get together people with needs and people available to meet them. As anyone who has worked with such programs knows, there are enormous problems to be overcome—lack of financial support, resistances of present job-holders, governmental job specifications, and concern over the political and social implications of kinds of people coming into positions of influence in organizations who are different from present incumbents. Still the concern for improving the lot of the poor led to many exploratory programs, often supported by the funds made available under the Economic Opportunity Act of 1964 and subsequently by the Office of Manpower Development and Training. By 1970 it was estimated that over a half-million nonprofessionals and aides had obtained employment in public services. Matarazzo (1971) in reviewing national developments in the utilization of nontraditional health manpower says: "A future historian or sociologist of the professions may be fascinated by his discovery of the professionals' slow paced, decades long diagnosis and search for solutions and the concurrent hundreds of haphazard, uncoordinated, community-initiated, seat-of-the-pants solutions to equal numbers of critical local mental health manpower shortage problems." (For a more extensive account of the community use of nonprofessional manpower, see Grosser, Henry, and Kelly, 1969.)

The programs were of several kinds. The most influential concept was that of *new careers*, promoted particularly by Pearl and Riessman (1965). As MacLennan (1969, p. 179) says: "The essence of New Careers is entry into the system without prior qualification and the creation and institutionalization of machinery and support for upward mobility." In a program at Howard University, new positions were created for aides in day care, recreation, and research. Youths, often without high school diplomas, were trained not only in specific job skills but also in social and organizational skills aimed at enabling them to succeed in the foreign culture of "the establishment." Many of these youths earned high school diplomas or passed equivalency tests. Early job placement was a distinctive feature of the program; academic credit was given wherever possible for work activity. The new careers idea spread widely, supported by federal funding, and hundreds of programs were organized. MacLennan points out that in the process of setting up these arrangements, the psychologists and other professionals had to learn to adopt the unfamiliar roles of lobbyist and salesman in order to contend with the clash of interests and the pressures that social change produces.

New careers programs and others like them do two things—employ "indigenous" citizens and develop *career ladders*. They have made special efforts to bring in minority and disadvantaged members of society. Other programs, such as model cities, worked toward the same end, and the effort was reinforced by federal legislation. But the second aspect is also important. Just bringing people into programs is not enough. They need opportunities to move ahead in their work. This requires that jobs be defined as rungs on career ladders, so that by obtaining additional training and experience an aide can become a teacher or a counselor or a nurse. The traditional procedures for obtaining credentials in the health professions and social service occupations discourages vertical movement. In a mental hospital, for example, it is almost impossible for a psychiatric aide to become a nurse, a social worker, or a psychologist without going back to school and starting all over. It is also difficult to move "horizontally" from one career to another—to shift from recreation, for instance, to social work. Perhaps "career lattice" would be a better term for the open job situation the new careers movement is promoting.

Another area of human resource development highlighted in the 1960s was the use of "mature women." As has been mentioned before, many capable women find themselves at loose ends when their "first career" of housewife and mother becomes less meaningful as children leave home. With thirty or forty years of life ahead of them, they still have much to contribute to society through a "second career." Most communities depend on "womanpower" for volunteer work in many organizations. Special programs were designed to make use of women more specifically for human services. Rioch's (1967) almost "classic" projects starting in 1960 demonstrated that after a rather intensive selection and two-year training program, housewives made excellent "mental health counselors." With support from NIMH, this idea has spread all over the country. Patterson and Ray and their colleagues (1968, 1972) demonstrated the feasibility of training housewives to become specialists in behavior modification; they, in turn can train parents to modify their children's behavior.

Efforts have also been made to make use of another underutilized section of the population—students. Jobs for the young are often hard to find and labor laws often constitute barriers to employment. This means that very capable and enthusiastic potentialities for human service are wasted. The early 1960s marked the development of unpaid and low-paid volunteer jobs which appealed to students as alternatives to college, programs such as the Peace Corps and VISTA (joined in 1971 into ACTION). Many of these positions were in community services. Other college students carried on volunteer work during their spare time—tutoring a few hours a week, or assisting in parks and recreation programs. More to the point were programs for field instruction in which students received credit for a mixture of academic and practical work. Holzberg, Knapp, and Turner (1967) and Rappaport, Chinsky, and Cowen (1971) have demonstrated the value of college students as companions for mental patients. The summer work—study mental health program of the Western Interstate Commission for Higher Education has led thousands of students to choose mental health careers or to deepen their commitment to such careers. Programs in human service have in some instances been extended downward to high school students.

The aged have been recognized as another underemployed group, and many elderly people are serving as foster grandparents for handicapped children, for instance.

ETHNIC AND CULTURAL ASPECTS OF COMMUNITY

One of the special meanings of "community" refers to groups of people with a particular ethnic or religious background. For instance, riots between Hindus and Muslims in India are called "communal" strife. Skin color in the United States has played a role like that of caste in India. Until recent decades, Americans of African descent have often been excluded from clubs and facilities open to whites. Pride in their ethnicity has arisen in the 1960s among blacks, American Indians, Mexican Americans, and Oriental Americans. As colonialism has declined, minorities and outcastes in many parts of the world have begun to assert the right of their ethnic group to a place in the sun. In community psychology, pluralism and regard for the special character of each locality is considered very important. Even in all-white communities, many people obtain real satisfaction in identifying themselves as Irishmen, Italians, Germans, Jews, Catholics, or Mayflower descendants. While deploring narrow bigotries, many people prize the variety of cultural contributions that different groups make to a community—special foods, music, and customs. Thus ethnic pluralism may enrich and enliven the lives of all the people.

Several admonitions seem appropriate for the community psychologist as he deals with cultural differences. For one thing, he should recognize that it will take quite awhile for some ethnic groups to accept him. Blacks or Chicanos often have strong hostile attitudes toward whites or "Anglos." Initial communication is likely to be impaired by stereotypes or by reserve. Black children may respond differently on tests administered by whites and blacks. People interviewed may respond differently to black and white interviewers. One needs to make use of local citizens and local leaders in developing and carrying out programs.

Ethnic differences also affect one's interpretation of research results and one's understanding of local conditions. White psychologists can learn something about black ghettos and Mexican-American migrant camps by reading about them, but not in the same way as by observing conditions directly. The psychologist must not assume, however, that he sees the situation in the same way as the inhabitants. To get closer to their point of view will require living with them and engaging in a great deal of honest give and take. Even then, many of the emotional meanings of events will not register with him as they would if he were born into the culture. More specifically, the psychologist must be wary of cultural idiosyncracies in the use of language, the definition of tasks, and the application of normative data based on a different cultural group. Cole and Bruner (1971) point out that intelligence tests and other cognitive measures reveal only current performance—not underlying competence. They warn the psychologist to inquire whether competence is really expressed in a particular test situation and what the significance of that situation is for the person's ability to cope with life in his own milieu. They point out that black children who have done poorly on school tests have been able to cope successfully with very complex verbal environments in the street. A caveat for psychologists is not to assume that their preferred way of carrying out professional activities is universally desirable or "scientific."

The authors have been concerned by the view of those psychologists who advocate active open encounter as the goal of therapy; sometimes they demonstrate highly aggressive interpersonal relations as the best way to help others. The life styles of people with different ethnic backgrounds probably require different ways of acting and communicating. A raised eyebrow of a reserved Britisher may be equivalent of a wide armswing and a torrent of expletives from an Italian. Making everyone into the image the psychologist holds is not the aim of improvement programs.

Nottingham (1970) proposes that the study of community psychology not stop at the boundaries of the United States. He argues that provincialism and ethnocentrism are harmful to the development of psychological knowledge. He therefore proposes the broadest possible view of community, citing four reasons: (1) as psychologists and as human beings, we need to care about all people; (2) we, as Americans, have contributed to several forms of instability in many countries, and, presumably, should demonstrate concern; (3) our interest in studying the world and in learning from it could benefit the community of nations by further demonstrating and sharing American qualities other than materialism, hedonism, and militarism; and (4) many countries are tackling common concerns such as racial prejudice, overpopulation, and individual and collective violence, and they might teach us or learn from us. As residents of the earthly spaceship, all of us need to think in terms of the systemic needs of the world community.

The psychologist can learn a great deal by studying how members of other cultures and subcultures view psychological matters and solve day-to-day problems. DeVos and Hippler (1969) report that treatments of psychological disorders by native practitioners in primitive societies are often at least as successful as Western methods, if not more successful. Partly this effectiveness might be because a shaman or medicine man is much more able to relate to the "patient" than an alien to the culture is. Also native practitioners may use catharsis, suggestion, and other techniques that Western psychiatrists or psychologists use, adapting them to their own cultural setting.

Another reason for becoming acquainted with other cultures is that some have developed excellent community mental health practices which we might wish to emulate. Furman (1965) has reported on the services available in Great Britain, the Netherlands, Denmark, and Sweden. It has often been noted that these countries seem far ahead of the United States in community care for deviant and disadvantaged citizens. Visitors to Copenhagen are able to make a tour of its social and rehabilitative agencies as well as tours of historical monuments. This concern for the quality of human living reflects a value in Danish society. Values are expressed in many ways—by what the government supports, by courtesy on the street, and by the whole social structure. Becoming aware of values of other societies gives us perspective on our own.

SOCIETY, PUBLIC POLICIES, AND PLANNING

Community systems operate as part of a larger society. There is commerce in ideas in and out of a town or country, just as much as there is commerce in material goods. Such events as war, depression, and national legislation are quickly reflected in behavior within communities. Other more subtle inputs with important effects are national advertising programs, organized crime, shifts in occupational patterns, and developments in technology. Problems of coordination with the metropolitan area surrounding a city are often complex and difficult. In working with such external influences, community psychologists ultimately become involved in larger political and social issues. As psychologists learn more about what helps communities they will have more to say about broader public policies.

Along with other social scientists, psychologists sometimes participate in the development of public policy and in social planning in extra-community systems. The most famous instance of such influence is the testimony of Kenneth B. Clark, later president of the APA, before the Supreme Court, testimony that helped to bring about its monumental 1954 decision about civil rights and school desegregation. As psychology and other social sciences build up a more certain knowledge base and greater skill in dealing with public problems, it is very likely that those psychologists who understand community needs will have more of an impact than they do now on policy formation.

One particular area of need is in social planning and social programming for cities. Edgerton (1971, p. 94) says, "The complex social, economic and political interdependence brought on by our increasing urbanism has increased the vulnerability of the individual to risks which take away his opportunities and freedom to realize his maximum potential." Urban problems of crime, mental illness, racial antagonisms, and alienation are enormous; cities have drastically deteriorated in the last few decades. Costello and Zalkind (1970), speaking from personal experience in New York, plead with social scientists to give more attention to problems of the cities, applying their knowledge about behavior and their skills in research and program development. They remind us that two out of three Americans live in or near one of the country's twenty major cities. They suggest as an illustration that psychologists attack the problem of violence in the cities. They point out that the average American child growing up in the 1960s and 1970s has seen the destruction of 13,000 individuals on television; they raise the question about the effect it would have on behavior if they were to view the same number of scenes of reconciliation and altruism. Costello and Zalkind also illustrate how different experimental approaches might be taken to a specific problem in the cities—that of false fire alarms. They suggest among other things observations systematically made of variations in the way alarm boxes operate, perhaps noting the effect on the person of a loud noise that starts when a person turns in an alarm.

Bard (1970), also working in New York City, noticed that a large percentage of the injuries and deaths sustained by police officers occurred in responding to calls for help coming out of "family beefs." Bard, working closely with the local police, devised a program—involving a good deal of role playing and socio-drama—to help police officers evolve the special skills needed to bring deescalation and permanent improvement to the potentially explosive situations.

Using police afforded 24-hour availability of the mobile service for troubled families, besides decreasing the danger to the officers. Bard has questioned the usefulness of the conventional 9-to-5 social and professional organizations after experiencing difficulty securing their cooperation with the project, as measured by lack of responsive services for referred families. His report of the project provides an excellent example of a clear, yet comprehensive account of a complex community project. Bard (1971) has pointed to the function of law enforcement in the helping system and called attention to the vital contributions of police and to the huge expectations and small resources given the police by the community.

In social planning, communities establish goals. Like locating criteria in studies of validity, goal setting gets tough once it gets beyond popular platitudes. In the area of positive mental health, Jahoda (1958) has formulated several general characteristics, such as attempting mastery of the environment, maintaining a stable yet flexible integration of personality, and perceiving the world independently of personal needs.

Psychologists can be of help by developing more specific social indicators of psychosocial disorder or effectiveness to use in community and societal planning. Even though exact goals are hard to define, the process of discussion of community goals and priorities may itself help communities develop a better understanding and perspective.

Defining objectives, estimating costs of programs, and formulating criteria of success are likely to occupy community psychologists more and more. Clinicians must undergo a revolution of thought as the public expects them to become more accountable. Sociopsychological services are no longer a private and confidential endeavor of several professions concerned only with a fraction of the population. The concern of the psychologist is for the public—for the community.

SUMMARY

Psychologists have a variety of roles in the community through which, in general, they give indirect service to individuals. Typical roles include consultant, program director, and participant-organizer or facilitator. Several theoretical perspectives, including general systems theory, epidemiology, ecology, role theory, and crisis theory have been used in thinking about communities. Sample guidelines for the development of community programs involve (1) focus on the living environment of the people involved; (2) work closely with the community, encouraging participation; (3) estimate and develop resources; (4) choose program points of entry fostering competence to prevent human breakdown; (5) be aware of and flexibly use both conflict and consensual problem solving strategies; (6) look beyond the immediate change to a new level of stability that provides for continuity of problem solving; and (7) be accountable to the community. Gathering information and evaluating activities are a vital part of community psychology. Outcome studies are valuable in themselves, but community psychology is badly in need of careful comparison and contrasting of natural or existing systems (e.g., churches, police, bartenders) with formally therapeutic ones of mental health. Not all the effects of formally therapeutic programs are positive, for instance labeling people or removing them from their natural community supports. New careers in helping people have sprung up in the community. The formalized professions have been slow to integrate or adjust to the new roles and to provide meaningful career ladders. Community psychologists must often work with cultural differences and must be aware that local customs and standards may differ radically from their own. The life styles of people with different ethnic backgrounds probably require different ways of acting and communicating in treatment. Some psychologists have produced programs that directly address widespread or pressing social problems, and an increasing number argue that psychological knowledge must be brought directly to bear on improving the quality of life in places such as the inner city.

SUGGESTED READINGS

Adelson, D., and Kalis, B. L. (eds.). *Community psychology and mental health.* San Francisco: Chandler, 1970.

Adelson and Kalis present an introduction plus eighteen articles covering a wide range of topics: the origins and development of community psychology from the Swampscott Conference near Boston in 1965, some theoretical frameworks, research and action programs, and issues in training.

Other good references are *Perspectives in Community Mental Health* by Bindman and Spiegel (1969), *Community Psychology* by Iscoe and Spielberger (1970), and the *Handbook of Community Mental Health* by Golann and Eisdorfer (1972).

Cox, F. M., Erlich, J. L., Rothman, J., and Tropman, J. E. (eds.). *Strategies of community organization.* Itasca, Ill.: Peacock, 1970.

This book of readings includes an excellent exposition of three models of community organization practice, a brief history of the social forces impinging on community organization, discussions of organizations, linkages between systems, and the strategies of social action, locality development, and social planning. The orientation is largely toward social work, from which community psychologists have a great deal to learn.

The reader may wish to compare this book with that of a leading community psychiatrist, Gerald Caplan (1970).

Klein, D. C. *Community dynamics and mental health.* New York: Wiley, 1968.

This is probably the first textbook on community psychology that is not a collection of articles. It is written by a man who was involved in the early development of community psychology in the Boston area. Klein affiliated with the National Training Laboratories, which grew out of Kurt Lewin's leadership in applied group dynamics. The author emphasizes the examination and change in the processes of community problem solving. For a review of the book, see Sundberg (1969a).

Kelly, J. G. The quest for valid preventive interventions. In C. D. Spielberger (ed.), *Current topics in clinical and community psychology*, Vol. 2. New York: Academic Press, 1970, pp. 183–207.

Emphasizing community psychology's special qualifications to test interventions, Kelly's excellent article outlines three methods for preventive programs: mental health consultation as a radiating process, organizational change as environmental restructuring, and community development as an evolutionary process. Illustrating various designs, Kelly views development of community knowledge as an ecological enterprise.

Keniston, K. How community mental health stamped out the riots (1968–78). *Trans-Action*, 1968, 5, 21–30.

Keniston, in this serious satire, points out the possibility that action in the name of mental health can be used to control not only deviant but also dissident citizens, camouflage genuine social injustice, and establish a new form of a police state.

Craik, K. H. Environmental psychology. In T. M. Newcomb (ed.), *New directions in psychology*, Vol. 4. New York: Holt, Rinehart and Winston, 1970, pp. 1–121.

Craik calls attention to the everyday physical environment that people move and use. He brings in relevant observations and research from geography, which field psychologists have heretofore largely ignored. He reviews the research procedures psychologists have used and might use. The community psychologist who finds himself conferring with planners will do well to become acquainted with Craik's work and with the extensive collection of readings of environment psychology by Proshansky, Ittelson, and Rivlin (1970). See also Craik (1971).

Ryan, W. (ed.) *Distress in the city: essays on the design and administration of urban mental health services.* Cleveland: Case Western Reserve Press, 1969.

This book presents a picture of Boston's handling of its mental health problems. The report of the survey and accompanying essays demonstrate the failure of conventional psychiatric programs to reach those who need help the most. Criticisms are raised about the medical model and the allocation of resources for mental health services. The book provides an important synthesis of survey data and theoretical discussion.

Feldman, S. E., and Jacobson, M., Intake policy as a community organization tool. *Community Mental Health Journal*, 1969, 5, 76–81.

The authors discuss three models of service: (1) direct service, which is generally very difficult because of the immediate overload experienced by an agency; (2) extended community management, through which an agency helps other resource people manage cases, which has the drawback that case responsibility is difficult to pin down and there is frequently much finger pointing between agencies; and (3) what they call the extensive community development model, in which they see direct service as secondary to trying to get treatment alternatives together. This alternative asserts that one agency cannot, need not, and should not provide every needed service and thus the most useful activity is to develop, communicate, and catalyze community organizations. The authors argue that people's objections and discomforts at service inadequacy can thus be used as an impetus for community organization.

Makita, K. The rarity of reading disability in Japanese children. *American Journal of Orthopsychiatry*, 1968, *38*, 599–614.

A study reported here indicates that the prevalence of dyslexia in Japan (0.98 percent) is some ten times lower than in Western countries. Transcultural epidemiology of reading disability is hardly found in psychiatric literature. No investigators refer to specific features of language script, the direct object of reading behavior. It is proposed . . . that the specificity of the used language is the most potent contributing factor in the formation of reading disability.

Brower, M. The emergence of community development corporations in urban neighborhoods. *American Journal of Orthopsychiatry*, 1971, *41*, 646–658.

In black and other nonwhite ghettos, there has been a rapid growth of community development corporations (CDCs) in answer to the demand for a shift of power to the local level. The economic, psychological, and political climate of the ghetto is examined. It is concluded that lack of power is corrupting and that this move toward community enterprise should be supported. Some early and innovative CDCs are described.

For additional readings concerning psychologists' roles or potential roles in urban planning and development, see Key (1969), Mordock (1971), and Rand (1969). For a systems approach, see Meier's *A Communications Theory of Urban Growth* (1962).

Clinebell, H. J. (ed.) *Community mental health: the role of church and temple.* Nashville: Abingdon Press, 1970.

Clinebell's collection of papers invites our attention to a potentially powerful force in the community—one often neglected by psychologists—namely the religious networks. Papers are presented in four sections: the church's roles in prevention, in treatment, the clergyman's role in mental health services, and training and organizing for mental health action. Not only does organized religion provide a readymade network of potential helpers, but it has in places done stimulating exploring of concepts of values and meaning. It also has unique experience with life crises.

Mechanic, D. *Mental health and social policy.* Englewood Cliffs, N.J.: Prentice-Hall, 1969.

Mechanic provides a sociologist's view of how the concepts of mental health are generated, transmitted, and ultimately enacted into social policy. He is particularly critical of the ideology of community psychiatry, which may, he feels, breed disappointment and frustration by making grandiose and unrealistic claims for healing a sick society.

RESEARCH EXAMPLES

Cook, P. E., and Josephs, P. O., The Community Adaptation Schedule and the California Psychological Inventory: a validational study with college students. *Community Mental Health Journal*, 1970, *6*, 366–373.

The Community Adaptation Schedule is designed to give a quantified measure of a person's adjustment to several facets of community living, a unifying community mental health concept which avoids notions of pathology and deviance. It consists of self-report items rated on a six-point scale. It is scored for total community adaptation, common question total, modes of response (affect, behavior, cognition); adaptation to work, family, larger social, commercial, and professional communities.

The authors investigated the relationship between the Community Adaptation Schedule and the CPI using fifty-seven advanced, undergraduate students. Significant and intelligible correlations gave evidence of the construct validity of the CAS.

Schedules such as the CAS will require validational studies taking community behavior as well as personality traits into account. Correlating the CAS with the Personal Attitude and Role Skills Inventory of Ellsworth (1968) might be a step in that direction.

Eisdorfer, C., Altrocchi, J., and Young, R. F., The principles of community mental health in a community setting: the Halifax County program. *Community Mental Health Journal*, 1968, *4*, 211–220.

The authors grapple with the problems of insufficient helping manpower and geographic vastness. They espouse a consultation approach to these problems, and, in presenting the history and structure of their program, state twenty principles or deductions from their experience. The paper presents sufficient details to serve both as an example of how to and how not to implement a similar wide-area consultation program. The paper serves also as a specimen of what is involved when the decision to use a consultation approach is made by a group that has faced the problems of manpower geographic vastness and decided against alternative schemes, such as limited direct service or referral educational programs.

Wagner, E. E., and Dobbins, R. D. MMPI profiles of parishioners seeking pastoral counseling. *Journal of Consulting Psychology*, 1967, *31*, 83–84.

This brief study attempts to throw some light on the question: What are people like who seek psychological help from their pastor? which is a vital question in the whole area of assessing psychological needs of a community. The MMPI was given by the minister of the Assembly of God church to every parishioner who routinely sought aid through pastoral counseling over a ten-month period. Forty subjects, thirteen males and twenty-seven females, were tested. A control group of forty parishioners not seeking help was selected to be similar to the experimental group in age, years of education, and mean income.

The null hypothesis between groups was rejected for all scales except Mf and Ma. The authors were able to get an idea of the variety of disturbance and their degree of seriousness by comparing the two groups on the number of subjects ranging 2SD or more above the mean. The psychological disturbances of those seen for pastoral counseling were not concentrated on a particular scale but (omitting Mf, Ma and Si) were rather evenly distributed across all clinical scales. (The authors feel that even distribution tends to contradict the assumption that the clergyman sees mainly discouraged or depressed people.) The results suggest that people seeking pastoral counseling might not differ greatly from those seen in clinical practice by psychologists or psychiatrists. The authors raise the question: Is the clergyman adequately trained to deal with such problems?

There are geographic social class and other limitations in sampling. Additionally, the MMPI is a very limited measure (we have no idea of overt behavior patterns or of community adjustment of the people); nonetheless it examines a segment of a functioning community helping mechanism. Perhaps the authors' next question should be: Is there evidence that mental health professionals do better with such problems?

Beier, E. G., Robinson, P., and Micheletti, G. Susanville: a community helps itself in mobilization of community resources for self help in mental health. *Journal of Consulting and Clinical Psychology*, 1971, *36*, 142–150.

The project at Susanville provides a first-class example of balanced attention to personal, family, organizational, and community systems. One local community figure felt that the community would benefit by using local resources rather than by relying on bringing in expensive consultants from outside. The plan for the project was developed with several sources sharing in the decision making and the implementation.

Eighteen adult trainees and fourteen high school students were trained to work with families having problem children in the schools or identified as being under stress. Training consisted of seventy hours of role play and supervised practicum over seven weeks. Trainees were immediately exposed to working with problem families using a communication model and the assumption that all family members contribute toward the problems.

Thirteen of the adult trainees were members of the local mental health power structure, one facet of the organizers' sensitivity to the difficulty ensuring the safety of a new organization in the established network of forces, tensions, and competing alignments. The adult trainees were each paid $100 for participating in the program.

The seven families seen by the adult trainees had come to the attention of school authorities for problems their children had been having in school. The families' role in helping the community was stressed rather than any "patienthood." They were told that the objective was to increase their ability to deal effectively with one another and the community. Fourteen high school students, apparently unpaid, were selected to work with four male counselees.

Trainees were taught eleven procedural pointers and principles, for example: "Do not accept 'I am as I am' statements (e.g., "I've always been happy go lucky: it's the way I am"). These are ways of stopping discussions. Consider people capable of changing, and these comments as excuses." Three major meetings were scheduled each week, including lectures, discussions, seminars, demonstrations, and individual appointments. From time to time, representatives of local community leadership or sponsorship participated as interested observers.

The evaluation phase collected four types of data: (1) interviews with participating trainees, (2) interviews with high school counselees and families, (3) videotaped and analyzed family interactions, and (4) information from various agencies in the community on type and frequency of community problems. Despite the brevity of the project, worthwhile results are reported both for trainees and families, along with suggestions for future research on community change.

The account of the Susanville project shows sensitivity to the courage and the preparation needed for new mental health behaviors to arise and survive in the community. Psychologists might ask, also, about the relationship of resource availability and innovation. How does innovation in resource-rich communities differ from that in resource-poor ones, and what do these differences imply for client well-being and for the direction of the profession?

Bard, M., *Training police as specialists in family crisis intervention.* Report PR 70-1, U. S. Department of Justice and Law Enforcement Assistance Administration, National Institute of Law Enforcement and Criminal Justice. Washington, D. C.: U. S. Government Printing Office, 1970.

Bard's project must rate as exemplary in the annals of community psychology. Besides having careful evaluation procedures and substantial scope, it carefully prepared the ground with the law-enforcement hierarchy before beginning. The project addressed a complicated problem involving a community resource usually neglected by human service workers: the role of law enforcement in family quarrels. As Bard (p. 30) says: "As a community mental health resource the police are an agency without parallel. In the interlocking network of helping agencies the police have stood in a unique position in the psychological front lines. By increasing the sensitivity and professional perception of police an unusual early warning mechanism for identifying psychological and social pathology is made available to the community."

The project attempted to modify family assaults and family homicides in a circumscribed area—a New York City precinct of some 85,000 residents—as well as to reduce personal damage to the police officers in such situations and equip them to be effective first-case finders. A neighboring precinct provided a comparison with the experimental group. Eighteen police volunteers were selected and trained in 160 hours of lectures, field trips, lab demonstrations, and role playing involving specially written plays and actors, and finally human-relation workshops. In the two-year operation phase, one radio car was reserved for family crisis work with continuous coverage provided by unit members. Weekly consultation to each member was provided by clinical psychology students.

The evaluation phase covered four months of the project but systematic data were collected throughout. Over the duration of the project, although there was an increase in family homicides in the experimental area consistent with a city-wide increase, there were no homicides in any of the 962 families seen on 1,388 occasions by the family crisis unit; family assaults decreased and there were no injuries to any unit member, despite the high probability of injury in such cases.

In the report the following were among the conclusions Bard stated:

1. Sensitive and skillful police intervention in family disturbances may serve to reduce the occurrence of family assaults and family homicides.

2. Personal safety of police officers can be greatly increased through the use of psychologically sophisticated techniques in dealing with highly charged human-conflict situations.

3. Policemen are in an unusual position for early identification of human behavioral pathology and, if trained, can play a critical role in crime prevention and preventive mental health.

4. Psychological education directed at specific police functions can enhance law enforcement in general and order maintenance in particular.

Bard commented on the great difficulty of getting traditional social service agencies to service police referrals or indeed to react to a police officer in a constructive open manner. Building effective bridges between police and other established agencies remains a critical important matter in communities. For this problem, the Bard project has made a valuable beginning. Readers wishing to pursue the topic further may wish to refer to Shellow and Roemer's "The Riot That Didn't Happen" (1966) and Bard's model for social action (1972).

part III

The Person and the Profession

chapter **18**

Development of the Clinician

In Chapters 18–20 we shall return to broader issues of the clinical psychologist and clinical psychology. Over earlier chapters of this book we have seen the wide variety of things that clinical psychologists do—observation, interviewing, testing, research, recommendations for case management, behavior modification, group therapy, organizational and community consultation, teaching and administration, and all of these in regard to many different kinds of clients and different sorts of settings. The occupation of clinical psychologist consists of a tremendously varied set of possibilities. Each individual must be prepared to choose only certain things to do. He or she may change tasks and settings from time to time; in fact, that is the rule, not the exception; but it is impossible to do all things at once. In this chapter we shall look at the shifting role mix that is a typical pattern for clinicians and we will bring to bear whatever findings are available from studies of the personal systems and social role of clinicians.

In addition to the "outside view" of the personal career field of the clinician, we will also take an "inside view" of his personal life. What is it like to work with dangerous or disturbed people? How does the clinician handle the tensions that he takes home from the office? How does the clinician try to reconcile the "hard" and "soft" sides his job requires—the scientific anaylsis versus the human caring, the organizational cost-benefit viewpoint versus the needs of the community? Do certain experiences contribute to professional growth? The clinician is not superhuman, and anyone considering going into the field, or who is already in it, must take account of his own personal needs and his own developing maturity.

WHO IS A CLINICIAN?

In our discussion so far in this book, we have not defined clearly what the training and qualifications of the clinical psychologist should be. We have mainly thought of the doctoral-level clinical psychologist as the model, but we have used the word "clinician" occasionally in a broad sense, applying it also to related occupations whose members would not technically be called clinical psychologists. As we shall see in Chapter 19, the profession of clinical psychology has moved a long way toward specifying the clinical psychologist as a person with a Ph.D. in psychology having several years of experience in clinical work. Certification and licensing have added legal force to that definition. There are many arguments for professional definition and regulation, as we will see in Chapter 19, but the viewpoint we have taken in this book is that clinical psychology (as contrasted with the clinical psychologist) is *an area of knowledge and practice* that is much broader than the specifically defined occupation. The principles of behavior modification are being taught and used by teachers, psychiatrists, and even by clients and people in the general public. Many group techniques are spreading widely throughout society. As G. A. Miller said in his APA presidential address (1969), we should "give psychology away" in order to help promote greater psychological effectiveness and human welfare. It is in this spirit that we view with welcome the development of ancillary and additional helping services at various levels of training.

For several decades the interest in clinical psychology has been very high. At the undergraduate level psychology is very popular. As many as fifty or more individuals may apply for each new opening in well-known doctoral training programs. Applicants have also been very numerous in counseling psychology doctoral programs, and many people are finding that counseling and clinical doctorates are equivalent for a large number of jobs. In addition, many trained at the master's level obtain positions and perform very similarly to Ph.D. psychologists. As we have seen in Chapter 17, many people are being trained as "mental health workers" or "counselors" with bachelor's degrees. If the massive need for psychosocial improvement of society is to be met, vast numbers must be involved in prevention and remediation of the "causalities of society." Whether nations are willing to pay for programs remedying "behavioral pollution" is an open question for the public and the political leadership.

The problem with clinical work broadly defined is that it is in danger of creating a chaos of titles and training programs. If governmental funding is reduced or experimental programs phased out, persons trained for positions and expecting to hold jobs cannot find them. In addition, the public needs some way of knowing who is an authentic, responsible, capable person in the areas of psychological assistance. The terms "psychologist" and "psychiatrist" are confusing enough to the layman.

Inevitably the clinical psychologist will be involved in this definition of the field of the helping professions. We will come back to this concern in Chapter 20 in a discussion of future manpower needs in clinical psychology. Although employment projections are complicated, it seems highly probable that jobs in academic circles are going to be more scarce in the United States as the downturn in births of the 1960s starts to hit colleges in the 1980s. The continuing popularity of education may result in more growth in community colleges than in universities. Students making decisions may want to keep such job projections in mind. (For further information, see the May 1972 issue of the *American Psychologist* on manpower—especially the short epilogue by the APA Executive Secretary, Kenneth Little, 1972.) For the remaining part of this chapter we shall refer to doctoral-level or highly experienced people when we refer to the clinical psychologist or clinician.

In summary, the clinical psychologist is viewed in this book (adapting a format from Bisno, 1969) as follows:

CLINICAL PSYCHOLOGISTS,

usually doctorates in psychology with several years of experience,
working within a sociocultural milieu
including a sponsoring organization
confront
problems of psychobiological and psychosocial distress and behavioral
disorder
with the goals
of maintaining and enhancing the function of persons,
singly and collectively,
through
occupying a variety of occupational roles in a variety of settings,
acting within a conceptual framework related to behavioral science,
and performing the tasks of
designing improvement plans,
through appraisal of clients and situations,
thereby providing realistic and constructive *image building* and
decision making,
implementing improvement programs
through communication and effective cooperation with clients and
their significant surroundings, and
use of such skills as psychotherapy, behavior modification, and consultation,
and
evaluating program effectiveness,
meanwhile contributing to
the *managing, teaching, and training* of others
and
the *furtherance of knowledge of the human condition.*

From this excruciating sentence, we can summarize again the varied roles of clinical psychologists as follows:

1. *Assessor* for the gathering, organizing, evaluating, and transmitting of information about persons and situations, including image making.

2. *Designer* and planner of improvement programs.
3. *Intervener—therapist* on an individual and small-group level.
4. *Consultant—facilitator* of organizational and community processes.
5. *Administrator* of programs—rule making and rule implementing.
6. *Teacher-facilitator* for conceptual and socioemotional growth.
7. *Evaluator* of programs.
8. *Knowledge developer* and researcher.

Most of these roles are reflected in the guidelines for evaluating clinicians who have reached the highest level of professional certification, the diplomate awarded by the American Board of Professional Psychology. Table 18-1 presents the check sheet used in recording the rationale for decisions by an ABPP examining board (personal communication from Mark Lewin, 1971).

TABLE 18—1   Check Sheet for Evaluation of the Performance of a Clinical Psychologist

A. **Assessment**
    Lacked a well-developed rationale for field examination assessment work
    Lacked a theoretical framework for assessment work in general
    Did not formulate adequate assessment impressions
    Limited depth in assessment thinking; did not formulate adequate recommendations for intervention
    Demonstrated limited range of assessment skills
    Did not use assessment time effectively
    Did not make efficient use of the assessment tools selected
    Seemed unaware of own limitations in assessment

B. **Constructive Interventions**
    Inadequate theoretical framework for intervention
    Inadequate rationale for intervention demonstrated
    Failed to establish adequate relationships with patient/client in case observed or reported
    Limited range of intervention skills
    Limited depth in intervention sample(s)
    Intervention work not effective
    Seemed unaware of own limitations in intervention
    Inadequate use of information available from assessment

C. **Ethical Practices**
    Inadequate knowledge of ethical principles
    Inadequate sensitivity to ethical problems
    Failed to intervene, report, or otherwise take appropriate action in unethical situation

D. **Psychology as a Profession**
    Too limited awareness of organized psychology
    Too limited participation in organized psychology

E. **Research**
Insufficient awareness of pertinent research
Insufficient understanding of implications of research
Insufficient ability in critical evaluation of research
Insufficient application of pertinent research in one's practice

F. **Miscellaneous**
Too limited scope of competencies to be boarded
Not sufficiently skillful in developing relations with patients/clients
Not sufficiently skillful or flexible in adapting to situations or to
patients/clients
Inadequate integration of assessment, ethics, and research

G. **Other**
Additional concerns about this candidate

Source: Adapted from the form used for negative decisions on ABPP examinations. By permission of the American Board of Professional Psychology, Inc.

CAREER DIRECTIONS

The book has already made clear the many patterns of clinical psychologists' lives. If anyone talks with several psychologists, he will soon find out that they have diversity of backgrounds and current concerns that all people have. The doctoral-level practicing clinician has made a series of choices, however, that have led to his profession. Figure 18-1 is a kind of road-map record of one clinical psychologist's decisions. It shows choice points throughout his life that have led to where he is now. It is possible that the results would have been far different if accidents or personal preferences had led to choosing other routes that were open at that time. The figure also indicates the shifting nature of the work of the clinician even after he obtains his highest degree. A professional career involves life-long learning—and choices.

Are there commonalities in diverse clinicians' lives? In the long process of moving from childhood to adulthood and old age, a small number of people out of the population of a country become psychologists, and of these only some practice clinical psychology throughout their professional lives. Can we detect any special characteristics of this particular kind of life history? Where are the special decisions points? What kind of a selection process goes on to winnow out a mature and effective clinican from the myriad possibilities?

Early Background and Characteristics
of Psychologists in General

One question psychologists frequently ask themselves is: "How did I get into this profession?" Some say they are miscarried ministers, writers, or physicians;

some say they came into psychology to try to solve their personal problems; some say they have always been curious about people—like the little boy in the *Peanuts* cartoon who says he wants to study people when he grows up because he's "just plain nosey."

The exact reasons any given person chose psychology are undoubtedly complex and multiply caused. Some light is thrown on the question from the survey of psychologists by the American Psychological Association (Clark, 1957). A large sample of psychologists who got their doctors' degrees in the 1930s and 1940s answered questionnaries about their backgrounds, training, and present situation. Concerning the family background of psychologists it is clear

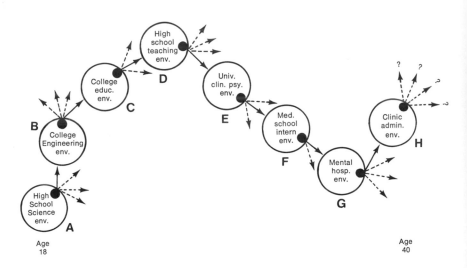

FIGURE 18-1 Map of the "career trip" of one clinical psychologist. Choice points: *A.* After a heavy emphasis on the physical sciences in his high school environment, CP (the clinical psychologist) chooses a college and is admitted to an engineering program on the advice of a favorite uncle, who is an engineer. *B.* Not doing well in engineering; after seeing a counselor in the college counseling center, he decides to shift to education. *C.* At the end of his college work, with a teaching certificate, he decides to accept one of three offers and enters the environment of a high school as a social science teacher; he marries and develops strong interests in child development and counseling. *D.* He decides to go back for graduate work in clinical psychology, and enters that environment. *E.* Among several possibilities for internships in the last year of graduate work, he chooses one in a medical school, where he becomes very interested in computerized diagnosis. *F.* CP chooses a mental hospital job paying the best money among the rather limited possibilities that year. *G.* Needing more money to support his growing family and ambitious life style, he takes the job of administrator of a small private clinic. *H.* After three successful years, at age 40, CP feels bored with his job, and is looking around for possibilities.

that education has been a vehicle of upward social mobility. Only about a third of the fathers of psychologists were professional men; another third were in managerial and office work, and the remaining third were in clerical work, sales, working-class occupations. At the time of Clark's study, one-third of the psychologists' fathers and mothers had only a grammer school education. This finding of upward mobility was also found by Henry, Sims, and Spray (1971) in their extensive study of psychotherapists (summarized at the end of this chapter). Roe has studied prominent research scientists in various scientific disciplines. In her study of psychologists (1952, 1953), she frequently found a family concern with social status, family patterns involving overprotection and firm control, and present resentment and difficulty with the parents.

In their religious backgrounds Clark reports that psychologists are very varied, but in comparison with the general population it is likely that psychology, like some other sciences, draws a higher proportion of persons with liberal Protestant and Jewish backgrounds and a smaller number of Catholics than would be expected from the proportion of such persons in the general population.

In the Henry et al. survey of therapists (1971) who were from New York, Chicago, and Los Angeles, 52 percent were Jewish in background. As with all professions, nonwhites are grossly underrepresented in psychology in proportion to the population. Boxley and Wagner (1971) reported a survey of faculty and students in clinical training programs showing that whereas blacks comprised 11 percent of the population, there were 2 percent black students and faculty. Spanish groups are also badly underrepresented. Astin's research (1972) on women psychologists indicated that about 13 percent of psychologists were women, and they were of lower status and less well paid than comparable men. Campbell and Soliman (1968) concluded from a retesting of women who had taken the Strong Vocational Interest Blank twenty-four years earlier that women's interests have not changed much and that psychology as a career continues to attract women who have more intellectual, scientific, and verbal interests than women in general.

A majority of the psychologists in the APA survey made their decision to go into psychology while in college. In undergraduate work the large majority were able to achieve high grades. They reported being influenced in their decision to enter psychology by a great variety of things. Prominent among them were good teachers and interesting courses, a scientific interest in human behavior, and a personal interest in knowing more about human beings. Roe's studies of psychologists (1952, 1953) led her to conclude that psychologists "are from childhood very much more concerned with other persons than are those who go into such fields as physics and biology. That personal relations loom so large in their lives may well have affected the theories of personality development now current" (1953, p. 171). The last comment seems a very important one for psychologists to keep in mind in judging the development of their field. In Gough's research with the California Psychological Inventory (1957), psychology graduate students show a characteristic profile. On the average, in comparison with the general population, they can be described as independent, more given to achieving by independence than conformance, intellectually superior, perceptive, ambitious, forceful, resourceful, quick, clever, spontaneous, insightful, flexible, adventurous, and showing social presence. Many of these characteristics would be true of graduate students in other fields as well. Among graduate students, psychologists obtain one of the highest average scores on tests of intellectual ability.

Characteristics of Psychologists Choosing the Clinical Speciality

So far we have been mainly concerned with all kinds of psychologists. Among people going into psychology, there is the question of who would go into clinical work. Entering graduate students in clinical work are very similar to other graduate students in psychology in possessing a high level of intelligence and professional and scientific interests (Kelly and Fiske, 1951). Kriedt (1949) was able to distinguish among the interests of several specialties which psychologists enter and has developed special scales for the Strong Vocational Interest Blank. Kriedt describes clinical psychologists as being differentiated from other psychologists by having stronger artistic, literary, teaching, verbal, and social service interests. It was found by Kelly and Fiske (1951) that clinical psychologists are quite similar in interests to psychiatrists.

Kelly and Goldberg (1959) in a follow-up of the 248 VA clinical psychologists who were studied at the time of their entrance into graduate work in 1947 and 1948 were also able to note some of their special characteristics. They found differences between those who subsequently engaged primarily in academic or research work and those who occupied administrative positions. They also tried to find the distinguishing characteristics of those who took up the practice of psychotherapy. The academic clinical psychologists were characterized as being bright, theoretically oriented, widely read but not socially active; their reported childhood backgrounds were characterized by considerable intrapsychic disturbance, lack of athletic ability and leadership, relative isolation and solitude, curiosity, and good school marks. Administrative clinical psychologists were characterized by extroversion, coming from a harmonious and religious family background, early participation in athletics, class leadership, somewhat less curiosity, good grades but somewhat lower measured intelligence. The overlap between academicians and administrators was quite low, but the therapists were not distinguished as a separate homogeneous group, contrary to the expectations of the experimenters. Like the academician, the therapist also had experienced family frictions and a sense of inferiority as a child; by the time he entered graduate school he already had pronounced interests in clinical work, and applied psychological work in general. Henry, Sims, and Spray (1971) found that the motivations reported by psychologists in psychotherapy as reasons for choosing their field were a desire to understand people, help people, and to understand and help themselves. Roe's review (1969) of research on the characteristics of therapists indicated higher "femininity" on the MMPI, less interest in mathematics, but more interest in people, the arts, and theoretical ideas than comparable groups. Thus we see a process of decision and differentiation among individuals going into clinical psychology.

Though it is possible to find differences among psychologists who go into different specialities, one major point of the clinical psychology assessment program should not be missed. It is very difficult to predict future success in clinical work from any of the traditional tests or from complex procedures aimed at the clinical evaluation of entering graduate students. The extensive assessment of VA trainees, reviewed at the end of this chapter, showed little relationship with criteria of later success (Kelly and Fiske, 1951). The most generally useful measures were two objective tests, the Miller Analogies (widely used as a test of ability to do graduate work) and the Strong Vocational Interest Blank. The best predictions were to intellectual aspects of success in graduate work, with correlations running from 0.35 to 0.60 even in the restricted range being studied. The monographs by Kelly and Fiske (1951) and Kelly and Goldberg (1959) clearly show that there is great diversity among the individuals who are later judged successful in psychodiagnosis, psychotherapy, and academic work in clinical psychology. It is also true that there was great diversity among the judges who served to establish criteria—that is, different universities and training centers adopt different criteria for judging candidates. A problem with some of these studies is that they were conducted a few decades ago on psychologists who grew up during the Depression and World War II. It is conceivable that a group growing up and trained in the 1960s and 1970s would have different characteristics. Studies using measures selected from the earlier research could test hypotheses about shifts in the professional culture.

TRAINING EXPERIENCES IN CLINICAL PSYCHOLOGY

Graduate school training is the essential formative experience for professional work. On the average, clinical psychologists take five years of graduate work to obtain the Ph.D. (Kelly and Goldberg, 1959), though the time varies greatly, with some individuals, who may hold part-time jobs, taking much longer. In their graduate years students develop their professional identity. They learn the principles, concepts, and skills of their vocation, which they will carry into future work. It is a period of intensive indoctrination to which they will react positively or negatively, in varying proportions, for the rest of their lives. During these years, they must clear many selective hurdles—course work, seminar papers, supervised clinical work, "preliminary" doctoral examinations, original research—all of which are used to appraise them as persons and as scholars and future practitioners. The cost in money, effort, and time is great. Many graduate students are married, putting extra burdens on wives and children. What is the effect of all these pressures, this selection? It is hard to give a clear answer, but certainly the program demands great motivation, persistence, ability, and general effectiveness of personality.

The early period of graduate school usually emphasizes general psychology, followed by a gradual turn to more and more specialized courses through the ensuing years. Preparation for clinical work often starts with observation, interviewing, and testing of normal people. Later in the practicum, the student is supervised in the assessment of actual clients and in taking a few cases in psychotherapy. In some universities community-clinical psychology is taught, emphasizing consultation and other work with organizations (Kelly, 1970a). This is apparently a growing emphasis (Simmons, 1971).

The introductory knowledge and skills learned in courses are put into practice under the supervision of psychologists in clinics, agencies, and hospitals. The detailed description of courses and practicum work in clinical psychology will not be undertaken here. Such descriptions have been published from time to time by the American Psychological Association, and more information is readily available by writing to any psychology department that offers graduate training in clinical psychology.

Along with the formal learning there is much to be learned informally. Many graduate schools have a unique traditional atmosphere and thrust which the new student quickly feels and usually identifies with. Prominent research psychologists emphasize the importance of learning from apprenticeship relationships with older research workers. Research assistantships and seminars with ongoing research projects provide valuable experience. Clinical practicum training often is a kind of apprenticeship under master diagnosticians or therapists. The graduate-student subculture is often a strong and formative influence. Students often say there is as much to be learned from associating closely with other graduate students facing similar problems as from any other source.

At the same time that contacts are being made with the many positive aspects of clinical training and experience, its negative aspects will become apparent. Training of this specialized kind increases the distance between the clinician and the "common man" with whom he will work. It requires a kind of compulsive delay of reward and an attention to books and abstract ideas that is sometimes almost neurosis-producing. Someone has said that the price of specialization is narrowness. Clinical psychologists are likely to overemphasize some things and overlook others. As an example, it has been shown in several studies that clinicians judging normal protocols accentuate the abnormal and pathological unrealistically (e.g., Soskin, 1954, 1959). Clinicians trained as they are today often fail to see the most obvious everyday influences on behavior and prefer to find or invent deep unconscious motives as explanations. In therapy, there are grounds for questioning seriously the effectiveness of clinicians from highly educated middle-class backgrounds in treating disturbed people with lower-class backgrounds or different subcultures. There seems to be too wide a disparity in values and understanding of each other's behavior. Also, many manual laborers and poorly educated people do not communicate well verbally and do not care for "talking therapy." Perhaps this is part of the reason Hollingshead and Redlich (1958) found that lower-class patients were more often given drug and shock treatments than middle-class patients. Also, in work with delinquent boys, some investigators have found that a counselor or social worker is more effective if he comes from a similar background, perhaps even to the extent of having had a police record himself when a youngster. The studies of clinical prediction, as we have previously seen, show that the people who can predict best are close to the norms of the group they are predicting.

These examples, and perhaps many others the reader can think of, point to the highly selective character and the training limitations of clinicians. So it becomes obvious that we need to become aware of our strengths and weaknesses—a difficult assignment. The fact that many highly educated clinicians cannot at present accomplish much with delinquents and lower-class patients does not end the problem. One solution may be to have these clinicians work through other people selected for their ability to undertake special methods and forms of contact. Another solution would be to improve training methods by some radical innovations. Yet another possibility arises from the research of Mitchell and Namenek (1970), who found that both psychiatrists and clinical psychologists tended to work with persons of socioeconomic backgrounds similar to their own. It might then seem particularly desirable to recruit more clinicians having lower-class backgrounds and to match backgrounds of lower-class clients as much as possible.

It is also true that no one can be all things to all persons. The clinical student and the practicing psychologist must choose their areas of knowledge and skill. Rioch (1970) has advocated thinking of oneself as like a teacher. Some teachers are good at working with kindergarten children, others become college professors. The area of clinical psychology is equally as broad and complex.

Training in clinical psychology is a source of continuous analysis. Few people are ever satisfied with the state of the then-current programs, and one sees the popular term "crisis in training" applied not only in psychology but also in psychiatry, medicine, social work, and to education in general. "Toward a Boulder model" is a term used frequently as a pun on the most influential of all the training conferences on clinical psychology—the conference in Boulder, Colorado, in 1949, which proclaimed the scientist—professional ideal for the clinician (Raimy, 1950). A more recent conference in Chicago (Hoch, Ross, and Winder, 1966) reaffirmed the Boulder model largely but added some moves toward more professionalism and recommended the establishment of psychologist-controlled centers for service and training. (For rather extensive critiques of the Chicago conference, see Shakow and Kovacs, 1968.) Most academic clinical psychologists support the scientist–practitioner model (Thelen and Ewing, 1970), but organizational moves have been underway to promote more frankly professional programs (Rothenberg and Matulef, 1969).

The most lively developments establishing a professionally oriented training program have been those of the University of Illinois (Peterson, 1968b, 1969) and the California School of Professional Psychology functioning both in San Francisco and Los Angeles (Pottharst, 1970). The Illinois program offers the degree of Doctor of Psychology (D.Psy.) instead of the Ph.D. A small number of students, equal in intellectual ability to the Ph.D. candidates, are selected on the basis of experience and orientation to action and service. The program does not require a research thesis. The California School is not housed in a university, avoiding the development of loyalty to academic models. It makes extensive use of practitioners for training and is trying, as mentioned elsewhere, to establish a career ladder from the Associate of Arts degree to the Ph.D. Although early reports were favorable, the programs will need to be in operation a considerable time before full evaluations can be made.

Another lively aspect of the debate on training is the continual attempt to make programs more relevant and up to date. Weissman, Goldschmid, and Stein (1971), in a survey sampling the APA Division of Clinical Psychology, found considerable discontent among clinicians about the training they had received. They concluded (p. 36) that "clinical psychologists appear to be least well trained in the areas most demanded by society's needs, that is, those involving a greater awareness of social-cultural-environmental aspects of mental health," as Albee (1968) and Hunt (1969) have also said. Proshansky (1972) sounds a similar theme, recommending that training programs open themselves to the community and orient themselves around problems and social issues. If such changes are to occur, which are desirable in our estimation, they cannot be added on to existing programs without lengthening them considerably. So careful attention must be given to what things in the present programs can be displaced. One area in which a deemphasis seems to have started is in the training for traditional assessment, especially projective techniques (Thelen, Varble, and Johnson, 1968; Shemberg and Keeley, 1970; Biederman and Cerbus, 1971).

THE CLINICAL PSYCHOLOGIST AT WORK

During graduate-school days and the years shortly thereafter, the identity and loyalties of the clinical psychologist have often become pretty firmly crystallized. Formative experiences in academic work and clinical training have pointed him or her to follow lines of effort in pursuit of certain values. The young psychologist may have become a devout adherent of social learning theory or existential psychology, of psychoanalysis or psychometrics. He discovers that certain kinds of research or service suit his interests and temperament. He has found his "heroes." His professional identity automatically ensures that he has a basis both for his positive choices and for his defenses against the onslaughts of people who adhere to other views. He tests out this identity against his experiences after graduate school. Whether the clinician's ideologies acquired in graduate school or later really are congruent with his behavior is an open question. Weissman, Goldschmid, and Stein (1971) conclude there is little consistency.

In these early postdoctoral years, there are many choice points at which he must answer questions that "set the switches" for later professional development. What kind of psychological work do I want to do? Where should I go? What lines of research interest me? What kinds of clinical problems should I work with? There is still considerable flexibility about changing lines and places of work. It is said that on the average a psychologist makes three moves before he settles down. One reason for the geographical mobility of psychologists is that their reference community is not limited to the city or region of residence. Professional literature, meetings, and correspondence keep them in touch with psychologists all over the country or even the world. The job market is thus a very wide one. When a psychologist goes into private practice, there is perhaps more need to remain in a given community, since building up an active practice depends on one's reputation and liaison with referral sources. Only a small percentage of psychologists are in full-time private practice, however; the vast majority are connected primarily with academic or clinical institutions.

These early years constitute the most likely ones for creative contributions to psychology (Lehman, 1960; Pressey, 1960). Yet this period is also a difficult one because of many demands upon the time of the new clinician. If we select publications as an index, the productivity of clinical psychologists is not highly impressive. In the Kelly and Goldberg follow-up of VA trainees (1959), only 30 percent of them had more than one publication to their credit during the first five years after the Ph.D. Levy (1962) found that 29 percent of the clinical psychologists obtaining degrees in 1948–1953 had published nothing seven to twelve years later. Ten percent accounted for almost half of the published research. Bednar and Shapiro (1970) mailed questionnaires asking for about 3 hours of time assisting in research on therapy. Less than 1 percent of practicing therapists (both psychiatrists and psychologists) were willing to participate. Furthermore, of those clinicians who do publish, only 20 percent do research that is action- or decision-oriented, the remainder being theoretical in orientation (Arthur, 1972). Wolff (1970) found little research being done by private practitioners but some very influential observations and theories. He points out the lack of rewards and organizational support for research.

There are many possible reasons (rationalizations?) for this state of affairs: poor research training, deficient motivation, heavy demands for service in clinical settings, and heavy academic teaching loads. Another possibility is that our expectations that clinical psychologists should publish are too high. It is true that much emphasis in psychological training is placed on research; yet many psychologists are primarily motivated for service and make their contribution through using psychological procedures to help people. Perhaps the conflict between research and service and the difficulty of achieving much along both lines is part of the reason that a large number of clinicians are dissatisfied. In the Kelly and Goldberg study (1959) 40 percent of the respondents stated that if they had their lives to live over again, they would choose either another field of psychology or some other profession, such as medicine or law. Again, without comparisons with other professional groups, it is difficult to interpret such a figure. In a survey of 158 psychologists in the state of Oregon, very few, only 8 percent, stated they would definitely go into another occupation if they were starting over again (Wiens et al., 1961).

The psychologist as well as his clients, is a creature of time. The young psychologist may find it difficult to acknowledge that, like older psychologists, and like those yet to decide to become psychologists, he or she will have a professional life cycle. Training, first job, other jobs, perhaps a major shift or two, a "peak" position, and then a shift to retirement or semiretirement—such details help cast the professional cycle of all of us. As the years go by there are shifts in the "role mix" of what a particular clinician does. One likely change is from direct work with patients to other activities. In Clark's APA survey (1957), clinicians who had been out of graduate school ten to twenty years reported that only a fourth of their time was devoted to straight clinical service; those out of graduate school for four years reported that a third of their time went into clinical work. The older clinicians reported more administrative work and teaching. Experienced clinicians also have more responsibility for supervising and training students. Of all these activities, administration is the most foreign to the clinician's previous training. As intimated in Chapters 16 and 17, the psychologist does bring to that role knowledge of people and some aspects of organizations, but he knows little about preparing budgets or doing cost-benefit analyses. Yet this activity can be seen as very important and exciting if it is viewed as it is in reality—a significant aspect of social change and programmatic creativity (Bindman, 1970; Felzer, 1970). Many psychologists seem to be doing well in administration, for a national survey shows their increasing acceptance as heads of public mental health programs (Dörken, 1970).

How stable the present roles of the clinical psychologist will be cannot be foreseen. Pressey (1960) has pointed out the impossibility of training adequately for future developments in any scientific field. Perhaps totally new kinds of activity will emerge. The increasingly large bulk of literature now published and the broadening of the work of psychologists into community consultation, applications to many fields, new research, and so on, make the field a dynamic, changing one. Time also brings extensive changes to professional organizations, governmental policies, and public attitudes, many of which will have far-reaching effects on the future shape of psychology. Social pressures, lobbies, minorities, international crises, and even the process of social maturation—all these may change the assumptions and tasks of those who would improve the quality of life. In particular, the national decisions about the degree and the extent of federal medical coverage or far-reaching legislation in welfare, education, or crime control could have the effect of creating or obviating whole classes of present problems. Certain types of psychological problems which seem related to the stresses of inadequate housing, overcrowding, poverty, and alienation may be greatly diminished by effective legislation. An adequate guaranteed income for everyone would radically alter the socioeconomic stresses which seem related to almost every study of mental illness and treatment. Yet it is certain that economic support, as important as it is for a sense of security and freedom of choice, will not eradicate psychological distress. In other areas legislation may make significant differences in the work of the psychologist. We can speculate, for instance, on the effects of legalizing marijuana or homosexuality. In contemplating needed changes in society, psychologists must be asking questions about the effects and the side effects of different sorts of legislation and public programs. Thus part of the work of the psychologist is to look beyond his immediate task and see the broader perspective of societal change.

THE CLINICIAN AS A PERSON

What is the personal life of the effective clinician like? What personal qualities contribute to his or her professional life? What might a beginning student of clinical psychology do to develop himself or herself?

These questions are important, because clinical psychology is frequently involved in the most intimate and emotion-charged aspects of life and because the most important ingredient in the helping relation is the clinician's personal influence. We wish that research had produced some clear answers, but findings are scattered and inconclusive. We must move ahead on the basis of our own knowledge of the field and personal experience.

At the outside, it would be repeated that we firmly believe that *a wide variety of persons can find satisfying and effective positions in clinical psychology.* Among our friends and acquaintances making significant contributions to clinical work, we know of many different life styles and life experiences— individuals from broken homes and traumatic backgrounds, persons with handicaps and unusual physical characteristics, people from all kinds of religions and ethnic origins, and a diversity of interpersonal styles. Partly this variety arises from the great many choices within the field—differing settings, differing clienteles, and differing activities. The psychologist who is a community activist may be very unlike the one doing research on psychoneurological disorders. With this diversity in mind, let us ask the questions: With what problems must the clinical psychologist learn to cope? And what experiences may be of help? We shall look at five areas of professional functioning:

Working with a Sense of Competence

How does the clinician develop, maintain, and advance a sense of competence in this difficult, changing, and uncertain field? Psychologists are taught, starting with their introductory psychology courses, that their science is an incomplete and complex one and that enormous amounts of research are necessary to clarify even simple problems. Although this attitude is appropriate, the applied psychologist must *act*, not stand still in a confusion of unanswered questions. So the practicing clinician must make decisions and interact with real people immediately facing real problems. Some people have observed that physicians are taught to give answers, and psychologists are taught to ask questions. Psychologists must retain a spirit of inquiry, but at the same time they must develop a sense of confidence in their ability to handle serious problems. Another aspect of this question of competence is knowing in what areas the psychologist is competent. Not an expert in everything, the psychologist must be wary of claiming more than he can do.

In addition to receiving the best graduate education that he can afford, the psychologist is likely to have many opportunities for continuing development of competence through workshops, professional meetings, and supervisory relations individually developed. The clinician needs to face frankly the fact that he cannot master every test or assessment device and every therapeutic theory and technique. He will feel much more confident if he can master some selected procedures very well and then develop variations on them. It is helpful to recognize that one cannot do certain things in clinical work and discuss these with supervisors and colleagues. It is also useful to study clinical cases on consultant work to see what worked well and what did not. The inquiring orientation of the psychologist is strengthening as well as deflating. By asking questions of himself and others he can learn what really works and what does not, thus eventually building up a confidence resting on reality.

Relating Empathically yet Realistically with Clients

How does the clinician develop and enhance an understanding and warm interaction with clients yet maintain sufficient objectivity? Most psychologists have a deep interest in people, and they want to be understanding and helpful. Most therapists in some way indicate that accurate empathy is very important—the ability to feel what the client feels. The ability to comprehend emotional communications has received some research attention as well as judgments and predicitions of others' responses, as mentioned elsewhere, but the field is still far from clear—especially the manner in which people might be trained to improve their understanding of others. In clinical work itself, the problem is not just accurate reception of communications, but accurate and helpful usage of one's understanding in therapeutic activity.

One simple way to develop empathy is to encourage the person to tell about himself and to listen with great interest, not judging, agreeing, or disagreeing. Training in such nonjudgmental, engrossed listening would seem to be a fundamental prerequisite for clinical education. Doing such listening with a variety of people may be very helpful, particularly with people for whom one has a hard time feeling a relationship. One male clinician told one of the authors about his difficulty in working with female homosexuals in a prison; he found it helpful when one of the women was willing to describe in detail how she felt about putting her breasts against another woman's breasts and proceeding with further descriptions of lesbian relationships. The clinician needs to put "part of himself" in the place of the other person—whether he is a mongoloid child or a nuclear physicist. This kind of "taking the role of the other" may be helped by psychodrama and role playing, by reading autobiographies and diaries, and by supervision. It is a high art.

Thinking and Acting Socioecologically

How does the clinical psychologist appreciate and use the complexity and ecological wholeness of the living situation of his clients and community? Part of the problem for a functioning psychologist is to adjust his manner of thinking such that he understands not only the client's feelings and thoughts but also the client's surroundings and the influences of them. The physical and social environment must be understood as well as the client. Just as there are areas of unconsciousness about feelings and fantasies, there are areas of unconsciousness about social and environmental conditions and forces.

In coping with this area of challenge, the clinician could learn a great deal if he could put himself physically into the environment of his clients. Living in a ghetto area or staying for several days as a patient on a hospital ward gives the psychologist experiences that could not easily be obtained by interview or superficial observation. (See Goldman, Bohr, and Steinberg, 1970, abstracted at the end of this chapter.) It is to be hoped that psychologists will do research on a variety of ways to teach people how to conceive of the living environment of clients. As mentioned in earlier chapters, asking the client or informant (such as a parent) to report carefully on his observations of behavior is another important way of establishing understandings and baselines of designing improvement programs.

Coping with Colleagues and Institutions

How should the clinician learn to function effectively within and with organizations? All of us are parts of or have to deal with large bureaucratic systems. Many psychologists work for hospitals, clinics, colleges, industries, governmental units, and other bureaucracies. In helping clients they often have to deal with such organizations. Professionals also have organized systems. Surviving and coping with bureaucracy is a necessary ability for clinical psychologists.

It helps the young psychologist learning to work in an organization to give some time specifically to learning about that organization and its environment. He should not only know the organization chart, but also the informal lines of communication and decision making. He needs to recognize that the institution is set up to ease decision making by impersonal rules, many of which may be as fair as possible but some of which are likely to work against some individual needs. His colleagues will be operating by a more or less similar understanding of procedures, but communication often breaks down and an enormous amount of time is put into meetings, memos, and other methods for ensuring wide understanding of the rules of the game. Taking an empathic point of view, role playing or other learning activities may be helpful. In any such situation, the clinician will be faced with the problem of allocating his professional time—how much should he give to meetings, clients, and so on. An understanding of priorities on usage of time is important, as well as an understanding of the formal and informal expectations of the job he takes. He should also recognize the great influence of the values of the financing organization on what is done—sometimes to the detriment of the original values for which the organization was set up. He will also be aware of internal tensions and squabbles among professional staff members, some of which may affect patient welfare.

Respecting and Understanding Oneself

How does the clinical psychologist develop an understanding of himself or herself? How does the clinician find a life style that both promotes client welfare and his own well-being? Since the use of self is a primary function in clinical work, be it as an observer, interviewer, therapist, or consultant, respect for oneself and self-development are fundamental to clinical effectiveness. The wise clinician appreciates his own needs for both involvement and distance from his work, for a balance between energetic expansion and consolidating withdrawal. He tries to understand himself whenever he finds that he is getting overly anxious or overly intimate in his relations to clients. He recognizes that he must have courage and take risks in order to enter the difficult and dark regions of human behavior and thought. He also recognizes that he cannot help everyone and that some people may find him objectionable or even hateful. He must then find his sources of deep conviction and belief and emotional satisfaction in a full life aside from his job.

The methods for understanding oneself have generally been through supervision in training or through counseling or therapy. Psychoanalysts require aspiring analysts to go through a didactic analysis. Most other training programs do not require personal therapy, but students are encouraged to voluntarily seek that experience for its learning value. Good supervision is particularly important for learning about oneself. In addition, the clinician may keep some kind of record of his behavior, such as a diary. Studying one's behavior by using video or audio tape recordings of one's clinical activities is often helpful. One area of special interest is the handling of personal tensions. Nearly everyone needs some confidante away from the place of work to discuss problems and release tensions—a wife or husband, or a good friend. Also in planning one's life, the clinician needs recreation and other means of "getting away from it all." Some clinicians particularly seek engrossing physical activity, since much of their working day involves sedentary mental work. The clinician needs to realize that his moods and anxieties are reflected in the manner in which he facilitates client growth. Gurman (1972), on the basis of his research, concludes that "therapists relatively free of emotional conflict, yet willing to acknowledge internal discomfort when it is present, are better able to understand, accept, and respond nondefensively to their patients" (p. 100).

Like the field in general, the clinician's personal development can be seen as involving psychobiological, personal, small-group, organization, and community systems. His professional life, like the clients' lives, can be viewed from any of these system levels and from different stages of development. The clinician's perspective should include this wide overview of development of systems over time.

CREATIVE DEVELOPMENT
FOR CLINICAL EFFECTIVENESS

Clinical psychology is a broad field wide open to those who wish to discover and invent. After all his centuries of struggle, man knows far too little about himself that is systematized and tested. Psychology as a science is less than a century old, and clinical psychology has arrived at a prominent position only in the last few decades; yet we promise much—sometimes too much. Human nature and its potentialities are great mysteries, the understanding of which seems now more important than ever before because of the perils attending the rapid development of technology. Also, in biological and psychological science the pace of development is becoming enormously fast—new drugs influencing the mind, biofeedback, a human embryo in a test tube, computer simulation of human problem solving. The range of possibilities for mass good and mass evil seems to have increased enormously. By comparison our socioclinical progress is very slow indeed.

Creativity can be called innovating problem solving. It is not just the production of something new or original, although certainly originality is involved. To be effectively creative, one must also be adaptive; the new device, method, or theory must contribute to the solution of a tangible and tough problem. There are many opportunities for real problem solving in clinical work itself. The development of a clear diagnostic picture of a person or the communication of an insightful and helpful interpretation to a patient in therapy is a creative act. There are problems to be solved creatively with clinical organization, administration, and leadership. There are problems in clinical research. All of these await a creative touch. Many creative solutions may be purely local phenomena known only to the clinical team and the patients involved, but they are nonetheless important. Some of these creative developments become systematized and communicated to others. Some of these creative contributions become so widely known and used that they influence the whole world. The prime example is the work of Sigmund Freud. His insights into human motives have changed man's view of himself so much that the world is not the same since he lived. There are other psychologists whose inventions of theories and procedures have had great influence—James, Jung, Galton, Watson, Binet, Lewin, and Maslow, to mention only a few. Some psychologists living today will have as much influence. There is little research directly dealing with creativity as it attacks clinical problems, although there has been a great deal of interest and research on creativity in recent years. (For reviews and bibliographies see Barron, 1968b; Hall, 1971; Stein, 1969; Tryk, 1968. Helson, 1967, has studied sex differences in creative styles.)

Concerning the *accomplishments* of psychologists in general, the studies of Roe (1952, 1953) have been mentioned and also some of Clark's findings (1957). Clark's study for the APA compared a general sample of psychologists with "significant contributors" to psychology nominated from a list of psychologists who have a high number of publications. These eminent psychologists tended to show an earlier preference for psychology, to have been trained at certain renowned universities, to be at present on university staffs, to be more active in the APA, to read more psychological literature, to have stronger interests in research and scholarly activities than in helping people, and to be working on long-term planned research programs. Chambers (1964) also found high initiative and motivation among both psychologists and chemists; eminence seems to relate to willingness to work hard! Bachtold and Werner (1970) found, among other things, that gifted women psychologists were more intelligent, adventuresome, flexible and self-sufficient, and aloof than college women in general.

The APA study points to the conflict that we have suggested earlier—the conflict between research and service interests of clinical psychologists. Each psychologist has to decide how his time is to be spent. Some prefer to work with the immediately pressing problems of clinical work, for which they seldom get credit through publication, though their work may be both valuable and creative. Others prefer to do research on clinical problems that are of more general and long-range significance. Clinical psychology needs both kinds of people.

Creativity also seems to be related to a stage in development. As mentioned before, the major creative contributions tend to come fairly early in the life of the scientist. Terman, the great student of giftedness, wrote (1954, p. 226): "In nearly all fields of science, the best work is done between ages 25 and 35, and rarely later than 40. The peak productivity for works of lesser merit is usually reached 5 to 10 years later... The lesson for us... is that the youth of high achievement potential should be well trained for his life work before too many of his most creative years have passed." Lehman's research on creativity in scientists (1960) confirms this conclusion. However, it must be remembered that there are variations in the age at which people are maximally creative. Freud was about forty before he turned to the study of mental disturbances and wrote his most important books. Anderson and Goodenough (1935) found a sex difference in number of publications of psychologists, with women reaching their peaks later than men. Psychologists do tend to keep up the quantitative output of publications even into their sixties and seventies. In a general survey of research on the older years, Anderson concluded that "aging results in efficiency or economy of effort at the cost of variability or versatility" (1959, p. 793). Whether the remaining energies of the elderly are turned to being less trifling or less brilliant is still an individual matter.

The conditions under which creativity in students will be best encouraged, and even trained, demand study. Pressey (1960) has urged that psychologists encourage gifted students to get into college earlier and give them early experience in research. The importance of scholarships and research fellowships is stressed by Clark (1957), although in later, postdoctoral years, financial support does not seem as important for researchers as in the graduate years. As mentioned elsewhere, a number of eminent research psychologists (APA Education and Training Board Ad Hoc Committee, 1959) believe that the *art of research* must not be overlooked. They asserted that a student may learn best through apprenticeship in an ongoing research program where he gets to see both the early groping efforts to formulate a problem along with intermediate steps and the completed products of research. They also wish to have variety in training for research encouraged rather than a highly standardized curriculum.

One of the most extensive studies of the personal characteristics of creative individuals has been conducted by the Institute of Personality Assessment and Research, in Berkeley, California, under the general direction of MacKinnon. A wide variety of artists and scientists have been studied. A number of the studies are still unpublished, but some general impressions can be stated. Creative persons seem to have the following traits (Crutchfield, 1961): cognitive flexibility, ideational fluency, originality of perceptions and thought, openness to experience both from the inner self and the outer world, tendencies to adopt an intuitive rather than a sense-dependent approach, strong theoretical and aesthetic interests, preference for complexity, freedom from excessive impulse control, interest in independent rather than conforming achievements, individualistic orientation, and a strong and sustained motivation for one's chosen field of work. The process of creating does not occur in a single dramatic flash. It requires a trained mind and persistence in seeking answers. Those who have chosen to face human problems are confronting the greatest challenges. Since new findings and insights often upset old beliefs, and since the great anxieties of human life often work to suppress honest search for answers, the creative clinical psychologist must possess much personal courage. (For further readings on creativity and the work of the assessment institute, see MacKinnon, 1962, 1965; Barron, 1968a.)

The clinical psychologist must also be concerned with continued learning throughout his professional life. As mentioned often elsewhere, it is difficult, if not impossible, to plan for conditions ten or even five years from now. A young clinician with a new Ph.D. can look forward to forty years of active professional life. What he can best learn are processes of learning and of developing himself. Also it is likely that the professional will develop more and more methods for providing continued up-grading of professional competence (Lewinsohn and Pearlman, 1972).

SUMMARY

In this chapter we have reviewed the research and ideas relevant to the personal development of the clinician and some of the more intimate and personal aspects of clinical work. We have mainly been referring to the doctoral-level clinician in this book and have pointed out the wide variety of settings, clients, and activities he or she engages in. In studies of the background of psychologists and clinical psychologists, there are some indications of early interest in intellectual pursuits, and in people and signs of upward socioeconomic mobility; but the overlap with other people and other professionals is great. The graduate training experiences are important in establishing a professional identity. Some advantages and disadvantages of increasing specialization are explored. Training for clinical psychology is an object of much continued concern, and every few years new conferences review educational programs. Recently there have been some efforts to develop genuinely professional programs, breaking away from the scientist—professional model prevalent since the Boulder conference in 1949. In his working years the clinical psychologist has many choices and is likely to find his professional life characterized by shifts in role mix and location. As a person, the psychologist needs to learn a sense of competence, realistic empathy with clients, a socioecological orientation, effective relating with colleagues and organizations, and an understanding of himself. Creativity and effectiveness in clinical work were reviewed. The practicing clinician thinks about continual development of himself or herself throughout his professional life.

SUGGESTED READINGS

Rogers, C. R. Carl R. Rogers. In E. G. Boring and G. Lindzey (eds.), *A history of psychology in autobiograpy*, Vol. 5. New York: Appleton-Century-Crofts, 1967.

There are surprisingly few accounts of the lives of clinical psychologists. Carl Rogers presents one, his autobiography, in this series of autobiographies. He reports his early memories growing up near Chicago, his early choice of scientific agriculture in college, followed by a shift to preparation for the ministry at Union Theological Seminary, and later to clinical and educational psychology. Rogers also tells of his work at Rochester, Ohio State, Chicago, Wisconsin, and the Western Behavioral Sciences Institute. He presents a personal analysis of this career, ending with the statement (p. 383): "Intellectually, I know . . . that I and my thinking may be shown to be completely erroneous; that the directions in which I am moving may prove to be blind alleys; but in spite of this openness of *mind*, I believe at the *feeling* level, in myself and in what I am doing. This degree of assurance I do have."

Other autobiographies that may be of interest to readers concerned with clinical psychology include that of Henry Murray in the same volume and Lewis Terman in the 1932 volume. The biography of Freud by Jones (1953) is also a very interesting presentation. There is a need to study clinicians, particularly more recent ones, to try to understand the important formative experiences that lead to humanitarian and scientific effectiveness.

Bugental, J. The person who is the therapist. In A. Z. Guiora and M. A. Brandwin (eds.), *Perspectives in clinical psychology*. New York: Van Nostrand Reinhold, 1968, pp. 45–58.

An experienced therapist, Bugental looks with a clear eye at the gratifications, pitfalls, and needed maturity of the person. He indicates, without deprecation, that the predecessors of the psychotherapist are the medicine man, sorcerer, priest, and family doctor. He notes the gratifications, some of them seductive and dangerous, in the work: one-way intimacy, a sense of omnipotence, vicarious mastery over life's problems, masculine tenderness, opportunities to express rebelliousness. Genuine maturity requires recognition of limited knowledge, selective participation, authentic encounter, continued conceptual growth, and some acceptance of guilt over failure to do better.

Wheelis (1958) frankly discusses the conflicts and disillusionments of a career in psychoanalysis. He shows the adolescent problems of identity and the loneliness and inadequacy that may underlie the choice of this career. He reports how training analyses do not live up to expectations and how deep and honest doubts about his effectiveness lead the practicing analyst into dogmatism or some other form of adjustment. He presents the feelings of the analyst in response to the hostility and love of the patient. This literary, and perhaps autobiographical, account by a psychoanalyst gives the reader an understanding of how many psychotherapists feel.

Shakow, D. On the rewards (and, alas, frustrations) of public service. *American Psychologist*, 1968, *23*, 87–96.

One of the great clinical psychologists tells of his experiences working in a state hospital, a university, and with the National Institutes of Health. He makes a number of insightful points about research and administration and identifies a number of improper acts or handicaps in these working situations. (He calls these *illegitimati*, after General Stillwell's celebrated motto, *Illegitimati non carborundum*—"Don't let the bastards grind you down.")

Henry, W. E., Sims, J. H., and Spray, S. L. *The fifth profession: becoming a psychotherapist*. San Francisco: Jossey-Bass, 1971.

The title of this book indicates the conclusion the authors came to after what was probably the most comprehensive study of psychotherapists to date.

Surveying the background of practitioners of psychiatric social work, psycho-analysis, psychiatry, and clinical psychology, Henry, Sims, and Spray found so few differences that they question the social and economic worth of keeping four distinct training programs. The research included a mailed questionnaire to mental health professionals in New York, Los Angeles, and Chicago and 100 interviews in each city. Among a multitude of results, they found that psychotherapists tend to be upwardly mobile, politically liberal, have early interests in medicine, and participate in personal therapy (74 percent of the total sample). For those interested in common education for the mental health professions, another source of information is the article by the psychiatrist Mariner (1967).

Hathaway, S. R. A study of human behavior: the clinical psychologist. *American Psychologist*, 1958, *13*, 257–265.

In a frank look at the development of clinical psychology, Hathaway points out the conflicts, frustrations, and struggles over prestige that have beset the science and the profession. He shows how clinical psychologists have tried to achieve a place as respected "doctors" while still avoiding the discomforts of being "on call" and having direct responsibility for patients; how psychologists have turned to research for security, although often the most satisfying rewards and the largest measure of personal recognition comes from clinical service that is frequently quite unscientific; how much of the training of psychologists is unneeded in practical clinical work; how many of the trappings of the psychologist, such as projective methods and personality "dynamics," have little if any scientific validity; how diagnostic testing is said to be important but the teaching faculty often does very little of it; how psychotherapy, thought prestigeful, is frequently dull and uninteresting; and how clinicians blur their specialty by trying to include all manner of human problems in their purview instead of concentrating on truly clinical problems. Hathaway concludes that clinical psychologists need to channel their energies into work with mental patients under a disciplined and recognizable training program; to explore the possible use of ancillary technicians for some psychological procedures; not to let themselves become overly involved in academic pursuits; to revive the respectability of testing, diagnosis, and the evaluation of psychopathology; and to attempt vigorously to meet the service needs in the expectation of which the public supports their profession. This article is reprinted in the book by Braun (1966), where the reader might find several other pertinent articles.

Goldman, A. R., Bohr, R. H., and Steinberg, T. A. On posing as mental patients: reminiscences and recommendations. *Professional Psychology*, 1970, *1*, 427–436.

Two of the authors spent periods up to one week as patients on wards with psychotics, neither ward personnel nor patients being aware of their nonpatient status. The observations and discussion in this short paper and the brief review of the literature are excellent introductions to the observational and training method. The pseudo-patients reported an overwhelming boredom in the impoverished ward situation and a surprising fear that they might be left in the hospital. They observed that patients' time perspectives were altered from normal and that small events assumed a disproportionate size. They also found an elaborate informal system of exchange and the use of rewards by psychiatric attendants for control of behavior without knowledge of behavior modification or token economy systems. With due attention to the ethics of disguised observation, this institutional living-in technique seems like a very powerful learning experience, stimulating many suggestions for improvement of patient care. Weitz (1972) used a living-in period to observe a ward using a token economy; he also experienced boredom and anger at the inhumane situation. Living in is one of the methods used for field instruction to improve the understanding of natural situations by undergraduates preparing for the human service professions (Sundberg, 1969b).

Mackler, B. Black on white or white on black: Harlem and white professionals. *Professional Psychology*, 1971, *2*, 247–250.

Mackler, a white psychologist, tells of his experiences working on a Neighborhood Model Cities planning project in Harlem. He says that he was always fearful of being mugged, and was especially frightened coming for evening meetings; he found that his black and Puerto Rican colleagues were also. He learned to admit his deficiencies and to stand up against nonwhites when he disagreed. He states that whites are often tested severely before nonwhites share the commonalities that are there all along.

Sarason, S. B. Toward a psychology of change and innovation. *American Psychologist*, 1967, *22*, 227–233.

Sarason reports personal observations on the problems of organizational creativity—the development of new programs in a community. Illustrating from the Psycho-Educational Clinic at Yale and Community Progress, Inc., in New Haven, he points out the lack of preparation of most psychologists for such social innovations and the need to develop an appreciation of the environment surrounding new ventures. Among other observations, he hypothesizes that "The fate of any single proposal for change will be determined in part by the number of changes which have been proposed but never implemented" (p. 229). Graziano (1969) also has written about innovation in the mental health field. He deplores the replacement of scientific and humanitarian goals by the professionals' pursuit of political power and points out the great resistance to change of entrenched interests. He illustrates with a case history of an attempt to start a treatment program for severely disturbed children. For a warm-hearted, nonprofessionalized report on a success story of organizational innovation, see the report on the Pearl Buck Center for retarded children (Buck, 1972). For more technical discussions of organizational change, see Schmuck et al. (1972), Lippitt et al. (1958), and others mentioned in Chapters 16 and 17.

RESEARCH EXAMPLES

Kelly, E. L., and Fiske, D. W. *The prediction of performance in clinical psychology*. University of Michigan Press, Ann Arbor, 1951.

This massive assessment program has had a profound effect on clinical psychology. It might be seen as the turning point in the optimism about clinical psychologists' abilities that prevailed following World War II. Along with the later book by Meehl (1954), it has forced psychologists to become more realistic, and therefore more modest, about their skills of clinical prediction. Although most of the effects were sobering, it also provided encouragement to those who have all along maintained that well-developed objective measures are of value.

This monograph reports on this five-year research program. Its primary purpose was the evaluation of a variety of procedures as predictors of later success in graduate training and professional function in clinical psychology. In 1947 and 1948 several hundred college graduates who were seeking admission to or actually entering the VA training program in clinical psychology in some 40 universities were evaluated by a wide variety of techniques. During the first year 137 subjects were brought to Ann Arbor in groups of 24 for a five-day stay at the assessment center. During the second year they were tested in other centers. The predictive measures were derived from a battery of objective tests, a battery of projective techniques, two interviews, and a series of situational tests. This large mass of data, including many judgments made by assessors possessing different kinds of information, formed the predictor variables. The criterion variables were the students' academic records and various ratings of success in clinical work.

Only a small portion of the very numerous findings of the study will be mentioned here. The subjects proved to be remarkably like other graduate students in psychology, differing mainly in possessing greater interest in people and persuasive activities. There were significant differences between various institutions in the interest and abilities of the graduate students. With respect to the criteria of success in clinical psychology, there was wide variation in the conceptions of the university professors and training supervisors. Ratings of clinical competence appeared to be as much a function of the role of the rater as of the person rated. When it came to predicting success in clinical psychology, intellectual aspects could be predicted surprisingly well, validities ranging from 0.35 to 0.60. The more clinical aspects of training were much less predictable. Social skills were predictable beyond chance but less so than the intellectual aspects. The validities of the 1947 group did not hold up well for the 1948 group. The criteria themselves were seen as very fallible.

Only a small proportion of the objective tests correlated with the criterion measures. The most generally useful of the objective tests were the Miller Analogies Test and the Strong Vocational Interest Blank. Predictions based on the credential file and the objective test profile were almost as accurate as those based on intensive study of the person with projective techniques and observation. Predictions of success based on single projective techniques tended to produce very low correlations with criteria. On follow-up none of the rated criterion measures differentiated students with less training from those who had more, and the authors concluded that it is an open question whether additional years of experience and present training procedures lead to any measurable improvement in clinical skill.

A summary of the study and additional information from a later follow-up study can be found in Kelly and Goldberg (1959). Another interesting subsequent publication is that of Carlson (1969). Using the original data, she was able to predict the VA trainees success or failure better than the Miller Analogies or the Strong did by the use of a Rorschach Index for optimal ego development.

Wispe, L., Ash, P., Awkard, J., Hicks, L. H., Hoffman, M., and Porter, J. The Negro psychologist in America. *American Psychologist*, 1969, *24*, 142–150.

The authors conducted a survey involving and extensive attempt to get names of black psychologists through 94 Negro colleges, 216 American psychology departments offering graduate work, large governmental departments, and other sources. A six-page questionnaire was mailed to 492 black psychologists. Of the 398 usable returns only 27 percent were members of APA.

The findings indicated with 51 percent of the respondents lived in the Southeastern part of the United States, almost exactly the percentage of blacks in the general population residing there. The median age was 38 years. Only 34 percent of the fathers of the respondents were manual laborers, compared with population estimates of 74 percent for blacks in general. Of Ph.D. psychologists, which comprised 42 percent of the respondents, few came from the highest-rated psychology departments. For the most part psychologists received their early training in Negro schools. The black psychologists with Ph.D.s earned as much as nonblack psychologists with Ph.D.s, but blacks with lower degrees appeared to be somewhat less well paid than their white cohorts. Nearly half of the respondents stated that race had limited their professional opportunities. The authors agree with one of the respondents that a serious problem is to make opportunities available for quality education.

The problem of recruiting minority-group members into careers in psychology is discussed by Bayton, Roberts, and Williams (1970). They conclude that more nonwhite students need to be brought into undergraduate programs in psychology and suggest that federal and private resources be directed to developing a small number of centers of excellence in predominately black colleges.

Cochrane, C. T. Effects of diagnostic information on empathic understanding by the therapist in a psychotherapy analogue. *Journal of Consulting and Clinical Psychology*, 1972, *38*, 359–365.

In the interest of improving training, Cochrane set out to explore the extent to which diagnostic information helps or interferes with the therapist's understanding of his client. She investigated the two principal types of empathy: (1) empathic communication, which she measured by ratings of subjects' taped responses to taped therapy sessions; and (2) empathic inference, which she measured by the correlation between the subjects' Q-sort descriptions of the client with the client's own Q-sort self-description. Thus the two principal dependent variables were quantified. The subjects were 18 graduate students in training. Under two conditions they were given diagnostic reports based on the Rorschach, sentence completion, and MMPI, one report being psychodynamically oriented (with emphasis on conflict areas, etiology, and pathology) and the other being phenomenologically oriented (attempting to show how the client saw his personal world). The third condition was without any diagnostic information. The information was derived from three clients, and each graduate student subject had each of the three conditions provided before he carried out the procedures yielding the measures of empathy.

The results showed no significant effects from the three conditions of diagnostic information. The author speculated that in the "real moment" of empathizing, the therapist "tunes out" additional information about the person. Cochrane also found that subjects' empathic communication behavior was fairly predictable from one client to another and concluded that it is a fairly stable characteristic. One interesting sidelight was the finding of a sex difference favoring females on empathic communication (similar to what Sundberg, 1966, found) but not on empathic inference.

In another study, Fish (1970) found a positive relationship between beginning therapists' empathy as judged from tapes and the empathic quality of written descriptions of their own emotions. Since empathy is a variable very frequently mentioned in regard to therapy and clinical work in general, it seems as if it should receive very careful consideration in the selection and training of clinical psychologists. For further readings on sensitivity to others and emotional communication, see Davitz (1964), A. G. Smith (1966), and H. C. Smith (1966).

Crow, W. J. The effect of training upon accuracy and variability in interpersonal perception. *Journal of Abnormal and Social Psychology*, 1957, 55, 355–359.

The purpose of this study, so arresting in its outcome, was to test the effect of training in interpersonal relations on ability to predict the responses of others. The subjects were seventy-two senior medical students randomly assigned either to an experimental or to a control group. The experimental group was instructed in physician–patient relationships and given training in more prolonged contact with patients than the control group was able to have. It was expected that the students in the experimental group would become more accurate in interpersonal perceptions of other persons.

At the beginning, during, and at the end of the year, students were asked to estimate the real status and self-ratings of patients presented in sound-film recorded interviews. Actual self-ratings and relevant MMPI scores were used as criteria for scoring the medical students' predictions.

Contrary to expectation, the experimental group became significantly less accurate than the control group. The variability of their estimates increased. The author suggests that training programs devoted to increasing interpersonal sensitivity run the risk of actually decreasing accuracy of perception. Increasing the trainee's responsiveness to individual differences apparently leads him to lose sight of stereotype or basic role data. A piece of research like this presents a sharp challenge to those engaged in the training of clinicians. We need to know much more about what goes into the various kinds of tasks clinicians perform. Also questions arise about the sorts of tasks for which accuracy of interpersonal perception would be useful and the kinds of tasks for which special sensitivity to individuals is needed.

In contrast to Crow's study, Bullmer (1972) was able to demonstrate improved accuracy of interpersonal perception through the use of programmed self-instruction. This area of research is of great importance for training in the human services and deserves much more attention.

For a further exploration of training, readers may see Goldberg's article on clinical judgment in the *American Psychologist* (1968b). Using immediate feedback on the accuracy of judgments about the same neurotic and psychotic profiles, he and his colleague, Rorer, compared the progress of MMPI experts, a middle group, and originally naïve students. Over nine weeks of training all judges trained on 4,000 profiles. Naïve judges improved their accuracy from 52 to 58 percent. Middle and expert judges were very similar, achieving an average accuracy of 65 percent. Goldberg and Rorer then showed some judges' predictions based on the actuarial formula mentioned above; those given the formula did improve to the level of the formula—70 percent—but not beyond it.

In another feedback study Sechrest, Gallimore, and Hersch (1967) found they could produce improvement of sentence-completion protocols by college students, but they concluded that most of the improvement was due to enhancement of motivation. Graham (1971), in a feedback study with the MMPI, did find an effect from correct feedback, as compared with random feedback, but the improvement was not great. Fancher's interesting study (1966) suggests that there are strong individual differences in ability to predict behavior and to profit from feedback. Schroeder (1972) found that judges who formed explicit hypotheses were more effective than those using "gut reactions," and those using hypotheses did learn from feedback. The challenge of changing the clinician's accuracy of judgment is at least as great as the challenge of changing client's behavior in therapy.

chapter 19

Professional Organization and Ethics

Becoming a professional psychologist, or becoming a member of any profession, carries with it certain implications of responsibility, a willingness to uphold standards of training and conduct, relationships with colleagues and professional societies—in general, both privileges and duties. In addition to such matters, there are the important personal concerns of one's prestige, economic status, and sense of professional identity. In this chapter we shall explore a number of these topics.

ORGANIZATIONS TO WHICH
CLINICAL PSYCHOLOGISTS BELONG

Clinical psychology, though a newly developed and still not crystallized specialty, clearly bears the marks of a profession—high standards of training, grave responsibilities for the welfare of clients, considerable independence in regard to policy making for itself, self-policing on ethical matters, and freedom to pursue creatively the problems that fall in its domain. The decade following World War II was certainly the most significantly formative period of the growing profession, one in which clinical psychology developed much of the character it has today and will doubtless keep for some time. During this period clinical psychologists shaped their professional organizations, adopted their first certification procedures, hammered out an official code of ethics, and set up the machinery for ensuring standards of training. The manifestations of clinical psychologists' concern for their professional development are chronicled in the official journals of the American Psychological Association, the *American Psychologist* and *Professional Psychology*, and in its monthly newspaper, the *APA Monitor*.

While clinical psychologists constitute the largest specialty group in the APA (about a third of the 35,000 members in 1972), the organization represents psychologists of all specialties as well as those who do not consider themselves specialists at all (Division 1 is called the Division of General Psychology). There has been among psychologists a strong conviction that science and practice should not be separated. Psychology is somewhat unique in this regard. The American Medical Association, for example, is an organization of practicing physicians. Physiologists and biochemists have their own scientific societies. Similarly, engineers and physicists do not usually belong to the same professional groups. But at the APA conventions clinical psychologists rub shoulders with experimental and industrial psychologists; psychotherapists and teachers, social and developmental psychologists interact with those whose specialties are hypnosis or measurement. A person becomes a member of the American Psychological Association first, and then joins one or more of its many divisions if he wishes to.

This heterogeneity gives rise to many conflicts and problems as well as advantages. The most persistent of these concerns arise from differences in the orientation of persons mainly interested in psychology as an organized body of knowledge, the researchers and educators, and persons mainly interested in professional practice. Yet, whenever it is suggested that the partnership between scientists and practitioners be dissolved, the majority of APA members reaffirm their decision to hold the two together.

The legislative body of the APA is the Council of Representatives, a group of somewhat more than 100 persons elected by divisions and state associations. The council meets briefly during the APA Convention in September and for a longer time about two months later to debate the issues that have arisen and to make policy decisions. A complex system of boards and committees under its jurisdiction pay special attention to particular aspects of psychology's business, such as scientific affairs, professional affairs, and education and training. An executive officer and a staff of some 100 persons at the central office in Washington, D.C., carry out the policies adopted by the council and handle the day-to-day work of the association, including the publication of a sizable number of journals, a monthly newspaper, and various books and pamphlets. These staff members answer a staggering number of letters from members and nonmembers, set up meetings of boards and committees, take care of the organization's finances, develop plans to be presented to committees and boards and to the Council for consideration, apply for research grants and direct the investigations such grants make possible, and do many other things as well. The APA with its board and committee structure, on the one hand, and its central office structure on the other, constitutes a large and very complex machine designed to carry out the wishes of its members, and while it is creaky at times and threatens to break down, it has continued to function quite well. Minor "tinkering" with the machine in the shape of by-law changes of course occurs almost every year.

There are several APA divisions besides the Division of Clinical Psychology (Division 12) to which clinical psychologists often belong: Personality and Social (8), Consulting (13), School Psychology (16), Counseling (17), Rehabilitation (22), Experimental Analysis of Behavior (23), Community (27), Psychotherapy (29), Hypnosis (30), and State Psychological Affairs (31). Many of them are elected to membership in the Council of Representatives and serve on the various boards and committees of the association. They often affiliate also with other organizations, such as the American Orthopsychiatric Association, the American Academy of Psychotherapists, the American Personnel and Guidance Association, or the American Association for the Advancement of Science. There is no dearth of opportunities for like-minded professional psychologists to join forces in the development of their specialty.

State and community associations also play an important part in maintaining professional standards and improving the quality of public services, and clinical psychologists have been very active in these groups. Many kinds of problems can best be tackled on a state or local level. The improvement of mental health resources in a particular state or region, the legal problems of psychology as they are affected by state laws, and civil service standards and rates of compensation have a vital bearing on psychologists' activity and welfare. Representatives of such organizations often work with the members of state legislatures in framing legislation bearing on the professional activities of psychologists and do what they can to facilitate the enactment of the laws they favor. This kind of political activity, although long familiar to other professions, has been a new experience for psychologists, who until recently were mostly content to remain in their academic "ivory towers."

CERTIFICATION AND LICENSURE

In order to maintain high professional standards, there must be methods for screening persons who believe themselves qualified to practice and making clear to the public which persons have met these standards. Otherwise, the lay person who seeks psychological help can have no way of knowing whether a self-styled "psychologist" is adequately trained and competent or just a quack. Since the demand for help with personal problems is great, many unqualified people have been able to pose as psychologists and even to make a good living out of doing so. A few years before legal steps were taken, the yellow-page section of the Los Angeles telephone directory contained several pages of advertising and a long list of self-styled psychologists, psychoanalysts, marriage counselors, and hypnotists. Several of them advertised, with such statements as this: "We can lift your burdens with one visit," and asserted that they could cure all manner of problems. Since any advertising of clinical services beyond a simple listing of name, degree, and field of specialization is condemned by professional organizations, we can be pretty certain that such high-sounding claims were made by quacks. [Establishing standards to apply to directory listings was one of the professional activities undertaken by the APA ethics committee (APA Ethics, 1969), so such misleading claims seldom appear any longer in reputable directories.]

On the national level, actions to raise and maintain standards of practice have been of two principal kinds. In the first place, the APA, through its Committee on Accreditation, publishes lists of universities approved for training in clinical or counseling psychology, and a list of approved internship agencies. In the second place, the American Board of Professional Psychology (ABPP) each year administers written and oral examinations on the basis of which diplomas are awarded to thoroughly qualified and experienced practitioners.

At the state level, thirty-eight of the fifty states (as of 1969) have passed laws certifying or licensing psychologists and specifying the standards they must meet in order to practice. One of the difficulties has been to define the services of a psychologist, especially those engaged in psychotherapy and counseling, in a way that will not restrict or infringe on the prerogatives of other professions, such as psychiatry and the ministry. Straight certification avoids this difficulty by limiting the use of the professional label only. Typically a certification law states that a person cannot call himself a "psychologist" or offer services designated as "psychological" to the public for remuneration unless he has met certain standards. These standards (excluding early "grandfather" provisions to authorize practice by experienced persons who may not have met the formal educational requirements) usually require the Ph.D. from a recognized university plus two years of experience. In a few states there is certification at the level of the master's degree.

In some states that do not yet have statutory certification the state psychological associations have set up programs of *self-certification*. As the name implies, the state organization itself voluntarily reviews the qualifications of its members who apply for certification and sees that proper standards are maintained.

There has been some criticism of the certification development within psychology itself (Deutsch, 1958), but most of the opposition has come from outside. The medical profession, especially psychiatry, has sometimes seen the recognition of psychology as an independent profession as a threat. In many states, however, psychiatrists have come to see the advantage of certification as a protection for the public and as valuable for promoting general professional development. There has been scattered opposition from other groups here and there, so that getting a bill through a legislature requires careful preparation and tactical skill.

As time has passed, many states have moved from certification to licensing in order to safeguard the interests of the public more adequately. A licensing law sets qualifications for persons who provide professional psychological services, such as testing or therapy, whether these practitioners call themselves psychologists or not.

ETHICAL STANDARDS OF PSYCHOLOGISTS

One of the accomplishments of the American Psychological Association of which psychologists can be justly proud is that over the years an official statement of ethical standards has been developed. An interesting aspect of this undertaking was its adoption of a semiinductive approach. A committee of psychologists went realistically to work on the project, drawing on their understanding of operational and experimental methods. They called upon their colleagues for descriptions of specific instances of psychologists at work where ethical issues had arisen. The following are examples of the "critical incidents" of good, poor, or undetermined ethical conduct which the committee gathered, all of them taken from the booklet entitled *Ethical Standards of Psychologists* (APA, 1953a):

A nonpsychologist colleague recently requested an endorsement for an article which he had written for a lay publication. The article dealt with the self-evaluation of parents and contained a "test," complete with item weights, which the reader could take and determine whether he or she was an "excellent, good, average, or poor" parent. The publisher requested an endorsement from a psychologist to the effect that this article was in accordance with psychological principles. The psychologist refused on the grounds that the article gave the impression of scientific validity, when none was there (p. 34).

At a social gathering composed mostly of nonpsychologists, a therapist in the group, when asked about his work, proceeded to discuss for apparent purposes of entertainment the details of several life histories of clients with whom he was working (p. 53).

A school examiner had used the Rorschach almost exclusively for estimating mental ability. Recommendations for grade placement and instructional treatment are based directly on these findings, without corroboration from other standardized instruments (p. 40).

A child is brought to a clinic because of difficulties in learning to read. It is found that his difficulties are due largely to low intelligence. Without unethical intent, but from a desire not to hurt the parent, a vague report is given which disguises the facts somewhat (p. 64).

A psychologist working for a clinic for veterans on a salary basis does personal counseling. On several occasions, veterans have offered money as an expression of their appreciation of the work of the psychologist. He refused to accept the gift with an explanation that the service is free and that acceptance of a gift would violate the fundamental basis on which the service is offered (p. 71).

A psychologist obtained results which he had reason to fear would discourage a form of democratic behavior in which he believed. He was unable to conduct further research on the problem. He withheld publication of his results while he tried to get other psychologists to repeat his work. Failing in this effort, he published his own study after two years (p. 119).

Some hundreds of situations were classified and studied by the committee. On the basis of these, the APA published a monograph of principles and illustrative cases (APA, 1953b). The statement was reexamined and updated in 1963 (and reissued in 1968) and is published in each issue of the biennial APA Biographical Directory for ready reference. Another book of illustrative cases was published in 1967, indicating how the Committee on Professional Ethics and Conduct has dealt with issues related to the code (APA, 1967). Golann (1970) has provided an enlightening historical account of the way in which the APA hammered out its codes and procedures during the thirty-year period from 1938 to 1968. In this and another paper (Golann, 1969) he also pointed out new ethical issues he saw emerging since 1963 when the present revision of the code was adopted.

The preamble of the ethical code sets the tone for the whole document (APA, 1968a, p. 357):

The psychologist believes in the dignity and worth of the individual human being. He is committed to increasing man's understanding of himself and others. While pursuing this endeavor, he protects the welfare of any person who may seek his service or of any subject, human or animal, that may be the object of his study. He does not use his professional position or relationships, nor does he knowingly permit his own services to be used by others, for purposes inconsistent with these values. While demanding for himself freedom of inquiry and communication, he accepts the responsibility this freedom confers: for competence where he claims it, for objectivity in the report of his findings, and for consideration of the best interests of his colleagues and of society.

The nineteen principles of the code specify general standards of responsibility, competence, representations to the public, relationships with clients, research participants, and with other professional people, the use of psychological tests, and credit for publications. For clinicians, the heart of the ethical code resides in statements about responsibility to the client. Two of the most important sections are reprinted below in their entirety (APA, 1968a, pp. 358–359):

Principle 6. Confidentiality. Safeguarding information about an individual that has been obtained by the psychologist in the course of his teaching, practice, or investigation is a primary obligation of the psychologist. Such information is not communicated to others unless certain important conditions are met.

  a. Information received in confidence is revealed only after most careful deliberation and when there is clear and imminent danger to an individual or to society, and then only to appropriate professional workers or public authorities.

  b. Information obtained in clinical or consulting relationships, or evaluative data concerning children, students, employees, and others are discussed only for professional purposes and only with persons clearly concerned with the case. Written and oral reports should present only data germane to the purposes of the evaluation; every effort should be made to avoid undue invasion of privacy.

   c. Clinical and other materials are used in classroom teaching and writing only when the identity of the persons involved is adequately disguised.
   d. The confidentiality of professional communications about individuals is maintained. Only when the originator and other persons involved give their express permission is a confidential professional communication shown to the individual concerned. The psychologist is responsible for informing the client of the limits of the confidentiality.
   e. Only after explicit permission has been granted is the identity of research subjects published. When data have been published without permission for identification, the psychologist assumes responsibility for adequately disguising their sources.
   f. The the psychologist makes provisions for the maintenance of confidentiality in the preservation and ultimate disposition of confidential records.

Principle 7. Client Welfare. The psychologist respects the integrity and protects the welfare of the person or group with whom he is working.
   a. The psychologist in industry, education, and other situations in which conflicts of interest may arise among various parties, as between management and labor, or between the client and employer of the psychologist, defines for himself the nature and direction of his loyalties and responsibilities and keeps all parties concerned informed of these commitments.
   b. When there is a conflict among professional workers, the psychologist is concerned primarily with the welfare of any client involved and only secondarily with the interest of his own professional group.
   c. The psychologist attempts to terminate a clinical or consulting relationship when it is reasonably clear to the psychologist that the client is not benefiting from it.
   d. The psychologist who asks that an individual reveal personal information in the course of interviewing, testing, or evaluation, or who allows such information to be divulged to him, does so only after making certain that the responsible person is fully aware of the purposes of the interview, testing, or evaluation and of the ways in which the information may be used.
   e. In cases involving referral, the responsibility of the psychologist for the welfare of the client continues until this responsibility is assumed by the professional person to whom the client is referred or until the relationship with the psychologist making the referral has been terminated by mutual agreement. In situations where referral, consultation, or other changes in the conditions of the treatment are indicated and the client refuses referral, the psychologist carefully weighs the possible harm to the client, to himself, and to his profession that might ensue from continuing the relationship.

f. The psychologist who requires the taking of psychological tests for didactic, classification, or research purposes protects the examinees by insuring that the tests and test results are used in a professional manner.

g. When potentially disturbing subject matter is presented to students, it is discussed objectively, and efforts are made to handle constructively any difficulties that arise.

h. Care must be taken to insure an appropriate setting for clinical work to protect both client and psychologist from actual or imputed harm and the profession from censure.

i. In the use of accepted drugs for therapeutic purposes special care needs to be exercised by the psychologist to assure himself that the collaborating physician provides suitable safeguards for the client.

During the late 1960s increasing concern was expressed about ethical issues that had arisen in research on human subjects. It was felt that Principle 16, Research Precautions, was not comprehensive enough to provide the guidelines that were needed. A new committee was set up to develop an ethical code to govern research involving human subjects. The procedures were similar to those used before. Members of the association were asked to submit examples of questionable or admirable decisions and practices. The committee distilled out of this material a set of principles. These were published and widely discussed, so that the final version would represent the best thinking of all psychologists on the issues before the report was acted upon by the Council of Representatives, the governing body of the American Psychological Association, in the fall of 1972. As a result of new psychological procedures like encounter groups and biofeedback, the Association also sets up methods to review and alter its ethical standards or issue special guidelines from time to time. One example of guidelines pertains to the use of drugs in research (APA Ad Hoc Committee, 1972).

The consideration of ethics does not stop with a statement of principles. The profession must enforce its ethical code. To this end, the APA reviews complaints about the professional conduct of its members and makes decisions. Arrangements are made for investigations and hearings, and a person found to be clearly in violation of the code is notified that his APA membership has been cancelled. This is a rare event, however; most of the actions of the APA Committee on Scientific and Professional Ethics and Conduct are educational or in the nature of reprimands.

RELATIONS WITH OTHER PROFESSIONS

Human behavior—complex and interrelated as it is with all sorts of phenomena—is naturally the object of study and practice by many disciplines and professions.

No one of these possesses an exclusive and proprietary right to the whole field of human life. Thus the psychologist will find that he will often cooperate closely with many other professional persons in working with patients and clients. This interdependence is perhaps most obvious in the case of children. For one thing, the life of the child is intimately tied in not only with his home but also with what happens in school. Teachers and principals are deeply concerned with the behavior problems of children. They are often the first to notice a child's disturbance. What is happening to the child in school must be understood in order to carry out many forms of treatment. In addition to the teachers, the pediatrician is concerned with the health of the child. When youngsters become delinquent, the juvenile court authorities are likely to enter the picture. If the child is in a foster home, or seriously deprived, the welfare department is likely to work with his case. Frequently the church connections of the family bring a clergyman into relationship with the clinic. In a hospital situation professions such as nursing, occupational therapy, and social work are involved. In such cases the psychologist sees that he needs to develop a number of different relationships that may be helpful to the patient or client and promote his mental health.

There are easy referrings back and forth among the professions in a community with good professional relationships. Very frequently psychologists receive referrals from schools, physicians, and ministers. In return the psychologist will consult with other professionals and make referrals when the case enters an area of their competence. The clinical psychologist should be aware of the limitations of his own skills and knowledge as well as the competence of others in his community to accomplish what he cannot alone. He will make sure that a case has been adequately studied medically. In most private clinical work he will insist on a physical examination to determine the role, if any, of organic factors before he embarks on psychotherapy (Blau, 1959). He will not work with a psychotic person unless in close liaison with a physician.

In some situations, as in vocational and educational counseling, it will not normally be necessary to have medical coverage, since this work is clearly labeled to the public as being restricted to problems such as occupational adjustment. Of course, if the psychologist does not have expert knowledge of occupations, and the client or patient needs special vocational guidance, the psychologist must then consult with or refer his client to an appropriate person in the community. The same is true of speech correction, reading disabilities, or legal and religious problems.

The extent of referral is, of course, limited by the community facilities. In a small town without special facilities, a psychologist may have to stretch a point and take on cases in which he has limited skill. But he should always know his community and the region well enough to know where to get the best available help for his client. He will have directories of professional services in his office so that he can make distant referrals when necessary. In the directories of the American Psychological Association and the American Psychiatric Association, he can readily check the names of psychotherapists. There are usually city or state directories of social welfare services. National directories are published by some national organizations.

The three largest kinds of institutional systems with which psychologists affiliate are education, industry, and medicine. In organizational units of these fields the psychologist consults, advises, or treats individuals and groups. He may have considerable influence, but the main job of the organization is usually something else—teaching children, supplying medical treatment, manufacturing, or carrying on a business. The psychologist needs to understand his position and role in relation to others. Each of these situations presents certain ethical and professional problems. All of them demand good human relationships. On the whole, the psychologist is welcomed in these situations.

The only professional groups with which psychologists have had any considerable amount of conflict have been with some representatives of medicine and psychiatry. The nub of the conflict has been over the entrance of clinical psychologists into independent practice of psychotherapy, a function in which the professions overlap in their offerings to the public. Nowadays, with so many groups doing so many different kinds of therapy, and with so many other types of intervention challenging the value of psychotherapy, the conflict over therapy has substantially subsided. There is practically no friction from the psychiatrist's side over the psychologist's private work in testing, doing research, or consulting with organizations. Furthermore, the psychologists do not question in the slightest the prerogatives of the medical profession where it is a matter of physical or organic disorders or where nonpsychological means of treatment, such as drugs or electroconvulsive therapy, are being used. These matters are legally under the physician's control.

It is useful to review the differing views and arguments that psychiatry and psychology offer when pressed on issues about jurisdiction, power, and economic gain. The argument of the psychiatric profession usually runs as follows: The treatment of human illness of all kinds traditionally and legally has been the responsibility of medical practitioners. Only the physician can be responsible for the diagnosis and treatment of mental illness. Physicians are experts on the functioning of the whole man, and it is always very difficult to disentangle the "mental" from the "physical." The medical profession welcomes the appropriate utilization of the psychological skills of other professional groups as long as they are under the supervision of physicians. Furthermore, among physicians it is the psychiatrist who is particularly competent by training and experience to deal with mental illness.

The psychologist's argument runs as follows: Psychologists by training and experience are qualified to deal with psychological problems, that is, problems that involve such processes as learning, motivation, personal development, and interpersonal relations. Granting psychiatric and medical responsibility for cases of organic disorder and psychosis, there remains over and above these a tremendous public need for psychological assistance. When psychologists have good training and experience, it is irrelevant and demeaning for them to be supervised by physicians regarding psychological matters. Moreover, many psychologists resent being excluded from the major American psychoanalytic associations, which through control by medical men in the early days restricted membership to those having the M.D. degree. This was done in spite of Freud's denial that medical training was important in psychoanalysis (Freud, 1950) and his defense of nonmedical colleagues. This restriction has been maintained in spite of the great contributions to psychoanalysis of distinguished nonmedical persons such as Anna Freud, Theodor Reik, Otto Rank, Erich Fromm, and Erik Erikson.

Underlying the dispute between the two professions are some other motives. The emergence of clinical psychology as an independent service to the public presents an *economic* challenge to medical interests. Most professional people are convinced that the demand for psychological services is so great that there is room for many more people to render these than are now doing so. Supposedly, too, the competition should result in more reduced fees for clients. One area in which this economic issue has been predominant is health insurance. Psychologists have made a determined effort to get policies written in such a way that reimbursement would cover psychological as well as psychiatric therapy.

Perhaps the central conflict is over *power* in an emerging area. More specifically the conflict is over the question of who is to lead or direct human service efforts in the next phase of their development—a phase that promises to give the leaders much power and prominence. Many who now exercise control naturally do not like to be faced with a demand that they share the authority over an important sector of human endeavor. However, psychologists feel that their background and training entitle them to a more independent position than that of supervisees of medicine. Some political control of services in a large area of human relationships is involved. Many people, including some within the ranks of psychiatry, see psychiatry as attempting to structure a health insurance scheme primarily for its own benefit; this is being done by defining psychiatrists as those in charge and by locking mental care into an expensive and outmoded model that favors traditional psychiatric practice. Again it would seem that both humanitarian needs and the vast number of human beings with psychological problems would argue for contributions from all who are capable.

Part of the conflict also arises from *the definition of what human problems and disorders are*. It seems largely a historical accident that the "mental illnesses" fell into the domain of medicine instead of education or theology. There have been a few spectacular associations between mental disturbances and organic causation, notably when syphilis was discovered to be the cause of general paresis. However, such psychiatric diagnostic categories as "personality trait disturbances," "adjustment problems," and "transient situational disorders" do not refer to organic causation. These problems arise in such areas as learning, personal development, and conscience. They are problems for behavioral scientists and specialists in learning and social psychology. They are also the concern of educators and clergymen. With the increasing tendency to question the relevance of the "medical model" and to replace it with other concepts about behavior and personality problems, a trend that has been discussed in some detail in earlier chapters, we may be approaching a time when the conflict between psychology and psychiatry over psychotherapy is a thing of the past. Certainly there is a great deal of real cooperation going on at the present time. The overriding fact of great public need suggests that it would be better if each profession would turn more of its energies toward solving human problems and less toward enhancing its own position.

THE DANGERS OF PROFESSIONALISM

The achievement of maturity by a profession requires self-knowledge. As we have suggested before, such knowledge should include a keen scrutiny of the groups with which it affiliates or identifies. Psychologists, as well as other professionals, need to be aware of the negative as well as the positive aspects of the development of the profession. In an excellent analysis of professionalism, Bisno (1960) recalls Tolstoy's admonition that any man can find good reasons to justify the way in which he makes his living.

Bisno first points out the great importance of professions in American life. When strangers meet, one of the first questions is: "What do you do?" Status, prestige, power, economic reward are tied in with professional affiliation. Although the stated goal of every profession is social good and the welfare of the client, Bisno finds striking evidence that this aim is often neglected in actual professional activity. Economic enhancement and maintenance of status take precedence over public needs when it comes to admitting candidates for training, setting up qualifications for professional membership, catering to wealthy and prestigeful clients, and emphasizing individual therapy as against preventive measures on a large scale.

Bisno, in a spirit of pseudo-profundity, proposes two "laws." The Law of Professional Velocity asserts the following (1960, p. 10): "The internal dynamics of the process of professionalization result in an upward and onward motion of the profession which is expressed in a continuous pressure toward extending the educational requirements for desired professional statuses irrespective of the absence of public clamor for such professional velocity." Bisno's second law, the Law of Professional Dissociation, is as follows (1960, p. 10): "As the process of professionalization goes on the professionals proceed to disassociate themselves from the uninitiated, respectfully referred to as subprofessionals, technicians, aides, the untrained, and laymen." By increasingly higher standards and the achievement of social distance for the elect, professionalism acts ultimately to restrict the situation and make it so rigid that public needs are no longer well served. The profession becomes more and more commercialized. The professional person is seen less and less as a dedicated humanitarian and more and more as a man with marketable skills. Vested interests begin to discourage social change. It is no secret that the American Medical Association has taken strong political stands and spent large sums of money on propaganda and lobbyists working against national health insurance legislation. Some professional groups, no less than labor unions and corporations, have developed great political power. Looking at themselves, some psychologists have become aware of the dangers in increasing professionalism and its concomitant shift to taking a political and social stance, which could be one outcome of the increase in private practice by clinical psychologists.

One of the persistent issues in APA boards and committees is the extent to which the association should try to influence legislation and take stands on matters of public policy. In 1971 a new organization, the Council for the Advancement of the Psychological Professions and Sciences (CAPPS), was formed to serve as an "action arm" of psychologists in promoting government policies they support and opposing those they disapprove.

Although the requirement for full professional status as a psychologist is a doctoral degree, with regard to the question of whether persons who have not obtained such degrees should be accepted as legitimate professional workers, spokesmen for psychology down through the years have shown a great deal of ambivalence. See, for example, the discussion at the 1965 Chicago conference on the training of clinical psychologists (APA, 1966a, p. 43):

> In trying to judge the correct course, the conferees seemed torn between recognizing current social needs and yet not reacting to them in what might later turn out to be socially irresponsible ways. The latter course was represented by some as promising more than the profession can offer and as overextending its resources. They viewed the training of fewer people at higher levels as the more responsible alternative. Others saw the latter as fine but unimaginative, pointing out that we now countenance, indeed advocate, roles which 10 years ago would have been looked on askance.

The solution the conference advocated was to approve M.A. level training but not to designate graduates of such programs as "psychologists." Many persons with and without Ph.D.s see such a policy as an evasion, and there is increasing support within the ranks of the APA for allowing non-Ph.D. persons to become voting members rather than restricting them to nonvoting *associate* status. The by-laws of the association have been amended to provide that associates can achieve voting privileges after five consecutive years of associate membership, and in 1971 the Council of Representatives voted to propose to the membership another by-law change that would set the minimum requirement for APA membership at the master's rather than the doctoral level.

Some of the movements and trends in present (1972) thinking about how society can best promote the psychological welfare of its members are in a direction away from past efforts to develop "helping professions." The extensive participation of persons without formal training in therapeutic efforts; self-help organizations of, by, and for alcoholics, drug addicts, or overeaters; attempts to promote human welfare through revolutionary changes in the structure of society—these and many other developments lead some psychologists—a small minority as yet—to oppose the whole movement toward the professionalization of psychology, a movement that has been going on for several decades. Such people view psychological concepts and techniques as assets and tools that should be made freely available to the public, not channeled through specially trained individuals. This challenge cannot be silenced by argument. It will be met as the future unfolds. It is recognized that with the extension of psychological services to more and more groups within the population, some way of utilizing the efforts of qualified persons with less than the doctor's degree—those with only bachelors' or associate degrees, as well as those with masters' degrees—must be found. To maintain the values of professionalism without overexclusiveness is one of the challenges of our time.

THE GOOD PROFESSION

Facing up to the problems of professionalism, the APA has approved a statement defining what a "good profession" should be like (APA, 1968b, p. 10):

> As members of a good profession, psychologists:
> 1. Guide their practices and policies by a sense of social responsibility;
> 2. Devote more of their energies to serving the public interest than to "guild" functions and to building ingroup strength;
> 3. Represent accurately to the public their demonstrable competence;
> 4. Develop and enforce a code of ethics primarily to protect the client and only secondarily to protect themselves;
> 5. Identify their unique pattern of competencies and focus their efforts to carrying out those functions for which they are best equipped;
> 6. Engage in cooperative relations with other professions having related or overlapping competencies and common purposes;
> 7. Seek an adaptive balance among efforts devoted to research, teaching, and application;
> 8. Maintain open channels of communication among "discoverers," teachers, and appliers of knowledge;
> 9. Avoid nonfunctional entrance requirements into the profession, such as those based on race, nationality, creed, or arbitrary personality considerations;
> 10. Insure that their training is meaningfully related to the subsequent functions of the members of the profession;
> 11. Guard against premature espousal of any technique or theory as a final solution to substantive problems;
> 12. Strive to make their services accessible to all persons seeking such services, regardless of social and financial considerations.

Psychologists are in a peculiar position in regard to the nature of a profession and its values. On the one hand, they are interested in the ethical conduct of their affairs as psychologists. On the other hand, they are interested in ethical conduct and values as objects of scientific study. In the latter role, psychologists can help to clarify and guide the development of the right values among people in general. Their psychological knowledge may contribute to the development of ways of behaving that flow from the possession of high values. Hobbs has made the following points (1959, p. 224): "Psychological knowledge should result in more ethical behaviors: (a) by clarifying the process of decision-making: (b) by divesting repressed responses already in the individual's repertory of their anxiety-producing potential, thus making them useful in problem-solving: and (c) by adding to the response repertory of the individual a number of alternative ways of behaving."

Because psychology has an enormous potential for good or evil as it develops into a more verified science of human behavior, the development of a good psychological profession is particularly important. Like the physicists with the atomic bomb, psychologists have already begun to develop techniques that have enormous power. Consider, for example, some of the implications of personal data banks, mass communication, stimulation of the "pleasure center," biofeedback, sensory deprivation, and operant conditioning. Aldous Huxley in *Brave New World* foresaw the early conditioning of children to fit them harmoniously into chosen kinds of roles in society. Orwell's *1984* showed how a totalitarian regime could impose nearly complete surveillance over individual behavior. These are forecasts of future potentialities which are awesome to consider. Faced with the possibility that they may decide to employ such powerful psychological methods, psychologists not only need to be loyal to the highest ethical standards, but they must also plan how they should relate themselves to the political forces which will decide just how psychology is to be utilized. In a democratic society, psychologists should be as committed to the development of independent thinking as the physician is to the preservation of life. All signs point to grave responsibilities for psychologists and their fellow behavioral scientists in the future.

SUMMARY

The development of a clinical psychologist involves his participation in professional organizations on national, state, and local levels. The American Psychological Association has a very active history of supporting and shaping standards of competence and training in clinical work. Through a number of years and a series of revisions the APA has provided statements of ethical standards to which clinical psychologists adhere. The primary and final interest of the clinician is the welfare of the client and of society. A growing number of states legally certify or license psychologists, thus preventing quacks and untrained persons from calling themselves psychologists or providing psychological service. Another approach followed by many state organizations is self-certification of their qualified members. In the many situations in which psychologists work, they cooperate with the members of several other professions. Good relations with others are important for the welfare of clients and patients. There has been considerable conflict, sometimes bitter, with medical organizations and especially psychiatry, centering around the practice of psychotherapy by clinicians. If the growth of the profession of clinical psychology is to be sound, the dangers of a rampant professionalism that loses sight of the public good must be guarded against. Since techniques for influencing human behavior may be misused, psychologists are likely to be faced with serious issues in the future, issues that will require them to become very clear about which values they should put first.

SUGGESTED READINGS

Moore, W. E. (in collaboration with G. W. Rosenblum). *The professions: roles and rules.* New York: Russell Sage Foundation, 1970.

This book, written by a sociologist, provides a good overview of professions in complex societies—how they emerge, what their defining characteristics are, how new members are "socialized" into them, and what their special responsibilities are. It is a balanced discussion, neither overly laudatory nor overly critical. A selected bibliography of 56 pages provides access to the most important other writings concerned with this topic.

American Psychological Association, Policy and Planning Board. Structure and function of APA: guidelines for the future. *American Psychologist,* 1972, *27,* 1–10.

This brief report outlines present and projected functions of the APA and some of its problems and alternative directions the association might go. It recommends a change to a structure of federated societies, as opposed to the present more centralized association, and the debate on that issue. Readers might also like to read about some of the issues in the earlier report by the Committee on Scientific and Professional Aims of Psychology (APA Professional Aims, 1967). That report of what has been called the "Clark Committee," after its chairman, Kenneth E. Clark, was the result of the extensive discussions of a committee appointed by the Board of Directors of APA in 1963 to examine the growing diversity in the APA. Attempting to arrive at common goals, it presented a diversity of opinions in the report. The distinguished committee members give differing opinions on such matters as scientific versus professional aims, the APA as a bureaucracy, clinical training, public responsibility, and graduate training.

American Psychological Association. Ethical standards of psychologists. *American Psychologist,* 1968, *23,* 357–361.

This is the most recent revision of the nineteen principles that constitute the official ethical code of the association. It has been published also as a separate, available from the APA Central Office, and in the early pages of successive editions of the APA *Biographical Directory*, where the by-laws of the association can also be found. The reader might like to review the rules and procedures of the APA ethics committee, which follows the standards, p. 362, in the *American Psychologist* (APA, 1968b).

American Psychological Association. *Casebook on ethical standards of psychologists.* Washington, D.C.: The Association, 1967.

The Casebook is organized around the nineteen principles of the code. The incidents are things that have actually happened, with the identity of the people involved disguised in various ways. The Committee on Ethical Standards for Psychology, who prepared the volume, indicate after each case their own opinion of the behavior, and in some instances tell what action was taken when the case was brought before them and the reason for the action.

Lakin, M. Some ethical issues in sensitivity training. *American Psychologist*, 1969, *24*, 923—928.

The enormous popularity of groups for training, personal "growth," and even entertainment raises many ethical questions. Poorly qualified people are advertising and selling group experiences and getting many customers. It is difficult to establish controls over qualifications of people because so many different professionals are practicing group techniques. Lakin points out many of the ethical problems (e.g., the need for responsible leadership, clarity of contract with persons coming to the group).

Specht, H. The deprofessionalization of social work. *Social Work*, 1972, *17*, 2, 3—15.

In a lively, even passionate, article, Specht discusses the dangers to the social work profession from four ideological currents: activism, antiindividualism, communalism, and environmentalism. He writes that the hallmark of the professional is not his readiness to identify with causes, but his desire and ability to offer help to all people within a framework of ethics and values. He argues for the importance of knowledge and research for the guidance of actions. Most of what Specht says would apply to clinical psychology, too, as it considers its place with regard to its broadening responsibilities in the community and society. Another article on the social work profession by Epstein (1970) explores effects of social action on role orientations. Epstein concludes that a bureaucratic orientation is conservatizing; a client orientation, radicalizing; and a professional orientation, flexible.

American Psychological Association. *Psychology as a profession.* Washington, D.C.: The Association, 1968.

One finds here some useful facts about the numbers and proportions of psychologists in different specialties and fields; an outline of the principles underlying the various roles psychologists play: research, teaching, service, and administration; a brief discussion of standards, rights, and responsibilities; and a list of 12 criteria of a good profession.

From material originally prepared for an APA committee on clinical psychology and the law, Shah (1969, 1970a, 1970b) presents a useful discussion of the important concerns: priveleged communications, confidentiality, and privacy.

Shore, M. F. and Golann, S. E. Problems of ethics in community mental health: a survey of community psychologists. *Community Mental Health Journal*, 1969, *5*, 452–460.

One area in which new ethical issues are showing up, as psychologists enlarge the scope of their professional activities, is community mental health. The replies received to three open-ended questions sent to all members of the Division of Community Psychology indicate that questions are arising about confidentiality of information, about consultant–consultee–client relationships, and about the competence of persons actually handling the therapeutic interventions. Psychologists are finding it difficult to separate their professional and citizen roles. The authors suggest that another casebook focusing on these issues would be useful.

Miller, G. A. Assessment of psychotechnology. *American Psychologist*, 1970, *25*, 991–1001.

Miller deals with some large questions that concern all psychologists, those relating to the evaluation of psychotechnology as a whole. He proposes a Code of Priorities to supplement the Code of Ethics to serve as guidelines in encouraging some kinds of development more than others. One of his important ideas, expressed here and elsewhere, is that the most valuable contributions psychology can make are those that can be put into the hands of the general public and not restricted to a knowledgeable elite.

In the psychological journals other important ethical and professional issues are presented by individuals. See, for instance, Smith's discussion of the ethics of population planning (1972).

chapter 20

The Future of Clinical Psychology

Where is clinical psychology going? In this last chapter, it is appropriate that we speculate about possibilities for the future. The value of conceptualizing the future is not that it enables us to *predict*, because prediction is almost impossible in the midst of the complex and conflicting influences of the modern world, but that it helps us *clarify* present values, delineate possibilities, and make choices. What the "futurists," as they are sometimes called, are doing is creating images of society, some of which may be used for designing and planning systems of human services. Because clinical psychology is part of the larger society, we need to look at the general context as we try to project on the screen pictures of what psychologists of the future may be doing.

SYSTEMATIC APPROACHES TO THE FUTURE

In the past, a number of brilliant thinkers have shown images to society, images that have been useful for discussion, conjecture, and even guidance. Plato's *Republic* was the first; Saint Augustine's *City of God*, Sir Thomas More's *Utopia*, and Samuel Butler's *Erewhon* were others. Some of the more recent visions of the future, such as Huxley's *Brave New World* and Orwell's *1984*, might be called anti-utopias. The most famous book of this sort by a psychologist is Skinner's *Walden Two*; it has even served as a model for several communes. Science fiction writers have also come out with futuristic views of society. All these pictures are of course speculative or imaginative, more like Rorschach perceptions than systematic reports based on a study of likelihoods and possibilities.

There are, however, several data-oriented approaches. One method is to develop *projections of past trends into the future*. An example is Little's (1972) assessment of the future academic marketplace for psychologists. He uses demographic data to relate current rates of Ph.D. production to future college enrollments and the number of graduates needed to maintain the 1969 percentage of college-employed psychologists. He concludes that by the mid-1980s there will be an oversupply of Ph.D.s in academic jobs. In this as with other projections of present trends into the future, the problem is that they usually take into account only a few variables. As we consider the future of clinical psychology, we find very few such studies based on projections available for our use, in any event.

Another approach to the future is to obtain *judgments of experts about likely events and conditions* and to combine these into a composite picture. Still another approach is the *simulation of future states of affairs* carried out by a computer into which data about past and present and decision rules have been entered. Sometimes this simulation takes the form of a game such as Buckminster Fuller's World Game. The Suggested Readings at the end of the chapter give further details about these techniques. So far there has been no systematic study of the future of clinical psychology or the human services by these methods, so that we must still proceed by speculation and opinion, encouraging the reader to engage in some speculation on his own.

EXTERNAL INFLUENCES

We can consider the trends on which the future of this psychological specialty rests under two main headings—external and internal influences, or trends in the outside world and trends within the profession itself. As we look first at the external factors, beginning with the most basic, we find that the most fundamental questions have to do with *the sheer survival of mankind*. Massive wars and the destruction of all complex life on this planet are distinct possibilities. Psychology and other social sciences may be able to develop ways of averting this doomsday. William James long ago called for a search for "moral equivalents of war" to challenge humankind for constructive efforts.

Assuming no massive wars, we can look to the trends that are apparent at the present time and likely to continue into the future. Caplow (1971) has provided two lists. The first one includes fifteen long-term trends that have persisted for a least a hundred years, are present in different degrees throughout the world, and can be extrapolated into the future with considerable confidence (pp. 629–630):

1. Technological progress
2. Technological diffusion
3. Increase of goods
4. Increase of services
5. Increase of symbols and images
6. Population expansion
7. Occupational specialization
8. Decreasing work effort
9. Equalization of the sexes
10. Urbanization and suburbanization
11. Intensified spatial mobility

12. Erosion of traditional cultures
13. Expansion of government
14. Increasing severity of war
15. Decreasing autonomy of the natural environment

To these fifteen might be added another—increasing bureaucratization, which applies not only to government but to businesses, schools, churches, and other institutions. All these trends are interconnected and interdependent and together produce a picture of massive movement of change in modern times.

In addition to the clear trends that will affect the future, Caplow (1971, pp. 647–648) identifies eleven unconfirmed trends more difficult to quantify or prove. These are very frequently the subject of discussion, and many people would judge them to be trends of the recent past that will continue into the future. Caplow's list is as follows:

1. Increasing anxiety
2. Breakdown of social values
3. Increasing anomie (alienation)
4. Increasing deviance
5. Increasing political violence
6. Decline of the family
7. Decline of religion
8. Status equalization
9. Cultural homogenization
10. Global interdependence
11. Accelerating rates of social change

Most of these, the reader will note, are psychological or social—psychological in nature. Whether the second list represents long-range movements in society is not clear, but even the presence of these concerns in people's minds suggests that there will be many who think of the need for psychological assistance in the near future. In the following discussion, we will select some trends for special attention.

A major factor in all future thinking, affecting all institutions and human interaction ultimately, is the problem of *population growth*. Various estimates of the world population (Ehrlich and Ehrlich, 1972, pp. 50, & 452; the Commission on Population Growth and the American Future, 1972, pp. 9, 11, 20) for the year 2000 place it at 5,400 to 7,500 million. The world had 1,500 million inhabitants in 1900 and 3,700 million in 1971. The U.S. population in the year 2000 is projected to be from 271 to 322 million, whereas in 1900 it was 76 million and in 1971, 207 million. Thus in the last 30 years of the twentieth century, it is expected that the world population will almost double in size, and the American population will increase by 50 percent. Even if extensive population-control procedures are put into effect, the number of people already living will put an enormous burden on the world's resources in the coming years.

Related problems such as urbanization and the demands for social services are formidable.

Another large class of external factors very important to the future of clinical psychology has to do with economic resources and the technology upon which they rest. The vast expansion of these resources in the United States and other postindustrial nations has provided support, on an unprecedented scale, for human services—education, medicine, legal assistance, entertainment, mass communication, and government—as well as giving individuals and families far more material goods than they ever had before. But serious problems have arisen in the distribution of the wealth that is being produced, unemployment has become a chronic plague in some sections of society, and a surfeit of material things has led to boredom and alienation in other sectors. The latter contributes to the popularity of psychotherapy, no doubt. While some nations fight famine, others consume excessive proportions of the earth's resources.

One of the broadest of the present trends that seems likely to affect the development of psychology even more strongly in the future is the attention to the quality of life, ecology, and the use of natural resources. National mentality is changing from the original "Go West, young man (for there are unlimited resources to be subdued and conquered)" toward the realization that "we are all passengers on the same spaceship." All the resources we can ever have access to we carry with us. If we damage some of the basic processes on which we rely, there may be no way to restore favorable balances. But changing society to be more in harmony with the national resources and ecological principles demands changes on the part of all of us as individuals—besides government, business, and industry. Psychologists have been slow to take up the study of how people may live more meaningful and satisfying lives with less emphasis on materialism. The changing of people's attitudes toward economic growth may be the toughest struggle in the ecology movement. To be sure, nowadays psychologists in their work as counselors and group leaders have entered the area of values, fulfillment, and clarification of personal goals. But in general the broader questions of how life may be lived, with what material props and toward what ends, have been addressed mainly by religionists and philosophers. A clinical or applied psychoecology is needed, to bring together our knowledge of specifics such as stress, overcrowding, and population problems and to combine such knowledge with a plan to allow individuals to work out their own future in socially productive ways. As humanity becomes increasingly aware of the threat to its sheer survival, a psychoecology—how man's biological, personal, interpersonal, and family systems can be compatible with the ecosystem—will become increasingly vital.

Meanwhile technology continues to progress (or at least change) at an accelerating rate, intensifying old problems and creating new ones. Drucker (1969) identified four new massive industries already on the horizon. The information industry, spawned by the computer and electronic communication, will lead to an enormous proliferation of not only formal educational devices but also adult and mass education. Homes and businesses will also have computer-assisted information processors as we now have notepads and books. Data banks, despite all the threats to privacy, are bound to proliferate. Platt (1972), recognizing that data banks are already in existence with private and governmental institutions, suggests that citizens must insist on the right to see any information kept on them and to have services to assist them in clarifying errors. The other three new industries Drucker lists would appear to have less impact on psychology and psychologists but are still important—the exploration and development of oceans, the increasing diversity and usefulness of new materials such as plastics, and the industries created by the rise of the megalopolis, such as mass transportation and new physical arrangements for living and working.

A great many specific technological developments have influenced and will influence psychology. Within the thirty years from 1940 to 1970, techniques that have become accepted as part of psychology include computers, video recordings, automated teaching machines, biofeedback instruments, and techniques for stimulating brain cells. A host of potential developments in biological technology—the coming power to alter genes and create new species, the ability to do cloning (the growing of a whole organism from a sample cell of an existing one, thus making carbon copies of individuals), transplantation of the nervous system, and the discovery of new chemicals and other techniques to stimulate the brain promise to further influence psychology profoundly.

Changes in the nature of human relationships have also been occurring and may occur with increasing rapidity. An important set of relationships that must be taken into consideration has to do with the nuclear family and alternatives to it that seem to be taking shape. In America, the isolated mother—father—children unit has been severely shaken by recent trends which seem likely to continue—geographical mobility, divorce, working parents, urban alienation. *Family supplementation* through group homes, substitute mothers, foster grandparents, cooperative nurseries, and other developments must be carefully evaluated if we are to provide the young child with the physical care and the intellectual and emotional stimulation he needs if he is to maximize his potentials. On the other end of the life cycle, special attention must be given to providing family-like conditions for the aged. In the middle of the life cycle, young mothers need relief from the heavy burden of housekeeping and child care, and overworked professionals and managers may achieve relief through more family life. What seems to be needed is an opportunity for the reformation of aspects of society so that women and men can take on different, more satisfying roles. The seeking of new relations by young people in "trial marriages" and communes is part of such explorations.

There is also the problem of the quality of parenthood. It has often been pointed out that people must be trained and licensed to do almost anything except one of the most important tasks a person can attempt, parenthood. We have failed to recognize the broad question of the wantedness of people. Socially acceptable parenthood, schooling, employment, and housing and economic possibilities must be provided if a prospective member of society is to escape the message that "you're really excess." One might speculate that the widespread disaffection among young people may have resulted from feeling unwanted and discovering at the same time that the American promise of power, that "you can change whatever you don't like," has been a seduction, misleading untruth, perpetrated by older generations.

The relationships among people that are especially important in psychology's future include the larger organizations or bureaucracies. The size and complexity of such organizations have increased tremendously during the last few decades, and seem likely to increase still more. Without going into detail, it would seem that psychology and other social sciences should have as a high priority the development of alternative possibilities for organizations keeping the needs of people in mind. One of the large dangers is the "top-down" planning mentality of many governmental and private commissions studying social problems; only the elite are involved, not people who represent ordinary citizens. Toffler (1970) has suggested "social future assemblies" for grass-roots participation in learning about trends and prospects and discussing where communities and nations should be going. In many places people would be playing "planning games " looking at different alternatives and expressing preferences.

As bureaucracies have functioned in the recent past in response to human needs, a major problem is what might be called *programism*. Social policy has been based on identifying a particular problem and dispatching a solution—a program—almost the way past military leaders dispatched cavalry to rescue a patrol overwhelmed by Indians. This lack of sensitivity and analysis of the wider system has led to some quite undesirable effects, among them the creation of divisiveness. For every eligible group, an ineligible group is automatically created. Not only do eligibilities depend on a wide variety of differing criteria, but it has become impossible for citizens or even legislators to keep track of the variety of programs that may apply to certain people. Besides excluding some citizens and creating divisions, programism tends to reward—often inadvertently—undesirable behaviors. In a recent financial crisis in one state, for example, the only two ways for a family to establish eligibility for public assistance were for a resident husband to leave home or for an unmarried daughter to become pregnant.

We have seen that it is possible for a program to make those it benefits more dependent. Perhaps the most serious charge to be leveled at programism is that programs can weaken existing systems by offering apparent short-term benefit. A program designed to provide foster or group homes for children in conflict with their parents may do harm as well as good. The very existence of such a program communicates to parents that they need not improve their techniques with successive children; thus family effectiveness is not strengthened. A program that tries instead to identify the system in difficulty and to strengthen it, as in this case by increasing the parenting skills of families, avoids this error.

But few programs even within behavioral-science areas have been examined to see how they affect related systems.

Other pertinent questions related to organizations and policy bear on the question of *opportunity structure*. If our present situation is characterized by both a bad opportunity structure and misperception by citizens of opportunities that do exist, should efforts focus only on changing opportunity structure, or should they also help people become aware of the existing opportunities? What does "equal opportunity" really mean? At what point does it enhance a person to be like the majority of society, and when does it begin to destroy his individuality? Clinical psychologists in correctional institutions will be confronted with this question when a single institution (and a single legal structure) tries to serve persons coming from widely differing subgroups (e.g., Kittrie, 1971). We have mentioned the example earlier of how newer institutions can become extremely attractive and pleasant for some deprived persons, and how such people may acquire—or be taught—behavior that is potentially dangerous to them in their community setting, such as forms of nonviolent or very atypical response: And so we must ask yet another question, can institutions such as correctional institutions really solve social problems? It certainly appears, for instance, that the debtor prisons of Dickens' time in England had little impact on the problem and that solution had to await economic reforms.

In addition to these broad, inclusive trends that are influencing the development of clinical psychology, there are other movements we might label *social concerns*. People in the second half of the twentieth century became concerned in a new way about poverty or *deprivation*. The word "deprived" has become as good a reason for action or a key to service as "disturbed" was in earlier times. Some critics of the social scene feel that the portents indicate that revolution is at hand; they view much of our social condition with alarm and forecast that far-reaching changes will come about in cataclysmic ways. Other observers feel that comments such as "this is the end of an era" are ways in which social critics traditionally attempt to achieve shaman status. Such observers tend to point to the ebb and flow of human affairs over the centuries and emphasize social evolution rather than revolution, and the fact that things have been worse as well as better in the past.

We see many persons (mature adults as well as the young) striving for a variety of social causes under a number of different banners. Most movements seem to contain large quantities of self-interest on the part of the members, a self interest embedded in the elaborate belief structure of the various groups. Social systems have been under attack from various sides, with some people vigorously testing new ways and others fervently clinging to their established order. As tensions mount, most groups emphasize their special interests and tend not to be concerned with producing or inventing types or forms of social order which might meet the needs of apparently conflicting groups.

Underlying all these specific concerns are philosophical questions about the quality of life and the nature of man. What do human beings want? What do human beings need? These two questions are very different ones and raise the question—who is to judge what is in the public interest? We are led back to different views of man—pessimistic or optimistic—and to differential trust in people to come up with good answers. Hardin (1968) was particularly concerned about the individual selfishness of people when he wrote of the "tragedy of the commons." In the English villages there used to be common pastures. But it was to the advantage of no single individual herdsman to be sparing of the pasture; adding one or two cows to his grazing herd was to his advantage. And so, each took more and more advantage of the commons, and eventually the source of food for all was gone. Likewise the world ecology is in danger of being ruined by abuse, overconsumption, and overpopulation. In a more poetic expression, Platt (1962, p. 62) indicates that human desires will shape what the future will bring: "To be warm and full and free, these are our first needs . . . but what dissolves and remolds societies unaware is that we also want, like children, to have sweet smells, music, pictures, entertainment, bright lights, and powerful servants. We want to make magic, to run like the wind and to fly like the birds and to talk across miles and be as beautiful as gods and to know how everything works."

Individuals do want these lovely things, but clinical psychologists also know that many with short-range perspectives also want the quick pleasure of an opiate trip, the sudden expression of murderous aggression, or the evasion of responsibility by embezzlement or child abandonment, and all of us should remember the prevalence of racism, sexism, the brutality of organized crime, and the exploitation of the poor in the name of profit. Alongside the rosy future view, we must consider the possibility of a new feudalism, where some people live in armed sanctuaries in city apartments, surrounded by roving guerrillas, where individuals easily disrupt the complex networks of energy transmission, transportation, and communication, and where "good" citizens are willing to accept dictatorial controls in order to gain security. At least the psychologist should be aware of these many individualistic and conflicting wants and should help as many people as possible gain nondestructive goals.

Some have expressed the hope that this age marks the beginning of man's ability—now that so many ancient enemies such as disease and hunger can be mastered—to be compassionate toward his fellows. Such a hope may reflect little more than a need to escape from the dehumanizing and brutalizing forces. But there is at least a possibility that we may be entering upon a new age.

TRENDS WITHIN THE FIELD

Some recent developments within the field of clinical psychology itself also constitute trends likely to influence its future directions. One of these is a resurgence of interest in *biological* variables. The relationship between genetics and behavior is being studied intensively and is likely to lead to new developments in clinical work. Treatment by medication is an important feature of many mental health programs, and research on psychopharmacology and other aspects of physiological psychology is actively in progress. The refinement of biofeedback techniques has opened new horizons in alteration and self-control of bodily processes.

Such developments would seem to point to the continuation—even the strengthening—of the traditional ties between clinical psychology and medicine.

Technological advances within psychology promise many further changes. Undoubtedly many new things of value for human research and service will be available between 1970 and the year 2000. Schwitzgebel (1970) points to such possibilities as electronic surveillance for parolees, automated public opinion sampling, and "behavioral prosthetics" to assist people to correct and improve behavior just as eyeglasses improve vision. Platt (1972) mentions the possibility of electronic aids in "personal programming for daily effectiveness"—providing reminders, reinforcement aids, and time planning. Lanyon (1971) has listed technology already available for mental health usage such as automation of psychological assessment, behavior-modification aids, and machine-aided counseling and therapy.

Another focus of increasing concern is the problem of *health care*. Federally assisted medical care, a National Health Service, and extended medical coverage by private insurance carriers all have champions. Eventually some extensions of federally guaranteed or prepaid service must take shape and psychologists will be faced with the dilemma of "going for their share of the money" versus thinking about, and perhaps protesting, the implications that psychological activity is a "service" to be "delivered."

Another salient trend that has become visible in recent years is the use of *nonprofessionals* in psychological assistance to people. New kinds of agencies, such as crisis clinics and suicide-prevention centers, are staffed very largely with nonprofessional volunteers, using them in ways that would have been considered improper in earlier times. The realization that existing and proposed mental health services can scarcely be staffed or financed with conventional manpower will prompt more of this shift in role patterns, training, and services. Such a shift will also be promoted by increased awareness that much of the traditional content of the field has questionable relevance to nonwhites and lower-class people who have been poorly served heretofore. Available to professionals and nonprofessionals alike, one of the most notable of newer tools, behavior modification, is likely to be expanded, "humanized," and diversified. Behavioral procedures will be having increasing impact in settings concerned with mental retardation, special education, child and family difficulties, and delinquency.

It has become clear that as society attempts to solve problems of human relations and of human service, we need to develop a practical conceptual framework for thinking about manpower (or, more properly, in many instances, "womanpower") and new systems of development, training, and career information. In planning for such occupations, one crucial aim would be to avoid dead-end or "boxed-in" jobs—to allow ready movement either horizontally (toward jobs with similar levels of responsibility, training, and pay) or vertically (toward jobs at higher levels). At the present time a psychiatric aide has no place to go. He cannot go very high in the pay scale, and he cannot readily move into the nursing line unless he goes back and takes a great deal of training. Similarly, a psychiatric nurse cannot readily become a psychologist without going back to college and taking a Ph.D. Although no doubt some people will need to return to college to make job shifts, flexibility in the whole system needs to be developed. Clinical psychology would be in a stronger position if it could provide for the use of the great amount of talent that develops through practical experience as a psychiatric aide, an employment counselor, a nurse's helper, or the like. The future will bring such systems into existence.

Service by nonprofessionals is also increasing as a result of the setting up of new organizations and agencies in which there are no professional staff members at all, except perhaps consultants and advisers. Many centers for youth, such as drop-in centers, contact operations and crash pads, and many helping institutions run by minority groups for their members are of this type. The widespread use of encounter groups run by nonprofessionals, even though it may be deplored, is another illustration of the "demystification" of psychiatric and psychological work. Thus the general rise of antiprofessional feeling acquires great impact because antiprofessionals are increasingly capable of questioning the relevance (in terms of social usefulness) of professionals and of bypassing their services. There is even a possibility that professional therapy will become obsolete. Indeed, Albee's (1970) APA Presidential Address, "The Uncertain Future of Clinical Psychology," pointed in that direction.

If the effect of the increased influence on biology is to bring clinical psychology closer to medicine, the influence of this movement away from professionalism would appear to be in the opposite direction. The medical concept of "delivery of services" is essentially what comes into question.

"Is it service that people need?" In general, the traditional medical establishment assumes that it is. Also, the widespread "sellability" of individual psychotherapy, group therapy, and encounter experiences is an endorsement of a marketing model. Certainly where the provision of gasoline or toilet paper or food is concerned, furnishing a network that makes available the product people want has proved to be commercially successful. But are "psychological services" really parallel? In the majority of cases we are faced with the problem of helping people live more productive lives, a problem for which the solution is to provide better opportunity structures, more stable relationships, or circumstances for learning or relearning. We know too that this same kind of process, based on a stable relationship or on learning or relearning goes on within people's ordinary lives in their communities, without any formal recognition that a psychological process is occurring. Thus an alternative to the concept of "delivery of services" seems to be the concept of "promoting effectiveness of functioning systems," or "increasing competence."

One advantage this concept holds is that the "delivery of services" notion seems to relegate people to a rather passive stance, suggesting that they themselves do not know what is good for them. Furthermore, the service must be delivered by specialized agencies, pervasive and expensive, and its operation may serve to weaken already-functioning systems. For example, suppose that a child welfare agency seeks to provide foster placement for all or most children who are involved in conflict at home. Before long every available space is filled, the "need" is discovered to be overwhelming, and several participating families are unconsciously getting ready to resolve conflicts with their younger children in the same way. Such a program does not improve the families themselves, and conflicts arise between parents and foster parents, families and agencies. Citizens complain about the taxes. The present trend toward self-help through nonprofessional organizations seems significant for the future.

THE UNCOMMON IMPORTANCE OF CHOICE

We have presented in Chapter 4 a sketch of a theory of possibilities, resting on the basic fact that for individual, group, or organization there are always multiple paths stretching into the future, but because time is limited, only a fraction of these possibilities can be actualized. What is becoming increasingly apparent to thoughtful futurists is that perhaps the most salient trend we can now discern is that possiblilities are multiplying, while time is still limited. Thus choice becomes a more and more essential human activity that cannot be avoided, and for many persons freedom becomes a wearisome burden rather than an ideal. The often-quoted remark of the preschooler in the *New Yorker* cartoon "Do we *have* to do what we want to again today?" has become a common complaint.

Toffler's enormously popular book *Future Shock*, cited in the Suggested Readings at the end of the chapter, has one section on diversity in which the author identifies the problem he calls *overchoice*. He describes in some detail the multiplication of products, organizations, information media, "fun" specialties, and life styles that has occurred as mass production has been replaced by the new technology. He shows how this situation gives rise to a "superabundance of selves" and makes the establishment of a firm personal identity increasingly difficult (p. 322): "Which of many potential selves shall we choose to be? What sequence of serial selves will describe us? How, in short, must we deal with overchoice at this, the most intensely personal and emotion-laden level of all? In our headlong rush for variety, choice, and freedom: we have not yet begun to examine the awesome implications of diversity."

Other sensitive observers of trends in modern society have perceived similar problems. The Swedish economist, Linder (1970), speaks of the "harried leisure class" and the cost of decision time in the postindustrial world. Drucker, in *The Age of Discontinuity* (1969) comments on the "burden of decision" in the new "society of organizations" (pp. 247–249).

It is, above all, the burden of decision imposed by the society of organizations which the young find frightening and against which they rebel. Suddenly there are career choices; the great majority only yesterday had their careers determined from birth on. Suddenly there are decisions on the direction and purpose of knowledge. Suddenly we have to have new economic policies; we can no longer trust either the automatic operation of Adam Smith's "complementary trade" or the "inevitability of history" of the Marxian schema. Suddenly we have acquired enough knowledge in medicine to have to make decisions—on heart transplants or artificial kidneys, for instance—about whom to keep alive and whom to let die.

The rhetoric of the young complains bitterly, about their being "manipulated." But their actions make it clear that it is the burden of decision that frightens them. . . For the society of organizations offers choices, and therefore imposes on the individual the burden of decisions. It demands of him the price of freedom: responsibility.

The significance of this aspect of postindustrial society is that it challenges the helping services to help individuals and groups deal more adequately with "overchoice" and the "burden of decision." To some extent, counseling psychology has always provided this sort of service to facilitate the choice of a career. These techniques and skills must be broadened and extended to cover more areas of life and more kinds of people.

But we are beginning to see other ways besides individual counseling to deal with this challenge. Computer technology may make it possible for individuals to obtain, before making decisions, a fairly complete picture of the probable consequences that would follow the choice of each alternative, along with a probability figure to indicate how likely the projected consequences are. Results based on the utilization of these sophisticated methods by government agencies, as, for example, in the choice of a policy to pursue in Vietnam, suggest that they are not yet satisfactory for general use. But they will undoubtedly be developed in the future, and it may become common procedure to run a series of computer simulations before arriving at any important life decision.

One of Toffler's proposals in the book cited above is that we deliberately create environments in which decision stress will be reduced. Individuals even now manage to surround themselves with personal "stability zones," aspects of their environments that they consciously decide not to change—homes, treasured possessions, old clothes. Society may learn to do this on a larger scale, creating new groupings of people who are moving in the same direction, new institutions like the halfway houses that help mental hospital patients handle the transition to community living, new "enclaves" of different sorts to which people who wish to live particular kinds of life with a certain consistency and even a "temporary tradition" can move.

Some parts of society do not have enough choice—or the right, competence-enhancing options. Among the option-deprived are the ghetto dwellers, those barred from positions by race, sex, or age, and the vast part of the developing world outside North America, Europe, and Japan. Whether people's lives are crippled by overchoice or absence of some alternatives, the problems of decision making and priorities on use of time are of central significance.

Undoubtedly other ways of easing the burden of choice and adjusting options for people will occur to creative designers of the future once the difficulty has been generally recognized. Clinical psychology will play a part in these developments.

PRIORITIES FOR CLINICAL PSYCHOLOGY

In the presence of many possibilities, priorities are needed for clinical psychology. To help guide the profession's choices, we would hope that working clinicians, instructors, students, and others will take time not only for conferences on training but also for the consideration of the needs of society and the goals of the clinical effort. Below are listed priorities we recommend for clinical psychology in the coming years.

Of highest importance is *the design and development of public programs for psychological well-being*. Clinical psychologists should assume leadership in planning for humane and realistic programs to enhance human resources. Such ambitious undertakings would involve working with others to promote such efforts as the following: A continuing study of future trends and alternatives, development of social indicators of "mental health" or psychological effectiveness, analyses of the relation of community and organizational systems to personal well-being, and information systems for transmitting findings and recommendations to decision makers. A special consideration is the optimal balance between private and public services. Planning should involve the consumers of psychological services—clients and patients—as well as other professionals and community leaders. Psychologists need to make special efforts to know the living conditions and needs of the less vocal members of society.

Improving the quality of life with people appears to rest on a more constructive model of man than does *delivering service to* them. Psychologists deal essentially in systems such as individuals, families, neighborhoods, and communities, and not in goods or narrowly conceived services. The basic job we face is to see that the naturally occurring systems, like individuals, families, and neighborhoods, increase in competence—in ability to help themselves and others, in ability to perceive and create opportunities and to select values. Our task is to promote human aspirations, human capacities, and human responsibility. The easy parallels of delivering cabbages or setting up a network to make gasoline easily available can be most misleading; "delivery" and "providing" in a narrow sense are not fit goals. Our priority must be to improve the quality of life.

Of great importance for the foregoing is the *study and support of natural problem solving in daily life*. If we are to develop programs for preventing behavioral disorders on a wide scale, we must know much more about the way people handle difficulties in families and communities; then we can assist in supporting the constructive forces and building up the natural reinforcement mechanisms. The carrying out of such programs would require a great deal of informal observation, field learning, and research in behavioral ecology and sophisticated analyses of level of intervention. Students should be learning directly in communities, especially from the major resources used in handling human problems—police, teachers, lawyers, physicians, and even bartenders and businessman. Such learnings are likely to lead to such widespread techniques as education of parents and teachers in community colleges, spot "commercials" and psychological problem-solving instruction on television, and family life education in schools, rather than just a proliferation of present services. It may be that annual psychological checkups will be developed for organizations and groups and that the natural curiosity of people about taking psychological tests may be useful. Such programs would aim at "giving psychology away" to help the public toward greater effectiveness.

The content of education, research, and service needs to reflect an *orientation to system developments over the life cycle*. Longitudinal studies already reveal great influences from early experiences on later phases of life; early childhood is a particularly important time and clinicians need to pay more attention to that period of life. Throughout the life cycle, the emphasis should be on analyzing and altering the system of daily living that envelops the person, not just the person himself. Theoretically it is likely that the cognitive functions will receive more emphasis as behavioral programs broaden to include more complex phenomena.

Within clinical and counseling psychology and in working with other professions, psychology needs to pay particular attention to *career development, career lattices, and occupational innovation for psychological assistance*. As psychological knowledge and skills grow, there will be many opportunities to develop new positions, to open up new career lines, and to break down present jobs in such a way that additional work will be available. Support for demonstration programs already has been given by national funding groups; additional support for well-thought-out programs is likely. Psychologists should recognize the generic quality of much of the helping enterprise and attempt to develop multidisciplinary support for training programs and joint efforts with social workers, physicians, lawyers, and educators. The field of environmental psychology will need a clinical sensitivity as it develops liaison with urban planning and architecture. Psychology already has many strengths in industrial, personnel, counseling, and clinical psychology to draw on as it looks at manpower and career problems.

Clinical psychology should retain a deep concern for *a humanized technology for improvement designs*. Trends already under way suggest a proliferation of techniques of assessment, learning, and therapy which will outdo but be more sophisticated than the intelligence-test movement of the 1920s and 1930s and the projective technique movement of the 1950s. Keeping the goal of improvement designs in mind, clinical psychologists will need to develop automated life history systems, situational assessment, systems for decision making in helping organizations, ways of communicating images of clients' potentials, community assessment systems, and aids to counseling and therapy. All of these must be designed with an eye toward their human consequences, the potential cost to privacy, and the values the methods convey to the users.

For more effective application of psychology, there should be an emphasis on *educational efforts that interrelate conceptual and practical learning and provide for periodic upgrading of knowledge and skill*. Future efforts are likely to include a mixture of self-instruction with classroom, simulation, and field learning. Each of these methods should be researched for its effectiveness. The new attention to the person *in situ* will result in new concepts about systems and the environment as well as new methodologies for understanding complex relationships.

Clinical psychologists should seek to heighten their knowledge and skills concerning *program evaluation*. Costs and payoffs for appraisal and intervention programs will be looked at as a whole and analyses of steps and subsystems will assist decision makers in improving their offerings to the public. Here again, clinicians should insist that criteria be humane and that long-term benefits not be overlooked. Large-scale program evaluation should look at the issue of "natural" versus "professional" systems in order to be open to the finding that, say, keeping a person in his home with medications may be better than any therapy the psychiatric hospital has. Further, as program evaluation findings accumulate, as with the increasingly frequently heard assertion that alternatives to psychiatric hospitalization are better than hospitalization, psychologists are challenged to make these publicly known for the benefit of both potential clients and taxpayers.

These, then, are seven priorities for coming years:—(1) broad-based design of public programs, (2) support for natural problem solving, (3) orientation to life-cycle systems, (4) occupational innovation, (5) humanized technology, (6) theory—practice integration and continued education, and (7) program evaluation. If these proposed emphases are supported by the profession and sources of funding, clinical psychology would be on a much more solid and effective basis before the year 2000.

TOWARD A PLURALISTIC CLINICAL PSYCHOLOGY

Ten years ago we suggested three alternative directions in which clinical psychologists might become specialists: medical psychology, psychological treatment, and the general area of human relations. The specialist in medical psychology might, we felt, take not just psychopathology, but the psychological side of all medical pathology as his province. The specialist in psychological treatment, while he might have several methods at his command, would focus primarily on being a psychotherapist. Finally, we speculated that the third possible direction, the clinical psychologist as a specialist in human relations, might entail emphasis on the role of the psychologist in social systems, for instance in planning and evaluating a therapeutic program within an institution.

INFLUENCES   POSSIBILITIES

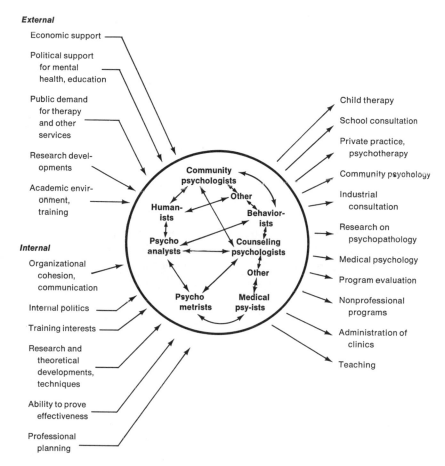

FIGURE 20-1 Influences and possibilities for clinical psychologists.

The three conventional activities of the clinical psychologist that have been recognized for decades are assessment, therapy, and research. As we look back over the past ten years, we see that these have been molded to fit not just one of the specialty areas, but all three, and others besides. To be sure, the medical psychology specialty has not expanded as much as the other two, and the decade has emphasized several other specializations and subspecializations as well. It seems, then, that clinical psychology has served as a general base from which diversification and specialization has proceeded.

It no longer seems feasible to sketch alternative directions in which the *whole profession* is likely to move. Individual psychologists and agencies are doing so many different things and considering so many others that it seems highly unlikely that they will agree upon any single direction of effort. Instead, we now assume that clinical psychology is increasingly a *pluralistic* profession and that it is individual psychologists rather than the professional group as a whole that must make choices about how energies and resources are to be deployed.

Figure 20-1 gives graphic form to this conception. Starting with a similar orientation and a common core of education and training, the body of individuals who constitute clinical psychology as a whole is subjected to the kinds of influences we have discussed in previous sections of the chapter. Individuals within the group react differently to these inputs, and out of the profession many separate lines of specialization are crystallized.

In thinking about the choices individuals must make among these specialties, we return to the perspective we described in the first chapter—settings, clients, and activities. These variables can be combined in a large number of ways, many of which have not yet been tried. One can choose to work, for example, in a small private clinic, a large institution, a school system, a community as a whole, or in his own office as a private practitioner. These are only a few of the settings in which clinical psychologists are already functioning. Each setting has its own advantages and disadvantages; each sensitizes those who work in it to some professional issues and ethical problems more than others.

One can choose to work with children or adults, with very disturbed or damaged persons, with only mildly maladjusted persons, or, in a preventive way, with people who are not disturbed at all. Distinctions between voluntary and involuntary clients, and between those able to pay for treatment and those who must obtain it through a public agency set up choices. One can choose whether his clients will be primarily individuals and groups whom he helps directly or organizations through which he helps individuals indirectly.

Even greater diversity confronts the chooser in the realm of activities. For example, he can emphasize assessment in the broad sense in which we have presented it in previous chapters, appraising individuals in context, or he can become an expert on one or a few tests. He can practice psychotherapy based on one particular theoretical orientation or several. He can devote most of his time to training volunteers. He can be a planner or a researcher of any one of a number of different varieties. These are only a few of the possibilities.

Obviously not all combinations of setting—client—activity some might prefer are feasible. A psychologist who wished, for example, to work in a small rural public clinic with mildly disturbed children doing nothing but research would find it difficult to locate his ideal position. But certainly a large number of setting—client—activity combinations does exist, and others may come into existence. And it will be good for the whole science and profession of clinical psychology to include this diversity of specializations.

It must be remembered that choice of specialization is always limited to some extent by economic factors. As we mentioned earlier, job prospects are not as bright in the early 1970s as they were in several preceding decades. The American Psychological Association has taken on the task of analyzing and reporting manpower trends so that more information about this aspect of choice will be available. (See, for instance, the May 1972 issue of the *American Psychologist*, which focused on such concerns.)

A pluralistic conception of clinical psychology will have implications for many aspects of professional organization and professional development. Some of these effects have already appeared. We mentioned in Chapter 19 that there are several divisions of the APA representing different professional specialties. The Accreditation Committee encourages diversity among training programs rather than standardization of a single pattern. We may see even more decentralization and diversification in the future within a general framework of agreement about the overall objectives and interest in other specialties besides one's own.

We must learn to work together as a profession in planning the future—to collect the sorts of data upon which sound evaluations and projections can be made, to set general goals, to develop long-range plans, and to modify them with changing circumstances. We need to anticipate the indirect as well as the direct consequences of the personal choices and the institutional decisions that we make. We need to consider the country as well as our own community, the welfare of the world as well as the welfare of the part of it in which we live. It is not enough to do one's own work well. Each of us must also play a part in designing the future.

SUMMARY

Throughout the ages men have produced images of the future based on speculation, projections of present trends, or judgment of experts. In considering the future of clinical psychology we must take into consideration such forecasts as they are appearing in our time. Certain facts and trends stand out—population growth, economic and technological progress, changes in social organization. The development of clinical psychology is being influenced by concern over poverty and deprivation; the demand for psychotherapy in the middle and upper classes; youth and its critical attack on institutions of society; the equalization of health care; and, more broadly, the whole quality of life.

Within the field itself, development is being influenced by the resurgence of interest in biological variables, the increasing participation of nonprofessionals in mental health work, and alternatives to professional psychotherapy.

The postindustrial society has created a proliferation of alternative products, subcultures, and life styles, making choice difficult, but imperative. Clinical psychology must set its own priorities.

In contrast with the outlook ten years ago, the charting of a few alternative directions for clinical psychology no longer seems feasible. Instead we look toward a pluralistic profession with many specialized kinds of work being carried out in many setting—client—activity situations. Professional organizations and training programs will evolve to facilitate such pluralistic development.

SUGGESTED READINGS

Toffler, A. *Future shock*. New York: Random House, 1970.

Toffler, writing in a lively style, presents forcefully many of the problems of our times and offers some suggestions for improvement. Future shock is the disorder of change—the disorientation, decision-tension, irrationality, and free-floating violence brought on by changes too rapid for human beings to cope with. The sources of future shock are the throwaway society, the new nomadism, the obsolescence of information, and the enormous diversity of things and people. Toffler demonstrates by historical references that the yearly novelty ratio is accelerating, altering the relation between the familiar and the unfamiliar. Human reactions include psychological breakdown, obsessive reversion to the past, and oversimplification. Toffler proposes strategies for survival such as personal stability zones, crisis counseling, enclaves of the past, technological control, education for the future, and widespread proliferation of councils and assemblies to study the future and involve decision makers. The book also has a large bibliography for further reading about futurism.

Future-interested readers also might like to read the psychologist Donald Michael's book *The Unprepared Society* (1968), Lundberg's *The Coming World Transformation* (1963) (which predicts that Western governments will become gigantic social service institutions), and Bell (1968), the editor of a progress report in Daedalus, *Toward the Year 2000*. One area of increasing importance for psychologists will be social planning and the development of social indicators; one reference is Bauer (1966). There are also some journals on studies of the future, *The Futurist* and *Futures, the Journal of Forecasting and Planning*.

Miller, G. A. Psychology as a means of promoting human welfare. *American Psychologist*, 1969, *24*, 1063–1075.

In this APA presidential address, George Miller made the already oft-quoted statement about giving psychology away (p. 1071): "Our responsibility is less to assume the role of experts and try to apply psychology ourselves than to give it away to the people who really need it—and that includes everyone." He indicates that the potential of psychology is nothing less than a revolution in the conception of man. He indicates that he prefers the goals of psychology to be understanding and prediction, not control; he advocates the principle of *habeas mentem*—the right of a man to his own mind. In the interests of a public psychology he sees the psychologist as assisting people in learning what they wish to know to make themselves competent.

Murphy, G. Psychology in the year 2000. *American Psychologist*, 1969, *24*, 523–530.

Gardner Murphy identifies ten areas that are likely to be important for the remainder of the century: psychophysiology (including fine localization, sensory deprivation, and psychopharmacology), internal scanning (ability to identify and condition fine muscular activities), confrontation of the unconscious world (increased differentiation of affective and impulsive states), voluntary control over processes hitherto thought involuntary (through feedback techniques), nameless states (discovery of many self-observed states and invention of language to cover them), parapsychology (acceptance of influences and communication not yet explained by physical laws), genetic developments (such as recognition of great individual differences and development of ways to counteract genetic anomalies), development of social ecology (increased importance of cross-cultural and cross-national communication and the study of ways of enriching the human environment especially for deprived children), the value of many new methods (which Murphy believes are largely the stimulus for new discoveries), and the importance in the human predicament of learning to look both inside and outside. Referring to the last point, Foa and Turner (1970) present the point of view that future research will show a correspondence between the inside and outside, in which the cognitive structure of the adult may turn out to be a counterpart of the institutional structure and the culture through the differential reinforcement patterns of significant others. They envision a psychology of organized components of behavior which will integrate a variety of psychological subdisciplines.

Bennis, W. G. A funny thing happened on the way to the future. *American Psychologist*, 1970, *25*, 595–608.

Warren Bennis presents a very stimulating comparison of his current thoughts about the future with those in a speech about organizational developments he made in 1964. In the intervening five years he had served as a college administrator in the period of student activism. He identifies the following new dilemmas: the problem of legitimacy of authority, the tensions between populism versus elitism and between interdependence and complicity, the need for fresh metaphors or symbolic rallying points, the discontinuities between microsystems and macrosystems, and the competition between forces that support and suppress democratic ideology and processes. He believes there will be more participation in governance by clients of organizations, more temporary societies, more quasi-legal processes of conflict resolution, more direct confrontations, more rapid turnover and varying relationships within institutions, and more attention to moral and ethical issues relative to technical efficiency goals. Bennis believes we must educate leaders to cope with information overload. He says (p. 607), "Marxist power was property. Today, power is based on control of relevant information." He also states that we must educate leaders to bring empathy and compassion and tolerance for ambiguity and differences to their organizations.

Schofield, W. The role of psychology in the delivery of health services. *American Psychologist*, 1969, *24*, 565–584.

Schofield, using a broad definition of health, demonstrates first that psychologists are heavily invested in the health enterprise. He points to expanded potentialities for involvement and contribution—especially in research and services oriented to psychological problems surrounding physical illness, development of subdoctoral specialties to work with psychologists, and improvement of diagnosis and assessment. He states (p. 578): "While our contributions as therapeutic conversationalists are not insignificant . . . they are likely to prove of considerably less value to society in the long run than contributions evolving from our expertise in the study of complex behavior and from our fundamental commitment to critical evaluation."

With another broad orientation Schulberg (1972) discusses the challenge to psychologists to contribute to human services and new care-giving systems. He notes that traditional distinctions between the mental health professions are becoming artificial and blurred. He points to four developments that seem to be arising at the community level for ensuring comprehensive human service: information and referral centers, diagnostic centers, multiservice centers, and human services networks. Like Schofield, Schulberg emphasizes the importance of evaluation and research. He predicts (p. 571): Psychologists can expect to face a series of crises in negotiating job roles and work relationships as they enter newly conceived human service programs." He concludes that training, therefore, should be broad, multidisciplinary, and community-based.

Albee, G. W. The uncertain future of clinical psychology. *American Psychologist*, 1970, *25*, 1071–1080.

In his presidential address to the American Psychological Association, Dr. Albee asserted that the present settings for clinical psychology—training in academic psychology departments and in psychiatry-dominated hospitals and clinics—are damaging, not promoting an independent profession nor attention to the serious problems of society. He points out sources of friction between scientists and professionals, such as the open-mindedness of science versus the jealous guarding of knowledge and status by the professionals. He identifies four future paths for clinical psychology—the perpetuation of the scientist—professional model; the establishment of separate professional programs; the development of a new major alliance, especially with education or social work; and the abandoning of clinical psychology.

Needless to say, Albee's talk, which was probably deliberately provocative, sent a shock wave through clinical psychology. One notable response is that of Schneider (1971), who refutes Albee's assertions point by point. Schneider's view is that clinical psychology is already in the process of change, incorporating a much more socially oriented concern, that the connection with science and inquiry is healthful for a profession and a source of strength ("The interplay between these aspects is psychology's trump card," p. 1064), and that Albee's last three alternative paths are improbable, difficult, or undesirable. Schneider is against the isolation suggested by Albee's proposals for separate psychological service centers and separate training programs. He sees clinical psychology as a lively, changing effort with the scientist—professional approach just coming into its prime. An earlier statement of the broadening concept of the scientist-professional role is that of Tyler and Speisman (1967).

A related proposal is that both scientists and professions be trained as polar ends of a role continuum and a third role be added in the middle based on a research and development model (Broskowski, 1971). The R and D clinician would be responsible for deliberate social problem solving, program evaluation, and applied technology, thus bridging the gap between the clinical scientist and clinical–professional. Thoreson et al. (1972) put forward a similar idea–the applied psychologist as a translator–teacher–evaluator between the discoveries of the scientist and the work of the practitioner. An alternative model by Guerney, Stollak, and Guerney (1971) proposes that the clinical psychologist frankly take the role of an educator–a teacher of personal and interpersonal attitudes and skills for solving psychological problems and enhancing life satisfaction. They argue cogently that such a role would take defect (ignorance) for granted and would emphasize motivation to acquire the know-how to pursue knowledge and skills to master the environment. The educative clinician would shift from a case orientation to designing and implementing a program for teaching for as wide a group as possible.

Major Journals and Series
Relevant to Clinical Psychology

MAJOR JOURNALS

American Journal of Mental Deficiency
American Journal of Orthopsychiatry
American Journal of Psychiatry
American Journal of Psychotherapy
American Psychologist
APA Monitor
Archives of General Psychiatry
Behavior Therapy
Behaviour Research and Therapy
British Journal of Medical Hypnotism
British Journal of Medical Psychology
British Journal of Psychiatry
British Journal of Social and Clinical Psychology
British Journal of Social Psychiatry and Community Health
Bulletin of the Menninger Clinic
The Clinical Psychologist
Clinical Psychology
Community Mental Health Journal
The Counseling Psychologist
The Family Coordinator
Family Process
Group Psychotherapy and Psychodrama
Hospital and Community Psychiatry
International Journal of Clinical and Experimental Hypnosis
International Journal of Group Therapy
International Journal of Mental Health
International Journal of Psychoanalysis

International Journal of Social Psychiatry
International Review of Applied Psychology
Journal of Abnormal Psychology
Journal of Applied Behavior Analysis
Journal of Applied Behavioral Science
Journal of Applied Psychology
Journal of Child Psychiatry
Journal of Child Psychology and Psychiatry and Allied Disciplines
Journal of Clinical and Experimental Hypnosis
Journal of Clinical Psychology
Journal of Consulting and Clinical Psychology
Journal of Counseling Psychology
Journal of the Experimental Analysis of Behavior
Journal of Humanistic Psychology
Journal of Marriage and the Family
Journal of Mental Deficiency Research
Journal of Nervous and Mental Disease
Journal of Personality Assessment
Journal of Psychiatric Research
Journal of Psychosomatic Research
Mental Health Digest
Mental Hygiene
Mental Retardation
Newsletter for Research in Psychology (VA)
Personnel and Guidance Journal
Professional Psychology
Psychiatric Quarterly
Psychiatry
Psychoanalytic Quarterly
Psychological Bulletin
Psychological Record
Psychological Reports
Psychological Review
Psychology Today
Psychosomatic Medicine
Psychotherapy: Theory, Research and Practice
Quarterly Journal of Studies on Alcohol
Rehabilitation Counseling Bulletin
Social Psychiatry
Social Work
Voices: The Art and Science of Psychotherapy

MAJOR SERIES AND ANNUALS

Advances in Child Development and Behavior, Academic Press
Advances in Experimental Clinical Psychology, Pergamon Press
Advances in Experimental Social Psychology, Academic Press
Advances in Psychological Assessment, Science & Behavior Books
Annual Progress in Child Psychiatry and Child Development, Brunner/Mazel
Annual Review of Psychology, Annual Reviews
Current Topics in Clinical and Community Psychology, Academic Press
Mental Measurements Yearbook, Gryphon Press
Minnesota Symposia in Child Psychology, University of Minnesota Press
Nebraska Symposium on Motivation, University of Nebraska Press
Proceedings of the Annual Convention of the American Psychological Association, American Psychological Association
Progress in Clinical Psychology, Grune & Stratton
Progress in Community Mental Health, Grune & Stratton
Progress in Neurology and Psychiatry, Grune & Stratton
Psychoanalytic Study of the Child, International Universities
Research in Psychotherapy, American Psychological Association

Classification of Mental Disorders

Society has labeled distressed and deviant people and their conditions in various ways—delinquents, lunatics, neurotics, criminals, psychosomatic disorders, behavior problems. Every century adopts its own system for describing those who are "different." An adequate system of description and classification which is likely to remain in favor indefinitely has not yet been devised.

One profession that has given particular attention to developing a classification system is medicine. Over the centuries medicine has had the responsibility of deciding whether a person is sick or not and, if he is sick, prescribing how he should be treated. The traditional approach has been to collect as many observations as possible of patients who seem to have similar symptoms or complaints. After a physician has seen a number of people who appear to have a similar disorder—perhaps a high fever followed by skin blotches which disappear in a few days—he reports this set of symptoms and gives it a name. Over the years many disorders have been pigeonholed in this way. (For a brief review of the history of classification in the medical sciences, see Temkin, 1965.)

Such collections of series of similar cases extended from physical symptoms to mental and behavioral disorders. Among the derangements thus labeled, the following are examples: *neurasthenia*, proposed by the American psychiatrist Beard in 1869; *paranoia*, by Vogel in 1764; *dementia praecox*, by Kraepelin; and others, such as *constitutional psychopathic inferiority* and *psychasthenia*. These are only a few of the terms proposed to describe one or another of the forms of mental illness. Many of them are rarely used today.

Many efforts to systematize the hodgepodge of psychiatric terms were made, culminating in the classification system of the German psychiatrist Kraepelin, a student of Wundt. Mainly using his system as a basis, the American Psychiatric Association produced a preliminary classification in 1939 and then the first official system of psychiatric nomenclature in 1952. We shall comment on the most current referred to as DSM II, from the second edition of the American Psychiatric Association's *Diagnostic and Statistical Manual* in 1968. The DSM II revision was developed to be compatible with the International Classification of Diseases (ICD-8), thus making American reporting of psychiatric problems similar to that used by other members of the World Health Organization.

546

DSM II, in order to achieve a measure of international compatibility, differs from DSM I by facilitating the recording of multiple diagnosis in almost descriptive fashion. Although the terms have been changed to sound more like fixed disease entities, (e.g., *schizophrenia* instead of the term *schizophrenic reaction* used in the 1952 system), the manual says that the committee "tried to avoid terms which carry with them *implications* regarding either the nature of a disorder or its causes . . . " (p. 122). The manual bolsters the idea of using the system as a way to describe problems when it states: "DSM II encourages clinicians to diagnose every disorder that is present, even if one is the symptomatic expression of another" (p. 124). DSM II abandons the three-part system of DSM I (organic, functional, mental retardation) for ten categories, Table B-1.

It is interesting to note that there is under each main heading a "catch-all" or miscellaneous category, to use for a patient who does not easily fit the given categories. This provision indicates how difficult it is to fit all kinds of abnormal behavior into definite classes.

Since the psychologist frequently works in psychiatric settings or is called upon to discuss psychiatric conditions, it is obligatory that he should have a knowledge of psychiatric terminology. We must also realize the need to have *some* set of commonly accepted terms for describing people. However, any shorthand system will have limited functional utility because of its necessary simplification of the complicated set of personal-environmental relations and personal characteristics involved in disorders.

Although the official psychiatric classification system is useful to the psychologist, it has serious disadvantages and inadequacies:

1. It does not refer directly to the specific etiology or causation of the different mental disorders, on the one hand, or specific treatments, on the other. It fails to specify relationships to theories of behavior or personality dynamics which the psychologist must always be thinking about.

2. As psychiatrists use the system, diagnosis is often for other than strictly descriptive purposes. A diagnosis may be used in a hospital for purposes of ward placement or the administrative handling of a patient. It may determine whether a disturbed veteran is classified as having a service-connected disability or not. For such reasons, administrative or legal considerations may sway the diagnostician.

3. The psychiatric system has the limitations of any typology. It identifies certain supposedly correlated clusters of symptoms which very few people actually fit. In real life people vary along many dimensions and from time to time. With almost every case there are certain exceptions which must be taken to the official diagnosis.

4. The psychiatric nomenclature is poorly developed in a scientific sense. An attempt is made at the description of disorders, but these are not specified in a concrete and operational way. As a result, considerable unreliability of diagnosis is to be expected, although one well-designed study (Schmidt and Fonda, 1956)

found that there was fair reliability for major categories. It makes inadequate recognition of genetic relationships and it presumes to pick some social/environmental problems—such as runaway reaction—to call psychiatric disorders, while ignoring all the rest, notably unwanted pregnancy.

5. But the most serious inadequacy of all from the psychologist's point of view is that it does not cover the wide range of problems with which psychologists deal. It has no categories in which to place the kinds of diagnosis that underlie the decisions clinics must make about children, such as placement of dependents in foster homes and recommendations about probation and parole for delinquents. It leaves out the large area of vocational maladjustments, the difficulties a person may run into in his job. It leaves out marital and sexual problems, except in their extreme sociopathic forms. The increasingly challenging problems relating to aging and retirement find no place in this system. Finally, it does not include any of the positive kinds of personality "deviation" that psychologists need to assess: high intelligence, creativity, and unusual stability and strength. For an extended discussion, see Mahrer (1970) and Phillips and Draguns (1971).

TABLE B-1   List of DSM-II Diagnoses and Code Numbers†

I		MENTAL RETARDATION
	310.	Borderline
	311.	Mild
	312.	Moderate
	313.	Severe
	314.	Profound
	315.	Unspecified

With each: Following or associated with

	.0	Infection or intoxication
	.1	Trauma or physical agent
	.2	Disorders of metabolism, growth, or nutrition
	.3	Gross brain disease (postnatal)
	.4	Unknown prenatal influence
	.5	Chromosomal abnormality
	.6	Prematurity
+	.7	Major psychiatric disorder
+	.8	Psycho-social (environmental) deprivation
	.9	Other condition

II		ORGANIC BRAIN SYNDROMES (OBS)
	A	PSYCHOSES

Senile and pre-senile dementia

	290.0	Senile dementia
	290.1	Pre-senile dementia

Alcoholic psychosis

| + | 291.0 | Delirium tremens |

+	291.1	Korsakov's psychosis
+	291.2	Other alcoholic hallucinosis
+	291.3	Alcohol paranoid state
+	291.4*	Acute alcohol intoxication*
+	291.5*	Alcoholic deterioration*
+	291.6*	Pathological intoxication*
	291.9	Other alcoholic psychosis

Psychosis associated with intracranial infection

292.0	General paralysis
292.1	Syphilis of CNS
292.2	Epidemic encephalitis
292.3	Other and unspecified encephalitis
292.9	Other intracranial infection

Psychosis associated with other cerebral condition

293.0	Cerebral arteriosclerosis
293.1	Other cerebrovascular disturbance
293.2	Epilepsy
293.3	Intracranial neoplasm
293.4	Degenerative disease of the CNS
293.5	Brain trauma
293.9	Other cerebral condition

Psychosis associated with other physical condition

	294.0	Endocrine disorder
	294.1	Metabolic and nutritional disorder
	294.2	Systemic infection
	294.3	Drug or poison intoxication (other than alcohol)
+	294.4	Childbirth
	294.8	Other and unspecified physical condition

| B | **NON-PSYCHOTIC OBS** |

	309.0	Intracranial infection
+	309.13*	Alcohol* (simple drunkenness)
+	309.14*	Other drug, poison or systemic intoxication*
	309.2	Brain trauma
	309.3	Circulatory disturbance
	309.4	Epilepsy
	309.5	Disturbance of metabolism, growth, or nutrition
	309.6	Senile or pre-senile brain disease
	309.7	Intracranial neoplasm
	309.8	Degenerative disease of the CNS
	309.9	Other physical condition

**III   PSYCHOSES NOT ATTRIBUTED
TO PHYSICAL CONDITIONS
LISTED PREVIOUSLY**

Schizophrenia

| 295.0 | Simple |

	295.1	Hebephrenic
	295.2	Catatonic
+	295.23*	Catatonic type, excited*
+	295.24*	Catatonic type, withdrawn*
	295.3	Paranoid
+	295.4	Acute schizophrenic episode
+	295.5	Latent
	295.6	Residual
	295.7	Schizo-affective
+	295.73*	Schizo-affective, excited*
+	295.74*	Schizo-affective, depressed*
	295.8*	Childhood*
	295.90*	Chronic undifferentiated*
	295.99*	Other schizophrenia*

Major affective disorders

	296.0	Involutional melancholia
	296.1	Manic-depressive illness, manic
	296.2	Manic-depressive illness, depressed
	296.3	Manic-depressive illness, circular
+	296.33*	Manic-depressive, circular, manic*
+	296.34*	Manic-depressive, circular, depressed*
	296.8	Other major affective disorder

Paranoid states

	297.0	Paranoia
+	297.1	Involutional paranoid state
	297.9	Other paranoid state

Other psychoses

	298.0	Psychotic depressive reaction

IV   **NEUROSES**

	300.0	Anxiety
	300.1	Hysterical
+	300.13*	Hysterical, conversion type*
+	300.14*	Hysterical, dissociative type*
	300.2	Phobic
	300.3	Obsessive compulsive
	300.4	Depressive
+	300.5	Neurasthenic
+	300.6	Depersonalization
+	300.7	Hypochondriacal
	300.8	Other neurosis

V   **PERSONALITY DISORDERS AND CERTAIN OTHER NON-PSYCHOTIC MENTAL DISORDERS**

Personality disorders

	301.0	Paranoid

	301.1	Cyclothymic
	301.2	Schizoid
+	301.3	Explosive
	301.4	Obsessive compulsive
+	301.5	Hysterical
+	301.6	Asthenic
	301.7	Antisocial
	301.81*	Passive-aggressive*
	301.82*	Inadequate*
	301.89*	Other specified types*

Sexual deviation

+	302.0	Homosexuality
+	302.1	Fetishism
+	302.2	Pedophilia
+	302.3	Transvestitism
+	302.4	Exhibitionism
+	302.5*	Voyeurism*
+	302.6*	Sadism*
+	302.7*	Masochism*
	302.8	Other sexual deviation

Alcoholism

+	303.0	Episodic excessive drinking
+	303.1	Habitual excessive drinking
+	303.2	Alcohol addiction
	303.9	Other alcoholism

Drug dependence

+	304.0	Opium, opium alkaloids and their derivatives
+	304.1	Synthetic analgesics with morphine-like effects
+	304.2	Barbiturates
+	304.3	Other hypnotics and sedatives or "tranquilizers"
+	304.4	Cocaine
+	304.5	Cannabis sativa (hashish, marihuana)
+	304.6	Other psycho-stimulants
+	304.7	Hallucinogens
	304.8	Other drug dependence

VI		**PSYCHOPHYSIOLOGIC DISORDERS**
	305.0	Skin
	305.1	Musculoskeletal
	305.2	Respiratory
	305.3	Cardiovascular
	305.4	Hemic and lymphatic
	305.5	Gastro-intestinal
	305.6	Genito-urinary
	305.7	Endocrine
	305.8	Organ of special sense
	305.9	Other type

VII		**SPECIAL SYMPTOMS**
	306.0	Speech disturbance
	306.1	Specific learning disturbance
+	306.2	Tic
+	306.3	Other psychomotor disorder
+	306.4	Disorders of sleep
+	306.5	Feeding disturbance
	306.6	Enuresis
+	306.7	Encopresis
+	306.8	Cephalalgia
	306.9	Other special symptom

VIII		**TRANSIENT SITUATIONAL DISTURBANCES**
	307.0*	Adjustment reaction of infancy*
	307.1*	Adjustment reaction of childhood*
	307.2*	Adjustment reaction of adolescence*
	307.3*	Adjustment reaction of adult life*
	307.4*	Adjustment reaction of late life*

IX		**BEHAVIOR DISORDERS OF CHILDHOOD AND ADOLESCENCE**
+	308.0*	Hyperkinetic reaction*
+	308.1*	Withdrawing reaction*
+	308.2*	Overanxious reaction*
+	308.3*	Runway reaction*
+	308.4*	Unsocialized aggressive reaction*
+	308.5*	Group delinquent reaction*
	308.9*	Other reaction*

X		**CONDITIONS WITHOUT MANIFEST PSYCHIATRIC DISORDER AND NON-SPECIFIC CONDITIONS**

Social maladjustment without manifest psychiatric disorder

+	316.0*	Marital maladjustment*
+	316.1*	Social maladjustment*
+	316.2*	Occupational maladjustment*
	316.3*	Dyssocial behavior*
+	316.9*	Other social maladjustment*

Non-specific conditions

+	317*	Non-specific conditions*

No mental Disorder

+	318*	No mental disorder*

XI		**NON-DIAGNOSTIC TERMS FOR ADMINISTRATIVE USE**
	319.0*	Diagnosis deferred*

319.1*   Boarder*
319.2*   Experiment only*
319.3*   Other*

Source: American Psychiatric Association, *Diagnostic and Statistical Manual, II,* 3rd ed, Table 1, p. 126. Reprinted by permission of the American Psychiatric Association.

† Many of the titles here as listed in abbreviated form.
+ These are new diagnoses, that do not appear in DSM-I.
* These diagnoses are for use in the U. S. only and do not appear in ICD-8.

Automated Interpretations
of the MMPI of Allen Ward

In Chapter 7 the case of Allen Ward was presented in considerable detail. The mental health center was trying out automated systems for interpretation of the Minnesota Multiphasic Personality Inventory. The scores obtained by Allen on the MMPI were as follows:

Validity-scale raw scores:

L,	2	F,	20	K,	14

Clinical scale T scores (K added):

Hs,	95	Pd,	88	Pt,	93	Si,	79
D,	96	MF,	86	Sc,	105		
Hy,	82	Pa,	85	Ma,	72		

Two MMPI interpretation services were provided with only the scores and the information that the person was twenty years old, male, and single. The report from the Mayo Clinic automated MMPI service was as follows:

Patient admits to a large number of unusual experiences, feelings, or symptoms. May have significant emotional problems.

Angry, dissatisfied with family life.

Restless or agitated. Active mentally or physically, but lacks sense of accomplishment.

Probable feelings of unreality. Bizarre or confused thinking and conduct. May have strange attitudes and false beliefs. Probably feels severely alienated and withdrawn.

Severely depressed, worrying, and pessimistic.

Great number of chronic physical complaints and preoccupation with bodily functions. Much functional pain, fatigue, and weakness likely.

Probably fussy, effeminate, dependent, and submissive. Strong artistic interests.

Resentful and suspicious of others. Blames others for own difficulties, delusional thinking likely.

Probably immature, egocentric, suggestible, and demanding.

Prone to develop circumscribed functional complaints such as headaches or backaches, which are usually presented in a dramatic and exaggerated manner. Lacks insight and is unlikely to accept a psychological explanation of symptoms.

Even though patients with this type of profile are prone to develop functional complaints, the possibility of organic disease cannot be excluded.

Introverted, shy, and socially inept.

For more information about the development and use of the Mayo computerized system, see Pearson and Swenson (1967) and Pearson et al. (1965).

The much longer report, from the Clinical Psychological Services headed by Alexander Caldwell in Los Angeles, was as follows:

Test-taking attitude

He made a moderate number of unusual and atypical responses to the MMPI. He was probably overstating the severity of his disturbance. However, this "plus-getting" approach also has been seen in patients with acute psychiatric illnesses that involved some intellectual confusion or disturbance of concentration. The scores appear overly elevated, but the pattern is probably appropriate.

Symptoms and personality characteristics

The pattern is often seen with an acute identity crisis including severe immaturity and confusion about his current and future goals. The profile indicates a serious vulnerability to a psychotic decompensation if not currently such a reaction. He tests as markedly fearful of emotional closeness with painful frustrations in his close relationships. He is apt to have many ways of keeping others at a distance. Chronic worrying, nervousness, fears, and anxieties are apt to have become overwhelming. He appears markedly self-preoccupied and prone to ruminate about his feelings of inferiority and inadequacy and about various threats to his security. Depression, apathy, and feelings of hopelessness are suggested. Disturbances of sleep are common with this pattern. Markedly shy and introverted, he tests as very lacking in poise and assurance, in social self-confidence, and in outgoing emotional responses.

The pattern predicts atypical physical symptoms that are secondary to his anxiety and expressive of his current conflicts. Conversion-like symbolizations of unreleased resentments, tensions, and aggressive impulses are particularly likely. At various times he could complain of dizziness, fainting, anorexia, atypical spells, or weakness, and possibly of being paralyzed. Distortions of his body image could prove to be borderline delusional. In addition the numerous physical preoccupations he expressed on the test suggest multiple chronic physical complaints lacking a sufficient organic basis. Recurrent gastrointestinal distress, headache, and fatigue would be typical, as would be concern about poor health and overreactions to minor physical dysfunctions. He is apt to get extensive "secondary gains" from his symptoms and to attribute many of his current difficulties to his health problems.

He may have been deeply hurt in past close relationships and be distrustful and questioning of the motives of others. His underlying anger and resentment appear moderate to severe. The profile suggests that his lack of warmth and inappropriate actions would drive others away from him. Lacking in longterm goals, he is apt to tolerate frustrations poorly and to overreact to anything he interprets as a demand on him. Underneath his self-blame or when less depressed, he appears prone to rationalize resentments and to feel that his difficulties cannot really be relieved unless other people or circumstances change. The test indicates that others would see him as passive-aggressive and as sometimes undependable and impulsive. Oversensitive and quick to feel unduly burdened, passivity and feelings of inferiority are apt to partly cover over the intensity of his anger.

He obtained the so-called "burnt child" pattern type for which the phrase, "The burnt child fears the fire", has aptly characterized the chronic fears of emotional closeness and involvement. Typical histories for this profile often include poor educational achievement relative to intelligence. He is prone to marry impulsively after a very brief courtship. However, he could then transfer his maternal dependency conflicts into the marriage.

His overall balance of masculine and feminine interests appears extremely passive, verbal, and esthetic. Severe self-doubts and male adequacy and a strong rejection of culturally defined masculine activities and pursuits are suggested.

Diagnostic impression

Schizo-affective and psychotic depressive diagnoses are common with this pattern. Other patients are seen as borderline psychotic without definitively schizophrenic symptoms.

Treatment considerations

The profile suggests a mild suicide risk; this could be serious if he became more depressed and saw his situation as increasingly hopeless. Tranquilizers and energizers have frequently been used with similar patients, often with good benefits from combinations of both. In some similar cases the intensity of the internal upheaval necessitated a careful following of the use and dosage of the tranquilizers and antidepressive medications prescribed. The profile suggests that contacts with relatives are likely to be of benefit in order to review the precipitating circumstances, adjustments to them that he may fail to mention, and ways of minimizing secondary gains.

Difficulties in trusting and in relating emotionally are likely to seriously handicap his response to treatment. Apathy and longterm schizoid trends would be prognostically negative. He tests as prone to get others to tell him what to do, but ambivalent if not negativistic to decisions made for him by someone else. Although responsibility for decisions should be gently but firmly encouraged, he is apt to need extensive support in order to take initiative and mobilize his energies. The shallowness of his longterm goals would also handicap his effort and persistence. He tests as prone to manipulate individual treatment passively if not overtly, and the character problems warn against involvements in his manipulations. He is particularly likely to provoke "rescue reactions" from those involved in his case. He would quickly verbalize a negativistic helplessness as soon as he feels obliged to "perform" in return for being rescued.

In many similar cases the precipitating circumstances involved increasing withdrawal and personal "binds" that were partly due to the patients' ambivalences and to their avoidance of decisions and responsibility. Although he may focus on sexual problems, the underlying confusions in identity appear to be the basic disturbance. Difficulties in assertiveness toward women are likely to be an important area in treatment. He is likely to require extended contact to let go of odd ideas and negative self-identifications. His awareness of the intensity of his hurt and angry feelings and of the indirectness of his ways of expressing them appears severly distorted. The profile recommends a relatively cautious and "here-now" handling of his anger since deeper interpretations could be disorganizing of his controls. Discovery of his personal ways of keeping others at a distance—perhaps especially as he uses them on the therapist—is apt to be of direct benefit in treatment.

As yet, there are few publications about the Caldwell system, but it makes extensive use of MMPI patterns, whereas the Mayo Clinic system emphasizes scale-by-scale interpretation.

The reader may wish to compare these "blind reports" with the full case presentation in Chapter 7. The psychologist who worked with Allen Ward informally judged the second report's emphasis on physical symptoms to be off the mark, but found the "burnt child" remarks and the statements about provoking "rescue relations" in others to be particularly apt.

Those wishing to read more about automated MMPI interpretation should see the Manning article (1971) mentioned at the end of Chapter 7 and the reviews of such systems in Buros (1972, pp. 250–266). Some of the pitfalls of computer interpretations are pointed out by O'Dell (1972), who found subjects rating generalized "Barnum" reports as being more accurate than real reports.

Guide for a History- Taking Interview

The following outline is a suggested guide for interviewing an adult client or patient regarding his own description of himself and of his life history (his anamnesis, or self-report). With some modification it would be an appropriate outline for interviewing adolescents and for obtaining information from the client's relatives. For other case-history outlines and discussions, see Hadley (1958), Menninger (1952), and Thorne (1955). Wells and Ruesch (1945) present a check sheet (reprinted in Berg and Pennington, 1966, pp. 55–58) for recording important events or descriptive terms which come up in the course of the interview. Peterson (1968a, pp. 121–122) gives a framework for an interview on problem behaviors for a social-learning approach to treatment. It is to be understood, of course, that the following list is a guide only, that often there will be neither time nor necessity for such an extensive case study, and that any actual interview is flexible. Nevertheless, this guide may serve to call to mind important material to be covered in understanding the client.

A. *Identifying data* (The details of this are usually dictated by routine procedures of the service or institution. In a hospital there will be a "face sheet" on a patient's chart with information on it. If the basic data are not available, it is important for the clinician to ascertain them. Included in such data would be the client's name, sex, address, date and place of birth, marital status, educational status, occupation, income, religion, names of close relatives, etc.)

B. *Reason for coming*
   1. Present problem, complaint, or concern.
   2. History of the concern, ideas about how it started.
   3. Nature of referral or how client learned about coming here.
   4. Previous experience with agencies, private practitioners, or hospitals about this problem.
   5. Expectations about how this service might help.

C. *Present situations*
   1. Description of an ordinary day in the client's life, from rising in the morning to going to bed; any major variations on weekends; etc.
   2. Descriptions of each member of present family, and other significant people.

3. Changes currently planned in situations—work or school, recreation, family.
D. *Family constellation* (family of orientation)
1. Description of mother and father (age now and at time of their marriage, general description of personality, and relationship with patient).
2. Description of each brother and sister (number of years older or younger than client, general description of personality, and relationship with client).
3. Client's role in the family (the "good little sister," "the black sheep," etc.).
4. Alliances and frictions in the family. Changes in family constellation such as divorce, death.
E. *Early recollections*
1. Descriptions of earliest events clearly recalled (noting age, people involved, and client's feelings about incident).
F. *Birth and development*
1. Term and conditions of birth.
2. Ages of walking and talking.
3. Problems of infancy and childhood (feeding difficulties, nailbiting, thumb sucking, fears, night terrors).
4. Social relations in childhood (outgoing or seclusive tendencies, lying, stealing, cruelty, truancy).
5. Client's view of own childhood (pleasant, unhappy).
G. *Health*
1. What childhood diseases and when.
2. Other illnesses, injuries, operations, handicaps.
3. Problems with drugs, alcohol.
4. Client's estimate of habitual degree of health and bodily weaknesses and strengths.
H. *Education and training*
1. Schools attended, dates of attendance, class standing.
2. Subjects of special interest, of strength and weakness.
3. Client's evaluation of adequacy of past training and present learning needs.
I. *Work record*
1. Descriptions of jobs in chronological sequence.
2. Reasons for changing jobs.
3. Attitudes toward work, responsibility, saving, indebtedness.
J. *Recreation, interests*
1. Nonpaid work (work around the home, volunteer work).
2. Interests, what client reads, what kinds of physical activities he pursues, membership in groups, religious activity, creative pursuits.
3. Client's evaluation of adequacy of self-expression.
K. *Sexual development*
1. First awareness (how learned about sex, attitude, and reactions).
2. Evolution of sex interest, sex pace, fantasies, dreams.
3. Kinds of sexual expression (masturbation, homosexual, and heterosexual).

      4. Client's evaluation of adequacy of his sexual expressions.

L. *Marital and family data*
      1. Date(s) and circumstances surrounding marriage(s) (where met, length of engagement, honeymoon).
      2. Pregnancies and children (ages, preferences).
      3. Major events in course of marriage, changes.
      4. Present family interaction (how decisions are made about buying major items, going on trips, etc.; amount and kind of communication; roles played by each member of family).
      5. Comparison between present family and family of orientation.
      6. Client's evaluation of present family strengths and problems.

M. *Self-description*
      1. Client's description of self as if writing a story about a person, or describing his role in a play.
      2. Outstanding characteristics—assets and limitations.
      3. Sources of worry, doubt, anxiety, remorse.
      4. Concrete difficulties would like to overcome in next few months or years; what adjustments have been tried.
      5. Client's description of what he would do if he were suddenly free of his symptoms, complaints, or problems.
      6. Client's description of two persons most like him and most unlike him.
      7. Client's ideal (the person he would like to be like).

N. *Choices and turning points in life*
      1. The most important turning points of life.
      2. How client went about making decisions at these turning points.
      3. A concrete illustration of a success and of a failure.
      4. Main resources of help and encouragement in times of crises, decisions, or uncertainty.

O. *Any additional points client sees as omitted in above history.*

Thirty Tests of Importance
in Clinical Psychology

Clinical psychologists are usually considered to be masters of psychological testing—particularly individual tests of intelligence and personality. As discussed in Chapter 9, the development of full competence in using tests requires a great deal of experience and knowledge. Probably few psychologists have detailed knowledge and skill with more than a dozen individual tests. Most tend to use only the few with which they are familiar. Still, clinicians will find that they need to be acquainted with a wide range of tests for several reasons: (1) Occasionally evaluations of clients or patients present problems that require unusual or specialized tests; (2) other psychologists will make referrals and mention other tests; (3) keeping up with new publications and research requires knowledge of a variety of tests; and (4) as the field evolves, new procedures address new questions. For such reasons it is important for students and practitioners of clinical psychology to know the major tests, including a few in each of the categories of testing activity.

In selecting tests for this appendix, we have been mindful of the great changes in assessment in recent years. As yet the movements of the 1960s and early 1970s—behavior modification, environmental psychology, humanistic psychology, and community psychology—have produced many new methods but few standard tests. As procedures emerge, they will be subject to the same questions of reliability and validity as the old tests have faced. For that reason and for the avoidance of the wasted energies in "reinventing the wheel," it is well for students to be familiar with a set of tests that have been important in the past. The following list does not provide evaluations. We suggest that students become acquainted with the tests by reading about them in Buros's *Mental Measurements Yearbook* and examining the tests and their manuals in the light of the discussion on test evaluation in Chapter 9. There are also many unpublished procedures. Johnson and Bommarito (1971) have collected many that pertain to children. In learning to give any test, we would do well to note the admonishment of Akhurst (1970, p. ix): "Intellectual assessments should never

561

be made unless the examiner is convinced that the information to be gained warrants the inconvenience caused and the intrusion into the privacy of the individual concerned. He is not competent to decide this unless he is able to administer tests efficiently and interpret their results accurately."

In deciding what tests to list, we have chosen a limited number and have mainly used systematic criteria. Thousands of standardized procedures exist, but we have arbitrarily decided to limit the basic list to thirty. Primarily we have required tests to meet two criteria of importance: *frequent usage*, which was obtained from the table reporting a survey of 251 clinical facilities in North America (Lubin, Wallis, and Paine, 1971), and a *high number of publications*, which was determined from the two latest *Mental Measurements Yearbooks* by Buros (1965, 1972). First we listed all tests used by at least half of the clinical agencies. In addition, we chose all tests used by at least 20 percent of the facilities and also having at least 100 publications in either *Yearbook*. (From 10 to 15 percent of the tests in the most relevant sections of the Buros's books—character and personality and individual intelligence tests have 100 publications). Thus a list of twenty-two tests was produced. (In passing, it might be noted that we checked ten major clinical textbooks published since 1962 for mentions of tests; all those tests mentioned by at least half of the books are included in the following list.)

For the total of thirty tests, we added eight selections to round out testing categories with practical clinical needs in mind. At the end of some categories we have listed all additional tests that were used by one-tenth of the clinical services in the survey by Lubin and his associates *and* were listed as having at least one hundred publications in the two latest Buros books. A number of research techniques and other interesting examples have been listed. Finally at the end some gaps in testing are covered. Tests named without references can be found in Buros's books. Unless otherwise indicated, tests usually are administered individually. The status of each test on the two criteria is indicated at the left of the title as follows:

(.2S)   Tests used by at least one-fifth of the clinical services.
(.5S)   Tests used by at least one-half of the clinical services.
(P)   Tests with 100 or more publications.

Intelligence and general ability

Bayley Scales of Infant Development (by Bayley in 1969; published by Psychological Corp.). A standardized and comprehensive measure of infant development from 2 months to 2.5 years. Involves a wide variety of items related to communication, concepts, responsiveness, and object manipulation. Has companion schedules for appraising motor development, interviewing the mother, and observing the infant's social behavior. Based on much research.

(P)   *Goodenough-Harris Drawing Test*—the "Draw-A-Man" Test (original by Goodenough in 1926; revision by Harris, 1963; Harcourt Brace). An old and simple procedure for obtaining a rough estimate of intelligence by scoring a child's drawing for details, proportion, and so on. Ages 5 to 15. See D. B. Harris (1963).

(.2S, P) *Peabody Picture Vocabulary Test* (Dunn, 1959–1970, American Guidance Service). Presented with pictures, the subject points to the appropriate representation when the examiner speaks a word. Useful with handicapped and retarded clients where expression of ideas may be more difficult than understanding them. Ages 2.5 to 18. Similar to the Peabody is the *Full-Range Picture Vocabulary Test*. A shorter instrument is the *Quick Test*.

(.2S, P) *Porteus Maze Test* (Psychological Corp.; 1914–1965). A series of printed labyrinths on which the subject draws the path from the starting place to the exit. A measure of directed attention, foresight, and planning. Gives both quantitative and qualitative scores. Has been found useful in studies of delinquents and brain-damaged persons. Ages 3 to adult.

(.2S, P) *Progressive Matrices* (Raven; H. K. Lewis in England; and Psychological Corp.; 1938–1963). A series of designs, each with a missing part, for which the subject is to choose among several alternatives. Simple oral directions. Can be used in groups. Developed and used widely in Great Britain. Ages 5 and over.

(.5S, P) *Stanford-Binet Intelligence Scale*, 3rd revision (Terman and Merrill; Houghton Mifflin; 1916–1964). A widely used and familiar individual intelligence test. Arranged by mental-age levels. This revision provides IQs as standard scores. Ages 2 to adult, but not standardized for older people.

(.5S, P) *Wechsler Adult Intelligence Scale*–the "WAIS" (Psychological Corp.; 1939–1955). Six verbal subtests (information, comprehension, arithmetic, similarities, digit span, and vocabulary) and five performance subtests (digit symbol, block design, picture completion, picture arrangement, and object assembly) provide a Verbal IQ, Performance IQ, and Full-Scale IQ. Ages 16 and over, with normative information up to 60 years of age and over. The *Wechsler-Bellevue Intelligence Scale* is the early form of the WAIS and WISC covering ages 10 to 70. See Matarazzo's extensive exposition of the Wechsler tests (1972).

(.5S, P) *Wechsler Intelligence Scale for Children*–the "WISC" (Psychological Corp.; 1949). The children's form of the Wechsler test, with norms for ages 5 to 15.

Additional: Also having 100 publications but being mentioned by only one-tenth of the clinical facilities surveyed by Lubin et al. (1971) was the *California Test of Mental Maturity*.

Intellectual deficit and brain damage

(.5S, P) *Bender-Gestalt Test* (or Visual-Motor Gestalt Test) (American Orthopsychiatric Association; 1938–1969). The subject's task is simply to copy nine designs as they are presented one at a time. The brief and nonthreatening task is used to study perceptual distortions suggesting brain damage, developmental retardation, and personality characteristics. Most common use, for differential diagnosis of organicity (Schulberg and Tolor, 1961). Scoring systems developed by Pascal and Suttell (1951), Hutt (1969), and others. Ages 4 and over.

(P) *Goldstein-Scheerer Tests of Abstract and Concrete Thinking* (Psychological Corp.; 1941–1951). A battery of five clinical techniques for testing a patient's ability to conceptualize, including the sorting of objects and copying of block designs, based on the theory that the main effect of brain damage is "concreteness." The Weigl color-form sorting task is sometimes used alone as a simple concept-formation task. No rigorous standardization, but offers good opportunities for clinical observation.

(.5S) *Memory-for-Designs Test* (Graham and Kendall; 1946–1960; Psychological Test Specialists). One of the most popular tests for the assessment of brain damage in children (8.5 years and older) and adults. After seeing a simple design for five seconds, the subject draws it from memory. There are fifteen designs and an objective scoring system.

(.2S, P) *Shipley-Institute of Living Scale for Measuring Intellectual Impairment* (distributed by Mrs. J. H. Boyle, 1939–1946). A paper-and-pencil test for adults that can be administered in a group as a quick screening device. Provides separate scores on vocabulary and abstractions sections. The conceptual quotient is based on the assumption that an unusually low abstraction score in comparison with vocabulary suggests intellectual deficit due to brain damage or a functional disorder.

Special abilities, aptitudes, and achievement

(.2S, P) *Differential Aptitude Tests* (Bennett, Bennett, Clendenen, Doppelt, Ricks, Seashore, and Wesman; Psychological Corp.; 1947–1969). A battery of eight tests including mechanical, clerical, spelling, and reasoning measures, requiring nearly four hours of testing. Intended primarily for high school counseling; used for grades 8 to 12 and adults.

(P) *General Aptitude Test Battery* (United States Training and Employment Service; U. S. Government Printing Office; 1946–1970). Eight paper-and-pencil tests and four tests with apparatus measure nine factors, such as manual dexterity, clerical perception, form perception, verbal and numerical ability. The GATB is given only by arrangements with state employment offices. Ages 16 and over. (Used by one-tenth of the clinical services.)

(.2S P) *Illinios Test of Psycholinguistic Abilities, Revised Edition*—the "ITPA" (Kirk, McCarthy, and Kirk; University of Illinois Press; 1961–1968). This test, somewhat misnamed, is intended to diagnose language abilities and cognitive functioning, but does not cover reading, writing, and spelling. Based on Osgood's theory of communication. Ages 2 to 10.

Additional: The following tests were used by one-tenth to one-fifth of the clinical services in the survey by Lubin et al. (1971) and also had at least 100 publications in the *Sixth* and *Seventh Mental Measurements Yearbooks*:

Bennett Mechanical Comprehension Test
Revised Minnesota Paper Form Board Test
Stanford Achievement Test

In addition, there were some other tests from the survey list which might occasionally be useful because of their special character:

Gray Oral Reading Test
Minnesota Clerical Test
Test of Color Blindness (Ishihara)

Interests, values, and attitudes

(.2S, P) *Kuder Preference Record—Vocational* (Science Research Associates; 1956–1963). The familiar and much-researched form of the Kuder is this one; there are other forms (the Kuder General Interest Survey, which is a downward extension of this, and the Kuder Preference Record—Occupational, which was developed like the Strong), with which this form is sometimes confused. A forced-choice technique providing scores on interests in the following kinds of activities: mechanical, computational, scientific, persuasive, artistic, literary, musical, social service, clerical, and outdoor activities. May be used for group testing. Grades 9 to 16 and adults.

(.2S, P) *Strong Vocational Interest Blank for Men*, and *for Women*—the "Strong" or "SVIB" (original by E. K. Strong; revision by David Campbell; Stanford University Press). Initiated in 1927, the Men's form of the Strong has recently been revised and given new scoring keys, and new Basic Interest Scales have been added. Widely used. For ages 10 and over. The Women's form (1933–1971) has also been revised recently. See manual (Campbell, 1971).

Additional: Used by one-tenth of the clinical services and having at least 100 publications is the *Study of Values* (Allport-Vernon-Lindzey). One new attitude scale that illustrates a direction which is likely to be pursued further as community psychology grows is the *Baker-Schulberg Community Mental Health Ideology Scale*.

Personality inventories

(.2S, P) *California Psychological Inventory*—the "CPI" (Gough; Consulting Psychologists Press; 1956–1969). Largely empirically derived by comparisons with criterion groups. Provides eighteen scales covering positive social characteristics, such as responsibility, social presence, socialization, tolerance, and achievement by independence, and including three scales to detect unusual test-taking attitudes. Can be given to groups. Ages 13 and over. For suggestions on applications and interpretation, see Gough (1968b) and Megargee's handbook (1972).

(.2S, P) *Edwards Personal Preference Schedule* (Psychological Corp.; 1953–1959). Developed in forced-choice format to control for social desirability. Provides fifteen scores of the subject's reports on his needs, such as achievement, intraception, dominance, abasement, and aggression. May be given in groups. College age and adults.

(.5S, P) *Minnesota Multiphasic Personality Inventory*—the "MMPI" (Hathaway and McKinley; Psychological Corp.; 1942–1967). Most widely used and researched inventory. Originally provided scores on four "validity" scales covering test-taking attitudes and nine "clinical" scales such as depression, hysteria, and schizophrenia. Now has many other scales developed from its pool of 550 items, several "cookbooks" for interpretation of patterns, and several automated interpretation systems. For ages 16 and over. Both individual and group forms. Butcher (1969) presents articles on clinical applications and research. For clinical interpretation, see Dahlstrom, Welsh, and Dahlstrom (1972).

Additional: Listed among the tests used by at least one-tenth of the clinical services and having at least 100 publications are the following:

Adjustment Inventory (Bell)
California Test of Personality
Guilford-Zimmerman Temperament Survey
Sixteen Personality Factor Questionnaire

An additional device for testing disturbed adolescents is the *Jesness Inventory*.

Personality-projective techniques

(.5S, P) *House-Tree-Person Projective Technique*—the "HTP" (Buck; Western Psychological Services; 1946–1964). After drawing a house, a tree, and a person, the subject is asked a series of guided questions. Although the manual provides quantitative scoring, it is mainly used impressionistically. Ages 5 and over.

(P) *Kent-Rosanoff Free Association Test* (Stoelting; 1910). Word association is a general technique for which the clinician might want to make up his own form. The subject is instructed to say the first word that comes to his mind when the examiner pronouces the stimulus word. The reaction time and emotionality of the subject are noted as well as the content. The best-known list of stimulus words (used by one-tenth of the clinical services) is the *Kent-Rosanoff*.

Words are classified on the basis of commonality and idiosyncracy. Jenkins and Russell (1960) presented norms and changes between 1910 and 1952. Children and adults.

(.5S, P) *Machover Draw-A-Person Test*—the "DAP" (Charles C Thomas, Publisher; 1949). The subject is asked to draw a person and then to draw a person of the opposite sex from the first one. Widely used. Children and adults. With the DAP the emphasis is on personality interpretation; with the Goodenough—Harris the concern is intellectual ability. Swenson (1968) has reviewed empirical studies. Adler's research (1970) led him to conclude that figure drawings are a one-factor test—a measure of cognitive sophistication or maturity.

(.5S, P) *Rorschach* (originated by Rorschach in 1921; Hans Huber in Switzerland, and Grune & Stratton). Very widely used and published. The subject tells what he sees in ten standard inkblots during the "free-association" phase, following which the examiner inquires regarding location of the perception and which blot characteristics suggested it. May be scored for form, color, and content by several systems, but often used impressionistically. Ages 3 and over. Many innovations and modifications on the method. For one comprehensive report on testing and interpretation see Goldfried, Stricker, and Weiner (1972). For a standardized version of the Rorschach already used by one-tenth of the clinical services and having a large number of publications, see the *Holtzman Inkblot Technique*, including the handbook of clinical applications of the HIT (Hill, 1972).

(.5S) *Rotter Incomplete Sentences Blank* (Rotter and Rafferty; Psychological Corp.; 1950). The most frequently used sentence completion form, consisting of two pages listing introductory words (stems) to be finished by subjects. May be given in groups to high school students and adults, but Rotter norms based only on college students. Other sentence-completion tests include Rohde (1957), Forer (1957), Loevinger's ego-development technique (Loevinger and Wessler, 1970; Loevinger, Wessler, and Redmore, 1970).

(.5S, P) *Thematic Apperception Test*—the "TAT" (originated by Murray and Morgan in 1935; Harvard University Press). A series of 20 pictures (from which a small number is often used for clinical work) to which the subject makes up stories. Scoring systems, including ones based on the original Murray need-press theory, are available, but clinical interpretation is usually impressionistic. See Murstein (1963, 1972). Many similar techniques use story telling in response to pictures (e.g., the *Children's Apperception Test* and research measures of achievement, affiliation, and power). The *Blacky Pictures* (see Blum, 1968) and the *Picture Arrangement Test* (Tomkins and Miner, 1957) are among other modifications.

Additional: Among those tests used by at least one-tenth of the clinical facilities and having at least 100 publications is the *Rosenzweig Picture Frustration Study*. The *Holtzman Inkblot Test* and the *Kent-Rosanoff Free Association Test* mentioned above also fit this category.

Miscellaneous and research techniques

(P) *Adjective Check List*—the "ACL" (Gough and Heilbrun; Consulting Psychologists Press; 1952–1965). An alphabetical list of 300 adjectives from "absent-minded" to "zany," which the subject simply checks to describe himself or others. The list can be scored for 24 variables, such as defensiveness, self-control, and need for achievement. High school and adults. Several similar tools exist, such as Lubin's *Depression Adjective Check List* and the *Multiple Affect Adjective Check List* by Zuckerman and Lubin.

(P) *Inpatient Multidimensional Psychiatric Scale*—the "IMPS" (Lorr, Klett, McNair, and Lasky; Consulting Psychologists Press; 1953–1966). A systematic means for rating behavior of hospitalized mental patients. (Used by one-tenth of the clinical services.) Produces 10 scores based on ratings following an interview, such as excitement, belligerence, and perceptual distortion. Several other rating scales based on observation of patients are available, such as the *Hospital Adjustment Scale*, the *MACC Behavioral Adjustment Scale*, and the *Boston City Hospital Behavior Checklist* (Martorano and Nathan, 1972). For children, see the *Devereux Behavior Rating Scales* and the *Jesness Behavior Checklist*.

Role Construct Repertory Test (Rep Test). After identifying significant persons in his life, the subject indicates their similarities and differences by comparing them. Analysis provides clues to the subject's personal constructs or ways of thinking about others. See Kelly (1955) and Bannister and Mair (1968). Group and individual forms.

(.5S, P) *Vineland Social Maturity Scale* (Doll; Educational Test Service; 1935–1953). Uses the reports of an informant, usually the mother, being interviewed by the clinician regarding the observed behavior of the patient or client in the areas of locomotion, communication, socialization, and occupation. Results are scored on social competence by age levels. Particularly useful in evaluating mental deficiency. Birth to adult.

Additional: Psychological assessment, despite its many procedures, still has important unfulfilled areas of potentiality. Some gaps, possibilities, and research techniques are as follows:

Behavior-modification assessment devices. Standardized procedures are only in the process of development for purposes of behavior change. Among testing techniques needed are measures to help select problem areas, desired outcomes, types of reinforcers, desensitization series, and surveys of significant environmental factors. Cautela and Kastenbaum (1967) have published a *Reinforcement Survey Schedule.* Lewinsohn uses a *Pleasant Events Schedule* to identify reinforcing activities (Lewinsohn and Libet, 1972). For other possibilities see Bijou and Peterson (1971), Goldfried and Pomeranz (1968), Kanfer and Phillips (1970), and Weiss (1968). A behavioral technology combining testing with learning seems to be in the process of development (Schwitzgebel, 1970).

Community and environmental assessment techniques. No well-developed devices exist yet for evaluation of the community, the environment, or of situations for clinical purposes. Craik (1971) reviews possibilities for appraising places and discusses situational assessment. Gough's *Home Index* (1949) is a research tool for assessing objects in the home and socioeconomic level. The *Stern Environment Indexes* are self-administering questionnaires for subjects to describe the characteristics of their environment, especially the college setting. The *Personal Adjustment and Role Skill Scales* (PARS) by Ellsworth (1968) are rater-report instruments developed as measures of community adjustment and have been the primary instruments in several program-evaluation studies. The *Community Adaptation Schedule* of Roen and Burnes is a research instrument for self-report of the person's relationships with his surroundings. The *Community-Oriented Programs Environment Scale* (COPES) assesses the psychosocial environments of treatment programs; see Moos (1972).

Family appraisal techniques. Some limited possibilities exist. See the review by Bodin (1968) and abstracts of published techniques by Straus (1969). One example, the *revealed differences* procedure, can be used to produce systematized data comparing people. Deriving from Strodtbeck's approach, it has been used mainly with married couples or families. Each person answers a set of questions individually, then meets with the others to decide on common answers for the group. Differences can be ascertained either by an observer or by the group itself. Another technique is the *Family Relations Test*, in which the child drops cards describing feelings into boxes attached to figures representing family members. See reports by Kauffman (1970, 1971). Another approach is the TAT-like *Family Story Technique.* See report by Kadushin, Waxenberg, and Sager (1971). Olson and Straus (1972) present a game called SIMFAM to be used as a diagnostic tool for marital and family therapy.

Interrelation of different views of a person. Few assessment devices attempt to detect similarities and differences between different reports about a person—what others say, what he says himself, what he reveals unconsciously. As mentioned in Chapter 9, one exception is the interpersonal diagnostic system of Leary (1957).

Life-history procedures. Although seldom standardized, case-history variables are often the most useful types of personal characteristics. One systematized approach is the *M-B History Record*, by Briggs. Lorei and Gurel (1972) report a biographical inventory for making employment decisions about schizophrenics. The *Social Readjustment Rating Scale* (Holmes and Rahe, 1967) has been used to study psychosomatic reactions to life changes.

Q-Sorts. The subject places a set of statements on cards in piles ranging from least characteristic to most characteristic of himself. Usually there are specified numbers for each pile, making statistical procedures simple. There are many kinds of Q-sorts. A well-researched one is Block's *California Q-Set*, which provides 100 carefully selected statements for comprehensively describing personality and psychodynamics. See Block (1961).

Semantic differential. Originally developed by Osgood, Suci, and Tannenbaum (1957) for research on the psychology of connotative meanings. Requires the subject to rate a given object or concept, such as "mother" or "sex" on many rating scales. These different concepts can then be compared for their connotative closeness or distance. Three major rating factors have emerged: evaluation, potency, and activity. Interesting application to the case of "The Three Faces of Eve" (Osgood and Luria, 1954).

Sociometry. A procedure to determine the relationships of individuals in a group from their statements of preferences. See Gardner and Thompson (1959) for a standardized approach with school children.

State versus trait measurement. Some characteristics of individuals are temporary and situation-related and others are more long-term and trans-situational. Measures that differentiate these and determine change over situation and time would be of potential clinical value. One step in this direction is the *State-Trait Anxiety Inventory* by Spielberger, Gorsuch, and Lushene.

Examples of Psychological Reports

The reports shown here are taken from the files of a variety of clinical settings. (Details have, of course, been altered so as to preserve the anonymity of the patient and the institution.) Although report writing is most conspicuous as a part of the clinical psychologist's task when clinicians function as members of psychiatric teams, the communication of appraisal information in some form is essential in all settings except those where a psychologist works completely alone. Even then it is necessary to keep some kind of record for himself. The student can learn from reading these examples how psychologists have handled this communication task.

As emphasized in the chapters on appraisal, it is helpful to organize the process around particular questions or reasons for referral. What the psychologist attempts to communicate is the image making he is engaged in while he worked with the client, keeping in mind that this leads to decisions and that the whole sequence constitutes the designing of an improvement program. In putting a report together, he immerses himself in the data, getting a clear idea of the whole case. Congruencies and discrepancies among test or observation elements and the person's typical behavior as well as his deviant behavior, are important. The form of the report, its style, tone, and intended message should consider the primary reader's circumstances and the alternatives open to him. The report must be sensitive to needs of secondary readers such as researchers and to possible "hidden agenda" tasks such as broadening a resource person's understanding or skill. Report writers need to tailor their product to help clients rather than serve tradition. They must beware of producing material that may be true of anyone. A psychological report represents a substantial investment of time, both the client's and the psychologist's. Clear functional utility is its only justification.

The illustrations that follow show a wide variety of psychological reports. At the end is a pseudo-report showing dangers to avoid in report writing.

Report on Sally Rhodes, a mental hospital inmate,
to the referring ward physician

This report was written by an experienced psychologist, the only psychologist in a very understaffed state hospital. With limited time available and forced to set himself a limited task, he administered just one test.

570

Psychological Evaluation

Name   Rhodes, Sally

Date _____

Age   29

Case number _____

Requested by Dr. _____ (physician)

Purpose   Evaluation of intellectual functioning

Ms. Rhodes is a short, heavy, squarely built blonde woman whose speech is like a rapid machine-gun flow of words in which she repeats herself again and again. She is very defensive about her low intellect, saying she isn't bright "in things like school," but maintaining that she is bright in other ways. She was very suspicious about the purpose of the test, is afraid it will cause her to be kept here in the hospital, and in general presents a very excited appearance. However, she denies her excitement, claims to be very calm, and does so in an excited argumentative voice. She feels she has been unfairly treated, is resentful of having her children taken from her, and cannot give a clear coherent logical account of the events leading up to her hospitalization. Her behavior appears definitely manic.

Tests administered.
Wechsler-Bellevue (I)
Verbal Scale IQ 73
Performance IQ 62
Full-Scale IQ 65

The subject is functioning at a defective intellectual level, and her present level of functioning is slightly below her potential, owing to the impairing effects of her excitement and the anxiety produced by the threat of the test situation. She relies heavily upon the defense of denial and is full of excuses for her errors. For example, when she misses a question she might say, "I could do it if I had more time," or "I have that question written down at home, and I could have learned it if I'd been told I was going to be tested," or "I could do it if I had a pencil; it's not being dumb if you have to use a pencil." She has a very low fund of general information, her thinking is quite concrete, and she is so excited that it was necessary to repeat almost every question. She doesn't interpret reality accurately, is very insecure with regard to her intellect. One feature was consistent throughout, and that was that she would never admit that she was as dull as she really is; she clings desperately to anything that will permit her to preserve her sense of being worthwhile and in so doing has to rely upon uneconomical, almost pathological, and very unstable defenses.

Diagnostic impression (from his limited observation).   Mental deficiency with hypomanic defense by denial, accompanied by some paranoid features that probably have a fairly realistic basis. Her social adjustment has always been about in line with the abovementioned intellectual level. She will probably always be a ward of the state, either in or out of the hospital.

(Name) _____

Psychologist _____

**Report on Chuck F., a child-guidance-clinic case,
to the clinic staff**

Report of Psychological Study

F., Charles N. ("Chuck")

Male, age 10, born _____

Clinic No. _____

Interviewed and tested _____

(Date) by (Name)

Reason for referral. Chuck was referred to the clinic by the school with a history of disobedience at home, running away from school, poor schoolwork, and taking or destroying other children's property. The family physician's report is essentially negative.

Previous tests. The school reports a Stanford-Binet IQ last year (date) of 91. He averages at the 3.1 grade level of achievement tests, although he is now near the end of the fourth grade.

Tests administered.   Wechsler Intelligence Scale for Children—six subjects

Rorschach

Michigan Picture Test—eight cards

Observation.   Chuck is a robust, healthy-appearing boy. This healthy appearance is at odds with his lethargic, "tired" manner (although he reported having a good night's sleep). Although he appears to have no motor or speech defects, the lack of energy was evidenced in his soft, colorless, and somewhat monotonous speech. He is left-handed, and although he does not wear glasses, his behavior on the coding subtests in the WISC (eyes within 2 inches of the pages) leaves some doubt as to his visual acuity.

When asked what the two activities he liked best and least were, Chuck said that he liked "going to the woods" and baseball best and "hated" school and cleaning his room. He claimed that no one had said anything about why he was coming here. When asked if his father had come with them he said, "No, he stays home and watches the ball game." This was the only reference to his stepfather.

Chuck gave up easily on items in the WISC and responded quickly but briefly on the projective tests. The general picture of low vitality was the central impression received from his behavior. It is difficult to assess the quality of the testing relationship. It was my feeling that Chuck was "going along" with anything suggested, patiently, but not enthusiastically.

Test results.   Intellectually Chuck has normal ability (WISC Full-Scale IQ 99), despite his poor school record. He was particularly poor on items having to do with practical reasoning about human problems (the Comprehension subtest). He shrugged his shoulders and said that he "didn't know." When I persisted with questions beyond the standard requirements, he was able to answer some of the items.

In regard to personality characteristics, aside from the indications of immaturity and unsettled sexual role that might be expected in boys of his age, the most notable feature is an interpersonal orientation of passive submission.

The general impression he gives is one of apathy, perhaps as a result of feelings of inadequacy and ineffectiveness. His stories reflected three themes: (1) sadness, (2) control by authority figures, and (3) being the recipient of action rather than the actor. These findings are consistent with the relationship with the examiner and the test-taking behavior. It also seems to fit in with the teacher's statement that he "seems afraid to let others like him." His quick response to the projective tests suggests, along with compliance, an adequate perception of reality and the possibility of a richer fantasy life than he ordinarily reveals.

Summary. Chuck gives the impression of a boy who feels uncertain of his own ability. He seems to have given up overt attempts to "control the situation" himself. His intellectual ability is such that he should not have too much difficulty in meeting the school's academic requirements. It is my opinion that Chuck is capable of entering into a warm relationship with others, if it is in an area in which he feels somewhat competent. In the light of his interests in outdoor life and in baseball, any organization, such as Boy Scouts or Little League, where he could have a successful experience in a social situation, would be advisable. The conflict between his parents reported in the social history is undoubtedly being reflected in his attempts to run away and in distracting fantasies. His behavior and the test results are not indicative of a typical predelinquent pattern. If psychotherapy is available, he would probably respond well. Perhaps a woman therapist might be able to relate with him more quickly in the light of his passive resistance with me and his very active problems with his father. It is also strongly recommended that Chuck's vision be carefully examined and that a careful medical examination and an analysis of the family's eating habits be conducted to explore reasons for his lethargic manner.

(Name) _____

Psychologist _____   _____

Report on Ms. C, a new patient at a psychiatric out-patient clinic, to the clinic staff

Ms. C is a 44-year-old divorced woman. She is a practical nurse but is currently unemployed. She is living with her 60-year-old mother, who helps take care of her two children. Her manner is noticeably reticent and somewhat depressive, and there is some degree of emotional withdrawal. She volunteers virtually no information, and even when she is directly questioned, her responses are guarded and cryptic, and she is generally uncommunicative. In the testing situation she was very cooperative, but her participation is more on the basis of submissiveness than of intrinsic interest in the proceedings. She was administered the Rorschach, Sentence Completion, Thematic Apperception Test, and the Minnesota Multiphasic Personality Inventory.

The Rorschach shows a basically hysterical type of personality structure, the presence of substantial obsessive trends, and significant indications of paranoid pathology. Sexual maladjustment is clearly evident and the indications of weakened reality contact seem to be related to the sexual problems. The patient is very resistant to attacking or even facing her basic problems, and this corroborates the impression one gets in attempting to interview her. There is a virtual absence of any insight. The MMPI shows significant peaks on the

Hysteria, Paranoia, and Depression scales. This kind of pattern has been found to be common with neurotic patients, although a significant degree of paranoid involvement is suggested. The TAT is, for the most part, rather bland except for the presence of a considerable number of themes involving highly aggressive acts. The most salient and pervasive feeling that emerges is the paranoid one of a defenseless person in a hostile and brutal world in which violent aggressive forces are always lurking and may strike one or one's loved one when they least expect it.

The Sentence Completion Test brings out most clearly the paranoid ideation suggested in the MMPI and Rorschach. She feels that she is extremely ill and that her condition is almost hopeless: I am very—"sick," and My greatest hope—"is almost gone." To further inquiries about these she says, "I feel that if my eyes, my ears, and my throat were thoroughly studied, they would find something wrong," and, "I don't think I'll ever be healthy and strong again." Although a nurse, she is unable to explain how a local eye, ear, and throat condition could cause her to be so severely and hopelessly sick, and she shows no interest in attempting to explain it. She is confused and baffled by many inexplicable experiences she has had and projects motives and interpretations into many common daily occurrences; for example, from sentence completions, I want to know—"why some people behave so strangely"; I secretly—"feel that something must have happened in 19-- that I don't know about"; If only—"people would tell me the truth." In the inquiry on these items she replies, "none of these things are too important, but so many of them happened to me. For example, when my brother-in-law's leg was broken, and I was present in the doctor's office, my brother-in-law remarked to the doctor, 'She's an excellent diagnostician,' referring to me. All the doctor said was, 'Well, I got you.' What did he mean by that? That's bothered and puzzled me ever since. The same kind of thing that's been happening that I can't explain is why the serious sick diabetic patient I was nursing was suddenly taken off all medication. And also the last patient that I had that none of the doctors or nurses did anything for. I can't understand these things." In the same vein, What puzzles me—"why one of the doctors talks about married men and men in high salaried positions." In the inquiry she responds, "The way he'd lower his voice or look at me when he'd get around to talking about those things. I don't know what his motive was, but I felt there was some reason behind it."

Along the same lines, and by dint of much probing, since the patient is very guarded and cryptic in all her responses, additional evidence of paranoid ideation was elicited. On both of two visits to fortune tellers, they told her about a particular man who would come into her life significantly. She relates many strange events which have happened around her house which she feels are all related to the return of this man into her life. She relates a recent experience in which she felt extremely good and symptom-free for a day or so, and she feels that this happened because she was given a massive amount of "dope" put in coffee returned to her by a girl in a neighboring apartment who had borrowed some coffee from her. These experiences, all of which are baffling and troubling to her seem to have increased in frequency since 19--, and she feels that the attitudes and feelings of her friends and associates toward her have changed. She is unable to account for these unusual experiences, but she feels that she is being used as a psychological experiment by someone who is causing these things to happen to her so that he can study her reactions to them.

Diagnostic impression. On first impression derived from an initial interview, Ms. C's superficial manner and guarded communicativeness conveys the picture of a person in good contact who is suffering from a reactive depressive state as a result of protracted and severe stress in a realistically difficult marital situation. The termination of the marriage in divorce and her stringent economic prospect of having to support her two children enhances this impression. On the basis of psychological testing and a searching and probing type of interview, however, evidence of substantial paranoid pathology, moving toward systematization, is elicited. It is felt that this patient is quite seriously ill, and the outlook is poor, inasmuch as her present level of communicativeness raises doubts about her availability for psychotherapy.

Psychological consultation report on Mr. Deeter, a patient in a general medical hospital, to the referring physician

Psychological Consultation Report

This 35-year-old man, Mr. Deeter, was referred to this service during October 19-- because of signs of mental deterioration associated with a 15-year history of *grand mal* seizures. In this evaluation the Rorschach, Wechsler Verbal Scale, and Memory-for-Design test were administered.

Although there is no previous IQ score for comparison it would appear that this patient shows little intellectual deficit. The earned score of 108 is in the normal range, and the ability he displays is generally good. There is a certain compulsiveness and occasional bizarreness to his responses, however, that can readily interfere with his ability to demonstrate his intellectual capacities. Similarly, there is little evidence that cerebral pathology is interfering with his skills or his ability to perceive accurately. In fact, he demonstrated surprisingly good visual-motor ability. However, Mr. Deeter does show some clear psychopathological signs. Beneath his rather controlled and benign exterior there is strong hostility. He does not show any overt psychotic indications, but he is capable of perceptual distortion and of bizarre thought. Psychologically he protects against overt manifestations by withdrawal and avoidance. In particular he shows little capacity for rewarding relationships with others. It is judged that at this time the patient does not present a very stable personality. Psychiatrically, the prognosis would appear to be poor. Diagnostically, this is not a clear picture inasmuch as the outstanding feature of the present evaluation is the personality instability. It may be that his seizures have a secondary effect in preventing any overt psychiatric symptoms from appearing. It is recommended that if possible this man be referred again in the near future for reevaluation by this service.

Diagnostic impression. Chronic brain syndrome associated with convulsive disorder.

a. Manifested by impaired reality testing and some bizarre thought and by social withdrawal and avoidance signs.
b. Precipitating stress undetermined.

c. Predisposition undetermined.

d. Impairment moderate to severe.

Report to a social worker in a remote small town about a small American Indian boy

The boy could be a prospect for adoption if the adoptive parents could be convinced that he wasn't retarded but had good potential. Note how the writer uses this opportunity to include didactic material. "Conferring about the report" thus became a consultation to the state welfare workers.

Psychological Report

Basis. Perry, age four years, two months, was seen at the request of State Department of Public Assistance, on (date), for general developmental evaluation and recommendations about resources and programs and the counseling of perspective adoptive parents.

Examination. The examination consisted of the Denver Developmental Screening Test and prolonged free-play interaction.

Appearance and manner. Perry's standard of appearance and physical care was a distinct credit to his foster mother. He was neatly dressed and well turned out. Slight initial shyness gave way to a style of simply proceeding to do what he wished and generally tending to ignore me rather than to interact with me. He obviously enjoyed some of our interaction, but did not seek it out.

Observations. Perhaps the area with closest-to-normal development is that of Gross Motor Skills. Perry's skills in walking, running, balancing, ball throwing and catching, general coordination, and so on, are not notably different from those of most four-year-olds.

Although few observations could be directly made in the area of personal and social skills, Perry's poor performances at hand washing and at putting on his coat lead to the inference that he is behind normal standards in learning such skills. Other factors within this area that might be discussed are buttoning buttons (90 percent of children Perry's age can), dressing with*out* supervision (76 percent of children Perry's age can; 90 percent of all children dress with supervision by 3.5 years). His separation from the social worker who brought him and his acceptance of the examiner were positive achievements and quite up to age standard.

Perry's repertoire of fine motor adaptive skills showed more definite slowness in its development. Many young children, when faced with tasks requiring copying or drawing, are able to concentrate on the design to be drawn. For Perry, the pencil itself proved a problem: Should he hold it in his fist, between fingers, or finger and thumb? Much in the area of visual-motor skills, traditionally sampled by copying and drawing, thus appeared below standard. Perry also "looked retarded" because of his reluctance to imitate the examiner when asked. He was unable to show any apprehension of concepts such as "longer than" which are age appropriate.

But the most striking area in which he is out of step with normal developmental patterns is in language skills. Compared to peers, Perry uses language less often, has a smaller vocabulary, less ability to construct coherent sentences, and fewer concepts such as "on," "under," "over," and "inside." At a grossly approximate estimate, Perry may have at least eighteen months progress to catch up in this area.

Perry conducted himself with reasonable self-control. He seemed to have a good range of interpersonal sensitivity, reacted well with a male figure, and can, in short, be said to have a distinctly favorable temperament.

Discussion. The process of evaluating Perry was, in effect, an effort to have Perry express some aspects of what he has learned and retained up to this time. Very low performances might be expected if he had difficulties with perceptual input (vision, hearing, etc.) or with internal processing (visual-motor incoordination, retardation, brain injury) or with expressive systems (poor speech, patterns of inattention to people, patterns of "turning people off"). Perry gave no gross signs of being in need of hearing or vision examination. But, "retardation" (slowed progress) is the ultimate label for symptoms of all the other classes.

Judging by the available history, there may be some familial predisposition toward slower development in Perry's case. But no gross problems in visual-motor coordination, psychomotor responsiveness, short-term memory, and so on, are evident, so this component must be regarded as minor. Most serious, on the other hand, is the array of expressive problems Perry has. He not only has a low level of such skills, he actually possesses strategies that work to keep his speech development down and tend to diminish verbal dialogue with adults. The whole range of expressive skills needs immediate attention.

In an effort to elicit Perry's best performance, he was given a raisin for any good effort at imitating a requested behavior. Even such a crude reinforcement schedule produced immediate and profound results. He did and said things unobtainable earlier in the session. Perry will obviously work hard for something he finds rewarding. The benefits of the approach are twofold: (1) he can be systematically taught an expanded repertoire of output—new words, new concepts, new syntax, plurals, drawing skills, etc., and (2) grownups working with him can avoid helping make the problem worse. Perry has a way of acting as if he has not heard or doesn't know, which forces the uncertain adult to the position of asking yes/no questions (to which he gestures and doesn't speak) or of doing the activity for him. Both these interactions directly harm his development, yet are usually quite inadvertent on the part of adults.

Recommendations. Perry can be helped by a variety of techniques, among them early schooling programs such as Head Start, well-designed and appealing television programs, experience-oriented (rather than custodial) preschools for normal children. Perhaps the most certain and the most potentially successful, however, is for interested adults to acquire the few simple techniques needed for teaching and some ideas of what to stress. (In this regard, sample materials are being made available. The programmed text for parents entitled *Living with Children* (Patterson and Gullion, 1971) is suggested as a second resource.

A completely blind analysis of the case of a schizophrenic veteran

Several miscarriages of communication are illustrated by a report written several years ago by one of the authors. The fictitious report was a completely blind analysis of the case of a schizophrenic veteran; it was written before the writer knew anything about the patient except that he was a new admission to a Veterans Administration hospital and his case was to be worked up for "A Case Study of Schizophrenia," a discussion by several psychologists at a state psychological association meeting. Nevertheless, it rang surprisingly true to the actual presentation of the case. The pseudo-report and some comments on it were as follows:

This veteran approached the testing situation with some reluctance. He was cooperative with the clinician, but mildly evasive on some of the material. Both the tests and the past history suggest considerable inadequacy in interpersonal relations, particularly with members of his family. It is doubtful whether he has ever had very many close relationships with anyone. Those few that he has had were tinged with a great deal of ambivalence. He has never been able to sink his roots deeply. He is immature, egocentric, and irritable, and often he misperceives the good intentions of the people around him. Projection is one of his prominent defense mechanisms. He tends to be basically passive and dependent, though there are occasional periods of resistance and rebellion against others. Although he shows some seclusiveness and autistic trends, he is in fair contact with reality. Vocationally, his adjustment has been very poor. Mostly he has drifted from one job to another. His interests are shallow and he tends to have poor motivation for his work. Also he has had a hard time keeping his jobs because of difficulty in getting along with fellow employees. Although he has had some relations with women, his sex life has been unsatisfactory to him. At present he is mildly depressed, although a great deal of affect is not shown. What physical complaints he has appear mainly to have a functional origin. His intelligence is close to average, but he is functioning below his potential. In summary, this is a long-time inadequate or borderline adjustment pattern. Test results and case history, although they do not give a strong clear-cut diagnostic picture, suggest the diagnosis of schizophrenic reaction, chronic undifferentiated type. Prognosis for response to treatment appears to be poor.

This completely blind analysis is based on the following assumptions:

1. The usual veteran referred for psychological testing is not likely to be an obvious or clear-cut diagnostic case. There is no need for testing unless there is indecision about what steps might be taken in his behalf. Consequently, hedging is to be expected in a report anyway.

2. There are some modal characteristics of patients coming to VA hosptials. In placing bets on what the patient is likely to be like, the best guess would be a description of the modal personality. For instance, most of the veterans coming to this hospital are chronic cases who have not succeeded in jobs or in family life. Also, the best guess on intelligence would obviously be average intelligence, but since the person is a psychiatric patient it is likely that he is not functioning at his best.

3. This is a schizophrenic case (according to the plan for the program). Given the general classification schizophrenia, one can work back to some of the characteristics that belong to such persons and have a fair chance of being right.

4. Certain modal behaviors of the clinical staff provide clues. They use certain words, resort to jargon. They have a preference for certain diagnoses. A large

percentage of the cases wind up with the diagnosis of schizophrenic reaction, chronic undifferentiated type.

5. There are some "universally valid" adjectives which are appropriate for almost any psychiatric patient, such as *dependent, immature, irritable,* and *egocentric.*

6. In the less clear areas where modal characteristics do not stand out, it is safe to write a vague statement or one that can be interpreted in various ways. Readers can be counted on to overlook a few vague misses and to select the descriptions that jibe with their own preconceptions.

7. All of this is intended to say that we have much in common with the old fortune teller, and that what we need are better ways of dealing with individuality. Knowing modal personalities is very useful; it certainly adds to ease of social communication; however, we are sometimes fooled into thinking that we know persons when actually all we know are our own stereotypes.

References

Aaronson, B., and Osmond, H. (eds.). *Psychedelics: the uses and implications of hallucinogenic drugs.* Garden City, N. Y.: Doubleday, 1970.

Abt, L. E., and Riess, B. F. (eds.). *Progress in clinical psychology*, Vol. 8. New York: Grune & Stratton, 1969.

Ackerman, N. W. *The psychodynamics of family life.* New York: Basic Books, 1958.

Adelson, D., and Kalis, B. L. (eds.). *Community psychology and mental health.* San Francisco: Chandler, 1970.

Adinolfi, A. A. Relevance of person perception research to clinical psychology. *Journal of Consulting and Clinical Psychology*, 1971, *37*, 167—176.

Adler, P. T. Evaluation of the figure drawing technique: reliability, factorial structure, and diagnostic usefulness. *Journal of Consulting and Clinical Psychology*, 1970, *35*, 52—57.

Adler, P. T. Ethnic and socioeconomic status differences in human figure drawings. *Journal of Consulting and Clinical Psychology*, 1971, *36*, 344—354.

Affleck, D. C., and Strider, F. D. Contribution of psychological reports to patient management. *Journal of Consulting and Clinical Psychology*, 1971, *37*, 177—179.

Akhurst, B. A. *Assessing intellectual ability.* New York: Barnes & Noble, 1970.

Albee, G. W. Conceptual models and manpower requirements in psychology. *American Psychologist*, 1968, *23*, 317—320.

Albee, G. W. The uncertain future of clinical psychology. *American Psychologist*, 1970, *25*, 1071—1080.

Allison, J., Blatt, S. J., and Zimet, C. N. *The interpretation of psychological tests.* New York: Harper & Row, 1968.

Allport, G. W. *Personality and social encounter.* Boston: Beacon Press, 1960.

Allport, G. W. *Letters from Jenny.* New York: Harcourt Brace, 1965.

American Institutes for Research. *Evaluative research: strategies and methods.* Pittsburgh: American Institutes for Research, 1970.

American Psychiatric Association. *Diagnostic and statistical manual of mental disorders*, Vol. 2, 3rd ed. Washington, D. C.: American Psychiatric Association, 1968.

American Psychological Association. *Ethical standards of psychologists.* Washington, D. C.: The Association, 1953. (a)

American Psychological Association. *Ethical standards of psychologists*, a *summary of ethical principles.* Washington, D. C.: The Association, 1953. (b)

American Psychological Association. *Professional preparation of clinical psychologists.* Washington, D. C.: The Association, 1966. (a)

American Psychological Association. *Standards for educational and psychological tests and manuals.* Washington, D. C.: The Association, 1966. (b)

American Psychological Association. *Casebook on ethical standards of psychologists.* Washington, D. C.: The Association, 1967.

American Psychological Association. Ethical standards of psychologists. *American Psychologist*, 1968, *23*, 357–361. (a)

American Psychological Association. *Psychology as a profession.* Washington, D. C.: The Association, 1968. (b) (*American Psychologist*, 1968, *23*, 195–200.)

American Psychological Association. Psychological assessment and public policy. *American Psychologist*, 1970, *25*, 264–266.

American Psychological Association, Ad Hoc Committee on Guidelines for the Use of Drugs and Other Chemical Agents in Research. Guidelines for psychologists for the use of drugs in research. *American Psychologist*, 1972, *27*, 335–336.

American Psychological Association, Committee on Scientific and Professional Aims of Psychology. *American Psychologist*, 1967, *22*, 49–76.

American Psychological Association, Committee on Scientific and Professional Ethics and Conduct. Rules and procedures. *American Psychologist*, 1968, *23*, 362–366.

American Psychological Association, Committee on Scientific and Professional Ethics and Conduct. Guidelines for telephone directory listings. *American Psychologist*, 1969, *24*, 70–71.

American Psychological Association, Education and Training Board Ad Hoc Committee. Education for research in psychology. *American Psychologist*, 1959, *14*, 167–179.

American Psychological Association, Policy and Planning Board. Structure and function of APA: guidelines for the future. *American Psychologist*, 1972, *27*, 1–10.

Amrine, M. Psychology in the news. *American Psychologist*, 1960, *15*, 630–631.

Anastasi, A. Psychology, psychologists, and psychological testing. *American Psychologist*, 1967, *22*, 297–306.

Anastasi, A. *Psychological testing*, 3rd ed. New York: Macmillan, 1968.

Anderson, J. E. The use of time and energy. In J. E. Birren (ed.), *Handbook of aging and the individual.* Chicago: University of Chicago Press, 1959, pp. 769–796.

Anderson, J. E., and Goodenough, F. L. Age and sex differences in productivity of American psychologists. *Psychological Bulletin*, 1935, *32*, 675–676.

Anderson, L. M. Personality characteristics of parents of neurotic, aggressive and normal preadolescent boys. *Journal of Consulting and Clinical Psychology*, 1969, *33*, 575–581.

Ard, B. N., Jr., and Ard, C. C. (eds.). *Handbook of marriage counseling.* Palo Alto, Calif.: Science & Behavior Books, 1969.

Ardila, R. Psychology in Latin America. *American Psychologist*, 1968, *23*, 567–574.

Argyris, C. T-groups for organizational effectiveness. *Harvard Business Review*, 1964, *42*, 60–74.

Argyris, C. Some unintended consequences of rigorous research. *Psychological Bulletin*, 1968, *70*, 185–197.

Argyris, C. *Intervention theory and method: a behavioral science view.* Reading, Mass.: Addison-Wesley, 1970.

Aronow, E., and Reznikoff, M. Application of projective tests to psychotherapy. *Journal of Personality Assessment*, 1971, *35*, 379–393.

Arthur, A. Z. Diagnostic testing and the new alternatives. *Psychological Bulletin*, 1969, *72*, 183–192.

Arthur, A. Z. Theory and action-oriented research. *Journal of Consulting and Clinical Psychology*, 1972, *38*, 129–133.

Association for Systems Management. *Management by objectives.* Cleveland: Association for Systems Management, 1971.

Astin, H. S. Employment and career status of women psychologists. *American Psychologist*, 1972, *27*, 371–381.

Astrachan, B. M. Towards a social systems model of therapeutic groups. *Social Psychiatry*, 1970, *5*, 110–119.

Atkinson, E. Four hours on the suicide phones. *Bulletin of Suicidology*, 1970, *7*, 38–41.

Ayllon, T., and Azrin, N. H. Reinforcement and instruction with mental patients. *Journal of Experimental Analysis of Behavior*, 1964, *7*, 327–331.

Bach, G. R., and Wyden, P. *The intimate enemy.* New York: Morrow, 1969.

Bachrach, A. J. (ed.). *Experimental foundations of clinical psychology.* New York: Basic Books, 1962.

Bachtold, L. M., and Werner, E. E. Personality profiles of gifted women psychologists. *American Psychologist*, 1970, *25*, 234–243.

Baller, W., and Schalock, H. D. Conditioned-response treatment of eneuresis. *Exceptional Children*, 1956, *22*, 233–236.

Banaka, W. H. *Training in depth interviewing.* New York: Harper & Row, 1971.

Bandura, A. *Principles of behavior modification.* New York: Holt, Rinehart and Winston, 1969.

Bannister, D., and Mair, J. M. *The evaluation of personal constructs.* New York: Academic Press, 1968.

Barber, T. X., DiCara, L. V., Kamiya, J., Miller, N. E., Shapiro, D., and Stoyva, J. (eds.). *Biofeedback and self control, 1970.* Chicago: Aldine-Atherton, 1971.

Bard, M. *Training police as specialists in family crisis intervention.* Washington: U. S. Government Printing Office, 1970 (LEAA Document PR 70-1).

Bard, M. The role of law enforcement in the helping system. *Community Mental Health Journal*, 1971, *7*, 151–160.

Bard, M. A model for action research. *Community Psychology Series*, 1972, *1*, 17–28.

Barker, R. G. (ed.). *The stream of behavior.* New York: Appleton-Century-Crofts, 1963.

Barker, R. G. *Ecological psychology.* Stanford: Stanford University Press, 1968.

Barker, R. G., Schoggen, M. F., and Barker, L. S. Hemerography of Mary Ennis. In A. Burton and R. E. Harris (eds.), *Clinical studies of personality.* New York: Harper & Row, 1955, pp. 768–808.

Barnes, M., and Berke, J. *Mary Barnes, two accounts of a journey through madness.* New York: Harcourt Brace, 1971.

Barron, F. *Personal soundness in university graduate students, an experimental study of young men in the sciences and professions.* Berkeley: University of California Press, 1954.

Barron, F. X. *Creativity and personal freedom.* New York: Van Nostrand Reinhold, 1968. (a)

Barron, F. X. The measurement of creativity. In D. Whitla (ed.), *Handbook of measurement in psychology and education.* Reading, Mass.: Addison-Wesley, 1968. (b)

Barry, J. R. Criteria in the evaluation of consultation. *Professional Psychology,* 1970, *1,* 363–366.

Bass, B. M., and Berg, I. A. (eds.). *Objective approaches to personality assessment.* New York: Van Nostrand Reinhold, 1959.

Bauer, R. A. (ed.). *Social indicators.* Cambridge, Mass.: MIT Press, 1966.

Baughman, E. E. A new method of Rorschach inquiry. *Journal of Projective Techniques,* 1958, *22,* 381–389. (a)

Baughman, E. E. The role of the stimulus in Rorschach responses. *Psychological Bulletin,* 1958, *55,* 121–147. (b)

Baughman, E. E. The effect of inquiry method on Rorschach color and shading scores. *Journal of Projective Techniques,* 1959, *23,* 3–7. (a)

Baughman, E. E. An experimental analysis of the relationship between stimulus structure and behavior on the Rorschach. *Journal of Projective Techniques,* 1959, *23,* 134–183. (b)

Bayton, J. A., Roberts, S. O., and Williams, R. K. Minority groups and careers in psychology. *American Psychologist,* 1970, *25,* 504–510.

Beck, S. J. How the Rorschach came to America. *Journal of Personality Assessment,* 1972, *36,* 105–108.

Becker, W. C. *Parents are teachers: a child management program.* Champaign, Ill.: Research Press, 1971.

Bednar, R. L., and Lawlis, G. F. Empirical research in group psychotherapy. In A. E. Bergin and S. L. Garfield (eds.), *Handbook of psychotherapy and behavior change.* New York: Wiley, 1971, pp. 812–838.

Bednar, R. L., and Shapiro, J. G. Professional research commitment: a symptom or a syndrome. *Journal of Consulting and Clinical Psychology,* 1970, *34,* 323–326.

Bee, H. L., Van Egeren, L. F., Streissguth, A. P., Nyman, B. A., and Leckie, M. S. Social class differences in maternal teaching strategies and speech patterns. *Developmental Psychology,* 1969, *1,* 726–734.

Beecher, H. K. Relation of significance of wound to pain experienced. *Journal of the American Medical Association,* 1956, *161,* 1609–1613.

Beier, E. G., Robinson, P., and Micheletti, G. Susanville: a community helps itself in mobilization of community resources for self help in mental health. *Journal of Consulting and Clinical Psychology,* 1971, *36,* 142–150.

Bell, D. (ed.). *Toward the year 2000. Work in progress.* New York: Houghton Mifflin, 1968. (Originally published in *Daelalus,* Summer 1967.)

Benjamin, A. *The helping interview.* Boston: Houghton Mifflin, 1969.

Bennett, C. C., Anderson, L. S., Cooper, S., Hassol, L., Klein, D. C., and Rosenblum, G. *Community psychology: a report of the Boston conference on the education of psychologists for community mental health.* Boston: Boston University, 1966.

Bennis, W. G. *Organizational development: its nature, origins and prospects.* Reading, Mass.: Addison-Wesley, 1969.

Bennis, W. G. A funny thing happened on the way to the future. *American Psychologist,* 1970, *25,* 595—608.

Berg, I. A., and Pennington, L. A. (eds.). *An introduction to clinical psychology,* 3rd ed. New York: Ronald Press, 1966.

Bergin, A. E., and Garfield, S. L. *Handbook of psychotherapy and behavior change: an empirical analysis.* New York: Wiley, 1971.

Bergin, A. E., and Strupp, H. H. New directions in psychotherapy research. *Journal of Abnormal Psychology,* 1970, *76,* 13—26.

Berlyne, D. E. American and European psychology. *American Psychologist,* 1968, *23,* 447—452.

Bernal, M. E., Duryee, J. S., Pruett, H. L., and Burns, B. J. Behavior modification and the brat syndrome. *Journal of Consulting and Clinical Psychology,* 1968, *32,* 447—455.

Berrien, F. K. *General and social systems.* New Brunswick, N. J.: Rutgers University Press, 1968.

Bertalanffy, L. von. *General systems theory: foundations, development, applications.* New York: Braziller, 1968.

Berzins, J. I., Ross, W. F., and Cohen, D. I. Relation of the A-B distinction and trust-distrust sets to addict patients' self-disclosures in brief interviews. *Journal of Consulting and Clinical Psychology,* 1970, *34,* 289—296.

Berzins, J. I., and Seidman, E. Subjective reactions of A and B quasi-therapists to schizoid and neurotic communications. *Journal of Consulting and Clinical Psychology,* 1968, *32,* 342—347.

Berzins, J. I., and Seidman, E. Differential therapeutic responding of A and B quasi-therapists to schizoid and neurotic communciations. *Journal of Consulting and Clinical Psychology,* 1969, *33,* 279—286.

Beveridge, W. E. *Problem solving interviews.* London: George Allen & Unwin, 1968.

Biederman, L., and Cerbus, G. Changes in Rorschach teaching. *Journal of Personality Assessment,* 1971, *35,* 524—526.

Bieri, J., Atkins, A. L., Briar, S., Leaman, R. L., Miller, H., and Tripodi, T. *Clinical and social judgment.* New York: Wiley, 1966.

Bigner, J. J. Parent education in popular literature: 1950—1970. *The Family Coordinator,* 1972, *21,* 313—319.

Bijou, S. W., and Peterson, R. F. Functional analysis in the assessment of children. In P. McReynolds (ed.), *Advances in psychological assessment,* Vol. 2. Palo Alto: Science & Behavior Books, 1971, pp. 63—78.

Bindman, A. J. The psychologist as a mental health administrator. *Professional Psychology,* 1970, *1,* 445—447.

Bindman, A. J., and Spiegel, A. D. (eds.). *Perspectives in community mental health.* Chicago: Aldine-Atherton, 1969.

Birnbaum, M. Sense about sensitivity training. *Saturday Review,* 1969, November, 82—97.

Birren, J. E. (ed.) *Handbook of aging and the individual.* Chicago: University of Chicago Press, 1959.

Bisno, H. Professional status and professional policies: a heterodox analysis. *Counseling News and Views*, 1960, *12*, 4—11.

Bisno, H. A theoretical framework for teaching social work methods and skills, with particular reference to undergraduate social welfare education. *Journal of Education for Social Work*, 1969, *5*, 5—17.

Black, M. *The social theories of Talcott Parsons*. Englewood Cliffs, N. J.: Prentice-Hall, 1961.

Blau, T. H. *Private practice in clinical psychology*. New York: Appleton-Century-Crofts, 1959.

Blazier, D. C., and Goosman, E. T. *A marriage analysis*. Saluda, N. C.: Family Life Publications, 1966.

Blizard, P. J. Beliefs about disease and alcoholism. *Mental Hygiene*, 1971, *55*, 184—189.

Block, J. *The Q-sort method in personality assessment and psychiatric research*. Springfield, Ill.: Charles C Thomas, 1961.

Block, J. *The challenge of response sets*. New York: Appleton-Century-Crofts, 1965.

Blum, G. S. Assessment of psychodynamic variables by the Blacky Pictures. In P. McReynolds (ed.), *Advances in psychological assessment*, Vol. 1. Palo Alto: Science & Behavior Books, 1968, pp. 150—168.

Bodin, A. M. Conjoint family assessment: an evolving field. In P. McReynolds (ed.), *Advances in psychological assessment*, Vol. 1. Palo Alto, Calif.: Science & Behavior Books, 1968, pp. 223—243.

Bolman, L. Some effects of trainers on their T-groups. *Journal of Applied Behavioral Science*, 1971, *7*, 309—325.

Bordin, E. S. Inside the therapeutic hour. In E. A. Rubinstein and M. B. Parloff (eds.), *Research in psychotherapy*. Washington, D. C.: American Psychological Association, 1959, pp. 235—246.

Borgatta, E. F. Sidesteps toward a nonspecial theory. *Psychological Review*, 1954, *61*, 343—352.

Boring, E. G. *A history of experimental psychology*, 2nd ed. New York: Appleton-Century-Crofts, 1950.

Boring, E. G. When is human behavior predetermined? *Science Monthly*, 1957, *84*, 189—196.

Boszormenyi-Nagy, I., and Framo, J. L. *Intensive family therapy, theoretical and practical aspects*. New York: Harper & Row, 1965.

Boucher, M. L. Effect of seating distance on interpersonal attraction in an interview situation. *Journal of Consulting and Clinical Psychology*, 1972, *38*, 15—19.

Boxley, R. and Wagner, N. N. Clinical training programs and minority groups, a survey. *Professional Psychology*, 1971, *2*, 75—81.

Bradford, L. P., Gibb, J. R., and Benne, K. D. (eds.). *T-group theory and laboratory method*. New York: Wiley, 1964.

Braginsky, B. M., and Braginsky, D. D. Schizophrenic patients in the psychiatric interview: an experimental study of their effectiveness at manipulation. *Journal of Consulting Psychology*, 1967, *31*, 543—547.

Braun, J. R. (ed.). *Clinical psychology in transition: selected readings*, rev. ed. New York: World, 1966.

Breger, L. (ed.). *Clinical-cognitive psychology: models and integrations.* Englewood Cliffs, N. J.: Prentice-Hall, 1969.

Bromer, J. A. Hawthorne counseling that failed. *Contemporary Psychology* 1968, *13*, 59–60.

Broskowski, A. Clinical psychology: a research and development model. *Professional Psychology*, 1971, *2*, 235–242.

Brotemarkle, R. A. (ed.). *Clinical psychology: studies in honor of Lightner Witmer to commemorate the thirty-fifth anniversary of the founding of the first psychological clinic.* Philadelphia: University of Pennsylvania Press, 1931.

Broverman, I. K., Broverman, D. M., Clarkson, F. E., Rosenkrantz, P. S., and Vogel, S. R. Sex-role stereotypes and clinical judgments of mental health. *Journal of Counsulting and Clinial Psychology*, 1970, *34*, 1–7

Brower, M. The emergence of community development corporations in urban neighborhoods. *American Journal of Orthopsychiatry*, 1971, *41*, 646–658.

Brown, B. B. Recognition of aspects of consciousness through association with EEG alpha activity represented by a light signal. *Psychophysiology*, 1970, *6*, 442–452.

Brown, B. B. Awareness of EEG-subjective activity relationships detected within a closed feedback system. *Psychophysiology*, 1971, *7*, 451–464.

Brozek, J. Spectrum of Soviet psychology, 1968 model. *American Psychologist*, 1969, *24*, 944–946.

Buck, P. S. *A community success story: the founding of the Pearl Buck Center.* New York: John Day, 1972.

Buckley, W. (ed.). *Modern systems research for the behavioral scientist: a sourcebook.* Chicago: Aldine-Atherton, 1968.

Bugental, J. The person who is the therapist. In A. Z. Guiora and M. A. Brandwin (eds.), *Perspectives in clinical psychology.* New York: Van Nostrand Reinhold, 1968, pp. 45–58.

Bullmer, K. Improving accuracy of interpersonal perception through a direct teaching method. *Journal of Counseling Psychology*, 1972, *19*, 37–41.

Buros, O. K. (ed.). *The fifth mental measurements yearbook.* Highland Park, N. J.: Gryphon Press, 1959.

Buros, O. K. (ed.). *The sixth mental measurements yearbook.* Highland Park, N. J.: Gryphon Press, 1965.

Buros, O. K. *Personality tests and reviews.* Highland Park, N. J.: Gryphon Press, 1970.

Buros, O. K. (ed.). *The seventh mental measurements yearbook*, Vols. 1, 2. Highland Park, N. J.: Gryphon Press, 1972.

Burton, A. (ed.). *Case studies in counseling and psychotherapy.* Englewood Cliffs, N. J.: Prentice-Hall, 1959.

Burton, A. (ed.). *Encounter.* San Francisco: Jossey-Bass, 1970.

Burton, A., and Harris, R. E. (eds.). *Clinical studies of personality.* New York: Harper & Row, 1955.

Bush, R. N., and Allen, D. W. Micro-teaching: controlled practice in the training of teachers. Paper presented at the Santa Barbara conference on teacher education of the Ford Foundation, Santa Barbara, April 1964.

Butcher, J. N. (ed.). *MMPI: research developments and clinical applications.* New York: McGraw-Hill, 1969.

Cahn, M. M. Poetic dimensions of encounter. In A. Burton (ed.). *Encounter.* San Francisco: Jossey-Bass, 1970, pp. 97–111.

Campbell, D. P. A counseling evaluation with a "better" control group. *Journal of Counseling Psychology*, 1963, *10*, 334–339.

Campbell, D. P. *The results of counseling: twenty-five years later.* Philadelphia: Saunders, 1965.

Campbell, D. P. *Handbook for the Strong Vocational Interest Blank.* Stanford: Stanford University Press, 1971.

Campbell, D. P., and Soliman, A. M. The vocational interests of women in psychology. *American Psychologist*, 1968, *23*, 158–163.

Campbell, D. T. Reforms as experiments. *American Psychologist*, 1969, *24*, 409–429.

Campbell, D. T., and Stanley, J. C. *Experimental and quasi-experimental designs for research.* Chicago: Rand McNally, 1963.

Campbell, J. P., and Dunnette, M. D. Effectiveness of T-group experiences in managerial training and development. *Psychological Bulletin*, 1968, *70*, 73–104.

Cannell, C. F., and Kahn, R. L. Interviewing. In G. Lindzey and E. Aronson (eds.). *Handbook of social psychology*, Vol. 2, 2nd ed. Reading, Mass.: Addison-Wesley, 1968, pp. 526–595.

Caplan, G. *Principles of preventive psychiatry.* New York: Basic Books, 1964.

Caplan, G. *The theory and practice of mental health consultation.* New York: Basic Books, 1970.

Caplow, T. *Elementary sociology.* Englewood Cliffs, N. J.: Prentice-Hall, 1971.

Carlson, E. T., and Dain, N. The psychotherapy that was moral treatment. *American Journal of Psychiatry*, 1960, *117*, 519–524.

Carlson, R. Rorschach prediction of success in clinical training. *Journal of Consulting and Clinical Psychology*, 1969, *33*, 699–704.

Carse, J. A district mental health service: the Worthing experiment. *Lancet*, 1958, *1*, 39–41.

Cashdan, S. Sensitivity groups–problems and promise. *Professional Psychology*, 1970, *1*, 217–224.

Cattell, R. B., and Warburton, F. W. *Objective personality and motivation tests.* Urbana, Ill.: University of Illinois Press, 1967.

Cautela, J. R., and Kastenbaum, R. A reinforcement survey schedule for use in therapy, training and research. *Psychological Reports*, 1967, *20*, 1115–1130.

Chambers, J. A. Relating personality and biographical factors to scientific creativity. *Psychological Monographs*, 1964, *78*, 1–20.

Chapman, L. J., and Chapman, J. P. Genesis of popular but erroneous psychodiagnostic observations. *Journal of Abnormal Psychology*, 1967, *72*, 193–204.

Chapman, L. J., and Chapman, J. P. Illusory correlation as an obstacle to the use of valid psychodiagnostic signs. *Journal of Abnormal Psychology*, 1969, *74*, 271–280.

Chartier, G. M. A-B therapist variable: real or imagined? *Psychological Bulletin,* 1971, *75*, 22–33.

Chassan, J. B. *Research design in clinical psychology and psychiatry.* New York: Appleton-Century-Crofts, 1967.

Chowdry, K., and Newcomb, T. M. The relative ability of leaders and nonleaders to estimate opinions of their own group. *Journal of Abnormal Social Psychology*, 1952, *47*, 51–57.

Clark, D. H. Response to Lakin. *American Psychologist*, 1970, *25*, 880–882.

Clark, K. E. *America's psychologists, a survey of a growing profession.* Washington, D. C.: American Psychiatric Association, 1957.

Clausen, J. A. Family structure, socialization and personality. In L. W. Hoffman and M. L. Hoffman (eds.), *Review of child development research*, Vol. 2. New York: Russell Sage Foundation, 1966, pp. 1–54.

Clinebell, H. J. (ed.). *Community mental health: the role of church and temple.* Nashville: Abingdon Press, 1970.

Cloward, R. A., and Ohlin, L. E. *Delinquency and opportunity: a theory of delinquent gangs.* New York: Free Press, 1960.

Cobb, S. Technique of interviewing a patient with psychosomatic disorder. In A. Weider (ed.), *Contributions toward medical psychology*, Vol. 1. New York: Ronald Press, 1953, pp. 225–233.

Cochrane, C. T. Effects of diagnostic information on empathic understanding by the therapist in a psychotherapy analogue. *Journal of Consulting and Clinical Psychology*, 1972, *38*, 359–365.

Cohen, H. L. Educational therapy: the design of learning environments. In J. M. Schlien (ed.), *Research in Psychotherapy*, Vol. 3. Washington, D. C.: American Psychiatric Association, 1968, pp. 21–53.

Cole, J. K., and Magnussen, M. G. Where the action is. *Journal of Consulting Psychology*, 1966, *30*, 539–543.

Cole, M., and Bruner, J. S. Cultural differences and inferences about psychological processes. *American Psychologist*, 1971, *26*, 867–876.

Collier, R. M. Independence: an overlooked implication of the open system concept. *Journal of Individual Psychology*, 1962, *18*, 103–113.

Commission on Population Growth and the American Future. *Population and the American Future.* New York: New American Library, 1972.

Constantine, L. L., Constantine, J. M., and Edelman, S. K. Counseling implications of comarital and multilateral relations. *The Family Coordinator*, 1972, *21*, 267–273.

Cook, P. E., and Josephs, P. O. The community adaptation schedule and the California Psychological Inventory: a validational study with college students. *Community Mental Health Journal*, 1970, *6*, 366–373.

Cooper, R., and Foster, M. Sociotechnical systems. *American Psychologist*, 1971, *26*, 467–474.

Costello, T. W., and Zalkind, S. S. Cities, behavioral research and community mental health. In D. Adelson and B. L. Kalis (eds.), *Community psychology and mental health.* San Francisco: Chandler, 1970, pp. 177–207.

Cowden, J. E., and Pacht, A. R. Predicting institutional and post release adjustment of delinquent boys. *Journal of Consulting Psychology*, 1967, *31*, 377–381.

Cowen, E. L., Gardner, E. A., and Zax, M. *Emergent approaches to mental health problems.* New York: Appleton-Century-Crofts, 1967.

Cox, F. M., Erlich, J. L., Rothman, J., and Tropman, J. E. (eds.). *Strategies of community organization.* Itasca, Ill.: Peacock, 1970.

Craik, K. H. Environmental psychology. In T. M. Newcomb (ed.), *New directions in psychology*, Vol. 4. New York: Holt, Rinehart and Winston, 1970, pp. 1—121.

Craik, K. H. The assessment of places. In P. McReynolds (ed.), *Advances in psychological assessment*, Vol. 2. Palo Alto, Calif.: Science & Behavior Books, 1971, pp. 40—62.

Crocetti, G. M., Spiro, H. R., Lemkau, P. V., and Siassi, I. Multiple models and mental illnesses: a rejoinder to "Failure of a moral enterprise: attitudes of the public toward mental illness" by T. R. Sarbin and J. C. Mancuso. *Journal of Consulting and Clinical Psychology*, 1972, *39*, 1—5.

Cronbach, L. J. *Essentials of psychological testing*, 2nd ed. New York: Harper & Row, 1960.

Cronbach, L. J. *Essentials of psychological testing*, 3rd ed. New York: Harper & Row, 1970.

Cronbach, L. J., and Furby, L. How should we measure change—or should we? *Psychological Bulletin*, 1970, *74*, 68—80.

Cronbach, L. J., and Gleser, G. C. *Psychological tests and personnel decisions*, 2nd ed. Urbana, Ill.: University of Illinois Press, 1965.

Cronbach, L. J., and Meehl, P. E. Construct validity in psychological tests. *Psychological Bulletin*, 1955, *52*, 281—302.

Crow, W. J. The effect of training upon accuracy and variability in interpersonal perception. *Journal of Abnormal and Social Psychology*, 1957, *55*, 355—359.

Crutchfield, R. S. The creative process. In *The creative person: Proceedings of a conference presented at the Tahoe Alumni Center, October 13—17, 1961.* Berkeley, Calif.: Institute of Personality Assessment and Research, 1961, pp. VI.1—VI.16.

Cuadra, C. A., and Albaugh, W. P. Sources of ambiguity in psychological reports. *Journal of Clinical Psychology*, 1956, *12*, 109—115.

Dahlstrom, W. G., Welsh, G. S., and Dahlstrom, L. E. *An MMPI handbook, Vol. 1, Clinical interpretation*, rev. ed. Minneapolis: University of Minnesota, 1972.

Dailey, C. A. The practical utility of the clinical report. *Journal of Consulting Psychology*, 1953, *17*, 297—302.

Dailey, C. A. *Assessment of lives.* San Francisco: Jossey-Bass, 1971.

Dallenbach, K. M. Phrenology versus psychoanalysis. *American Journal of Psychology*, 1955, *68*, 511—525.

Darbonne, A. R. Crisis: a review of theory, practice, and research. *Psychotherapy, Theory, Research and Practice*, 1967, *4*, 49—56.

Datel, W. E., and Gengerelli, J. A. Reliability of Rorschach interpretations. *Journal of Projective Techniques*, 1956, *19*, 372—381.

David, H. P. *International resources in clinical psychology.* New York: McGraw-Hill, 1964.

David, H. P. International trends in clinical psychology. In B. B. Wolman (ed.), *Handbook of clinical psychology.* New York: McGraw-Hill, 1965, pp. 1469–1506.

David, H. P. Behavioral research in population planning. *Professional Psychology,* 1970, *1,* 207–211.

Davids, A. Comparison of three methods of personality assessment: direct, indirect, and projective. *Journal of Personality,* 1955, *23,* 423–440.

Davidson, H. A psychiatric word clinic. *Mental Hospitals,* 1957, *8,* No. 9, 3–9; *8,* No. 10, 10–15; 1958, *9,* No. 1, 18–22; *9,* No. 3, 12–24.

Davidson, P. O., and Costello, C. G. (eds.). *N = 1: experimental studies of single cases.* New York: Van Nostrand Reinhold, 1969.

Davitz, J. R. (ed.). *The communication of emotional meaning.* New York: McGraw-Hill, 1964.

Dawes, R. M. A note on base rates and psychometric efficiency. *Journal of Consulting Psychology,* 1962, *26,* 422–424.

Demming, J. A., and Pressey, S. L. Tests "indigenous" to the adult and older years. *Journal of Counseling Psychology,* 1957, *4,* 144–148.

Dennis, W. *Readings in the history of psychology.* New York: Appleton-Century-Crofts, 1948.

Deutsch, C. P. After legislation—what price psychology? *American Psychologist,* 1958, *13,* 645–651.

Deutsch, M. Field theory in social psychology. In G. Lindzey and E. Aronson (eds.), *Handbook of social psychology,* Vol. 1, 2nd ed. Reading, Mass.: Addison-Wesley, 1968, pp. 412–567.

DeVos, G. A., and Hippler, A. T. Cultural psychology: comparative studies of human behavior. In G. Lindzey and E. Aronson (eds.), *Handbook of social psychology,* 2nd ed. Reading, Mass.: Addison-Wesley, 1969, pp. 323–417.

Diamond, S., Balvin, R., and Diamond, F. R. *Inhibition and choice.* New York: Harper & Row, 1963.

Dickson, W. J., and Roethlisberger, F. J. *Counseling in an organization: a sequel to the Hawthorne researches.* Boston: Division of Research, Harvard Business School, 1966.

Dittmann, A. T. Systematic psychoanalysis as research. [Review of D. M. Bullard (ed.), *Psychoanalysis and psychotherapy: selected papers of Frieda Fromm-Reichmann.* Chicago: University of Chicago Press, 1959.] *Contemporary Psychology,* 1960, *5,* 366–367.

Dollard, J., and Miller, N. E. *Personality and psychotherapy.* New York: McGraw-Hill, 1950.

Dörken, H. Utilization of psychologists in positions of responsibility in public mental health programs: a national survey. *American Psychologist,* 1970, *25,* 953–958.

Dörken, H. A dimensional strategy for community focused mental health services. In G. Rosenblum (ed.), *Issues in community psychology and preventive mental health.* New York: Behavioral Publications, 1971, pp. 75–88.

Dror, Y. Applied social science and systems analysis. In I. L. Horowitz (ed.), *The use and abuse of social science.* New Brunswick, N. J.: Transaction Books, 1971, pp. 109–132.

Drucker, P. F. *The effective executive.* New York: Harper & Row, 1967.

Drucker, P. F. *The age of discontinuity: guidelines to our changing society.* New York: Harper & Row, 1969.

Dubos, R. *So human an animal.* New York: Scribner's, 1968.

Dunnette, M. D. People feeling: joy, more joy, and the "slough of despond." *Journal of Applied Behavioral Science,* 1969, *5,* 25—44.

Dymond, R. F. Adjustment changes over therapy from self-sorts. In C. R. Rogers and R. F. Dymond (eds.), *Psychotherapy and personality change.* Chicago: University of Chicago Press, 1954, pp. 55—75.

Eddy, N. B., Halbach, H., Isbell, H., and Seevers, M. H. Drug dependence: its significance and characteristics. *Bulletin of the World Health Organization,* 1965, *32,* 721—733.

Edgerton, J. W. Evaluation in community mental health. In G. Rosenblum (ed.), *Issues in community psychology and preventive mental health.* New York: Behavioral Publications, 1971, pp. 89—108.

Ehrlich, P. R., and Ehrlich, A. H. *Population resources environment: issues in human ecology,* 2nd ed. San Francisco: W. H. Freeman, 1972.

Eisdorfer, C., Altrocci, J., and Young, R. F. The principles of community mental health in a community setting: the Halifax County program. *Community Mental Health Journal,* 1968, *4,* 211—220.

Eisenberg, L. Child psychiatry, the past quarter century. *American Journal of Orthopsychiatry,* 1969, *39,* 389—401.

Ellis, A. Neurotic interaction between marital partners. *Journal of Counseling Psychology,* 1958, *5,* 24—28.

Ellis, A. *Reason and emotion in psychotherapy.* New York: Lyle Stuart, 1962.

Ellsworth, R. B. *The MACC Behavioral Adjustment Scale* (Form II). Beverly Hills, Calif.: Western Psychological Services, 1962.

Ellsworth, R. B. *Nonprofessionals in psychiatric rehabilitation.* New York: Appleton-Century-Crofts, 1968.

Ellsworth, R. B., Foster, L., Childers, B., Arthur, G., and Kroeker, D. Hospital and community adjustment as perceived by psychiatric patients, their families, and staff. *Journal of Consulting and Clinical Psychology Monographs,* 1968, *32,* No. 5, Part 2, 1—41.

Ellsworth, R. B., Maroney, R., Klett, W., Gordon, H., and Gunn, R. Milieu characteristics of successful psychiatric treatment programs. *American Journal of Orthopsychiatry,* 1971, *41,* 427—441.

Elwood, D. L., and Griffin, H. R. Individual intelligence testing without the examiner. *Journal of Consulting and Clinical Psychology,* 1972, *38,* 9—14.

English, H. B., and English, A. C. *A comprehensive dictionary of psychological and psychoanalytical terms.* Essex, England: Longman Group, 1958.

Epstein, I. Professional role orientations and conflict strategies. *Social Work,* 1970, *15,* 87—92.

Erickson, E. H. *Childhood and society.* New York: Norton, 1950.

Erickson, E. H. *Identity and the life cycle.* New York: International Universities Press, *Psychological Issues Monograph, 1,* 1959.

Eysenck, H. J. The effects of psychotherapy: an evaluation. *Journal of Consulting Psychology,* 1952, *16,* 319—324.

Eysenck, H. J. *The effects of psychotherapy.* New York: International Science Press, 1966.

Eysenck, H. J. Behavior therapy as a scientific discipline. *Journal of Consulting and Clinical Psychology*, 1971, *36*, 314–319.

Fairweather, G. W. *Social psychology in treating mental illness.* New York: Wiley, 1964.

Fairweather, G. W. *Methods for experimental social innovation.* New York: Wiley, 1967.

Fairweather, G. W., Sanders, D. H., Cressler, D. L., and Maynard, H. *Community life for the mentally ill.* New York: Behavioral Science, 1970.

Fancher, R. E., Jr. Explicit personality theories and accuracy in person perception. *Journal of Personality*, 1966, *34*, 252–261.

Feifel, H. Attitudes toward death; a psychological perspective. *Journal of Consulting and Clinical Psychology*, 1969, *33*, 292–295.

Feigl, H. Philosophical embarrassments of psychology. *American Psychologist*, 1959, *14*, 115–128.

Feinberg, M. R. The powers and pitfalls of the clinical and industrial psychologist as an administrator. In L. Abt and B. Riess (eds.), *Progress in Clinical Psychology*, Vol. 9, *Clinical psychology in industrial organization.* New York: Grune & Stratton, 1971, pp. 106–114.

Feldman, S. Ideas and issues in community mental health. *Hospital and Community Psychiatry*, 1971, *22*, 17–21.

Feldman, S. E., and Jacobson, M. Intake policy as a community organization tool. *Community Mental Health Journal*, 1969, *5*, 76–81.

Felzer, S. B. The psychologist as an administrator in a local community mental health facility. *Professional Psychology*, 1970, *1*, 448–452.

Fenichel, O. *The psychoanalytic theory of neurosis.* New York: Norton, 1945.

Ferguson, E. A. *Social work*, 2nd. ed. Philadelphia: Lippincott, 1969.

Fiedler, F. E. A comparison of therapeutic relationships in psychoanalytic, nondirective, and Adlerian therapy. *Journal of Consulting Psychology*, 1950, *14*, 436–445. (a)

Fiedler, F. E. The concept of an ideal therapeutic relationship. *Journal of Consulting Psychology*, 1950, *14*, 239–245. (b)

Fiedler, F. E. Factor analyses of psychoanalytic, nondirective, and Adlerian therapeutic relationships. *Journal of Consulting Psychology*, 1951, *15*, 32–38.

Fish, J. M. Empathy and the reported emotional experiences of beginning psychotherapists. *Journal of Consulting and Clinical Psychology*, 1970, *35*, 64–69.

Fiske, D. W. *Measuring the concepts of personality.* Chicago: Aldine-Atherton, 1971.

Fiske, D. W., and Pearson, P. H. Theory and techniques of personality measurement. In P. H. Mussen and M. R. Rosenzweig (eds.), *Annual review of psychology.* Palo Alto, Calif.: Annual Reviews, 1970, pp. 49–86.

Flanagan, J. C. Evaluation and validation of research data in primary prevention. *American Journal of Orthopsychiatry*, 1971, *41*, 117–123.

Foa, U. G., and Turner, J. L. Psychology in the year 2000. *American Psychologist*, 1970, *25*, 244–247.

Ford, D. H., and Urban, H. B. *Systems of psychotherapy*. New York: Wiley, 1963.

Forer, B. R. The fallacy of personal validations: a classroom demonstration of gullibility. *Journal of Abnormal Social Psychology*, 1949, *44*, 118–123.

Forer, B. R. *The Forer Structured Sentence Completion Test*. Los Angeles: Western Psychological Services, 1957.

Foster, A. Writing psychological reports. *Journal of Clinical Psychology*, 1951, *7*, 195.

Foulkes, S. H., and Anthony, E. J. *Group psychotherapy: the psychoanalytic approach*, 2nd ed. Baltimore: Penguin Books, 1965.

Framo, J. L. Systematic research on family dynamics. In I. Boszormenyi-Nagy and J. Framo (eds.), *Intensive family therapy*. New York: Harper & Row, 1965, pp. 407–462.

Frankel, M. Effects of videotape modeling and self-confrontation techniques on micro-counseling behavior. *Journal of Counseling Psychology*, 1971, *18*, 465–471.

Frederiksen, N. Toward a taxonomy of situations. *American Psychologist*, 1972, *27*, 114–123.

Freud, S. *The interpretation of dreams*. New York: Macmillan, 1913.

Freud, S. *On the psychopathology of everyday life*. New York: Macmillan, 1914.

Freud, S. *New introductory lectures on psychoanalysis*. New York: Norton, 1933.

Freud, S. *Collected papers*, Vol. 3. *Case histories*. London: Hogarth, 1949. (Originally published in 1925.) (a)

Freud, S. *Outline of psychoanalysis*. New York: Norton, 1949. (b)

Freud, S. Postscript to a discussion on lay analysis. In *Collected papers*, Vol. 5. London: Hogarth, 1950, pp. 205–222. (Originally published in 1927.)

Freudenberger, H. J. Free clinics: what they are and how you start one. *Professional Psychology*, 1971, *2*, 169–173.

Furman, S. S. *Community mental health services in northern Europe*. Bethesda, Md.: National Institute of Mental Health, U. S. Department of Health, Education and Welfare, 1965.

Gardner, E. F., and Thompson, G. G. *Syracuse Scales of Social Relations*. New York: World, 1959.

Gardner, R. A. *The boys and girls book about divorce*. New York: Science House, 1970.

Garfield, S. L., Heine, R. W., and Leventhal, M. An evaluation of psychological reports in a clinical setting. *Journal of Consulting Psychology*, 1954, *18*, 281–286.

Garmezy, N. Vulnerability research and the issue of primary prevention. *American Journal of Orthopsychiatry*, 1971, *41*, 101–116.

Gauron, E. G., and Dickinson, J. K. Diagnostic decision making in psychiatry. *Archives of General Psychiatry*, 1966, *14*, 225–232.

Gendlin, E. T., Beebe, J., III, Cassens, J., Klein, M., and Oberlander, M. Focusing ability in psychotherapy, personality, and creativity. In J. M. Shlien (ed.), *Research in Psychotherapy*, Vol. 3. Washington, D. C.: American Psychological Association, 1968, pp. 217–241.

Ghiselli, E. E. The measurement of occupational aptitude. *University of California Publications in Psychology,* 1955, *8,* 100–216.

Gibb, J. R. The role of the consultant. *Journal of Social Issues,* 1959, *15,* 1–4.

Gibb, J. R. The effects of human relations training. In A. E. Bergin and S. L. Garfield (eds.), *Handbook of psychotherapy and behavior change.* New York: Wiley, 1971, pp. 839–862.

Gilberstadt, H., and Duker, J. *A handbook for clinical and actuarial MMPI interpretation.* Philadelphia: Saunders, 1965.

Glasscote, R. M., Cumming, E., Rutman, I., Sussex, J. N., and Glassman, S. M. *Rehabilitating the mentally ill in the community.* Washington, D. C.: Joint Information Service of the American Psychiatric Association and the National Association for Mental Health, 1971.

Glasscote, R. M., and Gudeman, J. E. *The staff of the mental health center.* Washington, D. C.: American Psychiatric Association, 1969.

Glasser, W. *Reality therapy, a new approach to psychiatry.* New York: Harper & Row, 1965.

Goethals, G. W., and Klos, D. S. (eds.). *Experiencing youth: first person accounts.* Boston: Little, Brown, 1970.

Goffman, E. *The presentation of self in everyday life.* Garden City, N. Y.: Doubleday, 1959.

Goffman, E. *Asylums.* Garden City, N. Y.: Doubleday, 1961.

Golann, S. E. Emerging areas of ethical concern. *American Psychologist,* 1969, *24,* 454–459.

Golann, S. E. Ethical standards for psychology: development and revision, 1938–1968. *Annals of the New York Academy of Science,* 1970, *169,* 398–405.

Golann, S. E., and Eisdorfer, C. (eds.). *The handbook of community mental health.* New York: Appleton-Century-Crofts, 1972.

Goldberg, C. Group sensitivity training. In J. Aronson (ed.), *International Journal of Psychiatry,* Vol. 9. New York: Science House, 1970, pp. 165–192.

Goldberg, L. R. The effectiveness of clinicians' judgments: the diagnosis of organic brain damage from the Bender Gestalt Test. *Journal of Consulting Psychology,* 1959, *23,* 25–33.

Goldberg, L. R. Diagnosticians versus diagnostic signs: the diagnosis of psychosis versus neurosis from the MMPI. *Psychological Monographs,* 1965, *79* (9, Whole No. 602).

Goldberg, L. R. Seer over sign: the first "good" example? *Journal of Experimental Research in Personality,* 1968, *3,* 168–171. (a)

Goldberg, L. R. Simple models or simple processes? Some research on clinical judgments. *American Psychologist,* 1968, *23,* 483–496. (b)

Goldberg, L. R. Man versus model of man: a rationale, plus some evidence, for a method of improving on clinical inferences. *Psychological Bulletin,* 1970, *73,* 422–432.

Goldberg, L. R. Five models of clinical judgment: an empirical comparison between linear and nonlinear representations of the human inference process. *Organizational Behavior and Human Performance,* 1971, *6,* 458–497.

Goldberg, L. R. Man versus mean: the exploitation of group profiles for the construction of diagnostic classification systems. *Journal of Abnormal Psychology*, 1972, *79*, 121–131.

Goldfried, M. R., and D'Zurilla, T. J. A behavioral-analytic model for assessing competence. In C. D. Spielberger (ed.), *Current topics in clinical and community psychology*, Vol. 1. New York: Academic Press, 1969, pp. 151–196.

Goldfried, M. R., and Pomeranz, D. M. Role of assessment in behavior modification. *Psychological Reports*, 1968, *23*, 75–87.

Goldfried, M. R., Stricker, G., and Weiner, I. B. *Rorschach handbook of clinical and research applications.* Englewood Cliffs, N. J.: Prentice-Hall, 1972.

Goldiamond, I. Stuttering and fluency as manipulable operant research classes. In L. Krasner and L. P. Ullman (eds.), *Research in behavior modification.* New York: Holt, Rinehart and Winston, 1966, pp. 106–156.

Golding, S. L., and Rorer, L. G. "Illusory correlation" and the learning of clinical judgment. *Journal of Abnormal Psychology*, 1972, in press.

Goldman, A. R., Bohr, R. H., and Steinberg, T. A. On posing as mental patients: reminiscences and recommendations. *Professional Psychology*, 1970, *1*, 427–436.

Goldman, L. *Using tests in counseling*, 2nd ed. New York: Appleton-Century-Crofts, 1971.

Goldschmid, M. L., Stein, D. D., Weissman, H. N., and Sorrells, J. A survey of the training and practices of clinical psychologists. *The Clinical Psychologist*, 1969, *22*, 89–94, 107.

Gomberg, W. The trouble with democratic management. *Trans-Action*, 1966, *3*, 30–35.

Goodwin, D. L., Garvey, W. P., and Barclay, J. R. Microconsultation and behavior analysis: a method of training psychologists as behavioral consultants. *Journal of Consulting and Clinical Psychology*, 1971, *37*, 355–363.

Goodwin, H., and Mudd, E. Marriage counseling: methods and goals. In B. Ard and C. Ard (eds.), *Handbook of marriage counseling.* Palo Alto, Calif.: Science & Behavior Books, 1969. pp. 93–105.

Gordon, J. E. (ed.). *Handbook of clinical and experimental hypnosis.* New York: Macmillan, 1966.

Gottschalk, L. A., and Auerbach, A. H. (eds.). *Methods of research in psychotherapy.* New York: Appleton-Century-Crofts, 1966.

Gough, H. G. *California Psychological Inventory Manual.* Palo Alto, Calif.: Consulting Psychologists Press, 1957.

Gough, H. G. Cross-cultural studies of the socialization continuum. *American Psychologist*, 1960, *15*, 410 (abstract). (a)

Gough, H. G. Theory and measurement of socialization. *Journal of Consulting Psychology*, 1960, *24*, 23–30. (b)

Gough, H. G. An interpreter's syllabus for the California Psychological Inventory. In P. McReynolds (ed.), *Advances in psychological assessment*, Vol. 1. Palo Alto, Calif.: Science & Behavior Books, 1968, pp. 55–79. (a)

Gough, H. G. *Manual for the California Psychological Inventory.* Palo Alto, Calif.: Consulting Psychologists Press, 1968. (b)

Gough, H. G. Scoring high on an index of social maturity. *Journal of Abnormal Psychology*, 1971, *77*, 236–241. (a)

Gough, H. G. Some reflections on the meaning of psychodiagnosis. *American Psychologist*, 1971, *26*, 160–167. (b)

Gough, H. G., and Sandhu, H. S. Validation of the CPI socialization scale in India. *Journal of Abnormal and Social Psychology*, 1964, *68*, 544–547.

Graham, J. R. Feedback and accuracy of clinical judgments from the MMPI. *Journal of Consulting and Clinical Psychology*, 1971, *36*, 286–291.

Graziano, A. M. Clinical innovation and the mental health power structure. *American Psychologist*, 1969, *24*, 10–18.

Greenspoon, J. The reinforcing effect of two spoken sounds on the frequency of two responses. *American Journal of Psychology*, 1955, *68*, 409–416.

Greenspoon, J., and Gersten, C. D. A new look at psychological testing: psychological testing from the standpoint of a behaviorist. *American Psychologist*, 1967, *22*, 848–853.

Gregory, C. C., and Downie, N. M. Work history of schizophrenics and alcoholics. *Rehabilitation Counseling Bulletin*, 1970, *13*, 355–363.

Grossberg, J. M. Behavior therapy: a review. *Psychological Bulletin*, 1964, *62*, 73–88.

Grosser, C., Henry, W. E., and Kelly, J. G. (eds.). *Nonprofessionals in the human services.* San Francisco: Jossey-Bass, 1969.

Group for the Advancement of Psychiatry, Committee on the Family. *The field of family therapy*, Vol. 7. (Report 78). New York: Group on the Advancement of Psychiatry, 1970.

Guerney, B., Stollak, G., and Guerney, L. The practicing psychologist as educator—an alternative to the medical practitioner model. *Professional Psychology*, 1971, *2*, 276–282.

Gurel, L. A forward looking backward glance: an overview of past, present, and projected program evaluation staff research. Proceedings of 12th Annual Conference, Veterans Administration, Denver, 1967.

Gurman, A. S. Therapists' mood patterns and therapeutic facilitativeness. *Journal of Counseling Psychology*, 1972, *19*, 169–170.

Guttentag, M., and Struening, E. L. (eds.). *Handbook of evaluation research* (in press).

Hadley, J. M. *Clinical and counseling psychology.* New York: Knopf, 1958.

Haley, J. *Strategies of psychotherapy.* New York: Grune & Stratton, 1963.

Haley, J. Family therapy. In J. Aronson (ed.), *International Journal of Psychiatry*, Vol. 9. New York: Science House, 1970, pp. 233–241.

Haley, J. *Changing families.* New York: Grune & Stratton, 1971.

Hall, C. S., and Lindzey, G. *Theories of personality*, 2nd ed. New York: Wiley, 1970.

Hall, E. T. *The hidden dimension.* New York: Doubleday, 1966.

Hall, J., and Williams, M. S. Group dynamics training and improved decision making. *Journal of Applied Behavioral Science*, 1970, *6*, 39–68.

Hall, J., and Williams, M. S. Personality and group encounter style: a multi-variate analysis of traits and preferences. *Journal of Personality and Social Psychology*, 1971, *18*, 163–172.

Hall, R. V., Lund, D., and Jackson, D. Effects of teacher attention on study behavior. *Journal of Applied Behavior Analysis*, 1968, *1*, 1–12.

Hall, W. B. Creativity: a selective annotated bibliography. *Professional Psychology*, 1971, *2*, 307–312.

Halstead, W. C. *Brain and intelligence.* Chicago: University of Chicago Press, 1947.

Hammond, K. R., and Allen, J. M. *Writing clinical reports.* Englewood Cliffs, N.J.: Prentice-Hall, 1953.

Hanvik, L. J. *Some psychological dimensions of low back pain* (unpublished doctoral dissertation, University of Minnesota). Minneapolis, Minnesota, 1949.

Hardin, G. The tragedy of the commons. *Science*, 1968, *162*, 1243–1248.

Harper, R. A. Marriage counseling as rational process-oriented psychotherapy. *Journal of Individual Psychology*, 1960, *16*, 192–207.

Harris, C. W. *Problems in measuring change.* Madison: University of Wisconsin Press, 1963.

Harris, D. B. *Children's drawings as measures of intellectual maturity: a revision and extension of the Goodenough Draw-A-Man Test.* New York: Harcourt Brace, 1963.

Harrison, R. Research on human relations training: design and interpretation. *Journal of Applied Behavioral Science*, 1971, *7*, 771–785.

Hathaway, S. R. A study of human behavior: the clinical psychologist. *American Psychologist*, 1958, *13*, 257–265.

Hathaway, S. R., and Meehl, P. E. *An atlas for the clinical use of the MMPI.* Minneapolis: University of Minnesota Press, 1951.

Hathaway, S. R., and Monachesi, E. D. (eds.). *Analyzing and predicting juvenile deliquency with the MMPI.* Minneapolis: University of Minnesota Press, 1953.

Hathaway, S. R., Reynolds, P. C., and Monachesi, E. D. Follow-up of the later careers and lives of 1,000 boys who dropped out of high school. *Journal of Consulting and Clinical Psychology*, 1969, *33*, 370–380.

Helson, R. Sex differences in creative style. *Journal of Personality*, 1967, *35*, 214–233.

Henry, W. E., Sims, J. H., and Spray, S. L. Mental health professionals in Chicago: some preliminary observations on origin and practice. In J. M. Schlien (ed.), *Research in psychotherapy*, Vol. 3. Washington, D. C.: American Psychological Association, 1968, pp. 547–572.

Henry, W. E., Sims, J. H., and Spray, S. L. *The fifth profession: becoming a psychotherapist.* San Francisco: Jossey-Bass, 1971.

Hill, E. F. *The Holtzman inkblot technique.* San Francisco: Jossey-Bass, 1972.

Hills, D. A., and Williams, J. E. Effects of test information upon self-evaluation in brief educational-vocational counseling. *Journal of Counseling Psychology*, 1965, *12*, 275–281.

Hinckley, R. G., and Hermann, L. *Group treatment in psychotherapy.* Minneapolis: University of Minnesota Press, 1951.

Hobbs, N. Science and ethical behavior. *American Psychologist*, 1959, *14*, 217–225.

Hobbs, N. Helping disturbed children: psychological and ecological strategies. *American Psychologist*, 1966, *21*, 1105–1115.

Hoch, E., Ross, A. O., and Winder, C. L. (eds.). *Professional preparation of clinical psychologists*. Washington, D. C.: American Psychological Association, 1966.

Hoffman, P. J. The paramorphic representation of clinical judgment. *Psychological Bulletin*, 1960, *57*, 116–131.

Hollingshead, A. B., and Redlich, F. C. *Social class and mental illness: a community study*. New York: Wiley, 1958

Holmes, T. H., and Rahe, R. H. The social readjustment rating scale. *Journal of Psychosomatic Research*, 1967, *11*, 213.

Holsti, O. R. Content analysis. In G. Lindzey and E. Aronson (eds.)., *Handbook of social psychology*, Vol. 2, 2nd ed. Reading, Mass.: Addison-Wesley, 1968, pp. 596–692.

Holt, R. R. Yet another look at clinical and statistical prediction: or, is clinical psychology worthwhile? *American Psychologist*, 1970, *25*, 337–349.

Holzberg, J. D., Knapp, R. H. and Turner, J. L. College students as companions to the mentally ill. In E. L. Cowen, E. A. Gardner and M. Zax (eds.). *Emergent approaches to mental health problems*. New York: Appleton-Century-Crofts, 1967. pp. 91–109.

Holtzman, W. H. The changing world of mental measurement and its social significance. *American Psychologist*, 1971, *26*, 546–553.

Hook, S. (ed.). *Psychoanalysis, scientific method, and philosophy*. New York: New York University Press, 1959.

Horowitz, I. L. (ed.). *The use and abuse of social science*. New Brunswick, N. J.: Transaction Books, 1971.

Hovey, H. B. The questionable validity of some assumed antecedents of mental illness. *Journal of Clinical Psychology*. 1959, *15*, 270–272.

Howard, K. I., and Orlinsky, D. E. Psychotherapeutic processes. In P. Mussen and M. Rosenzweig (eds.), *Annual review of psychology*, Vol. 23. Palo Alto, Calif.: Annual Reviews, 1972, pp. 615–668.

Howard, K. I., Orlinsky, D. E., and Hill, J. A. Content of dialogue in psychotherapy. *Journal of Counseling Psychology*, 1969, *16*, 396–404.

Huber, J. T. *Report writing in psychology and psychiatry*. New York: Harper & Row, 1961.

Hull, C. *Principles of behavior, an introduction to behavior theory*. New York: Appleton-Century-Crofts, 1943.

Hunt, J. M. Traditional personality theory in the light of recent evidence. *American Scientist*, 1965, *53*, 80–96.

Hunt, J. M. Graduate training: some dissents and suggestions. *The Clinical Psychologist*, 1969, *22*, 182–188.

Hurley, J. R. Parental malevolence and children's intelligence. *Journal of Consulting and Clinical Psychology*, 1967, *31*, 199–204.

Hurvitz, N. Marital problems following psychotherapy with one spouse. *Journal of Consulting Psychology*, 1967, *31*, 38–47.

Hutt, M. *The Hutt adaptation of the Bender-Gestalt Test*, 2nd ed. New York: Grune & Stratton, 1969.

Inglis, J. Psychological investigations of cognitive deficit in elderly psychiatric patients. *Psychological Bulletin*, 1958, *55*, 197–214.

Iscoe, I. and Spielberger, C. D. *Community psychology: perspectives in training and research.* New York: Appleton-Century-Crofts, 1970.

Ives, M. Psychology at Saint Elizabeth's–1907–1970. *Professional Psychology*, 1970, *1*, 155–158.

Jackson, D. D. Family rules. *Archives of General Psychiatry*, 1965, *12*, 589–594.

Jackson, D. N., and Messick, S. (eds.). *Problems in human assessment.* New York: McGraw-Hill, 1967.

Jacobson, E. *Progressive relaxation.* Chicago: University of Chicago Press, 1929.

Jahoda, M. *Current concepts of positive mental health.* New York: Basic Books, 1958.

James, W. *Principles of psychology*, Vol. 1. New York: Holt, Rinehart and Winston, 1890.

Jellinek, E. M. *The disease concept of alcoholism.* New Haven: College and University Press, 1960.

Jenkins, J. J., and Russell, W. A. Systematic changes in word association norms: 1910–1952. *Journal of Abnormal and Social Psychology*, 1960, *60*, 293–304.

Jessor, R., and Feshbach, S. (eds.). *Cognition, personality and clinical psychology: a symposium held at the University of Colorado.* San Francisco: Jossey-Bass, 1967.

Johnson, D. T., and Spielberger, C. D. The effects of relaxation training and the passage of time on measures of state-and-trait-anxiety. *Journal of Clinical Psychology*, 1968, *24*, 20–23.

Johnson, O. G., and Bommarito, J. W. *Tests and measurements in child development: a handbook.* San Francisco: Jossey-Bass, 1971.

Joint Commission on Mental Illness and Health. *Action for mental health.* New York: Basic Books, 1961.

Jones, E. *The life and work of Sigmund Freud*, Vol. 1. *1856–1900, The formative years and the great discoveries.* New York: Basic Books, 1953.

Jones, M. C. A study of the emotions of preschool children. *School and Society*, 1925, *21*, 755–758.

Jourard, S. M. *The transparent self: self-disclosure and well-being.* Princeton, N. J.: Van Nostrand, 1964.

Kadushin, P., Waxenberg, S. E., and Sager, C. J. Family Story Technique changes in interactions and effects during family therapy. *Journal of Personality Assessment*, 1971, *35*, 62–71.

Kahana, B., and Kahana, E. Changes in mental status of elderly patients in age-integrated and age-segregated hospital milieus. *Journal of Abnormal Psychology*, 1970, *75*, 177–181.

Kahn, R. L., and Cannell, C. F. *The dynamics of interviewing: theory, technique and cases.* New York: Wiley, 1957.

Kamiya, J., Barber, T. X., DiCara, L. V., Miller, N. E., Shapiro, D., and Stoyva, J. (eds.). *Biofeedback and self control.* Chicago: Aldine-Atherton, 1971.

Kanfer, F. H. Self-regulation: research, issues, and speculations. In C. Neuringer and J. L. Michael (eds.), *Behavior modification in clinical psychology*. New York: Appleton-Century-Crofts, 1970, pp. 178–220.

Kanfer, F. H., and Phillips, J. S. Behavior therapy: a panacea for all ills or a passing fancy? *Archives of General Psychiatry*, 1966, *15*, 114–128.

Kanfer, F. H., and Phillips, J. S. *Learning foundations of behavior therapy*. New York: Wiley, 1970.

Kanfer, F. H., and Saslow, G. Behavioral analysis: an alternative to diagnostic classification. *Archives of General Psychiatry*, 1965, *12*, 529–538.

Kaplan, B. (ed.). *The inner world of mental illness*. New York: Harper & Row, 1964.

Kaspar, J. C., Millichamp, J. G., Backus, R., Child, D., and Schulman, J. L. A study of the relationship between neurological evidence of brain damage in children and activity and distractibility. *Journal of Consulting and Clinical Psychology*, 1971, *36*, 329–337.

Kaspar, J. C., and Schulman, J. L. Organic mental disorders: brain damages. In B. B. Wolman (ed.), *Psychopathology of childhood*. New York: McGraw-Hill, 1971.

Kastenbaum, R., and Aisenberg, R. *The psychology of death*. New York: Springer, 1972.

Kaswan, J. W., Love, L. R., and Rodnick, E. H. Information feedback as a method of clinical intervention and consultation. In C. D. Spielberger (ed.), *Current topics in clinical and community psychology*, Vol. 3. New York: Academic Press, 1971, pp. 123–161.

Katz, D., and Kahn, R. L. *The social psychology of organizations*. New York: Wiley, 1966.

Kauffman, J. M. Validity of the Family Relations Test. *Journal of Projective Techniques and Personality Assessment*, 1970, *34*, 186–189.

Kauffman, J. M. Family Relations Test responses of disturbed and normal boys: additional comparative data. *Journal of Personality Assessment*, 1971, *35*, 128–138.

Kavanaugh, J. The new salvationists. *Playboy*, 1971, *18*, 131–132, 134, 146, 148, 150.

Keehn, J. D. Reinforcement of alcoholism: schedule control of solitary drinking. *Quarterly Journal of Studies on Alcohol*, 1970, *31*, 28–39.

Kelly, E. L. Clinical psychology—1960: a report of survey findings. *Newsletter, Division of Clinical Psychology of the APA*, 1961, *14* (Winter issue), 1–11.

Kelly, E. L., and Fiske, D. W. *The prediction of performance in clinical psychology*. Ann Arbor, Mich.: University of Michigan Press, 1951.

Kelly, E. L., and Goldberg, L. R. Correlates of later performance and specialization in psychology, follow-up study of the trainees assessed in the VA Selection Research Project. *Psychological Monographs*, 1959, *73*, No. 12 (Whole No. 482).

Kelly, G. A. *The psychology of personal constructs*, Vol. 1. *A theory of personality*, Vol. 2. *Clinical diagnosis and therapy*. New York: Norton, 1955.

Kelly, J. G. Antidotes for arrogance: training for community psychology. *American Psychologist*, 1970, *25*, 524–531. (a)

Kelly, J. G. The quest for valid preventive interventions. In C. D. Spielberger (ed.). *Current topics in clinical and community psychology*, Vol. 2. New York: Academic Press, 1970, pp. 183–207. (b)

Kelly, J. G. Qualities for the community psychologist. *American Psychologist*, 1971, *26*, 897–903.

Keniston, K. How community mental health stamped out the riots (1968–78). *Trans-Action*, 1968, *5*, 21–30.

Key, W. H. Urban renewal and the problems of community involvement. In M. F. Shore and F. V. Mannino (eds.), *Mental health and the community: problems, programs and strategies*. New York: Behavioral Publications, 1969, pp. 23–40.

Kiesler, F. More than psychiatry: a rural program. In M. F. Shore and F. V. Mannino (eds.), *Mental health and the community: problems, programs and strategies*. New York: Behavioral Publications, 1969, pp. 103–122.

Kittrie, N. N. *The right to be different: deviance and enforced therapy*. Baltimore: Johns Hopkins University Press, 1971.

Klein, D. C. *Community dynamics and mental health*. New York: Wiley, 1968.

Klein, D. F., and Davis, J. M. *Diagnosis and drug treatment of psychiatric disorders*. Baltimore: Williams & Wilkins, 1969.

Kleinmuntz, B. *Personality measurement*. Homewood, Ill.: Dorsey Press, 1967.

Klett, C. J., and Pumroy, D. K. Automated procedures for psychological assessment. In P. McReynolds (ed.), *Advances in psychological assessment*, Vol. 2. Palo Alto, Calif.: Science & Behavior Books, 1971, pp. 14–39.

Klopfer, W. G. *The psychological report: use and communication of psychological findings*. New York: Grune & Stratton, 1960.

Klopfer, W. G. The blind leading the blind: psychotherapy without assessment. *Journal of Projective Techniques and Personality Assessment*, 1964, *28*, 387–392.

Kluckhohn, C., and Murray, H. A. Personality formation: the determinants. In C. Kluckhohn, H. A. Murray, and D. M. Schneider (eds.), *Personality in nature, society and culture*, 2nd ed. New York: Knopf, 1955, pp. 53–67.

Knapp, D. L., and Schafer, W. E. *Social science and public policy*. Eugene, Ore.: Wallace School of Community Service and Public Affairs, 1970.

Koch, S. (ed.). *Psychology, a study of a science*, Vols. 3, 5. New York: McGraw-Hill, 1959 (Vol. 3), 1963 (Vol. 5).

Koch, S. The image of man implicit in encounter group therapy. *Journal of Humanistic Psychology*, 1971, *11*, 109–128.

Koester, G. A. A study of the diagnostic process. *Education of Psychological Measurements*, 1954, *14*, 473–486.

Koontz, H., and O'Donnell, C. *Principles of management: an analysis of managerial functions*, 5th ed. New York: McGraw-Hill, 1972.

Korsch, B. M., and Negrete, V. F. Doctor-patient communication. *Scientific American*, 1972, *227*, 66–74.

Kostlan, A. A method for the empirical study of psychodiagnosis. *Journal of Consulting Psychology*, 1954, *18*, 83–88.

Krasner, L., and Ullman, L. P. (eds.). *Research in behavior modification.* New York: Holt, Rinehart and Winston, 1966.

Krauss, H. H., and Tesser, A. Social contexts of suicide. *Journal of Abnormal Psychology*, 1971, *78*, 222–228.

Kriedt, P. H. Vocational interests of psychologists. *Journal of Applied Psychology*, 1949, *33*, 482–488.

Kubler-Ross, E. *On death and dying.* New York: Macmillan, 1969.

Kulik, J. A., Stein, K. B., and Sarbin, T. R. Dimensions and patterns of adolescent antisocial behavior. *Journal of Consulting and Clinical Psychology*, 1968, *32*, 375–382.

Ladd, C. E. Record-keeping and research in psychiatric and psychological clinics. *Journal of Counseling Psychology*, 1967, *14*, 361–367.

Lakin, M. Some ethical issues in sensitivity training. *American Psychologist*, 1969, *24*, 923–928.

Langsley, D. G , and Kaplan, D. M. *The treatment of families in crisis.* New York: Grune & Stratton, 1968.

Lanyon, R. I. Mental health technology. *American Psychologist*, 1971, *26*, 1071–1076.

Lanyon, R. I. Technological approach to the improvement of decision making in mental health services. *Journal of Consulting and Clinical Psychology*, 1972, *39*, 43–98.

LaPointe, F. H. Origin and evolution of the term "psychology." *American Psychologist*, 1970, *25*, 640–646.

Lazarus, A. A. *Behavior therapy and beyond.* New York: McGraw-Hill, 1971.

Leary, T. *The interpersonal diagnosis of personality.* New York: Ronald Press, 1957.

Lederer, W. J., and Jackson, D. D. *The mirages of marriage.* New York: Norton, 1968.

Ledvinka, J. Race of interviewer and the language elaboration of black interviewees. *Journal of Social Issues*, 1971, *27*, 185–197.

Leeper, R. W. *Lewin's topological and vector psychology: a digest and a critique.* Eugene, Ore.: University of Oregon Press, 1943.

Lehman, H. C. The age decrement in outstanding scientific creativity. *American Psychologist*, 1960, *15*, 128–134.

Leifer, R. The medical model as ideology. *International Journal of Psychiatry*, 1970, *9*, 13–21.

Leighton, A. H. *My name is legion: foundations for a theory of man in relation to culture.* New York: Basic Books, 1959.

Leighton, D. C., Leighton, A. H., and Armstrong, R. A. Community psychiatry in a rural area: a social psychiatric approach. In L. Bellak (ed.), *Handbook of community psychiatry.* New York: Grune & Stratton, 1964, pp. 166–176.

Lemkau, P. V. The planning project for Columbia. In M. F. Shore and F. V. Mannino (eds.), *Mental health and the community: problems, programs and strategies.* New York: Behavioral Publications, 1969, pp. 193–204.

Lennard, H. L., and Bernstein, A. *Patterns in human interaction: an introduction to clinical sociology.* San Francisco: Jossey-Bass, 1969.

Lennard, H. L., and Bernstein, A. Dilemma in mental health program evaluation. *American Psychologist*, 1971, *26*, 307–310.

Lennard, H. L., Epstein, L. J., Bernstein, A., and Ransom, D. C. *Mystification and drug misuse*. San Francisco: Jossey-Bass, 1971.

Lentz, R. J., Paul, G. L., and Calhoun, J. F., Reliability of three measures of functioning with "hard core" chronic mental patients, *Journal of Abnormal Psychology*, 1971, *78*, 69–76.

Lester, D. Attempts to predict suicidal risk using psychological tests. *Psychological Bulletin*, 1970, *74*, 1–17.

Levine, D. Why and when to test: the social context of psychological testing. In A. I. Rabin (ed.), *Projective techniques in personality assessment: a modern introduction*. New York: Springer, 1968, pp. 553–580.

Levine, M., and Levine, A. *A social history of helping services*. New York: Appleton-Century-Crofts, 1970.

Levinson, H. The clinical psychologist as organizational diagnostician. *Professional Psychology*, 1972, *3*, 34–40.

Levy, L. H. The skew in clinical psychology. *American Psychologist*, 1962, *17*, 244–249.

Levy, L. H. *Psychological interpretation*. New York: Holt, Rinehart and Winston, 1963.

Levy, L. H., and Orr, T. B. The social psychology of Rorschach validity research. *Journal of Abnormal and Social Psychology*, 1959, *58*, 79–83.

Levy, M. R. Issues in the personality assessment of lower class patients. *Journal of Projective Techniques and Personality Assessment*, 1970, *34*, 6–9.

Lewin, K. Forces behind food habits and methods of change. *Bulletin of the National Research Council*, 1943, *108*, 35–65. (Reprinted in K. Lewin, *Field theory in social science*. New York: Harper & Row, 1951.)

Lewinsohn, P. M., and Libet, J. Pleasant events, activity schedules, and depressions. *Journal of Abnormal and Social Psychology*, 1972, *79*, 291–295.

Lewinsohn, P. M., and Pearlman, S. Continuing education for psychologists. *Professional Psychology*, 1972, *3*, 48–52.

Lewis, W. W. Project Re-ED: Educational intervention in discordant child rearing systems. In E. L. Cowen, E. A. Gardner, and M. Zax (eds.), *Emergent approaches to mental health problems*. New York: Appleton-Century-Crofts, 1967, pp. 352–368.

Lindemann, E. Symptomatology and management of acute grief. *American Journal of Psychiatry*, 1944, *101*, 141–148.

Linder, S. B. *The harried leisure class*. New York: Columbia University Press, 1970.

Lindzey, G., Loehlin, J., Manosevitz, M., and Thiessen, O. Behavioral genetics. In P. Mussen and M. Rosenzweig (eds.), *Annual review of psychology*, Vol. 22. Palo Alto, Calif.: Annual Reviews, 1971, pp. 39–94.

Lippitt, R., Watson, J., and Westley, B. *The dynamics of planned change*. New York: Harcourt Brace, 1958.

Litman, R. E. Suicide prevention: evaluating effectiveness. *Life-Threatening Behavior*, 1971, *1*, 155–162.

Little, K. B. Problems in the validation of projective techniques, *Journal of Projective Techniques*, 1959, *23*, 287–290.

Little, K. B. Epilogue: academic marketplace, 1984. *American Psychologist*, 1972, *27*, 504–506.

Little, K. B., and Shneidman, E. S. Congruencies among interpretations of psychological test and anamnestic data. *Psychological Monographs*, 1959, *73*, No. 6 (Whole No. 476).

Loevinger, J., and Wessler, R. *Measuring ego development*, Vol. 1, *Construction and use of a sentence-completion test*. San Francisco, Jossey-Bass, 1970.

Loevinger, J., Wessler, R., and Redmore, C. *Measuring ego development*, Vol. 2, *Scoring manual for women and girls*. San Francisco: Jossey-Bass, 1970.

Lofquist, L. H., and Davis, R. V. *Adjustment to work: a psychological view of man's problems in a work-oriented society*. New York: Appleton-Century-Crofts, 1969.

Lorei, T. W., and Gurel, L. Use of a biographical inventory to predict schizophrenics' posthospital employment and readmission. *Journal of Consulting and Clinical Psychology*, 1972, *38*, 238–243.

Lorsch, J. W., and Lawrence, P. R. *Studies in organizational design*. Homewood, Ill.: Dorsey Press, 1970.

Louttit, C. M. Publication trends in psychology: 1894–1954. *American Psychologist*, 1957, *12*, 14–21.

Lovaas, O. I. Some studies on the treatment of childhood schizophrenia. In J. M. Shlien (ed.), *Research in psychotherapy*, Vol. 3. Washington, D. C.: American Psychological Association, 1968, pp. 103–121.

Lubin, B., and Levitt, E. E. (eds.). *The clinical psychologist*. Chicago: Aldine-Atherton, 1967.

Lubin, B., Wallis, R. R., and Paine, C. Patterns of psychological test usage in the United States: 1935–1969. *Professional Psychology*, 1971, *2*, 70–74.

Luborsky, L., Chandler, M., Auerbach, A. H., Cohen, J., and Bachrach, H. M. Factors influencing the outcome of psychotherapy: a review of quantitative research. *Psychological Bulletin*, 1971, *75*, 145–185.

Lundberg, F. *The coming world transformation*. Garden City, N. Y.: Doubleday, 1963.

Luria, A. R. *Higher cortical functions in man*. New York: Basic Books, 1966.

Lyden, F. J., and Miller, E. G. (eds.) *Planning-programming-budgeting: a systems approach to management*, 2nd ed. Chicago: Markham, 1972.

Lyerly, S. B. and Abbott, P. S. *Handbook of Psychiatric Rating Scales, 1950–1964*, PHS Pub. # 1495, Washington, D. C.: Government Printing Office, 1966.

MacCorquodale, K., and Meehl, P. E. On a distinction between hypothetical constructs and intervening variables. *Psychological Review*, 1948, *55*, 95–107.

Macht, L. B., Scherl, D. J., and English, J. T. Not as a patient: psychological development in a job training program. *American Journal of Orthopsychiatry*, 1970, *40*, 142–150.

MacKinnon, D. W. The nature and nurture of creative talent. *American Psychologist*, 1962, *17*, 484–495.

MacKinnon, D. W. Personality and the realization of creative potential. *American Psychologist*, 1965, *20*, 273–281.

Mackler, B. Black on white or white on black: Harlem and white professionals. *Professional Psychology*, 1971, *2*, 247–250.

MacLennon, B. W. New careers: Program development and the process of institutional change. In M. F. Shore and F. V. Mannino (eds.), *Mental health and the community: problems, programs and strategies*. New York: Behavioral Publications, 1969, pp. 179–192.

Macleod, R. K. Program budgeting works in nonprofit institutions. *Harvard Business Review*, 1971, *49*, 46–56.

Madison, P. *Freud's concept of repression and defense, its theoretical and observational language*. Minneapolis: University of Minnesota Press, 1961.

Madison, P. *Personality development in college*. Reading, Mass.: Addison-Wesley, 1969.

Mahrer, A. R. (ed.). *New approaches to personality classification*. New York: Columbia University Press, 1970.

Makita, K. The rarity of reading disability in Japanese children. *American Journal of Orthopsychiatry*, 1968, *38*, 599–614.

Manis, J. G., and Melzer, B. N. (eds.) *Symbolic interaction: a reader in social psychology*. Boston: Allyn and Bacon, 1967.

Mannheim, K. *Ideology and utopia: an introduction to the sociology of knowledge*. New York: Harcourt Brace, 1936.

Manning, H. M. Programmed interpretation of the MMPI. *Journal of Personality Assessment*, 1971, *35*, 162–176.

Manson, M. P., and Lerner, A. *The marriage adjustment sentence completion survey*. Beverly Hills, Calif.: Western Psychological Services, 1962.

March, J. G. (ed.). *Handbook of organizations*. Chicago: Rand McNally, 1965.

Mariner, A. S. A critical look at professional education in the mental health field. *American Psychologist*, 1967, *22*, 271–281.

Marks, P. A., and Seeman, W. *The actuarial description of personality: an atlas for use with the MMPI*. Baltimore: Williams & Wilkins, 1963.

Martorano, R. D., and Nathan, P. E. Syndromes of psychosis and nonpsychosis: the factor analysis of a systems analysis. *Journal of Abnormal Psychology*, 1972 (in press).

Masling, J. The influence of situational and interpersonal variables in projective testing. *Psychological Bulletin*, 1960, *57*, 65–85.

Masling, J. Role-related behavior of the subject and psychologist and its effect upon psychological data. In D. Levine (ed.), *Nebraska symposium on motivation, 1966*. Lincoln, Nebr.: University of Nebraska Press, 1966, pp. 67–103.

Maslow, A. H. *Motivation and personality*. New York: Harper & Row, 1954.

Maslow, A. H. *Toward a psychology of being*, 2nd ed. New York: Van Nostrand Reinhold, 1968.

Maslow, A. H. *The farther reaches of human nature*. New York: Viking Press, 1971.

Massimo, J. L., and Shore, M. F. The effectiveness of a comprehensive, vocationally oriented psychotherapeutic program for adolescent delinquent boys. *American Journal of Orthopsychiatry*, 1963, *33*, 634–642.

Massimo, J. L., and Shore, M. F. Comprehensive vocationally-oriented psychotherapy for adolescent delinquent boys: a follow-up study. *American Journal of Orthopsychiatry*, 1966, *36*, 609–615.

Masters, W. H., and Johnson, V. *Human sexual inadequacy*. Boston: Little, Brown, 1970.

Matarazzo, J. D. The interview. In B. B. Wolman (ed.), *Handbook of clinical psychology*. New York: McGraw-Hill, 1965, pp. 403–450. (a)

Matarazzo, J. D. Some national developments in the utilization of nontraditional mental health manpower. *American Psychologist*, 1971, *26*, 363–372.

Matarazzo, J. D. A postdoctoral residency program in clinical psychology. *American Psychologist*, 1965, *20*, 432–439. (b)

Matarazzo, J. D. *Wechsler's measurement and appraisal of adult intelligence*, 5th ed. Baltimore: Williams & Wilkins, 1972.

Matarazzo, J. D., and Wiens, A. N. *The interview: research on its anatomy and structure*. Chicago: Aldine-Atherton, 1972.

May, P. R. A. *Treatment of schizophrenia: a comparative study of five treatment methods*. New York: Science House, 1968.

May, R. *Love and will*. New York: Norton, 1969.

McClelland, D. C. Opinions predict opinions: so what else is new? *Journal of Consulting and Clinical Psychology*, 1972, *38*, 325–326.

McClelland, J. N., and Rhodes, F. Prediction of job success for hospital aides and orderlies from MMPI scores and personal history data. *Journal of Applied Psychology*, 1969, *53*, 49–54.

McClelland, W. *Selection for secondary education*. London: University of London Press, 1942.

McNair, D. M., Callahan, D. M., and Lorr, M., Therapist "type" and patient response to psychotherapy. *Journal of Consulting Psychology*, 1962, *26*, 425–429.

McReynolds, P. (ed.). *Advances in psychological assessment*. Vol. 1. Palo Alto, Calif.: Science & Behavior Books, 1968.

McReynolds, P. (ed.). *Advances in psychological assessment*. Vol. 2. Palo Alto, Calif.: Science & Behavior Books, 1971.

Mechanic, D. *Mental health and social policy*. Englewood Cliffs, N. J.: Prentice-Hall, 1969.

Meehl, P. E. *Clinical versus statistical prediction*. Minneapolis: University of Minnesota Press, 1954.

Meehl, P. E. Wanted—a good cookbook. *American Psychologist*, 1956, *11*, 263–272.

Meehl, P. E. A comparison of clinicians with five statistical methods of identifying psychotic MMPI profiles. *Journal of Counseling Psychology*, 1959, *6*, 102–109. (a)

Meehl, P. E. Some ruminations of the validation of clinical procedures. *Canadian Journal of Psychology*, 1959, *13*, 102–128. (b)

Meehl, P. E. The cognitive activity of the clinician. *American Psychologist*, 1960, *15*, 19–27.

Meehl, P. E. Specific genetic etiology, psychodynamics, and therapeutic nihilism. *International Journal of Mental Health*, 1972, *1*, 10–27.

Meehl, P. E., and Rosen, A. Antecedent probability and the efficiency of psychometric signs, patterns, or cutting scores. *Psychological Bulletin*, 1955, *52*, 194–216.

Megargee, E. I. (ed.) *Research in clinical assessment.* New York: Harper & Row, 1966.

Megargee, E. I. *The California Psychological Inventory handbook.* San Francisco: Jossey-Bass, 1972.

Meier, R. L. *A communications theory of urban growth.* Cambridge, Mass.: MIT Press, 1962.

Meltzoff, J., & Kornreich, M. *Research in psychotherapy.* Chicago: Aldine-Atherton, 1970.

Menninger, K. A. *A manual for psychiatric case study.* New York: Grune & Stratton, 1952.

Menninger, K., Mayman, M., and Pruyser, P. *The vital balance: the life process in mental health and illness.* New York: Viking Press, 1963.

Mensh, I. N. *Clinical psychology, science and profession.* New York: Macmillan, 1966.

Meyer, P. R. Counseling and adjustment after long mental illness. *Journal of Counseling Psychology*, 1960, *7*, 275–277.

Meyer, V. The treatment of phobic patients on the basis of learning principles. *Journal of Abnormal and Social Psychology*, 1957, *55*, 261–266.

Michael, D. N. *The unprepared society: planning for a precarious future.* New York: Basic Books, 1968.

Milgram, S. The experience of living in cities. *Science*, 1970, *167*, 1461–1468.

Miller, G. A. Psychology as a means of promoting human welfare. *American Psychologist*, 1969, *24*, 1063–1075.

Miller, G. A. Assessment of psychotechnology. *American Psychologist*, 1970, *25*, 991–1001.

Miller, G. A., Galanter, E., and Pribram, K. H. *Plans and the structure of behavior.* New York: Holt, Rinehart and Winston, 1960.

Miller, J. G. The nature of living systems. *Behavioral Science*, 1971, *16*, 277–301.

Miller, L. C. School behavior checklist: an inventory of deviant behavior for elementary school children, *Journal of Consulting and Clinical Psychology*, 1972, *38*, 134–144.

Miller, N. E. Learning of visceral and glandular responses. *Science*, 1969, *163*, 434–445.

Mills, C. W. The professional ideology of social pathologists. *American Journal of Sociology*, 1943, *49*, 165–180.

Mintz, J. Survey of student therapists' attitudes toward psychodiagnostic reports. *Journal of Consulting and Clinical Psychology*, 1968, *32*, 500.

Mintz, J., Luborsky, L., and Auerbach, A. H. Dimensions of psychotherapy: a factor-analytic study of ratings of psychotherapy sessions. *Journal of Consulting and Clinical Psychology*, 1971, *36*, 106–120.

Minuchin, S., Montalvo, B., Guerney, B. G., Jr., Rosman, B. L., and Schumer, F. *Families of the slums: an exploration of their structure and treatment.* New York: Basic Books, 1967.

Mischel, W. *Personality and assessment.* New York: Wiley, 1968.

Mischel, W. Direct versus indirect personality assessment: evidence and implications. *Journal of Consulting and Clinical Psychology,* 1972, *38,* 319–324.

Mitchell, K. M., and Namenek, T. M. A comparison of therapist and client social class. *Professional Psychology,* 1970, *1,* 225–230.

Mitchell, K. R. Repeated measures and the evaluation of change in the individual client during counseling. *Journal of Counseling Psychology,* 1969, *16,* 522–527.

Mittler, P. (ed.) *The psychological assessment of mental and physical handicaps.* New York: Barnes & Noble, 1970.

Mizushima, K., and DeVos, G. An application of the California Psychological Inventory in a study of Japanese delinquency. *Journal of Social Psychology,* 1967, *71,* 45–51.

Molish, H. B. Projective methodologies. In P. H. Mussen and M. R. Rosenzweig (eds.), *Annual review of psychology.* Palo Alto, Calif.: Annual Reviews, 1972, pp. 577–614.

Money, J. Sex reassignment. In J. Aronson (ed.), *International Journal of Psychiatry.* Vol. 9. New York: Science House, 1970.

Moore, G. H., Bobbitt, W. E., and Wildman, R. W. Psychiatric impressions of psychological reports. *Journal of Clinical Psychology,* 1968, *24,* 373–376.

Moore, W. E. (in collaboration with G. W. Rosenblum). *The professions: roles and rules.* New York: Russell Sage Foundation, 1970.

Moos, R. Assessment of the psychosocial environments of community-oriented psychiatric treatment programs. *Journal of Abnormal Psychology,* 1972, *79,* 9–18.

Mordock, J. B. Urban renewal agencies: guidelines for mental health consultation. *Professional Psychology,* 1971, *2,* 155–158.

Moreno, J. L. Psychodrama. In S. Arieti (ed.), *American handbook of psychiatry.* Vol. 2. New York: Basic Books, 1959.

Morgan, H., and Cogger, J. *The interviewer's manual.* New York: Psychological Corporation, 1972.

Mowrer, O. H. (ed.). *Morality and mental health.* Chicago: Rand McNally, 1967. (a)

Mowrer, O. H. A revolution in integrity. *Voices,* 1967, *3,* 26–33. (b)

Murphy, G. Psychology in the year 2000. *American Psychologist,* 1969, *24,* 523–530.

Murphy, G., and Murphy, L. B. (eds.) *Asian psychology.* New York: Basic Books, 1968.

Murstein, B. I. *Theory and research in projective techniques: emphasizing the TAT.* New York: Wiley, 1963.

Murstein, B. I. (ed.) *Handbook of projective techniques.* New York: Basic Books, 1965.

Murstein, B. I. Normative written TAT responses for a college sample. *Journal of Personality Assessment,* 1972, *36,* 109–147.

Myrdal, G. *The political element in the development of economic theory.* Cambridge, Mass.: Harvard University Press, 1965.

Nathan, P. E. *Cues, decisions and diagnoses.* New York: Academic Press, 1967.

Nathan, P. E., Samaraweera, A., Ausberg, M. M., and Patch, V. D. Syndromes of psychosis and psychoneurosis. *Archives of General Psychiatry*, 1968, *19*, 704–716.

Neuringer, C., and Michael, J. L. (eds.). *Behavior modification in clinical psychology.* New York: Appleton-Century-Crofts, 1970.

Nottingham, J. A. Where's the fence?–the psychologist's limits of community. *Professional Psychology*, 1970, *1*, 477–481.

O'Dell, J. W. P. T. Barnum explores the computer. *Journal of Consulting and Clinical Psychology*, 1972, *38*, 270–273.

Odiorne, G. *Management by objectives.* Englewood Cliffs, N. J.: Prentice-Hall, 1969.

Office of Strategic Services Staff. *Assessment of men.* New York: Holt, Rinehart and Winston, 1948.

Olson, D. H. Marital and family therapy: integrative review and critique. *Journal of Marriage and the Family*, 1970, *32*, 501–538.

Olson, D. H., and Straus, M. A. A diagnostic tool for marital and family therapy: the SIMFAM technique. *The Family Coordinator*, 1972, *21*, 251–258.

Osgood, C. E., and Luria, Z. A blind analysis of a case of multiple personality using the Semantic Differential. *Journal of Abnormal and Social Psychology*, 1954, *49*, 579–591.

Osgood, C. E., Suci, G. J., and Tannenbaum, P. H. *The measurement of meaning.* Urbana, Ill.: University of Illinois Press, 1957.

Ossorio, A. G., and Fine, L. Psychodrama as a catalyst for social change in a mental hospital. In J. H. Masserman and J. L. Moreno (eds.), *Progress in psychotherapy*, Vol. 5, *Review and integrations.* New York: Grune & Stratton, 1960.

Overall, J. E. Associations between marital history and the nature of manifest psychopathology. *Journal of Abnormal Psychology*, 1971, *78*, 213–221.

Pallone, N. J., Rickard, F. S., and Hurley, R. B. Key influencers of occupational preference among black youth. *Journal of Counseling Psychology*, 1970, *17*, 498–501.

Palmer, J. O. *The psychological assessment of children.* New York: Wiley, 1970.

Pandey, R. E. Psychology in India. *American Psychologist*, 1969, *24*, 936–939.

Parker, C. A. As a clinician thinks . . . . *Journal of Counseling Psychology*, 1958, *5*, 253–261.

Parsons, F. *Choosing a vocation.* Boston: Houghton Mifflin, 1906.

Parsons, O. A. Clinical neuropsychology. In C. D. Spielberger (ed.), *Current topics in clinical and community psychology.* Vol. 2. New York: Academic Press, 1970, pp. 1–60.

Pasamanick, G., Scarpitti, F. R., and Dinitz, S. *Schizophrenics in the community: an experimental study in the prevention of hospitalization.* New York: Appleton-Century-Crofts, 1967.

Pascal, G. R. Psychological deficit as a function of stress and constitution. *Journal of Personality*, 1951, *20*, 175–187.

Pascal, G. R., and Suttell, B. J. *The Bender-Gestalt Test: quantification and validity for adults.* New York: Grune & Stratton, 1951.

Patterson, G. R. *Families: applications of social learning to family life.* Champaign, Ill.: Research Press, 1971.

Patterson, G. R., Cobb, J. A., and Ray, R. S. A social engineering technology for retraining the families of aggressive boys. In H. E. Adams and I. P. Unikel (eds.), *Issues and trends in behavior therapy.* Springfield, Ill.: Charles C Thomas, 1972, in press.

Patterson, G. R., and Gullion, M. E. *Living with children: new methods for parents and teachers,* rev. ed. Champaign, Ill.: Research Press, 1971.

Patterson, G. R., McNeal, S. Hawkins, N., and Phelps, R. Reprogramming the social environment. *Journal of Child Psychology and Psychiatry,* 1967, *8,* 181–195.

Patterson, G. R., Ray, R. S., and Shaw, D. A. Direct intervention in families of deviant children. *Oregon Research Institute Research Bulletin,* 1968, *8,* 9.

Patterson, G. R., and Reid, J. B. Reciprocity and coercion: two facets of social systems. In C. Neuringer and J. L. Michael (eds.), *Behavior modification in clinical psychology.* New York: Appleton-Century-Crofts, 1970, Chap. 7.

Paul, G. L. *Insight versus desensitization in psychotherapy: an experiment in anxiety reduction.* Stanford: Stanford University Press, 1966.

Paul, G. L. Insight versus desensitization in psychotherapy two years after termination. *Journal of Consulting Psychology,* 1967, *31,* 333–348.

Peak, H. Problems of objective observation. In L. Festinger and D. Katz (eds.), *Research methods in the behavioral sciences.* New York: Holt, Rinehart and Winston, 1953.

Pearl, A., and Riessman, F. *New careers for the poor.* New York: Free Press, 1965.

Pearson, J. S., Rome, H. P., Swenson, W. M., Mataya, P., and Brannick, T. L. Development of a computer system for scoring and interpretation of Minnesota Multiphasic Personality Inventories in a medical clinic. *Annals of the New York Academy of Sciences,* 1965, *126,* 684–695.

Pearson, J. S., and Swenson, W. M. *User's guide to the Mayo Clinic automated MMPI program.* New York: Psychological Corporation, 1967.

Perls, F. S. *Gestalt therapy verbatim.* Lafayette, Calif.: Real People Press, 1969.

Perls, F. S., Hefferline, R. E., and Goodman, P. *Gestalt therapy: excitement and growth in the human personality.* New York: Dell, 1965 (originally published in 1951).

Persons, R. W., and Marks, P. A. Self-disclosure with recidivists: optimum interviewer-interviewee matching. *Journal of Abnormal Psychology,* 1970, *76,* 387–391.

Peskin, H. Multiple prediction of adult psychological health from preadolescent and adolescent behavior. *Journal of Consulting and Clinical Psychology,* 1972, *38,* 155–160.

Peterson, D. R. Behavior problems of middle childhood. *Journal of Consulting Psychology,* 1961, *25,* 205–209.

Peterson, D. R. *The clinical study of social behavior.* New York: Appleton-Century-Crofts, 1968. (a)

Peterson, D. R. The Doctor of Psychology program at the University of Illinois. *American Psychologist,* 1968, *23,* 511–516. (b)

Peterson, D. R. Attitudes concerning the Doctor of Psychology Program. *Professional Psychology*, 1969, *1*, 44–47.

Peterson, D. R. Status of the Doctor of Psychology Program, 1970. *Professional Psychology*, 1971, *2*, 271–275.

Phares, E. J. and Campbell, J. P. Sensitivity training in industry: issues and research. In L. E. Abt and B. F. Riess (eds.), *Progress in clinical psychology*, Vol. 9, *Clinical psychology in industrial organization*. New York: Grune & Stratton, 1971, pp. 176–190.

Phillips, L. *Human adaptation and its failures.* New York: Academic Press, 1968.

Phillips, L., and Draguns, J. G. Classification of the behavior disorders. In P. H. Mussen and M. R. Rosenzweig (eds.), *Annual review of psychology*, Vol. 22. Palo Alto, Calif.: Annual Reviews, 1971, pp. 447–482.

Pittenger, R. E., Hockett, C. F., and Danehy, J. J. *The first five minutes, a sample of microscopic interview analysis.* Ithaca, N. Y.: Paul Martineau, 1960.

Platt, J. R. *The excitement of science.* Boston: Houghton Mifflin, 1962.

Platt, J. R. What's ahead for 1990. *The Center Magazine*, 1972, *5*, 21–28.

Pohlman, E. *The psychology of birth planning.* Cambridge, Mass.: Schenkman, 1969.

Pope, B., and Scott, W. H. *Psychological diagnosis in clinical practice.* New York: Oxford University Press, 1967.

Portes, A. Behavior therapy and critical speculation. *Journal of Consulting and Clinical Psychology*, 1971, *36*, 320–324. (a)

Portes, A. On the emergence of behavior therapy in modern society. *Journal of Consulting and Clinical Psychology*, 1971, *36*, 303–313. (b)

Pottharst, K. E. To renew vitality and provide a challenge in training—The California School of Professional Psychology. *Professional Psychology*, 1970, *1*, 123–130.

Pratt, S. Gurus or Gurkhas. *Contemporary Psychology*, 1971, *16*, 453–454.

Premack, D. Reinforcement theory. In D. Levine (ed.), *Nebraska symposium on motivation.* Lincoln, Nebr.: University of Nebraska Press, 1965, pp. 123–180.

Pressey, S. L. Toward earlier creativity in psychology. *American Psychologist*, 1960, *15*, 124–127.

Proshansky, H. M. For what are we training our graduate students? *American Psychologist*, 1972, *27*, 205–212.

Proshansky, H. M., Ittelson, W. H., and Rivlin, L. G. (eds.) *Environmental psychology.* New York: Holt, Rinehart and Winston, 1970.

Psychological Corporation. *Test Service Bulletin*, No. 56. New York: Psychological Corporation, 1966.

Quay, H. C. Personality patterns in pre-adolescent delinquent boys. *Educational and Psychological Measurement*, 1966, *26*, 99–110.

Rabin, A. I. *Projective techniques in personality assessment: a modern introduction.* New York: Springer, 1968.

Rabkin, L. Y. (ed.) *Psychopathology and literature.* San Francisco: Chandler, 1966.

Rahe, R. H., Mahan, J. L., and Arthur, R. J. Prediction of near-future health change from subjects' preceding life changes. *Journal of Psychosomatic Research*, 1970, *14*, 401.

Raiffa, H. *Decision analysis: introductory lectures on choices under uncertainty.* Reading, Mass.: Addison-Wesley, 1968.

Raimy, V. C. (ed.) *Training in clinical psychology.* Englewood Cliffs, N. J.: Prentice-Hall, 1950.

Rand, G. What psychology asks of urban planning. *American Psychologist*, 1969, *24*, 929–935.

Rapaport, D., Gill, M. M., and Schafer, R. In R. R. Holt (ed.), *Diagnostic psychological testing.* New York: International University Press, 1968.

Rappaport, J., and Chinsky, J. M. Behavior ratings of chronic hospitalized patients: cross-situational and cross-rater agreement. *Journal of Consulting and Clinical Psychology*, 1970, *34*, 394–397.

Rappaport, J., Chinsky, J. M., and Cowen, E. L. *Innovations in helping chronic patients: college students in a mental institution.* New York: Academic Press, 1971.

Razin, A. M. A-B variable in therapy: a critical review. *Psychological Bulletin* 1971, *75*, 1–21.

Redl, F. Strategy and techniques of the life-space interview. *American Journal of Orthopsychiatry*, 1959, *29*, 1–18.

Reich, C. *The greening of america.* New York: Random House, 1970.

Reiff, R. Psychology and public policy. *Professional Psychology*, 1970, *1*, 315–330.

Reisman, J. M. *The development of clinical psychology.* New York: Appleton-Century-Crofts, 1966.

Reitan, R. M., and Fitzhugh, K. B. Behavioral deficits in groups with cerebral vascular lesions. *Journal of Consulting and Clinical Psychology*, 1971, *37*, 215–223.

Reiterman, C. (ed.) *Abortion and the unwanted child.* New York: Springer, 1971.

Rempel, P. R. The use of multivariate statistical analysis of MMPI scores in classification of delinquent and nondelinquent high school boys. *Journal of Consulting Psychology*, 1958, *22*, 17–23.

Rich, J. *Interviewing children and adolescents.* New York: St. Martin's Press, 1968.

Richards, T. W. *Modern clinical psychology.* New York: McGraw-Hill, 1946.

Richardson, S. A., Dohrenwend, B. S., and Klein, D. *Interviewing: its forms and functions.* New York: Basic Books, 1965.

Rioch, M. J. Pilot projects in training mental health counselors. In E. L. Cowen, E. A. Gardner, and M. Zax (eds.), *Emergent approaches to mental health problems.* New York: Appleton-Century-Crofts, 1967, pp. 110–127.

Rioch, M. J. Should psychotherapists do psychotherapy? *Professional Psychology*, 1970, *1*, 139–142.

Robins, L. N. *Deviant children grown up.* Baltimore: Williams & Wilkins, 1966.

Robinson, J. *Economic philosophy.* Chicago: Aldine-Atherton, 1962.

Roe, A. Analysis of group Rorschachs of psychologists and anthropologists. *Journal of Projective Techniques*, 1952, *16*, 212–224.

Roe, A. A psychological study of eminent psychologists and anthropologists and a comparison with biological and physical scientists. *Psychological Monographs*, 1953, *67*, No. 2.

Roe, A. Individual motivation and personal factors in career choice. In F. N.

Arnoff, E. A. Rubinstein, and J. C. Speisman (eds.), *Manpower for mental health*, 1969, pp. 131–148.

Roen, S. R. Evaluative research and community mental health. In A. E. Bergin and S. L. Garfield (eds.), *Handbook of psychotherapy and behavior change: an empirical analysis.* New York: Wiley, 1971, pp. 776–811.

Roethlisberger, F. J., and Dickson, W. J. *Management and the worker.* Cambridge, Mass.: Harvard University Press, 1939.

Roff, M. Childhood social interactions and young adult bad conduct. *Journal of Abnormal and Social Psychology*, 1961, *63*, 333–337.

Rogers, C. R. The necessary and sufficient conditions of therapeutic personality change. *Journal of Consulting Psychology*, 1957, *21*, 95–103.

Rogers, C. R. A theory of therapy, personality, and interpersonal relationships, as developed in the client-centered framework. In S. Koch (ed.), *Psychology: a study of a science*, Study I, *Conceptual and systematic*, Vol. 3, *Formulations of the person and the social context.* New York: McGraw-Hill, 1959, pp. 184–256.

Rogers, C. R., Carl R. Rogers. In E. G. Boring and G. Lindzey (eds.), *A history of psychology in autobiography*, Vol. 5. New York: Appleton-Century-Crofts, 1967. pp. 343–384.

Rogers, C. R. *Carl Rogers on encounter groups.* New York: Harper & Row, 1970.

Rohde, A. R. *The sentence completion method.* New York: Ronald Press, 1957.

Rorer, L. G. The great response-style myth. *Psychological Bulletin*, 1965, *70*, 1–19.

Rosenthal, D. *Genetic theory and abnormal behavior.* New York: McGraw-Hill, 1970.

Rosenthal, R., and Jacobsen, L. *Pygmalion in the classroom: teacher expectation and pupils' intellectual development.* New York: Holt, Rinehart and Winston, 1968.

Roszak, T. *The making of a counter culture.* Garden City, N. Y.: Doubleday, 1969.

Rothenberg, P. J., and Matulef, N. J. Toward professional training. *Professional Psychology*, 1969, *1*, 32–37.

Rotter, J. B. *Clinical psychology*, 2nd ed. Englewood Cliffs, N. J.: Prentice-Hall, 1971.

Rubinstein, E. A., and Parloff, M. B. (eds.) *Research in psychotherapy*, Vol. 1. Washington, D. C.: American Psychological Association, 1959.

Rudestam, K. E. Stockholm and Los Angeles: a cross-cultural study of the communication of suicidal intent. *Journal of Consulting and Clinical Psychology*, 1971, *36*, 82–90.

Runkel, P. J., and McGrath, J. E. *Research on human behavior.* New York: Holt, Rinehart and Winston, 1972.

Russell, E. W., Neuringer, C., and Goldstein, G. *Assessment of brain damage.* New York: Wiley, 1970.

Ryan, W. (ed.) *Distress in the city: essays on the design and administration of urban mental health services.* Cleveland: Case Western Reserve University, 1969.

Sacks, J. M., and Kirtley, D. D. Some personality characteristics related to response to subtle and obvious items of the MMPI. *Journal of Consulting and Clinical Psychology*, 1972, *38*, 66–69.

Salter, A. *Conditioned-reflex therapy*. New York: Creative Age, 1949.

Sandron, L. Two opposing models for a self-following prophecy. *Counseling Psychologist*, 1971, *2*, 82–87.

Sarason, S. B. Toward a psychology of change and innovation. *American Psychologist*, 1967, *22*, 227–233.

Sarason, S. B. *The creation of settings and the future societies*. San Francisco: Jossey-Bass, 1972.

Sarbin, T. R. A contribution to the study of actuarial and individual methods of prediction. *American Journal of Sociology*, 1943, *48*, 593–602.

Sarbin, T. R. A role-theory perspective for community psychology: The structure of social identity. In D. Adelson and B. L. Kalis (eds.), *Community psychology and mental health*. San Francisco: Chandler, 1970, pp. 89–113.

Sarbin, T. R., and Allen, V. L. Role theory. In G. Lindzey and E. Aronson (eds.), *Handbook of social psychology*, Vol. 1, 2nd ed. Reading, Mass.: Addison-Wesley, 1968, pp. 488–567.

Sarbin, T. R., and Mancuso, J. C. Failure of a moral enterprise: attitudes of the public toward mental illness. *Journal of Consulting and Clinical Psychology*, 1970, *35*, 159–173.

Sarbin, T. R., and Mancuso, J. C. Paradigms and moral judgments: improper conduct is not disease. *Journal of Consulting and Clinical Psychology*, 1972, *39*, 6–8.

Sarbin, T. R., Taft, R., and Bailey, D. E. *Clinical inference and cognitive theory*. New York: Holt, Rinehart and Winston, 1960.

Sargent, H. D., and Mayman, M. Clinical psychology. In S. Arieti (ed.), *American handbook of psychiatry*, Vol. 2. New York: Basic Books, 1959, pp. 1711–1732.

Satir, V. *Conjoint family therapy*, 2nd ed. Palo Alto, Calif.: Science & Behavior Books, 1967.

Satz, P., Fennell, E., and Reilly, C. Predictive validity of six neurodiagnostic tests: a decision theory analysis. *Journal of Consulting and Clinical Psychology*, 1970, *34*, 375–381.

Sawyer, J. Measurement *and* prediction, clinical *and* statistical. *Psychological Bulletin*, 1966, *66*, 178–200.

Schafer, R. *Psychoanalytic interpretation in Rorschach testing*. New York: Grune & Stratton, 1954.

Schein, E. H. *Process consultation: its role in organization development*. Reading, Mass.: Addison-Wesley, 1969.

Schein, E. H., and Bennis, W. G. *Personal and organizational changes through group methods: the laboratory approach*. New York: Wiley, 1965.

Scherer, S. E., Ettinger, R. F., and Mudrick, N. J. Need for social approval and drug use. *Journal of Consulting and Clinical Psychology*, 1972, *38*, 118–121.

Schmidt, H. O., and Fonda, C. P. Reliability of psychiatric diagnosis: a new look. *Journal of Abnormal and Social Psychology*, 1956, *52*, 262–267.

Schmidt, W. H. *Organizational frontiers and human values.* Belmont, Calif.: Wadsworth, 1970.

Schmuck, R. A., Runkel, P. J., Saturen, S. L., Martell, R. T., and Derr, C. B. *The handbook of organization development in schools.* Palo Alto, Calif.: National Press Books, 1972.

Schneider, S. F. Reply to Albee's "The uncertain future of clinical psychology." *American Psychologist*, 1971, *26*, 1058–1070.

Schofield, W. *Psychotherapy: the purchase of friendship.* Englewood Cliffs, N. J.: Prentice-Hall, 1964.

Schofield, W. The role of psychology in the delivery of health services. *American Psychologist*, 1969, *24*, 565–584.

Schofield, W., and Balian, L. A comparative study of the personal histories of schizophrenic and nonpsychiatric patients. *Journal of Abnormal and Social Psychology*, 1959, *59*, 216–225.

Schroder, H. M., Driver, M. J., and Streufert, S. *Human information processing: individuals and groups functioning in complex social situations.* New York: Holt, Rinehart and Winston, 1967.

Schroeder, H. E. Use of feedback in clinical prediction. *Journal of Consulting and Clinical Psychology*, 1972, *38*, 265–269.

Schulberg, H. C. Challenge of human service programs for psychologists. *American Psychologist*, 1972, *27*, 566–573.

Schulberg, H. C., and Tolor, A. The use of the Bender-Gestalt in clinical practice. *Journal of Projective Techniques*, 1961, *25*, 347–351.

Schulman, J. *Remaking an organization: innovation in a specialized psychiatric hospital.* Albany, N. Y.: State University of New York Press, 1969.

Schultz, K. V. *Marriage personality inventory.* Oakland, Calif.: Psychological Services Press, 1966.

Schwartz, E. K. To group or not to group. *Contemporary Psychology*, 1971, *16*, 423–424.

Schwitzgebel, R. L. Behavior instrumentation and social technology. *American Psychologist*, 1970, *25*, 491–499.

Scott, F. G., and Brewer, R. M. (eds.). *Confrontations of death: a book of readings and a suggested method of instruction.* Corvallis, Ore.: Continuing Education Books, 1971.

Scott, W. A., and Johnson, R. C. Comparative validities of direct and indirect personality tests. *Journal of Consulting and Clinical Psychology*, 1972, *38*, 301–318. (a)

Scott, W. A., and Johnson, R. C. Determinants of differential test validity. *Journal of Consulting and Clinical Psychology*, 1972, *38*, 327–328. (b)

Scrimshaw, N. S. Early malnutrition and central nervous system function. *Merrill Palmer Quarterly of Behavior and Development*, 1969, *15*, 375–388.

Sears, R. R. *Survey of objective studies of psychoanalytic concepts.* New York: Social Science Research Council, 1943.

Sechrest, L. Incremental validity: a recommendation. *Educational and Psychological Measurement*, 1963, *23*, 153–158.

Sechrest, L., Gallimore, R., and Hersch, P. D. Feedback and accuracy of clinical predictions. *Journal of Consulting Psychology*, 1967, *31*, 1–11.

Seifert, J. A., Draguns, J. G., and Caudill, W. Role orientation, sphere dominance, and social competence as bases of psychiatric diagnosis in Japan. *Journal of Abnormal Psychology*, 1971, *78*, 101–106.

Selye, H. *The stress of life*. New York: McGraw-Hill, 1956.

Shah, S. A. Privileged communications, confidentiality, and privacy. *Professional Psychology*, 1969, *1*, 56–69.

Shah, S. A. Privileged communications, confidentiality, and privacy: confidentiality. *Professional Psychology*, 1970, *1*, 159–164. (a)

Shah, S. A. Privileged communications, confidentiality and privacy: privacy. *Professional Psychology*, 1970, *1*, 243–245. (b)

Shakow, D. On the rewards (and, alas, frustrations) of public service. *American Psychologist*, 1968, *23*, 87–96.

Shakow, D. *Clinical psychology as science and profession—a forty-year odyssey*. Chicago: Aldine-Atherton, 1969.

Shakow, D., and Kovacs, A. L. Troubled clinical waters. *Contemporary Psychology*, 1968, *13*, 225–231.

Shapiro, M. B. The single case in clinical-psychological research. *Journal of General Psychology*, 1966, *74*, 3–23.

Sharma, S. L. A historical background of the development of nosology in psychiatry and psychology. *American Psychologist*, 1970, *25*, 248–253.

Shellow, R., and Roemer, D. V. The riot that didn't happen. *Social Problems*, 1966, *14*, 221–233.

Shemberg, K., and Keeley, S. Psychodiagnostic training in the academic setting: past and present. *Journal of Consulting and Clinical Psychology*, 1970, *34*, 205–211.

Shibutani, T. *Society and personality, an interactionist approach to social psychology*. Englewood Cliffs, N. J.: Prentice-Hall, 1961.

Shlein, J. M. *Research in psychotherapy*. Vol. 3. Washington, D. C.: American Psychological Association, 1968.

Shneidman, E. S., Farberow, N. L., and Litman, R. E. *The psychology of suicide*. New York: Science House, 1970.

Shoben, E. J. Toward a concept of the normal personality. *American Psychologist*, 1957, *12*, 183–189.

Shore, M. F., and Golann, S. E. Problems of ethics in community mental health: a survey of community psychologists. *Community Mental Health Journal*, 1969, *5*, 452–460.

Shore, M. F., and Massimo, J. L. Five years later: a follow-up of comprehensive vocationally oriented psychotherapy. *American Journal of Orthopsychiatry*, 1969, *39*, 769–773.

Shostrom, E. L. Group therapy: let the buyer beware. *Psychology Today*, 1969, *2*, 36–45.

Shostrom, E. L. *Pair Attraction Inventory*. San Diego, Calif.: Educational and Industrial Service, 1971.

Silverman, L. H. A Q-sort study of the validity of evaluations made from projective techniques. *Psychological Monographs*, 1959, *73*, No. 7.

Simmons, W. L. Clinical training programs, 1964–1965 and 1968–1969: a characterization and discussion. *American Psychologist*, 1971, *26*, 717–721.

Simon, L. J. The political unconsciousness of psychology: clinical psychology and social change. *Professional Psychology*, 1970, *1*, 331–342.

Sines, L. K. The relative contribution of four kinds of data to accuracy in personality assessment. *Journal of Consulting Psychology*, 1959, *23*, 483–492.

Skinner, B. F. *The behavior of organisms.* New York: Appleton-Century-Crofts, 1938.

Skinner, B. F. *Science and human behavior.* New York: Macmillan, 1953.

Skinner, B. F. *Beyond freedom and dignity.* New York: Knopf, 1971.

Slovic, P., Rorer, L. G., and Hoffman, P. J. Analyzing use of diagnostic signs. *Investigative Radiology*, 1971, *6*, 18–26.

Small, L. The uncommon importance of psychodiagnosis. *Professional Psychology*, 1972, *3*, 105–110.

Smart, R. G., and Jones, D. Illicit LSD users: their personality characteristics and psychopathology. *Journal of Abnormal Psychology*, 1970, *75*, 286–292.

Smith, A. G. (ed.) *Communication and culture.* New York: Holt, Rinehart, 1966.

Smith, H. C. *Sensitivity to people.* New York: McGraw-Hill, 1966.

Smith, M. B. Personal values in the study of lives. In R. W. White (ed.), *The study of lives.* Englewood Cliffs, N. J.: Prentice-Hall, 1963, pp. 324–347.

Smith, M. B. Ethical implications of population policies. *American Psychologist*, 1972, *27*, 11–15.

Smith, M. B., and Hobbs, N. *The community and the community mental health center.* Washington, D. C.: American Psychological Association, 1966.

Smyth, R., and Reznikoff, M. Attitudes of psychiatrists toward the usefulness of psychodiagnostic reports. *Professional Psychology*, 1971, *2*, 283–288.

Sommer, R. *Personal space, the behavioral basis for design.* Englewood Cliffs, N. J.: Prentice-Hall, 1969.

Soskin, W. F. Bias in postdiction from projective tests. *Journal of Abnormal and Social Psychology*, 1954, *49*, 69–74.

Soskin, W. F. Influence of four types of data on diagnostic conceptualization in psychological testing. *Journal of Abnormal and Social Psychology*, 1959, *58*, 69–78.

Sowles, R. C., and Gill, J. H. Institutional and community adjustment of delinquents following counseling. *Journal of Consulting and Clinical Psychology*, 1970, *34*, 398–402.

Specht, H. The deprofessionalization of social work. *Social Work*, 1972, *17*, 2, 3–15.

Speer, D. C. Behavior problem checklist (Peterson-Quay): baseline data from parents of child guidance and nonclinic children. *Journal of Consulting and Clinical Psychology*, 1971, *36*, 221–228.

Spilken, A. Z., Jacobs, M. A., Muller, J. J., and Knitzer, J. Personality characteristics of therapists: description of relevant variables and examination of conscious preferences. *Journal of Consulting and Clinical Psychology*, 1969, *33*, 317–326.

Spitzer, R. L., and Endicott, J. Diagno II: further development in a computer program for psychiatric diagnosis. *American Journal of Psychiatry*, 1969, *125*, 12–21.

Sprague, R. L., Barnes, K. R., and Werry, J. S. Methylphenidate and thioridazine: learning, reaction time, activity, and classroom behavior in disturbed
children. *American Journal of Orthopsychiatry*, 1970, *40*, 615–627.

Squire, M. B. (ed.) *Current administrative practices for psychiatric services.*
Springfield, Ill.: Charles C Thomas, 1970.

Srole, L., Langner, T. S., Michael, S. T., Opler, M. K., and Rennie, T. A. *Mental
health in the metropolis: the midtown Manhattan Study.* New York:
McGraw-Hill, 1962.

Stanton, A. H., and Schwartz, M. S. The mental hospital. New York: Basic
Books, 1954.

Steele, B. F. *Helping the battered child and his family.* Chicago: University of
Chicago Press, 1970.

Steele, B. F., and Pollock, C. B. Psychiatric study of parents who abuse infants
and small children. In R. E. Helfer and C. H. Kempe (eds.), *The battered
child.* Chicago: University of Chicago Press, 1968, pp. 103–147.

Stein, K. B., Sarbin, T. R., and Kulick, J. A. Further validation of antisocial
personality types. *Journal of Consulting and Clinical Psychology*, 1971, *36*,
177–182.

Stein, M. I. Creativity. In E. F. Borgatta, and W. W. Lambert (eds.), *Handbook
of personality theory and research.* Chicago: Rand McNally, 1969, pp.
900–942.

Stotsky, B. A., Daston, D. G., and Vardack, C. N. An evaluation of the
counseling of chronic schizophrenics. *Journal of Counseling Psychology*,
1955, *2*, 248–255.

Straus, M. A. *Family measurement techniques: abstracts of published instruments, 1935–1965.* Minneapolis: University of Minnesota Press, 1969.

Strupp, H. H., and Luborsky, L. (eds.) *Research in psychotherapy.* Vol. 2.
Washington, D. C.: American Psychological Association, 1962.

Stuart, R. B. Operant interpersonal treatment for marital discord. *Journal of
Consulting and Clinical Psychology*, 1969, *33*, 675–682.

Suchman, E. A. *Evaluative research: principles and practice in public service and
social action programs.* New York: Russell Sage Foundation, 1967.

Sundberg, N. D. A note concerning the history of testing. *American Psychologist*, 1954, *9*, 150–151.

Sundberg, N. D. The acceptability of "fake" versus "bona fide" personality test
interpretations. *Journal of Abnormal and Social Psychology*, 1955, *50*,
145–147.

Sundberg, N. D. The practice of psychological testing in clinical services in the
United States. *American Psychologist*, 1961, *16*, 79–83.

Sundberg, N. D. A method for studying sensitivity to implied meanings. *Gawein*
(Journal of Psychology, University of Nijmegen, Netherlands), 1966,
15, 1–8.

Sundberg, N. D. The communal sources of well-being. (A review of D. C. Klein,
Community Dynamics and Mental Health.) *Contemporary Psychology*,
1969, *14*, 407–409. (a)

Sundberg, N. D. Toward systematic learning in natural settings. In W. Sheppard (ed.), *Proceedings of the Conference on Instructional Innovations in Undergraduate Education*. Eugene, Ore.: University of Oregon, 1969. (b)

Sundland, D. M., and Barker, E. N. The orientation of psychotherapists. *Journal of Consulting Psychology*, 1962, *26*, 201–212.

Swenson, C. H. Empirical evaluations of human figure drawings. *Psychological Bulletin*, 1968, *70*, 20–44.

Szasz, T. S. *The myth of mental illness*. New York: Harper & Row, 1961.

Talland, G. A. *Deranged memory*. New York: Academic Press, 1965.

Tallent, N. On individualizing the psychologists' clinical evaluation. *Journal of Clinical Psychology*, 1958, *14*, 243–245.

Tallent, N. Psychological consultation in psychiatry. *Diseases of the Nervous System*, 1960, *21*, 1–7.

Tallent, N., and Reiss, W. J. Multidisciplinary views on the preparation of written clinical psychological reports: III. The trouble with psychological reports. *Journal of Clinical Psychology*, 1959, *15*, 444–446.

Tannenbaum, R., Wechsler, I. R., and Massarik, F. *Leadership and organization: a behavioral science approach*. New York: McGraw-Hill, 1961.

Tanner, J. M. The regulation of human growth. *Child Development*, 1963, *34*, 817–847.

Taplin, J. Crisis theory: critique and reformulation. *Community Mental Health Journal*, 1971, *7*, 13–23.

Temkin, O. The history of classification in the medical sciences. In M. M. Katz, J. O. Cole, and W. E. Barton (eds.), *Classification in psychiatry and psychopathology*. Chevy Chase, Md.: National Institute of Mental Health, 1965.

Terman, L. M. The discovery and encouragment of exceptional talent. *American Psychologist*, 1954, *9*, 221–230.

Terreberry, S. The evolution of organizational environments. *Administrative Science Quarterly*, 1968, *12*, 590–613.

Thelen, M. H., and Ewing, D. R. Roles, functions, and training in clinical psychology: a survey of academic clinicians. *American Psychologist*, 1970, *25*, 550–554.

Thelen, M. H., Varble, D. L., and Johnson, J. Attitudes of academic clinical psychologists toward projective techniques. *American Psychologist*, 1968, *23*, 517–521.

Thomas, H. F. Encounter, the game of no game. In A. Burton (ed.), *Encounter*. San Francisco: Jossey-Bass, 1970, pp. 69–80.

Thoreson, R. W., Krauskopf, C. J., McAleer, C. A., and Wenger, H. D. The future for applied psychology. *American Psychologist*, 1972, *27*, 134–139.

Thorne, F. C. *Principles of psychological examining*. Brandon, Vt.: *Journal of Clinical Psychology*, 1955.

Thorne, F. C. *Integrative psychology*. Brandon, Vt.: Clinical Psychology Publishing Co., 1967.

Tipton, R. M. Relative effectiveness of two methods of interpreting ability test scores. *Journal of Counseling Psychology*, 1969, *16*, 75–80.

Toffler, A. *Future Shock*. New York: Random House, 1970.

Tomkins, S. S., and Miner, J. B. *The Tomkins-Horn Picture Arrangement Test*. New York: Springer, 1957.

Trachtman, J. P. Socio-economic class bias in Rorschach diagnosis: contributing psychosocial attributes of the clinician. *Journal of Personality Assessment*, 1971, *35*, 229–240.

Trexler, L. D., and Karst, T. O. Rational-emotive therapy, placebo, and no-treatment effects on public-speaking anxiety. *Journal of Abnormal Psychology*, 1972, *79*, 60–67.

Truax, C. B., and Carkhuff, R. R. *Toward effective counseling and psychotherapy*. Chicago: Aldine-Atherton, 1967.

Truax, C. B., Shapiro, J. G., and Wargo, D. G. The effects of alternate sessions and vicarious therapy pre-training on group psychotherapy. *International Journal of Group Psychotherapy*, 1968, *18*, 186–198.

Tryk, H. E. Assessment in the study of creativity. In P. McReynolds (ed), *Advances in psychological assessment*. Palo Alto, Calif.: Science & Behavior Books, 1968.

Turner, R. J., Dopkeen, L. S., and Labreche, G. P. Marital status and schizophrenia: a study of incidence and outcome. *Journal of Abnormal Psychology*, 1970, *76*, 110–116.

Tyler, F. B., and Speisman, J. C. An emerging scientist-professional role in psychology. *American Psychologist*, 1967, *22*, 839–847.

Tyler, L. E. Towards a workable psychology of individuality. *American Psychologist*, 1959, *14*, 75–81.

Tyler, L. E. *The work of the counselor*, 3rd ed. New York: Appleton-Century-Crofts, 1969.

Tyler, L. E. *Tests and measurements*, 2nd ed. Englewood Cliffs, N. J.: Prentice-Hall, 1971.

Tyler, L. E., Sundberg, N. D., Rohila, P. K., and Greene, M. M. Patterns of choices in Dutch, American, and Indian adolescents. *Journal of Counseling Psychology*, 1968, *15*, 522–529.

Ullman, L. P. *Institution and outcome: a comparative study of psychiatric hospitals*. Elmsford, N. Y.: Pergamon Press, 1967.

United States Department of Labor. *Manual for the USTES General Aptitude Test Battery, Section 1*. Washington, D. C.: U. S. Department of Labor, 1970.

United States Commission on Population Growth and the American future. *Population and the American Future: The Report of the Commission on Population Growth and the American Future*. Washington, D. C.: Government Printing Office, 1972.

Urban, H. B., and Ford, D. H. Some historical and conceptual perspectives on psychotherapy and behavior change. In A. E. Bergin and S. L. Garfield (eds.), *Handbook of psychotherapy and behavior change*. New York: Wiley, 1971, pp. 3–35.

Veith, I. Psychiatric nosology: from Hippocrates to Kraepelin. *American Journal of Psychiatry*, 1957, *114*, 385–391.

Veith, I. On the "principles of the heart" and the psychiatric insights of Zen. *New England Journal of Medicine*, 1971, *285*, 1458–1480.

Verden, P., and Shatterly, D. Alcoholism research and resistance to understanding the compulsive drinker. *Mental Hygiene*, 1971, *55*, 331–336.

Verplanck, W. S. How do you track down rumors? *American Psychologist*, 1970, *25*, 106—107.

Voegtlin, W. L., and Lemere, F. An evaluation of the aversion treatment of alcoholism. *Quarterly Journal of Studies of Alcoholism*, 1950, *11*, 199—204.

Wagner, E. E., and Dobbins, R. D. MMPI profiles of parishioners seeking pastoral counseling. *Journal of Consulting Psychology*, 1967, *31*, 83—84.

Wallace, J. An abilities conception of personality: some implications for personality measurement. *American Psychologist*, 1966, *21*, 132—138.

Wallace, R. K., and Benson, H. The physiology of meditation. *Scientific American*, 1972, *226*, 84—90.

Ward, R. F., and Faillace, L. A. The alcoholic and his helpers: a systems view. *Quarterly Journal of Studies of Alcoholism*, 1970, *31*, (3).

Watson, D. L., and Tharp, R. G. *Self-directed behavior: self-modification for personal adjustment.* Monterey, Calif.: Brooks/Cole, 1972.

Watson, R. I. Psychology: a perscriptive science. *American Psychologist*, 1967, *22*, 435—443.

Watt, N. F., Stolorow, R. D., Lubensky, A. W., and McClelland, D. C. School adjustment and behavior of children hospitalized for schizophrenia as adults. *American Journal of Orthopsychiatry*, 1970, *40*, 637—657.

Webb, E. J., Campbell, D. T., Schwartz, R. D., and Sechrest, L. *Unobtrusive measures: nonreactive research in the social sciences.* Chicago: Rand McNally, 1969.

Weick, K. E. Systematic observational methods. In G. Lindzey and E. Aronson (eds.), *The handbook of social psychology*, Vol. 2, 2nd ed. Reading, Mass.: Addison-Wesley, 1968, pp. 357—451.

Weiss, C. H. (ed.). *Evaluating action programs: readings in social action and education.* Boston: Allyn and Bacon, 1972.

Weiss, R. L. Operant conditioning techniques in psychological assessment. In P. McReynolds (ed.), *Advances in psychological assessment*. Vol. 1. Palo Alto, Calif.: Science & Behavior Books, 1968, pp. 169—190.

Weissman, H. N., Goldschmid, M. L., and Stein, D. D. Psychotherapeutic orientation and training: their relation to the practices of clinical psychologists. *Journal of Consulting and Clinical Psychology*, 1971, *37*, 31—37.

Weitz, W. A. Experiencing the role of a hospitalized psychiatric patient: a professional's view from the other side. *Professional Psychology*, 1972, *3*, 151—154.

Wells, F. L., and Ruesch, J. *Mental examiners' handbook*, 2nd ed. New York: Psychological Corporation, 1945.

Wender, P. H. *Minimal brain dysfunction in children.* New York: Wiley, 1971.

Weyant, R. G. Lycurgus: the father of applied psychology. *American Psychologist*, 1967, *22*, 432—434.

Wheeler, L. Predictions of brain damage from an aphasia screening test: an application of discriminant functions and a comparison with a nonlinear method of analysis. *Perceptual and Motor Skills*, 1963, *17*, 63—80.

Wheeler, L. Complex behavioral indices weighted by linear discriminant functions for the prediction of cerebral damage. *Perceptual and Motor Skills*, 1964, *19*, 907—923.

Wheelis, A. *The quest for identity*. New York: Norton, 1958.

White, R. W. Motivation reconsidered: the concept of competence. *Psychological Review*, 1959, *66*, 297–333.

White, S. H. The national impact study of Head Start. In J. Helmuth (ed.), *Disadvantaged child*, Vol. 3, *Compensatory education: a national debate*. New York: Brunner/Mazel, 1970, pp. 163–184.

Whitehorn, J. C., and Betz, B. J. A study of psychotherapeutic relationships between physicians and schizophrenic patients. *American Journal of Psychiatry*, 1954, *111*, 321–331.

Whittaker, J. O. Psychology in China: a brief survey. *American Psychologist*, 1970, *25*, 757–759.

Whittington, H. G. The development of an urban comprehensive community mental health program. In M. F. Shore and F. V. Mannino (eds.), *Mental health and the community: problems, programs, and strategies*. New York: Behavioral Publications, 1969, pp. 65–82.

Whyte, W. H., Jr. *The organization man*. New York: Simon & Schuster, 1956.

Wiener, D. N. Subtle and obvious keys for the Minnesota Multiphasic Personality Inventory. *Journal of Consulting Psychology*, 1948, *12*, 164–170.

Wiens, A. N., Brody, D. S., Matarazzo, J. D., and Warnath, C. F. The habits and practices of professional psychologists in Oregon. Report of the Oregon Psychological Association Board of Examiners, 1961.

Wiggins, J. S. *Personality and prediction: principles of personality assessment*. Reading, Mass.: Addison-Wesley, 1972.

Wiggins, N., and Kohen, E. S. Man versus model of man revisited: the forecasting of graduate school success. *Journal of Personality and Social Psychology*, 1971, *19*, 100–106.

Williams, J. E. Changes in self and other perceptions following brief educational-vocational counseling. *Journal of Counseling Psychology*, 1962, *9*, 18–28.

Williamson, E. G., and Bordin, E. S. Evaluating counseling by means of a control group experiment. *School and Society*, 1940, *52*, 434–440.

Winch, R. F., and More, D. M. Does TAT add information to interviews? Statistical analysis of the increment. *Journal of Clinical Psychology*, 1956, *12*, 316-321.

Winter, W. D. Family therapy: research and theory. In C. C. Spielberger (ed.), *Current topics in clinical and community psychology*, Vol. 3. New York: Academic Press, 1971, pp. 95–122.

Wirt, R. D., and Briggs, P. F. Personality and environmental factors in the development of delinquency. *Psychological Monographs*, 1959, *73*, No. 15 (Whole No. 485).

Wispe, L., Ash, P., Awkard, J., Hicks, L. H., Hoffman, M., and Porter, J. The Negro psychologist in America. *American Psychologist*, 1969, *24*, 142–150.

Witmer, L. Clinical psychology. *Psychological Clinic*, 1907, *1*, 1–9.

Wittson, C. L., and Hunt, W. A. The predictive value of the brief psychiatric interview. *American Journal of Psychiatry*, 1951, *107*, 582–585.

Wohlwill, J. F. The emerging discipline of environmental psychology. *American Psychologist*, 1970, *25*, 303–312.

Wolberg, L. R. *The technique of psychotherapy*, 2nd ed. New York: Grune & Stratton, 1954.

Wolff, W. M. Private practice research. *Journal of Consulting and Clinical Psychology*, 1970, *34*, 281–286.

Wolpe, J. *Psychotherapy by reciprocal inhibition.* Stanford, Calif.: Stanford University Press, 1958.

Yalom, I. D. *The theory and practice of group psychotherapy.* New York: Basic Books, 1970.

Yalom, I. D., and Lieberman, M. A. A study of encounter group casualties. *Archives of General Psychiatry*, 1971, *25*, 16–30.

Zajonc, R. B. Cognitive theories in social psychology. In G. Lindzey and E. Aronson (eds.), *Handbook of social psychology*, Vol. 1, 2nd ed. Reading, Mass.: Addison-Wesley, 1968.

Zax, M., and Cowen, E. L. Research on early detection and prevention of emotional dysfunction in young school children. In C. D. Spielberger (ed.), *Current topics in clinical and community psychology.* New York: Academic Press, 1969.

Zubin, J. Classification of the behavior disorders. *Annual Review of Psychology*, 1967, *18*, 373–406.

Zuckerman, M. Breaking out of the trait bag, or the state of the trait. Paper for a symposium: revolutionary implications of the state-trait distinction for psychological theory. Meeting of the American Psychological Association, Washington, D. C., 1971.

Zuckerman, M., and Lubin, B. *Manual for the Multiple Affect Adjective Check List.* San Diego, Calif.: Educational and Industrial Testing Service, 1965.

Zuckerman, M., Persky, H., Eckman, K. M., and Hopkins, T. R. A multi-trait multimethod measurement approach to the traits (or states) of anxiety, depression and hostility. *Journal of Projective Techniques*, 1967, *31*, 2, 39–48.

Zurcher, L. A. Implementing a community action agency. In M. F. Shore and F. V. Mannino (eds.), *Mental health and the community: problems, programs and strategies.* New York: Behavioral Publications, 1969, pp. 7–22.

Name Index

Subject Index

Minnesota Multiphasic Personality Inventory (MMPI) 119, 230, 231, 236, 237, 247, 306, 349, 481, 554–557, 565, 573, 574
Minnesota Paper Form Board Test, Revised, 564
Mistaken ideas, in cognitive change therapy, 78, 305, 307, 327, 333, 367, 402
Modeling, 323, 400
Moral
  responsibility, in therapy, 89
  treatment, 396
Motivation, 76, 97, 293
Multiple Affect Adjective Checklist, 567
Multipotentiality, 104

Natural caretakers, 324
Natural problem solving, 532–533
Needs hierarchy, 440
Negative instances, 115
Neo-Adlerians, 77
Neo-Freudians, 77
Neurosis. See Psychoneurosis
Nomological net, 241
New careers, 457
Nonprofessionals, 456–458, 528
  in community work, 467–468
  as key staff, 397
Nonverbal communication, 205
Nonverbal exercises, 402
Nonvoluntary clients, 25–27, 387
  families, 359, 377–380
Norms
  local, 250
  organizational, 425
  statistical aids in interpretation, 345–346
  subjective, 346–347
  tests, 235, 239

Observation, 199–202, 373–374
  erroneous, 167–168
  samples versus signs, 201–202
  by self, 201
  See also Controlled observation
Old age, intelligence, 257
Operant conditioning, 319, 321–324
Opportunity
  structure, 526
  theory, 456
Organization development, 398
Organizational
  effectiveness, 436
  variables, 419, 424–426
Organizations
  appraisal, 423–428
  consultation outcome criteria, 423, 426–427
  cost effectiveness, 427–428

evaluating effectiveness, 426–428
factors in staff morale, 418–423
goal setting, 428–430
internal change, 430–432
intervention, 296–297
level of system 414–415
limitations, 415–416
psychologist's need to understand, 414–416
roles of consultant, 416–418
roles of psychologists, 416–418
Oriental perspectives of man, 86–87
Outcome
  assessment recommendations, 249–252
  of assessment research, 159–162
  behavior change, 333–334
  counseling, research, 350–352
  psychotherapy research, 307–308
  See also Effectiveness
Outcome criteria, nonvoluntary clients, 26
Outcome research, 113, 116
  See also Research, evaluative
Overchoice, 530

Pair Attraction Inventory, 368
Paramorphic representation, 168
Pathognomonic signs, 201
Pathologizing bias, 247, 349–350, 425
Pathology. See Psychopathology
Patient(s)
  attitude toward change, 153
  attitude toward interview, 202–206
  determining who is, 149–150
  factors in selection, 429–430
  and systems, 93–108
  use of the term by psychologists, 13
  voluntary-nonvoluntary issue, 25–27, 359, 387
  See also Clients
Pattern(s)
  traits, 259–261
  See also Choice patterns
Payoff, 161
  See also Outcome
Peabody Picture Vocabulary Test, 230, 563
Peak experience, 86
Perception, 74, 216, 295, 297
Personal Adjustment and Role Skills Scales (PARS), 568
Personal Data Sheet (Woodward), 35
Personal understanding, 490–491
Personality
  importance of early experience, 76–77
  interpersonal approach, 77, 79–82
  intrapsychic or intrapersonal, 77
  plural nature, 105
  psychoanalytic theory, 75–78

Index of Research Examples

Index of Illustrations from Cases

655